Illustrator CC

2014 release

FOR WINDOWS AND MACINTOSH

ELAINE WEINMANN
PETER LOUREKAS
CHAD CHELIUS

Peachpit Press

Visual QuickStart Guide
Illustrator CC (2014 release)
Elaine Weinmann and Peter Lourekas

Peachpit Press
www.peachpit.com

To report errors, please send a note to errata@peachpit.com
Peachpit Press is a division of Pearson Education

Senior Production Editor: Lisa Brazieal
Composition: Chad Chelius and WolfsonDesign
Cover Design: RHDG/Riezebos Holzbaur Design Group, Peachpit Press
Interior Design: Elaine Weinmann
Interior llustrations: Elaine Weinmann and Peter Lourekas, except as noted

ISBN-13: 978-0-133-98703-4

ISBN-10: 0-133-98703-5

9 8 7 6 5 4 3 2 1
Printed and bound in the United States of America

Acknowledgments

Chad Chelius for jumping in and helping us to fully update and tech edit this edition. We could not have completed this without him!

Nancy Aldrich-Ruenzel has enthusiastically supported our projects since her tenure began as the publisher of Peachpit Press.

Susan Rimerman, our editor, keeps the many wheels in motion for us at Peachpit.

Lisa Brazieal, production editor, did an expert job of preparing our files for printing by RR Donnelley.

Among the other staff members at Peachpit Press who contribute their talents on an ongoing basis are Nancy Davis, editor in chief; Sara Todd, marketing manager; and Alison Serafini, contracts manager.

Elaine Soares, photo research manager, and Lee Scher, photo research coordinator, both of the Image Resource Center at Pearson Education (the parent company of Peachpit Press), quickly procured the stock graphics from Shutterstock.com that we requested.

Chris Lyons, Adobe Illustrator maestro, graciously allowed us to reproduce his artwork on several pages of this book (visit chrislyonsillustration.com).

We package our own books, which means that in addition to writing and testing the text and creating the illustrations, we design and produce press-ready InDesign files. To help us finish this title, Steve Rath generated a comprehensive index, and Scout Festa did a meticulous job of proofreading.

We commend the Illustrator CC prerelease team for producing a great product and for welcoming user input via the beta forum.

Recently, we moved our household and offices from the coast of New England to the mountains of Asheville, North Carolina. We are grateful to our friends and family who have encouraged and supported us in this journey.

Elaine Weinmann and Peter Lourekas

In this table of contents and throughout this book, new or improved Illustrator CC features are identified by red stars. ★

Contents

© Chris Lyons

NOTE TO OUR READERS

Before going to press with this book, we tested (and retested) our text to ensure that it accurately describes the options and features we viewed in the prerelease version of Illustrator CC (2014 release). Due to the nature of the Creative Cloud, however, some features may change or update at a later date. If there are any significant changes to Illustrator, we will post an addendum in the Access Bonus Content link below this book title at Peachpit.com, so be sure to register the book (see the directions above). Also, we may post supplemental information about Illustrator on our blog at elaineandpeter.com.

In this chapter, we'll show you how to get up and running in Adobe Illustrator. After learning how to launch the program, you'll learn how to create a new document; preview, open, and create document templates; create and modify multiple artboards; save and close your document; and quit/exit Illustrator.

Launching Illustrator

Note: To create a document after launching Illustrator, see the following page.

To launch Illustrator in Macintosh:

Do one of the following:

On the startup drive, open the Applications > Adobe Illustrator CC 2014 folder, then double-click the Adobe Illustrator CC 2014 application icon.

Click the Illustrator application icon  in the Dock. (To create an icon, drag the application icon from the application folder to the Dock.)

To launch Illustrator by opening a file, double-click an Illustrator file icon or drag an Illustrator file icon over the application icon in the Dock.

To launch Illustrator in Windows:

Do one of the following:

In Windows 7, click the Start button, choose All Programs, then click Adobe Illustrator CC 2014.

In Windows 8, display the Start screen, then click the tile for Adobe Illustrator CC 2014.

Double-click an Illustrator file icon (the file will open and Illustrator will launch).

➤ In Windows 8, to enable Illustrator to be launched from the Desktop, right-click the Illustrator tile in the Start screen, then choose Pin to Taskbar.

CREATE (SAVE) RELATED

1

IN THIS CHAPTER

A NOTE TO WINDOWS USERS

Most of the screen captures in this book were shot in the Mac OS. Although the Illustrator interface looks slightly different in Windows than in the Mac OS, the vast majority of the Illustrator features and options in dialogs, panels, menus, etc., are the same in both platforms. Where they differ, we have included screen captures of the Windows interface and/or noted accordingly in the text.

FINDING THE NEW STUFF IN THIS BOOK

This symbol ★ identifies Illustrator features that are new or improved.

Creating a new document

To create a new document:

1. Choose File > **New** (Cmd-N/Ctrl-N).

2. The New Document dialog opens.**A** Type a **Name** for the new document.

3. From the **Profile** menu, choose a preset for the medium in which you plan to output the file.

4. Each artboard in a document defines a separate printable area (see pages 7–12). Do either of the following:

   For your first document, set the **Number of Artboards** value to 1 (**A**, next page).

   For multiple artboards, choose the desired **Number of Artboards**, click a **Grid** order icon, choose a **Spacing** value for the spacing between artboards, and choose a number of **Columns** (**B**, next page).

5. Do either of the following:

   From the **Size** menu, choose a preset that matches your output device.

   Enter **Width** and **Height** values (if desired, you can change the measurement unit via the Units menu).

6. For the document **Orientation**, click the Portrait 🔲 or Landscape 🔲 button.

7. The **Bleed** values control the width of the print area for items that extend beyond the artboard. Ask your print shop what values to enter. Note: If you don't enter Bleed values here, you can do so later in the File > Document Setup or Print dialog.

8. If the Advanced options aren't showing, click the arrowhead, then do the following:

   Choose a **Color Mode** for the document: CMYK for print output; RGB for Web, devices, or video output.

   Choose a resolution for **Raster Effects**, depending on your output requirements (effects are covered in Chapter 15). For high-end print output, choose High (300 ppi).

   If you chose the Video And Film document profile, choose a **Transparency Grid** option.

   Leave the **Preview Mode** setting as Default.

   For Web output, to have the horizontal and vertical segments of objects align to the pixel grid so they look as crisp as possible, check **Align New Objects to Pixel Grid**.

9. Click OK. A new document window opens.

A *In the New Document dialog, type a name, then choose either a preset or custom settings.*

BASING A NEW FILE ON THE SETTINGS OF AN EXISTING ONE

To make the settings for an existing file appear in the New Document dialog, choose Browse from the Profile menu. In the Select File dialog, locate the file containing the desired settings, then click Open.

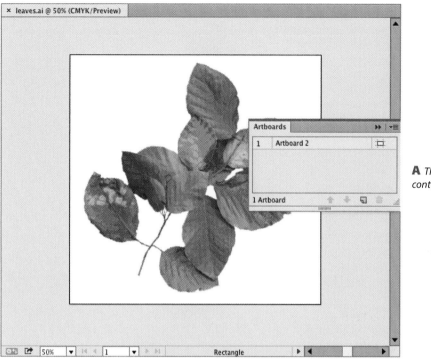

A *This document contains one artboard.*

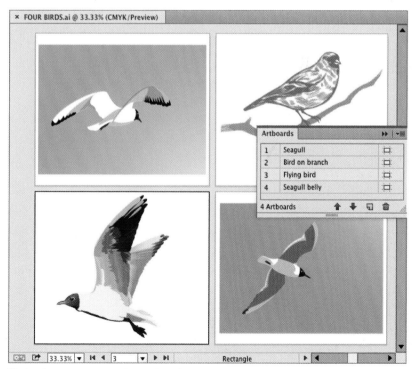

B *This document contains four artboards. Each artboard defines a separate printable area.*

Using templates

A template is an Illustrator document that opens auto-matically as a new, unsaved copy. Illustrator supplies a few industry-standard templates that you can use as a starting point for creating custom projects; we show you how to access them in the steps below. Following that, we show you how to open a standard Illustrator document as a template, then how to create a custom template.

To preview and open an Illustrator template:

1. Launch Bridge by clicking the Go to Bridge button **Br** on the Application bar in the Mac OS or to the right of the Help menu in Windows.

2. Click the Folders tab in the left panel. In the Mac OS, navigate to and open the Adobe Illustrator CC 2014/Cool Extras/en_US/Templates folder; in Windows, navigate to and open Program Files\Adobe\Adobe Illustrator CC 2014\Cool Extras\en_US\Templates.

3. Double-click the Blank Templates folder in the Templates folder. Find a template that interests you, then double-click it.

4. A copy of the template opens as a new, untitled document. The original file is left intact. Save the new file (see page 13).

You're not limited to using the templates that ship with Illustrator. One alternative is to open any existing Illustrator file as an untitled, unsaved document.

To open an existing Illustrator file as an untitled document:

1. Choose File > **New from Template** (Cmd-Shift-N/Ctrl-Shift-N).

2. The New from Template dialog opens. Locate and select an existing Illustrator file, then click **New** to open the file as an untitled document.

3. If the Font Problems dialog or a missing profile alert dialog appears, see the sidebar on page 63.

4. Save the new file (see page 13).

You can also save your own Illustrator files as templates. Regardless of what kind of project you're working on — CD label, business card, book cover, Web graphic, package design, etc. — you will find templates to be great timesavers.

When setting up a file to be saved as a template, you can choose document settings, layout aids such as guides, and multiple artboards, and you can also incorporate many Illustrator features, such as brushes, swatches, symbols, graphic styles, and of course, paths and type objects. Note: You'll probably want to revisit these instructions later, when you're better acquainted with Illustrator and have some experience in creating artwork under your belt.

To create a document template:

1. Create a new file or open an existing file.

2. Do any or all of the following — or anything else you can think of that might be useful to save in your template:

   Create Illustrator objects, such as paths and type.

   Create solid-color, gradient, or pattern swatches; brushes; graphic styles; character and paragraph styles; symbols; etc. Delete any of the above that won't be needed. You could also load or drag and drop objects containing those elements into the current document from another Illustrator document.

   Choose specifications for one or more artboards.

   Set the zoom level.

   Create ruler or object guides, choose ruler units (see page 413), and choose View menu options.

   Create and save custom views.

   Choose default settings for tools.

   Create layers and choose Layers panel options.

   Create crop or trim marks.

   Create transparency flattener, PDF, and print presets.

   Create text boxes containing instructions for users of the template.

3. Choose File > **Save as Template**. In the dialog, enter a name, keep the format as Illustrator Template (ait), keep the default location for templates (the folder that we listed in step 2 on the facing page) or choose a folder, then click Save.

THE ANATOMY OF AN ILLUSTRATOR DOCUMENT

Artwork that you want to export or print from Illustrator must be on an artboard (see the next page). To compare the currently active artboard to the paper size for the currently chosen printer, choose View > Fit Artboard in Window or press Cmd-0/Ctrl-0 (zero), then choose View > Show Print Tiling (the page size can be larger than the artboard size). To display the artboard boundaries if they are hidden, choose View > Show Artboards (Cmd-Shift-H/Ctrl-Shift-H). To learn more about the Illustrator workspace, see Chapter 3.

The following information is listed in the title bar: the current document name, zoom level, color mode (CMYK or RGB), and view (Outline, Preview, Overprint Preview, or Pixel Preview). And if View > Proof Colors is on, the current proof profile is also listed.

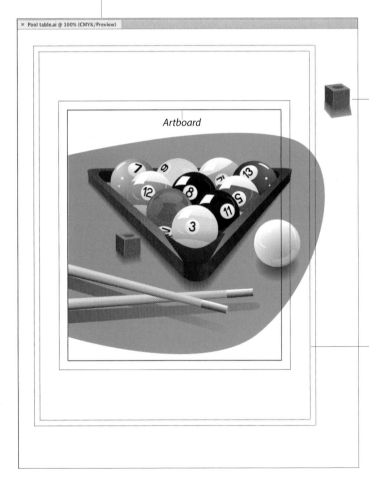

× Pool table.ai @ 100% (CMYK/Preview)

Artboard

The region outside the artboards is called the canvas.* You can create and stash objects in the canvas and drag them into any artboard when needed; they will save with the document.

To be part of a bleed, your artwork must extend from an artboard into the canvas. The red rectangle defines the bleed region, which can be specified in the New Document dialog when you create your file, in the Document Setup dialog for an existing document, or in the Print dialog upon output.

The inner dotted rectangle represents the actual printable area. It takes into account the printer's nonprintable margins at the edge of the paper, and is controlled by the specifications of the currently chosen printer (see Chapter 31). The outer dotted rectangle represents the paper size.

In Illustrator, the artboard is called the "live" area, and the "nonlive" area surrounding it is called the canvas. In Adobe Photoshop, the image is contained in what is called the canvas.

Adding artboards to a document

By default, every Illustrator document contains one artboard, and its dimensions are chosen in the New Document dialog. Using the Artboard tool, you can add more artboards to your document, scale them individually, change their orientation, and reposition them within the canvas area. Only one artboard can be active at a time. Artboards can be printed and exported individually or sequentially.

If you were to create an identity package for a client, for example, you could create a business card, stationery, and a brochure on separate artboards within the same document. Or you could create a series of separate but related graphics for the same website or animation project, a multipage PDF file, or components of a package design — all within one document. Any colors or graphic, paragraph, or character style definitions that you create will be available for all the artboards in the document.

To add an artboard with the Artboard tool: ★

1. Choose the **Artboard** tool  (Shift-O).

2. Do either of the following:

   To create an artboard of a preset size, drag using the **Artboard** tool to create a new artboard, then from the **Presets** menu on the Control panel, choose an option that fits your output medium.

   If you don't see sufficient blank canvas area in the document to accommodate the new artboard, press Cmd--/Ctrl-- (minus) to zoom out. You can

also hold down the Spacebar and drag the canvas area in the document window to make room. Drag to create an artboard. To draw an artboard from its center, hold down Option/Alt while dragging. To constrain the proportions of the artboard, hold down Shift while dragging.

➤ On the View menu, check Smart Guides and uncheck Pixel Preview and Snap to Grid, then align the new artboard via alignment guides as you drag (read about Smart Guides on pages 102–103 and 415).**A** To scale or reposition an artboard, see page 10.

3. To exit artboard-editing mode, either press Esc (the last selected tool reselects) or click a different tool.

➤ Artboards are assigned numbers automatically based on the sequence in which they are created.

USING THE STATUS BAR

Depending on which category you select from the Show submenu on the Status bar menu at the bottom of the document window, the bar will list the current Artboard Name, Current Tool, Date and Time, Number of [available] Undos, or Document Color Profile.

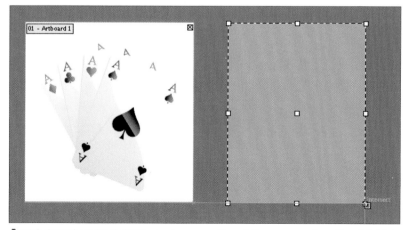

A *With the Artboard tool, drag to create a new artboard. Here, we are using a Smart Guide to align a new artboard with an existing one (see pages 102–103).*

To duplicate an artboard and its contents:

Do either of the following:

On the Artboards panel, A drag an artboard listing to the **New Artboard** button. In the document, the duplicate artboard will appear to the right of the existing ones.

Choose the **Artboard tool** (Shift-O), activate the **Move/Copy Artwork with Artboard** button on the Control panel, then Option-drag/Alt-drag an artboard.**B–C** (To use Smart Guides for alignment, see the first tip on the prior page). Press Esc.

➤ To rename an artboard, double-click the artboard name on the Artboards panel, enter a name, then click outside the name field or press Return/Enter. Another option is to click the Artboard tool, click an artboard in the document, then change the name in the Name field on the Control panel.

Artboards for the current document   *Orientation icon (click to open the Artboard Options dialog)*

Artboards		▶▶ / ▾≡
1	Letterhead	
2	Envelope	
3	Small label	
4	Large label	
5	business card	
6	Logo	

Order of artboards

6 Artboards   ⬆ ⬇ 🗔 🗑

Move Up   *Move Down*   *New Artboard*   *Delete Artboard*

A *Via the Artboards panel, you can create, select, duplicate, rename, and delete artboards; change their sequence; and open the Artboard Options dialog.*

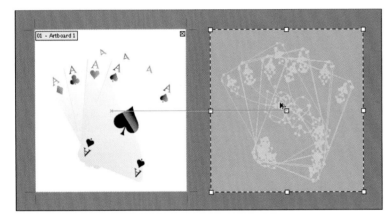

B *To copy an artboard and its contents, activate the Move/Copy Artwork with Artboard button on the Control panel, then with the Artboard tool, Option-drag/ Alt-drag the artboard.*

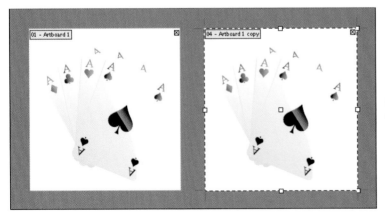

C *The duplicate artboard and its contents appear.*

To duplicate an artboard but not its contents:

Do one of the following:

On the Artboards panel, click the artboard to be duplicated, then click the **New Artboard** button. **A** The duplicate artboard will appear to the right of all the existing ones.

Choose the **Artboard** tool (Shift-O), deactivate the **Move/Copy Artwork with Artboard** button on the Control panel, then Option-drag/Alt-drag an artboard (to use Smart Guides for alignment, see the first tip on page 7). Press Esc to exit artboard-editing mode.

Choose the **Artboard** tool, click in an existing artboard, click the **New Artboard** button on the Control panel, position the artboard preview rectangle in the document window, then click to make the artboard appear (or hold down Option/Alt and click to produce multiple copies). Press Esc to exit artboard-editing mode.

➤ To create an artboard from a rectangular path, select the path, then choose Convert to Artboards from the Artboards panel menu.

Deleting artboards

To delete an artboard but not its contents:

Do either of the following:

Choose the **Artboard** tool (Shift-O), then click the Delete icon in the upper right corner of the artboard to be deleted. You could also click the artboard to be deleted, then press Delete/Backspace or click the Delete Artboard button on the Control panel. Press Esc.

On the Artboards panel, click the listing for the artboard to be deleted (or Cmd-click/Ctrl-click multiple listings), then click the **Delete Artboard** button.

➤ To delete all the empty artboards in a document (except for the original artboard, which must remain) from the Artboards panel menu, choose Delete Empty Artboards.

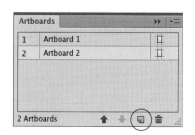

A *We clicked an artboard, then clicked the New Artboard button on the Artboards panel. A new blank artboard appeared, the same size as the original.*

FITTING AN ARTBOARD TO ARTWORK

➤ To fit the currently selected artboard to all the artwork in your document, choose Object > Artboards > Fit to Artwork Bounds. Note: If your document contains multiple artboards, after choosing the command, you will probably want to delete any extraneous artboards or reposition any overlapping ones.

➤ To fit an artboard around specific artwork, choose the Selection tool (V), then drag a marquee around (or Shift-click) that artwork. Activate the artboard by clicking its listing on the Artboards panel, then choose Object > Artboards > Fit to Selected Art.

The two commands mentioned above are also available on the Presets menu on the Control panel when the Artboard tool is selected.

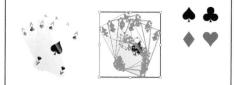

With a group of objects selected, we chose Object > Fit to Selected Art.

Modifying artboards

To change the location, scale, or orientation of an artboard:★

1. To display all the artboards in the document window, choose View > **Fit All in Window** or press Cmd-Option-0/Ctrl-Alt-0 (zero).

2. Choose the **Artboard** tool ⬚ (Shift-O), then click an artboard to select it.

3. To reposition the artboard and its contents, activate the **Move/Copy Artwork with Artboard** button ⬒ on the Control panel, then drag the artboard. Or, to reposition the artboard but not the artwork, deactivate the Move/Copy Artwork with Artboard button before dragging **A** (reactivate the button when you're done).

4. To scale the artboard, do any of the following:

   From the **Preset** menu on the Control panel, choose a predefined size.

   Drag a side or corner handle of the artboard.**B** To scale the artboard proportionally, hold down Shift while dragging. To resize an artboard from its center, hold down Option/Alt while dragging, and to resize an artboard proportionately from its center, hold down Option/Alt and Shift while dragging.

➤ When you scale an artboard manually, the exact dimensions are listed in a label next to the pointer. If the readouts aren't displaying, turn on View > Smart Guides, and in Illustrator/Edit > Preferences > Smart Guides, make sure Measurement Labels is checked.

Enter new values in the **W** and/or **H** fields on the Control panel (check the Constrain Width and Height Proportions button first, if desired).

5. To change the orientation of the artboard, click the **Portrait** 📱 or **Landscape** 📱 button on the Control panel. Or to rotate the artboard on a touchscreen device or touchpad, rotate two spread-out fingers, such as your thumb and forefinger. (You can also pan the document by dragging with two fingers, or zoom by pinching two fingers.)

6. Press Esc.

➤ You can also change the size and orientation of an artboard in the Artboard Options dialog (see page 12).

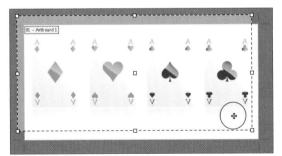

A *To move an artboard while keeping its contents stationary, deactivate the Move/Copy Artwork with Artboard button on the Control panel; then, with the Artboard tool, drag the artboard.*

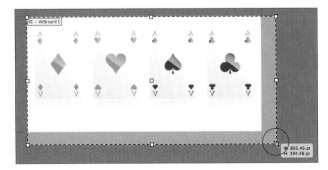

B *To scale an artboard manually, drag one of its handles with the Artboard tool.*

Aligning and rearranging artboards

If you prefer not to align your artboards manually, you can use the Rearrange Artboards dialog to quickly arrange them in neat rows or columns. If you change the order of the artboard listings on the Artboards panel before opening the dialog, the artboards will be rearranged automatically based on that new sequence.

To rearrange or realign multiple artboards:

1. *Optional:* To control the order in which the dialog will arrange the artboards, change the order of any artboard listing on the Artboards panel by dragging it upward or downward (or by clicking a listing, then clicking the Move Up ⬆ or Move Down ⬇ button on the panel).

2. From the Artboards panel menu, choose **Rearrange Artboards**.

3. In the dialog, **A–B** click a **Layout** icon: Grid by Row, Grid by Column, Arrange by Row, or Arrange by Column.

   If desired (and depending on which options are available), change the number of **Rows** or **Columns**, or change the **Spacing** value for the distance between the rows and columns.

   Check **Move Artwork with Artboard** to have your artwork stick with the artboards as they're moved (unless for some reason you want the artboards to move and the art to remain stationary).

4. Click OK. **C** All the artboards will display in the document window in their new configuration (and also in a new order, if you followed step 1).

➤ To cycle among multiple artboards when the Artboard tool is selected, hold down Option/Alt and press an arrow key on your keyboard. To fit an artboard in the document window, see page 28.

A *The original document contains four artboards in a row.*

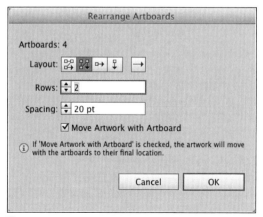

B *You can use the Rearrange Artboards dialog to realign the artboards in your document, or to rearrange them based on the current order of listings on the Artboards panel. We clicked the second Layout button and chose a Rows value of 2.*

C *Now the artboards are arranged in two columns and two rows.*

Choosing artboard options

Note: The options provided in the Artboard Options dialog are also available on the Control panel when the Artboard tool is selected.

To choose artboard options:

1. To open the Artboard Options dialog,**A** do either of the following:

   On the Artboards panel, double-click the orientation icon for an artboard listing.

   Choose the **Artboard** tool, click an artboard in the document, then click the **Artboard Options** button on the Control panel.

2. For the currently selected artboard, you can change the artboard Name, choose a Preset size or enter new Width and/or Height values (check Constrain Proportions if you want to preserve the current aspect ratio), change the artboard Orientation, or change its x/y location.

3. For video output, check which guides you want to Display: **Show Center Mark** displays crosshairs in the center of the artboard; **Show Cross Hairs** displays a line at each of the four midpoints of the artboard; and **Show Video Safe Areas** displays guides that mark the viewable area of the artboard. (See also the sidebar on this page.)

4. Check **Fade Region Outside Artboard** to have the area outside all the artboards display as dark gray (not white) when the Artboard tool is selected. Check **Update While Dragging** to have the artboard area display as a medium gray while an artboard is being dragged.

5. Click OK. If the Artboard tool is selected, press Esc.

➤ *Beware!* The Delete button in the Artboard Options dialog deletes the currently selected artboard, not the current values in the dialog.

A Use the Artboard Options dialog to scale, and choose display options for, the current artboard.

Artboard Options

Name: Four Cards

Preset: Custom

Width: 845.96 pt   X: 446.47 pt

Height: 446.98 pt   Y: 767.45 pt

Orientation:

☐ Constrain proportions   ⓘ Current proportions: 1.89

Display

☐ Show Center Mark

☐ Show Cross Hairs

☐ Show Video Safe Areas

Video Ruler Pixel Aspect Ratio: 1

Global

☑ Fade region outside Artboard

☑ Update while dragging

ⓘ Artboards: 2

ⓘ To create a new artboard within an artboard, press Shift. Option+Drag to duplicate artboard.

Delete   Cancel   OK

ENABLING GUIDE MARKS VIA THE CONTROL PANEL

When the Artboard tool is selected, you can quickly turn guide (Display) marks on or off for the currently selected artboard via buttons on the Control panel.

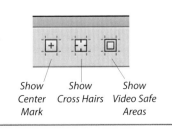

Show Center Mark   Show Cross Hairs   Show Video Safe Areas

Saving a document in the Adobe Illustrator (.ai) format

An Illustrator file can be saved in these six formats: Adobe Illustrator (.ai), Illustrator EPS (.eps), Illustrator Template (.ait), Adobe PDF (.pdf), SVG Compressed (.svgz), or SVG (.svg). Files in these formats can be reopened and edited in Illustrator.

You should keep your file in the Adobe Illustrator (.ai) format if you're going to print it directly from Illustrator or if you're going to import it into a program that reads this format, such as InDesign. If you're going to display the file online or export it to an application that doesn't read Illustrator (.ai) files, you will need to save a copy of it in a different format, such as Adobe PDF (see Chapter 31).

To save a file in the Adobe Illustrator (.ai) format:

1. If the file has never been saved, choose File > Save (Cmd-S/Ctrl-S). If the file has already been saved, choose File > Save As. In either case, the Save As dialog opens.

2. Enter a name in the Save As/File Name field.

3. Navigate to the desired drive and folder.

4. From the Format/Save as Type menu, choose **Adobe Illustrator (ai)/Adobe Illustrator (*AI)**.

5. Click Save. The Illustrator Options dialog opens.**A** Keep Illustrator CC as the choice on the Version menu. (For legacy formats, see the sidebar on the next page.)

6. Under **Options**, check any or all of the following:

    Create PDF Compatible File to save a PDF representation along with the file, to enable the file to be read by other applications that support the PDF format (e.g., Photoshop, InDesign), to enable Bridge to preview individual artboards, and to activate the Fonts option in this dialog. We recommend checking this option, despite the fact that it increases the file size.

    Include Linked Files (if available) to save a copy of any linked files with the document (see Chapter 22).

    If you chose a profile in the Edit > Assign Profile dialog, check **Embed ICC Profiles** to embed those profiles in the file, for better color management.

    Use Compression to compress vector data (and PDF data, if included) to help reduce the file size. With this option checked, the Save command may process more slowly.

Save Each Artboard to a Separate File, then click All or enter a Range. With this option off, multiple artboards will be saved in one file.

7. If you checked Create PDF Compatible File, under Fonts, enter a percentage in the **Subset Fonts When Percent of Characters Used Is Less Than** field to specify what percentage of the fonts used in the artwork will be embedded in the document. If not all the characters in a particular font are being used, you can have Illustrator embed just a subset of the font characters, as opposed to the whole font, to help reduce the file size. For example, at a setting of 50%, the entire font will be embedded only if more than 50% of its characters are used in the file, or just a subset of fonts if fewer than 50% of the font characters are used in the file. Characters in embedded fonts will display and print on any system, even those in which they aren't installed. Note that the higher the Subset Fonts percentage, the more characters will be embedded, increasing the file size. At a setting of 100%, all the characters in a font are embedded.

8. Click OK. The file with the new name remains open onscreen; the file with the original name closes but is preserved on disk.

A When saving a file in the Illustrator (.ai) format, choose settings in the Illustrator Options dialog.

The prior version of your document is overwritten each time you use the Save command. Do yourself a favor and save often — don't be shy about it! And be sure to create backups of your work frequently, too.

To resave a file:

Choose File > **Save** (Cmd-S/Ctrl-S).

When you use the Save a Copy command, the original version of the file stays open onscreen and a copy of it is saved to disk (the opposite of the Save As command).

To save a copy of a file:

1. Choose File > **Save a Copy** (Cmd-Option-S/ Ctrl-Alt-S). The Save a Copy dialog opens.

2. To save the file in the Illustrator (.ai) format, follow steps 2–8 on the preceding page. Or for other formats, see Chapter 31.

To revert to the last saved version of a file:

1. Choose File > **Revert**.

2. When the alert dialog appears, click Revert.

Ending a work session

To close a document:

1. To close a tabbed document, click the ✖ on the window tab or press Cmd-W/Ctrl-W.

    To close a floating document in the Mac OS, click the close (red) button in the upper left corner of the document window.

    To close a floating document in Windows, click the close box in the upper right corner of the document window.

2. If the file contains unsaved changes, an alert dialog will appear.**A** Click Don't Save to close the file without saving your edits, or click Save to resave the file before closing it (or click Cancel).

➤ To learn the difference between tabbed and floating windows, see page 25.

To quit/exit Illustrator:

1. In the Mac OS, choose Illustrator > **Quit Illustrator** (Cmd-Q).

    In Windows, choose File > **Exit** (Ctrl-Q) or click the close box for the application window.

2. All open Illustrator files will close. If any of the open files contain unsaved changes, an alert will appear. To resave the file(s), click Save, or to quit/exit Illustrator without saving your edits, click Don't Save.

A *If you try to close a file that contains unsaved changes, this alert will appear.*

SHORTCUTS FOR THE SAVE DIALOGS

	Mac OS	Windows
Save the edits in a previously saved file (no dialog opens), or open the Save As dialog for an unsaved file	Cmd-S	Ctrl-S
Open the Save As dialog	Cmd-Shift-S	Ctrl-Shift-S
Open the Save a Copy dialog	Cmd-Option-S	Ctrl-Alt-S

CLOSING OPEN FILES QUICKLY

Close all tabbed windows	Right-click a window tab and choose Close All from the context menu
Close all floating windows (Mac OS only)	Option-click the close button on one of the document windows
Close all tabbed and floating windows	Press Cmd-Option-W/ Ctrl-Alt-W

SAVING FILES IN EARLIER VERSIONS

To save a CC 2014 file in a previous Illustrator format, in the Illustrator Options dialog, choose the desired format from the Version menu (see step 5 on the preceding page). Note that saving to a previous version can cause unexpected text reflows. Avoid saving a file in a pre-CS version of Illustrator, as those versions can't save such document features as multiple artboards, live effects, Live Paint groups, and transparency.

   If you save a document that contains multiple artboards to an earlier version of Illustrator (such as CS3) and check Save Each Artboard as a Separate File in the Illustrator Options dialog, the result will be a separate file for each artboard, along with a master file in which each artboard has been converted to a guide.

Choosing the proper color settings for Illustrator is a crucial step before creating artwork. In this chapter, you'll learn how to use color settings to manage and maintain color consistency among documents and output devices, synchronize the color settings of all your Adobe Creative Cloud programs, change document color profiles, and finally, soft-proof your artwork onscreen for the chosen output device.

Introduction to color management

Problems with color can creep up on you when the various hardware devices and software packages you use treat color differently. If you were to open an Illustrator graphic in several different imaging programs or Web browsers, the colors might look completely different in each case, and might not look the same as they did onscreen in Illustrator. Print the graphic, and the results could be different yet again. In some cases, you might find such discrepancies to be slight and unobjectionable, but in other cases, they could wreak havoc with your design and turn your project into a disaster.

A color management system can solve most of these problems by acting as a color interpreter. Such a system knows how each device and program understands color and, by using color profiles (mathematical descriptions of the color space of each device), makes the proper adjustments so the colors in your files look the same as you move them from one program or device to another. Illustrator, Photoshop, and other programs in the Adobe Creative Cloud use the standardized ICC (International Color Consortium) profiles to tell your color management system how specific devices use color. Whether you're planning a traditional print run or will be using the same artwork for multiple purposes (such as for Web and print), your work will benefit from color management.

In Illustrator, you'll find most of the color management controls in the Edit > Color Settings dialog. It gives you access to preset management settings for various publishing situations, including press and Web output, and also lets you choose custom settings. There are two main areas in the basic dialog:

➤ The **Working Spaces** options govern how RGB and CMYK colors are displayed in your document and serve as the default color profiles for new Illustrator documents.

➤ The **Color Management Policies** options for RGB and CMYK color files govern how Illustrator manages color when you open a document that doesn't have

Continued on the following page

MANAGE COLOR

2

an attached color profile, or if the document's profile doesn't match the current color settings in Illustrator.

Choosing the correct color settings will help keep your document colors consistent from the onscreen version to final output. The options in the Color Settings dialog may appear complex at first, but you and your documents will benefit if you take the time to learn about them.

Note: For commercial print output, ask your print shop to recommend specific color management settings to ensure a smooth color management workflow.

Calibrating your display

In an LCD (liquid crystal, or flat panel) display, a grid of fixed-size liquid crystals filters color from a light source in the back. Although the color profile that is provided with a typical LCD display (and that is installed in your system automatically) describes the display characteristics accurately, over time — a period of weeks or months — the colors you view onscreen will gradually become less accurate and will need adjustment.

The first step toward achieving color consistency is to calibrate your display. Although you can adjust the brightness setting on an LCD monitor, it's best to leave that setting alone and give your display a periodic tune-up using an external calibration device instead. This device, or calibrator, will produce a profile containing the proper settings (white point, black point, and gamma) for your particular display. The Adobe color management system, in turn, will interpret the colors in your Illustrator document and display them more accurately based on that profile.

Calibrators range widely in cost, from a $100-to-$300 colorimeter to a much more expensive (but more precise) high-end professional gadget, such as a spectrophotometer. Even with a basic colorimeter and its simple step-by-step wizard, you will be able to calibrate your display more precisely than by using subjective "eyeball" judgments.

Among moderately priced calibrators, some currently popular and reliable models include Spyder4Pro and Spyder4ELITE by Datacolor and i1Display Pro by X-Rite.

➤ On our blog, at www.elaineandpeter.com, we show you how to use a Spyder device.

Note: Don't be tempted to use the calibration utility that's built into your computer system — it's not going to give you accurate results. If you want to achieve good output from Illustrator, you owe it to yourself to invest in a hardware calibrator. Even the least expensive external device is superior to the internal controls.

WHAT ARE COLOR SPACES AND PROFILES?

➤ Each device, such as a camera or computer display, is able to capture and reproduce a particular range (or gamut) of color, known as its color space.

➤ The mathematical description of the color space of each device is called the color profile. The color management system uses the color profile to define the colors in a document.

➤ Illustrator uses the document profile to display and edit artwork colors, or if the document doesn't have a profile, Illustrator uses the current working space profile (the profile you will choose in the Color Settings dialog) instead.

CALIBRATE YOUR DISPLAY, AND KEEP IT CALIBRATED!

➤ Computer displays become uncalibrated gradually, and you may not notice the change until the colors are way off. To maintain the color consistency of your display, stick to a regular monthly calibration schedule. (Our calibration software reminds us to recalibrate via a monthly onscreen alert. If yours offers this option, you should take advantage of it.)

➤ Also, be sure to recalibrate your display if you adjust its brightness and contrast settings (intentionally or not), change the temperature or amount of lighting in your office — or repaint your office walls!

Choosing color settings for Illustrator

To choose color settings for Illustrator:

1. Choose Edit > **Color Settings** (Cmd-Shift-K/ Ctrl-Shift-K). The Color Settings dialog opens (**A**, page 19).

2. Choose a preset from the **Settings** menu. Briefly, the five basic presets are as follows:

   Monitor Color sets the RGB working space to your display profile. This is a good choice for video output, but not for print output.

   North America General Purpose 2 meets the requirements for screen and print output in the United States and Canada. All profile warnings are off.

   North America Newspaper manages color for output on newsprint paper stock.

   North America Prepress 2 manages color to conform with common press conditions in the United States and Canada. This is the recommended preset for commercial print output. The default RGB color space that is assigned to this setting is Adobe RGB (1998). When CMYK documents are opened, their color values are preserved.

   North America Web/Internet is designed for online output. All RGB images are converted to the sRGB IEC61966-2.1 color space.

3. At this point you can click OK to accept the predefined settings or you can proceed with the remaining steps to choose custom settings.

4. The **Working Spaces** menus govern how RGB and CMYK colors will be treated in documents that lack an embedded profile. You can either leave these settings as they are or choose custom options. The RGB options that we recommend using are discussed below (see also the third tip after step 7 on the following page). For the CMYK setting, you should ask your output service provider which working space to choose.

   Adobe RGB (1998) encompasses a wide range of colors and is useful when converting RGB images to CMYK images. This working space is recommended for inkjet and commercial printing, but not for online output.

   ProPhoto RGB contains a very wide range of colors and is suitable for output to high-end dye sublimation and inkjet printers.

   sRGB IEC61966-2.1 is a good choice for Web output, as it reflects the settings for an average computer display. Many hardware and software manufacturers use it as the default space for scanners, low-end printers, and software.

5. From the RGB and CMYK menus in the Color Management Policies area, choose a color management policy for Illustrator to use when the profile in a document doesn't match the current color settings you have chosen for Illustrator:

   Off to prevent files from being color-managed when imported or opened.

   Preserve Embedded Profiles if you will be working with both color-managed and non-color-managed documents and you want each document to keep its own profile.

   Convert to Working Space if you want all your documents to be converted to the current color working space. This is usually the best choice for Web output.

   Choose **Preserve Numbers (Ignore Linked Profiles)** to have Illustrator preserve embedded profiles (and the numeric values of colors used in the file) for CMYK documents but ignore profiles for linked CMYK imagery.

   For **Profile Mismatches**, check **Ask When Opening** to have an alert appear if the color profile in a file you're opening doesn't match the working space for Illustrator. If you choose this option, you can override the current color management policy via an alert dialog upon opening a document.

   Check **Ask When Pasting** to have Illustrator display an alert when a color profile mismatch crops up as you paste or drag and drop a color image into your document. If you choose this option, you can override the current color management policy via an alert dialog when pasting.

Continued on the following page

For files that have **Missing Profiles**, check **Ask When Opening** to have Illustrator display an alert offering you the opportunity to assign the current working spaces profile or a custom profile to files as you open them.

6. *Optional:* If you've chosen custom color settings that you want to save for later use, click Save. To have your custom settings file appear on the Settings menu, save it in the default location.

7. Click OK.

➤ To learn about the various alert dialogs that may appear onscreen as you open a file, see page 63.

➤ To reuse your saved settings, choose the file name from the Settings menu in the Color Settings dialog. To load a settings file that wasn't saved in the Settings folder (the default location) and therefore isn't listed on the Settings menu, click Load, locate the desired file, then click Open.

➤ We recommend that you avoid the Working Spaces settings of Apple RGB and ColorMatch RGB, which were designed for displays that are no longer standard. Also avoid the Monitor RGB [current display profile] and ColorSync RGB profiles, both of which rely on the viewer's display and system settings, a situation that can undermine color consistency.

DESIGNING FOR THE COLOR-BLIND

At some point in your career, you may be hired to design graphics, such as signage, that are fully accessible to color-blind viewers. In fact, some countries require signage in public spaces to comply with the Color Universal Design (CUD) guidelines. The View > Proof Setup > Color Blindness – Protanopia-Type and Color Blindness – Deuteranopia-Type commands in Illustrator simulate how your document will look to viewers who have common forms of color blindness.

In case you're not familiar with those two terms, for a protanope, the brightness of red, orange, and yellow is dimmed, making it hard for such a person to distinguish red from black or dark gray. Protanopes also have trouble distinguishing violet, lavender, and purple from blue because the reddish components of those colors look dimmed. Deuteranopes are unable to distinguish between colors in the green-yellow-red part of the spectrum and experience color blindness similar to that of protanopes, without the problem of dimming.

Adobe Illustrator Help offers these tips for creating accessible signage:

➤ Give the objects a wide stroke in black, white, or a dark color.

➤ Apply patterns.

➤ Use orange-red instead of pure red.

➤ Use bluish green instead of yellowish green.

➤ Avoid gray.

➤ Avoid the color combinations of red and green, yellow and bright green, light blue and pink, and dark blue and violet.

Color Settings

Synchronized: Your Creative Cloud applications are synchronized using the same color settings for consistent color management.

Settings: North America Prepress 2 ▾   Load...   Save...

Working Spaces

RGB: Adobe RGB (1998) ▾

CMYK: U.S. Web Coated (SWOP) v2 ▾

The Working Spaces options govern the display of RGB and CMYK colors and serve as the default color profiles for new documents.

Color Management Policies

RGB: Preserve Embedded Profiles ▾

CMYK: Preserve Numbers (Ignore Linked Profiles) ▾

Profile Mismatches: ☑ Ask When Opening   ☑ Ask When Pasting

Missing Profiles: ☑ Ask When Opening

The Color Management Policies govern how colors are treated when you open a file that lacks a color profile or when a file's profile conflicts with the currently chosen color settings.

Description:

Provides a fairly large gamut (range) of RGB colors and is well-suited for documents that will be converted to C Use this space if you need to do print production work with a broad range of colors.

Rest the pointer over a menu or option, and read information about it here in the Description area.

More Options   Cancel   OK

A *When you choose a preset from the Settings menu in the Color Settings dialog, the other options are chosen for you automatically. You can customize any preset by choosing settings.*

Synchronizing the color settings

If the color settings differ among the Adobe Creative Cloud programs that you have installed on your system (such as between Illustrator and Photoshop or InDesign), the words "Not Synchronized" will display at the top of the Edit > Color Settings dialog in Illustrator.**A** If you have a Creative Cloud subscription or have installed multiple Adobe programs (including Adobe Bridge), you can use the Color Settings dialog in Bridge to synchronize the color settings of all the color-managed Adobe programs in your system.

Note: Before using Bridge to synchronize the color setting among your Adobe programs, make sure you've chosen the proper settings in Illustrator (see pages 17–19).

To synchronize the color settings among your Adobe Creative Cloud applications:

1. On the Application bar in Illustrator, click the **Go to Bridge** button. [Br]

2. In Bridge, choose Edit > **Color Settings** (Cmd-Shift-K/ Ctrl-Shift-K). The Color Settings dialog opens,**B** showing the same list of settings as found in the Color Settings dialog when Advanced Mode is unchecked.

3. Click the settings preset you chose in Illustrator, then click Apply. Bridge will change (synchronize) the color settings of the other Adobe Creative Cloud applications to match the selected preset.

A This alert in the Color Settings dialog informs us that the color settings in our Creative Cloud applications aren't synchronized with one another.

B Use the Color Settings dialog to synchronize the color settings of all the Adobe Creative Cloud applications that are installed in your system.

Changing the document profile

When a file's profile doesn't match the current working space or the file is missing a color profile altogether, you can use the Assign Profile command to assign the correct one. You may notice visible color shifts if the color data of your file is reinterpreted to match the new profile, but rest assured, the color data in the actual document is preserved.

To change or delete a document's color profile:

1. With a file open in Illustrator, choose Edit > **Assign Profile**. The Assign Profile dialog opens.**A**

2. Do one of the following:

   To remove the color profile from the document, click **Don't Color Manage This Document**. The current working space will now control the appearance of colors in the artwork.

   If your document doesn't have an assigned profile or if its profile is different from the current working space, click **Working** [document color mode and the name of the current working space] to assign that profile.

   To assign a different profile to your document, click **Profile**, then choose the desired profile from the menu. This won't change or convert any color data in your artwork.

3. Click OK.

➤ The profile chosen in the Assign Profile dialog is also listed as the Document Profile in the Color Management panel of the File > Print dialog.

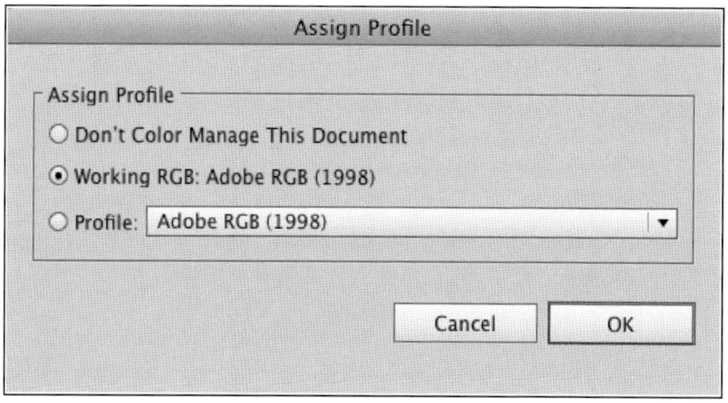

EMBEDDING A COLOR PROFILE WHEN SAVING A FILE

When you use the File > Save As command to save a file in the Adobe Illustrator (.ai) format, the Illustrator Options dialog opens. In that dialog, you can check Embed ICC Profiles to embed a profile into the document, if one has been assigned.

A Use the Assign Profile dialog to either delete a file's color profile or assign a new one.

Proofing a document onscreen

Another step in color management is to get an idea of how your artwork is going to look in print or online. You can do this by viewing a soft proof of your document onscreen. Although this method is less accurate than viewing a press proof or viewing the file in a browser, it can give you a general idea of how your artwork would look if it were printed using CMYK inks or displayed online on a Windows or Macintosh display.

To proof colors onscreen for commercial printing or online output:

1. From the View > **Proof Setup** submenu, choose a type of output display to be simulated:

   Working CMYK [current working space] to simulate colors for the commercial press that is currently chosen on the CMYK menu under Working Spaces in the Edit > Color Settings dialog in Illustrator.

   For an RGB document, choose **Legacy Macintosh RGB (Gamma 1.8)** to simulate colors for online output using the legacy Mac gamma (1.8) or **Internet Standard RGB (sRGB)** to simulate colors using Windows gamma (2.2) as the proofing space.

   For an RGB document, choose **Monitor RGB** to simulate colors using the custom display profile for your monitor.

   For the **Color Blindness** options, see the sidebar on page 18.

   To create a proofing model for a specific output device, choose **Customize**. The Proof Setup dialog opens.**A** Check Preview. From the **Device to Simulate** menu, choose the color profile for your target output device, then uncheck **Preserve CMYK (or RGB) Numbers**. With this option off, Illustrator colors will appear as though converted, and you'll need to choose a **Rendering Intent** (see the sidebar). The Display Options (On-Screen) are available for some profiles. **Simulate Paper Color** simulates the soft white of actual paper, based on the current proof profile, and **Simulate Black Ink** simulates the dark gray that many printers produce when printing black. Click OK.

2. The View > Proof Colors command will be checked automatically, enabling you to see the soft proof onscreen. The name of the device being simulated will be listed in the document tab. Uncheck the command when you're done.

A *Use the Proof Setup dialog to choose custom options for soft-proofing your Illustrator files.*

THE RENDERING INTENTS

► **Perceptual** changes colors in a way that seems natural to the human eye, while attempting to preserve the appearance of the overall document. This is a good choice for documents that contain continuous-tone images.

► **Saturation** changes colors with the intent of preserving vivid colors, but in doing so may compromise color fidelity. Nevertheless, it's a good choice for charts and business graphics, which normally contain fewer colors than continuous-tone images.

► **Absolute Colorimetric** maintains the color accuracy only of colors that fall within the destination color gamut (i.e., the color range of your printer), but in doing so sacrifices the accuracy of colors that are outside that gamut.

► **Relative Colorimetric** is the default intent for all the Adobe presets in the Color Settings dialog. It compares the white, or highlight, of your document's color space to the white of the destination color space (the white of the paper, in the case of print output) and shifts colors where needed. This is the best Rendering Intent option for documents in which most of the colors fall within the color range of the destination gamut, because it preserves most of the original colors.

In this chapter, you will become acquainted with basic features of the Illustrator interface, such as the Application bar, document tabs, and panels. You will learn how to arrange document windows, change the document zoom level, bring a different part of a document into view, fit an artboard in the document window, change the screen display mode and document views, save and choose custom view settings, reconfigure the panel groups and docks, and save and manage your custom workspaces. By the end of the chapter, you will know how to configure your workspace to suit your usual workflow — and even better, you will have the skills to create custom workspaces for various kinds of tasks.

The Hello screen ★

When you launch Illustrator CC for the first time, you'll notice a new screen that is reminiscent of the old Welcome screen you might be used to: the Hello Screen.

The Hello screen is designed to help you discover, learn, and use Illustrator features. The screen is divided into four tabbed categories: Create, New Features, Getting Started, and Tips & Techniques. The Create tab provides an easy way to create a variety of different types of documents as well as quick access to recently opened documents. The remaining tabs provide access to videos that teach you how to use Illustrator features to their fullest. The content displayed is relevant to your subscription and use of Illustrator and will update accordingly.

Features of the Illustrator workspace

In Windows — and when displayed in the Mac OS — an Application frame houses the Application bar, tabbed document windows, the Control panel, and all the other panels. For Mac OS users, we recommend keeping the frame visible (see the next page). Note: We also refer to the application window in Windows as the "Application frame." The Application frame cannot be hidden in Windows.

Although you have the option to float individual document windows onscreen or dock them as multiple tabs within a floating window, we recommend docking them as tabs within the Application frame instead. First, the Application frame conveniently blocks out any Desktop clutter, and second, your documents will fit neatly inside the frame without blocking or being obscured by any of the Illustrator features (such as the panels).

WORKSPACES 3

To show the Application frame in the Mac OS:

To show the Application frame if it's hidden, choose Window > **Application Frame. A**

➤ You can resize the Application frame by dragging an edge or a corner.

➤ To minimize the Application frame in Windows, click the Minimize button; or to do this in the Mac OS, click the yellow Minimize button.

CHANGING THE SHADES OF THE ILLUSTRATOR INTERFACE

You will notice that some of the screen captures in this chapter show a dark interface and some show a light interface. To change the interface colors in Illustrator, see page 418.

A In the Mac OS, we strongly recommend that you work with the Application frame showing.

To use the Application bar:

Use the button and menus on the Application bar to manage your workspace.**B** In Windows, the main Illustrator menus also display on the Application bar.

To search Adobe and Community Help for information, enter a keyword or phrase in the Search for Help field, then press Return/Enter.

Go to Adobe Bridge   Arrange Documents menu for arranging multiple documents onscreen   The current workspace   Menu for accessing, saving, and managing workspaces

B These controls are available on the Application bar in the Mac OS.

Using tabbed document windows

We recommend that you always dock your open document windows into the Application frame as tabs. You can display any document easily by clicking its tab.

To set a preference so all documents you subsequently open will dock as tabs:

Go to Illustrator/Edit > Preferences > User Interface, check **Open Documents as Tabs**, then click OK.

If you inadvertently float a document window (by dragging the tab away from the Application bar and Control panel), you can easily redock it as a tab.

To dock floating windows into the Application frame:

To dock one floating document window as a tab, drag its title bar to the tab area (just below the Control panel) of the Application frame, and release the mouse when the blue drop zone bar appears.**A–B**

To dock all currently floating document windows as tabs, on the Arrange Documents menu ▼ on the Application bar, click the **Consolidate All** (first) icon.■ If one or more documents are already docked as tabs and other windows are floating, another option is to right-click a tab and choose **Consolidate All to Here** from the context menu.**C**

➤ To cycle among the currently open documents, press Cmd-~ (tilde)/Ctrl-Tab.

➤ To fit an artboard in the document window, see page 28.

➤ You can dock one floating document window into another by dragging the title bar of one document below the title bar of the other document. (Frankly, we prefer, and recommend, docking documents as tabs in the Application frame.)

A *To dock a floating document window as a tab, drag its title bar to the tab area of the Application frame, and release the mouse when the blue drop zone bar appears.*

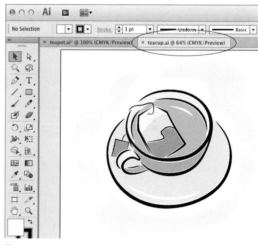

B *The tab appears at the top of the document window.*

C *To dock all floating documents into the Application frame, right-click a document tab and choose Consolidate All to Here.*

Arranging document windows

By using icons on the Arrange Documents menu on the Application bar, you can quickly tile multiple documents in various layouts, such as two documents arranged side by side or vertically, or four or six documents in a grid formation.

To display multiple tabbed document windows:

On the Application bar, click the **Arrange Documents** menu icon 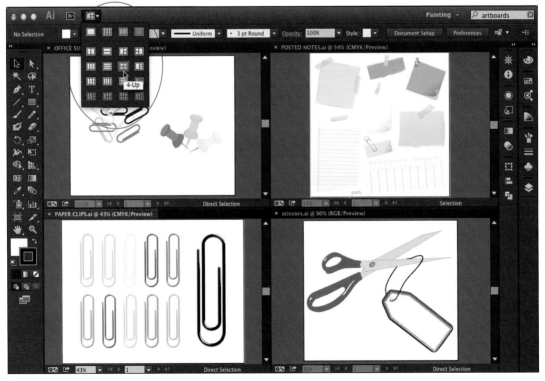 to open the menu, then click one of the available icons (the availability of icons depends on the number of open documents).**A**

Note: You can choose a different zoom level for each open document window, even when multiple documents are displayed (see the next page).

▶ If any open documents are floating when you click an option on the Arrange Documents menu, they will be docked as tabbed windows automatically.

Just as easily, you can go back to displaying just one document at a time.

To redisplay one tabbed document window:

Do either of the following:

Right-click a document tab and choose **Consolidate All to Here** from the context menu.

On the Arrange Documents menu on the Application bar, click the **Consolidate All** (first) icon.

A *Choose a tiling option from the Arrange Documents menu.*

Changing the zoom level

When changing the zoom level for your document, you can zoom out to display multiple artboards, fit one artboard in the document window, or zoom in to magnify a detail of your artwork. The current zoom level is listed as a percentage between 3.13% and 6400% on the document tab and in the lower left corner of the document window. (The zoom level has no bearing on the output size.)

There are many ways to change the zoom level in Illustrator. The most efficient way is via one of the keyboard shortcuts. You can use them while performing other tasks — regardless of which tool is currently selected.

A *You can choose a preset percentage from the zoom menu in the lower left corner of the document window.*

To change the zoom level:

Do any of the following:

Use any of the shortcuts that are listed in the sidebar at right.

Choose a preset percentage from the zoom menu in the lower left corner of the document window.**A** Or choose Fit on Screen from that menu to fit the entire active artboard within the current document window size.

Make sure no objects are selected, then right-click in the document and choose Zoom In or Zoom Out.

Double-click the zoom field in the lower left corner of the document window, type the desired zoom level, then press Return/Enter.

Display the Navigator panel. ✳ Click the Zoom Out or Zoom In button, or move the Zoom slider, or Cmd-drag/Ctrl-drag across a section of the preview to magnify that area of the document.

On a touchscreen device or touchpad, pinch inward with two fingers or spread two fingers outward.

➤ To move a different part of your magnified artwork into view, see the next page.

➤ You can change the zoom level while the screen is redrawing.

SHORTCUTS FOR ZOOMING IN AND OUT

	Mac OS	Windows
Fit current artboard in the window	Cmd-0 (zero)	Ctrl-0 (zero)
Fit all artboards in the window	Cmd-Option-0 (zero)	Ctrl-Alt-0 (zero)
Actual size	Cmd-1	Ctrl-1
Zoom in	Cmd- + (plus) or Cmd-Spacebar click or drag	Ctrl- + (plus) or Ctrl-Spacebar click or drag
Zoom out	Cmd- – (minus) or Cmd-Option-Spacebar click	Ctrl- – (minus) or Ctrl-Alt-Spacebar click

USING THE ZOOM TOOL

We think the Zoom tool 🔍 (Z) is less convenient to use than the other methods described on this page, but if you want to use it, select it, then do any of the following:

➤ In the document window, click in the center of, or drag a marquee across, the area to be magnified. The smaller the marquee, the higher the zoom level.

➤ Option-click/Alt-click in the document window to reduce the zoom level.

➤ Drag a marquee and then, without releasing the mouse, press and hold down the Spacebar, move the marquee over the area to be magnified, then release the mouse.

Moving an area of a document into view

To move a different area of a document into view:

Do one of the following:

Choose the **Hand** tool 🖑 (H) or hold down the Spacebar to turn the current tool into a temporary Hand tool, and drag the document to the desired position.

Display the Navigator panel, ✳ then drag the Proxy Preview area (red outlined box) on the panel.

On a touchscreen device or touchpad, drag with two fingers. Or to navigate between artboards, swipe with three fingers.

➤ If your cursor is inserted in a type object, pressing the Spacebar will add spaces to the text. If you're using a type tool and you want to move the document in the window without switching tools, see the sidebar on page 253.

Fitting an artboard in the document window

There are two ways to fit an artboard to the bounds of the document window. (To learn more about artboards, see pages 7–12.)

To fit an artboard within the document window:

Do either of the following:

On the Artboards panel, 🗗 double-click an artboard listing (next to the name).**A–B** Or if the chosen artboard is already displaying, click the listing just once.

Using the artboard navigation controls at the bottom of the document window, do either of the following: From the **Artboard Navigation** menu, choose an artboard number,**C** or click the First, Previous, Next, or Last arrow.

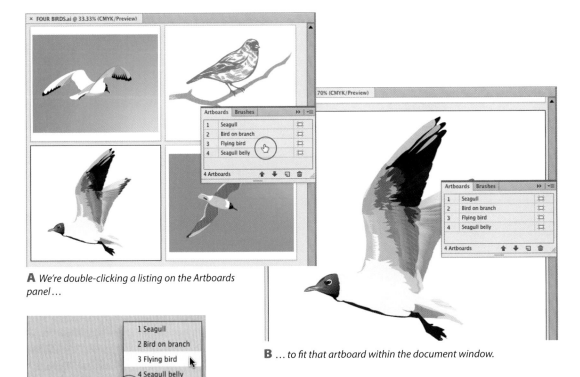

A *We're double-clicking a listing on the Artboards panel…*

B *… to fit that artboard within the document window.*

C *We're choosing an artboard number from the Artboard Navigation menu.*

Changing the screen mode

The three screen modes control the display of various features of the Illustrator interface.

To choose a screen mode for Illustrator:

Press (and keep pressing) F to cycle through the three screen modes, or from the **Screen Mode** menu at the bottom of the Tools panel, **A** choose one of the following:

Normal Screen Mode B (the default mode) to display the Application frame (if that option is on), menu bar, Application bar, document tabs, and panels, with the Desktop visible behind everything.

Full Screen Mode with Menu Bar C to display the document in a maximized window with the menu bar, Application bar, scroll bars, and panels visible, but not the document tabs.

Full Screen Mode to display the document in a maximized window with the zoom and artboard controls showing at the bottom of the screen but all the other Illustrator features (and the Dock/taskbar) hidden.

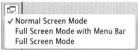

A *Choose from the Screen Mode menu at the bottom of the Tools panel.*

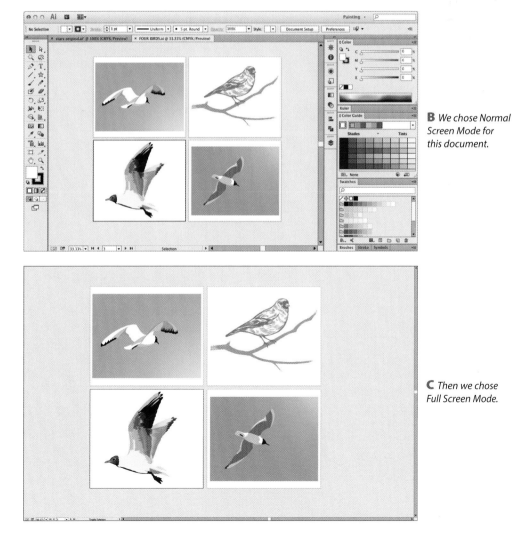

B *We chose Normal Screen Mode for this document.*

C *Then we chose Full Screen Mode.*

Switching document views

A document can be displayed and edited in four different views: Preview, Outline, Pixel Preview, and Overprint Preview. In all the views, the other View menu commands — Hide/Show Edges, Artboard, Print Tiling, Slices, Guides, and Grid — are accessible. (For Overprint Preview view, see page 432.)

To switch document views:

Do either of the following:

Press Cmd-Y/Ctrl-Y to toggle between **Preview** view **A** and **Outline** view **B** (View > Preview and View > Outline). In Preview view, all fill and stroke colors and all placed images are visible; in Outline view, objects display as wireframes without fill or stroke colors, and placed images display as an X in a white box. Another option is to deselect (click a blank area of the document), then right-click in the document and choose Outline or Preview from the context menu. The screen redraws more quickly in Outline view.

To activate a 72-ppi view so you can see what your vector graphics would look like if you were to rasterize them for display in a Web browser, choose View > **Pixel Preview C** (or press Cmd-Option-Y/ Ctrl-Alt-Y), and also choose View > Actual Size (Cmd-1/Ctrl-1). See also the sidebar below.

➤ Cmd-click/Ctrl-click the visibility icon 👁 for a layer (not an individual object) on the Layers panel 📚 to toggle Preview and Outline views for just that layer. See also the sidebar on page 193.

MORE ABOUT THE PIXEL GRID

➤ To view a representation of the pixel grid in Pixel Preview view, go to Illustrator/Edit > Preferences > Guides & Grid and check Show Pixel Grid (Above 600% Zoom), and choose a document zoom level of 600% or higher.

➤ To align objects to the pixel grid, see "Creating pixel-perfect artwork for the Web," on page 84.

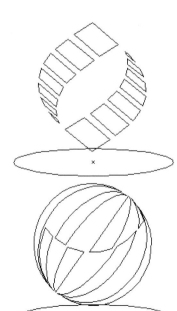

A *This artwork is displayed in Preview view.*

B *Here it's displayed in Outline view.*

C *And here it's displayed in Pixel Preview view.*

Creating custom views

You can save up to 25 custom views for the current document, and you can switch among them via the View menu. Each custom view can include a zoom level, the display of a specific artboard, and a choice of either Preview or Outline view.

To save a custom view:

1. Do all of the following:

   Choose a **zoom** level for your document.

   If the document contains multiple artboards, display the one for which you want to choose a view (see page 28).

   Choose **Preview**, **Outline** (Cmd-Y/Ctrl-Y), or **Pixel Preview** (Cmd-Option-Y/Ctrl-Alt-Y) view.

2. Choose View > **New View**. The New View dialog opens.**A**

3. In the Name field, type a descriptive name for the new view, for easy identification (as in "160% view, Preview, Artboard 4").

4. Click OK. The view is now listed on, and can be chosen from, the bottom of the View menu.

➤ Unfortunately, custom views can be created only for a specific document — not for the application. However, custom views can be saved as part of a document template (see page 5).

To rename or delete a custom view:

1. Choose View > **Edit Views**.

2. In the Edit Views dialog, click the view to be renamed or deleted.**B**

3. Do either of the following:

   Change the name in the **Name** field.

   Click **Delete** to delete the view.

4. Click OK. The View menu will update to reflect your edits.

➤ If you want to rename more than one view, you have to click OK and then reopen the dialog for each one individually. It's a simple little system.

A *Type a Name for a custom view in the New View dialog.*

B *In the Edit Views dialog, click a view name, then change the Name; or to delete a selected view, click Delete.*

Configuring the panel groups and docks

In Illustrator, the panels are as indispensable as the tools. You can easily minimize, collapse, or hide them so they don't intrude on your document space when you're not using them, and expand or display them when you need to access them.

In the predefined workspaces (see page 34), the panels are arranged in docks on the right side of your screen — except for the Tools panel, which is docked on the left side. The panels are stored in groups within the docks (**A**, next page). In this section, we'll show you how to open and close the panels, and reconfigure the panel groups and docks to suit your workflow. (For a description and illustration of the individual panels, see the next chapter.)

To show or hide the panels:

To show a panel: Choose the panel name from the Window menu. The panel will display either in its default group and dock or in its last open location (floating or in a dock). To bring a panel to the front of its group, click its tab (the panel name). Some panels can also be opened temporarily via a link on the Control panel or Appearance panel; see the sidebar on page 42.

Close a panel or group: To close (not collapse) a panel, right-click the panel tab or icon and choose Close from the context menu. To close a whole panel group, choose Close Tab Group from the same context menu.

Hide or show all the panels: Press Tab to hide or show all the open panels, including the Tools panel, or press Shift-Tab to hide or show all the panels except the Tools panel.

Make hidden, docked panels reappear: After you have hidden the panels via the Tab or Shift-Tab shortcut, move the pointer just inside the right edge of the Application frame. The panel docks (but not freestanding panels) will redisplay temporarily. Move the pointer away from the panels, and they'll disappear again. Note: If this isn't working, redisplay the panels, then right-click any panel icon or tab and choose Auto-Show Hidden Panels from the context menu.

➤ Every panel has a menu ▨ in the upper right corner, from which you can choose options specifically for that panel.

To reconfigure the panels:

Expand a panel that's collapsed to an icon: Click the icon or panel label. If Auto-Collapse Iconic Panels is checked in Illustrator/Edit > Preferences > User Interface and you open a panel from an icon, it will collapse back to the icon when you click elsewhere. With this preference unchecked, the panel will remain expanded; to collapse it back to an icon, click the Collapse to Icons button, ▨▨ or click the panel icon or label in the dock.

➤ To quickly access the Auto-Collapse Iconic Panels option from a context menu, right-click any panel tab, bar, or icon.

Maximize or minimize an expanded panel or group (vertically): Double-click the panel name or tab bar (next to the names). For some panels, such as Character, Color, Color Guide, and Stroke, you can display more or fewer options by clicking the expand/collapse arrow icon ▨ on the tab.

Collapse a whole dock to icons or to icons with labels: Click the Collapse to Icons button ▨▨ at the top of the dock (**B**, next page), or double-click the topmost bar. Repeat to expand it.

Change the width of an expanded dock; or expand icons to icons with labels, or vice versa: Position the mouse over the vertical left edge of the dock (◀▨ cursor), then drag horizontally (**C**, next page).

Move a panel to a different slot in the same group: Drag the panel tab to the left or right.

Move a panel into a different group: Drag the panel tab over the tab bar of the desired group, and release the mouse when the blue drop zone border appears (**D**, next page).

Change the location of a panel group in a dock: Drag the tab bar upward or downward, and release the mouse when the horizontal blue drop zone bar is in the desired location (**E**, next page).

Create a new dock: Drag a panel tab or tab bar sideways over the vertical left edge of a dock (**F**, next page), and release the mouse when the blue vertical drop zone bar appears.

Reconfigure a dock that's collapsed to icons: The methods are similar to those for an expanded group. Drag the gripper bar ▨▨▨▨ to the edge of a dock to

Instructions continue on page 34

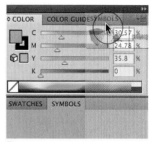

A *The panels in the left dock are collapsed to icons with labels (in three groups), whereas the ones in the right dock are expanded (in four groups). The Layers/Artboards group is minimized vertically.*

D *A blue drop zone border appears as we drag the Symbols panel to the title bar of the Color/Color Guide group.*

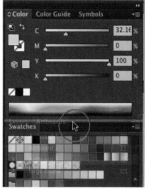

B *We clicked the Collapse to Icons button to collapse the whole right dock to icons. The panel groups were preserved.*

E *A blue horizontal drop zone bar appears as we move a panel group upward to a new slot in the same dock.*

C *We dragged the edge of the left dock to the right to shrink it to just icons (no labels).*

F *A blue vertical drop zone bar appears as we drag a panel out of a dock to create a new dock for it.*

create a new dock; or drag the bar upward or downward between groups to restack the group (look for a horizontal drop zone line); or drag it into another group to add to that group (look for a blue drop zone border).**A–B**

Float a docked panel or group: Drag the panel tab, icon, or bar out of the dock. To stack floating panels or groups, drag the tab bar of one so it meets the bottom of another, and release the mouse when a blue drop zone bar appears.

➤ To reset the panels to their default visibility states and locations, choose Essentials from the Workspace menu on the Application bar.

➤ To prevent a floating panel from docking as you move it around onscreen, hold down Cmd/Ctrl.

➤ If you inadvertently take the panel docks out of the Application frame, drag the top bar to the right edge of the Application frame, and release the mouse when a vertical blue drop zone line appears.

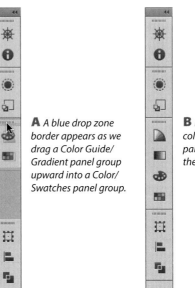

A *A blue drop zone border appears as we drag a Color Guide/ Gradient panel group upward into a Color/ Swatches panel group.*

B *Now the four color-related panels are in the same group.*

Choosing, saving, managing, and resetting workspaces

When you choose a predefined Illustrator workspace, the panels and panel groups that are most suited to a particular sphere of work appear onscreen. On the following page, you'll learn how to create and save custom workspaces for different purposes.

To choose a workspace:

From the **Workspace** menu on the Application bar, choose a workspace.**C** User-defined workspaces (if any) are listed at the top of the menu, followed by the eight preset workspaces.

➤ The arrangement of panels on a computer that is hooked up to dual displays is saved as a single workspace. You could put all the panels on one display, or put the ones you use most often on one display and those you use less often in the other.

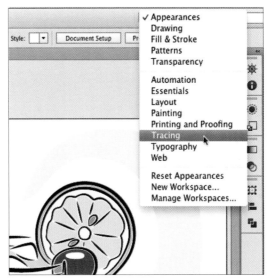

C *Choose a workspace from the Workspace menu on the Application bar. (User-saved workspaces are listed at the top of the menu.)*

If the predefined workspaces don't suit your needs exactly, you can hide, show, collapse, or expand any of the panels or docks. Even better, instead of tediously repeating those steps at the beginning of each work session, you can save custom workspaces for different kinds of work that you do in Illustrator. Saved workspaces are available on the Workspace menu (on the Application bar) for all documents.

To save a custom workspace:

1. Open a document, so settings will display in panels.

2. If you like, you can use any of the preset workspaces on the Workspace menu as a starting point. Configure the Illustrator workspace by doing any or all of the following:

   Position the panels that you normally use where you want them, including the Tools panel tearoff toolbars and any library panels (e.g., any of the PANTONE PLUS color books). Put them in the desired groups in one or more docks.

   Expand any of the panel docks, or collapse them to icons or icons with labels. For instance, you could expand the panels that you use frequently in one dock, and collapse the ones you use less frequently to icons in another dock.

   Resize any of the temporary panels, including any of those that open from the Control panel, such as the temporary Swatches panel. For the Swatches panel, you can choose a display option from the Show Swatch Kinds menu.

   For any panel, choose a View (e.g., a thumbnail or list view) from the panel menu.

   Open any tearoff toolbars for tool groups that you use frequently (such as for the type tools or for the Rectangle and its related tools).

3. From the Workspace menu on the Application bar, choose **New Workspace**.

4. In the New Workspace dialog, **A** enter a descriptive Name for the workspace.

5. Click OK. Your workspace (and any other user-saved workspaces) will be listed on, and can be chosen from, the Workspace menu on the Application bar.

➤ To edit an existing workspace, follow the steps above, except in step 4, enter the same name (an alert will appear in the dialog). **B**

➤ You can't save an artboard number, zoom level, or custom view as part of a workspace.

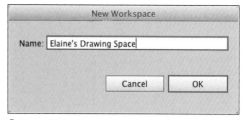

A *Type a Name for a new custom workspace in the New Workspace dialog.*

B *To replace an existing workspace, reenter the same name (an alert appears in the dialog).*

To rename, delete, or duplicate a saved workspace:

1. From the Workspace menu on the Application bar, choose **Manage Workspaces**.

2. In the Manage Workspaces dialog, **A** do any of the following:

   To **rename** a workspace, click the workspace name, then type the desired name in the field.

   To **duplicate** a workspace, click an existing workspace, then click the New Workspace button. Rename the duplicate workspace, if desired (a good idea).

   To **delete** a user-created workspace, click the workspace name, then click the Delete Workspace button. If you try to delete a user-created workspace that is currently displayed in your document, an alert dialog will appear. Click Yes to confirm.

3. Click OK.

➤ If no workspaces are selected in the Manage Workspaces dialog when you click the New Workspace button, the new workspace will include the current state of the panels and other features of the Illustrator interface.

You can reset any predefined or user-defined workspace to its saved settings.

To reset a workspace:

1. Via the Workspace menu on the Application bar or the Window > Workspace submenu, display the workspace to be reset.

2. From either the menu or the submenu listed in the preceding step, choose **Reset** [workspace name].

A *Use the Manage Workspaces dialog to rename or delete any of the custom workspaces that you have saved.*

This chapter will help you become more intimately acquainted with the Illustrator interface features that you will be using continually as you work: the panels. In the preceding chapter, you learned how to arrange them onscreen. Here you will see what the individual panels look like and be briefly introduced to their specific functions — from choosing color swatches (Swatches panel) to switching among artboards (Artboards panel) to editing layers (Layers panel). Note: In-depth instructions for using specific panels are amply provided throughout this book.

The Illustrator panels that are used in this book*

You can read through this chapter with or without glancing at or fiddling with the panels onscreen, and also use it as a reference guide as you work. Panel icons are shown on the next page. Following that, you'll find instructions for using the Tools panel, a brief description of each tool, an introduction to the Control panel, then a description and illustration of all the other Illustrator panels that are used in this book (in alphabetical order). Note: To open a panel that isn't already in a dock, choose the panel name from the Window menu.

CHOOSING VALUES IN A PANEL OR DIALOG

To change a value incrementally, click in a field in a panel or dialog, then press the up or down arrow key on the keyboard.

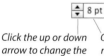

Click the up or down arrow to change the value incrementally. *Or enter a new value in the field.* *Or choose a preset value from the menu.*

SHORTCUTS FOR ENTERING VALUES IN ILLUSTRATOR PANELS

Apply a value and highlight the next field	Tab
Apply a value and highlight the previous field	Shift-Tab
Apply a value and exit the panel	Return/ Enter

---

*The Actions, SVG Interactivity, and Variables panels aren't covered in this book.

4

Identifying the panel icons

Each panel in Illustrator has a unique icon.**A** If you keep the panels collapsed to conserve screen space, you can identify them by their icons. If you don't recognize a panel icon, use the tool tip to identify it.

Align		Kuler	
Appearance		Layers	
Artboards		Links	
Attributes		Magic Wand	
Brushes		Navigator	
Character		OpenType	
Character Styles		Paragraph	
Color		Paragraph Styles	
Color Guide		Pathfinder	
CSS Properties		Pattern Options	
Document Info		Separations Preview	
Flattener Preview		Stroke	
Glyphs		Swatches	
Gradient		Symbols	
Graphic Styles		Tabs	
Image Trace		Transform	
Info		Transparency	

A When collapsed, each panel has a unique icon.

OPENING THE PANELS FOR EDITING TYPE

Illustrator provides seven panels for editing type: Character, Character Styles, Glyphs, OpenType, Paragraph, Paragraph Styles, and Tabs. All of them can be opened via the Window > Type submenu; the Glyphs panel can also be opened via the Type menu. Four of them can also be opened via a shortcut, as listed below.

	Mac OS	Windows
Character	Cmd-T	Ctrl-T
OpenType	Cmd-Option-Shift-T	Ctrl-Alt-Shift-T
Paragraph	Cmd-Option-T	Ctrl-Alt-T
Tabs	Cmd-Shift-T	Ctrl-Shift-T

USING THE CONTEXT MENUS

When you right-click in the document, depending on where you click and which tool happens to be selected, a menu of context-sensitive commands pops up onscreen. If a command is available on a context menu (or can be executed quickly via a keyboard shortcut), we let you know in our instructions, to spare you a trip to the main menu bar.

Note to Mac OS users: If your mouse doesn't have a right-click button, hold down Control and click to open the context menu.

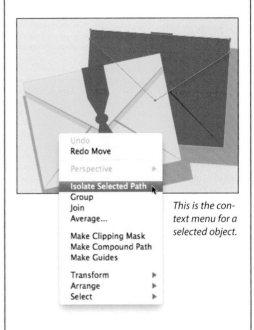

This is the context menu for a selected object.

HIDING AND SHOWING PANELS AND TOOLS

Hide or show all the currently open panels, including the Tools panel and tearoff toolbars	Tab
Hide or show all the currently open panels but not the Tools panel or tearoff toolbars	Shift-Tab

Using the Tools panel

In addition to the tools on the Tools panel, which are used for creating and editing objects, you will also find color controls, a menu or icons for choosing a drawing mode, and a menu for choosing a screen mode. If the panel is hidden, choose Window > Tools to display it. To convert the panel layout from single column to double column or vice versa, either click the double arrowhead at the top or double-click the top bar.

Click once on a visible tool to select it, or click and hold on a tool that has a tiny arrowhead to choose a related tool from a fly-out menu. You can cycle through tools on the same menu by Option/Alt clicking the visible tool.

To create a tearoff toolbar for a group of related tools, press and hold on the arrowhead for a tool, then click the vertical tearoff bar on the right edge of the menu.**A–B** To dock tearoff toolbars together, drag one tearoff toolbar to the side of an existing one and release when the vertical drop zone line displays.**C–D** To make a tearoff toolbar vertical instead of horizontal, click the double-arrow **E–F** or double-click the top bar. To close a docked tearoff toolbar, drag it by its gripper bar out of its dock, then click its close button (x).

To access a tool quickly, use the letter shortcut that is assigned to it. The shortcuts are listed in parentheses on the next two pages, and also in the tool tips onscreen.**G** (Note: If the tool tips aren't displaying, go to Illustrator/Edit > Preferences > General and check Show Tool Tips.)

Some tools can also be accessed temporarily via a toggle key. For example, pressing Cmd/Ctrl turns the current tool into a temporary selection tool. You'll learn many tool toggles as you proceed through this book.

To turn the tool pointer into a crosshairs icon for more precise positioning, go to Illustrator/Edit > Preferences > General and check Use Precise Cursors. Or if you prefer to keep that preference off, you can turn the pointer to a crosshairs icon temporarily by pressing the Caps Lock key.

You can choose options for the current tool from the Control panel (see page 43). Some tools, such as the Paintbrush and Pencil tools, have a related options dialog, which opens when you double-click the tool or when you click the tool and then press Return/Enter.

A We're creating a tearoff toolbar.

B Tearoff toolbars can be moved anywhere onscreen.

C We're docking a second tearoff toolbar to the first one.

D The two tearoff toolbars are docked together.

E We're clicking the double arrow on a tearoff toolbar to switch its orientation from horizontal...

F ...to vertical.

G Via the tool tip, you can identify a tool and learn its shortcut.

The Tools panel illustrated

Gripper bar, for moving the panel

Selection (V) *Selects, moves, and transforms entire objects*

Direct Selection (A) *Selects and reshapes objects by their anchor points and segments*

Magic Wand (Y) *Selects objects based on their color and opacity attributes*

Lasso (Q) *Selects individual points and segments on a path by dragging around them*

Pen (P) *Draws paths that are composed of curved and/or straight segments*

Type (T) *Creates and edits horizontal type*

Line Segment (\) *Draws separate straight lines at any angle*

Rectangle (M) *Draws rectangles and squares*

Paintbrush (B) *Creates Calligraphic, Scatter, Art, Bristle, or Pattern brush strokes*

Pencil (N) *Draws freehand paths*

Blob Brush (Shift-B) *Creates closed freehand shapes (or reshapes them)*

Eraser (Shift-E) *Erases sections of objects*

Rotate (R) *Rotates objects*

Scale (S) *Enlarges and shrinks objects*

Width (Shift-W) *Reshapes an object's stroke*

Free Transform (E) *Rotates, scales, reflects, shears, distorts, or applies perspective to objects*

Shape Builder (Shift-M) *Combines objects*

Perspective Grid (Shift-P) *Puts objects into one-, two-, or three-point perspective*

Mesh (U) *Creates and edits multicolored mesh objects*

Gradient (G) *Changes the position, length, radius, or angle of existing gradients*

Eyedropper (I) *Samples and applies paint or type attributes*

Blend (W) *Creates shape and color blends between objects*

Symbol Sprayer (Shift-S) *Sprays symbol instances into a set*

Column Graph (J) *Creates column graphs*

Artboard (Shift-O) *Creates and document artboards*

Slice (Shift-K) *Defines slice areas of a document*

Hand (H) *Moves the document in its window*

Zoom (Z) *Changes the zoom level of a document*

Fill (*press* **X** *to toggle or click to activate*) *The color, gradient, or pattern that fills the inside of a path*

Swap Fill and Stroke (Shift-X) *Swaps the current fill and stroke colors*

Default Fill and Stroke (D) *Sets the fill color to white and the stroke to black 1 pt.*

Stroke (*press* **X** *to toggle or click to activate*) *The color or pattern that's applied to a path*

Gradient (>) *Resets the fill or stroke to the last gradient*

None (/) *Sets the current stroke or fill color to None*

Color (<) *Resets the fill or stroke to the last solid color*

Drawing modes: *Draw Normal, Draw Behind, or Draw Inside (Shift-D)*

Screen modes (F) *Change the size of the document window and control the display of Illustrator features*

The tearoff toolbars*

Convert Anchor Point (Shift-C) *Converts corner points to smooth points, and vice versa*

Add Anchor Point (+)   **Delete Anchor Point (–)**

Polar Grid *Creates circular grids*

Arc *Creates curve segments*   **Spiral** *Creates spiral lines*   **Rectangular Grid** *Creates rectangular grids*

Reflect (O) *Creates a mirror reflection of an object*

LIQUIFY TOOLS *(apply distortion)*

Warp (Shift-R) *Distorts objects*   **Pucker**   **Scallop**   **Wrinkle**
Twirl   **Bloat**   **Crystallize**

Live Paint Selection (Shift-L) *Selects sections of a Live Paint group*

Live Paint Bucket (K) *Recolors faces and edges in a Live Paint group*

Measure *Measures the distance between two points*

SYMBOLISM TOOLS *(edit symbol instances)*

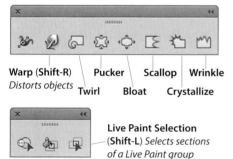

Symbol Styler

Symbol Shifter   **Symbol Scruncher**   **Symbol Sizer**   **Symbol Stainer**   **Symbol Screener**
Symbol Spinner

Print Tiling *Positions the printable page*

Group Selection *Selects whole groups (and nested groups)*

Area Type *Creates and edits type horizontally inside an object*   **Vertical Area Type** *Creates and edits type vertically inside an object*   **Touch Type (Shift-T)** *Scales, rotates, and shifts characters manually*

Type on a Path *Creates and edits type horizontally along a path*   **Vertical Type** *Creates and edits vertical type*   **Vertical Type on a Path** *Creates and edits type vertically along a path*

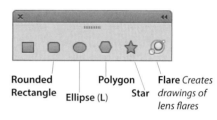

Rounded Rectangle   **Ellipse (L)**   **Polygon**   **Star**   **Flare** *Creates drawings of lens flares*

Path Eraser *Erases sections of paths*

Smooth *Smooths path segments*

Knife *Carves up paths*

Scissors (C) *Splits paths*

Reshape *Reshapes sections of paths*

Shear *Skews objects*

Slice Selection *Selects slices, for Web output*

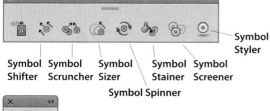

The tearoff toolbars for the Perspective Grid and Graph tools aren't illustrated here.

Creating custom tools panels

To conserve space on your screen and for more efficient editing, you can create separate, custom tools panels in which you store just the tools that you use for specific kinds of tasks. For example, you could create separate panels for drawing tools, reshaping tools, or tools for creating gradients and blends. You can open any custom tools panel from the Window > Tools submenu.

To create a custom tools panel: ★

1. Choose Window > Tools > **New Custom Tools Panel**.
2. In the dialog, enter a name for your tools panel,**A** then click OK. A new panel appears onscreen.**B**
   Note: All custom tools panels contain a Fill square and a Stroke square, which cannot be deleted.
3. To add tools to your custom panel, drag any tool individually from the standard Tools panel into the tools (top) area of your panel (plus sign pointer).**C**

   ➤ To copy a tool that is in a group but isn't currently visible on the Tools panel, select the tool first to make it the topmost tool. To quickly cycle through the tools within the current group, hold down Option/Alt and click the topmost tool. Or if you prefer to display all the tools in a group on a separate tearoff toolbar, press and hold on the arrowhead for a tool to open its menu, release, then click the vertical tearoff bar on the right edge of the menu.

4. To delete a tool from the custom panel, drag it out of the panel (a minus sign appears in the pointer).
5. To relocate a tool within a custom panel, drag it to the desired slot, then release it when the vertical drop zone bar appears.

To rename, copy, or delete a custom tools panel: ★

1. Choose Window > **Manage Tools Panel**.
2. The Manage Tools Panel dialog opens.**D** Click the name of the panel that you want to rename, copy, or delete.
3. Do one of the following:

   To rename the panel, change the name in the field, then click OK.

   To duplicate the panel, click the New Custom Tools panel button,⬚ type the desired name, then click OK.

   To delete the panel, click Delete.

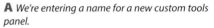

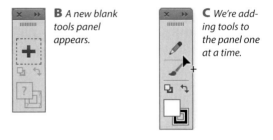

A *We're entering a name for a new custom tools panel.*

B *A new blank tools panel appears.*

C *We're adding tools to the panel one at a time.*

D *Use the Manage Tools Panel dialog to rename, duplicate, or delete a custom tools panel.*

OPENING A TEMPORARY PANEL

➤ Click a link (word or letter that has a blue underline) on the Control panel to open a related panel. For example, you could click Stroke to open a temporary Stroke panel, or click Opacity to open a temporary Transparency panel.

➤ Click the Stroke or Fill color square on the Control panel to open a temporary Swatches panel, or Shift-click either square to open a temporary Color panel.

➤ You can open other temporary panels by clicking a thumbnail or arrowhead. For example, you could click the Style thumbnail or arrowhead to open a temporary Graphic Styles panel.

The Control panel

The Control panel houses many frequently used controls conveniently under one roof, and changes contextually depending on what tool and kind of object are selected. Two of the many variations are shown below. For example, you can use this panel to apply fill and stroke colors; change an object's variable width profile, brush stroke definition, or opacity; apply basic type attributes, such as the font family and point size; align and distribute multiple objects; access controls for editing symbols, Image Trace, and Live Paint objects; and embed or edit linked images.

When no objects are selected, you can use this panel to choose default fill, stroke, brush, style, and opacity settings for the current document and quickly access the Document Setup or Preferences dialog by clicking the button with that name.

To move the Control panel to the top or bottom, respectively, of the Application frame, choose Dock to Top or Dock to Bottom from the menu at the right end of the panel. Or if you prefer to make the panel free-floating, drag the gripper bar on the far left side. To control which options display on the panel, uncheck or check any of the items on the panel menu.

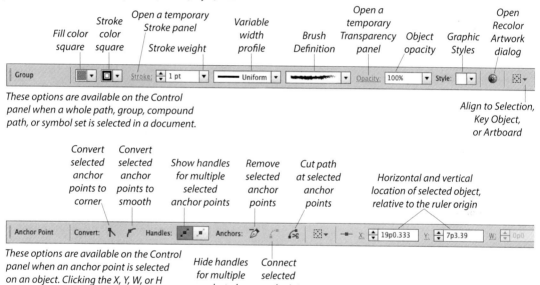

These options are available on the Control panel when a whole path, group, compound path, or symbol set is selected in a document.

These options are available on the Control panel when an anchor point is selected on an object. Clicking the X, Y, W, or H opens a temporary Transform panel.

Artboards panel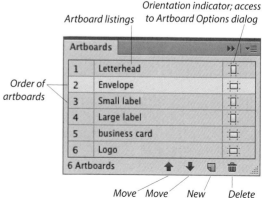

In addition to listing all the artboards in the current document, the Artboards panel lets you display, create, rename, and duplicate artboards; change their order; rearrange them in the document; choose options for them; change their orientation; and delete them. The Artboard Options dialog opens when you double-click the artboard orientation icon, which is located to the right of the artboard name. See pages 7–12 and 28.

Align panel

The buttons on the top two rows of the Align panel align and/or distribute two or more objects along their centers or along their top, left, right, or bottom edges. Objects can be aligned to a selection, an artboard, or a key object (one of the selected objects). Buttons in the lower part of the panel redistribute (equalize) the spacing among three or more objects. See pages 107–108. This panel can also be used to align anchor points (see page 174). Align buttons also appear on the Control panel when two or more objects are selected.

Appearance panel

The appearance attributes of an object consist of its fill and stroke color, Stroke panel settings, effects, and Transparency panel settings. The Appearance panel lists the specific appearance attributes and settings for whichever layer, group, or object is currently targeted on the Layers panel. You can use the panel to add extra fill or stroke attributes, edit or remove attributes, apply and edit effects, and edit individual attributes within an applied graphic style.

Using convenient in-panel features, you can edit attributes quickly. For example, you can click a link (blue underlined word) to open a dialog or a temporary panel: Click Stroke to open the Stroke panel, Opacity to open the Transparency panel, or the name of an effect to open its dialog. To open a temporary Swatches panel, click the Stroke or Fill color square, then click the thumbnail or arrowhead (or Shift-click the latter to open a temporary Color panel). See Chapter 14.

Attributes panel

The Attributes panel lets you choose overprint options for an object (see page 431), show or hide an object's center point (see page 105), switch the fill between color and transparency in a compound path (see page 361), or change an object's fill rule.

You can also use this panel to create a hotspot for Web output. Assign an image map shape and a URL to a selected object, then to verify the URL in the Web browser that is currently installed on your system, click the Browser button.

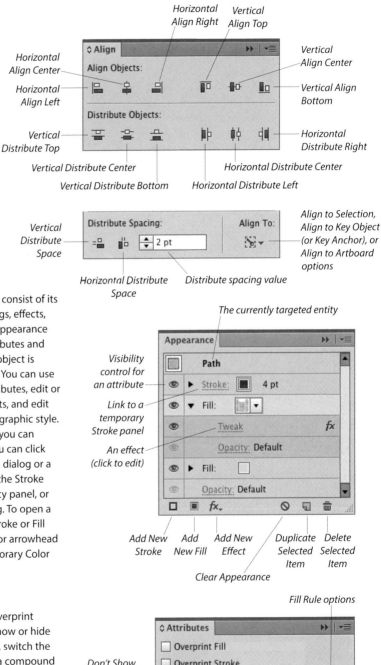

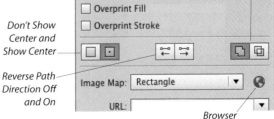

Brushes panel

There are five varieties of decorative brushes that you can apply to paths: Calligraphic, Scatter, Art, Bristle, and Pattern. You can apply a brush either by choosing the Paintbrush tool and a brush and then drawing a shape, or by applying a brush to an existing path.

To personalize your brush strokes, you can create and edit custom brushes. If you modify a brush that's being used in a document, you'll be given the option via an alert dialog to update the paths with the revised brush. Brushes on the Brushes panel save with the current document. See Chapter 23.

To open a temporary Brushes panel, click the Brush Definition thumbnail on the Control panel, or for a selected Stroke listing on the Appearance panel, click the Brush Definition thumbnail.

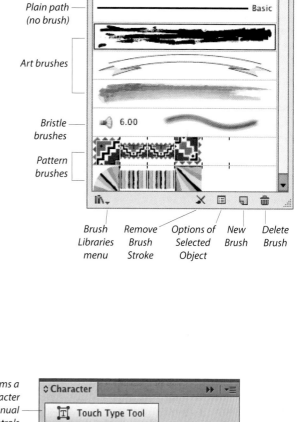

Calligraphic brushes
Scatter brushes
Plain path (no brush)
Art brushes
Bristle brushes
Pattern brushes

Brush Libraries menu — Remove Brush Stroke — Options of Selected Object — New Brush — Delete Brush

SHOWING OR HIDING PANEL OPTIONS

Some of the panels in Illustrator have extra options, which you may or may not see at first. To display or show a panel's full options, click the double arrow on its tab (once or twice).

Character panel

You will use the Character panel to apply type attributes: font family, font style, font size, leading, kerning, tracking, horizontal scale, vertical scale, baseline shift, character rotation, and special glyphs. You can also use this panel to access the Touch Type tool, choose a language for hyphenation, and set the anti-aliasing method. See pages 267–272, 286, and 287.

When a type tool or a type object is selected, the Control panel also provides some basic type controls. To open a temporary Character panel, click Character on the Control panel.

Transforms a type character via manual controls
Font Family
Font Style
Font Size
Kerning
Vertical Scale
Baseline Shift
All Caps, Small Caps, Superscript, Subscript, Underline, and Strikethrough

Leading
Tracking
Horizontal Scale
Character Rotation
Anti-aliasing method

Hyphenation language for the current document

Character Styles panel

A character style is a collection of settings for type characters, including a font family, font style, font size, leading, tracking, and kerning. Unlike paragraph styles, which apply to whole paragraphs, character styles are used to quickly format small amounts of type (such as bullets, boldfaced words, italicized words, or large initial caps) to distinguish them from the main text. When you edit a character style, any text in which it is being used updates accordingly.

Using the Character Styles panel, you can create, apply, edit, duplicate, and delete styles. See pages 284–287. (Compare this panel with the Paragraph Styles panel, which is shown on page 51.)

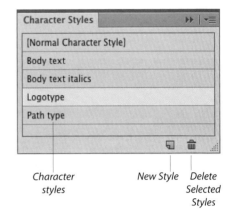

Character styles   New Style   Delete Selected Styles

Color panel

In Illustrator, colors are applied to an object's fill (interior) or stroke (edge). Use the Color panel to mix a global process color, enter a hexadecimal code, or set a tint percentage for a spot or global color. Choose a color model for the panel, such as RGB or CMYK, from the panel menu. Quick-select a color by clicking in the spectrum bar at the bottom of the panel, or click the black, white, or None button. You can expand the bar by dragging the bottom edge downward. See page 117.

To open a temporary Color panel, Shift-click the Fill or Stroke square or arrowhead on the Control panel or the Appearance panel.

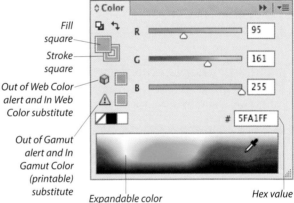

Fill square
Stroke square
Out of Web Color alert and In Web Color substitute
Out of Gamut alert and In Gamut Color (printable) substitute
Expandable color spectrum bar
Hex value

Color Guide panel

Use the Color Guide panel to generate color schemes from a base color by choosing a harmony rule and/or a variation type (Tints/Shades, Warm/Cool, or Vivid/Muted). You can click any variation swatch to apply it as a fill or stroke color to one or more selected objects. You can also save variations from the Color Guide panel as a group to the Swatches panel, or edit the current color group via the Edit Colors dialog. See pages 115 and 128–130.

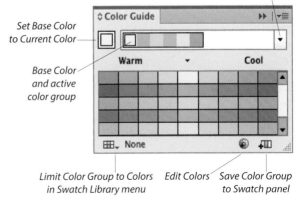

Harmony Rules menu

Set Base Color to Current Color
Base Color and active color group

Limit Color Group to Colors in Swatch Library menu   Edit Colors   Save Color Group to Swatch panel

CSS Properties panel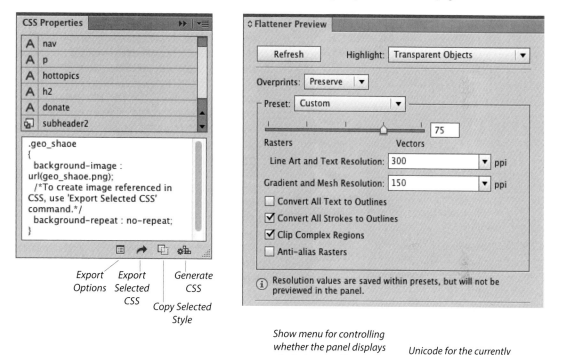

The CSS Properties panel lists all the character and graphic styles that are being used in the current Illustrator document, as well as the CSS code for the currently selected object(s). If you're designing a Web page and you want to ensure that it is styled correctly, you or a Web developer can copy the CSS code from this panel, and then paste the code into the HTML file. See pages 452–454.

Flattener Preview panel

Artwork that contains semitransparent objects must be flattened before it is printed. Using the Highlight menu options in the Flattener Preview panel, you can preview which objects in your document will be affected by flattening, adjust the flattening settings, then click Refresh to preview the effect of the new settings in your artwork. See page 436.

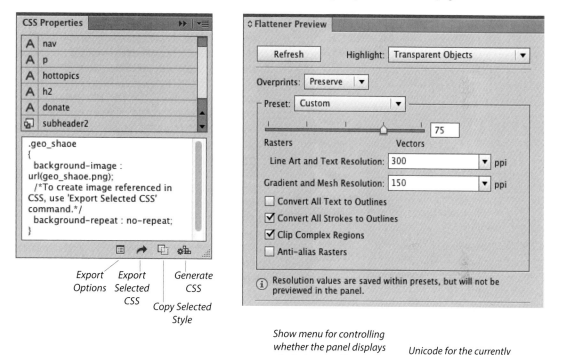

Export Options | Export Selected CSS | Generate CSS
Copy Selected Style

Show menu for controlling whether the panel displays glyphs in a specific category or for the entire font

Unicode for the currently selected character

Glyphs panel

Using the Glyphs panel, you can find out which character variations (alternate glyphs) are available for any given character in a specific OpenType font, and insert specific glyphs from that font into your document (including glyphs that can't be entered via the keyboard). See page 279.

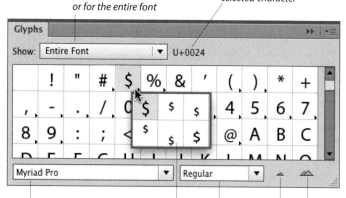

Font family | Pop-up showing alternate glyphs for a specific character | Font style | Zoom Out | Zoom In

For the Document Info panel, see page 447.

Gradient panel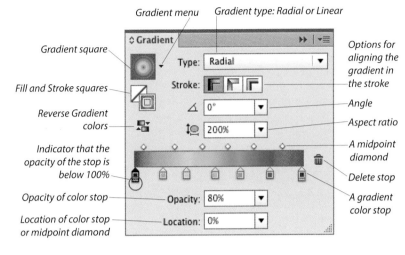

The Gradient panel lets you create, apply, and edit gradients, which are soft, gradual blends between two or more colors. You can use the panel to apply a gradient to an object's fill or stroke, adjust the amount of a color by dragging its stop, choose a different color or opacity value for a selected stop, click below the gradient slider to add new colors, move a midpoint diamond to change the location where two adjacent colors are mixed equally, reverse the gradient colors, change the overall gradient type or angle, or change the alignment of a gradient in an object's stroke. See Chapter 24.

Graphic Styles panel

The Graphic Styles panel enables you to store and apply collections of appearance attributes, such as multiple solid-color fills or strokes, transparency and overprint settings, blending modes, brush strokes, and effects. Using graphic styles, you can apply attributes quickly and create a cohesive look among multiple objects or documents (similar to how paragraph styles are used with type). See Chapter 16. To open a temporary Graphic Styles panel, click the Style thumbnail or arrowhead on the Control panel.

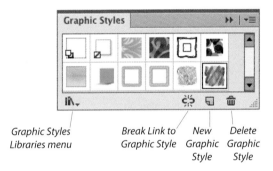

Graphic Styles Libraries menu
Break Link to Graphic Style
New Graphic Style
Delete Graphic Style

Info panel

If no objects are selected in the current document, depending on the current tool, the Info panel lists the x/y (horizontal and vertical) location of the pointer. If an object is selected, the panel lists the location of the object, its width and height, and data about its fill and stroke colors (the color components; or the name of a pattern or gradient; or a color name or number, such as a PANTONE PLUS number). While an object is being transformed via a transform tool, the panel lists pertinent information, such as a percentage value for a scale transformation or an angle of rotation. When a type tool and type object are selected, the panel displays type specifications. When the Measure tool is used, the Info panel opens automatically and lists the distance and angle the tool has just calculated.

Image Trace panel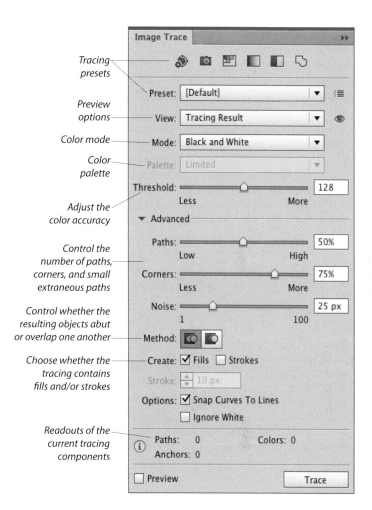

The Image Trace feature detects and traces areas of color and shade in a raster image that is opened or placed into Illustrator, such as a Photoshop, TIFF, or JPEG image or scanned artwork, and converts those areas to Illustrator paths.

You can choose from a wide array of tracing options on the Image Trace panel prior to the tracing — and because a tracing is "live," you can also use the panel to fine-tune the results. You can use a built-in tracing preset (predefined settings) as a starting point, or create and apply custom presets. Among the numerous settings that you can specify are a mode (black and white, grayscale, or color), a color palette, the number of resulting colors, whether fill and/or stroke colors are produced, and the precision with which the image is traced. See Chapter 17.

Tracing presets

Preview options

Color mode

Color palette

Adjust the color accuracy

Control the number of paths, corners, and small extraneous paths

Control whether the resulting objects abut or overlap one another

Choose whether the tracing contains fills and/or strokes

Readouts of the current tracing components

Kuler panel

Kuler (pronounced "cooler") is a free, Web-hosted Adobe application that lets users create, upload, and comment on color groups, called color themes. The Kuler panel in Illustrator displays the themes that you have created or designated as favorites on Kuler.adobe.com or that you have created using the Adobe Kuler app on an iPhone. Via the panel, you can apply colors directly to objects, or you can add colors to the Swatches panel for later use. To show the panel, choose Window > Kuler. See pages 133–135.

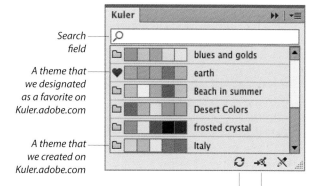

Search field

A theme that we designated as a favorite on Kuler.adobe.com

A theme that we created on Kuler.adobe.com

Refresh the panel

Launch the Kuler website

Layers panel

The indispensable Layers panel lets you add and delete layers and sublayers in a document, and create layer groups. You can also use this panel to select, target, restack, duplicate, delete, hide, show, lock, unlock, merge, change the view for, or create a clipping set for a layer, sublayer, group, or individual object. When your artwork is finished, you can use a command on the panel menu to flatten the document into one layer or release all the objects to separate layers for export as a Flash animation. See Chapter 13.

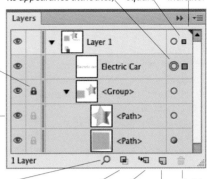

Icon for targeting an object or group (to edit its appearance attributes) — *Selection square* — *Current Layer indicator*

Lock icon (makes the entity uneditable)

Visibility icon (hides or shows the entity)

Locate Object — *Make/Release Clipping Mask* — *New Sublayer* — *New Layer* — *Delete Selection*

Links panel

When you place an image from another application, such as Photoshop, into an Illustrator document, you can opt to have Illustrator embed a copy of the image into the file (and thereby increase the file size but allow the program to color-manage it) or merely link the image to your document (and minimize the file size but require the original file to be available for print output). Using the Links panel, you can monitor the status of linked images, convert a linked image to an embedded one (or vice versa), open a linked image in its original application for editing, update an edited image, restore the link to an image that is missing or modified, and view image data. See pages 314–317.

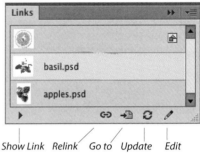

Show Link Info — *Relink* — *Go to Link* — *Update Link* — *Edit Original*

Magic Wand panel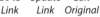

The Magic Wand tool selects objects that have the same or a similar fill color, stroke color, stroke weight, opacity, or blending mode as the currently selected object. Using the Magic Wand panel, you specify which attributes the tool may select and set a tolerance value for each attribute. For example, if you were to check Opacity, choose an opacity Tolerance of 10%, then click an object that has an opacity of 50%, the tool would find and select objects in the document that have an opacity between 40% and 60%. See page 99.

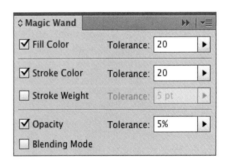

Navigator panel

The Navigator panel has two main functions. To use it to move the current document in its window, drag or click in the proxy preview area (red outlined box). To change the document zoom level, use the zoom controls at the bottom of the panel. To both zoom to, and bring a specific area of, a document into view, Cmd-drag/Ctrl-drag in the proxy preview area.

Proxy preview area

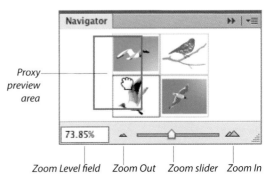

Zoom Level field — *Zoom Out* — *Zoom slider* — *Zoom In*

OpenType panel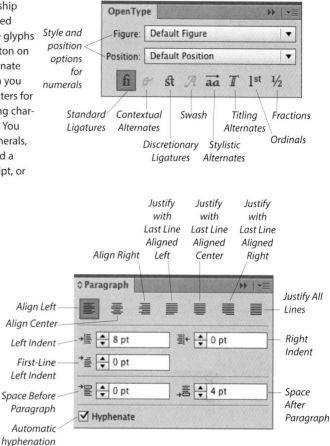

Among the Roman OpenType font families that ship with Illustrator, the fonts that contain an expanded character set and a large assortment of alternate glyphs are labeled with the word "Pro." By clicking a button on the OpenType panel, you can specify which alternate characters (glyphs) will appear in your text when you type the requisite key or keys. The special characters for a given font may include ligatures, swashes, titling characters, stylistic alternates, ordinals, and fractions. You can also use the panel to specify options for numerals, such as a style (e.g., tabular lining or oldstyle) and a position (e.g., numerator, denominator, superscript, or subscript). See page 280.

Paragraph panel

Use the Paragraph panel to apply settings that affect entire paragraphs, such as horizontal alignment, indentation, spacing before or after, and automatic hyphenation. Via the panel menu, you can choose hanging punctuation and composer options and open a dialog for choosing justification or hyphenation options. See pages 273, 277–279, and 284.

The Align Left, Align Center, and Align Right buttons are also available on the Control panel when a type object is selected. To open a temporary Paragraph panel, click Paragraph on the Control panel.

Paragraph Styles panel

A paragraph style is a collection of paragraph specifications (including horizontal alignment, indentation, spacing before or after, word spacing, letter spacing, hyphenation, and hanging punctuation), as well as character attributes, such as the font family, font style, and font size. When you apply a paragraph style to one or more selected paragraphs, the type is reformatted with the specifications in that style. When you edit a paragraph style, the type in which it is being used updates accordingly. With paragraph (and character) styles, you can typeset text quickly and ensure that the formatting is consistent. Use the Paragraph Styles panel to create, store, apply, edit, duplicate, and delete paragraph styles for the current document. See pages 284–287.

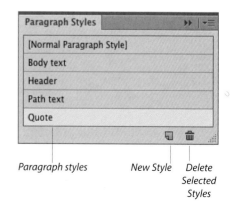

Pathfinder panel

Depending on how they are applied, the Shape Mode commands on the top row of the Pathfinder panel combine selected, overlapping objects into one or more standard paths or into a compound shape. The Expand button converts a compound shape into either a path or a compound path (the latter if the command originally produced a cutout shape). The Pathfinder buttons on the bottom row of the panel produce flattened, cut-up shapes from multiple selected objects. See pages 362–364.

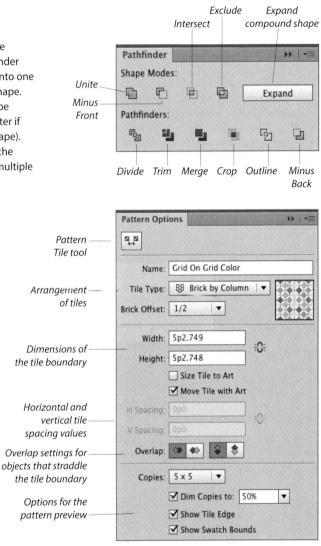

Exclude

Intersect

Expand compound shape

Unite

Minus Front

Divide Trim Merge Crop Outline Minus Back

Pattern Options panel

Via the Pattern Options panel, along with some intuitive on-image controls, you can create and edit seamless patterns. When you create a pattern, it appears automatically on the Swatches panel for the current document. You can apply any pattern swatch in the Swatches panel to an object's fill (interior) or stroke (edge).

The Pattern Options panel lets you change the pattern tiling configuration (Grid, Brick, or Hex); adjust the spacing between tiles; and for objects that straddle the tile boundary and overlap one another, control which objects are in front. You can also choose preview options for pattern-editing mode, including the number of copies that display, to what extent the copies are dimmed, and whether the tile and/or swatch boundaries display. See pages 137–144.

Pattern Tile tool

Arrangement of tiles

Dimensions of the tile boundary

Horizontal and vertical tile spacing values

Overlap settings for objects that straddle the tile boundary

Options for the pattern preview

Separations Preview panel

The Separations Preview panel gives you an idea of how the individual C, M, Y, and K color components in a CMYK document will separate to individual plates during the commercial printing process. You can use the panel to check that a color is properly set to knock out colors beneath it in your artwork, or to check whether a color is properly set to overprint on top of the other colors. Other uses for the panel are to monitor the use of spot colors in the artwork, to verify that any spot color is set to knock out colors beneath it, and to determine whether a specific black is a rich black (a mixture of C, M, Y, and K inks) or a simple black that contains only the K component. See pages 432–433.

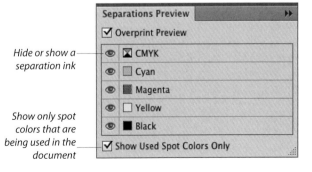

Hide or show a separation ink

Show only spot colors that are being used in the document

Stroke panel

Stroke settings control the appearance of an object's path (edge). By using the Stroke panel, you can specify a stroke weight (thickness), cap (end) style, and corner (join) style, and an alignment option to control the position of the stroke on the path. You can also use the panel to create a dashed (or dotted) line or border, apply an arrowhead and/or tail style, and change the stroke width profile. See pages 122–124 and 166. To open a temporary Stroke panel, click Stroke on the Control or Appearance panel.

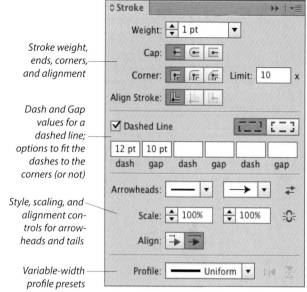

Stroke weight, ends, corners, and alignment

Dash and Gap values for a dashed line; options to fit the dashes to the corners (or not)

Style, scaling, and alignment controls for arrowheads and tails

Variable-width profile presets

Swatches panel

Use the Swatches panel to choose, store, and apply solid colors, patterns, gradients, and color groups. If you click a swatch, it becomes the current fill or stroke color (depending on whether the Fill or Stroke square is active on the Tools panel and Color panel), and it is applied to all currently selected objects.

Double-clicking a swatch opens the Swatch Options dialog, in which you can change the swatch name or change its type to global process, nonglobal process, or spot. See pages 116, 118, 120, 126–129, and 136. To open a temporary Swatches panel, click the Fill or Stroke square or arrowhead on the Control or Appearance panel.

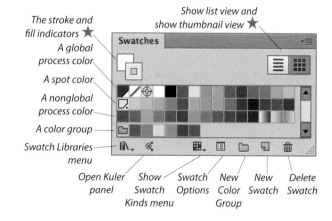

Show list view and show thumbnail view

The stroke and fill indicators

A global process color

A spot color

A nonglobal process color

A color group

Swatch Libraries menu

Open Kuler panel

Show Swatch Kinds menu

Swatch Options

New Color Group

New Swatch

Delete Swatch

Symbols panel

Symbols are Illustrator objects that are stored on the Symbols panel and save with the current document. Using symbols, you can quickly and easily create a complex collection of objects, such as a bank of trees or clouds. To create one instance of a symbol, you simply drag from the Symbols panel onto the artboard; to assemble multiple instances quickly into what is called a symbol set, you use the Symbol Sprayer tool.

The other symbolism tools let you change the position, stacking order, proximity, size, rotation angle, or transparency of multiple instances in a set, or gradually apply a color tint or graphic style — while maintaining the link to the original symbol on the panel. If you edit the original symbol, all instances of that symbol in the document update automatically. See Chapter 28.

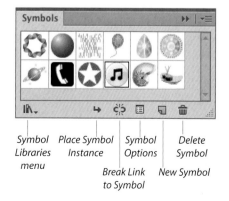

Symbol Libraries menu

Place Symbol Instance

Symbol Options

Delete Symbol

Break Link to Symbol

New Symbol

Transparency panel

You can use the Transparency panel to change the blending mode or opacity of a layer, group, or individual object. The Make Mask button applies the opacity value and grayscale equivalent of a color (or colors), gradient, or pattern in the topmost object to underlying selected objects, and optionally hides sections of those objects that extend beyond its edges. See Chapter 27.

To open a temporary Transparency panel, click the Opacity link on the Control or Appearance panel. You can also change the opacity of an object directly via the Control panel.

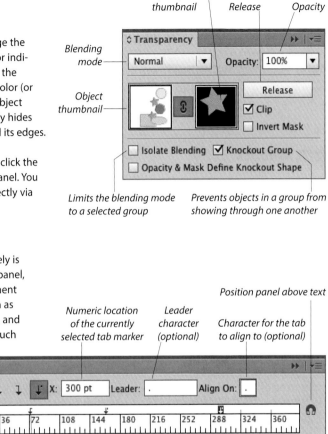

Opacity mask thumbnail

Make Mask/ Release

Object Opacity

Blending mode

Object thumbnail

Limits the blending mode to a selected group

Prevents objects in a group from showing through one another

Tabs panel

The only way to align columns of text precisely is by using tabs and the Tabs panel. Using the panel, you can insert, move, and change the alignment of custom tab markers, specify a leader (such as a period character, to produce a dotted line), and specify a character for your text to align to (such as a decimal point). See page 288.

Left-, Center-, Right-, and Decimal-Justified alignment buttons for horizontal type (or Top-, Center-, Bottom-, and Decimal-Justified buttons for vertical type)

Numeric location of the currently selected tab marker

Leader character (optional)

Position panel above text

Character for the tab to align to (optional)

A tab marker

Transform panel

The Transform panel lists the location, width, height, rotation angle, and shear angle of the currently selected object, and can be used to change those values. By clicking a reference point, you can control what part of the object the transformations are calculated from. The panel can also be used to align selected objects to the pixel grid. Via commands on the panel menu, you can control whether just the object, the object and a fill pattern, or just the fill pattern is transformed. See pages 152–153.

A reference point icon and X, Y, W, and H fields also appear on the Control panel when one or more paths are selected. To open a temporary Transform panel, click the X, Y, W, or H link (or if those fields aren't showing, click the word "Transform").

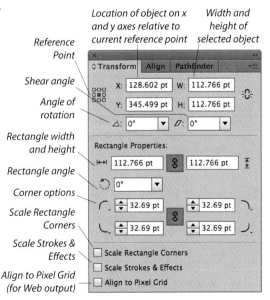

Reference Point

Shear angle

Angle of rotation

Rectangle width and height

Rectangle angle

Corner options

Scale Rectangle Corners

Scale Strokes & Effects

Align to Pixel Grid (for Web output)

Location of object on x and y axes relative to current reference point

Width and height of selected object

In this chapter, you will open files via the Open command and via Bridge, a separate application that serves as a conduit among programs in the Adobe Creative Cloud. You will also learn how to customize the Bridge window and use it to preview, open, label, rate, group, find, rename, delete, move, copy, and assign keywords to files. (Bridge is included with Illustrator.)

Note: Adobe Bridge must be downloaded and installed separately from Illustrator.

Opening files from Illustrator

Follow the instructions below if you want to open Illustrator files using the Open command in Illustrator. Or if you prefer to use Bridge to open files — as we do and recommend — turn the page and start reading from there. (To learn how to import files from other programs into Illustrator, see Chapter 22.)

To open a file from Illustrator:

1. To display the Open dialog, choose File > **Open** (Cmd-O/Ctrl-O).

2. In the Mac OS, to list files only in the formats that Illustrator can read, choose Enable: All Readable Documents. In Windows, to list all files, both readable and not, from the menu next to the File Name field, choose All Formats, or choose a specific format.

3. Locate and click a file name, then click Open. If an alert dialog about a color profile or missing font appears, see page 63; if an alert dialog pertaining to imported images appears, see page 309.

➤ To reopen a recently opened file, choose the file name from the File > Open Recent Files submenu.

To open an Illustrator file from the Macintosh Finder or Windows Explorer:

Double-click the icon for an Illustrator file. The file name may include one of the following extensions: .ai, .ait, .eps, or .idea. Illustrator will launch if it isn't already running.

In the Mac OS, you can also open a file by dragging its icon over the Adobe Illustrator CC 2014 application icon in the Dock. And you can open an Illustrator file that has an .svgz or .svg extension by this method or by double-clicking.

BRIDGE

5

Launching Adobe Bridge

The excellent navigation controls and large thumbnail previews in Bridge make locating and opening files a snap. There are many useful features in Bridge to explore, such as the ability to organize file thumbnails into collections and collapsible stacks, assign keywords to files, and filter the display of thumbnails by various criteria.

To launch Adobe Bridge:

To launch Adobe Bridge, do one of the following:

In the Mac OS or Windows, on the Application bar in Illustrator, click the **Go to Bridge** icon [Br] (Cmd-Option-O/Ctrl-Alt-O).

In the Mac OS, double-click the **Adobe Bridge CC** application icon [Br] or click the **Bridge** icon [Br] in the Dock.

In Windows 8, display the Start screen, then click the tile for **Adobe Bridge CC** (**64bit**).

Features of the Bridge window

First, we'll identify the main sections of the Bridge window (**A**, next page). The two rows of buttons and menus running across the top of the window are referred to jointly as the toolbar. The second row of the toolbar is called the Path bar.

In the default workspace, Essentials, the main window is divided into three panes: a large pane in the center and a vertical pane on either side. Each pane contains one or more panels, which are accessed via their tabs: Favorites, Folders, Filter, Collections, Content, Preview, Metadata, and Keywords. Using panels in the side panes, you can manage files, filter the display of thumbnails, and display file data; the Content panel displays document thumbnails. You can hide, show, or resize any of the panels or move any panel into a different pane. At the bottom of the Bridge window are controls for changing the thumbnail size and layout. To customize the Bridge workspace, see pages 58–59 and 64–65.

We'll explore the toolbar features and most of the panels in depth in this chapter. To help you get oriented, here is a brief description of the panels:

The **Favorites** panel displays a list of folders that you've designated as favorites, for quick access (see page 61).

The **Folders** panel contains a scrolling window with a hierarchical listing of all the top-level and nested folders on your hard disk. See page 60.

By clicking various criteria in the **Filter** panel, you can filter which file thumbnails in the current folder display in the Content panel. See page 72.

The **Collections** panel lists all your collections, which are groups that you have made of file thumbnails. Using collections, you can organize and access your file thumbnails without having to relocate the actual files. See pages 69–70.

The **Content** panel displays thumbnails for files (and, optionally, for nested folders) within the current folder. In the lower right corner of the Bridge window, you can click a View Content As button to control whether, and in what format, metadata pertaining to the current files displays in the Content panel (see page 65). The Content panel is used and illustrated throughout this chapter.

The **Preview** panel displays a large preview of one or more document (or folder) thumbnails that are selected in the Content panel. If a document you are previewing contains multiple artboards, controls are provided for navigating through them. If the thumbnail for a video file is selected in the Content panel, a controller for previewing the video displays in this panel. Or if a multipage PDF file is selected, you can click the left or right arrow to preview pages in the file. See pages 60–61.

In the **Metadata** panel, you can find detailed information about the currently selected file, within expandable categories. The File Properties category, for example, lists such data as the file name, format, date created, and date modified. For a close-up of this panel, see the sidebar on page 61 (see also Bridge Help).

Use the **Keywords** panel to assign one or more descriptive keywords to your files, such as the client or project name or the subject matter of the artwork. You can search for file thumbnails based on the keywords that are assigned to them, and filter thumbnails by checking specific keywords in the Filter panel (see page 73).

Note: The Inspector panel isn't covered in this book.

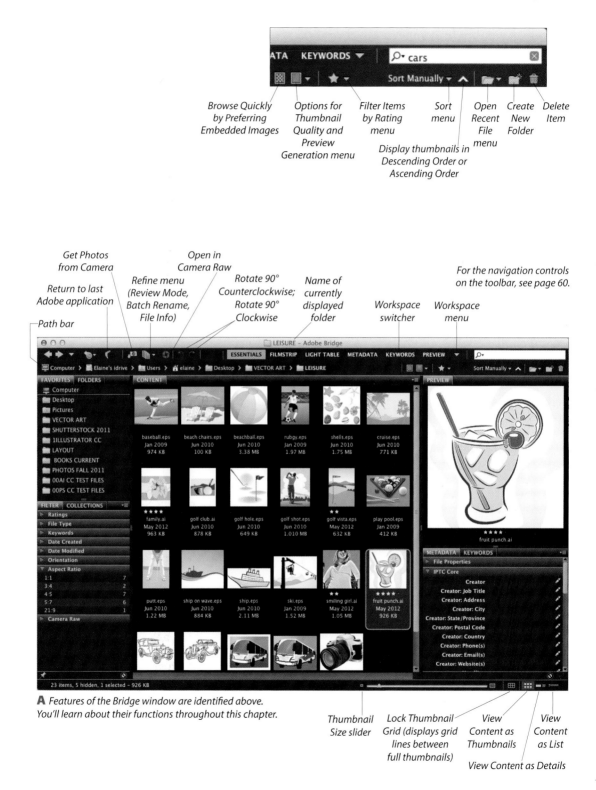

Browse Quickly by Preferring Embedded Images

Options for Thumbnail Quality and Preview Generation menu

Filter Items by Rating menu

Sort menu

Open Recent File menu

Create New Folder

Delete Item

Display thumbnails in Descending Order or Ascending Order

Get Photos from Camera

Open in Camera Raw

Return to last Adobe application

Refine menu (Review Mode, Batch Rename, File Info)

Rotate 90° Counterclockwise; Rotate 90° Clockwise

Name of currently displayed folder

For the navigation controls on the toolbar, see page 60.

Workspace switcher

Workspace menu

Path bar

A Features of the Bridge window are identified above. You'll learn about their functions throughout this chapter.

Thumbnail Size slider

Lock Thumbnail Grid (displays grid lines between full thumbnails)

View Content as Thumbnails

View Content as List

View Content as Details

Choosing a workspace for Bridge

To reconfigure the Bridge window quickly, choose one of the predefined workspaces. (To create and save custom workspaces, see pages 64–66.)

To choose a workspace for Bridge: ★

Do one of the following:

In the workspace switcher on the upper toolbar, click **Essentials**, **Filmstrip**, **Metadata** (List View for the thumbnails), **Keywords**, **Preview**, **Light Table**, **Folders**, or a user-saved workspace.**A** (If there's room on the toolbar and you want to display more workspace names, pull the gripper bar to the left.)

From the **Workspace** menu on the workspace switcher, choose a workspace **B–C** (and **A–C**, next page).

Press the shortcut for one of the first six workspaces on the switcher (as listed on the Workspace menu): Cmd-F1/Ctrl-F1 through Cmd-F6/Ctrl-F6. The shortcuts are assigned automatically to the first six workspaces on the switcher, based on their current order from left to right.

➤ To resize the thumbnails for any workspace, see page 64.

To change the order of workspaces on the switcher:

Do either of the following:

Drag a workspace name to the left or right.

Right-click a workspace name and choose a different name from the context menu.

To reveal more workspace names, drag the gripper bar to the left.

A To change workspaces, click a workspace name on the switcher …

B … or choose a workspace name from the Workspace menu.

C The Filmstrip workspace features a large preview of the currently selected thumbnail(s), and the thumbnails are displayed horizontally.

A *In the Essentials workspace, all the panels are showing.*

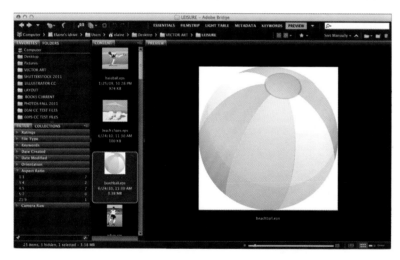

B *In the Preview workspace, the Metadata and Keywords panels are hidden to make room for a large preview, and the thumbnails are displayed vertically.*

C *The Output workspace allows you to generate a PDF containing thumbnails of the selected images (a contact sheet) or a Web gallery that can be uploaded to a web server to present images online. Note: The Output workspace does not ship with Bridge CC by default but can be downloaded separately from the Adobe website by going to http://helpx.adobe.com/bridge/kb/install-output-module-bridge-cc.html. Although it requires a few minutes to install, it is well worth it!* ★

Previewing graphics in Bridge

For navigating to and opening folders, Bridge provides controls on the toolbar and in the Folders and Favorites panels.

To select and preview graphics in Bridge:

1. Do any of the following:

   In the **Folders** panel, navigate to the folder to be opened. You can use the scrolling arrows, and you can expand or collapse any folder by clicking its arrowhead. Display the contents of a folder by clicking its icon in the **Folders** panel or by double-clicking its thumbnail in the **Content** panel. Note: For folder thumbnails to display in the Content panel, View > Show Folders must be checked.

   Click the **Go Back** button ◄ on the toolbar **A** to step back through the last folders viewed, or the **Go Forward** button ► to reverse those steps.

   Click a folder name in the **Favorites** panel.

   From the **Go to Parent or Favorites** menu ◢ on the toolbar, choose a parent or favorites folder.

   Click a folder name on the **Path** bar (if the bar isn't showing, choose Window > Path Bar).

   From one of the menus ▶ on the Path bar, choose a folder. If another submenu displays, click another folder; repeat until you reach the desired folder.

➤ To display thumbnails for files in all the nested subfolders inside the current folder, choose Show Items from Subfolders from its menu.▶ To restore the normal view, click the Cancel button ◙ on the Path bar.

2. In the **Content** panel, do either of the following:

   Click a thumbnail. A colored border will appear around it, and data about the file will be listed in the Metadata panel. An enlarged preview of the graphic will also display in the Preview panel, if that panel is showing.

   To select multiple files, Cmd-click/Ctrl-click nonconsecutive thumbnails; or click the first thumbnail in a series of consecutive thumbnails, then Shift-click the last one you want to select.**B**

3. If the file for the currently selected thumbnail contains multiple artboards, you can cycle through

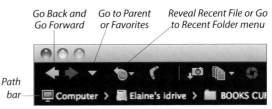

Go Back and Go Forward   Go to Parent or Favorites   Reveal Recent File or Go to Recent Folder menu

Path bar

A These are the navigation controls in Bridge.

The Preview panel displays an enlargement of one or more selected thumbnails, so you can shop and compare.

B Cmd-click/Ctrl-click multiple thumbnails in the Content panel to compare them in the Preview panel.

them by clicking the left or right arrow below the preview or by entering the desired artboard number in the field and then pressing Return/Enter.**A**

➤ A number in the upper left corner of a document thumbnail indicates that it's in a stack (user-created group). To display all the document thumbnails in a stack, click the number; to collapse the stack, click the number again. To learn more about stacks, see page 67.

➤ To cycle through thumbnails in the same folder, press the left or right arrow key. To quickly locate and select a particular thumbnail, start typing the file name (you don't need to click anywhere first).

To add a folder to the Favorites panel:

Do either of the following:

Drag a folder icon from the Content panel or from the Desktop into the Favorites panel.

Right-click a folder in the Folders or Content panel and choose **Add to Favorites** (or click the folder, then choose File > Add to Favorites).

A *In the Preview panel, you can cycle through multiple artboards in an Illustrator document by clicking the left or right arrow or by entering the desired artboard number in the field.*

➤ To remove a folder from the list of Favorites, right-click it and choose Remove from Favorites.

➤ Via check boxes in the Favorite Items area of Adobe Bridge CC/Edit > Preferences > General, you can control which system-defined folders appear in the top part of the Favorites panel.

VIEWING THE METADATA OF A FILE

When you click the thumbnail for an Illustrator document, information about the file displays in expandable categories in the Metadata panel. You can use the IPTC Core category in this panel to attach creator, description, copyright, and other information to the currently selected file: Click the field next to a listing, enter or modify the file description information, press Tab to cycle through and edit other data, then click the Apply button ◾ in the lower right corner.

Opening files from Bridge

You can open as many files in Illustrator as the currently available RAM and scratch disk space on your computer will allow. (To learn how to import files from other programs into Illustrator, see Chapter 22.)

To open files from Bridge into Illustrator:

1. In the Content panel, display the thumbnails for the documents you want to open.

2. Do either of the following:

   Double-click a thumbnail.

   Click a thumbnail or select multiple thumbnails, then double-click one of them or press Cmd-O/Ctrl-O.

   Illustrator will launch, if it isn't already running, and the chosen document(s) will appear onscreen.

3. If the Font Problems dialog or an alert about a color profile appears, see the next page. If an alert about a linked image file appears, see the sidebar on page 309 and the first task on page 316.

➤ You can also open a file by right-clicking its thumbnail, then choosing Open (or Open With > Adobe Illustrator CC 2014) from the context menu.

➤ To locate a file in Finder/Explorer, right-click its thumbnail in Bridge and choose Reveal in Finder/Reveal in Explorer from the context menu. The folder that the file resides in will open in a window in Finder/Explorer and the file icon will be selected.

➤ By default, the Bridge window stays open after you use it to open a file. To have the Bridge window close/minimize as you open a file, hold down Option/Alt while double-clicking the file thumbnail.

To reopen a recently opened file:

To reopen a file that was recently opened and then closed, do one of the following:

Choose from the **Open Recent File** menu on the right side of the Path bar.

Choose from the File > **Open Recent** submenu.

From the **Reveal Recent File or Go to Recent Folder** menu on the toolbar, choose Adobe Illustrator > **Recent Adobe Illustrator Files**, then in the Content panel, click the thumbnail for a file to open it. To redisplay an "actual" folder when you return to Bridge, click the Go Back arrow or a Favorites folder.

RESPONDING TO ALERT DIALOGS UPON OPENING A FILE

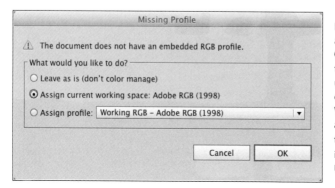

If you open a file in Illustrator that is using a missing font (the font isn't available or isn't installed), the Adobe Typekit dialog will appear. Typekit is an online set of fonts available to Creative Cloud subscribers. If the missing font is available via Typekit (indicated by a check mark next to the font name), you can simply press the Sync Fonts button to activate it. If you click Close to let the document open with a substitute font and that missing font subsequently becomes available in the system, that font will also become available on the font menus in Illustrator and the type will re-display correctly in the document. If you'd like to replace the missing font, click the Find Fonts button to choose a replacement font for the missing font. ★

If the color profile in a file that you open doesn't match the current working space for Illustrator, the Embedded Profile Mismatch alert dialog will appear. Click Use the Embedded Profile (Instead of the Working Space) if you must keep the document's current profile; or to convert the profile to the current working space (and for better consistency with your color management workflow), click Convert Document's Colors to the Working Space. Click OK. (See also pages 17–19 and 21.)

If the Missing Profile alert dialog appears as you open a file, click Assign Current Working Space. Listed next to this option will be the profile that is used in the Color Settings preset you chose for Illustrator on pages 17–19. With North America Prepress 2 chosen as the preset (for an RGB workflow), that profile will be Adobe RGB (1998); in a CMYK workflow, the profile will be U.S. Web Coated (SWOP) v2.

Customizing the Bridge window

To display or hide the panels:

On the **Window** menu, check which panels you want to show or hide.

➤ To hide (and then show) the side panes, press Tab. To hide one side pane, double-click the dark vertical bar between that pane and the middle pane.

To configure the panes and panels manually:

Do any of the following:

To make a panel or panel group taller or shorter, drag its horizontal gripper bar upward or downward.**A**

To make a whole pane wider or narrower, drag its vertical gripper bar to the left or right;**B** the adjacent pane will resize accordingly.

You can minimize/maximize some panels by double-clicking the panel tab.

To move a panel into a different group, drag the panel tab, and release the mouse when the blue drop zone border appears around the desired group.

To display a panel as a separate group, drag its tab between two panels, and release the mouse when the horizontal blue drop zone line appears.

➤ To save a Bridge layout as a user-created workspace for easy access in the future, see page 66.

To resize the document thumbnails:

At the bottom of the Bridge window, drag the **Thumbnail Size** slider **C** or click the **Smaller Thumbnail Size** button ☐ or **Larger Thumbnail Size** button.☐

➤ To display only full thumbnails, with grid lines between them, click the Lock Thumbnail Grid button ▦ at the bottom of the Bridge window. With this option on, the thumbnails won't reshuffle if you resize the Content panel.

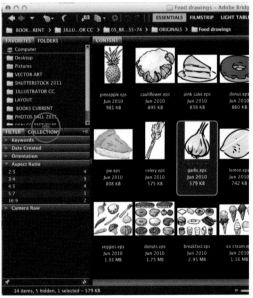

A We are moving the gripper bar upward to shorten the Favorites panel group and lengthen the Filter panel group.

B We are moving the gripper bar for the right pane to the left to widen the Preview and Metadata panels.

C Use the Thumbnail Size slider to resize the thumbnails in the Content panel.

To control the format in which metadata displays in the Content panel:

1. In the lower right corner of the Bridge window, click one of these buttons: **A** **View Content as Thumbnails** (minimal file data), **View Content as Details** (more file data),**B** or **View Content as List** (small thumbnails with columns of data).

    ➤ If the View Content as List button is activated, you can change the column order by dragging any column header to the left or right.

2. To control which categories of metadata display below or next to the file thumbnails when the View Content as Thumbnails button is activated, go to Adobe Bridge CC/Edit > Preferences > Thumbnails, then select from any or all of the **Show** menus. For example, to have Bridge list file sizes, choose Size.

➤ When the View Content as Thumbnails button is activated, you can toggle the display of data on and off by pressing Cmd-T/Ctrl-T.

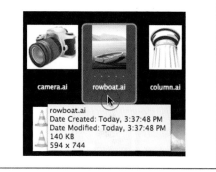

METADATA IN THE TOOL TIPS

If Show Tooltips is checked in Adobe Bridge CC/ Edit Preferences > Thumbnails, and you rest the pointer on a document thumbnail, the tool tip will list the metadata for that file. Uncheck the option if the tool tips become annoying.

View Content   *View Content*   *View Content*
as Thumbnails   *as Details*   *as List*

    A *These buttons control the display of metadata in the Content panel.*

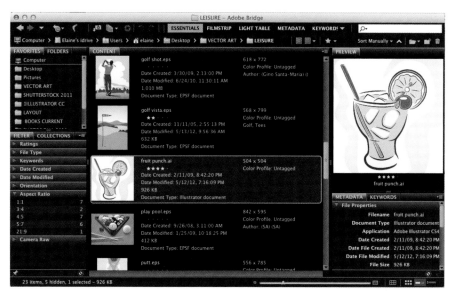

B *When the View Content as Details button is activated, metadata displays next to the file thumbnails.*

Saving custom workspaces

By saving each workspace that you customize, you will be able to access those settings again quickly at any time. For example, you could save one workspace that is designed for locating files (a large Favorites/Folders panel), another workspace that is set up for browsing many thumbnails (a variation on the Light Table workspace), and yet another workspace that is geared toward creating and applying keywords (a lengthened Keywords panel).

To save a custom workspace for Bridge:

1. Do all of the following:

   Choose a size and location for the overall Bridge window.

   Arrange the panel sizes and groups as desired.

   Choose a thumbnail size for the Content panel.

   Choose a sorting order from the Sort menu at the top of the Bridge window (see page 72).

   Click a View Content button.

2. From the **Workspace** menu on the workspace switcher, choose **New Workspace**.

3. In the New Workspace dialog,**A** enter a Name for the workspace, check Save Window Location as Part of Workspace and/or Save Sort Order as Part of Workspace (both are optional), then click Save.

   Note: Your new workspace will be listed first on the workspace switcher, and will be assigned the first shortcut (Cmd-F1/Ctrl-F1). To change the order of the workspaces on the bar, drag any workspace name horizontally to a different slot. When you do this, the shortcuts will be reassigned based on the new order.

➤ To delete a user-saved workspace, from the Workspace menu, choose Delete Workspace. From the menu in the dialog, choose the workspace to be deleted, then click Delete.

Resetting the Bridge workspace

When you make a manual change to a saved workspace, the change sticks with the workspace, even if you switch to a different one. For instance, if you were to change the thumbnail size for the default Filmstrip workspace, click a different workspace, then click back on the Filmstrip workspace, the new thumbnail size would still display. Via the commands for resetting workspaces, you can restore the default settings to any individual predefined (standard Adobe) or user-saved workspace or to all the predefined workspaces.

To reset the Bridge workspace:

Do either of the following:

To restore the default settings to one workspace, right-click the workspace name on the switcher and choose **Reset**.

To restore the default settings to all the Adobe predefined workspaces, choose **Reset Standard Workspaces** from the Workspace menu.

A *In the New Workspace dialog, enter a Name for your custom workspace and choose options for it.*

CHOOSING COLORS FOR THE BRIDGE INTERFACE

In Adobe Bridge CC/Edit > Preferences > General (Cmd-K/Ctrl-K), you can choose a User Interface Brightness (gray) value for the side panes; a different Image Backdrop value for the Content and Preview panels and for the background behind files when displayed in Full Preview View, Slideshow, or Review Mode; and an Accent Color for the border around selected folders, thumbnails, and stacks.

GETTING TO ILLUSTRATOR QUICKLY

If Illustrator was the last Adobe application you were using, you can get back to it quickly from Bridge by clicking the Return to Adobe Illustrator (boomerang) button 🔳 on the toolbar. Illustrator will launch, if it isn't already running.

Using thumbnail stacks

Before learning about stacks, you need to know how to rearrange file thumbnails in the Content panel.

To rearrange thumbnails manually:

Drag any thumbnail (or select, then drag multiple thumbnails) to a new location. Okay, that was a no-brainer. The header on the Sort menu switches to "Sort Manually."

➤ Thumbnails remain where you place them unless you change the sorting order or perform a stacking operation.

One method for controlling how many thumbnails display at a given time is to group them into stacks. You can select the thumbnails for a stack based on any characteristic, such as a client or project, or the subject matter of the artwork.

To group thumbnails into a stack:

1. Shift-click or Cmd-click/Ctrl-click to select multiple thumbnails.**A** The first thumbnail in the selection is going to become the "stack thumbnail" (will display on top of the stack).

2. Press Cmd-G/Ctrl-G or right-click one of the selected thumbnails and choose Stack > **Group as Stack.B** A stack looks like a couple of playing cards in a pile, with the stack thumbnail on top. The number in the upper left corner (called the "stack number") indicates how many thumbnails the stack contains.

To select the thumbnails in a stack:

To expand, display, and select all the thumbnails in a stack, click the stack number (click it again to collapse the stack).

To select all the thumbnails in a stack while keeping the stack collapsed, click the stack border (the bottom "card") or Option-click/Alt-click the stack thumbnail (the top one in the stack). Note that although the stack is collapsed, because it is selected, all the thumbnails it contains are displaying in the Preview panel, if that panel is showing.

To rearrange thumbnails within a stack:

To move a thumbnail to a different position in an expanded stack, click it to deselect the other selected thumbnails, then drag it to a new spot (as shown by the vertical drop zone line).

To move a whole stack:

1. Collapse the stack, then Option-click/Alt-click the stack thumbnail. The borders of both "cards" in the stack should now be highlighted.

2. Drag the document thumbnail (not the border).

➤ If you drag the top thumbnail of an unselected stack, you'll move just that thumbnail, not the whole stack.

To add a thumbnail to a stack:

Drag a thumbnail over a stack thumbnail, or if the stack is expanded, to the desired position.

To remove a thumbnail from a stack:

1. Click the stack number to expand the stack.

2. Click a thumbnail to be removed (to deselect the other thumbnails), then drag it out of the stack.

To ungroup a stack:

1. Click the stack number or stack thumbnail.

2. Press Cmd-Shift-G/Ctrl-Shift-G (Stacks > Ungroup from Stack) or right-click a stack thumbnail and choose Stack > **Ungroup from Stack**. The stack number and border will disappear.

A We selected six thumbnails to be grouped in a stack…

B …then chose the Group as Stack command.

Searching for files

To find files via Bridge:

1. In Bridge, choose Edit > **Find** (Cmd-F/Ctrl-F). The Find dialog opens.**A**

2. From the **Look In** menu in the Source area, choose the folder to be searched (by default, the current folder is listed). To select a folder that's not on the list, choose Look In: Browse, locate the desired folder, then click Open.

3. From the menus in the **Criteria** area, choose search criteria (e.g., Filename, Date Created, Keywords, or Rating), choose a parameter from the adjoining menu, and enter data in the field. To add another criterion to the search, click the ⊕ button, or to remove a row of fields, click ⊖.

4. From the **Match** menu, choose "If any criteria are met" to find files based on one or more of the criteria you have specified, or choose "If all criteria are met" to confine the selection to files that meet all of the criteria.

5. Check **Include All Subfolders** to let Bridge search through any of the subfolders that are contained within the folder you chose in step 2.

6. *Optional:* Check Include Non-indexed Files to let Bridge search files that it hasn't yet indexed (files that Bridge has yet to display). This could slow down the search.

7. Click Find. The results of the search will display in the Content panel.**B** The parent folder will be listed on the Path bar and on the Reveal Recent File or Go to Recent Folder menu.

8. To create a collection from the search results, see the following page.

➤ To discard the current search results and initiate a new search, click New Search, or to dismiss the results, click the Cancel button.

Find dialog

Find

Source

Look in: ART for SCREENSHOTS

Criteria

| Filename | contains | eggs | ⊖ ⊕ |
| Keywords | contains | cooking | ⊖ ⊕ |

Results

Match: If any criteria are met

☑ Include All Subfolders
☐ Include Non-indexed Files (may be slow)

Find   Cancel

A *Use the Find dialog to search for and locate files based on various criteria.*

QUICK SEARCH FOR A FILE

In the Favorites panel, click Computer, then double-click the thumbnail for your hard disk; or navigate to a particular folder. In the search field 🔍▾ on the Bridge toolbar, type the name of the file you're looking for, then press Return/Enter.

B *The search results from the Find command display in the Content panel. The parameters that you used for the search and the name of the folder that was searched will be listed as the Find Criteria.*

Creating and using collections

The collection features in Bridge provide a useful way to catalog and access files without your actually having to relocate them. There are two kinds of collections: a Smart Collection, which is created from the results of a Find search, and what we call a "nonsmart" collection, which is created by dragging thumbnails manually to a collection icon.

To create a Smart Collection:

1. Click the tab for the Collections panel. (If it's hidden, choose Window > Collections Panel.)

2. Perform a search via the Edit > Find command (see the preceding page). When the search is complete, click the **Save as Smart Collection** button at the top of the Content panel.**A**

3. A new Smart Collection icon appears in the Collections panel. Type a name in the highlighted field, then press Return/Enter.**B**

➤ To add a collection to the Favorites panel, right-click the icon and choose Add to Favorites.

➤ To delete a collection, click it, then click the Delete Collection button. If an alert appears, click Yes. Not to worry: This won't delete the actual files.

To display the contents of a collection:

Click an icon in the Collections panel.

If you edit an existing Smart Collection based on altered criteria in a new search, the collection contents will update automatically.

To edit a Smart Collection:

1. In the Collections panel, click the icon for an existing Smart Collection.

2. At the top of the Content panel or in the lower left corner of the Collections panel, click the **Edit Smart Collection** button. **C**

3. The Edit Smart Collection dialog opens. It looks like the Find dialog, which is shown on the preceding page. To add another criterion, click the next ⊕ button, choose and enter the criterion, and choose "If any criteria are met" from the Match menu. You can also change the source folder and/or change the original criteria.

4. Click Save. The results of the new search will display in the Content panel.

   Note: If you move a thumbnail from a Smart Collection into a folder that wasn't used in the search (or move the actual file), it will be removed from the collection, but not from your hard disk. Don't *delete* a thumbnail from a Smart Collection however, unless you want Bridge to delete it from your hard disk!

A *To create a Smart Collection, click the Save as Smart Collection button in the Content panel.*

B *A new Smart Collection appears on the Collections panel. Type a name for it in the field.*

C *To edit a Smart Collection, click a Smart Collection icon on the Collections panel, then click the Edit Smart Collection button at the bottom of the panel.*

You can also create a collection without running a search first. We call this a "nonsmart" collection. You can add to a nonsmart collection by dragging thumbnails into it (you cannot do this for a Smart Collection).

To create a nonsmart collection:

1. On the Content panel, select the document thumbnails to be placed into a collection. On the **Collections** panel, click the **New Collection** button, ⊞ then click Yes in the alert dialog.

2. On the Collections panel, rename the collection,**A** then press Return/Enter. The number of thumbnails the collection contains is listed next to the name.

To add thumbnails to a nonsmart collection:

1. Display the Collections panel.

2. Drag one or more thumbnails from the Content panel over a nonsmart collection icon. ⊞ **B**

➤ You can copy and paste, or drag, thumbnails from a Smart Collection into a nonsmart one, or from one nonsmart collection into another.

To remove thumbnails from a nonsmart collection:

1. On the Collections panel, click the icon for a nonsmart collection ⊞ to display its contents.

2. Select the thumbnails to be removed, then click **Remove from Collection** at the top of the Content panel.**C**

If you rename a file in Finder/Explorer or move a file from its original location on disk, it may be listed as missing from any standard collections it is a part of, and Bridge will try to relink it to those collections. If Bridge is unsuccessful, do as follows.

To relink a missing file to a nonsmart collection:

1. On the Collections panel, click the collection to which you need to relink one or more files.

2. Next to the Missing File Detected alert at the top of the Content panel, click **Fix.D**

3. In the Find Missing Files dialog, click Browse, locate and select the missing file, then click Open. Click OK to exit the dialog.

A *To create a new collection, click the New Collection button, then type a name for it in the highlighted field.*

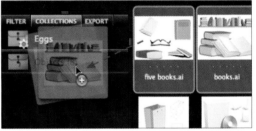

B *Drag one or more thumbnails to a nonsmart collection listing to add them to that collection.*

C *To take selected thumbnails out of the currently selected collection, click Remove from Collection.*

D *To relink a file that's missing from a collection, click Fix.*

Rating and labeling thumbnails

If you assign each thumbnail a star rating and/or a color label, you'll be able to use that criterion to sort thumbnails in the Content panel, display them via the Filter panel (see the following page), and locate them via the Find command. In addition, you can apply a Reject rating to any thumbnails that you want to hide from the Content panel (but aren't ready to delete from your hard drive).

To rate and label thumbnails:

1. Select one or more thumbnails in the Content panel.

2. When you do any of the following, either a specific number of stars, a "Reject" label, or a colored label appears below the image thumbnail:

   From the Label menu, choose a **Rating** (number of stars) and/or a **Label** (color-coded strip).**A**

   Right-click a thumbnail in the Content panel, and from the Label submenu on the context menu, choose a category.

   Right-click in the Preview panel and choose a star rating and/or a label.

   Click a thumbnail, then click any one of the five dots below it; stars will appear.**B** To remove a star, click the star to its left. To remove all the stars from a thumbnail, click to the left of the first star.**C** (If you don't see the dots or stars, enlarge the thumbnails via the Thumbnail Size slider, and they should appear.)

   Press one of the keyboard shortcuts that are listed on the Label menu.

   To label the losers with a red "Reject" label, choose Label > **Reject** (Option-Delete/Alt-Del).**D** If Show Reject Files is unchecked on the View menu, all rejected thumbnails will be hidden.

➤ If tool tips get in the way of your adding or removing stars, go to Adobe Bridge CC/Edit > Preferences > Thumbnails and uncheck Show Tooltips.

➤ You can rename the Label categories in the Labels panel of the Preferences dialog for Bridge.

To remove ratings or labels from thumbnails:

1. Select one or more document thumbnails in the Content panel.

2. Do either or both of the following:

   Choose Label > **No Rating** or press Cmd-0/Ctrl-0 (zero).

   Choose Label > **No Label**.

A This thumbnail has an Approved (green) rating.

B We clicked the third dot on this thumbnail to assign a three-star rating…

C …but then we changed our minds, so we clicked to the left of the stars to remove them.

D This poor thumbnail has a Reject rating.

Filtering the display of thumbnails

The Filter panel lists data that is specific to files in the current folder, such as their label, star rating, date created, or keywords. When you check specific criteria in the panel, only thumbnails meeting those criteria display in the Content panel. (Note that thumbnails within stacks are ignored.)

To filter the display of thumbnails:

Do either of the following:

On the **Filter Items by Rating** menu 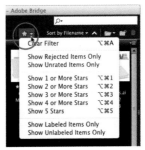 on the Bridge toolbar,**A** check the desired criteria.

On the **Filter** panel, click the arrowhead to expand any category, such as Labels or Ratings, then check a criterion.**B** For example, to display only files that have a three-star rating, check the three-star listing under Ratings. To require that additional criteria be met, check more listings, either in the same category or in other categories. (To remove a criterion, click the listing again.)

➤ To prevent the current filters (check marks) from clearing when you display other folders, click the Keep Filter When Browsing 📌 button on the panel. When active, the button will have a highlight color.

➤ To remove all check marks from the Filter panel, click the Clear Filter ◯ button at the bottom of the panel or press Cmd-Option-A/Ctrl-Alt-A.

➤ The categories in the Filter panel (e.g., Ratings, Keywords) change dynamically depending on what categories are checked on the panel menu and on the metadata in files in the currently selected folder. For instance, if you haven't applied ratings to any files in the current folder, there won't be a Ratings category; if you apply a rating to one of the thumbnails, a Ratings category will appear.

B Because we checked the three-star ranking in the Filter panel (Ratings category), only thumbnails matching that criterion (that have three stars) are displaying in the Content panel.

Choosing a sorting order for thumbnails

The criterion that is checked on the Sort menu controls the order in which thumbnails display in the Content panel (regardless of which folder is currently displayed). By applying ratings, labels, and keywords (see the next page), choosing a sorting order, and checking categories in the Filter panel (see below), you'll be able to locate and display just the files you need. The sorting order also affects the batch and automate commands in Bridge, because those commands process files based on the current sequence of thumbnails.

To choose a sorting order for thumbnails:

From the **Sort** menu on the Path bar, choose a sorting order (such as By Date Created).**C** All the thumbnails in the Content panel will be re-sorted. To restore the last manual sort (rearrangement of thumbnails by dragging), choose Manually on the menu. If you display a different folder, the current sorting order will apply. Note: Sorting doesn't change the order of thumbnails within stacks.

➤ To reverse the current order, click the Ascending Order 🔼 or Descending Order 🔽 arrowhead.

A You can filter the display of thumbnails via the Filter Items by Rating menu.

C From the Sort menu on the Path bar, choose a sorting order for thumbnails.

Assigning keywords to files

Keywords (words that are assigned to files) are used by search utilities to locate files and by file management programs to organize them. In Bridge, you can create parent keyword categories (for events, people, places, etc.), as well as nested subkeywords within those categories, and then assign them to your files. You can locate files by entering keywords as search criteria in the Find dialog, build a Smart Collection based on a search for keywords, or display files by checking Keywords listings in the Filter panel.

To create keywords and subkeywords:

1. Display the Keywords panel. To create a new parent keyword category, click the **New Keyword** button, ⊞ then type a keyword.

2. To create a nested subkeyword, click a parent keyword, click the **New Sub Keyword** button, ⊞ type a word, then press Return/Enter.**A** Each time you want to add another subkeyword, click the parent keyword first. You can also create nested sub-subkeywords.

➤ You can move (drag) any subkeyword from one parent keyword category into another.

To assign keywords to files:

1. Select one or more document thumbnails in the Content panel. If keywords are already assigned to any of the files in your selection, those words will be listed next to Assigned Keywords at the top of the Keywords panel; you can assign more.

2. Check the box for one or more subkeywords (and, if desired, keywords).**B** To remove a keyword or subkeyword from a file, uncheck the box.

➤ The keywords that are assigned to the files in the current folder are also listed in the Keywords category in the Filter panel.

➤ To assign keywords via the File Info dialog, select one or more thumbnails, then from the Refine menu ⌸ on the Bridge toolbar, choose File Info (Cmd-I/Ctrl-I). In the Keywords field of the Description tab, enter keywords, separated by semi-colons or commas. Be on the alert for typing errors!

➤ If you click the thumbnail for a file to which keywords were assigned outside of Bridge, those keywords will display temporarily in the Keywords panel, under Other Keywords. To convert a tempo-rary keyword to a permanent one, right-click it and choose Make Persistent from the context menu.

A *We created a new parent keyword called "Office Supplies," kept that category selected, then via the New Sub Keyword button, added some subkeywords to it.*

B *We selected multiple file thumbnails, then assigned a subkeyword to them by checking the box.*

USING THE KEYWORDS PANEL

Rename a parent keyword or subkeyword	Right-click the word, choose Rename from the context menu, then type a name (this won't alter data that is already embedded).
Delete a parent keyword or subkeyword	Click the word, then click the Delete Keyword button. ⌶ If that keyword is assigned to any files, it will now be listed in italics. (To reinstate an itali-cized word, choose Make Persistent from the context menu.)
Find a keyword or subkeyword	Type the word in the search field at the bottom of the panel. Choose a search parameter from the menu. ⌕

Exporting the Bridge cache

When the contents of a particular folder are displayed in the Content panel in Bridge for the first time, Bridge creates hidden cache files pertaining to those files and places them in the same folder. Bridge uses the cache to display program features, such as ratings, labels, and high-quality thumbnails. The thumbnails in a given folder redisplay more quickly once the cache has been created. Note: These hidden cache files can be read and used only by Bridge.

Setting the following preference will ensure that Bridge includes its cache data with any files that you copy to a removable disk or to a shared folder on a network.

To set a preference to have Bridge export the cache automatically:

1. In Bridge, choose Adobe Bridge CC/Edit > Preferences (Cmd-K/Ctrl-K) > Cache.

2. Under Options, check **Automatically Export Cache to Folders When Possible**, then click OK.

If for some reason the cache preference is turned off and you need to export the cache for the files in a specific folder, follow these steps. The hidden cache files will be placed in the current folder and will also be included if you move or copy the Illustrator files.

To export the Bridge cache for the current folder:

1. Display the contents of a folder in Bridge.

2. Choose Tools > Cache > **Build and Export Cache**.

3. In the Build Cache dialog, keep the Build 100% Previews option off, but do check **Export Cache to Folders**, then click OK.

➤ To display the cache file icons for the currently displayed folder, choose View > Show Hidden Files.

If Bridge is having trouble displaying a particular folder of thumbnails, try purging the cache for those thumbnails. This will prompt Bridge to rebuild the cache.

To purge cache files:

Do either of the following:

To purge all the cache files from the current folder, choose Tools > Cache > **Purge Cache for Folder** "[current folder name]."

To purge the cache files just for specific thumbnails, select them, then right-click one of them and choose **Purge Cache for Selection**.

Managing files via Bridge

To create a new folder:

Navigate to the folder to which you want to add a folder, then click the **New Folder** button 📁 at the right end of the Bridge toolbar. Type a name to replace the highlighted one; press Return/Enter.

You can move files to a different folder on your hard disk either by dragging them or via a command.

To move or copy files between folders:

Method 1 (by dragging)

1. Select one or more thumbnails (Content panel).

2. In the Folders panel, navigate to (but don't click) the folder or subfolder into which you want to move the selected files.

3. To move the selected files, drag them over the folder name in the Folders panel; or to copy them, do the same, except hold down Option/Ctrl while dragging (a + symbol will appear in the pointer). Or if you want to move (not copy) files to another hard disk, hold down Cmd/Shift while dragging.

Method 2 (via the context menu)

1. Select one or more thumbnails (Content panel).

2. Right-click one of the selected thumbnails, then from the **Move To** or **Copy To** submenu on the context menu, do either of the following:

Select a folder under **Recent Folders** or **Favorites**.

Select **Choose Folder**, locate a folder in the Open dialog, then click Open.

➤ To copy files via the Clipboard, select one or more thumbnails, press Cmd-C/Ctrl-C (copy), click the desired folder, then press Cmd-V/Ctrl-V (paste).

To delete a file or folder:

1. Click an image or folder thumbnail or Cmd-click/Ctrl-click or Shift-click multiple thumbnails.

2. Press Cmd-Delete/Ctrl-Backspace. If an alert dialog appears, click OK.

➤ To retrieve a deleted file or folder, choose Edit > Undo *immediately*. Or drag it from the trash for your operating system into the Content panel.

To rename a file or folder:

1. Click a thumbnail, then click the file or folder name; the name becomes highlighted.

2. Type a new name (keep the extension), then either press Return/Enter or click outside the name field.

In Illustrator, all paths consist of straight and/ or curved line segments that are connected by anchor points. Paths can be closed, such as polygons and ovals, or open, such as lines and spirals. In the instructions below, we show you how to select and delete unwanted objects. Following that are instructions for using the Rectangle, Rounded Rectangle, Ellipse, Polygon, Star, Line Segment, and Spiral tools, with which you can produce geometric objects quickly and easily. In addition, you'll learn how to further refine shapes using the Live Shapes feature.

In the next chapter, you will learn to draw in a loose, freehand manner. Once you master these basics, you will learn how to select paths for editing (Chapter 8), copy and align them (Chapter 9), apply colors to them (Chapter 10), and change their shape (Chapters 11 and 12). Other methods for creating objects, such as by using the Pen tool, type tools, and tracing commands, are covered in later chapters.

Selecting and deleting objects

You'll be creating many different shapes in this chapter, and your artboard may soon become crowded with junk. To remove an object you've just created, choose Edit > Undo (Cmd-Z/Ctrl-Z). To remove an object that's been around for a while, do the following.

To select and delete objects:

1. Choose the **Selection** tool (V), then click the object to be deleted, or drag a marquee around multiple objects to be deleted.

2. Press Delete/Backspace.

➤ If you use the Direct Selection tool to select points on an object, you can press Delete/Backspace twice to delete the whole object.

THINGS TO DO BEFORE CREATING OBJECTS!

➤ From the Tools panel, choose the drawing mode of Draw Normal. On the occasion that you want a new object to appear behind an existing selected one, choose Draw Behind mode instead. For Draw Inside mode, see pages 371 and 375. To cycle through the modes, press Shift-D.

➤ If your document contains multiple artboards, via the Artboards panel or via the Artboard Navigation menu at the bottom of the document window, display and select the artboard to which you want to add new objects.

➤ If your document contains multiple layers, click a layer to contain the new object (see Chapter 13).

GEOMETRIC OBJECTS

6

CHOOSING COLORS QUICKLY

Methods for choosing and applying fill and stroke colors are explained fully in Chapter 10. In the meantime, if you want to choose a fill and a stroke color for the tools you will be using in this chapter, see "A quick color primer" on page 85.

Creating rectangles and ellipses

To create a rectangle or an ellipse by dragging:

1. Choose the **Rectangle** tool 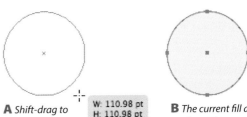 (M) or the **Ellipse** tool (L).

2. Drag diagonally.**A** As you drag, a wireframe representation of the rectangle or oval will display. When you release the mouse, the rectangle or oval will be selected, and the current fill and stroke settings will be applied to it.**B–C**

   You can also use these modifiers while dragging:

   To draw the object from its center, Option-drag/Alt-drag.

   To move the rectangle or ellipse as you draw it, before releasing the mouse, Spacebar-drag.

   To draw a square with the Rectangle tool or a circle with the Ellipse tool, Shift-drag.

To create a rectangle or an ellipse by specifying dimensions:

1. Choose the **Rectangle** tool (M) or the **Ellipse** tool (L), then click on an artboard. The Rectangle or Ellipse dialog opens.**D**

2. *Optional:* To preserve the ratio of the last-used values, click the **Constrain Proportions** button.

3. Enter **Width** and **Height** values, then click OK.**E**

➤ To choose measurement units for Illustrator, see page 413.

A *Shift-drag to draw a perfect circle.*

W: 110.98 pt
H: 110.98 pt

B *The current fill and stroke settings are applied to the new object automatically.*

C *To put type on a circle, see pages 265–266.*

Ellipse

Width: 14 pt

Height: 14 pt

[Cancel] [OK]

D *Enter values in the Ellipse (or Rectangle) dialog.*

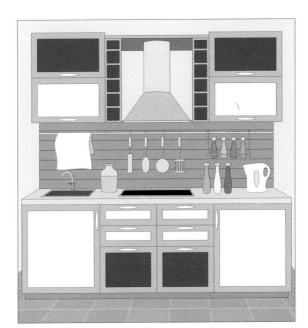

E *The cabinetry in this art was created using rectangles. To duplicate objects, see page 104.*

To create a rounded rectangle:

1. Choose the **Rounded Rectangle** tool.

2. Drag diagonally. As you drag, a wireframe representation of the rounded rectangle will display.**A** When you release the mouse, the rounded rectangle will be selected and the current fill and stroke settings will be applied to it.**B–C**

➤ As you create an object with the Rounded Rectangle tool, keep the mouse button down and press (and keep pressing) the up arrow to make the corners more round, or press and hold the down arrow to make them more square. Or press (don't hold) the left or right arrow to toggle between square and round corners.

➤ To draw a rounded rectangle of a specific size, choose the Rounded Rectangle tool, click on an artboard, then enter Width, Height, and Corner Radius values. The Corner Radius value, which controls the degree of curvature in the corners of rounded rectangles, can also be specified in Illustrator/Edit > Preferences > General. When changed in one location, the value updates in the other location automatically.

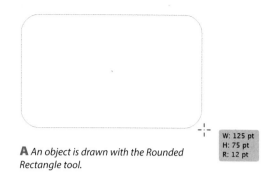

W: 125 pt
H: 75 pt
R: 12 pt

A *An object is drawn with the Rounded Rectangle tool.*

B *The rounded rectangle remains selected after it's drawn.*

C *This retro pattern contains rounded rectangles of various sizes and colors. (To create fill patterns, see pages 139–146.)*

DISPLAYING ON-OBJECT READOUTS

Turn on View > Smart Guides (the command should have a check mark), turn off View > Pixel Preview, and in Illustrator/Edit > Preferences > Smart Guides, check Measurement Labels. With these settings in place, the following will occur:

➤ As you create an object, its exact Width and Height dimensions will display in a readout.

W: 4.61 in
H: 3.72 in

➤ When the Selection or Direct Selection tool is above an anchor point or the center point of an object, a readout indicating its exact X (horizontal) and Y (vertical) location will display.

anchor
X: 22.85 in
Y: 1.13 in

If the Construction Guides preference is checked for Smart Guides and you move your pointer over the anchor point of an existing object while drawing a new one, a guide will extend from that anchor point. You can specify angles for Smart Guides in the Preferences dialog (see page 415).

Reshaping a path using Live Corners and Live Shapes

Using the Live Shapes feature for rectangles and rounded rectangles, you can change the style of one or more corners of a rectangle and the corners will maintain their radius as the rectangle or rounded rectangle is scaled (even non-proportionately). You can change the corner type and radius by dragging a corner widget or by adjusting the values in the Transform panel. On an open or closed path of any shape, you can change the corner type to a rounded, inverted rounded (concave), or beveled (chamfer) segment. Shapes other than rectangle and rounded rectangle are not live and will not maintain their corner radius when scaled non-uniformly.

To modify corners after drawing a shape ★

1. Using the Rectangle or Rounded Rectangle tool, draw a shape. Corner widgets will appear at each corner of the shape, **A** and the Transform panel will display showing the properties of the shape.**B** This is referred to as a Live Shape.

2. Drag a corner widget to adjust the corner radius. Press the up or down arrow keys on your keyboard to change the corner type as you drag, or Option-click/Alt-click a corner widget to change the corner type. You can also change the corner type in the Transform panel.

A All corner widgets are active after drawing a rectangle or rounded rectangle.

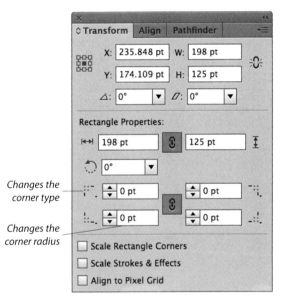

Changes the corner type

Changes the corner radius

B The Transform panel displays automatically by default after drawing a live shape.

KEEPING LIVE CORNERS LIVE ★

► Live Shapes (and their widgets) are preserved when you scale an object (rectangle or rounded rectangle) using the Scale or Free Transform tool, via the Scale tool dialog, or by dragging a handle on the object's bounding box (even when scaled non-proportionately).

► Live Corners (and their widgets) are preserved only when scaling the object proportionately. These objects can lose their corner editability if scaled non-proportionately.

► Some edits will convert a Live Corner to a standard anchor point with direction handles (make the corner "non-live"), such as if you move or drag a direction handle on an anchor point of a Live Shape or Live Corner.

► Rectangles from a file opened from a previous version of Illustrator will not contain Live Rectangles. To convert a standard rectangle to a Live Rectangle, simply choose Object > Shape > Convert to Rectangle.

To reshape the corners on a path: ★

1. Deselect all objects in your document. Choose the **Direct Selection** tool (A).

2. Click a corner anchor point on a path, or Shift-click multiple corner anchor points on one or more paths. The path(s) can be open or closed. A corner widget displays near each selected corner.**A**

   Note: If you don't see the widget(s), choose View > Show Corner Widget (the command on the menu should now be called Hide Corner Widget).

3. Do any of the following:

   Drag the widget toward or away from the anchor point.**B** While dragging, you can press the up or down arrow key on the keyboard to cycle through the three corner styles. One or more segments will be added to the corner of the object(s).

   ➤ To cycle through the corner styles a different way, hold down Option/Alt and click (and keep clicking) a corner widget.**C**

   Click the underlined **Corners** link on the Control panel, or double-click a corner widget on the path. In the dialog, click a different **Corner** style button, or change the **Radius** value, or click the other **Rounding** button (relative rounding or absolute rounding).**D** You can also change the Corner Radius value directly on the Control panel. Absolute rounding uses the exact numerical value to generate the corner for the selected widget(s), whereas relative rounding produces a corner that is relative to the angle creating the corner, which generally produces a sharper curve.

   Note: When a corner has the maximum Radius setting, the corner widget and corresponding path segment display a red highlight. **E**

➤ In Illustrator/Edit > Preferences > Selection & Anchor Display, you can check Hide Corner Widget for Angles Greater Than, then specify an angle value for corners above which you want Illustrator to hide the widget.

A *We selected an anchor point with the Direct Selection tool; the corner widget displays near it.*

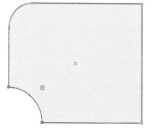

B *We're dragging the widget inward to create a rounded corner.*

C *We dragged the lower left widget inward, then pressed the up arrow to make the corner concave.*

D *The Corners dialog provides two rounding options, relative and absolute.*

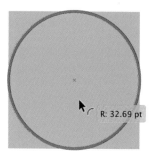

E *When you drag a corner to its maximum radius amount, the segment(s) are highlighted in red.*

Here's a quick introduction to one of the many commands on the Effect menu: Round Corners. Effects produce appearances, which are nonpermanent, editable changes. To learn more about effects, see Chapter 15.

To round the corners of an existing object using an effect:

1. Select one or more objects.**A**

2. On the Effect menu, under Illustrator Effects, choose Stylize > **Round Corners**.

3. In the dialog, check Preview. Choose a **Radius** value for the radius of the curve **B** (if you enter a value, press Tab to preview the new setting).

4. Click OK.**C** If you want to edit the Round Corners setting for the object at any time, display the Appearance panel, ⬤ then click Round Corners.

5. Make sure the New Art Has Basic Appearance option is checked on the Appearance panel menu, so any new objects you create won't have the Appearance panel settings that you have chosen.

Creating polygons

With the Polygon, Star, and Spiral tools, as with the other tools discussed in this chapter, all you have to do is drag in an artboard or enter values in the tool dialog.

To create a polygon by clicking:

1. Choose the **Polygon** tool. ⬡

2. Click where you want the center of the polygon to be located. The Polygon dialog opens.**D**

3. Enter a **Radius** value for the distance from the center of the object to the corner points (then press Tab).

4. Choose a number of **Sides** for the polygon by clicking the up or down arrow or by entering a number—3 for a triangle, 4 for a rectangle, etc. The sides will be of equal length.

5. Click OK.**E** A polygon will appear where you clicked, and the current fill and stroke settings will be applied to it automatically (see Chapter 10).

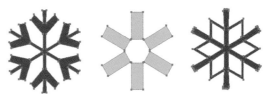

A *Three objects are selected.*

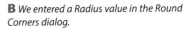

B *We entered a Radius value in the Round Corners dialog.*

C *Now the corners are rounded.*

D *We entered Radius and Sides values in the Polygon dialog.*

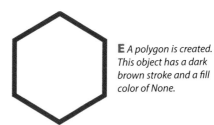

E *A polygon is created. This object has a dark brown stroke and a fill color of None.*

To create a polygon by dragging:

1. Choose the **Polygon** tool.

2. Drag in an artboard, starting from where you want the center of the polygon to be located.

   While dragging, do any of the following:

   To scale the polygon, drag away from or toward the center.

   To rotate the polygon, drag in a circular direction.

   To constrain the bottom edge of the polygon to the horizontal axis, hold down Shift.

   To add sides to or delete sides from the polygon, press the up or down arrow key.

   To move the polygon without scaling it, hold down the Spacebar.

3. When you release the mouse, the polygon will be selected, and the current fill and stroke settings will be applied to it.

➤ To align a new object with an existing object while drawing it, use Smart Guides (see pages 102–103.

Creating stars

To create a star by clicking:

1. Choose the **Star** tool.

2. Click where you want the center of the star to be located. The Star dialog opens.**A**

3. Enter **Radius 1** and **Radius 2** values, in points. The higher value is the distance from the center of the star to its outermost points; the lower value is the distance from the center of the star to the innermost points. The greater the difference between the two values, the narrower the arms of the star.

4. Choose a number of **Points** for the star by clicking the up or down arrow, by clicking in the field and then pressing the up or down arrow key, or by entering a number.

   ➤ To create a star that looks similar to the one shown in figure **B**, make the Radius 1 value twice the value of Radius 2, and choose 5 as the Points value.

5. Click OK.

➤ You can rotate the completed star (or any other object) via its bounding box. See page 147.

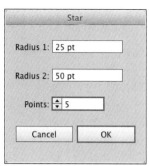

A *We entered Radius and Points values in the Star dialog.*

B *A star is born.*

CREATING ART FROM BASIC BUILDING BLOCKS

You can create illustrations like this one by using basic geometric objects as building blocks, such as ellipses, rectangles, and rounded rectangles.

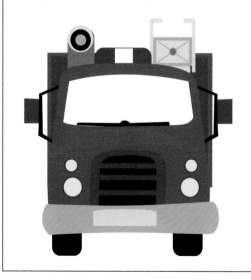

To create a star by dragging:

1. Choose the **Star** tool.

2. Drag in an artboard, starting from where you want the center of the star to be located.

   While dragging, do any of the following:

   To scale the star, drag away from or toward its center.

   To rotate the star, drag in a circular direction.

   To constrain two points of the star to the horizontal axis, drag with Shift held down.**A**

   To add points to or delete points from the star, press the up or down arrow key.**B**

   To move the star, drag with the Spacebar held down.

   To keep each pair of shoulders (opposing segments) parallel to each other, hold down Option/Alt.

   To increase or decrease the length of the arms of the star while keeping the inner radius points constant, drag away from or toward the center of the star with Cmd/Ctrl held down.**C**

3. When you release the mouse, the star will be selected and the current fill and stroke settings will be applied to it.**D**

➤ Hold down ~ (tilde) while dragging quickly with the Star or Polygon tool to create progressively larger (separate) copies of the object. The more rapidly you drag, the farther apart the copies will be from one another. You can apply new stroke colors and settings to the copies afterward. (See also the Offset Path command on page 106.)

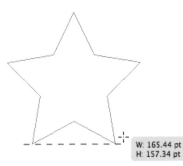

A *While dragging with the Star tool, we are holding down Shift to constrain two points of the star to the horizontal axis.*

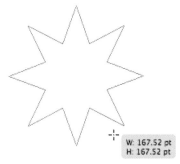

B *We pressed the up arrow key to add points to the star.*

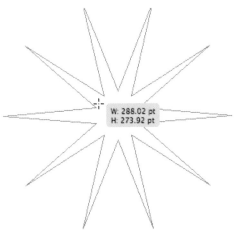

C *We dragged with Cmd/Ctrl held down to elongate the arms of the star.*

D *To apply gradients to objects, see Chapter 24. To move (extend) the points on a star, see page 158.*

Next, we'll show you how to use the Line Segment and Spiral tools (on the Line Segment tool pop-out menu), which create independent objects or groups of objects.

Creating line segments

The Line Segment tool creates straight lines. Each time you release the mouse and drag again with this tool, a new, separate path is created.

To draw a line segment by dragging:

1. Choose the **Line Segment** tool ✎ (\).

2. Drag to draw a line.**A–B** As you do so, you can do any of the following:

   To have the line extend outward from the point of origin, drag with Option/Alt held down.

   To constrain the line to the nearest 45° increment, drag with Shift held down.

   To move the line, drag with the Spacebar held down.

➤ To create multiple separate lines of varied lengths from the same center point but at different angles, drag in a circular direction with ~ (tilde) held down. Move the mouse rapidly as you create the copies to spread them apart.

To create a line segment by entering values:

1. Choose the **Line Segment** tool ✎ (\).

2. Click where you want the segment to begin. The Line Segment Tool Options dialog opens.

3. Enter the desired line **Length**, then press Tab.

4. Enter an **Angle** or move the dial.

5. *Optional:* Check Fill Line to assign the current fill color to the line, in addition to the current stroke color, which is assigned automatically (see Chapter 10). The fill color won't be revealed unless you reshape the line into a curve or an angle. With Fill Line unchecked, the line will have a fill of None, but you can apply a fill color (and also change the stroke color) after exiting the dialog.

6. Click OK.

➤ To restore the default settings to the Line Segment Tool Options dialog, Option-click/Alt-click the Reset button (Cancel becomes Reset).

> **DÉJA VU**
>
> When you open the options dialog for the Rectangle, Ellipse, Rounded Rectangle, Polygon, Star, Line Segment, or Spiral tool (by clicking an artboard with the tool), the last-used settings display — whether the last object was created by dragging or by using the dialog. To quickly create additional objects using the current options settings, click an artboard with the tool, then press Return/Enter to exit the dialog.

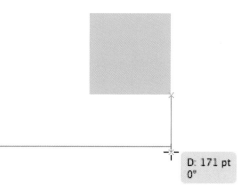

A *Shift is held down as a line is drawn, to constrain it to the horizontal axis. A Smart Guide (in green) is also being used to align the line to another object (see pages 102–103).*

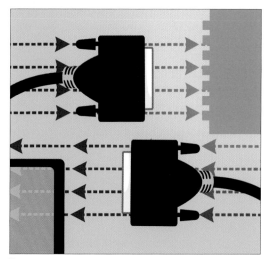

B *To create a dashed line, see page 124. To add an arrow-head to a line, see page 123.*

Creating spirals

To create a spiral by dragging:

1. Choose the **Spiral** tool.

2. Drag in the document window, starting from where you want the center of the spiral to be.

3. While dragging, do any of the following: **A**

   To scale the spiral, drag away from or toward the center.

   To control how tightly the spirals wind toward the center (the Decay value), Cmd-drag/Ctrl-drag slowly away from or toward the center.

   To add segments to or delete segments from the center of the spiral, press the up or down arrow key.

   To rotate the spiral, drag in a circular direction.

   To move the spiral, drag with the Spacebar down.

4. When you release the mouse, the spiral will be selected, and the current fill and stroke settings will be applied to it. **B–C**

Creating pixel-perfect artwork for the Web

➤ To make your artwork look as crisp as possible onscreen, particularly any straight horizontal or vertical edges, check **Align New Objects to Pixel Grid** in the Advanced area of the New Document dialog when you create your document. If you forgot that step, you can align objects that you subsequently create to the pixel grid by choosing the same option on the Transform panel menu.

➤ To align existing objects (except type objects) to the pixel grid, select them, then check **Align to Pixel Grid** on the full Transform panel. As you move or transform the objects or change their stroke weight, they will snap to the grid. To quickly select all the objects in your document that aren't aligned to the pixel grid, choose Select > Object > **Not Aligned to Pixel Grid**. Note: If you move pixel-aligned and non-pixel-aligned objects simultaneously, their relative positions will be preserved.

➤ To see a representation of the pixel grid onscreen, choose a zoom level of 600% or greater. In Illustrator/Edit > Preferences > Guides & Grid, check **Show Pixel Grid (Above 600% Zoom)**, and also turn on View > **Pixel Preview**. See also page 30.

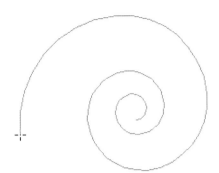

A *We drew this spiral with the Spiral tool.*

B *We applied the Streamer brush from the Borders_Novelty brush library to the spiral. To learn about brushes, see Chapter 23.*

C *Spirals can be altered in several ways, such as by applying brush strokes, a shear transformation, or effects. You will learn those techniques later in this book.*

If you enjoy sketching in a loose, freehand manner, the Pencil, Paintbrush, and Blob Brush tools will be right up your alley. Each tool has its own special attributes, which we explore in this chapter. Paths drawn with these tools can be reshaped using any of the techniques described in Chapters 11 and 12. In fact, in addition to being used to create objects, the Pencil and Blob Brush tools also have a reshaping function.

A quick color primer

Before exploring the freehand drawing tools, learn how to quickly set the fill color, stroke color, and stroke weight. Do this via either the Control panel or the in-panel editing feature of the Appearance panel.

To choose a fill or stroke color:

1. Choose the **Selection** tool ▶ (V), then click an object or drag a marquee around multiple objects.

2. Do either of the following:

   On the Control panel, click the Fill or Stroke square or arrowhead,**A** then on the temporary Swatches panel, click a swatch.

   On the Appearance panel, ◉ click the square for the Fill or Stroke listing, click the color square or arrowhead, then on the temporary Swatches panel, click a swatch.**B**

   Note: To choose a fill or stroke color of None, click the **None** button ▢ on the Swatches panel.

To choose a stroke weight:

   Do either of the following:

   On the Control panel, click the up or down Stroke Weight arrow.

   On the Appearance ◉ panel, click the Stroke link, then click the up or down Stroke Weight arrow on the temporary Stroke panel.

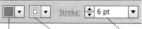

Fill square   Stroke square   Stroke
Weight

A *To open a temporary Swatches panel, click the Fill or Stroke square on the Control panel…*

B *…or on the Appearance panel.*

FILL AND STROKE DEFINED

► The fill displays inside a closed or open object or on a face within a Live Paint group. The stroke displays on the path of a closed or open object.

► The fill or stroke can be a solid color, a pattern, a gradient, or None (of the above).

► A stroke can be dashed or continuous. A Scatter, Calligraphic, Art, Bristle, or Pattern brush can also be applied to a stroke.

Note: To learn more about choosing and applying fill and stroke colors, see Chapter 10.

Note: For optimal results when using the Pencil, Paintbrush, or Blob Brush tool, draw with a pressure-sensitive tablet and a stylus. (Not to worry — although it's recommended, it's not mandatory.)

Drawing with the Pencil tool

The Pencil tool has three distinct functions: You can drag in a blank area of the artboard to create a new, open path (as described in the steps below); drag along the edge of an existing, selected path to reshape it (see page 165); or drag from an endpoint of an existing open path to add segments to it (see page 163).

Note: To choose options for the Pencil tool, see page 88.

To draw with the Pencil tool:

1. Choose the **Pencil** tool 🖉 (N).

2. Choose a stroke color and weight, and a fill color of None.

3. Draw lines (a proxy line will appear while you draw). You can release the mouse between strokes. That's all there is to it. (Well, except for the artistic part!)

4. Press Cmd-Y/Ctrl-Y to toggle the display of the artwork with its current color settings (Preview view) **A** and a wireframe representation (Outline view).

5. *Optional:* To apply a brush to a selected path, keep the artwork selected, show the Brushes panel 🖌 or click the Brush Definition menu on the Control panel, then click a brush. To learn about brushes, see Chapter 23.

6. *Optional:* To change the contour of a selected path, choose from the Variable Width Profile menu on the Control panel **B–C** (see page 166).

➤ To create a closed path with the Pencil tool, start drawing the path, then return to the start of the path and release the mouse button when you see the 🖉° icon. ★

➤ To close an existing path with a straight segment, select the path, then hold down the Option/Alt key and drag from one anchor point to the next with the Pencil tool. Alternatively, choose the Selection tool (V), click the line, then press Cmd-J/Ctrl-J. ★

➤ If you want to draw perfectly straight lines, hold down the Option/Alt key as you draw with the Pencil tool, release the Option/Alt key, and continue dragging to draw freehand again. ★

➤ If you want to draw precision curves, your best bet is the Pen tool (see Chapter 21) instead.

A *An iPod is drawn with the Pencil tool. If you don't know what subject matter to draw, observe the objects around you, and draw the contour of one that interests you.*

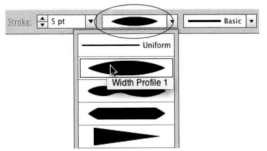

B *You can choose a contour for a selected path from the Variable Width Profile menu.*

C *We applied Width Profile 1 to these paths.*

Drawing with the Paintbrush tool

If you use a stylus and a pressure-sensitive tablet, the Paintbrush tool will respond to pressure. The harder you press on the tablet, the wider the stroke.

Note: To choose options for the Paintbrush tool, see the following page.

To draw with the Paintbrush tool:

1. Choose the **Paintbrush** tool ✎ (B).

2. Choose a stroke color and weight, and a fill color of None.

3. Show the Brushes panel ✋ or click the Brush Definition menu ⬛ Basic ▾ on the Control panel, then click a brush. We recommend choosing a Bristle or Art brush (see Chapter 23).

4. Do either of the following:

    To draw open paths, draw separate lines.**A–B**

    To draw a closed path, drag to draw the path, then Option-drag/Alt-drag to close it (release Option/Alt last).

5. *Optional:* To change the contour of the stroke on a selected path, choose from the Variable Width Profile menu on the Control panel (see page 166).

➤ To change the width of a Bristle brush between strokes, press [or]. To change the brush opacity between strokes, press a number key (e.g., 5 for 50% opacity, 9 for 90% opacity, or 0 for 100% opacity).

When you remove a brush stroke from a path, it is given a plain, basic shape. Similarly, if you remove a width profile from a path, it is given a uniform width.

To remove a brush stroke or width profile from a path:

1. Choose the **Selection** tool ▹ (V), then click a path.

2. On the Control panel, do either or both of the following:

    To restore the default width profile, on the **Variable Width Profile** menu, click **Uniform**.

    To remove a brush, on the **Brush Definition** menu, click the **Basic** brush.

➤ When an object that contains a brush stroke is selected, you can click the Stroke listing on the Appearance panel to make a Brush Definition menu appear. And if you click the Stroke link on that panel, a variable width Profile menu displays on a temporary Stroke panel.

A *These objects were drawn with an Art brush chosen for the Paintbrush tool.*

B *We applied assorted fill colors to the objects.*

A CHECKLIST OF THINGS TO DO BEFORE YOU BEGIN DRAWING (A FRIENDLY REMINDER)

➤ Display an artboard.

➤ Choose a drawing mode (usually Draw Normal ◉) from the bottom of the Tools panel.

➤ If your document contains multiple layers, click a layer.

Choosing options for the Pencil and Paintbrush tools

The Pencil and Paintbrush tools can be customized in two ways: by choosing settings on the Control panel or via an options dialog. Changes to the tool options affect only lines you subsequently draw, not existing ones. The 2014 release of Illustrator CC provides significant improvements to how paths are generated when drawn with the Pencil, Paintbrush, Smooth, and Blob Brush tools.

To choose options for the Pencil or Paintbrush tool:

1. Do either of the following:

   Double-click the **Pencil** tool ✏ (or press N to choose the tool, then press Return/Enter).

   Double-click the **Paintbrush** tool ✔ (or press B to choose the tool, then press Return/Enter).

2. In the Fidelity area of the options dialog: **A**

   Choose a **Fidelity** value.**B–C** An Accurate Fidelity setting produces many anchor points and paths that accurately follow the movement of your mouse, whereas a Smooth setting produces fewer anchor points and smoother paths.★

3. Check any of the following options:

   Fill New Pencil Strokes or **Fill New Brush Strokes** to have new paths (whether they are open or closed) fill automatically with the current fill color. The default setting for this option is off.

   Keep Selected to have the paths stay selected after they're created. This saves you a step if you tend to edit your paths right after drawing them.

   Option key toggles to Smooth Tool to provide a quick way to access the Smooth tool when the Option/Alt key is held down and the Pencil tool is active. With this option chosen, you can't draw a straight line using the Pencil tool.

   Edit Selected Paths to activate the reshaping function of the tool (see page 165). The Within: [ ] Pixels value is the minimum distance the pointer must be from a path for the tool to reshape it. Uncheck this option if you want to be able to draw multiple lines or brush strokes near one another without reshaping any existing selected paths.

4. Click OK.**D**

➤ Click Reset in the Pencil or Paintbrush Tool Options dialog to restore the default settings for the tool.

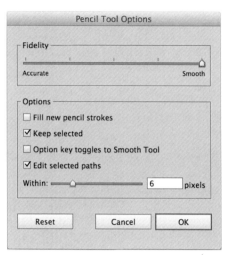

A The Pencil tool has its own options dialog ★.

B This line was drawn with the Pencil tool at an Accurate Fidelity setting.

C This line was drawn with the Pencil tool at a Smooth Fidelity setting.

D Each stroke in this drawing is a separate path.

Using the Blob Brush tool

The Blob Brush is a versatile, dual-purpose tool. It lets you draw closed paths in a loose, freehand style, and also lets you reshape existing closed paths, regardless of which tool they were created with. The tool is similar to a traditional felt-tip marker, with two advantages: It enables you to reshape your strokes after they're drawn, and it's odor-free! If you like to draw artwork "by hand," you'll probably take an instant liking to it. "Blob Brush tool" is a cumbersome name to say aloud, but it's a fun tool to use.

On this page, you'll learn how to create objects with the Blob Brush tool; on the next page, you'll choose options for the tool; and on page 179, you'll master its reshaping function.

To draw with the Blob Brush tool:

1. Choose the **Blob Brush** tool ![icon] (Shift-B).

2. On the Control or Appearance panel, click the **Stroke** thumbnail or arrowhead ![icon] to open a temporary Swatches panel, then click a solid-color swatch on the panel.

3. Position the brush cursor over an artboard. Press [to decrease the brush tip size or] to increase it.

4. Draw lines, as you might with a traditional marking pen.**A–B** Let the lines crisscross or touch one another. When you release the mouse, a new closed path or compound path is created (unlike the stroked paths that are produced by the Paintbrush and other freehand drawing tools).

5. *Optional:* Without changing the stroke color, draw a connecting line from one end of a Blob Brush shape to the other end, to connect them.

6. Choose the Selection ![icon] or Direct Selection ![icon] tool, then click the new shape. Illustrator applies the current stroke color to the inside of the object and gives the object a stroke color of None.

7. *Optional:* For the selected Blob Brush path, via the Appearance or Control panel, change the Opacity percentage.

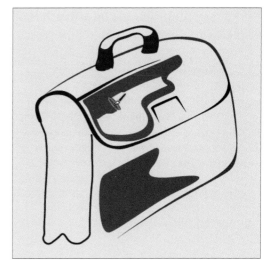

A *A briefcase is drawn with the Blob Brush tool.*

B *Other areas of "shading" were drawn with the Blob Brush.*

To choose options for the Blob Brush tool: ★

1. Double-click the **Blob Brush** tool. 🖌 The Blob Brush Tool Options dialog opens.**A**

2. Check **Keep Selected** to have the Blob Brush objects remain selected after they are created. We check this option so we can see more easily when our Blob Brush objects are being merged.

3. Check **Merge Only with Selection** to permit new Blob Brush strokes to merge only with selected unstroked objects, or uncheck this option to allow new strokes to merge with any unstroked objects that have the same fill color as the brush, whether they are selected or not. (To merge shapes with this tool, see page 170.)

4. Under Fidelity, choose an Accurate **Fidelity** setting to produce many anchor points and paths that follow your mouse movements more accurately, or a Smooth setting to produce fewer anchor points and smoother paths. ★

5. For the brush **Size**, **Angle**, and **Roundness** options,**B–C** see steps 4–7 in the steps for editing a Calligraphic brush on pages 324–325.

6. Click OK.

A You can customize the behavior of the Blob Brush tool via its options dialog.

B A Roundness setting of 100% for the Blob Brush tool produced the rounded ends on this object…

C …whereas an Angle setting of –45° and a Roundness setting of 22% produced ends that look more calligraphic.

As a prerequisite to learning editing techniques in Illustrator, you need to master the methods for selecting and deselecting objects. The simple fact is that an object must be selected before it can be edited. The many selection controls in Illustrator include five tools, an assortment of Select menu commands, and a selection area on the Layers panel. In this chapter, in addition to learning all the selection methods, you will learn how to group objects, isolate groups and objects for editing, and save your selections for future access. Once you master these fundamental skills, you'll be ready to learn how to move, copy, and align objects (in the next chapter) and then plunge into the fun stuff, such as recoloring, transforming, reshaping, and applying effects.

The five selection tools ★

The basic functions of the selection tools are introduced here. Step-by-step instructions for using these tools are given elsewhere in this chapter.

Use the **Selection** tool ▶ (V) to select or move a whole object or group **A** and to select all of an object's points (see page 93). This tool can also be used to scale, reflect, or rotate an object via its bounding box (see page 147).

Continued on the following page

A *The Selection tool selects entire objects.*

SELECT

Use the **Direct Selection** tool to select one or more individual anchor points or segments on a path and to display the Live Corner widget if applicable.**A** If you click a curve segment with this tool, the direction handles and anchor points for that segment become visible (see page 94). (The anchor points on straight segments don't have direction handles — they just have anchor points.)

Although the **Group Selection** tool ![icon] can be used to select all the anchor points on an individual path, the main purpose of this tool is for selecting groups (of objects) that are nested inside larger groups. Click once with this tool to select an object in a group, click a second time to select the entire group that the object belongs to, click a third time to select the parent group it's nested within, and so on. The Group Selection tool can be selected from the Direct Selection tool fly-out menu or accessed temporarily when using the Direct Selection tool by holding down Option/Alt.

➤ Instead of using the Group Selection tool, we prefer to edit a group in isolation mode. An advantage of this method is that it makes other objects temporarily uneditable. See page 96.

Use the **Lasso** tool ![icon] (Q) to select anchor points and segments by dragging a free-form marquee around them (see page 98).**B**

The **Magic Wand** tool ![icon] (Y) selects objects that contain the same or a similar fill color, stroke color, stroke weight, opacity, or blending mode as the object you click, depending on the current tool settings on the Magic Wand panel (see page 99).**C**

Note: In the illustrations on these pages, we turned off the display of the bounding box (the bounding box surrounds whichever objects are selected). If you want to do the same for your document, press Cmd-Shift-B/ Ctrl-Shift-B.

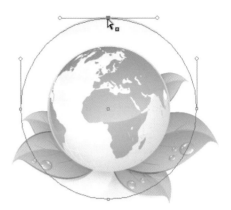

A *The Direct Selection tool selects individual anchor points and segments on a path.*

B *The Lasso tool selects anchor points and segments via a free-form marquee.*

C *The Magic Wand tool selects objects that have the same or a similar fill color, stroke color, stroke weight, opacity, or blending mode as an object you click.*

Using the Selection tool

To select one or more objects:

1. Make sure the View > **Smart Guides** option has a check mark (Cmd-U/Ctrl-U). Also go to Illustrator/Edit > Preferences > Smart Guides, and make sure the **Object Highlighting** option is checked.

2. Choose the **Selection** tool  (V).

3. Do one of the following:

   Because Smart Guides are on (with the Object Highlighting preference enabled), the edge of a path will be highlighted as you move the pointer over it. Click the path.**A**

   If the object has a color fill, your document is in Preview view, and the Object Selection by Path Only option is off (see the sidebar at right), you can click the object's fill.

   Position the pointer outside one or more objects to be selected, then drag a marquee across all or part of them. The whole path will become selected, even if you marquee just a portion of it.**B–C**

With the Selection tool, you can add objects to or subtract objects from a selection.

To add objects to or subtract objects from a selection:

Choose the **Selection** tool (V), then Shift-click on or Shift-drag a marquee around any unselected objects to add them to the selection, or do the same for any selected objects to deselect them.

SELECTING OBJECTS BY PATH ONLY

If Object Selection by Path Only is checked in Illustrator/Edit > Preferences > Selection & Anchor Display, in order to select an object, you must click a segment or anchor point on the path. When this option is unchecked, you don't have to be as precise about where you click: If the object contains a fill (not None) and the document is in Preview view, you can click the fill or the path.

SELECTING UNDERLYING OBJECTS

If Command/Control Click to Select Objects Behind is checked in Preferences > Selection & Anchor Display and you want to select objects that are hidden behind other objects at the current pointer location, Cmd-click/Ctrl-click (and keep clicking).

A *We selected a path with the Selection tool (for the figures on this page, the bounding box is hidden).*

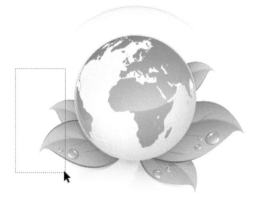

B *We marqueed a few paths with the Selection tool.*

C *The paths within the marquee became selected.*

Using the Direct Selection tool

As a prerequisite to reshaping objects (which you will do in Chapter 12), you need to learn how to select individual points and segments. It's important to be precise about which components of an object you select.

To select or deselect anchor points or segments with the Direct Selection tool:

1. Open the Illustrator/Edit > Preferences dialog. In the Selection & Anchor Display panel, check Highlight Anchors on Mouse Over (for other Anchor Point and Handle Display preferences, see page 411). And in the Smart Guides panel of the same dialog, check Object Highlighting and Anchor/Path Labels. Click OK.

2. Turn on View > **Smart Guides** (Cmd-U/Ctrl-U). (The command should have a check mark.)

3. Choose the **Direct Selection** tool (A).

4. Do one of the following:

   To select a segment, click the path.**A**

   To select an anchor point, pass the pointer over an anchor point (the point enlarges temporarily), then click.**B–C**

   Position the pointer outside one or more objects, then drag a marquee across the anchor points or segments you want to select.**D** Only the points or segments you marquee will become selected.**E**

5. *Optional:* To select additional anchor points or segments, or to deselect individual selected anchor points or segments, Shift-click them or Shift-drag a marquee around them.

➤ To access the Selection or Direct Selection tool temporarily (whichever one was used last) when using a nonselection tool, hold down Cmd/Ctrl.

Selecting objects via a command

The Select commands select objects whose characteristics are similar to those of either the last selected object or the currently selected one.

To select objects via a command:

Do any of the following:

Select an object on which to base the search, or deselect all objects to base the search on the last object that was selected. From the Select > **Same** submenu, choose one of the available commands, such as Fill & Stroke, Fill Color, Opacity, Stroke Color,

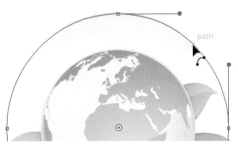

A *A curve segment is clicked with the Direct Selection tool.*

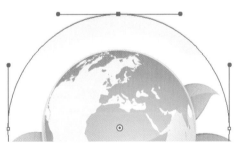

B *As you move the pointer over an anchor point, it becomes enlarged temporarily. Click the point to select it.*

C *Selected anchor points are solid; unselected anchor points are hollow.*

D *A marquee is made with the Direct Selection tool.*

E *Only anchor points within the marquee became selected.*

or Stroke Weight.**A** Most of these commands are also found on the **Select Similar Options** menu on the Control panel **B** (the menu isn't available for some kinds of objects). Read about the Select Same Tint % preference on page 408.

Select one or more objects, then from the Select > **Object** submenu,**C** choose **All on Same Layers** to select all the objects on the layer the object resides in (or if the currently selected objects are on more than one layer, from those layers), or choose **Direction Handles** to select all the direction handles on the currently selected object or objects (see page 157).

With or without selecting an object first, from the Select > **Object** submenu, choose one of the following: **Bristle Brush Strokes** or **Brush Strokes** to select all objects that have those types of brush strokes; **Clipping Masks** to select masking objects (to display their edges); **Stray Points** to select lone points that don't belong to any paths (for deletion); or for text, choose **All Text Objects**, **Point Type Objects**, or **Area Type Objects**.

Via the Select Similar Objects button on the Control panel, you can quickly reapply the last command that you chose from the Select Similar Options menu.

To reapply the last chosen Select Similar Options command:

Select an object, then click the **Select Similar Objects** button (next to the menu).

Selecting objects via the Layers panel

To select objects via the Layers panel:

1. Display the Layers panel.

2. Do either of the following:

   If the listing for the object to be selected isn't visible on the Layers panel, reveal it by clicking the expand/collapse triangle for its top-level layer, sublayer, or group. Next, at the far right side of the panel, click the selection area for the object. A colored square appears (each top-level layer is assigned a different color automatically).**D**

   To select all the objects on a layer or sublayer, click in the selection area for the whole layer or sublayer.

➤ To learn more about selecting objects via the Layers panel, see pages 188–189.

A *Choose from the Select > Same submenu …*

B *… or choose from the Select Similar Options menu on the Control panel …*

C *… or choose from the Select > Object submenu.*

D *Click the selection area for an object on the Layers panel.*

Working with groups

When objects are in a group, you can select, isolate, copy, paste, or edit them as a unit. You can group different kinds of objects (e.g., type objects with placed images), and you can edit individual objects in a group without having to ungroup them first.

To put objects into a group:

1. Do either of the following:

   Choose the **Selection** tool (V). In the document, Shift-click or drag a marquee around all the objects to be grouped.

   Shift-click the selection area at the far right side of the Layers panel to make a selection square appear for each object to be put in a group (click the expand/collapse arrow, if necessary, to reveal the object listings). Or if you want to select all the objects on a layer, click the selection square for the layer.

2. Right-click in the document window and choose **Group** from the context menu (Cmd-G/Ctrl-G).**A** All the objects in the group will be moved to the layer of the topmost selected object.

The easiest and quickest way to edit individual objects in a group is to put the group into isolation mode.

To edit grouped objects in isolation mode:

1. In Illustrator/Edit > Preferences > General, make sure **Double Click to Isolate** is checked.

2. Choose the **Selection** tool (V), then double-click a group in your artwork.**B**

3. Objects within the group are shown in full color and are editable; objects outside the group are temporarily dimmed and uneditable. A gray isolation mode bar appears at the top of the document window, which lists the name of the selected layer and group. An Isolation Mode listing also appears on the Layers panel.

4. You can click and edit objects in an isolated group with the Selection tool, or click and edit individual points or segments in objects with the Direct Selection tool.**C** With the Selection tool, you can also double-click any nested group to isolate it from its parent group; to reselect the parent group, click <Group> on the isolation mode bar.

5. To exit isolation mode, click the isolation mode bar or press Esc.

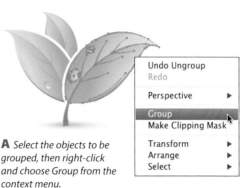

A *Select the objects to be grouped, then right-click and choose Group from the context menu.*

Isolation mode bar

B *We double-clicked the leaf group on the right to put it into isolation mode; the other objects are temporarily dimmed.*

C *We double-clicked an object in the group to further isolate it. The name of the object appears on the isolation mode bar.*

Before creating an object or placing an image into an Illustrator document, you can specify which group it will be added to.

To add a new object to a group:

1. Choose the **Selection** tool (V), then double-click a group to isolate it.**A**

2. Draw a new object or objects.**B** A listing for each new object you create will appear within the group listing on the Layers panel.

3. *Optional:* On the Layers panel, expand the listing for the group to which you added an object, then drag the new object listing to the desired stacking position within the group.

4. To exit isolation mode, click the isolation mode bar at the top of the window or press Esc.

To add an existing object to a group:

1. With the **Selection** tool (V), click the object to be added to a group.

2. Choose Edit > **Cut** (Cmd-X/Ctrl-X).

3. Double-click the group to isolate it.

4. Choose Edit > **Paste** (Cmd-V/Ctrl-V). Drag the object to the desired location, then click the isolation mode bar at the top of the document window to exit isolation mode.

➤ To add an existing object to a group via the Layers panel, see page 191.

Sometimes a group has to be disbanded — er, ungrouped.

To ungroup a group:

1. To select a group, choose the **Selection** tool (V), then either click the group in the document window or click the selection area for the group listing on the Layers panel.

2. Do either of the following:

   Right-click the artboard and choose **Ungroup** from the context menu.

   Choose Object > **Ungroup** (Cmd-Shift-G/Ctrl-Shift-G).

   The group listing disappears from the Layers panel, but the objects remain selected.

➤ Keep choosing the same command to ungroup nested groups (groups within parent groups).

➤ To learn how to select groups and grouped objects via the Layers panel, see page 191.

A *We double-clicked the leaf group on the right to isolate it. The other objects are temporarily dimmed.*

B *We added another water droplet to the isolated group.*

Isolating individual objects

Not only can you put a whole group into isolation mode, but you can also edit individual objects in this mode, whether they're in a group or not. This option is useful for isolating objects in complex artwork.

Note: Throughout this book, when we instruct you to select an object for editing, remember that in most cases you can simply isolate the object instead.

To isolate one object:

1. Do either of the following:

    In Illustrator/Edit > Preferences > General, make sure **Double Click to Isolate** is checked. Choose the Selection tool (V) then double-click an object.

    To isolate an object in a group, choose the Direct Selection tool (A), then click the object. Next, click the **Isolate Selected Object** button on the Control panel or right-click the object and choose **Isolate Selected Path**.

2. A dark gray **isolation mode** bar appears at the top of the document window, bearing the name of the selected object. **A**

3. Edit the object.

4. To exit isolation mode, click the gray isolation mode bar at the top of the window or press Esc.

Using the Lasso tool

Say you need to select a few points on one path and a few points on a nearby path. With the Direct Selection tool, you could click the points individually (tedious), or if the points in question happen to fall conveniently within a rectangular area, you could marquee them. To select points in complex artwork, our preferred method is to drag around them with the Lasso tool. Don't use this tool to select whole paths.

To select or deselect points or segments with the Lasso tool:

1. Deselect (click a blank area of the artboard).

2. Choose the **Lasso** tool (Q), then drag to encircle segments or points. **B–C** You can drag right across any path. You don't need to close the selection; just release the mouse when the desired points have been lassoed.

3. *Optional:* Shift-drag around any unselected points or segments to add them to the selection, or Option-drag/Alt-drag around any selected points or segments to deselect them.

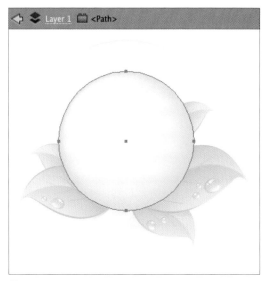

A *We double-clicked a circle object to isolate it.*

B *We are winding our way around parts of objects with the Lasso tool.*

C *Only the points and segments we marqueed became selected.*

Using the Magic Wand tool

The Magic Wand tool selects all the objects in a document that have the same or a similar fill color, stroke color, stroke weight, opacity, or blending mode as the object you click, depending on which options are checked on the Magic Wand panel.

To choose options for the Magic Wand tool:

1. To show the Magic Wand panel, double-click the **Magic Wand** tool 🖌 or choose Window > **Magic Wand**.

   If all three sections of the panel aren't showing, click the up/down arrowhead on the panel tab to make them appear.

2. On the left side of the panel,**A** check the attributes you want the tool to select: **Fill Color**, **Stroke Color**, **Stroke Weight**, **Opacity**, or **Blending Mode**.

3. For each option you checked in the preceding step (except Blending Mode), choose a **Tolerance** value. Choose a low value to select only objects whose colors, weights, or opacities match (or are very similar to) the one you will click with the tool, or choose a high value to allow the tool to select a broader range of those attributes. For Fill Color or Stroke Color, choose a Tolerance (0–255 for an RGB document or 0–100 for a CMYK document); for the Stroke Weight, choose a weight Tolerance (0–1000 pt); for the Opacity, choose a percentage (0–100).

4. To permit the Magic Wand tool to select objects on all layers, check **Use All Layers** on the panel menu (the default setting), or uncheck this option to limit the selection to objects on just the current layer.

➤ The Reset command on the Magic Wand panel menu resets all fields on the panel to their default values and unchecks all the options except Fill Color.

IN THE CROSSHAIRS

If Use Precise Cursors is checked in Illustrator/ Edit > Preferences > General, or if the Caps Lock key is enabled on your keyboard, the pointer for the Lasso and Magic Wand tools (among other tools) will be a crosshairs icon ⌖ instead of the tool icon. Use the crosshairs when a task requires precise positioning of the pointer.

To use the Magic Wand tool:

1. Choose the **Magic Wand** tool 🖌 (Y).

2. To create a new selection, click an object in the document window. Depending on the current settings on the Magic Wand panel, other objects containing the same or a similar fill color, stroke color, stroke weight, opacity, or blending mode may become selected.**B–C**

3. Do either of the following:

   To add to the selection, Shift-click another object.

   To subtract from the selection, Option-click/ Alt-click one of the selected objects.

A *Choose settings for the Magic Wand tool on its panel.*

B *The first two water droplets have an opacity of 100%; the third one has an opacity of 50%. We checked Fill Color and Opacity for the Magic Wand tool, then clicked the fill of the leftmost object. Only the middle droplet, which has the same fill color and opacity as the first one, became selected.*

C *This time we used the Magic Wand tool with the Opacity option off. All three objects became selected because their opacity settings were ignored as a factor.*

Saving selections

Via the Save Selection command, you can save any selection under a custom name. To reselect the same objects quickly, simply choose the name of your saved selection on the Select menu.

To save a selection:

1. Select one or more objects.

2. Choose Select > **Save Selection**.

3. In the Save Selection dialog,**A** enter a descriptive name, then click OK.

4. To reselect the objects at any time, choose your custom selection name from the bottom of the **Select** menu.

➤ To rename or delete a saved selection, choose Select > Edit Selection. Click a selection name, change it or click Delete,**B** then click OK.

A *If you save your selections, they will be easy to access for future use.*

B *Use the Edit Selection dialog to rename or delete any of your saved selections.*

Selecting and deselecting all objects

To select all the objects in a document:

Choose Select > **All** (Cmd-A/Ctrl-A). All unlocked objects in your document will become selected, regardless of whether they're located on an artboard or in the scratch area. This command won't select locked objects or objects on hidden layers (for which the visibility icon on the Layers panel is off).

➤ If a text cursor is flashing in a text block when you choose the Select > All command, all the text in the object, and any other objects it's threaded to, will become selected (instead of all the objects in your document).

To select all the objects on just the current artboard:

1. On the Artboards panel, click an artboard listing.

2. Choose Select > **All on Active Artboard** (Cmd-Option-A/Ctrl-Alt-A).

To prevent objects from being modified, you must make sure they're deselected.

To deselect all the objects in a document:

Do either of the following:

Choose Select > **Deselect** (Cmd-Shift-A/Ctrl-Shift-A).

Choose any selection tool (or hold down Cmd/Ctrl), then click a blank area of the document.

➤ To deselect an individual object in a selection of multiple objects, Shift-click it with the Selection tool. To deselect an object in a group, see page 191.

The Inverse command deselects all selected objects and selects all the unselected ones.

To invert a selection:

Choose Select > **Inverse**.

Once you have created multiple objects in a document, you'll undoubtedly find a need to reposition, copy, or realign them. In this chapter, you'll learn how to move objects with the assistance of Smart Guides; duplicate, align, and distribute objects; and create and use ruler guides, guide objects, and the grid to position objects manually.

Moving objects

In these instructions, you will learn the simplest and most straightforward method for moving objects: by dragging. In conjunction with a great feature called Smart Guides (see pages 102–103), dragging will take care of most of your moving needs.

To move an object or group by dragging:

1. Choose the **Selection** tool ▸ (V).

2. Do either of the following:

   Drag the object's path (this can be done in Outline or Preview view).

   If the document is in Preview view, the object has a fill, and the Object Selection by Path Only feature is off in Illustrator/Edit > Preferences > Selection & Anchor Display, you can drag the object's fill.**A** This can also be done with the Direct Selection tool.

➤ Hold down Shift while dragging an object to constrain the movement to a multiple of 45°.

➤ If you begin dragging an object and change your mind, perhaps because you selected the incorrect object, you can cancel the drag operation by pressing the Escape key on your keyboard.★

➤ If you like to work with the bounding box feature off (except when transforming objects), choose View > Hide Bounding Box.

➤ To learn other techniques for moving objects, such as the Transform panel, Control panel, and Transform Each command, see pages 152–155.

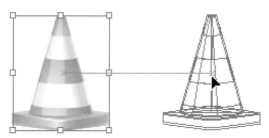

A With the aid of a Smart Guide, a group is dragged along the horizontal axis.

Aligning objects with the help of Smart Guides

Smart Guides are various kinds of nonprinting labels or lines that appear onscreen temporarily when you create, move, duplicate, or transform an object. For example, "magnetic" alignment guides appear onscreen when you move an object. You can use them, say, to align an object along the horizontal or vertical axis, or to align the edge of an object to the edge of an artboard or to the edge of another object. You can also use Smart Guides when repositioning artboards. This feature is easier done than said, so give it a try.

To align objects with the help of Smart Guides:

1. Confirm that the View > Pixel Preview and Snap to Grid features are off, and the View > **Smart Guides** (Cmd-U/Ctrl-U) and View > **Snap to Point** features are on (are checked on the menu).

2. To establish the necessary preferences for Smart Guides, go to Illustrator/Edit > Preferences (Cmd-K/Ctrl-K) > Smart Guides, and check all six Display Options boxes.**A** Switch to the Selection & Anchor Display panel, check Snap to Point, then click OK.

   Note: Although you won't be using all of the different kinds of Smart Guides in this task, we recommend activating all of them so they will be available for other tasks.

3. Choose the **Selection** tool (V).

4. Drag an object, releasing the mouse when the object snaps to any of the following:

   An **alignment guide** that denotes the edge or midpoint of another object.**B**

   The **center point** of another object.**C**

   An **anchor point** on the edge of another object (**A**, next page).

   The edge of an **artboard**.

   ➤ The measurement label (in the gray rectangle) lists the current horizontal distance (dX) and vertical distance (dY) that you have moved your selection from its original location.

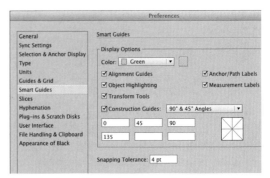

A Check all six of the Display Options check boxes in the Smart Guides panel of the Preferences dialog.

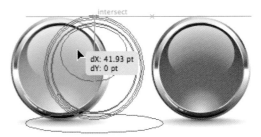

B A horizontal alignment guide appears at the moment when the edge of the group we're moving aligns with the top edge of another group.

C We're aligning the center point of a group with the intersection of two alignment guides — in this case, to the center point of another object. The measurement label (in the gray box) lists the distance we dragged the group.

➤ Smart Guides vanish as quickly as they appear. To create guides that remain onscreen, see page 111.

➤ The Smart Guides preferences are described in detail on page 415. For example, you can establish specific angles for Smart Guides or change their color to make them contrast better with colors in your artwork. To use the Transform Tools option for Smart Guides, see pages 148–149.

➤ Smart Guides provide useful information even if the mouse is merely hovering over an object.**B**

A *Because the Snap to Point option is on (in the Selection & Anchor Display panel of the Preferences dialog), when the pointer of an object we drag is over an anchor point on another object, it becomes a white arrowhead.*

HIDING OR SHOWING THE BOUNDING BOX

On page 147, you will learn how to transform an object or group via its bounding box. In the meantime, if you want to hide (or show) the bounding box, which displays on all selected objects, choose View > Hide Bounding Box (or Show Bounding Box) or press Cmd-Shift-B/Ctrl-Shift-B.

The Bounding Box feature is on for Illustrator, so the bounding box displays around this selected group.

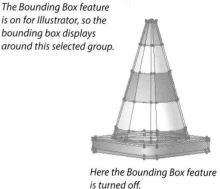

Here the Bounding Box feature is turned off.

B *Object highlighting (the blue border) and anchor/path labels (the green text labels) display when the pointer is over the edge or an anchor point of an object, with the mouse button up. The measurement label on the right lists the x/y location of that anchor point.*

Copying objects

To copy an object or group, you can use any of the following techniques:

➤ Dragging (instructions below)

➤ Arrow keys (sidebar on this page)

➤ The Clipboard (facing page)

➤ The Offset Path command (page 106)

➤ The Rotate, Reflect, Scale, or Shear tool (pages 148–149)

➤ The Transform panel (sidebar on page 152)

➤ The Transform Each command (page 154)

➤ The Transform effect (page 155)

➤ The Layers panel (page 192)

To copy an object or group in the same document by dragging:

1. Choose the **Selection** tool ▶ (V).

2. Option-drag/Alt-drag an object's path or fill (not its bounding box, if showing),**A–B** release the mouse, then release Option/Alt. To constrain the copy to an increment of 45°, include Shift in the shortcut (learn about the Constrain Angle on pages 408–409). To use Smart Guides for alignment while creating the copy, see the previous two pages.

➤ To repeat the last transformation (such as the creation of a duplicate), press Cmd-D/Ctrl-D.

➤ To copy an object in a group and make the copy a member of the group, Option-drag/Alt-drag it with the Direct Selection tool. Or if you want the duplicate to appear outside the group, select it with the Direct Selection tool, choose Edit > Copy, then choose Edit > Paste.

When you drag an object from one document to another, a copy of the object appears in the target document automatically.

To drag-copy an object or group to another document:

1. Open two documents.

2. Choose the **Selection** tool ▶ (V).

3. Click in the source document, drag an object or group to the tab of the target document, pause until the target document displays, then release the mouse where you want the duplicate to appear.

➤ To drag-copy an object that is in a group, use the Direct Selection tool.

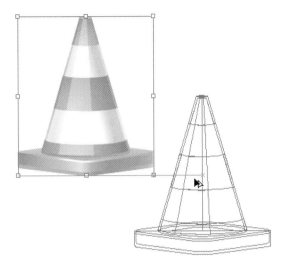

A *The quickest way to copy a group or an object is simply to Option-drag/Alt-drag it. Note the double-arrowhead pointer.*

B *A copy of the group is made.*

COPYING OBJECTS BY USING AN ARROW KEY

Choose the Selection tool, select an object, then press Option-Shift-arrow/Alt-Shift-arrow to copy the object and move the copy in the direction of the arrow by 10 times the current Keyboard Increment value in Illustrator/Edit > Preferences > General (or press Option-arrow/Alt-arrow to move the copy by the current increment). The default increment is 1 pt.

If you select an object or a group and choose the Cut or Copy command, the object or group is placed onto the Clipboard, which is a temporary storage area in your computer's system memory. The contents of the Clipboard are replaced each time you choose Cut or Copy. The Paste command places the current Clipboard contents on the currently selected layer in the center of the document window. The current Clipboard contents can be pasted an unlimited number of times.

To learn about the PDF and AICB formats, which control how Illustrator copies content to the Clipboard for transfer to other applications, see page 419.

To copy or move objects between documents using the Clipboard:

1. Open two documents, then display the source document.

2. Via the Selection tool ⚓ (V) or the Layers panel, select the object(s) or group to be copied or moved.

3. Do either of the following:

   To put a copy of the object(s) or group onto the Clipboard while leaving the original(s) in place, choose Edit > **Copy** (Cmd-C/Ctrl-C).

   To put the object(s) or group onto the Clipboard and delete it from the current document, choose Edit > **Cut** (Cmd-X/Ctrl-X).

4. Click the tab of the target document.

5. Choose Edit > **Paste** (Cmd-V/Ctrl-V). The Clipboard contents will appear in the center of the document window. If the document is in Draw Normal mode, the contents will appear within the current layer. For the other paste commands, see the sidebar at right.

   Note: If an object is selected and the document is in Draw Inside mode, the Clipboard contents will paste inside that object (see page 367). Or if the document is in Draw Behind mode, the Clipboard contents will be stacked behind the currently selected object.

➤ To restack an object in front of or behind another object, use the Layers panel (see page 191).

PASTING TO THE ORIGINAL LAYER

To ensure that the Clipboard contents always paste to the top of the same layer or sublayer from which they were copied or cut, turn the Paste Remembers Layers option on via the Layers panel menu. To allow the Clipboard contents to paste onto whichever layer happens to be selected at the time, leave this option off. Note: If this option is on and you copy or cut an object, then delete the object's layer and use the Paste command, the object will paste onto a brand new layer.

OTHER PASTE COMMANDS ON THE EDIT MENU

➤ Paste in Front (Cmd-F/Ctrl-F) and Paste in Back (Cmd-B/Ctrl-B) paste the Clipboard contents in the current artboard, at the same horizontal and vertical (x/y) location from which they were copied or cut, stacked in front of or behind the current selection, respectively.

➤ Paste in Place (Cmd-Shift-V/Ctrl-Shift-V) pastes the Clipboard contents in the current artboard, at the same x/y coordinates from which they were copied (instead of in the center of the document window).

➤ Paste in all Artboards (Cmd-Option-Shift-V/Ctrl-Alt-Shift-V) pastes the Clipboard contents at the same x/y coordinates in every artboard in the current document. We recommend using the Cut command first (instead of Copy) because Paste in All Artboards will paste a copy of the object on top of the original. Note: The contents may land outside any artboards that are smaller than the one from which the object was cut.

HIDING OR SHOWING THE CENTER POINT

To hide (or show) the center point on one or more selected objects, display the Attributes panel, 🔲 then click the Don't Show Center button (or the Show Center button) on the panel. To hide or show the center point for all objects in the current document, choose Select > All (Cmd-A/Ctrl-A) before clicking the button. Note: If you don't see the Show Center buttons on the panel, click the up/down arrowhead in the panel tab.

The Offset Path command copies a path and offsets the duplicate around or inside the original object by a specified distance. The copy is given the same fill and stroke attributes as the original object. The command also reshapes the copy automatically so it fits perfectly around the original path. You might not use this command on a regular basis, but it can come in handy if you happen to need a precisely scaled copy of an object.

To offset a copy of a path:

1. Select one or more objects.

2. Choose Object > Path > **Offset Path**. The Offset Path dialog opens.**A** Check Preview.

3. In the Offset field, enter the distance the duplicate path is to be offset from the original. Make sure this value is larger or smaller than the stroke weight of the original path, so the copy will be visible.

   For a closed path, a positive offset value will create a new path that is larger than the original one, and a negative value will create a path that is smaller than the original one. For an open path, both positive and negative values create a wider closed path, in the same shape as the original stroke.

4. Choose a **Joins** (bend) style for the shape of the joints in the duplicate: **Miter** (pointed),**B Round** (rounded),**C** or **Bevel** (beveled).

5. *Optional:* Change the Miter Limit value for the point at which a mitered (pointed) corner becomes a beveled one. A high Miter Limit (13 or greater) creates long, pointy corners; a low Miter Limit (4 or less) creates beveled corners.

6. Click OK. The offset path will be a separate path from, and will be stacked behind or in front of, the original path.**D** Regardless of whether the original object was open or closed, the resulting offset path will be closed.

➤ The Offset Path command can also be applied as an editable effect via Effect > Path > Offset Path. To learn about effects, see Chapter 15.

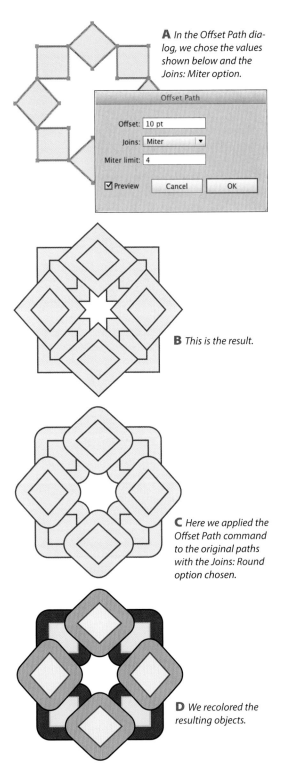

A *In the Offset Path dialog, we chose the values shown below and the Joins: Miter option.*

B *This is the result.*

C *Here we applied the Offset Path command to the original paths with the Joins: Round option chosen.*

D *We recolored the resulting objects.*

Aligning and distributing objects via buttons

To line up objects neatly in a row or column (such as buttons for a Web page or blocks of point type), rather than trying to position them by eye, use the convenient controls on the Align or Control panel.

To align or distribute objects:

1. For alignment, select two or more objects or groups; or for distribution, select three or more objects. (If all the objects are in the same group, you can isolate the group before selecting the objects.)

2. Do either of the following:

    Display the Align panel. ▬ **A** To display the full panel, click the arrows on the panel tab.

    Display the Control panel. **B** The align buttons may not display if the Application frame is too narrow; enlarge the frame and the buttons should appear. If you still don't see the buttons, confirm that Align is checked on the panel menu.

3. On the Align panel menu or in Illustrator/Edit > Preferences > General, check **Use Preview Bounds** to have Illustrator factor in an object's stroke weight and any applied effects when calculating an alignment or distribution command, or turn this option off to have Illustrator ignore the stroke weight and any effects. (By default, the stroke thickness extends halfway outside the path.)

4. Do either of the following:

    From the **Align To** menu, ▦ ▼ choose **Align to Selection** (the default setting) to confine any repositioning of objects to the bounding box of the overall selection, depending on which Align Objects button you click in the next step.

    To specify an object in the selection that is to remain stationary (called the "key" object), click an object; it will display a thicker border. Or to have the topmost of the selected objects (according to the stacking order on the Layers panel) become

Continued on the following page

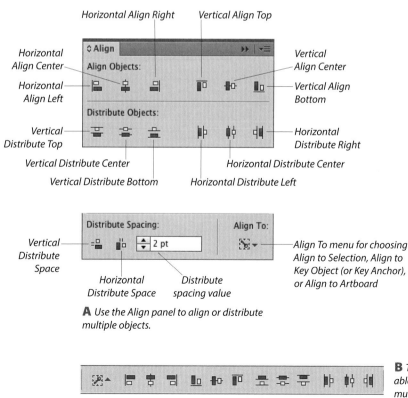

Horizontal Align Right   Vertical Align Top

Horizontal Align Center

Horizontal Align Left

Vertical Align Center

Vertical Align Bottom

Vertical Distribute Top

Horizontal Distribute Right

Vertical Distribute Center

Vertical Distribute Bottom   Horizontal Distribute Left

Horizontal Distribute Center

Vertical Distribute Space

Horizontal Distribute Space   Distribute spacing value

Align To menu for choosing Align to Selection, Align to Key Object (or Key Anchor), or Align to Artboard

A Use the Align panel to align or distribute multiple objects.

B These align features are available on the Control panel when multiple objects are selected.

the key object, choose **Align to Key Object** from the Align To menu.

➤ To cancel the key object at any time, choose Align to Selection from the Align To menu, or choose Cancel Key Object from the panel menu, or click the object again.

5. Do either of the following:

On the Align or Control panel, click one or more of the **Align Objects** buttons **A–B** and/or **Distribute Objects** buttons.**C**

On the Align panel, click either or both of the two **Distribute Spacing** buttons. If you want to specify the desired spacing between the objects, designate a key object, then choose a value via the Distribute Spacing menu or field before clicking a button.

➤ Change your mind? To apply a different Align panel option, first nix the last one by using the Undo command (Cmd-Z/Ctrl-Z).

➤ If you choose Align to Artboard from the Align To menu ▦ ▾ on the Align or Control panel, depending on which Align Objects or Distribute Objects button you click, at least two of the selected objects will align with the top, right, bottom, or left edge of the current artboard. If you were to click, say, the Vertical Distribute Top button, the top of the topmost object would align to the top of the artboard, the bottom of the bottommost object would align to the bottom of the artboard, and the remaining objects would be distributed evenly between them.

➤ To align objects to the pixel grid, see "Creating pixel-perfect artwork for the Web" on page 84.

➤ If the objects don't align perfectly, make sure they all have the same Align Stroke setting on the Stroke panel (see page 122).

➤ To align multiple anchor points on one or more objects, see page 174.

A *These are the original objects.*

B *We clicked the Vertical Align Bottom button first.*

C *Then we clicked the Horizontal Distribute Center button.*

Creating ruler guides

For most purposes, Smart Guides work quite well for arranging objects, but they're fleeting. If you need guides that stay onscreen (except when you hide them intentionally), and that also have magnetism, create ruler guides as in the steps below. Ruler guides don't print.

To create ruler guides:

1. Choose View > Guides > **Show Guides** (Cmd-;/Ctrl-;), or if the command is listed as Hide Guides, leave it be.

2. *Optional:* To create a new top-level layer to contain the guides you're about to create, Option-Shift-click/Alt-Shift-click the New Layer button 🔲 on the Layers panel. In the Layer Options dialog, name the layer "Guides," then click OK. Keep the new Guides layer selected.

3. If the rulers aren't showing at the top and left sides of the document window, choose View > Rulers > **Show Rulers** (Cmd-R/Ctrl-R).

4. Drag one or more guides from the horizontal or vertical ruler onto your artboard,**A–B** noting its location by the dotted line on the opposite ruler as you do so. (The higher the zoom level, the finer the ruler increments.) Each guide is listed individually on the Layers panel as a <Guide>.

   Position the pointer over the desired location on the horizontal or vertical ruler, then double-click.

   To create a pair of intersecting guides, hold down Cmd/Ctrl and drag from the ruler origin, which is the corner where the two rulers meet.

   Note: If you want to limit a guide to a particular artboard rather than have it extend across the whole canvas, choose the Artboard tool, click the artboard, then drag to create the guide.

➤ To control whether the ruler origin and increments apply to just the current artboard or stretch across all the artboards in your document (are global), right-click a ruler and choose Change to Artboard Rulers or Change to Global Rulers from the context menu. To switch between the two options quickly, press Cmd-Option-R/Ctrl-Alt-R.

➤ Option-drag/Alt-drag from the horizontal ruler to create a vertical guide, or from the vertical ruler to create a horizontal guide.

➤ You can choose a different color for guides in Illustrator/Edit > Preferences > Guides & Grid.

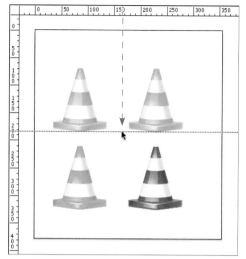

A *A guide is dragged from the horizontal ruler.*

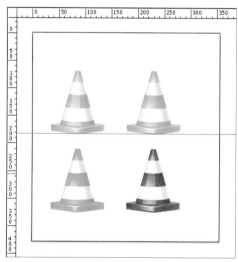

B *Ruler guides remain onscreen unless you choose to hide or delete them.*

MAKE IT SNAPPY ★

Turn on View > Snap to Point. Next, drag the edge, the fill, an anchor point, or the center point of an object near a guide or near an anchor point on another object; the object snaps to the guide or point, but the directional handles for the anchor point will not snap to the point and will remain completely unrestricted. In Preferences > Selection & Anchor Display, you can change the Snap to Point value (the maximum distance between the pointer and the target within which the snap occurs); the default value is 2 px.

Creating guides from objects

Thus far we have shown you how to work with two kinds of guides: Smart Guides and ruler guides. Here you will learn how to convert a standard path into a guide. The process is reversible, meaning the guide can be converted back to a standard object at any time. Like ruler guides, guides that are made from objects don't print.

To create a guide from an object:

1. Click the selection square on the Layers panel for an object,**A** a group of objects, or an object in a group. The object can't be a symbol, type, an object in a blend or distortion envelope, or a Live Paint group. You can copy the object and work with the copy, if you like. Note: If the object you convert to a guide is part of a group, the guide listing is going to appear within that group.

2. Do either of the following:

   Choose View > Guides > **Make Guides** (Cmd-5/ Ctrl-5).**B**

   Right-click the artboard and choose **Make Guides** from the context menu.

➤ You can transform or reshape an object guide, provided the guides in your document aren't locked (see "To lock or unlock all guides" on the next page). The object guide can also be selected (and hidden) via the Layers panel (see pages 189 and 194); look for the <Guide> listing. Remember to relock the guide after editing it.

When you release an object guide, the object regains its former fill and stroke attributes.

To release a guide that was made from an object:

1. On the Layers panel, make sure none of the guides to be released has a lock icon.

2. Do either of the following:

   To release one guide, in the document window, Cmd-Shift-double-click/Ctrl-Shift-double-click the edge of the guide.

   To release one or more guides, make sure guides aren't locked (see the first task on the next page). Select the guide to be released, either manually or by clicking the selection area on the Layers panel (Shift-click for multiple selection squares), then right-click in the artwork and choose **Release Guides** from the context menu (Cmd-Option-5/Ctrl-Alt-5).

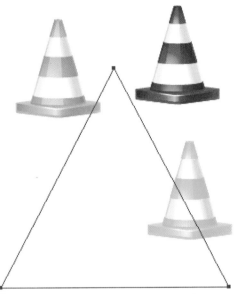

A We selected a three-sided polygon (a triangle).

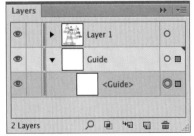

B We used the Make Guides command to convert the polygon to a guide, then aligned the traffic cone object groups within the guide. (We put our guide on a separate layer.)

Locking and unlocking guides

To select or move ruler or object guides, you must make sure they're unlocked first.

To lock or unlock all guides:

Deselect all objects, then right-click in the document and choose **Lock Guides** from the context menu (Cmd-Option-;/Ctrl-Alt-;).

➤ To hide (or show) guides, choose Hide Guides (or Show Guides) from the context menu.

You can easily lock or unlock (as well as hide or show) ruler and object guides individually, because each one has its own <Guide> listing on the Layers panel.

To lock or unlock guides individually:

1. Make sure the Lock Guides command is off (see the instructions above).

2. On the Layers panel, click in the edit (lock) column for any guide to lock or unlock it. The padlock icon appears or disappears.

Clearing guides

To clear one guide:

1. Verify that either all guides are unlocked or that the guide you want to remove is unlocked.

2. Choose the **Selection** tool (V), then click the ruler guide or guide object to be removed.

3. In the Mac OS, press Delete; in Windows, press Backspace or Del.

4. To relock all the remaining guides, deselect all objects, then right-click in the document window and choose Lock Guides.

The Clear Guides command removes all ruler and object guides from your document.

To clear all guides:

Choose View > Guides > **Clear Guides**.

TIPS FOR WORKING WITH GUIDES

➤ If you drag all your guides into a separate layer that you create specifically just for the guides, you will be able to lock or unlock all of them at once by clicking the edit icon for that layer, or lock or unlock any guide individually via its own edit icon.

➤ If the current color assigned to the guides is similar to the selection color for the layer that contains the <Guide> listings, it may be hard to tell when the guides are selected. To change the layer selection color, double-click the layer listing, then in the Layer Options dialog, choose a Color from the menu. Or to change the color that is assigned to the guides instead, use the Guides: Color menu or swatch in Illustrator/Edit > Preferences > Guides & Grid.

Using the grid

The grid is like nonprinting graph paper. You can use it as a framework to arrange objects on, either by eye or by using the Snap to Grid feature. The first step, logically, is to display the grid.

To show the grid:

Do either of the following:

Choose View > **Show Grid** (Cmd-"/Ctrl-").**A**

Deselect, then right-click and choose **Show Grid** from the context menu.

To hide the grid, either choose View > Hide Grid or choose Hide Grid from the context menu.

➤ You can change the grid color, style (lines or dots), or spacing in Illustrator/Edit > Preferences > Guides & Grid. With the Grids in Back preference checked (the default setting), the grid displays behind all objects rather than in front of them.

To snap objects to the grid:

1. Choose View > **Snap to Grid** (Cmd-Shift-"/ Ctrl-Shift-") to make the check mark appear.

2. With the Selection tool ▶ (V), drag an object near a gridline; the edge of the object will snap to the gridline. This feature works whether the grid is showing or not.

   Note: When the Snap to Grid feature is on, Smart Guides won't display (even if the Smart Guides option is on). If you like to use Smart Guides to align objects, as we do, when you're done using the grid, hide it and also turn off the Snap to Grid feature.

➤ If the View > Pixel Preview feature is on, View > Snap to Grid changes to View > Snap to Pixel, which is turned on automatically. See the sidebar on page 30. Note that Smart Guides don't display when the Pixel Preview option is on.

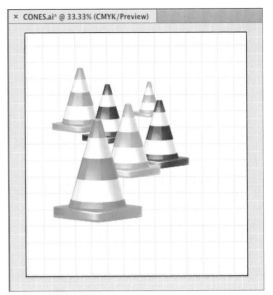

× CONES.ai* @ 33.33% (CMYK/Preview)

A *The grid is showing in this document.*

In the preceding four chapters you mastered creating, selecting, and positioning objects. Here you will add colors and patterns. You will learn what kinds of colors are suitable for print or Web output. You will fill the inside or edge of an object with a solid color or pattern using numerous panels and tools, save and organize swatches in the Swatches panel, copy swatches between files, choose stroke attributes, use the Color Guide panel, use the Kuler apps and panel, replace colors in your artwork, invert colors, colorize a grayscale image, blend fill colors between objects, and create and edit fill patterns using the Pattern Options panel.

Using color in Illustrator

The fill, which is applied to the inside of an object or an area in a Live Paint group, can be a solid color, a pattern, or a gradient (or a color of None). The stroke, which is applied to an object's path, can be a solid color, a pattern (or None), or a gradient, and it can be dashed or continuous. You can apply a brush to an object's stroke, make a stroke into an arrow, or as we describe on page 166, change the width profile. The path to which you apply a fill and/or stroke can be open or closed.

The fill and stroke colors in the current or last selected object — or new colors that you choose when no objects are selected — display on the Tools, Color, Control, and Appearance panels.**A** The two current colors are applied to new objects automatically.

Continued on the following page

Continued on the following page

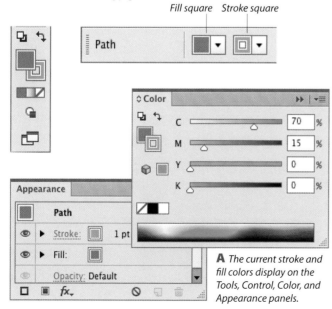

Fill square   Stroke square

A The current stroke and fill colors display on the Tools, Control, Color, and Appearance panels.

In this chapter, you will use the Color, Swatches, Color Guide, Kuler, Appearance, Pattern Options, and library panels; the Color Picker; and the Eyedropper tool to create and apply colors and patterns. You will also use the Control, Stroke, and Appearance panels to change the weight, style (dashed or solid), alignment (position on the path), and endcaps of a stroke, and create arrows.

Beyond this chapter, there are other fill and stroke features to explore. In Chapter 12, you will create nonuniform stroke widths using variable width profiles and the Width tool; in Chapter 14, you will apply multiple fill and stroke attributes; in Chapter 18, you will apply colors with the Live Paint Bucket tool; in Chapter 24, you will create and save gradients; and in Chapter 29, you will use the Recolor Artwork dialog to assign new colors or color groups to your artwork.

Colors for your output medium

Before delving into the specific coloring features of Illustrator, you need to know what types of colors are suitable for your artwork and your target output medium.

Colors for print output

A **solid** color (also called a spot color) is a predefined mixture of specific inks that is printed via a separate printing plate. To create PANTONE PLUS number 7489C (a medium green), for instance, your print shop would mix ink percentages of 60 cyan, 0 magenta, 80 yellow, and 7 black. To choose a solid color, you need to flip through a printed guide for a matching system (such as the PANTONE PLUS Solid Chips guide); pick a named, numbered color; then locate that color in Illustrator. You can use just solid colors if your document doesn't contain any photos, gradients, or other continuous-tone elements. Each solid color incurs a cost, so remember to factor that into your budget.

In commercial **process** printing, minute dots of the four process colors — cyan (C), magenta (M), yellow (Y), and black (K) — are printed from four separate plates. When viewing the print, your eyes (and mind) blur the dots together and read them as solid colors. (If you examine a photograph in a magazine or catalog with a magnifying lens or loupe, you will see the actual dots.) You can choose premixed process colors from a matching system, such as TRUMATCH or PANTONE PLUS Color Bridge, or enter specific process color percentages in the Color panel **A** or Color Picker.**B**

QUICK ACCESS TO THE COLORING PANELS

To quickly open a color-related panel, either click its icon in a dock or use one of these methods:

Appearance panel ⬤	Press Shift-F6
Color panel 🎨	Shift-click the Fill or Stroke square or arrowhead on the Control panel;* or click, then Shift-click the Fill or Stroke square on the Appearance panel; or press F6
Swatches panel ▦	Click the Fill or Stroke square or arrowhead on the Control panel, or click the Fill or Stroke square on the Appearance panel twice*

*When opened from the Control or Appearance panel, these panels stay open only temporarily.

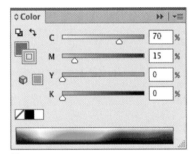

A For print output, choose colors in the CMYK color model. CMYK colors can be mixed on the Color panel ...

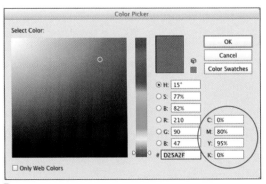

B ... or in the Color Picker.

The four-color process printing method must be used if your artwork contains continuous tones.**A**

In Illustrator, you can create and apply nonglobal process colors, which can only be edited individually in selected objects, or global process colors, which can be changed either individually in selected objects or globally in all objects in which they are being used (by editing the color swatch). This is explained on page 136.

If your budget allows, you can print a file using process colors and also add a solid (spot) color or two, say, for a key graphic, such as a logo.

Colors for Web output

For Web and video output, you should either choose **RGB** colors (percentages of red, green, and blue) or enter **hexadecimal** values.**B** Hexadecimal colors (hex colors for short) are described using a total of six characters from among the digits 0 through 9 and the letters A through F. Following the hash symbol (#), the first two characters indicate the amount of red, the second two indicate the amount of green, and the third two indicate the amount of blue.

Note: For more accurate color matching between a document that you view onscreen and the medium in which it will be published, make sure you have chosen the proper color management settings (see Chapter 2).

In the New Document dialog (Advanced options showing), when creating a document, you can choose CMYK or RGB as the document color mode. Any colors you mix or choose in that document will conform automatically to the chosen mode. If you change the document color mode, all the colors in the artwork will be converted to the new mode. Note that the gamut of RGB colors is larger than the gamut of CMYK colors.

Note: If the final output for your file will be an inkjet print (the inkjet print won't merely be used as a mockup or proof before commercial proofing and printing), choose RGB Color as the document mode.

To change the color mode of a document:

1. To be on the safe side, copy your file via the File > Save As command (Cmd-Shift-S/Ctrl-Shift-S).

2. Choose File > Document Color Mode > **CMYK Color** (for commercial print output) or **RGB Color** (for inkjet printing, or for Web or device output). The current document color mode is listed in the document tab.

➤ If you need to reverse a document color mode change, don't choose the former mode. Instead, choose Edit > Undo immediately.

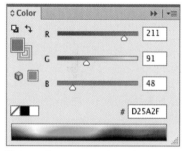

A *The extended Info panel lists the components or swatch name of the fill (on the left) and stroke (on the right) in the currently selected object. If multiple selected objects contain a nonmatching fill or stroke color, that readout area will be blank.*

B *For Web output, use the RGB color model or enter hexadecimal values.*

STAYING IN THE MODE

➤ You can create either process CMYK colors or RGB colors in an Illustrator document, but not both. Any process colors that you create in a document will conform automatically to the current document color mode, regardless of which mode you choose for the Color panel (see page 119). This is also true of the Color Mode menu in the Swatch Options dialog when you edit a swatch (see page 136).

➤ Embedded placed and pasted images are converted to the current document color mode automatically.

IGNORING THE "OUT OF WEB" ALERT

When designing Web graphics, you don't need to restrict yourself to Web-safe colors, which were formulated for earlier computer systems that couldn't display millions of colors. Disregard the Out of Web color warning ⬡ if it appears in the Color panel or Color Picker, and in the picker, keep the Only Web Colors option unchecked.

Using the basic color controls

Note: To choose new default colors for future objects, deselect all before choosing fill and stroke colors.

To apply a fill or stroke color, gradient, or pattern via a temporary Swatches panel:

1. Select one or more objects, or isolate an object.

2. Do any of the following:

   On the Control panel, click the Fill or Stroke square or arrowhead,**A** then on the temporary Swatches panel that opens, click a solid-color, gradient, or pattern swatch.**B–C** (To learn more about applying a gradient to an object's stroke, see page 345.)

   On the Appearance panel, click the Fill or Stroke listing,**D** click the color square or arrowhead,**E** then on the temporary Swatches panel, click a swatch.

   ➤ You can also change the stroke weight via the Control or Appearance panel; see page 122.

To apply a fill or stroke color of None:

1. Select one or more objects, or isolate an object.

2. Do one of the following:

   On the Tools panel or the Color panel, click the Fill or Stroke square, then either click the **None** button ☐ or press /.

   On the Control panel, click the Fill or Stroke square or arrowhead, then click the **None** button ☐ on the temporary Swatches panel.

   On the Appearance panel, click the Fill or Stroke listing, then press /.

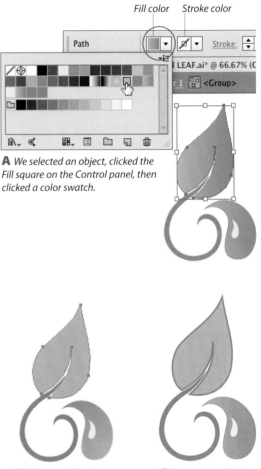

Fill color   Stroke color

A *We selected an object, clicked the Fill square on the Control panel, then clicked a color swatch.*

B *The new fill color appeared in the object.*

C *Next, we applied a stroke color to the same object.*

D *Click the Fill or Stroke listing on the Appearance panel.*

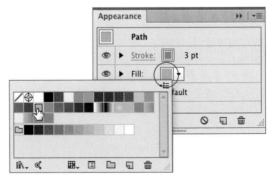

E *Click the Fill or Stroke square or arrowhead to open a temporary Swatches panel, then click a swatch.*

You can also apply a solid color to objects by using the Color Picker dialog or the Color Guide panel.

To apply a solid fill or stroke color using the Color Picker:

1. Select one or more objects, or isolate an object.

2. On the Tools or Color panel, double-click the Fill or Stroke square. The Color Picker opens.

3 Click a hue on the vertical bar in the middle of the dialog (or drag the slider), then click a brightness and saturation value of that hue in the large square.**A** You can also define a color by entering HSB, RGB, hexadecimal, or CMYK values.

If your document is going to be printed and the Out of Gamut icon ⚠ appears in the dialog, click the swatch below the icon to replace the chosen color with the closest printable one.

4. Click OK.

➤ If the fill or stroke colors differ among selected objects, a question mark **?** appears in the Fill and/or Stroke square on the Tools, Color, and Control panels. The new color you choose will apply to all the selected objects.

To apply a variation of a current color via the Color Guide panel:

1. Select one or more objects, or isolate an object.

2. On the Tools or Color panel, click the Fill or Stroke square.

3. Display the Color Guide panel.

4. Click the **Set Base Color to Current Color** button ▣ in the upper left corner of the panel, then click a color variation swatch in the panel.**B** For more about this panel, see pages 130–132.

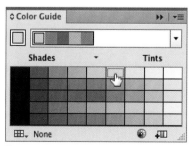

A *In the Color Picker, click a hue on the vertical bar, then click a variation of that color in the large square.*

B *On the Color Guide panel, click a variation of the current color.*

APPLYING BLACK OR WHITE

➤ To apply a white fill *and* a black stroke of 1 pt. to a selected object, click the Default Fill and Stroke button ▣ on the Tools panel or press D.

➤ To apply a white or black fill or stroke separately to a selected object, click the Fill or Stroke square on the Color panel, then click the White or Black selector on the Color panel (shown below) or click the White or Black swatch on the Swatches panel.

Saving colors as swatches

The Swatches panel is used for storing and applying process and solid colors, patterns, gradients, and color groups. Swatches that you add to the panel save only with the current file. To learn more about this panel, see pages 126–129.

To save the current fill or stroke color as a swatch:

1. Click the Fill or Stroke square on the Color 🎨 panel.

2. Do either of the following:

   Select or isolate an object that contains the color to be saved as a swatch.

   Deselect, then choose a color via the Color Picker, click a color on the Color Guide panel (see the preceding page), or specify values via the Color panel (see the facing page).

3. Display the Swatches panel 🎨 so it stays open, either expanded in a dock or floating.

4. Hold down Option/Alt and click the **New Swatch** button 🔲 on the Swatches panel.**A–B**

➤ To rename a swatch, double-click it, then enter a name in the Swatch Name field; or put the panel into list view (via the panel menu or the Show List View button in the upper-right corner of the panel), then double-click the name on the panel.★

To save the colors being used in a document as swatches:

Do either of the following:

Deselect, then from the Swatches panel menu, choose **Add Used Colors**.

Select one or more objects, then from the Swatches panel menu, choose **Add Selected Colors**.

Note: Both commands convert nonglobal process colors 🔲 to global process colors 🔲 (see page 136).

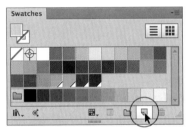

A Click the color square on the Color or Tools panel, then Option/Alt click the New Swatch button on the Swatches panel.

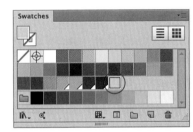

B The new swatch appears on the panel.

SHORTCUTS FOR COLORING OBJECTS

Toggle the Fill and Stroke squares (Tools and Color panels)	Press X
Make the fill color the same as the stroke color, or vice versa	Drag one square over the other on the Tools panel or Color panel
Swap the current fill and stroke colors	Press Shift-X or click the Swap Fill and Stroke button 🔄 on the Tools panel
Apply a fill of None	Click the None button ▱ on the Color or Tools panel, or press /
Reapply the last solid color after applying a gradient, pattern, or None	Click the Last Color button 🔲 on the Color panel or the Color button 🔲 on the Tools panel, or press <
Reapply the last gradient after applying a solid color, pattern, or None	Click the Gradient button 🔲 on the Tools panel, or press >

Default Fill and Stroke (D) — Swap Fill and Stroke (Shift-X)

Fill square — Stroke square

Color (<) — None (/)

Gradient (>)

These color controls are located at the bottom of the Tools panel.

Choosing colors via the Color panel

Via the Color panel, you can choose an RGB or hexa-decimal color for Web output or a CMYK color for print output.

To apply a color via the Color panel:

1. Select one or more objects, or isolate an object — or to choose colors for an object to be created, deselect.

2. Do one of the following:

   On the Color panel, 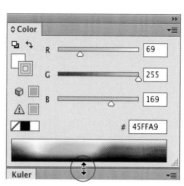 click the Fill or Stroke square.

   On the Control panel, Shift-click the Fill or Stroke square or arrowhead to open a temporary Color panel.

   On the Appearance panel, ⬤ click the Fill or Stroke listing, then Shift-click the square or arrowhead for that listing to open a temporary Color panel.

3. To choose a color for video or Web output, from the Color panel menu, choose **RGB** (not Web Safe RGB). For greater accuracy in sampling, expand the color spectrum bar by dragging the left or bottom edge of the panel.**A** Click a color in the spectrum bar, then, if desired, tweak the color by moving the sliders.

   For video or Web output, from the Color panel menu, choose **RGB**, then enter a hexadecimal value in the # field. Note: You can copy and paste this value into another application.

   To define a specific process color for print output, from the Color panel menu, choose **CMYK**. Refer to a printed guide (such as a PANTONE PLUS Color Bridge guide) for exact values, then enter C, M, Y, and K percentages.**B**

4. Optional (but recommended): To save the new color as a nonglobal process color swatch, Option-click/Alt-click the New Swatch button 🔲 on the Swatches panel. To save as a global process color swatch, Option-Shift-click/Alt-Shift-click the New Swatch button 🔲 on the Swatches panel.

▶ To specify a shade on a gray spectrum, choose Grayscale from the panel menu. Or to define a color by hue (location on the color wheel), saturation (purity), and brightness values, choose HSB.

▶ To cycle through the color models for the Color panel, Shift-click the spectrum bar at the bottom of the panel.

▶ Colors can also be defined numerically via the Color Picker (see page 117).

A To expand the Color panel, drag the bottom (or left) edge.

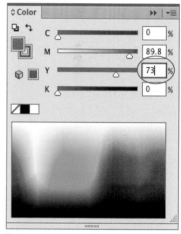

B For print output, choose CMYK from the panel menu, then enter percentage values.

SELECTING TYPE OR A TYPE OBJECT FOR RECOLORING

▶ To recolor all the type in a block, select it with the Selection tool or the Layers panel first.

▶ To recolor just a portion of the type in a block, select that passage with a type tool first.

▶ To recolor an object that contains path or area type (not the type), select the path with the Direct Selection tool first.

SUBSTITUTING AN IN-GAMUT COLOR

If the current RGB or HSB color has no CMYK equivalent (and therefore can't be printed on a commercial press), an Out of Gamut warning ⚠ displays on the Color panel. If you click the icon or swatch, Illustrator will replace it with the closest equivalent printable color.

Applying colors from a library

In these instructions, we'll show you how to access and apply solid or process colors from a matching system (such as PANTONE PLUS) or swatches from one of the predefined Adobe color libraries.

To access swatches from a library:

1. *Optional:* To apply a color to artwork, select one or more objects or isolate an object, and click the Fill or Stroke square on the Tools or Color panel.

2. From the **Swatch Libraries** menu 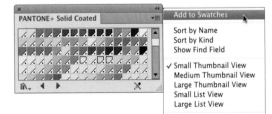 on the Swatches panel (or from a submenu on that menu), choose a library name. If you want to open a library from a matching system (for print output), choose it from the Color Books submenu (see the sidebar on this page); or to reload the default swatches, choose from the Default Swatches submenu.

   The chosen library will open in a floating panel. You can scroll in or enlarge the panel, if necessary, to reveal more colors.

3. If you click a swatch in a Color Books library or click a color group icon in a library, that color or color group will appear on the Swatches panel immediately. For other colors, do either of the following:

   On the library panel, click a swatch or hold down Cmd/Ctrl or Shift and click multiple swatches, then choose **Add to Swatches** from the panel menu. **A**

   Drag a swatch or a selection of multiple swatches from the library panel to the Swatches panel.

➤ Once you have opened a library, you can cycle through other libraries by clicking the Load Next Swatch Library or Load Previous Swatch Library button.

➤ To control whether a library panel reappears when you relaunch Illustrator, check or uncheck Persistent on the library panel menu. From that menu, you can also choose a thumbnail or list view for the panel (the larger views are helpful for viewing gradients and patterns).

➤ To close a whole library panel, click its close box. To close just one library on a panel, right-click its tab and choose Close from the context menu.

➤ You can't modify swatches on a library panel (note the non-edit icon in the lower right corner). However, you can edit any swatch once you add it to the Swatches panel.

➤ Although it is advised that you use the latest swatch colors, in Illustrator CC, both PANTONE PLUS and legacy PANTONE swatches can be used in the same file; the original formula of each swatch is preserved. More information can be found by going to Illustrator Help > Pantone Plus Color Libraries.

ABOUT THE COLOR BOOK BRANDS

ANPA colors are used in the newspaper industry.

DIC Color Guide and TOYO Color Finder colors are used in Japan.

FOCOLTONE process colors are designed to help prevent registration problems and lessen the need for trapping.

HKS process colors and HKS spot colors (without the word "Process" in the name) are used in Europe.

PANTONE PLUS colors are widely used in the commercial print industry in North America.

TRUMATCH process colors include 40 tints/shades of each hue (organized differently from PANTONE colors).

AVOIDING NASTY COLOR SURPRISES

As you learned in Chapter 2, the Color Settings command in Illustrator uses monitor and printer device profiles and output intents in conjunction with the system's color management utility to achieve better color matching between the onscreen display of artwork and the final output. Unfortunately, even with a good color management system in place, you can't proof spot colors for commercial printing onscreen (don't be tempted to trust what you see). Instead, pick spot colors and evaluate their appearance in a printed guide for a color matching system that is used in your locale. And before authorizing a print run, also request and examine at least one color proof from your print shop.

A *Select one or more swatches or color groups on a library panel, then choose Add to Swatches from the panel menu to make them appear on your document's Swatches panel.*

Changing the tint percentage

If you need to output a design to a commercial press using just one black and one spot color printing plate (perhaps as a cost-saving measure), you can achieve a pleasing range of tints by applying an assortment of tint percentages of a spot (solid) color. You can also choose a percentage for any global process color (to learn more about global process colors, see page 136).

To change the tint percentage of a spot or global process color:

1. Select one or more objects that contain the same spot or global process color. Note: On the Swatches panel, spot color swatches have a dot in the lower right corner, whereas global process color swatches have a white triangle in the corner.

2. Do one of the following:

   On the Color panel, click the Fill or Stroke square, then drag the **T** (Tint) slider or enter a value.**A**

   On the Color panel, click the Fill or Stroke square, then hover your cursor over the tint slider and scroll up or down using the scroll wheel on your mouse to change the tint percentage of the current fill color.★

To open a temporary Color panel, Shift-click the Fill or Stroke square on the Control panel; or on the Appearance panel, click, then Shift-click the Fill or Stroke square. Drag the **T** (Tint) slider or enter a value.**B**

➤ If Select Same Tint % is checked in Illustrator/ Edit > Preferences > General, the Fill Color, Stroke Color, and Fill & Stroke Color commands on the Select Similar Options menu on the Control panel will select only objects that contain the same color and tint percentage as the currently selected object. With this preference unchecked, the above-mentioned commands will select all tint percentages of the same color.

➤ If selected objects contain the same spot or global process color in different tint percentages, a question mark will display in the Fill or Stroke square. The tint percentage you choose will apply to all the selected objects.

QUICKLY RECOLOR AN OBJECT BY DRAGGING

You can quickly apply a fill or stroke color, gradient, or pattern without having to select an object first. Click the Fill or Stroke square on the Tools or Color panel, then drag a swatch from the Swatches panel or Color Guide panel, or from the Fill square on the Color panel, onto any object (it doesn't matter which tool is selected).

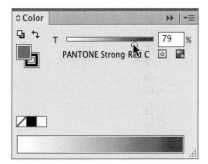

A On the Color panel, drag the Tint slider, scroll using the scroll wheel on your mouse, or enter a value.

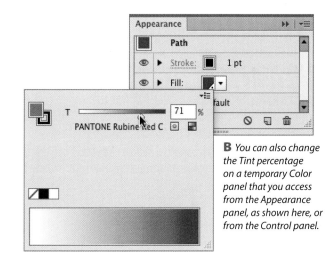

B You can also change the Tint percentage on a temporary Color panel that you access from the Appearance panel, as shown here, or from the Control panel.

Changing the stroke weight, alignment, caps, and joins

In addition to changing the color of a stroke, you can change the stroke weight, the position of the stroke on the path, and the style (dashed or solid, rounded or sharp corners, flat or rounded ends). And you can choose settings to turn it into an arrow. (To use the Profile options on the Stroke panel, see page 166.)

To change the weight of a stroke:

1. Select one or more objects, isolate an object, or select some type.

2. In any of these locations, change the stroke weight by clicking the up or down arrow, by entering a value, or by choosing a value from the menu:

   In the **Weight** area of the Stroke panel. **A**

   In the **Stroke Weight** area of the Control panel.

   Using the **Stroke Weight** controls on the Appearance panel (click the Stroke square to display them).**B**

   ➤ Shift-click the up or down Stroke Weight arrow to change the value by a larger interval.

To change the alignment of a stroke on a path:

1. Select one or more closed paths, or isolate a closed path. To see the effect of the align options, make the stroke fairly wide or zoom in on your artwork.

2. Display the full Stroke panel (see the sidebar on this page).

3. Click the **Align Stroke to Center** (the default setting), **Align Stroke to Inside**, or **Align Stroke to Outside** button.**C–E**

   Note: To apply a variable width profile to a path (see page 166), to use the Width tool (see pages 167–168), or to apply a gradient along or across an object's stroke (see page 345), the path must have the Align Stroke to Center setting. If you apply a brush stroke to a path, the Align Stroke to Center setting is applied automatically.

To change the stroke cap or corner style:

1. Select one or more objects or isolate an object, and apply a fairly wide stroke to it.

2. Display the full Stroke panel.

3. To modify the endpoints of aan open path or all the dashes in a dashed line, click one of the **Cap** buttons: (**A–B**, next page).

DISPLAYING THE STROKE PANEL

➤ Click the Stroke panel icon in the panel dock. To display the full set of options, click the double arrowheads on the panel tab once or twice.

➤ To open a full but temporary Stroke panel, click the underlined Stroke link on the Control panel (objects with mixed stroke attributes can be selected).

➤ To open a full but temporary Stroke panel when one object is selected or when multiple objects that have the same stroke attributes are selected, click the underlined Stroke link on the Appearance panel.

A *To change the stroke weight of an object, you can use the controls on the Stroke panel …*

B *… or on the Appearance panel.*

C *Align Stroke to Center*

D *Align Stroke to Inside*

E *Align Stroke to Outside*

Butt Cap ⊏ to create squared ends, in which the stroke stops at the endpoints, or to create short, rectangular dashes. Use this option when you need to align your paths very precisely.

Round Cap ⊏ to create semicircular ends or elliptical dashes.

Projecting Cap ⊏ to create squared ends, in which the stroke extends beyond the endpoints (by half the current stroke weight), or to create longer dashes.

4. To modify the joins on the corner points (not the curve points) of the path, click a **Corner** button:

Miter Join ⌐ to produce pointed bends.

Round Join ⌐ to produce semicircular bends.

Bevel Join ⌐ to produce beveled bends. The sharper the angle in a path, the wider the bevel.

5. *Optional:* Change the Limit value for the minimum length of a mitered (pointed) corner for it to become a beveled corner. Don't fret over how this works; just use a very low Limit value if you want to create beveled corners.

➤ To learn the difference between corner and curve points, see page 299.

Creating arrows

To add an arrowhead and/or tail to a path:

1. Select one or more objects or isolate an object — preferably an open path. Apply a stroke color to it and choose a weight.

2. Display the full Stroke panel. ≡

3. From the **Arrowheads** pickers, choose an arrowhead style for the starting point of the path and a tail style for the endpoint of the path.

   ➤ To swap the two styles on the path, click the Swap Start and End Arrowheads button. ⇄

4. *Optional:* To scale the arrowhead or tail on the object, use the respective Scale controls. Or to scale both ends at once, click the link icon ⚙ first.**C** Note: If you change the stroke width, you may need to adjust the scale of the arrowhead and tail.

5. *Optional:* To change the alignment of the arrowhead and tail on the path, click the Extend Arrow Tip Beyond End of Path button ➜ or the Place Arrow Tip at End of Path button. ➜

➤ To remove an arrowhead or tail from a selected path, choose None from the menu.

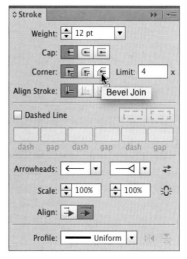

A *To identify the Cap and Corner buttons on the Stroke panel, use the tool tips.*

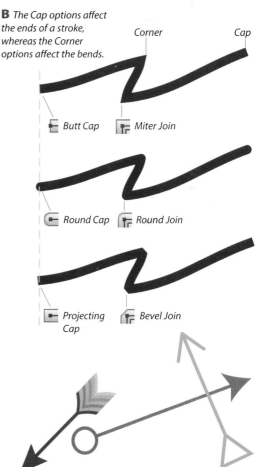

B *The Cap options affect the ends of a stroke, whereas the Corner options affect the bends.*

Corner   Cap

⊏ Butt Cap   ⌐ Miter Join

⊏ Round Cap   ⌐ Round Join

⊏ Projecting Cap   ⌐ Bevel Join

C *Arrowheads and tails are applied to these paths.*

Creating a dashed stroke

Using the Dashed Line controls, you can easily create a dashed stroke that has either uniform or varied dash lengths and spacing.

To create a dashed (or dotted) stroke:

1. Select one or more objects, or isolate an object. Make sure the stroke has a color and that its weight is 1 pt. or greater.

2. Display the full Stroke panel.

3. Click a **Cap** button for the shape of the ends of the dashes (see the preceding page).

4. Check **Dashed Line.**

5. Enter a value in the first **Dash** field for the length of the first dash, then press Tab.**A**

6. *Optional:* Enter a value in the first Gap field (for the length of the first gap following the first dash), then press Tab to proceed to the next field or press Return/Enter to exit the panel. If you don't enter a Gap value, the Dash value will also be used as the Gap value.

7. *Optional:* To create dashes of more than one length, enter values in the other Dash fields. If you don't do this, the first Dash value will be used for all the dashes, and all the dashes will have a uniform length. Ditto for the gaps.

8. To control how the dashes fit around the corners of the object, click the **Preserves Exact Dash and Gap Lengths** button ⌐‗⌐ for no adjustment at the corners, or click the **Aligns Dashes to Corners and Path Ends, Adjusting Lengths to Fit** button ⌐‗⌐ (that's a mouthful!) to have the dashes adjust to fit symmetrically at the corners. We chose the first option for the top two objects in figure **B** and the second option for the bottom two objects.

➤ To create a dotted line, click the second Cap button (Round Cap), enter a Dash value of 0, and enter a Gap value that is equal to or greater than the stroke weight. For example, for a stroke weight of 15 pt., enter a Dash value of 0 and a Gap value between 20 and 30 pt.

➤ To save a dashed stroke as a graphic style, drag a path to which that stroke is applied into the Graphic Styles panel (see page 225).

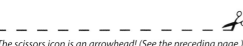

The scissors icon is an arrowhead! (See the preceding page.)

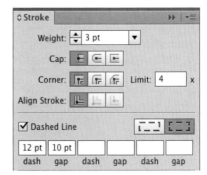

A *These Dashed Line settings will produce dashes that are 12 pt. long and are separated by 10-pt. gaps.*

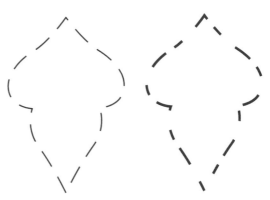

Weight 1 pt., Dash 14, Gap 9, Butt Cap

Weight 2 pt., Dash 8, Gap 15, Dash 15, Gap 8, Butt Cap

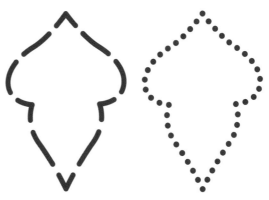

Weight 4 pt., Dash 24, Gap 8, Round Cap

Weight 4.6 pt., Dash 0, Gap 7.8, Round Cap and Join

B *These dashed strokes were created using various settings.*

Using the Eyedropper tool

When you click an object with the Eyedropper tool, it samples the object's color and stroke attributes, displays them on the Color, Stroke, and Appearance panels, and applies them to selected objects — in one quick and easy step. Note: This tool doesn't pick up or apply variable width profiles or brush strokes.

To sample and apply colors with the Eyedropper tool:

1. *Optional:* To specify default settings for the attributes that you want the Eyedropper tool to pick up and apply, double-click the tool ✐ (or click the tool, then press Return/Enter). In the Eyedropper Options dialog, check the attributes that the tool is to pick up and apply (the default setting is all options checked), uncheck the attributes to be ignored, then click OK.

2. *Optional:* Select one or more objects. They will be recolored instantly with the attributes you are going to sample with the Eyedropper in step 4.

3. Choose the **Eyedropper** tool ✐ (I).

4. Click an object in your artwork that contains the desired attributes.**A** It can be any kind of object (even a color in a placed image), and it can contain a solid color, pattern, or gradient. The object doesn't have to be selected. Depending on the current Eyedropper Options settings, the sampled colors may appear in the Fill and/or Stroke squares on the Tools, Color, Appearance, and Control panels, and the sampled stroke settings may appear on the Stroke panel.

   If you selected any objects before using the Eyedropper tool, the sampled attributes will be applied to those objects.**B**

➤ Option-click/Alt-click an object to do the opposite of the above — that is, apply color attributes from the currently selected object to the object you click.**C–D**

➤ To have the Eyedropper tool sample just the color you click in a solid color, gradient, or pattern (no other attributes), click the Fill or Stroke square on the Tools or Color panel, then Shift-click the color to be sampled.

➤ To save the sampled color, drag it from the Fill or Stroke square on the Color panel to the Swatches panel.

A *Select one or more objects, then with the Eyedropper tool, click an object that contains the desired attributes.*

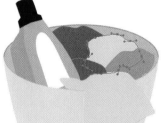

B *The attributes you sample will be applied instantly to the selected object(s).*

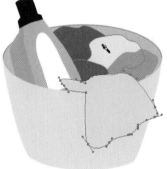

C *Another method is to Option-click/ Alt-click with the Eyedropper tool to apply attributes from the currently selected object to the one you click.*

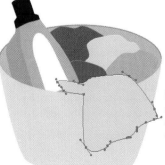

D *This is the result after we Option/ Alt clicked with the Eyedropper tool.*

Using the Swatches panel

Via the Swatches panel menu, you can control which categories and size of swatches the panel displays.

To choose display options for the Swatches panel:

1. Display the Swatches panel.

2. To control which categories of swatches display on the panel, from the **Show Swatch Kinds** menu, choose Show All Swatches for all types (colors, gradients, patterns, and color groups),**A** Show Color Swatches for just solid colors and color groups, Show Gradient Swatches for just gradients, Show Pattern Swatches for just patterns, or Show Color Groups for just color groups.

3. From the panel menu, choose a view for the currently displayed category of swatches. The medium and large thumbnail views are useful for identifying gradients and patterns. In the two list views, solid colors have icons that identify their type and mode.**B** You can also switch easily between list view and thumbnail view using the icons in the upper-right corner of the Swatches panel.★

4. *Optional:* From the panel menu, choose Sort by Name to sort all nongrouped swatches alphabetically by name or numerically by their color contents; or choose Sort by Kind (when all categories are displayed) to sort swatches in the following order: solid colors, gradients, patterns, color groups.

➤ You can drag a swatch, or multiple selected swatches, to another location on the panel. Color groups are always listed last.

To search for a swatch on the Swatches panel or a library panel:

1. If the search field isn't showing on the Swatches panel or a library panel, check Show Find Field on the panel menu.

2. In the field, type a color number or name (e.g., a number from a color book or the name of a custom color); or type between one and four specific color values (e.g., C=0 M=100 Y=50 K=0). Illustrator will find the swatch that has the closest match (but the program won't fill in the rest of the color name).**C**

3. To redisplay all the swatches, click the ⊠.

➤ To access the search field in the Color Picker, double-click the Fill or Stroke square on the Tools or Color panel to open the picker, then click Color Swatches.

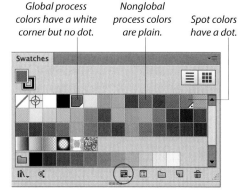

Global process colors have a white corner but no dot.　*Nonglobal process colors are plain.*　*Spot colors have a dot.*

A *All four varieties of swatches (color, gradient, pattern, and color groups) are displayed on this Swatches panel because Show All Swatches is chosen on the Show Swatch Kinds menu. Note: To learn the difference between global and nonglobal colors, see page 138.*

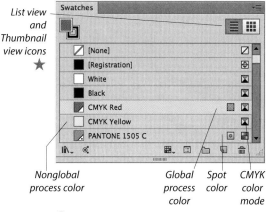

List view and Thumbnail view icons ★

Nonglobal process color　*Global process color*　*Spot color*　*CMYK color mode*

B *When the Swatches panel is in a list view, icons representing the color type and document color mode display on the right side.*

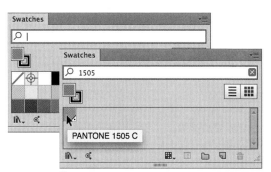

C *We clicked in the Find Field ... then typed the number of a PANTONE color; the color was found.*

A convenient way to organize swatches on the Swatches panel is by putting them in color groups. If you're coordinating a group of colors for a specific client, project, or whatever, you will be able to locate and display them more easily if they're in groups.

When the panel is in a thumbnail view, the colors in each group are lined up in a row, beginning with the folder icon, and each group name can be identified via its tool tip. When the panel is in a list view, the name of the color group is listed next to the folder icon, followed by a nested listing of the colors in the group.

To create a color group from swatches:

1. Deselect.

2. On the Swatches panel, ▦ Shift-click to select contiguous swatches or Cmd-click/Ctrl-click to select multiple non-contiguous swatches (sorry, no gradients, patterns, or the color None).**A**

3. Click the **New Color Group** button ▢ at the bottom of the panel.

4. In the New Color Group dialog, enter a Name, then click OK. The new group appears on the Swatches panel.**B**

    Note: To add a swatch to an existing color group, drag the swatch from the Swatches or Color Guide panel into the group or onto the group icon.

➤ You can also create a color group via the Color Guide panel (see pages 130–132), the Kuler panel (see pages 133–135), or the Recolor Artwork or Edit Colors dialog (see Chapter 29). To edit any color group via the Edit Colors dialog, double-click the group icon on the Swatches panel.

➤ To rename a color group, click its icon, then choose Color Group Options from the panel menu; or if the panel is in a list view, double-click the group name.

➤ To restack a color group among other color groups, drag its icon upward or downward.

To create a color group from artwork:

1. Select the artwork that contains the colors to be put into a new color group.**C**

2. Click the **New Color Group** button ▢ on the Swatches panel.

3. In the New Color Group dialog, enter a name for the group; click **Selected Artwork**; if desired, check Convert Process to Global and/or Include Swatches for Tints; then click OK.**D**

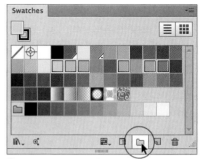

A With several swatches selected, the New Color Group button is clicked.

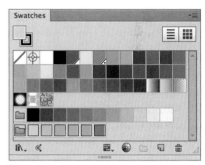

B The new color group appears on the panel.

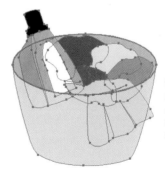

C We selected artwork in a document, then clicked the New Color Group button on the Swatches panel.

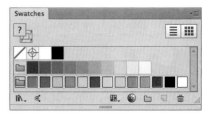

D The new color group appears on the panel.

To copy swatches between Illustrator files:

1. Open the file into which you want to load swatches.

2. From the **Swatch Libraries** menu at the bottom of the Swatches panel, choose **Other Library**. The Select a Library to Open dialog opens.

3. Locate and click the Illustrator file from which you want to copy swatches, then click Open. A library of swatches opens, bearing the name of the source file.

4. In the library panel that was generated from the source file, do either of the following:

   Click a swatch or color group icon.**A–B**

   Cmd-click/Ctrl-click or Shift-click multiple swatches or click a swatch in a color group, then choose Add to Swatches from the panel menu.

5. If the Swatch Conflict dialog appears, see the sidebar at right.

➤ To quickly append spot or global process colors from one file to another, do either of the following: Copy and paste an object or group that contains those colors from one document to another, or drag the object or group from one Illustrator document window onto the tab, and then into the window, of the other document. To append nonglobal process colors, do the same, then drag from the Fill and/or Stroke square on the Color panel to the Swatches panel.

RESOLVING A SWATCH CONFLICT

➤ The Swatch Conflict dialog will appear as you copy swatches or objects between files if a global process color has the same name as an existing swatch in the current document, but different color percentages. Click Merge Swatches to have the incoming swatch adopt the color values of the existing one, or click Add Swatches to add the incoming swatch to the document (Illustrator appends a number to its name). Note: To apply the current Options setting to any other name conflicts that crop up and prevent the alert dialog from opening repeatedly, check Apply to All.

➤ If a conflict arises between spot colors, Illustrator will merge the new swatch into the existing one.

A We opened a library of swatches from another file, then clicked a color group.

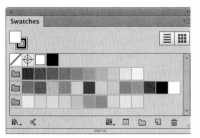

B The color group appeared on the Swatches panel for the current document.

To duplicate a swatch:

1. On the Swatches panel, click the swatch to be duplicated, then click the **New Swatch** button 🔲 on the panel.

2. The New Swatch dialog opens. Change the swatch name, if desired, check Global or not (see page 136), then click OK.

➤ To bypass the dialog as you duplicate a swatch, click the swatch, then Option-click/Alt-click the New Swatch button (or drag the swatch over the button).

To delete swatches from the Swatches panel:

1. On the Swatches panel, 🔳 do one of the following:

   Click a swatch.

   Click the icon for a color group.

   Cmd-click/Ctrl-click (or Shift, then Shift-click) multiple swatches or color groups.

   To select only the swatches that aren't being used in your artwork, choose **Show All Swatches** from the **Show Swatch Kinds** menu, 🔳▾ then choose **Select All Unused** from the panel menu.

2. Click the **Delete Swatch** button 🗑 at the bottom of the Swatches panel, then click Yes in the alert dialog; or to bypass the prompt, Option-click/Alt-click the Delete Swatch button.

➤ If you delete the swatch for a spot or global process color (or for a pattern or gradient that contains a spot or global process color) that is currently in use in your document, a nonglobal process color equivalent of the deleted color is applied to those objects automatically (see page 136).

➤ To restore a swatch that you have just deleted, choose Undo. If it's too late to use the Undo command but the deleted color is still in use in your artwork, select an object that contains the color, click the Fill and/or Stroke square on the Tools or Color panel, then Option-click/Alt-click the New Swatch button on the Swatches panel. If the swatch was a global process or spot color, you will need to reset it to Global or Spot via the Swatch Options dialog (see page 136).

➤ To restore swatches from a default library or any other library, see page 120.

Swatches and color groups that you load onto the Swatches panel will save with the current document but will disappear from the panel if you replace them with another library (such as one of the default preset libraries). Thankfully, you can collect the swatches and color groups currently on the panel into a library, for access and use in any document.

To create a custom library of swatches:

1. Make sure the Swatches panel contains only the swatches or color groups to be saved in a library.

   ➤ To delete all the swatches that aren't being used in your artwork, choose Show All Swatches from the Show Swatch Kinds menu, 🔳▾ choose Select All Unused from the Swatches panel menu, then click the Delete Swatch button. 🗑

2. From the top of the **Swatch Libraries** menu 📚▾ on the Swatches panel, choose **Save Swatches**.

3. The Save Swatches as Library/Save As dialog opens. Type a name for the library in the Save As/File Name field. In Windows 8, keep the Save as Type option set to Swatch Files (*.ai). Keep the default location, and click Save.

4. User-saved libraries are listed on, and can be opened from, the User Defined submenu on the Swatch Libraries menu.

SAVING SWATCHES FOR OTHER ADOBE APPLICATIONS

To save the swatches that are currently on the Swatches panel in Illustrator for use in other Adobe Creative Cloud applications, choose Save Swatch Library as ASE from the panel menu. Type a name (keep the .ase extension), choose a location, then click Save.

Using the Color Guide panel

Use the Color Guide panel to generate color schemes from a base color by choosing a harmony rule and/ or a variation type (Tints/Shades, Warm/Cool, or Vivid/ Muted). You can apply any resulting swatch as a fill or stroke color, save variations from the panel as a group to the Swatches panel, and edit the current color group via the Edit Colors dialog.

This panel might prove useful if you want to apply a set of coordinated colors quickly, if your projects require you to work with an approved group of colors, or if you simply want to see how your artwork might look in a different range of hues, tints, or saturation values. To get acquainted with the panel, start by choosing options for it.

To choose variation options for the Color Guide panel:

1. Show the Color Guide panel, 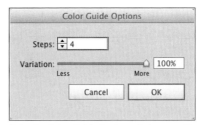 then choose **Color Guide Options** from the panel menu. The Color Guide Options dialog opens.**A**

2. Click the up/down arrow to set the number of variation **Steps** (columns of colors) to be displayed on either side of the colors in the central column, and move the **Variation** slider to control how much the colors can vary from those in the central column.

3. Click OK.**B**

➤ To make the swatches wider, enlarge the Color Guide panel by dragging its left or right edge.

To apply color variations via the Color Guide panel:

1. From the **Limit Color Group to Colors in Swatch Library** menu at the bottom of the Color Guide panel, choose None.

2. To set the base color and initial variations, do either of the following:

   Select an object,**C** then click the Fill or Stroke square on the Tools or Color panel. To have the panel generate variations based on that fill or stroke color, click the **Set Base Color to Current Color** button in the upper left corner of the Color Guide panel.

   Deselect, click the Fill or Stroke square on the Tools or Color panel, then click a swatch or color group on the Swatches panel, or click a swatch or color theme on the Kuler panel (see pages 133–135), or select a color via the Color panel.

A *In the Color Guide Options dialog, specify the number of Steps (variation columns) to be displayed on the Color Guide panel, and a degree of Variation for those colors.*

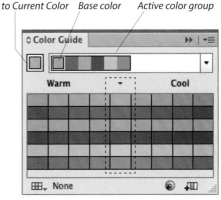

B *The original colors from the active color group display in the central column of the Color Guide panel. The options for this panel are set to 4 Steps (four columns on either side of the central one) and the maximum Variation percentage.*

C *We selected an object.*

3. The active color group displays at the top of the Color Guide panel. To control what types of variations are derived from the active color group, choose a variation type from the panel menu:

Show Tints/Shades adds progressively more black to the variations on the left side of the central column and progressively more white to the variations on the right.**A**

Show Warm/Cool adds progressively more red to the variations on the left and progressively more blue to the variations on the right.

Show Vivid/Muted progressively reduces the saturation of colors on the left and progressively increases the saturation of colors on the right.**B**

4. To apply a color variation, do either of the following:

To recolor the currently selected object, click a color in the active group at the top of the panel or click a variation swatch in the main part of the panel.

Drag a variation swatch over any selected or unselected object.**C**

Note: When you click a variation on the Color Guide panel, that color appears in the Set Base Color to Current Color button. If you then click that button, the active color group changes and new variations are generated.

➤ To limit the harmony and variation colors on the Color Guide panel to colors in a library, from the Limit Color Group to Colors in Swatch Library menu, choose a library name (e.g., Earthtone or Color Books > PANTONE + Solid Coated). The library name will be listed at the bottom of the Color Guide panel, and only colors from that library will display as variations on the panel and on the Harmony Rules menu (see the next page). To remove the current restriction, choose None from the same menu.

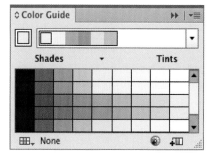

A *The Show Tints/Shades option produced these colors.*

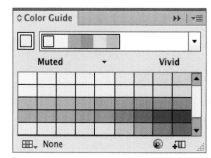

B *Here the Show Vivid/Muted option is chosen instead.*

C *We dragged variation swatches from the Color Guide panel over a few of the objects in the artwork.*

Another easy way to change the variations on the Color Guide panel is by choosing a harmony rule, such as Complementary, Analogous, or High Contrast. A new color group and variations are generated from the same base color, in accordance with the chosen rule. We could spend hours exploring the endless variations.

To create a color group and variations based on a harmony rule:

1. To establish a base color on the Color Guide panel, 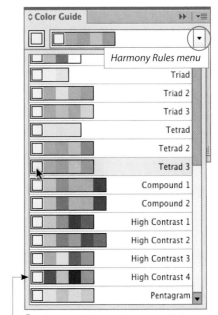 follow step 2 in "To apply color variations via the Color Guide panel" on page 130.

2. On the Color Guide panel, click to open the **Harmony Rules** menu (to the right of the active color group), **A** then click a rule. A new color group displays at the top of the panel. Below that, you will see the variations that Illustrator generated from the new color group. **B**

3. *Optional:* To produce a new color group and variations based on the chosen harmony rule, click a variation or a color in the active color group, then click the Set Base Color to Current Color button. You can also choose a different rule.

4. To recolor an object, select it, click the Fill or Stroke square on the Color panel, then click a color variation swatch, or drag a swatch over any selected or unselected object. **C**

The color group and variations on the Color Guide panel are transitory. They change as soon as you reset the base color, choose a different harmony rule, or click a swatch on the Swatches panel. Thankfully, you can save either the active color group or selected variations as a color group to the Swatches panel.

To add colors from the Color Guide panel to the Swatches panel:

1. On the Color Guide panel, 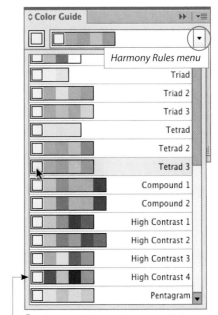 do either of the following:

   To save the active color group, deselect any selected variations by clicking the blank area.

   Cmd-click/Ctrl-click (or click, then Shift-click) the desired color variations.

2. Click the **Save Color Group to Swatch Panel** button. The new group appears on the Swatches panel.

➤ To save a single variation instead of a color group, select it, then hold down Option/Alt and click the New Swatch button on the Swatches panel.

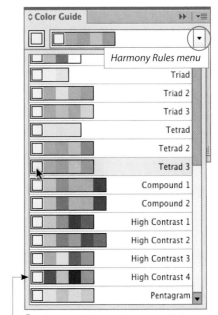

Base color

A *When you choose a harmony rule from the menu on the Color Guide panel, the base color stays the same, but the color group changes to abide by the new rule.*

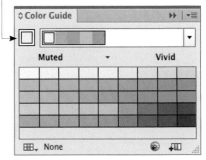

B *A new color group and variations appear on the panel, based on the new harmony rule.*

C *We dragged some new color variations onto objects in our artwork.*

Using Kuler

Using your Adobe Creative Cloud ID at Kuler.adobe.com (pronounced "cooler"), you can locate, comment on, and create groups of colors, called color themes, for use in Illustrator and other Adobe programs.

To browse Kuler color themes:

1. In Illustrator, display the **Kuler** panel, 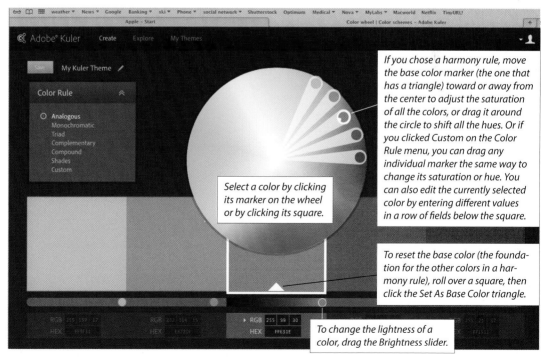 then click the **Launch Kuler Website** button to get to Kuler.adobe.com.

2. Click **Explore**. Click a category under **View**, then click Week, Month, or All; or in the **Search** field, enter a general topic or tags, or a specific creator name or user id number, then press Return/Enter.

3. To designate a theme as a favorite, roll over the theme, then click the **Favorite** button.

4. To view all your favorite themes, click **My Themes** at the top of the window, then click **My Favorites**. (To remove a favorite theme, roll over it and click the Info button, then click the **Favorite** button; or if the theme was created by another user, you can simply roll over it and click the Favorite button.

➤ To comment on a theme, roll over it and click the Info button, type a comment in the field, then click **Add Comment**. To view other themes by the same creator, click their link under Info, next to Created By.

To create or edit a Kuler theme:

1. Follow step 1, at left.

2. Do either of the following:

   On the menu bar, click **Create**.

   Find a theme that you like, either via a search or under My Favorites, roll over the theme, then click **Edit**.

3. To create or edit the theme based on a harmony rule, click an option under **Color Rule** (the color markers will move as a unit); or to allow the markers to move independently of one another, click Custom.

4. To edit the theme, see the callouts in figure **A**.

5. When you're done editing the theme, click **My Kuler Theme** or **Copy of** [theme name], enter a name in the field, then click **Save**.

6. To view all your themes (or to cancel editing your own theme), click **My Themes**.

If you chose a harmony rule, move the base color marker (the one that has a triangle) toward or away from the center to adjust the saturation of all the colors, or drag it around the circle to shift all the hues. Or if you clicked Custom on the Color Rule menu, you can drag any individual marker the same way to change its saturation or hue. You can also edit the currently selected color by entering different values in a row of fields below the square.

Select a color by clicking its marker on the wheel or by clicking its square.

To reset the base color (the foundation for the other colors in a harmony rule), roll over a square, then click the Set As Base Color triangle.

To change the lightness of a color, drag the Brightness slider.

A *Use the controls on the Create page on Kuler.adobe.com, to create or edit a color theme.*

To create a color theme from a photo: ★

1. From the Kuler home page, choose Create from the menu at the top of the screen, then click the Create From Image icon 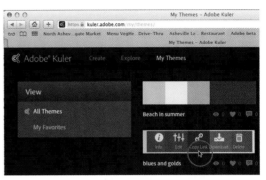 in the upper right corner.

2. Click one of your photos, then choose a mood from the Color Mood menu. Give the theme a name if desired. Click Save.

3. Colors from the photo display on the Create page on Kuler.adobe.com and in My Themes. Follow steps 3–5 in the preceding task.

To manage your Kuler themes:

1. Click **My Themes**, then click **All Themes** or **My Favorites**.

2. Roll over a theme to display a menu of options,**A** then do any of the following:

   Click **Copy Link** to copy the URL for the theme, which you can then paste (e.g., into an email).

   To generate an Adobe Swatch Exchange File of colors in the theme for use in Adobe applications, click **Download**.

   To delete the theme permanently from Kuler, click **Delete**, then click Delete again.

3. To access more options (in addition to the Edit, Copy Link, Download and Delete buttons), click the **Info** button, then do any of the following: **B**

   To make your theme available to the Kuler community, click **Private;** the label changes to "Public." If you change your mind, click Public.

   To enable users to find your theme via a search, under Info, in the **Tags** window, enter one or more words that describe your theme. Press Return/Enter after entering each tag.

➤ To use a downloaded theme, from the Swatch Libraries menu on the Swatches panel in Illustrator, choose Other Library, locate the theme in the Downloads folder, then click Open. The theme will open in a separate panel (see page 120).

➤ The symbols and numbers below each theme indicate how many times the theme has been viewed, designated as a favorite (either by you or by others), and commented upon.

Via your Adobe Creative Cloud ID, the Kuler panel **C** in Illustrator is synced automatically to your My Themes page at Kuler.adobe.com (provided you're signed into your account). All the themes that are on your My Themes page on Kuler appear on the panel, including

A *On your My Themes or My Favorites page, roll over a theme to display this menu of options.*

B *Click the Info button for a theme on your My Themes or My Favorites page to display the Actions and Info panels.*

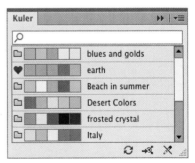

C *Via the Kuler panel, you can browse your Kuler themes, then add colors or themes to the Swatches panel for your document, or apply colors directly to selected objects.*

the ones that you have designated as favorites. You can add themes from the Kuler panel to the Swatches panel, or apply colors from the panel to your artwork.

To use the Kuler panel in Illustrator:

1. In Illustrator, open a document. To display the Kuler panel, choose Window > **Kuler** or click the **Open Kuler Panel** button on the Swatches panel.

2. If the panel doesn't display all the themes from your My Themes page, click the **Refresh** button. (Via the panel menu, you can verify which Kuler account is being used, as well as the date and time the panel was last refreshed.)

   ➤ The themes you have created have a folder icon; your favorite themes have a heart icon.

3. To add colors from the Kuler panel to the Swatches panel, do one of the following:

   Click the folder or heart icon for a theme. The theme appears as a color group on the Swatches panel.

   To add multiple swatches or themes, Cmd-click/ Ctrl-click those swatches or folder/heart icons, then from the panel menu, choose **Add to Swatches**.

4. To apply a color directly to one or more selected objects, click the Fill or Stroke square on the Color panel, then click a swatch on the Kuler panel.

   ➤ The theme or color you click on the Kuler panel also displays on the Color Guide panel.

Color themes that you capture on an iPhone via the Adobe Kuler app are synced (via your Creative Cloud account) to your My Themes page at Kuler.Adobe.com as well as to the Kuler panel in Illustrator.

To use the Adobe Kuler app on an iPhone:

1. Install the free **Adobe Kuler** app on your iPhone, then launch the app. If the scene in front of you doesn't display onscreen, tap the camera icon.

2. To create a color theme, do either of the following:

   To capture colors without taking a photo, move the bar to the eye icon, hold up your phone to the desired area, then tap the screen. (If you want to capture a different area, tap the screen to unfreeze it first.) If desired, you can move any color dot to a different location. Tap the **Save Theme** icon.

   To create a color theme from a photo, drag the bar to the left, and hold up the phone to frame the shot. (If desired, you can tap the flash icon, then tap the no flash, flash, or auto flash icon.)

Tap the camera icon to capture the photo. If desired, you can move any color dot to a different location; or tap the My Moods icon, then tap a mood. Tap the **Save Theme** icon.

3. To edit a theme, click the theme (bar of colors) to collapse it partially, then click the **Edit** icon. Do either or both of the following:

   Tap a color to select it, then move any of the bars upward or downward.

   Click the **color wheel** icon. Tap the **Harmony Rule** icon, then on the menu, tap a named rule to have the color markers on the color wheel move as a unit, or tap Custom to allow the markers to move independently of one another. Move any marker inward to change the saturation, or in a circular direction to change the hue. Rotate the rim of the wheel to change the lightness.

   ➤ To undo all your edits, tap the Cancel icon.

4. To save your edits, tap the **Save Theme** icon, then tap **Save a Copy** or **Save Changes** (or tap the screen to return to editing).

5. When a theme is partially collapsed, you can manage it by doing any of the following (optional):

   To rename or attach tags to the theme, tap the Info icon. To make the theme available to the public, drag the Public Theme bar to the right (you must be signed in to Kuler). Tap Save Changes.

   To share the theme, tap the Share Theme icon; you must be signed in to Kuler.

   To delete the theme, tap the Delete icon, then tap Delete.

   ➤ To return to the capture screen at any time, tap the camera icon.

6. To display your iPhone themes in Illustrator, show the Kuler panel, then click the **Refresh** button.

➤ To view the Kuler photos on your iPhone, on your Home Screen, tap Photos, then Albums > Kuler. If your photos don't appear in your album, go to the Kuler App, tap the settings icon, then Preferences, then under Saving Photos, check Save Images to the "Kuler" Album. The new setting will affect only future photos.

Replacing colors in your artwork

Via the Select Similar Options menu on the Control panel, you can quickly select multiple objects that have a common attribute, such as the same fill color, then apply a replacement color to all the selected objects.

To replace a color, stroke attribute, or opacity setting throughout a document:

1. Select an object that contains a spot color(s), nonglobal process color(s), stroke weight, or other attribute that you want to change, and that is also in use in other objects.

2. From the **Select Similar Options** menu ▦ ▾ on the Control panel, choose an option, such as Fill Color, Stroke Color, or Fill & Stroke Color.

3. To change an attribute in the selected objects, such as an attribute that you chose in the prior step, do any of the following:

   Click the Fill or Stroke square on the Tools or Color panel, then select a different color via the Swatches, Color Guide, or Color panel, or in a swatch library panel. Tint percentages for spot colors will remain the same.

   Choose a new stroke weight or other stroke attributes on the Stroke or Appearance panel.

   Change the Opacity percentage on the Control or Appearance panel.

4. Deselect (Cmd-click/Ctrl-click a blank area of an artboard).

A global process color swatch is one for which Global is checked in the Swatch Options dialog. When you edit the values of a global process color swatch, the color updates automatically in all objects in which it is being used — whether or not those objects are selected.

To change a process color from nonglobal to global:

1. Double-click a nonglobal process color swatch on the Swatches panel. Note: Global process color swatches have a white corner and no dot; nonglobal process colors are plain (no corner and no dot).

2. The Swatch Options dialog opens. **A** Check **Global**, then click OK.

➤ To make a global swatch nonglobal, uncheck Global in the Swatch Options dialog.

To edit the values of a global process color:

1. Double-click a global process color swatch on the Swatches panel.

2. In the Swatch Options dialog, check Preview, edit the color by moving the sliders, then click OK. Existing tint percentages are preserved.

To replace a global process color that's being used in multiple objects, instead of recoloring one object at a time, you simply replace the current color swatch with a new one, and the replacement color appears in all the objects (even if they're not selected). Existing tint percentages are preserved.

To replace a global process color swatch:

1. Deselect all objects.

2. Do one of the following:

   From the Swatch Libraries menu ▨▾ on the Swatches panel, choose a library name. Click a color on the library panel, then Option-drag/Alt-drag it over the global process color swatch on the Swatches panel that you want to replace.

   Click the Fill or Stroke square on the Color panel, then choose a new color via the Color panel (or double-click either square and mix a color via the Color Picker); or click a color on the Color Guide panel. Option-drag/Alt-drag the Fill or Stroke square over the global process color swatch on the Swatches panel that you want to replace.

   On the Swatches panel, Option-drag/Alt-drag one global color swatch over another.

➤ If you Option-drag/Alt-drag a nonglobal process color swatch over a global process swatch, the resulting swatch will be a global process color.

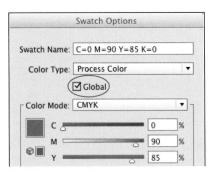

A *Double-click a swatch to open the Swatch Options dialog, then check or uncheck Global.*

Inverting colors

The Invert Colors command converts solid colors, gradients, and patterns in selected objects to their opposite values on the color scale. The command doesn't convert spot colors or global process colors.

To invert colors in your artwork:

1. Select one or more objects (Note: to invert colors in an imported image, follow step 1 in the next task before completing this task).**A**

2. Choose Edit > Edit Colors > **Invert Colors.B**

Colorizing grayscale images

To colorize a grayscale image:

1. Do either of the following:

   Import a grayscale or color BMP, JPEG, PCX, PDF, PSD, or TIFF image into an Illustrator document via the File > **Open** command, or via the File > **Place** command with the Link option unchecked.**C**

   Note: To learn about the File > Open and File > Place commands, see Chapter 22.

2. If you imported a color image, convert it to grayscale by choosing Edit > Edit Colors > **Convert to Grayscale**.

3. With the grayscale image selected in your Illustrator document, click the Fill square on the Color panel, then apply a color via the Color, Swatches, or Color Guide panel.**D**

A *This is the original placed, embedded image.*

B *We applied the Invert Colors command.*

C *We placed this grayscale Photoshop image into an Illustrator document.*

D *We colorized the image by clicking a solid brown color on the Swatches panel.*

Blending fill colors

To blend fill colors between objects:

1. Select three or more objects that contain fill colors, or isolate a group.**A** None of the objects should have a fill of None. The more objects you use, the more gradual the blend.

   Note the following restrictions:

   ➤ The two objects that are either farthest apart or frontmost and backmost can contain different nonglobal colors or different tints of the same global process or spot color.

   ➤ Among the selected objects, those that are either frontmost or backmost or are topmost, bottommost, leftmost, or rightmost cannot contain a pattern, gradient, global process color, spot color, or graphic style; nor can they be type objects or symbol instances.

   ➤ The objects may contain different stroke settings, including a brush stroke or a nondefault width profile, but those attributes will remain only in the original objects, because the Edit Colors commands change only fill colors.

2. From the Edit > **Edit Colors** submenu, choose one of the following commands:

   Blend Front to Back to use the fill colors of the frontmost and backmost objects as the starting and ending colors in the blend. This works irrespective of the x/y location of the objects in the artwork.**B**

   Blend Horizontally to use the fill colors of the leftmost and rightmost objects as the starting and ending colors in the blend.

   Blend Vertically to use the fill colors of the topmost and bottommost objects as the starting and ending colors in the blend.

   Selected objects that are stacked between the frontmost and backmost objects or between the two outermost objects will be assigned intermediate colors. The original stroke colors and weights will remain the same, and the objects will remain on their respective layers.

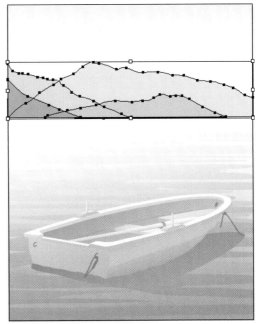

A We put a group into isolation mode.

B We applied the Blend Front to Back command.

Creating a pattern

If you tried to create patterns in a previous version of Illustrator, you will be especially delighted by the new pattern-making features. Not only is it amazingly simple to create patterns and apply them, but editing them is a cinch, too. Illustrator even takes care of making seamless repeats. Best of all, you can see your changes live throughout the whole process.

To create a pattern:

1. Select one or more Illustrator objects (or a group). The objects may contain fill and stroke colors, including a gradient (but not a pattern). For suggestions, see the sidebar at right.

2. Do either of the following:

   Choose Object > Pattern > **Make**. The Pattern Options panel displays.

   Show the Pattern Options panel, ▦ **A** then choose **Make Pattern** from the panel menu.

   The document is put into pattern-editing mode (it's like isolation mode), **B** and a new pattern swatch appears on the Swatches panel. **C**

Continued on the following page

OBJECTS YOU CAN USE IN A PATTERN

➤ Geometric objects created with the Ellipse, Rectangle, Polygon, Line, Spiral, Star, or Pen tool.

➤ Objects drawn with the Blob Brush, Pencil, or Paintbrush tool, or a Live Paint group.

➤ Type (it will be editable in pattern editing mode).

➤ A raster image that you place into Illustrator with the Link option unchecked, such as a Photoshop .psd file (see Chapter 22).

➤ The expanded results of a tracing (see Chapter 17).

➤ A clipping mask or a compound path.

➤ The objects may contain nondefault opacity and blending mode settings (see Chapter 27).

➤ The objects may contain brush strokes (see Chapter 23), symbols (see Chapter 28), or effects (see Chapter 15), but as an alert will inform you, those "live" elements will be expanded by the pattern feature. An expanded brush can't be edited via the Brushes panel; an expanded symbol or symbol set can't be edited via the Symbols panel.

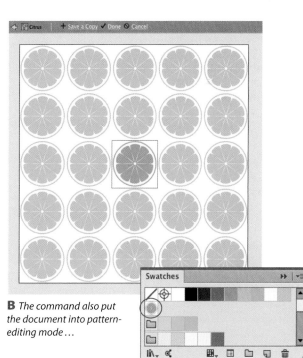

A *We selected an object, then chose Make Pattern from the Pattern Options panel menu. The artwork appeared in the swatch on the panel.*

B *The command also put the document into pattern-editing mode…*

C *… and created a pattern swatch immediately on the Swatches panel.*

Note: By default, an alert will inform you that Illustrator added the new swatch to the Swatches Panel. Click "Don't Show Again" if you want to prevent the alert from reappearing; click OK.

➤ The blue (default color) tile edge in the center of the artboard defines the edge of the pattern tile.

3. On the Pattern Options panel, do the following:

Enter a **Name** for the pattern.

From the **Tile Type** menu, choose a tiling configuration.**A** If you choose a Brick option, also choose a Brick Offset option.

4. To change the spacing between the tiles, check **Size Tile to Art**, and if desired, click the Maintain Spacing Proportions button. Click in the **H Spacing** or **V Spacing** field, then press the up or down arrow on the keyboard (use a positive value to increase the spacing, or a negative value to decrease it).**B**

5. If your artwork contains multiple objects, uncheck **Size Tile to Art**, then try dragging an object, and see how the pattern changes immediately in the preview.

If you move any object so it overhangs the tile edge, Illustrator will replicate that object on the opposite side of the tile, to create a continuous, seamless pattern. To control the stacking position of the overhanging objects, click one of the **Overlap** buttons in each pair: Left in Front or Right in Front, and Top in Front or Bottom in Front (**A–B**, next page).

Check **Move Tile with Art** to force the tile edge to move if you drag all the pattern object(s), or uncheck this option when you need to move all the objects separately from the tile edge.

6. To scale the tile separately from the artwork, do either of the following:

To specify dimensions, uncheck **Size Tile to Art**; if desired, click the Maintain Width and Height Proportions button to maintain the current aspect ratio; then enter **Height** and **Width** values (press Tab to apply) or click in either field and press the up or down arrow.

Click the **Pattern Tile** tool in the panel, then adjust any handle (Shift-drag to maintain the proportions of the tile) (**C**, next page). When you're done, click the tool again to deselect it.

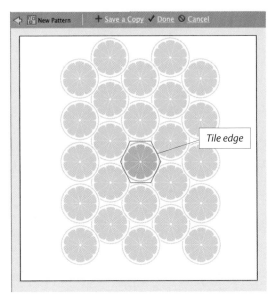

A *We chose the Hex by Column option from the Tile Type menu.*

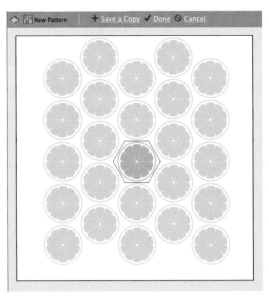

B *We increased the H Spacing and V Spacing values to 12 pt.*

➤ Shrinking the tile will cause some objects to straddle the tile edge. Double-check that you're still happy with the Overlap settings.

➤ At any time if you want to remove the custom scaling and refit the tile edge to the objects, check Size Tile to Art.

7. For the preview, do any of the following (these options affect how the pattern previews, not how it looks or repeats when used in your artwork):

From the **Copies** menu, choose how many times you want the pattern to repeat in the preview (the default setting is 5 x 5).

To make it easier to differentiate between the actual object(s) used to produce the pattern and the copies produced by the pattern feature, check **Dim Copies To**, then enter or choose an opacity value (In **A**, the copies are dimmed to 60%).

Check **Show Tile Edge** to display the tile edge. This option isn't available when the Pattern Tile tool is selected.

Check **Show Swatch Bounds** to display a swatch boundary, which marks the outermost area of objects that will be repeated in the tile.

8. To exit pattern-editing mode and accept the swatch, at the top of the document window, click **Done** (or press Esc) or click the bar.

(To exit pattern-editing mode and delete the new swatch from the Swatches panel, click Cancel.)

Continued on the following page

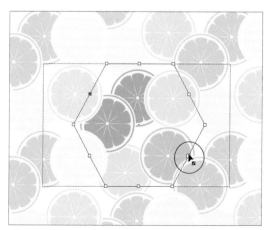

Swatch boundary   *Tile edge*

A *To add some variation to the pattern, we duplicated the original orange slice (group of objects) a few times, then recolored some of the copies. We unchecked Size Tile to Art, then dragged a couple of objects so they straddled the tile edge. This is the default Overlap option of Top in Front. (Here both the tile edge and swatch boundary are displayed.)*

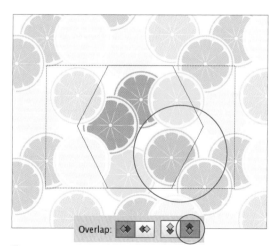

B *Here the Overlap option of Bottom in Front was clicked.*

C *With the Pattern Tile Tool, the tile edge can be resized manually (separately from the artwork).*

Note: If objects in the pattern contain "live" appearances, an alert may inform you that Illustrator must expand those items in order to create a pattern swatch.**A** If you click OK, the live aspect of those objects will no longer be editable (e.g., a brush can't be edited via the Brushes panel), but that's not necessarily a problem. If you prefer to edit or eliminate any live items from the pattern, click Cancel, edit or discard those objects, then exit pattern-editing mode.

9. You can apply the pattern to any object as a fill **B** and/or as a stroke (**A–B**, next page).

➤ You can also create a pattern by choosing the Make Pattern command with no objects selected, then creating some artwork within the tile edge.

A *This alert informs you that your pattern artwork contains live objects.*

KEEPING THE PATTERN OPTIONS PANEL OPEN

By default, the Pattern Options panel closes when you exit pattern-editing mode (when you click Done or Save a Copy). To keep the panel open even while you're not creating or editing a pattern, uncheck Auto-Close on Exiting Edit Mode on the panel menu.

CHANGING THE PATTERN TILE EDGE COLOR

To change the color of the pattern tile edge, choose Tile Edge Color from the Pattern Options panel menu (or choose Object > Pattern > Tile Edge Color). In the dialog, choose a color from the menu, or click the swatch and choose a color from the picker. To establish your color choice as the new default color, check Use as Default.

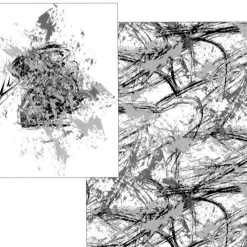

B *You don't necessarily have to create geometric or hard-edged patterns — you can also create textures. Loosely drawn paths (with brush strokes), top left, were used to create a pattern, which is used as a fill in the object above. Our pattern settings are shown on the panel at right.*

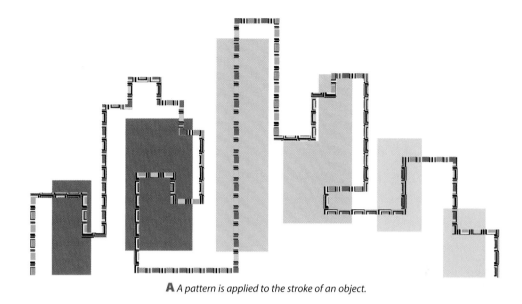

A *A pattern is applied to the stroke of an object.*

B *Patterns are applied to the fill in these objects.*

Editing a pattern

Once you have mastered creating a simple pattern, for added interest, try throwing in a few more objects, transforming some of the objects, changing their transparency settings, or applying an effect. In pattern-editing mode, all the controls are available that you would normally use to edit objects in Illustrator. You can reposition, reshape, recolor, or add a brush stroke or variable width profile to any object, and add and delete objects.

To edit a pattern:

1. On the Swatches panel, do either of the following:

   Double-click a pattern swatch.

   Click a pattern swatch, then click the **Edit Pattern** button.

2. The Pattern Options panel displays and the document is put into pattern-editing mode.

3. *Optional:* To preserve a copy of the original swatch, click Save a Copy, enter a name in the New Pattern dialog, then click OK. An alert may appear, informing you that the original pattern (not the copy) will remain onscreen, ready for editing. Click OK.

4. Edit the components of the pattern using any Illustrator features or tools:

   Recolor or reposition any of the objects, or apply transformation edits, such as scaling or rotation.**A–C**

   Add objects to the pattern.

   Change any settings on the Pattern Options panel as per steps 4–7 on pages 140–141 (e.g., decide whether you want Size Tile to Art on or off).

   Change the opacity (**A–B**, next page) or blending mode for any object via the Appearance panel; see Chapter 27.

   Apply an effect (**C**, next page); see Chapter 15. See the Note in step 8 on page 141.

   ➤ The swatch thumbnail on the Pattern Options panel updates as you edit the pattern.

   Adjust the stacking of objects that straddle the tile edge via the Overlap buttons on the Pattern Options panel (or via the Layers panel).

5. To exit pattern-editing mode and apply your edits to the swatch, at the top of the document window, click **Done** (or press Esc) or click the bar.

   ➤ You can load and edit patterns from any Illustrator library. To copy pattern swatches between

A *Some patterns (especially geometric ones) look best in a basic grid (Tile Type option), with all the objects oriented vertically. If it's working, don't mess with it!*

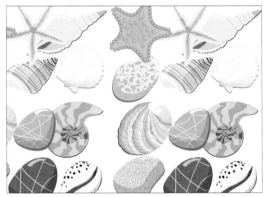

B *The orientation, scale, and placement of these objects is fairly uniform, which doesn't suit the naturalistic subject matter.*

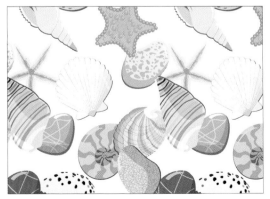

C *Some objects were repositioned to extend beyond the tile edge, and some were rotated or scaled. Better.*

Illustrator documents, see the steps on page 128 (or for a quick approach, copy and paste an object that contains a pattern from one document to another). Pattern swatches from previous versions of Illustrator can be edited using the Pattern Options panel.

➤ Any object that you want to include in a pattern must be situated at least partially within the tile edge. Illustrator won't discard any objects that are fully outside the tile; they just won't be included.

➤ If you're having trouble seeing the edits you're making to selected objects in pattern-editing mode, hide the selection borders temporarily by pressing Cmd-H/Ctrl-H (View > Hide Edges). Be sure to re-enable the display of edges when you're done.

REPOSITIONING A PATTERN IN AN OBJECT

To reposition a pattern fill or stroke within an object while keeping the object stationary, hold down ~ (tilde) and drag inside it with the Selection or Direct Selection tool. To learn about settings for transforming patterns, see the sidebars on pages 149 and 153.

A *This is the original pattern.*

B *We lowered the Opacity setting for some of the objects in this pattern.*

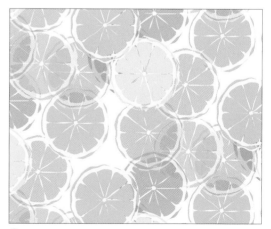

C *We applied the Roughen effect to all the objects (and clicked the OK button in the alert dialog to allow Illustrator to expand the effect).*

Blank areas in a pattern are transparent.**A** In fact, this can be an asset if you want to layer multiple pattern fills in separate objects in your artwork. On the other hand, if you want to build an opaque, solid-colored background into the pattern, follow these steps.

To add a background to a pattern:

1. On the Swatches panel, do either of the following:

   Double-click a pattern swatch.

   Click a pattern swatch, then click the **Edit Pattern** button.

2. With the Rectangle tool, ▢ draw a rectangle to fit the tile edge. To prevent gaps from appearing in the pattern, let it overhang the tile edge slightly on the top or bottom and on one side. Apply a fill color.

3. With the rectangle selected, on the Layers panel, drag the rectangle listing downward to the bottom-most position in the stack of pattern objects.

4. Because the background object extends to the tile edge, Illustrator will calculate it as part of the overlap, and parts of other objects that overhang the tile edge may become blocked.**B** To prevent this from happening, make sure no objects straddle any corners of the tile edge (in other words, an object can extend off only one side).**C**

5. To exit pattern-editing mode and apply your edits to the swatch, at the top of the document window, click **Done** (or press Esc) or click the bar.

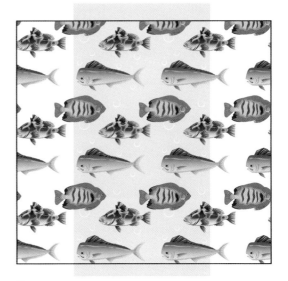

A *Empty areas in a pattern are transparent. An aqua blue object is stacked behind an object containing a pattern fill.*

B *If you add a colored background object that meets the tile edge, some parts of objects could be hidden due to overlap limitations.*

C *For the best results when adding a background, allow objects to overhang the tile edge on just the left or right edge or just the top or bottom edge.*

Illustrator provides several ways to rotate, scale, reflect, distort, shear, or apply perspective to an object. These methods include manipulating the object's bounding box and using the Free Transform tool, individual transformation tools, the Transform panel, the Control panel, the Transform Each command, and the Transform effect.

Transforming an object via its bounding box

One of the simplest ways to transform an object is via its bounding box. Note that this method doesn't allow you to make copies, as other methods do.

To transform an object via its bounding box:

1. With the Selection tool, ▸ select one or more objects or a group, or double-click an object or group to isolate it. If the bounding box feature is off, press Cmd-Shift-B/Ctrl-Shift-B (View > Show Bounding Box). If you isolated a group, click an object in the group to display its bounding box.

2. Do either or both of the following:

   As you drag a handle to **scale** the object, you can hold down Shift to scale it proportionally, or Option/Alt to scale it from its center, **A–B** or both Shift and Option/Alt to scale it proportionally from its center.

   To **rotate** the object, move the pointer slightly outside a corner handle (the pointer will become a curved double arrow), then drag in a circular direction.

W: 5.59 in
H: 4.84 in

A *Option-drag/Alt-drag an object or group to scale it from its center.*

B *The group is enlarged.*

Using the Free Transform tool

With the versatile Free Transform tool, you can scale, rotate, reflect, shear, apply perspective to, or distort one or more objects. Handles on the bounding box, buttons on a floating bar, and unique pointers help make the job easy. You can use a mouse — or on a touchscreen device, use your finger. The only limitation of this tool is that (unlike with the other transform tools) you can't copy the object(s) while applying the transformation.

To use the Free Transform tool:

1. With the Selection tool, select one or more objects or a group,**A** or double-click a nongrouped object to isolate it.

2. *Optional:* If you want to preserve the original object or group, duplicate it, and keep the copy selected.

3. Choose the **Free Transform** tool (E). A bounding box displays around the selected object(s), and a vertical bar with buttons appears. On the bar, the Free Transform button is selected automatically. You can drag the bar so it's near the selected object(s).

4. As you apply any of the following transformations, if you want to constrain the edit to the current Constrain Angle (see the sidebar on the next page), activate the **Constrain** button on the Free Transform bar before either dragging a handle with a mouse or using your finger on a touchscreen device. (If you're using a mouse, you can also constrain a transformation by holding down Shift while dragging a handle; to transform the object from its center, also hold down Option/Alt).

   To **scale** just the height or width of the object, drag a midpoint handle on the bounding box, or to scale both the height and width of the object, drag a corner handle.**B–C**

   To **rotate** the object, drag a corner handle in a circular direction.

   To **reflect** the object, drag a handle all the way across it.

   To **shear** (slant) the object, drag the top or bottom midpoint handle horizontally or a side midpoint handle vertically.**D–E**

   To apply **perspective** to the object, click the Perspective Distort button on the Free Transform bar, then drag a corner handle (**A-B**, next page).

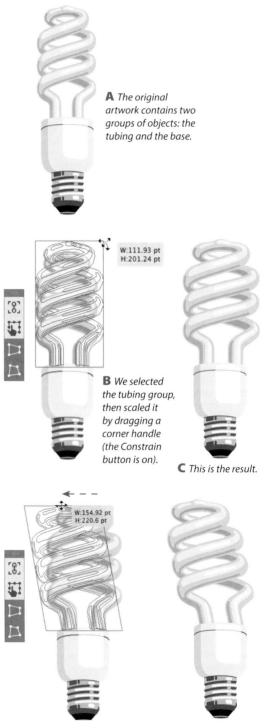

A *The original artwork contains two groups of objects: the tubing and the base.*

W:111.93 pt
H:201.24 pt

B *We selected the tubing group, then scaled it by dragging a corner handle (the Constrain button is on).*

C *This is the result.*

W:154.92 pt
H:220.6 pt

D *To shear the group, we dragged a midpoint handle.*

E *This is the result.*

To **distort** the object, click the Free Distort button on the Free Transform bar, then drag a corner handle. **C–D**

Note: Perspective and distort transformations can't be applied to editable type.

➤ To change the location from which an object is transformed, drag the reference point away from the center. To reset the reference point to its default location, either drag it manually, or deselect and reselect the object with the Selection tool.

➤ Pinch and swipe gestures aren't supported while the Free Transform tool is selected.

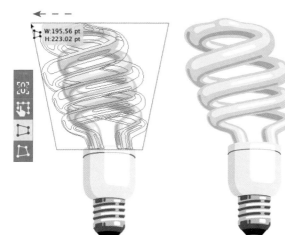

CHOOSING PREFERENCES FOR TRANSFORMATIONS

When performing transformations, there are three options in Illustrator/Edit > Preferences (Cmd-K/Ctrl-K) > General you should be aware of:

➤ When you transform an object, the default horizontal angle is 0° and the default vertical angle is 90°. The default starting point for measuring the degree of an angle is the horizontal (x) axis (the three o'clock position). In the Constrain Angle field, you can enter a custom setting.

➤ If Transform Pattern Tiles is checked when you transform an object that contains a pattern fill or stroke, the pattern will also transform. Note: If you subsequently fill the object with a different pattern, the current transform values will apply to the replacement pattern. If you want to restore the default values to the pattern, apply a solid color, then reapply the pattern.

➤ Via the Scale Strokes & Effects check box, you can control whether an object's stroke and effects also scale when an object is scaled.

Note: For the Scale Strokes & Effects check box on the Transform panel, see page 152. To control whether the panel will transform patterns, see the sidebar on page 153.

A *We clicked the Perspective Distort button, then dragged a corner handle.*

B *This is the result.*

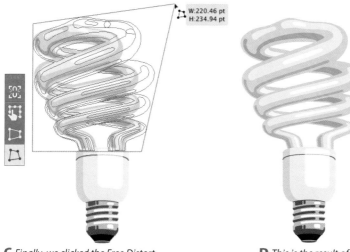

C *Finally, we clicked the Free Distort button, then dragged a corner handle.*

D *This is the result of all our transform edits.*

Using the Scale, Rotate, Shear, and Reflect tools

As we showed you on pages 102–103, Smart Guides can be helpful when aligning objects or points to one another. Here Smart Guides are used while an object is transformed.

To transform an object with the Scale, Rotate, Shear, or Reflect tool:

1. Go to Preferences (Cmd-K/Ctrl-K) > **Smart Guides**, make sure the Alignment Guides, Measurement Labels, and Transform Tools options are checked, then click OK. Also make sure View > **Smart Guides** is on (Cmd-U/Ctrl-U) and View > Snap to Grid and Pixel Preview are off.

2. With the Selection tool, select one or more objects or a group, or double-click an object or group to isolate it. If you isolate a group, click an object in the group.

3. When using one of the transform tools that you will choose next, you can either let the object transform from its center (the default behavior) or set a custom reference point for Illustrator to transform the object from by clicking near the object (the pointer will turn into an arrowhead). In either case, before dragging, position the mouse (button up) far away from the center or reference point, for better control.**A**

   Note: As you drag to transform the object, Smart Guides will appear onscreen temporarily. Move the pointer along a Smart Guide to apply the transformation on that axis. The angle of rotation or other transformation data will display in the measurement label.**B–C**

   Do any of the following:

   Choose the **Scale** tool (S), then drag away from or toward the object (**A**, next page).

   Choose the **Rotate** tool (R), then drag around the object.

Continued on the following page

A *We clicked to establish a reference point (away from the center) with the Rotate tool, repositioned the mouse, and are dragging in a circular direction.*

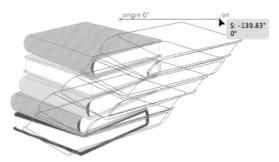

B *A Smart Guide is being used with the Shear tool.*

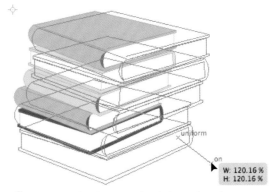

C *A Smart Guide is being used with the Scale tool.*

Choose the **Shear** tool, ⍁ then drag away from the object.**B**

Choose the **Reflect** tool ⧉ (O), click to establish a reference point, then click or drag to define the axis of reflection.**C–D**

These are some additional options:

To transform a copy of the object, start dragging, then hold down Option/Alt and continue to drag (release Option/Alt last).

To transform the object at an increment of 45°, or to scale it proportionally, or to constrain a shear to the current Constrain Angle (the horizontal or vertical axis, by default), start dragging, then hold down Shift and continue to drag; release the mouse before releasing Shift.

To transform a copy of the object along an increment of 45°, or to copy and scale it proportionally, start dragging, then hold down Option-Shift/Alt-Shift and continue to drag.

To flip and scale the object simultaneously, drag completely across it with the Scale tool.

➤ To transform a pattern but not the object when using the Scale, Rotate, Shear, or Reflect tool, drag with ~ (tilde) held down.

➤ To reset an object's reference point to the default location, choose the Selection tool, ⬉ deselect, then reselect the object.

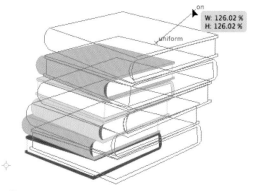

A *We clicked to establish a reference point with the Scale tool, repositioned the mouse, and are dragging toward the upper right with Shift held down.*

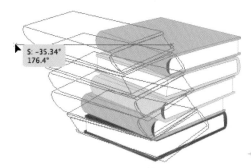

B *We clicked to establish a reference point with the Shear tool, repositioned the mouse, and are dragging diagonally to the left.*

C *We clicked to establish a reference point with the Reflect tool…*

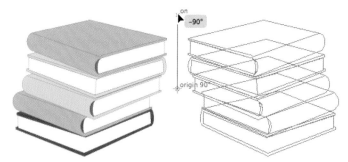

D *… then dragged upward with Shift held down.*

Using the Transform and Control panels

Use the Transform panel to move, scale, rotate, or shear an object by an absolute amount or a percentage.

To move, scale, rotate, or shear an object using the Transform panel:

1. With the Selection tool, select one or more objects or a group, or double-click an object or group to isolate it. If you isolate a group, click an object in the group to display its bounding box.

2. Do either of the following:

   Show the Transform panel. 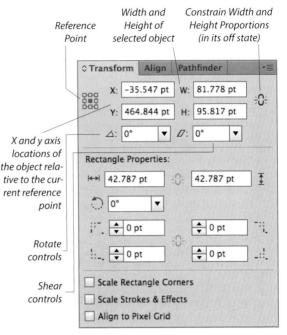**A**

   To open a temporary Transform panel, click the blue X, Y, W, or H link on the Control panel. Or if the Application frame is too narrow for those letters to display, click Transform.

3. To control the part of the object from which the X and Y values are calculated, click a **reference point** on the upper left side of the panel. (The other values will be calculated relative to the object's bounding box.)

4. If the object contains a pattern, from the Transform panel menu, choose **Transform Object Only**, **Transform Pattern Only**, or **Transform Both**.

5. If you're going to scale the object, check or uncheck **Scale Strokes & Effects** on the extended panel to control whether the object's stroke and any applied effects will also scale. This option can also be turned on or off in Illustrator/Edit > Preferences > General.

6. As you enter or choose values, use one of the shortcuts listed in the sidebar (above right) to apply them:

   To move the object to the right, increase the **X** value, or to move it to the left, reduce the X value.

   To move the object downward, increase the **Y** value, or to move it upward, lower the Y value.

   To scale the object, enter percentage or absolute **W** (width) and/or **H** (height) values. To scale the object proportionally, either click the Constrain Width and Height Proportions button first or, if the button is deactivated, press Cmd-Return/Ctrl-Enter after entering the value.

   Enter or choose a positive **Rotate** value to rotate the object counterclockwise, or a negative value to rotate it clockwise.

Reference Point | Width and Height of selected object | Constrain Width and Height Proportions (in its off state)

X and y axis locations of the object relative to the current reference point

Rotate controls

Shear controls

A *Use the Transform panel to apply precise transformation values to objects.*

APPLYING TRANSFORMATIONS VIA A DIALOG

➤ To apply a transformation via a dialog, select one or more objects or a group, then right-click the selection and choose Transform > Rotate, Reflect, Scale, or Shear from the context menu. In the dialog that opens, check Preview, then enter values and choose options. If you want to transform a copy of the selected object(s), exit the dialog by clicking Copy instead of OK.

➤ To transform an object from a user-defined reference point instead of from the center, with the Rotate (R), Reflect (O), Scale (S), or Shear tool, Option-click/Alt-click on or near the object, then follow the instructions above.

➤ If an object's fill or stroke contains a pattern and you want the pattern to transform along with the object, check both Transform Objects and Transform Patterns in the transform dialog; or to scale the pattern but not the object, uncheck Objects.

To shear the object to the right, enter or choose a positive **Shear** value; or to shear to the left, enter or choose a negative Shear value.

7. From the panel menu, you can choose the **Flip Horizontal** or **Flip Vertical** command.

➤ To apply a transformation as an editable and removable effect, see page 155.

➤ With Use Preview Bounds checked in Illustrator/ Edit > Preferences > General (the default setting), the W and H values on the Transform, Control, and Info panels are calculated based on the full dimensions of an object, including the weight and width of its stroke and any applied effects. With this option off, the dimensions of the basic path are listed instead.

➤ To learn about the Align New Objects to Pixel Grid option on the Transform panel menu, see page 84.

Note: If your Application frame is too narrow to display the X, Y, W, and H controls on the Control panel and it can't be widened, follow the steps on the preceding page instead of the steps below.

To move or scale an object using the Control panel:

1. Select an object or group, or isolate an object.

2. On the Control panel, **A** do either or both of the following:

   To move the object, choose or enter new **X** (horizontal) and/or **Y** (vertical) values.

   To scale the object, choose or enter **W** (width) and/ or **H** (height) values. To scale the object proportionally, click the Constrain Width and Height Proportions button ⚙ first.

➤ You can click in a field on this (or any other) panel and press the up or down arrow on the keyboard to change the value incrementally. You can also position your cursor over the **W** or **H** fields and use the scroll wheel on your mouse to scale an object.

Here the Constrain Width and Height Proportions button is in its on state.

LETTING ILLUSTRATOR DO THE MATH

In the W, H, X, or Y field on the Transform or Control panel, you can let Illustrator perform simple math (see below). When entering values, you can use any of these units of measure: p, pt, ", in, mm, cm, q, or px. To apply a new value, press Tab or Return/Enter.

➤ To perform addition, to the right of the current number and unit, enter a plus sign, then a number (as in "+2"). For example, to move an object horizontally to the right, you would enter a plus sign after the current X value and unit, followed by the amount you want it to move. To perform subtraction, enter a minus sign (as in "–2") instead of a plus sign.

➤ To multiply the current value, after the current value and unit, type an asterisk (*), then a number. For example, to reduce an object's scale by half, click to the right of the current value and unit, then type "*.5" (e.g., 4p would become 2p). For division, enter / instead of an asterisk.

➤ To multiply a value by a percentage, select the current value and unit, then enter a number and the percent symbol (%). To reduce the width or height to three-quarters of its current value, for example, enter "75%" (e.g., 4p would become 3p).

TRANSFORMING A PATTERN IN AN OBJECT

To control whether a pattern can be transformed via the Transform panel, check Transform Object Only, Transform Pattern Only, or Transform Both on the panel menu.

SHORTCUTS FOR APPLYING TRANSFORM PANEL VALUES

Apply the value and exit the panel	Return/Enter
Apply the value and select the next field	Tab
Apply the value, exit the panel, and copy the object	Option-Return/ Alt-Enter

A *Reposition an object or group by changing the X and/or Y values on the Control panel, or scale it by changing the W and/or H values.*

Using the Transform Each command

The transformation tools transform multiple objects relative to a single, common reference point, whereas the Transform Each command transforms objects relative to their individual center points. **A–C** If you want your artwork to look less regular and more hand-drawn, apply this command to multiple objects with the Random option checked.

To perform multiple transformations via the Transform Each command:

1. Select one or more objects (preferably two or more). If you're going to use the Random option (see step 4), select objects that aren't in a group.

2. Right-click one of the objects and choose Transform > **Transform Each** (Cmd-Option-Shift-D/ Ctrl-Alt-Shift-D).

3. Move the dialog out of the way, if necessary, and check Preview.

4. Do any of the following (**A**, next page):

   Click a different **reference point** ▦ (the point from which the transformations will be calculated).

   Move the **Scale: Horizontal** or **Vertical** slider (or enter a percentage value, then press Tab) to scale the objects horizontally or vertically from their individual reference points.

   Increase the **Move: Horizontal** value to move the objects to the right, or decrease it to move them to the left; increase the **Vertical** value to move the objects downward, or decrease it to move the objects upward.

   Move the **Angle** dial; or enter a value, then press Tab.

   Check **Reflect X** to flip the objects horizontally, or **Reflect Y** to flip them vertically.

   Check **Random** to let Illustrator apply random transformation values within the range that you have chosen for Scale, Move, or Rotate. For example, at a Rotate Angle of 35°, a different angle between 0° and 35° will be used for each selected object. Keep unchecking and rechecking Preview to get different random effects.

5. Check which parts of the objects you want Illustrator to transform: **Scale Strokes & Effects**, **Transform Objects**, or **Transform Patterns**.

6. Click OK or Copy.

A *This is the original arrangement of objects.*

B *With the Rotate tool, we rotated all the objects 15°.*

C *Here the original objects were rotated 15° via the Transform Each command instead, with the Random option unchecked.*

Transform Each

Scale
Horizontal: 125%
Vertical: 65%

Move
Horizontal: 30 pt
Vertical: 0 pt

Rotate
Angle: 0°

Options
☐ Reflect X ☑ Scale Strokes & Effects
☐ Reflect Y ☑ Transform Objects
☐ Random ☐ Transform Patterns

☑ Preview Copy Cancel OK

A *The Transform Each dialog lets you Scale, Move, Rotate, or Reflect an object according to random or fixed values.*

Transform Effect

Scale
Horizontal: 130%
Vertical: 100%

Move
Horizontal: –24 pt
Vertical: 0 pt

Rotate
Angle: 54

Options
☐ Reflect X ☐ Scale Strokes & Effects
☐ Reflect Y ☑ Transform Objects
☐ Random ☐ Transform Patterns
Copies 0

☐ Preview Cancel OK

Using the Transform effect

When applied via the Transform Effect dialog, your transformation settings can be modified long after you close the dialog, and even after you close and reopen your document.

To use the Transform effect:

1. Select one or more objects.

2. From the Add New Effect menu *fx.* on the Appearance panel, ⬤ or from the Effect menu on the Illustrator menu bar, choose Distort & Transform > **Transform**.

3. The Transform Effect dialog looks and functions like the Transform Each dialog, with two exceptions. In the Transform Effect dialog, you can specify a number of **Copies**. And when the **Random** box is checked, the same random value for each option (Scale, Move, and Rotate) is applied to every selected object, which produces less random results than the Random option of the Transform Each command.**B** With these exceptions in mind, follow steps 4–5 on the preceding page, then click OK to exit the dialog.

4. To edit the transformation at any time, select the object, then reopen the Transform Effect dialog by clicking Transform on the Appearance panel.**C** (To learn more about this panel, see Chapter 14.)

B *Use the Transform Effect dialog to apply editable transformations.*

Appearance
Path
👁 ▶ Stroke: ■ 1 pt
👁 ▶ Fill: ▼
👁 Transform *fx*
☐ ◼ *fx.* Click to Edit Effect 🗑

C *To edit a Transform effect, click the Transform listing on the Appearance panel.*

Repeating a transformation

By using the Transform Again command, you can quickly repeat the last transformation on any selected object(s); the last-used values are applied. If the last object was cloned as it was transformed, Transform Again will produce another transformed copy.

To repeat a transformation:

1. Transform an object or a group.**A**

2. Keep the object selected, or select another object or group.

3. Press Cmd-D/Ctrl-D or right-click the object or group and choose Transform > **Transform Again.B–C**

REORIENTING THE BOUNDING BOX

If you rotate an individual object (not a group) via any method except the Transform effect, the bounding box will no longer align with the x/y axes of the page (this result is most evident on a nonrectangular object). If you like, you can square off the bounding box to the horizontal axis while preserving the new orientation of the object: Select the rotated object, then right-click and choose Transform > Reset Bounding Box (or choose Object > Transform > Reset Bounding Box). Note: To hide or show the bounding box, press Cmd-Shift-B/Ctrl-Shift-B.

A *To create a sunburst, our first step was to rotate and copy a triangle at a 24° angle via the Rotate dialog.*

B *Next, we applied the Transform Again command 13 times by pressing Cmd-D/Ctrl-D.*

C *We positioned three curved objects in front of the sunburst.*

➤ *To clip the outer edges in this illustration via a clipping mask, we drew a rectangle over the objects, selected all the objects, then pressed Cmd-7/Ctrl-7 (see Chapter 26).*

In Chapters 6 and 7 you learned how to draw paths without needing to think about their individual components. In this important chapter, you'll learn how to reshape a path's contour by manipulating the nuts and bolts that all paths are composed of: direction handles, anchor points, and segments. Once you learn how to change the position, number, or type (smooth or corner) of anchor points on a path, you'll be able to create just about any shape imaginable.

Other techniques covered in this chapter include learning how to quickly reshape all or part of a path with the Pencil, Anchor Point, Paintbrush, Blob Brush, Path Eraser, Eraser, and Reshape tools; change the profile and width of a stroke; align anchor points; join endpoints; reshape objects via an Effect command; combine paths; and split and cut paths. This chapter also includes three practice exercises.

The building blocks of a path

In Illustrator, all paths are composed of straight and/or curved segments that are connected by anchor points. A path can be open, with two endpoints, or closed, with no endpoints. Smooth anchor points have a pair of direction handles that move in tandem, whereas corner anchor points have no direction handles, one direction handle, or a pair of direction handles that move independently.**A** By dragging the end of a direction handle, you can change the shape of the curve it's connected to. The angle of a direction handle controls the slope of the curve that leads into the anchor point; the length of a direction handle controls the height of the curve.

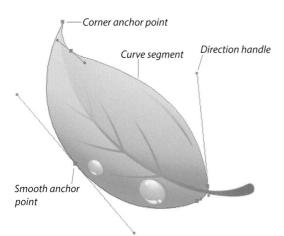

Corner anchor point

Curve segment

Direction handle

Smooth anchor point

A *You can manipulate the basic components of a path manually by dragging, or by using a tool or command.*

Moving points and segments

If you move an anchor point, the segments that are connected to it reshape, lengthen, or shorten accordingly. If you move a straight segment, the anchor points it's connected to move with it, whereas if you move a curve segment, the curve reshapes but the connecting anchor points remain stationary.

Note: For the instructions in this chapter, make sure Highlight Anchors on Mouse Over is checked in Illustrator/Edit > Preferences > Selection & Anchor Display. And while that dialog is open, you can also choose preferences for the display of anchor points and handles (see page 411).

To move an anchor point or a segment:

1. Choose the **Direct Selection** tool (A), and click a blank area of the document to deselect.

2. Move the pointer over the edge of an object, and do any of the following: Drag an anchor point (it will enlarge when the pointer is over it);**A** drag a segment (it will reshape the segment);**B** or click an anchor point or segment, then press an arrow key. For the first two methods, you can use the alignment guides feature of Smart Guides for precise positioning.

➤ Shift-drag a point or segment to constrain the movement to a multiple of 45°.

➤ You can move more than one point or segment at a time, even if they're on different paths. To select them first, Shift-click them individually or drag a marquee around them.

Reshaping curves

In the instructions above, you learned that you can drag an anchor point or a curve segment to reshape a curve. Another — and more precise — way to reshape a curve is to lengthen, shorten, or change the angle of the direction handles on a curve point.

To reshape a curve segment:

1. Choose the **Direct Selection** tool (A).

2. Click an anchor point or a curve segment.**C**

3. Do either of the following:

   Drag the end of a direction handle toward or away from the anchor point.**D**

   Rotate the end of a direction handle around the anchor point. You can use Shift to constrain the angle of the handle, or position the handle using the alignment guides feature of Smart Guides.

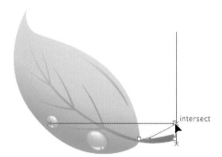

A *We moved an anchor point, with the help of Smart Guides for positioning.*

B *We moved a segment.*

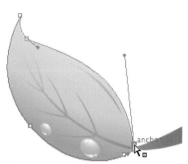

C *We selected an anchor point on a shape.*

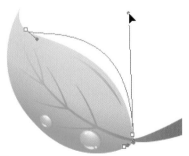

D *We dragged the end of a direction handle away from the anchor point, to reshape the curve.*

Converting points

Corner anchor points either have no direction handles, or have direction handles that move independently of each other. The pair of direction handles on a smooth point always stay in a straight line and rotate in tandem (although they can be different lengths). With a click of a button, you can convert any corner point to a smooth point.

To convert a corner anchor point to a smooth anchor point:

1. In Illustrator/Edit > Preferences > Selection & Anchor Display, make sure **Highlight Anchors on Mouse Over** is checked. Click OK.

2. Choose the **Direct Selection** tool ▸ (A), and deselect.

3. Pass the pointer over a corner anchor point on a path, and when a point becomes highlighted (enlarged), click to select it.**A**

4. On the Control panel, click the **Convert Selected Anchor Points to Smooth** button.◤ **B–C** Direction handles will appear on the selected point, and the segments that are connected to it will become curved.

5. *Optional:* To reshape the curve, with the Direct Selection tool, drag either one of the direction handles.**D**

➤ You can also convert a corner point to a smooth point by using the Convert Anchor Point tool (Shift-C). Move the pointer over a corner point, and when it becomes highlighted, drag away from it. Direction handles will appear as you drag.

➤ To learn more about converting points, see pages 303–305.

➤ To round the corners on a selected path by using an editable and removable effect, use the Effect > (Illustrator Effects) Stylize > Round Corners command.**E–F** Once you have applied the effect, you can click the effect listing on the Appearance panel to reopen the Round Corners dialog at any time, and change the Radius value. See page 206. (To straighten out the rounded corners, delete the effect listing from the Appearance panel.)

CREATING A TEAROFF TOOLBAR

To practice the techniques in this chapter, we recommend tearing off the toolbar for the Pen tool so the Pen and its cohorts are easily accessible. (Once you memorize the shortcuts for accessing these tools, you won't need to display the toolbar.)

A *To convert a corner point to a smooth one, click it with the Direct Selection tool...*

B *... then click the Convert Selected Anchor Points to Smooth button on the Control panel.*

C *Direction handles appear for the selected anchor point.*

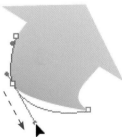

D *You can drag either direction handle to modify the curve.*

E *All the objects in this original artwork have sharp corners.*

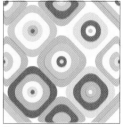

F *The Effect > Stylize > Round Corners command rounded all the corners.*

To convert a smooth anchor point to a corner anchor point:

1. Choose the **Direct Selection** tool (A), and deselect.

2. Pass the pointer over a smooth anchor point on a path, and when it becomes highlighted, click it.**A**

3. On the Control panel, click the **Convert Selected Anchor Points to Corner** button.**B** The direction handles will disappear from the anchor point.

➤ You can also convert a smooth point to a corner point (or vice versa) by clicking it with the Convert Anchor Point tool (Shift-C).

In these steps, you will convert direction handles that stay in a straight line into handles that can be rotated independently of each other.

To rotate direction handles independently:

1. Choose the **Direct Selection** tool (A).

2. Deselect, click the edge of an object to display its anchor points, then click a smooth point.**C**

3. Choose the **Convert Anchor Point** tool (Shift-C).

4. Drag one of the direction handles on the point. The curve segment it is connected to will reshape as you drag.**D**

5. Choose the **Direct Selection** tool again (A), click the anchor point, then drag the other direction handle for the same anchor point.**E**

➤ To restore a corner point with direction handles that rotate independently to a smooth point, follow the steps on the preceding page.

➤ When the Pen tool (P) is selected, you can hold down Option/Alt to turn it into a temporary Convert Anchor Point tool.

➤ To select all the direction handles on one or more selected objects, from the Select > Object submenu, choose Direction Handles.

A *Click a smooth anchor point, then click the Convert Selected Anchor Points to Corner button on the Control panel.*

B *The smooth point is converted to a corner point.*

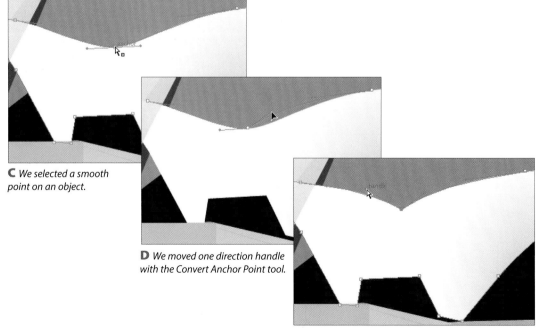

C *We selected a smooth point on an object.*

D *We moved one direction handle with the Convert Anchor Point tool.*

E *We moved the second direction handle.*

Adding points

Another way to reshape a path is by adding anchor points to it manually.

To add anchor points to a path manually:

1. Choose the **Selection** tool ▶ (V), then select or isolate an object.

2. Do either of the following:

   Choose the **Add Anchor Point** tool 🖊 (+).

   Choose the **Pen** tool 🖊 (P), and make sure **Disable Auto Add/Delete** is unchecked in Illustrator/Edit > Preferences > General (yes, it's a confusing double negative).

3. Click the edge of the object. A new, selected anchor point appears.**A** Repeat to add more points to the path, if desired.

   ► To locate the edge of a path, make sure Object Highlighting is checked in Illustrator/Edit > Preferences > Smart Guides, and turn on the Smart Guides feature (Cmd-U/Ctrl-U). As you move the pointer over the edge of an object, the path outline will appear as a Smart Guide.

   Logically, an anchor point that you add to a curve segment will be a smooth point with direction handles, whereas an anchor point that you add to a straight segment will be a corner point with no direction handles.

4. *Optional:* With the Direct Selection tool (A), move the new anchor point.**B** If it's a smooth point, you can also lengthen or rotate its direction handles.

► If you don't click precisely on a segment with the Add Anchor Point tool, an alert dialog may appear. Click OK, then try again.

► Hold down Option/Alt to turn the Add Anchor Point tool into a temporary Delete Anchor Point tool, or vice versa.

A *We clicked a segment to add a new point.*

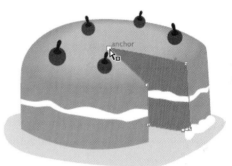

B *Then we moved the new point.*

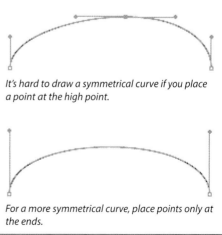

GETTING A GOOD CURVE

By paying attention to the placement of points, you can produce smoother curves. When reshaping paths (and while drawing them, as you will see in Chapter 21), place points at the ends of a curve instead of at the middle.

It's hard to draw a symmetrical curve if you place a point at the high point.

For a more symmetrical curve, place points only at the ends.

The Add Anchor Points command inserts one point between each pair of existing anchor points in a selected object.

To add anchor points to a path via a command:

1. Choose the Selection tool ⬆ (V), then select the object(s) to which points are to be added.

2. Choose Object > Path > **Add Anchor Points.A–C** If desired, repeat to add yet more points.

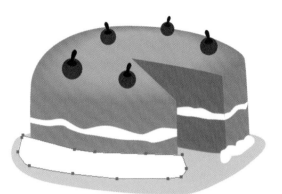

A We added this simple white object to this artwork.

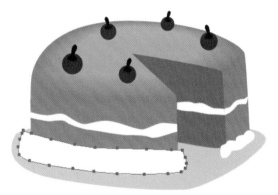

B We applied the Add Anchor Points command to the object.

C We applied Effect > Distort & Transform > Roughen to alter the shape. Because points were added to the path, we were able to keep the Roughen settings low, which produced less overall distortion.

You can add segments to a path with the Pencil tool, regardless of which tool was used to draw the path, and whether or not the path has an applied brush stroke. If a path does have a brush stroke, you can also add to it by using the Paintbrush tool.

To add to an open path with the Pencil or Paintbrush tool:

1. Choose the Selection tool ▶ (V), then select or isolate an open path.

2. Double-click the **Pencil** tool ✐ (N) to open the options dialog for that tool. Or if the path has a brush stroke, you can double-click the **Paintbrush** tool ✐ instead.

3. In the tool preferences dialog, make sure **Edit Selected Paths** is checked, then click OK.

4. Position the pointer directly over the path, then draw an addition to the path.**A–B**

➤ If you end up with a new, separate path instead of an addition to an existing path, delete the new one. On your next try, make sure the pointer is directly over the path before you begin drawing. Or when using the Paintbrush tool, verify that the path to which you're adding a segment has a brush stroke.

To add to an open path with the Pen tool:

1. Choose the **Pen** tool ✐ (P).

2. Position the pointer over the endpoint of an open path (the path doesn't have to be selected). A slash appears next to the Pen icon when the tool is positioned correctly.**C**

3. Click the endpoint to make it a corner point, or drag from it to make it a smooth point. The point will become selected.**D**

4. Position the pointer where you want the next anchor point to appear, then click or drag.

5. If desired, continue to click to create more corner points or drag to create more smooth points.**E** Switch to another tool when you're done adding to the path, or Cmd-click/Ctrl-click a blank area of the artboard to deselect.

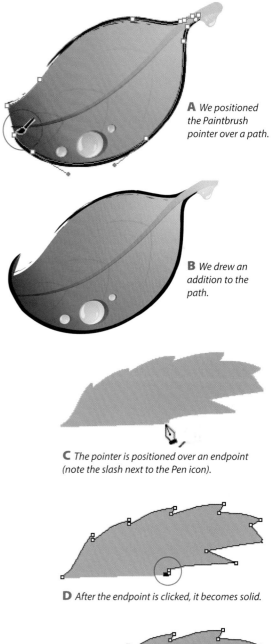

A *We positioned the Paintbrush pointer over a path.*

B *We drew an addition to the path.*

C *The pointer is positioned over an endpoint (note the slash next to the Pen icon).*

D *After the endpoint is clicked, it becomes solid.*

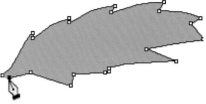

E *More points are then added to the same path.*

Deleting points

If you delete points from a closed path, it remains closed.

To delete anchor points from a path:

Method 1 (Pen tool)

1. Do either of the following:

    Choose the **Delete Anchor Point** tool  (-).

    Choose the **Pen** tool (P), and make sure Disable Auto Add/Delete is unchecked in Illustrator/Edit > Preferences > General.

2. Cmd-click/Ctrl-click the edge of the object from which you want to delete anchor points.

3. Click an anchor point (don't press Delete!).**A** The point will be deleted.**B** Repeat to delete other anchor points, if desired.

➤ If you don't click precisely on an anchor point with the Delete Anchor Point tool, an alert dialog may appear. Click OK and try again.

Method 2 (Control panel)

1. Choose the **Direct Selection** tool (A).

2. Deselect, click the edge of an object to display its anchor points, then click a point (or Shift-click multiple points).

3. On the Control panel, click the **Anchors: Remove Selected Anchor Points** button.

A *We clicked an anchor point with the Delete Anchor Point tool (we could have used the Pen tool instead).*

B *We deleted the point.*

Reshaping objects with the Pencil or Paintbrush tool

With the Pencil and Paintbrush tools, you can reshape a path by dragging along its edge.

To reshape a path with the Pencil or Paintbrush tool:

1. Do either of the following:

    To reshape a path that doesn't have an applied brush stroke, choose the **Pencil** tool (N).

    To reshape a path that does have a brush stroke, choose the **Pencil** tool (N) or the **Paintbrush** tool (B).

2. Cmd-click/Ctrl-click a path to select it.

3. Position the pointer directly over the edge of the path, then drag along it.**C** The path will reshape instantly.**D**

    Note: Be sure to position the pointer precisely on the edge of the path when you begin *and finish* dragging. If you don't, you will create a new path instead of reshaping the existing one.

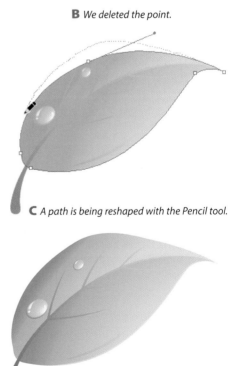

C *A path is being reshaped with the Pencil tool.*

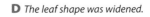

D *The leaf shape was widened.*

Reshaping segments

You can convert an existing straight segment to a curved segment — or reshape a curved segment — by dragging it with the Pen or Anchor Point tool.

To reshape a path segment with the Anchor Point or Pen tool: ★

1. Do either of the following:

   Choose the **Anchor Point** tool (Shift-C).

   Choose the **Pen** tool (P) and hold down Option/Alt.

2. Let the pointer hover over an existing path segment (the path doesn't have to be selected); the pointer changes to the Reshape Segment cursor. **A**

3. Do either of the following;

   Drag the segment. If the segment was curved, it will reshape according to the direction in which you drag; **B** if the segment was straight, it will become curved. **C–D**

   To make the segment into a symmetrical curve (make its direction handles parallel to each other), drag it with Shift held down. **E**

➤ You can also use the above technique to reshape a segment while drawing a new path with the Pen tool. To resume drawing, release Option/Alt.

By default, when you drag a curved segment on a path, the handles are unconstrained — or if you prefer, you can constrain the handles to parallel alignment by holding down Shift.

To reshape a curved path segment with the Direct Selection tool: ★

1. Choose the **Direct Selection** tool (A). Deselect, then click a path.

2. Drag a segment; the cursor changes to the Reshape Segment cursor. The edits will be unconstrained, just as they are when you use the Anchor Point tool or Pen tool. If you want to make a symmetrical curve with parallel direction handles, drag with Shift held down.

   Note: If you drag a straight segment with the Direct Selection tool, the segment will move without being reshaped (this is the legacy behavior).

➤ To copy a path segment while reshaping it with the Direct Selection tool, drag it with Option/Alt held down. The copy will be a new, separate path.

A *We're positioning the Anchor Point tool over a curved segment on a path.*

B *We're dragging the segment.*

C *We're positioning the Anchor Point tool over a straight segment*

D *We're dragging the straight segment upward, converting it to a curve.*

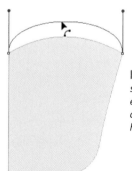

E *Here we're dragging the same straight segment upward, except this time with Shift held down, to make the direction handles parallel to each other.*

Applying a variable width profile preset to an object's stroke

Using the new Profile options, you can quickly apply a preset, nonuniform width to an object's stroke, to make it look more hand drawn.

To apply a variable width profile preset to an object's stroke:

1. Select or isolate a path and apply a stroke color.

2. Display the full Stroke panel, ≣ then do all of the following:

   Choose a stroke **Weight** of 6 pt. or greater. **A**

   Make sure the **Align Stroke to Center** button is active.

   From the **Profile** menu, choose a width profile. **B–C**

3. *Optional:* To flip the width profile along the path, click the Flip Along button. ⋈ **D** (The change will be noticeable only if you apply a profile in which the starting and ending widths are different, such as in Width Profile 2, Width Profile 4, or Width Profile 5.)

   ➤ You can also choose a profile from the Variable Width Profile menu on the Control panel.

   Note: To restore the default stroke profile at any time, select or isolate the object, then choose Uniform from the Profile menu (Stroke panel) or the Variable Width Profile menu (Control panel).

   ➤ If an object that you have selected or targeted has a variable width profile, an asterisk will display next to the stroke weight value on the Appearance panel.

A *The stroke widths in the original artwork are uniform and boring.*

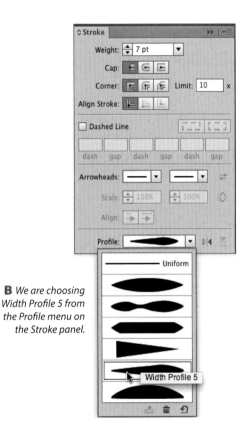

B *We are choosing Width Profile 5 from the Profile menu on the Stroke panel.*

C *The variable width profile gives the line work pizzazz.*

D *We clicked the Flip Along button to flip the starting and ending thicknesses of the current stroke profile .*

Changing an object's stroke width using the Width tool

Using the Width tool, you can change the width profile of an object's stroke manually.

To reshape an object's stroke using the Width tool:

1. Select or isolate a path, and apply a stroke color and Weight (not 0). (It can have an Art or Pattern brush applied to it, but not another type of brush.) On the Stroke panel, ☰ make sure the **Align Stroke to Center** button is active.

2. Choose the **Width** tool 🖉 (Shift-W).

3. Move the pointer over a segment of a closed or open path, or over the endpoint of an open path. Click to make a width point (hollow diamond) appear, then drag outward from the path to lengthen the handles or inward to shorten them, **A–B** or Option-drag/Alt-drag one of the handles to change its length independently of its mate.**C**

4. Do any of the following optional steps:

   Drag any width point along the path to a new location, or Shift-drag a point to move that point along with other width points.

   To duplicate a point, drag it with Option/Alt held down.

   To delete a point, click it, then press Delete/Backspace.

   ➤ To move multiple width points, Shift-click those points, release Shift, then drag with the Width tool. To deselect a selected width point, press Esc.

To adjust the stroke width by entering values:

1. Follow steps 1 and 2 above. Create width points or choose a width profile preset.

2. Double-click the path or an existing width point to open the Width Point Edit dialog.**D**

3. Click the Adjust Widths Proportionately icon, ⚙ if desired, to lengthen or shorten both handles simultaneously, then change the **Side 1** and/or **Side 2** values for the length of one or both handles; or choose a **Total Width** value for the combined length of both handles. For a more gradual change in width, allow handles on neighboring width points to adjust along with the selected one by checking **Adjust Adjoining Width Points**.

4. Click OK.

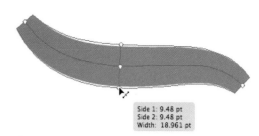

A *To widen this path symmetrically, we dragged outward from it using the Width tool.*

B *To flare the end of the stroke, we dragged from an endpoint outward using the Width tool.*

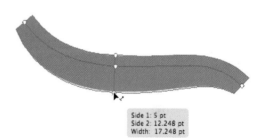

C *Here we are holding down Option/Alt while dragging a handle to move it independently of its mate.*

D *To move both handles outward, we are entering a Total Width value in the Width Point Edit dialog.*

On the preceding page you produced continuous width points using the Width tool. Here you will produce discontinuous points, for more abrupt changes in the stroke width.

To create a discontinuous width point:

1. Follow one of the tasks on the preceding two pages to make the stroke width on a path nonuniform, using three or more width points.

2. Select the **Width** tool  (Shift-W), then click an existing width point on the path or create a new one. For the sake of this exercise, drag outward from the path to make the stroke fairly wide.**A**

3. Drag an adjacent width point **B** on top of the one for which you just lengthened the handles.**C** It is now a discontinuous width point.**D–E**

4. A discontinuous width point has two pairs of handles. To adjust the length of either pair, position the Width tool on the edge of the narrower or wider part of the stroke to locate a handle, then drag inward or outward from the path.

➤ You can double-click a discontinuous point with the Width tool to open the Width Point Edit dialog (**A**, next page), then enter specific values to adjust the length of each pair of handles. If you want to remove a pair of handles, check Single Width Only.

➤ To convert one discontinuous width point back into two standard continuous ones, with the Width tool, drag the point along the path; it will separate into two points.

A *We used the Width tool to add a width point to this path, then lengthened its handles.*

B *We located an adjacent width point on the same path with the Width tool…*

C *… then dragged that adjacent point over the point we had created. It is now a discontinuous point.*

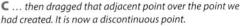

D *The result is an abrupt change in the stroke width.*

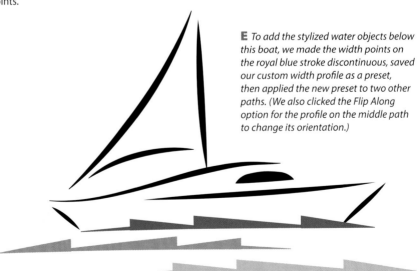

E *To add the stylized water objects below this boat, we made the width points on the royal blue stroke discontinuous, saved our custom width profile as a preset, then applied the new preset to two other paths. (We also clicked the Flip Along option for the profile on the middle path to change its orientation.)*

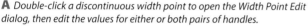

A *Double-click a discontinuous width point to open the Width Point Edit dialog, then edit the values for either or both pairs of handles.*

If you create a custom profile preset that you like, you can save it for future use.

To create a width profile preset:

1. Use the **Width** tool 🖊 to alter the stroke width of a path, and keep the path selected.**B**

2. At the bottom of the Variable Width Profile menu on the Control panel or the Profile menu on the extended Stroke panel, click the **Add to Profiles** button.🔽 **C** Enter a name for the profile in the dialog, then click OK.

3. The new profile appears at the bottom of both menus, and is available for all documents.**D**

➤ You can restore all the default profiles to the Variable Width Profile and Profile menus by clicking the Reset Profiles button ↻ on either menu, but be aware that when you click OK in the alert dialog,**E** Illustrator will discard all custom profiles on the menus. *Ouch!*

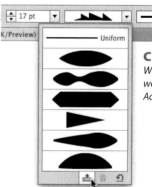

B *We created a custom stroke width on the blue path, and kept the path selected.*

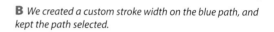

C *On the Variable Width Profile menu, we are clicking the Add to Profiles button.*

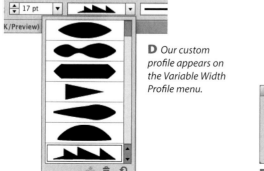

D *Our custom profile appears on the Variable Width Profile menu.*

E *If you click the Reset Profiles button, this alert dialog will display.*

Reshaping objects with the Blob Brush tool

In addition to being a great tool for producing "magic marker" type drawings, as we showed you on page 89, you can drag with the Blob Brush tool to reshape or smooth the edges of existing closed paths. It can be used on any object that has a stroke of None: an ordinary path, a compound path, a masked object within a clipping mask, or the start or end object of a live blend.

To reshape an object with the Blob Brush tool:

1. Select or isolate an object that was created with any tool except a type or symbol tool, **A** and make sure it has a stroke color of None. ☑ It can contain a solid fill color, a pattern, a gradient, or a graphic style.

2. Choose the **Blob Brush** tool 🖌 (Shift-B).

3. To add to the object, draw strokes that cross it at some point. Your strokes will merge with the closed path. **B** Note: If you create a hole with the tool (e.g., draw a loop), the resulting object will be a compound path; to learn about compound paths, see pages 364–366.

   To smooth the edge of the object by eliminating anchor points, make sure the path is selected and hold down Option/Alt to access the Smooth tool temporarily, then drag along an edge of the object.

➤ Press [or] to decrease or increase the diameter of the Blob Brush tool. To choose other options for the tool, see page 90.

The versatile Blob Brush tool can also be used to merge multiple objects, but in a unique way — by drawing strokes across them.

To combine objects using the Blob Brush tool:

1. Arrange two or more closed paths near or overlapping each other (no type objects), and select them. They must have the same solid fill color, pattern, or gradient and a stroke of None, and they must be on the same layer (to restack objects, see page 191). They may not contain a graphic style.

2. With the **Blob Brush** tool, 🖌 draw strokes that cross the objects. Note: If your strokes produce a hole (as in a loop), the result will be a compound path.

A To add shading to the cup, we created a basic polygon shape to use as a starting point, and kept it selected.

B We used the Blob Brush tool to reshape the new object, to make it fit better on the side of the cup.

EXERCISE: Draw and reshape objects in a freehand style

To master the art of drawing shapes by hand, you can use the Blob Brush tool to draw and reshape an object, **A–B** then erase any unwanted parts of it with the Eraser tool. **C** Finally, you can use the Smooth tool to smooth out any rough edges. **D** By using this great trio of tools, you can reshape a path without having to fiddle with any anchor points or direction handles.

A *To create foam on the top of a glass, we double-clicked the Blob Brush tool, checked Merge Only with Selection, clicked OK, then drew some shapes with the Blob Brush tool.*

B *We selected each new shape and used the Blob Brush tool to fill them in. We also reshaped the tan object to create "drips."*

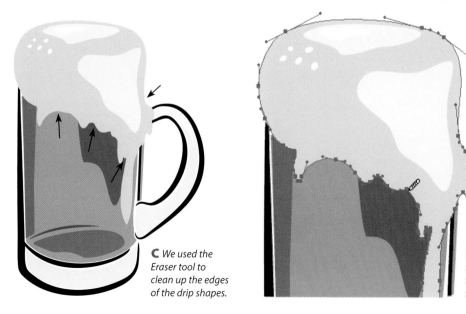

C *We used the Eraser tool to clean up the edges of the drip shapes.*

D *Finally, we used the Smooth tool to smooth some of the rough edges.*

Using the Reshape tool

The Reshape tool does a nice job of changing the contour of a path gently without distorting its shape. Give it a try and see if you like it. Note: Unfortunately, Smart Guides don't work with this tool.

To use the Reshape tool:

1. Choose the **Direct Selection** tool (A), deselect, then click the edge of a path. Only one point or segment should be selected.

2. Choose the **Reshape** tool (it's on the same fly-out menu as the Scale tool).

3. Do one of the following:

    Drag any visible **anchor point** on the path. A tiny square border will display around the point when you release the mouse.

    Drag any **segment** of the path. A new square border point is created.

    Shift-click or marquee **multiple anchor points** on the path (a square will display around each one), then drag one of the square points. The selected portion of the path will maintain its overall contour as it elongates or contracts, and the rest of the path will stay put.

EXERCISE: Create a brush with the Reshape tool

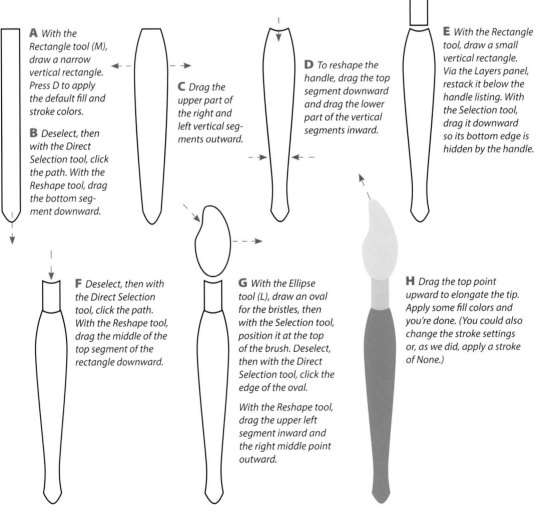

A With the Rectangle tool (M), draw a narrow vertical rectangle. Press D to apply the default fill and stroke colors.

B Deselect, then with the Direct Selection tool, click the path. With the Reshape tool, drag the bottom segment downward.

C Drag the upper part of the right and left vertical segments outward.

D To reshape the handle, drag the top segment downward and drag the lower part of the vertical segments inward.

E With the Rectangle tool, draw a small vertical rectangle. Via the Layers panel, restack it below the handle listing. With the Selection tool, drag it downward so its bottom edge is hidden by the handle.

F Deselect, then with the Direct Selection tool, click the path. With the Reshape tool, drag the middle of the top segment of the rectangle downward.

G With the Ellipse tool (L), draw an oval for the bristles, then with the Selection tool, position it at the top of the brush. Deselect, then with the Direct Selection tool, click the edge of the oval.

With the Reshape tool, drag the upper left segment inward and the right middle point outward.

H Drag the top point upward to elongate the tip. Apply some fill colors and you're done. (You could also change the stroke settings or, as we did, apply a stroke of None.)

Erasing sections of objects

The Eraser tool removes parts of objects that it passes over. The remaining parts of the objects are reconnected automatically to form closed paths.

To erase parts of objects:

1. If you want to limit the effect of the Eraser tool to specific objects (perhaps if there are many objects close together in your artwork, and you want to erase only some of them), select those objects first or put an object into isolation mode. Otherwise, deselect all.**A**

   Note: The object can be a Live Paint object or a compound path, it can be in a clipping mask, and it may contain gradients or patterns. It cannot be a type object, an object in a blend, or an object in a distortion envelope.

2. Choose the **Eraser** tool ![eraser icon] (Shift-E).

3. Do either of the following:

   Drag across parts of objects to be erased.**B–C** Hold down Shift while dragging to draw straight strokes at increments of 45°.

   Option-drag/Alt-drag to create a temporary rectangle. Any parts of the artwork that fall within the rectangle will be erased.

➤ Press [or] to decrease or increase the diameter of the Eraser tool. Double-click the tool icon to choose options for the tool shape.

➤ If you drag with the Eraser tool on the inside of an object — without crossing over the edge — the result will be a compound path.

A *We drew this mountain range with the Pencil tool.*

B *With the Eraser tool, we erased sections of the object to create details in the mountains and lake.*

USING THE PATH ERASER TOOL

To erase parts of a path without having to click points, choose the Path Eraser tool ![path eraser icon] (the last tool on the Pencil tool fly-out menu). Select a path, then drag the eraser of the pencil pointer along the path.

C *With a smaller diameter chosen for the Eraser tool, we made more erasures. Finally, we placed two colored rectangles behind the mountain layer.*

Aligning points

The Align buttons on the Control panel precisely realign selected endpoints or anchor points along the horizontal and/or vertical axis, and as a result, the paths to which those points belong are reshaped.

To align points:

1. Choose the **Lasso** tool ⌖ (Q).

2. Drag to select two or more endpoints or anchor points **A** on the same path or on different paths.

3. On the Control panel, do any of the following:

   To align the points by moving them along the horizontal (x) axis, click one of the three **Horizontal Align** buttons.

   To align the points by moving them along the vertical (y) axis, click one of the three **Vertical Align** buttons.

   To overlap the points along both the horizontal and vertical axes, click a **Horizontal Align** button, then click a **Vertical Align** button. Use this method if you're planning to join the points into one point (see "To join two endpoints into one point" on the facing page).

   If you click a Left, Right, Top, **B** or Bottom **C** Align button, points will align to the leftmost, rightmost, topmost, or bottommost selected point, respectively. If you click a Center Align button, **D** points will align to a location that is equidistant between the points.

➤ If you Shift-select points with the Direct Selection tool (instead of selecting them via dragging) before clicking an align button, points will align with and move toward the last point you select (called the key anchor point), regardless of which Horizontal or Vertical Align button you click.

➤ To align selected points via a command, right-click and choose Average (Cmd-Option-J/Ctrl-Alt-J), then click Axis: Horizontal, Vertical, or Both in the dialog (the Control panel provides more options).

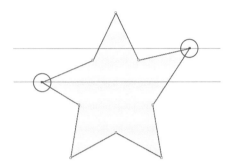

A *We selected two anchor points.*

B *We clicked the Vertical Align Top button.*

C *We clicked the Vertical Align Bottom button.*

D *We clicked the Vertical Align Center button.*

Joining endpoints

You can use the join controls in Illustrator to connect nonoverlapping endpoints with a new straight segment, or to join overlapping endpoints into one anchor point. Endpoints can be joined on the same open path (to close the path) or on separate open paths (to join them together).

To connect two endpoints with a segment:

1. Do either of the following:

    With the Direct Selection tool ⬙ (A) or the Lasso tool ⬙ (Q), drag to select two (or more) endpoints. **A**

    With the Selection tool ⬙ (V) or the Layers panel, select one or more open paths. The objects can be in a group but they can't be compound paths, paths in a Live Paint group, or type objects.

2. Do one of the following: **B**

    Press Cmd-J/Ctrl-J (Object > Path > Join).

    Right-click in the document and choose **Join**.

    If you selected endpoints (not whole objects), you can click the **Connect Selected End Points** button ⬙ on the Control panel.

    Note: If you select multiple whole open paths with the Selection tool, the Join command will join the endpoints that are closest to each other. The attributes from the upper path (as listed on the Layers panel) will be applied to the newly combined object.

To join two endpoints into one point:

1. With the Direct Selection tool ⬙ (A) or the Lasso tool ⬙ (Q), drag to select two endpoints.

2. Do either of the following: **C**

    Press Cmd-Option-Shift-J/Ctrl-Alt-Shift-J.

    On the Control panel, click one of the three Horizontal Align buttons and one of the three Vertical Align buttons to position the two selected endpoints directly on top of each other, then do one of the following: Press Cmd-J/Ctrl-J, or click the **Connect Selected End Points** button ⬙ on the Control panel, or right-click in the document and choose **Join**.

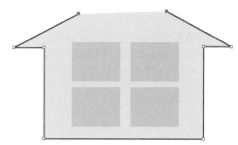

A *We selected two endpoints.*

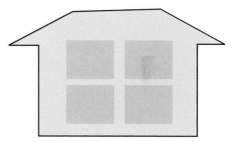

B *The Connect Selected End Points button created a straight segment between them.*

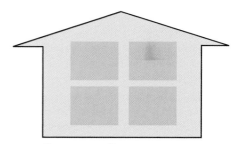

C *This is figure **A** after we clicked the Horizontal Align Center and Vertical Align Center buttons, then clicked the Connect Selected End Points button on the Control panel.*

Reshaping objects using commands

Some of the commands on the Effect menu can be used to explode simple shapes into more complex ones, with practically no effort on your part. For example, the Zig Zag effect, used in the steps below, adds anchor points to a path and then moves those points to produce waves or zigzags. Best of all, the Effect menu commands don't alter the actual path, so the results are both editable and removable. To explore effects more in depth, see Chapter 15.

To apply the Zig Zag effect:

1. Select an object. On the Appearance panel, ⊙ click below the Opacity listing to make sure the Stroke and/or Fill listings are deselected.

2. From the **Add New Effect** menu *fx.* on the Appearance panel, choose Distort & Transform > **Zig Zag**.

3. The Zig Zag dialog opens.**A** Check Preview. Click Points: **Smooth** (at the bottom of the dialog) to create curvy waves, or **Corner** to create sharp-cornered zigzags.

4. Do either of the following:

   To move the added points by a percentage relative to the size of the object, click **Relative**, then move the Size slider.

   To move the added points by a specified distance, click **Absolute**, then specify that distance via the **Size** slider or field.

5. Choose a number of **Ridges Per Segment** for the number of anchor points to be added between existing points. The greater the number of ridges, the more complex the resulting object. If you enter a number, press Tab to preview its effect.

6. Click OK.**B–E**

► To edit the settings for the effect at any time, select the object, then click Zig Zag on the Appearance panel.

► To apply the Zig Zag effect to just an object's stroke, select the object, click the Stroke listing on the Appearance panel, then follow steps 2–6 above.**F–G** You could also try this with the Distort & Transform > Pucker & Bloat or Twist effect. To view the effect listing on the Appearance panel, click the expand arrowhead for the Stroke listing.

A *Choose settings for the Zig Zag effect.*

B *The original object is a star.*

C *The Zig Zag effect is applied (Size 20%, Relative, Ridges 4, Smooth).*

D *The original object is a circle.*

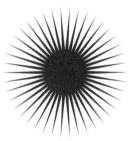

E *The Zig Zag effect is applied (Size 24%, Relative, Ridges 20, Corner).*

F *The original object is a circle.*

G *The Zig Zag effect is applied to just the object's stroke (Size 9%, Relative, Ridges 4, Smooth).*

If you use one of the "easy" tools to create objects, such as the Rectangle, Ellipse, Star, Blob Brush, Pencil, or Paintbrush, followed by any of the simpler reshaping techniques that are covered in this chapter, you will be able to create artwork that looks complex without having to painstakingly draw it with the Pen tool. One of the easiest ways to create illustrations is to combine objects via a command on the Pathfinder panel. For example, to combine whole objects, rather than joining points one pair at a time, you can simply click the Unite button on the Pathfinder panel, as in the following steps.

To combine objects using a command:

1. Position two or more objects so they overlap one another at least partially.**A**

2. With any selection tool, marquee at least some portion of all the objects.

3. Display the Pathfinder panel.

4. Click the **Unite** (first) button on the panel. Voilà! The individual objects are now combined into one closed object or compound path. It will automatically be given the attributes of the object that was originally on top.**B–F**

➤ To learn more about this panel, and also about the Shape Builder tool, see Chapter 25.

➤ To learn about compound paths, see pages 365–367.

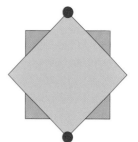

A Arrange two or more objects so they overlap, then select them.

B The Unite button on the Pathfinder panel was clicked to combine the separate shapes into one compound shape.

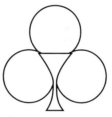

C The original artwork consists of four objects.

D The Unite command is applied.

E The original artwork consists of four objects.

F The Unite command is applied (Macintosh becomes Granny Smith!).

Slicing and dicing

The Scissors tool either opens a closed path or splits one open path into two. You can split a path either at an anchor point or in the middle of a segment.

To split a path with the Scissors tool:

1. Choose any selection tool, then click an object to display its points.

2. Choose the **Scissors** tool ✂ (C).

3. Click the object's path: If you click once on a closed path, it will turn into a single open path; if you click once on an open path, it will be split into two paths.

    If you click a segment, two new endpoints will appear, one on top of the other. If you click an anchor point, a new anchor point will appear on top of the existing one, and it will be selected.**A**

4. To move the new endpoints apart, choose the **Direct Selection** tool ▷ (A), then either drag the selected endpoint away from its mate or press an arrow key.**B**

To split a path via the Control panel:

1. Choose the **Direct Selection** tool ▷ (A).

2. Click a path to display its anchor points, then click an anchor point to select it.

3. Click the **Cut Path at Selected Anchor Points** button 🔲 on the Control panel. A new anchor point will appear on top of the existing one, and it will be selected.

4. To move the two new endpoints apart, drag the selected one.

A *We clicked an anchor point with the Scissors tool. You can click an anchor point or a segment.*

There is no segment, and therefore no stroke, between these two endpoints.

B *We moved the new endpoint on our newly opened path.*

The Divide Objects Below command uses an object like a cookie cutter to cut the objects below it, then deletes the cutting object.

To cut objects via the Divide Objects Below command:

1. Create or select an object to be used as a cutting shape. It can't be a group or a Live Paint group.

   Optional: The Divide Objects Below command is going to delete the cutting object, so you may want to Option-drag/Alt-drag it to copy it first.

2. Place the cutting object on top of the object(s) to be cut.**A**

3. Make sure only the cutting object is selected.

4. Choose Object > Path > **Divide Objects Below**. The topmost shape (the cutting object) is deleted and the underlying objects are cut into separate paths where they met the edge of the cutting object.**B–C**

5. Deselect. You can use the Selection tool to select or isolate, then recolor or move, any of the resulting (newly cut) objects. Any cut objects that were originally in a group will remain so.

➤ To prevent an object that is stacked below the cutting shape from being affected by the Divide Objects Below command, you can either lock it (see page 193) or hide it (see page 194).

A *The white leaf shape will be used as a cutting object (there are three objects below it).*

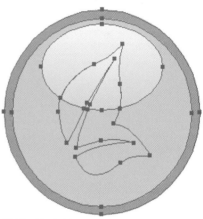

B *The Divide Objects Below command used the leaf shape to cut through the underlying objects.*

DIVIDE VERSUS DIVIDE OBJECTS BELOW

The Divide Objects Below command (this page) deletes the cutting object and leaves the resulting objects ungrouped (if they weren't originally in a group), whereas the Divide button on the Pathfinder panel preserves the paint attributes of all the objects, including the topmost (cutting) object, and puts the resulting paths in a group (see page 360). Divide tends to produce smaller pieces than Divide Objects Below.

C *We applied different fill colors to the resulting divided paths.*

EXERCISE: Draw a glass of beer (or cream soda!)

1. With the Ellipse tool ⬤ (L), draw a vertical oval that is approximately 3.5" wide by 5.5" high, and also a smaller horizontal oval. With the Rectangle tool ⬛ (M), draw a rectangle at the bottom of the vertical ellipse.

2. With the Selection tool, �', select all three shapes. Open the Art History > Impressionism library of swatches, then apply a pale blue-gray fill and a black stroke.**A** On the Pathfinder panel, click the Unite button. 🔳

3. With the Delete Anchor Point tool ✏️ (-), click to delete the points shown in **B**.

4. With the Direct Selection tool ▲ (A), drag to select the four bottom points of the stem. Click the Convert Selected Anchor Points to Smooth button ⌐ on the Control panel. Deselect. To reshape the stem, as shown in,**C** click each point, then press an arrow key; move two points inward and two points outward. Use the Reshape Segment cursor ↱ to reshape the bottom curve of the stem. ★

5. With the Ellipse tool, Option-drag/Alt-drag to create an oval the same width as the glass top, scale it to fit the glass, and fill it with a cream color.**D** With the Add Anchor Point tool ✏️ (+), add five new points along the top of the oval. With the Direct Selection tool, select and drag each point separately to make the oval look more like foam.**E**

6. With the Selection tool (V), select the glass object. With the Scale tool 🔲 (S), start dragging, then hold down Option/Alt and drag diagonally inward to create a slightly smaller copy. Apply a light tan fill color and a stroke of None. With the Delete Anchor Point tool (–), click the bottom two points on the scaled copy. With the Direct Selection tool (A), move the top two corner points on the scaled copy closer to the top corners of the original glass shape.**F**

7. Deselect. Double-click the Blob Brush tool. 🖌️ Set the Size to 40 pt, the Angle to 40°, and the Roundness to 22%; click OK. Choose a darker tan fill color (and a Stroke of None), then drag vertically along the right edge of the glass to create shading. Double-click the tool again, change the Angle value to –40°, then click OK. Drag inside the left edge of the glass.**G**

8. With the Ellipse tool (L), draw an oval for the base of the glass, and apply the same colors as the glass. Via the Layers panel, restack it below the glass object.

9. Reset the angle for the Blob Brush to 0. Create more areas of shading and highlights on the glass and stem. Cheers! **H**

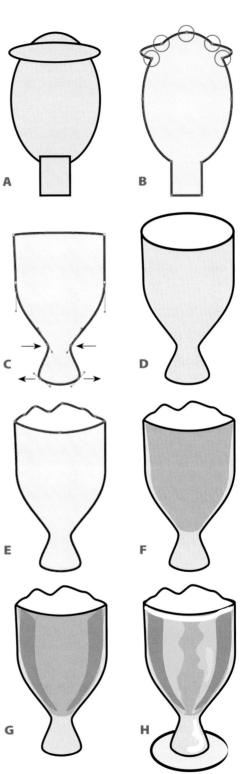

A
B
C
D
E
F
G
H

Until this point (unless you snuck ahead to this chapter!), you've been creating objects on a single, default layer that was created automatically when you created your document, and each new path was stacked above the last one automatically. In this chapter, you'll learn how to purposely change the stacking order of objects via the Layers panel. A You will use the panel to create top-level layers and sublayers; delete layers and objects; select layer listings; select objects; restack, duplicate, lock, unlock, hide, and show layers; collect objects onto a new layer; release objects to layers; and finally, merge and flatten layers.

Getting to know the Layers panel

With a document open, click the Layer 1 arrowhead on the Layers panel to expand the list of objects on that layer. Layer 1 is a top-level layer, meaning it isn't nested within another layer.

You can add as many layers as you like to a document, depending on available system memory, and you can also create sublayers (nested layers) within any top-level layer.

Continued on the following page

Layers panel

A top-level layer — *Torn sheet front*
A sublayer — *Layer 7*
A group — *<Group>*
An object — *<Path>*, *<Path>*

Visibility icon (click to show or hide a layer, sublayer, group, or object)

Current Layer indicator

Selection square (in the selection area)

Lock or unlock a layer, sublayer, group, or object

Pen, Mini notepad, Notepad, Torn sheets back, Background

6 Layers

Make/Release Clipping Mask   New Sublayer   New Layer   Delete Selection

A *The objects in this document are nested within top-level layers and sublayers, at various stacking levels (the artwork is shown at the top of the page).*

The actual objects that make up your artwork — paths, type, images, etc. — are nested within one or more top-level layers, or in groups or sublayers within top-level layers. The backmost layer in the document is listed last on the Layers panel.

When you create an object, it appears on the currently selected layer, but it can be moved to a different layer at any time, either individually or by restacking the whole layer or sublayer it resides in. The stacking order of objects in a document is unaffected by the number and the arrangement of artboards.

The Layers panel also has other important functions beyond enabling you to restack objects. You can use it to select, target (for appearance changes), show or hide, and lock or unlock any layer, sublayer, group, or individual object.

By default, each new vector object you create is listed as <Path> on the Layers panel, each placed raster image or rasterized object is listed as <Image> or by the name of the image file, each individual symbol instance is listed by the symbol name, each symbol set is listed as a generic <Symbol Set>, and each type object is listed by characters in the object. Similarly, object groups are listed by such names as Live Paint, Compound Path, etc.

Although you may say "Whoa!" when you first see the number of listings on the Layers panel, once you become accustomed to working with it, you will appreciate how much easier it makes even the simplest tasks, such as selecting and locking objects.

Different Layers panel options can be chosen for each Illustrator document.

To choose Layers panel options:

1. Choose **Panel Options** from the Layers panel menu. The Layers Panel Options dialog opens.**A**

2. Keep **Show Layers Only** unchecked; otherwise the panel will list only top-level layers and sublayers, not individual objects.

3. For the size of the layer and object thumbnails, click a **Row Size** of Small (12 pixels), Medium (20 pixels), or Large (32 pixels), or click Other and enter a custom size (12–100 pixels).**B**

4. Check the kinds of listings you want the panel to display as **Thumbnails**: Layers, Groups, or Objects. If you check Top Level Only for layers, thumbnails will display for top-level layers but not for sublayers.

5. Click OK.

ONE CATCHALL NAME

In this book, we often refer to the elements of an Illustrator document (paths, type, raster images, etc.) generically as objects, but when necessary, we identify specific kinds of objects (e.g., "symbol instances" or "clipping masks").

A *Via the Layers Panel Options dialog, you can customize the Layers panel for each file.*

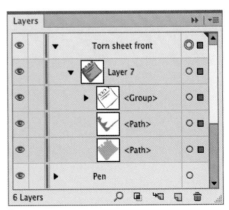

B *For this Layers panel, we chose the Row Size of Large and turned Thumbnails off for Layers.*

Creating layers

In these instructions, you'll learn how to create the granddaddy of layers—top-level layers.

To create a new top-level layer:

Method 1 (without choosing options)

1. On the Layers panel, ❧ click the listing for a top-level layer. The new layer is going to appear above the one you click.

2. Click the **New Layer** button 🖵 at the bottom of the panel. To the new layer, Illustrator will assign the next number in sequence and the next available color, as listed on the Color menu in the Layer Options dialog.

Method 2 (choosing options)

1. On the Layers panel, click the listing for a top-level layer. The new layer is going to appear above the one you click.

2. Option-click/Alt-click the **New Layer** button. 🖵 **A** The Layer Options dialog opens.

3. Do any of the following:

   Change the layer **Name**.

   Via the **Color** menu, choose a highlight color for selection borders on the layer and for the vertical bar in the listing on the Layers panel. Colors are assigned to new top-level layers automatically based on their order on this menu, from the top color down.

   ➤ If the fill or stroke colors of objects on the layer are similar to the selection color, consider choosing a contrasting selection color.

   Choose other layer options (see the sidebar on page 195).

4. Click OK. **B**

➤ Objects always reside in a top-level layer or sublayer (or in a group within either of the above)—they can't float around unassigned.

➤ To create a new top-level layer in the topmost position on the panel, regardless of which layer listing is currently selected, Cmd-click/Ctrl-click the New Layer button on the Layers panel. (Or if your document is in Draw Behind mode, 🖵 the same shortcut will create a new top-level layer at the bottom of the stack.)

Continued on the following page

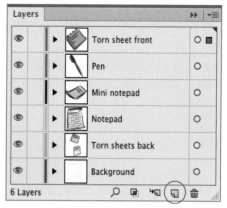

A *Click a layer, then Option-click/Alt-click the New Layer button. When the Layer Options dialog opens, choose options for, or rename, the new layer.*

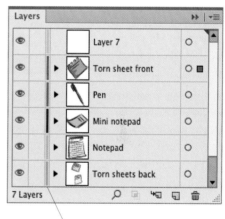

Layer color

B *The new layer (Layer 7) appears above the "Torn sheet front" layer, which was previously selected.*

ADDING LAYERS BELOW EXISTING ONES

If your document is in Draw Behind mode 🖵 (Tools panel) when you create a new layer, the new layer will appear directly below the currently active one.

➤ To rename a layer listing, double-click the name, type the desired name, then click elsewhere or press enter/return.

➤ Layers and sublayers are numbered in the order in which they're created, regardless of their indent level or their position in the stacking order.

Once you become accustomed to adding and using top-level layers, you'll be ready to add another tier to the hierarchy: sublayers. Every sublayer is nested within (indented within) either a top-level layer or another sublayer. If you create a new object or group of objects when a sublayer is selected, the new object or group will be nested within that sublayer. You don't necessarily have to create or use sublayers, but you may find they help you keep the panel organized, especially for complex documents.

By default, every sublayer is given the generic name "Layer," but as with layers, you can rename them so they will be easier to identify (e.g., "green logo" or "saxophone" or "tyrannosaurus").

To create a sublayer:

1. On the Layers panel 🎨 click the top-level layer (or sublayer) in which the new sublayer is to appear.

2. Do either of the following:

   To create a new sublayer without choosing options for it, click the **New Sublayer** button. 🔲 **A–B**

   To choose options as you create a new sublayer, Option-click/Alt-click the **New Sublayer** button. 🔲 In the Layer Options dialog, enter a Name, check or uncheck any of the options (see the sidebar on page 195), then click OK.

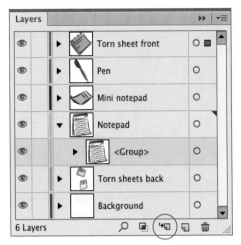

A *Click a layer listing, then click the New Sublayer button.*

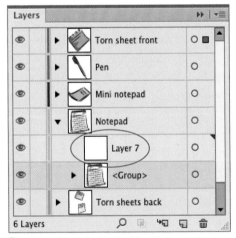

B *A new sublayer listing (in this case, Layer 7) appeared within our "Notepad" layer.*

Deleting layers and objects

You know how to make 'em. Now you need to learn how to get rid of 'em.

Beware! When you delete a top-level layer or sublayer, all the objects that were residing in that layer are removed from the document.

To delete a layer, sublayer, group, or object:

1. On the Layers panel, 🗁 click the layer, sublayer, group, or object to be deleted, or Cmd-click/Ctrl-click multiple listings.

   Note: Multiple selected objects must be in the same layer, sublayer, or group; selected sublayers or groups must be in the same top-level layer. You may click multiple listings at the same indent level (e.g., all top-level layers or all groups), but not listings from different indent levels (e.g., not ungrouped objects plus objects in a group).

2. Do either of the following:

   Click the **Delete Selection** button 🗑 at the bottom of the Layers panel.**A–C** If you are deleting a top-level layer that contains objects, an alert dialog will appear; click Yes to proceed.

➤ To retrieve a deleted layer and the objects it contained, use the Undo command immediately.

A *This is the original artwork.*

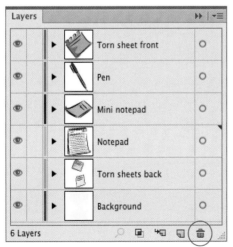

B *We highlighted the "Notepad" layer, then clicked the Delete Selection button.*

C *This is the artwork after we deleted the "Notepad" layer.*

Selecting listings on the Layers panel

If you want to control the stacking level at which a new object will appear in a document, before drawing the object, in addition to being aware of the current drawing mode of your document and whether any objects are selected, you need to click a top-level layer, sublayer, group, or object listing on the Layers panel. The same holds true for objects that you paste, drag and drop, or place into a document.

If you select an object, the listing for its top-level layer or sublayer becomes selected automatically on the Layers panel, but the converse isn't true: Simply clicking a listing doesn't cause objects to become selected in the document window. Think of selecting layer listings (which is discussed on this page and the next) as a layer management technique, and of selecting the objects themselves (making their anchor points, and possibly their bounding box, appear) or targeting objects for appearance changes, as an essential first step in the editing process.

Note: To learn how to select objects via the Layers panel, see pages 188–190. To learn how to target objects for appearance changes, see the sidebar on page 188 and Chapter 14.

If your document is in Draw Normal mode ▣ (Tools panel) and you create a new object (or place, paste, or drag and drop an object into your document), you will get different results depending on what you select first on the Layers panel:

➤ If you click a top-level layer or group listing first (but not a sublayer in that layer), the new object will be listed at the top of that top-level layer.

➤ If you click a sublayer listing first (and no objects are selected), the new object will appear within that sublayer.

➤ If you select an object first, the new object will appear at the top of the same layer or sublayer as the selected object, but outside any group on that layer or sublayer.

To select a layer, sublayer, group, or object listing on the Layers panel:

Click the name (or to the right of the name) of a top-level layer, sublayer, group, or object — not the circle or the selection area at the far right side of the panel. The Current Layer indicator (black triangle) **A** moves to the layer or sublayer in which the item you clicked resides.

USING DRAW BEHIND MODE

If your document is in Draw Behind mode ▣ (Tools panel), the following will occur:

➤ If an object is selected when you create a new object, the new object will appear behind (and will be listed below) the selected object on the current layer.

➤ If no objects are selected when you create a new object, the new object will appear behind (and be listed below) all the artwork on the layer that has the Current Layer indicator.

You can press Shift-D to cycle through the available drawing modes.

To learn about Draw Inside mode, see page 371.

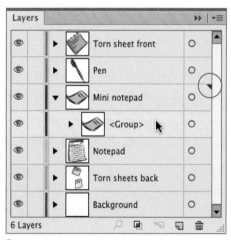

A When a group is clicked, the Current Layer indicator moves to the top-level layer that the group resides in.

If multiple layer listings (layers, sublayers, groups, or objects) are selected, you can restack them on the panel simultaneously or apply the same layer options to them. There are some rules to remember for this as well:

➤ You can select multiple sublayer listings within the same top-level layer, provided they're at the same nesting level, but you can't select multiple sublayer listings in different top-level layers.

➤ You can select multiple listings of the same category (e.g., multiple top-level layers) and nesting level, but you can't select multiple listings from different nesting levels (e.g., not both top-level layers and objects on another layer).

➤ You can select multiple object listings (such as a path and type) in the same top-level layer, but not from different top-level layers.

To select multiple layer listings:

1. On the Layers panel, click the listing for a top-level layer, sublayer, or object.

2. Do either of the following:

   Shift-click the name of another top-level layer, sublayer, or object. The listings you click, plus any items of a similar kind that are stacked between them, will become selected.

   Cmd-click/Ctrl-click the names of other contiguous or noncontiguous top-level layers, sublayers, or objects.**A**

➤ Cmd-click/Ctrl-click to deselect any individual listings when multiple listings are selected.

➤ Although you can select multiple layer or sublayer listings, the Current Layer indicator displays for only one top-level layer or sublayer at a time.

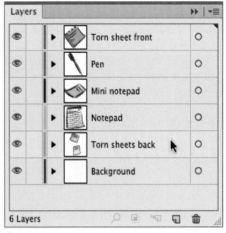

A *Two noncontiguous top-level layer listings are selected.*

Selecting objects via the Layers panel

In Chapter 8, you learned how to select objects using tools and commands. Here you will learn how to select paths or groups via the Layers panel. The result is the same — the object's anchor points (and its bounding box, if that feature is on) become visible in the document window, and the object is ready for editing.

To select all the objects in a layer:

At the far right side of the Layers panel, click the **selection area A** for a top-level layer or sublayer. A colored selection square appears for every sublayer, group, and object on that layer (if the layer list is expanded), and every object on the layer, regardless of its indent level, becomes selected in the document window. The bounding box for the objects will also display, if that feature is on (View menu).**B** And unless the items are in a group, the target circle for each path and group will also become selected.

➤ To deselect an individual object, expand the list for its top-level layer or sublayer, then Shift-click the object's selection square.

To deselect all the objects in a layer:

Shift-click the selection square for the layer containing the objects you want to deselect. All the objects in the layer will be deselected, including the objects in any nested sublayers or groups.

THE CIRCLE OR THE SQUARE?

The difference between selecting and targeting should become clearer to you by the end of the next chapter. Here is an introduction:

➤ If you click either the target circle ⃝ on the right side of the Layers panel for an object or group or the selection area next to the circle, that object or group becomes selected and targeted and its generic name (e.g., "Path," "Type," or "Group") is listed at the top of the Appearance panel. ◉

➤ If you click the selection area for a top-level layer, all the objects or groups on the layer become selected and targeted for appearance changes, and its generic name (e.g., "Mixed Objects") is listed on the Appearance panel. If you click the target circle for a top-level layer, all the objects on the layer become selected, but only the top-level layer is targeted, and "Layer" is listed at the top of the Appearance panel.

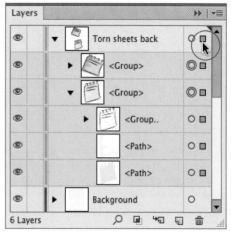

A If you click the selection area for a layer, all the paths and groups within it become selected in the document. The selection squares appear in the color that is currently assigned to that layer.

B All the paths and path groups on the "Torn sheets back" layer became selected in this artwork.

To select an object via the Layers panel:

1. On the Layers panel, expand the top-level layer, sublayer, or group for the object to be selected.

2. At the far right side of the panel, click the selection area or target circle for the entity you want to select.

Via the Layers panel, you can select multiple groups or objects on different top-level layers or sublayers.

To select multiple objects on different layers:

1. On the Layers panel, make sure the listings for all the nested objects to be selected are visible (expand any layer or group lists, if necessary).

2. Click the selection area or target circle for any object, then Shift-click any other individual groups or objects to add them to the selection. The items don't have to be listed consecutively.**A–B**

➤ To deselect any selected object individually, Shift-click its selection square or target circle.

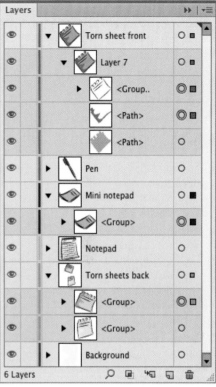

A *Objects from nonconsecutive stacking levels are selected (note the colored selection squares on the far right).*

B *Objects that we selected from different stacking levels are shown selected in the artwork.*

LOCATING A LISTING ON THE LAYERS PANEL FOR A SELECTED OBJECT

When the number of listings on the Layers panel grows long, it can be hard to locate a particular object listing. Organizing them into sublayers can help, as does the Locate Object button. With the Selection tool, select an object, then click the Locate Object button on the Layers panel. The list for that object's layer expands, if it's not already expanded, and its listing is highlighted.

On pages 96–97, you learned how to create, isolate, and add a new object to (and ungroup) a group. Here you will select objects in a group via the Layers panel.

To select a whole group via the Layers panel:

1. *Optional:* To put the group in isolation mode, double-click it in the document with the Selection tool ▲ (V).**A** Note: If this doesn't work, make sure Double Click to Isolate is checked in Illustrator/ Edit > Preferences > General.

2. To select all the objects in the group (including any groups nested within it), click the selection area or the target circle ◯ for the group listing on the right side of the Layers panel.

➤ When a document isn't in isolation mode, you can also select a whole group by clicking any object in the group with the Selection tool (V). If you want to display the bounding box (which appears around the current selection), press Cmd-Shift-B/ Ctrl-Shift-B.

➤ To select an object in a deselected group (or to select individual anchor points or segments), use the Direct Selection tool (A).

To select two or more objects in a group:

1. Deselect all (Cmd-Shift-A/Ctrl-Shift-A).

2. Do either of the following:

   The group can be in isolation mode for this method, or not. Expand the group list on the Layers panel, then Shift-click the selection area or the target circle ◯ at the far right side of the panel for each object in the group that you want to select.**B**

   With the group in isolation mode, choose the **Selection** tool ▲ (V), click an object, then Shift-click additional objects.

➤ To deselect any selected item, Shift-click the object or the selection square again.

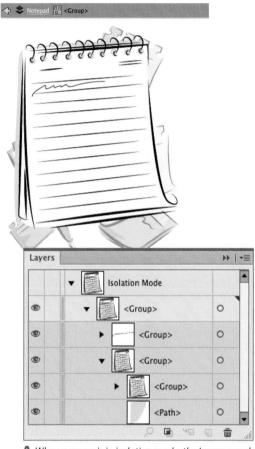

A *When a group is in isolation mode, the Layers panel lists only that group and its objects.*

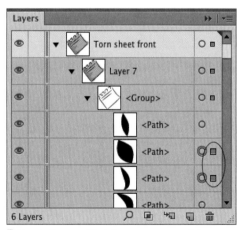

B *To select some objects in a group, expand the group list, then Shift-click the selection area for those objects.*

Restacking layers and objects

The order of objects (and layers) on the Layers panel matches the front-to-back order of objects (and layers) in the artwork. If you move a group, object, sublayer, or top-level layer upward or downward on the list, the artwork will redraw accordingly. You can restack objects and layers by dragging (see below) or by using a command (see the next page).

To restack a layer, group, or object via the Layers panel:

Drag a top-level layer, sublayer, group, or object upward or downward on the Layers panel, either within the same indent level (say, to restack a group within its own top-level layer) **A–C** or to a different group or layer. The document will redraw according to the new stacking position.**D**

➤ On page 97, you learned how to add an existing object to a group via the Cut and Paste commands. You can also move an existing object into (or out of) a group by restacking the listing, as described above.

➤ If you move an object that's part of a group or clipping mask to a different top-level layer, the object will be released from that group or mask.

A *This is the original artwork.*

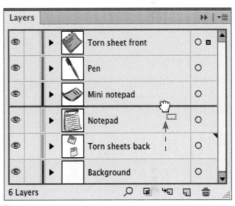

B *We are dragging a layer listing upward to a new stacking position (note the dotted rectangle next to the hand icon).*

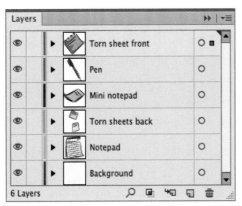

C *The "Torn sheets back" layer is now in front of the Notepad layer.*

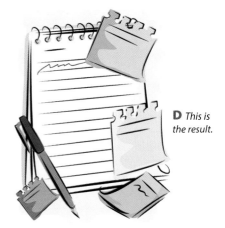

D *This is the result.*

When the Layers panel contains many layers and a long list of objects, it can be tedious to expand and collapse layers each time you need to restack an object. For a faster method, use the Send to Current Layer command.

To move an object to a layer via a command:

1. Select one or more objects.

2. On the Layers panel, click the layer to which you want to move the selected object(s).

3. Right-click one of the selected objects in the document and choose Arrange > **Send to Current Layer** (or choose the command from the Object > Arrange submenu). Note: If the selected object was in a group, the entire group will be moved to the selected layer.

➤ To reverse the order of specific layers, groups, and objects on the Layers panel, Cmd-click/Ctrl-click nonconsecutive listings (or click and then Shift-click a series of consecutive listings), then choose Reverse Order from the panel menu.

Duplicating layers and objects

Duplicate objects appear in the same x/y location as, and directly on top of, the objects from which they are duplicated. If you duplicate a layer or sublayer, the word "copy" is appended to the duplicate name.

To duplicate a layer, sublayer, group, or object:

Do one of the following:

Hold down Option/Alt and drag a layer, sublayer, group, or object listing upward or downward to the desired top-level layer or sublayer, or within a group.**A–B**

Drag a layer, sublayer, group, or object listing over the **New Layer** button.

On the Layers panel, click the layer, sublayer, group, or object to be duplicated, then choose **Duplicate** [layer or object name] from the Layers panel menu.

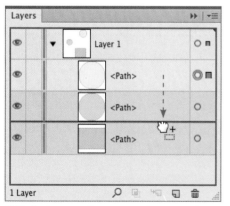

A *To duplicate an object, we are dragging its listing with Option/Alt held down.*

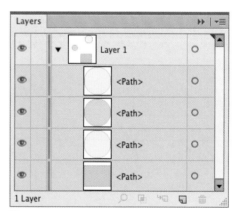

B *A copy of the object appears.*

Locking layers and objects

Locked objects can't be selected or modified, but they do remain visible. When a whole layer is locked, none of the objects within it can be edited. When you save, close, and reopen a file that contains locked objects, the objects remain locked.

Note: As an alternative way to make some objects uneditable temporarily, you can isolate an object or group without locking it.

To lock or unlock layers or objects:

Do one of the following:

On the Layers panel, click in the edit (second) column for a layer,**A** sublayer, group, or object. The lock icon 🔒 appears. Click the icon to unlock the item.

To lock multiple layers, sublayers, groups, or objects, drag upward or downward in the edit column. Drag back over the lock icons to unlock the items.

Option-click/Alt-click in the edit column for a top-level layer to lock or unlock all the other top-level layers except the one you click.

➤ If you lock an object and then lock its top-level layer, but later decide to unlock the object, you will have to unlock the top-level layer first.

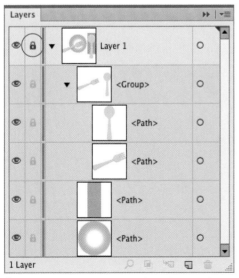

A When a layer is locked, none of the objects within it can be selected or edited. You can also lock groups or individual objects.

Hiding layers and objects

When you hide the objects you're not working on, your artwork looks less complex temporarily, and the screen redraws faster. You can hide a top-level layer (with all its nested layers), a group, or an individual object. Hidden objects are invisible in both Outline and Preview views. When you save, close, and reopen a file that contains hidden objects, they remain hidden.

To hide or show layers or objects:

Do one of the following:

Click the **visibility** icon  for a top-level layer, sublayer, group, or object.**A–D** To redisplay the hidden items, click in the same slot.

Drag upward or downward in the visibility column to hide multiple, consecutive top-level layers, sublayers, groups, or objects. To redisplay the hidden items, drag again.

Display all layers, then Option-click/Alt-click in the visibility column for a top-level layer to hide or show all the top-level layers except the one you click.

Note: If you want to redisplay a hidden object but its top-level layer is also hidden, you must redisplay its top-level layer first.

➤ To hide layers via a command, make sure all layers are visible (choose Show All Layers from the Layers panel menu if they're not), click a top-level layer or layers to remain visible, then choose Hide Others from the panel menu.

➤ To learn more about printing layers, see page 422.

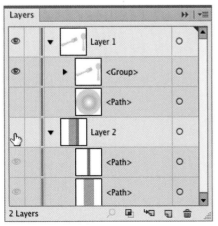

C You can also hide or show an entire layer.

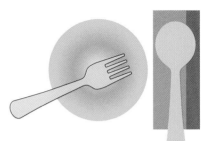

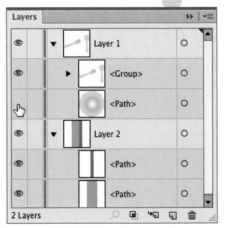

A You can hide or show an individual object or group.

B The plate layer is hidden.

D The napkin layer is hidden.

Collecting objects into a new layer

The Collect in New Layer command moves all the currently highlighted top-level layers, sublayers, groups, or objects to a brand new layer.

To collect multiple layers, sublayers, groups, or objects into a new layer:

1. Deselect all objects.

2. Cmd-click/Ctrl-click the listings for the layers, groups, or objects to be put on a new layer.**A** They must all be at the same indent level (e.g., all objects from the same sublayer or on consecutive sublayers). Don't click the selection area.

3. From the Layers panel menu, choose **Collect in New Layer**. If you selected sublayers, groups, or objects in the preceding step, they will now reside in a new sublayer within the same top-level layer;**B** or if you selected top-level layers, they will now be nested as sublayers within a newly named top-level layer.

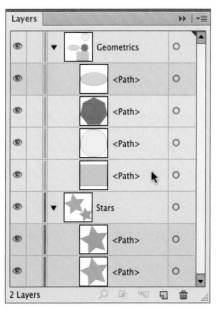

A *We selected three path listings.*

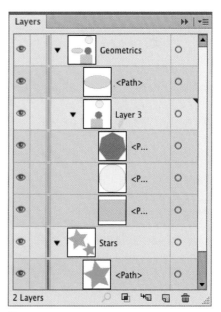

B *The Collect in New Layer command gathered the selected listings into a new sublayer (and labeled it Layer 3).*

Releasing objects to layers

The two Release to Layers commands are useful when you need to prepare an Illustrator file for export to Adobe Flash Professional to be used as the contents of an object, frame, or Web animation. The commands disperse all objects or groups residing within the currently selected top-level layer to new, separate layers within the same layer. After placing the file in Flash, you can convert the layers into separate objects or into a sequence.

Read step 2 carefully before deciding which command to use.

To move objects to new, separate layers:

1. On the Layers panel, click a top-level layer, sublayer, or group (not an object).**A**

2. From the Layers panel menu, choose either of the following:

   Release to Layers (Sequence) to nest each object from the selected layer or group in a separate new layer within the original top-level layer.**B** Any former groups are nested in a new layer or sublayer. The original stacking order of the objects is preserved.

   Release to Layers (Build) if you're going to build a cumulative frame sequence in an animation program by adding objects in succession.**C** The bottommost layer will contain just the bottommost object; the next layer above that will contain the bottommost object plus the next object above it; the next layer above that will contain the two previous objects plus the next object above it, and so on.

➤ If you release a layer or sublayer that contains a clipping mask that you created via the Layers panel, the clipping mask will remain in effect.

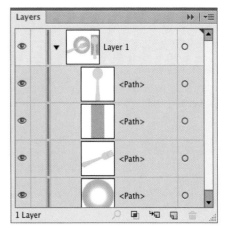

A *We selected a top-level layer on the Layers panel.*

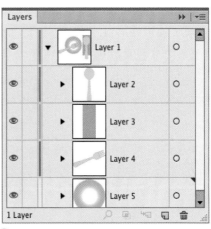

B *These are the results we got from the Release to Layers (Sequence) command…*

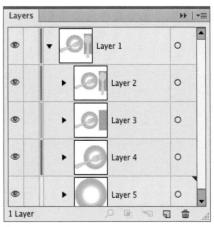

C *…versus the Release to Layers (Build) command.*

Merging layers and groups

If the layers and sublayers on your Layers panel grow to an unwieldy number, you can consolidate them at any time by using the Merge Selected command. Unlike the Flatten Artwork command, which flattens an entire document (see the next page), the Merge Selected command merges just the listings that you select.

In addition to merging layers (or sublayers) with one another, you can merge two or more groups, or merge a group with a sublayer, provided the selected listings reside within the same top-level layer. In the case of a group being merged with a sublayer, the objects will be ungrouped and will be placed on the selected sublayer. You can't merge objects with one another.

To merge layers, sublayers, or groups:

1. *Optional:* Use File > Save As to preserve a copy of your file, with its layers.

2. As you Cmd-click/Ctrl-click the listings for two or more layers, sublayers, or groups, click last on the listing that you want the selected items to merge into.**A** You can merge locked and/or hidden layers.

3. Choose **Merge Selected** from the Layers panel menu.**B**

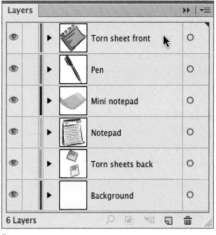

A *As you select the layers (or sublayers or groups) to be merged, click last on the layer you want the items to merge into.*

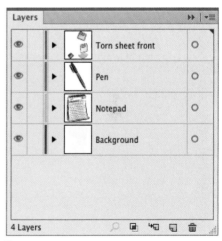

B *The Merge Selected command merged the three selected layers into one.*

Flattening layers

The Flatten Artwork command moves all the sub-layers, groups, and objects in a document to just one top-level layer, and discards all other top-level layers. Objects remain fully editable. If your document contains any hidden top-level layers when you choose this command, you can opt via an alert dialog to either preserve the hidden artwork (by clicking No) or allow Illustrator to discard the hidden layers (by clicking Yes).

To flatten all the layers in a document:

1. *Optional:* Use File > Save As to preserve a copy of your file, with its layers.

2. Display any hidden top-level layers that you want to preserve.

   Note: Any object that you hide by clicking its individual visibility icon will be preserved by the Flatten Artwork command, and will remain hidden.

3. By default, if no layers are selected, the Flatten Artwork command merges all the currently visible layers into whichever top-level layer is displaying the Current Layer indicator. If you prefer to flatten the document into a layer of your choosing, click that layer now.

4. Choose **Flatten Artwork** from the Layers panel menu.

5. If the document contains artwork on hidden top-level layers, an alert dialog will appear.**A–C** Click Yes to discard the hidden artwork, or click No to preserve it. If you click No, all the artwork on hidden top-level layers will become visible. Regardless of which button you click, the result will be a flattened file.

➤ The Flatten Artwork command can be undone if you choose Undo immediately.

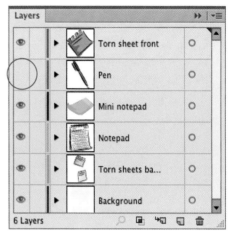

A *One of the layers in this file is hidden.*

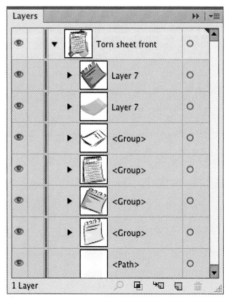

B *Because the hidden layer contains artwork, this alert dialog appeared when we chose the Flatten Artwork command (it's always nice to be given a second chance).*

C *Because we clicked Yes, the Flatten Artwork command flattened the artwork into the selected layer ("Torn sheet front") and completely discarded the hidden layer.*

Appearance attributes consist of an object's fill, stroke, effect, and transparency settings.
In this chapter, you'll learn how to use the Appearance panel ◉ to apply, edit, copy, and restack appearance attributes for a layer, sublayer, group, or object. You can create additional fill and stroke attributes to alter an object's appearance, change its opacity or blending mode, or apply effects. When an object is selected, its attributes are listed on the panel.**A–B**

Appearance attributes change how an object looks and prints, not its actual underlying path. You can save, close, and reopen a document, and the existing appearance attributes will remain editable and removable. Appearance attributes add speed and flexibility — but also some complexity — to object editing. When you're finished with this chapter, be sure to continue with the next two chapters, which are closely related: Chapter 15 (Effects) and Chapter 16 (Graphic Styles).

A *A circle is selected. Its attributes are listed on, and can be edited via, the Appearance panel (shown below).*

Link to a temporary Color or Swatches panel *Stroke Weight*

An added Stroke attribute

Link to a temporary Stroke panel

Link to a temporary Transparency panel

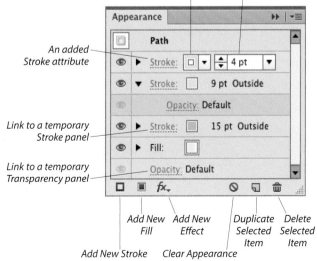

Add New Fill *Add New Effect* *Duplicate Selected Item* *Delete Selected Item*

Add New Stroke *Clear Appearance*

B *This is the Appearance panel for the object shown in figure* **A**.

Applying appearance attributes

You can apply appearance attributes to individual objects one at a time, or you can target a whole top-level layer or group for appearance changes, in which case the attributes will apply to all the objects that are nested within the targeted layer or group. For example, if you target a layer and then change its opacity or blending mode, all the objects on that layer will adopt that opacity or blending mode. When an object has more than just the basic fill and stroke attributes, its listing on the Layers panel has a gray target circle.**A**

Appearance attributes can be modified or removed at any time, even after you save, close, and reopen your file. To edit an attribute, you simply retarget the object. Via convenient links and menus right on the Appearance panel, you can change an object's fill color, stroke attributes, opacity, blending mode, or brush stroke, and apply effects.

To apply appearance attributes via in-panel links:

1. Do either of the following:

   In the document window, select an object.**B**

   On the Layers panel, ⬙ click the target circle ⬤ for a layer, group, or object. A ring appears around the circle, signifying that it's now an active target. If you click the target circle for a layer, all the objects on the layer will become selected, and the word "Layer" will appear at the top of the Appearance panel.

2. Show the Appearance panel. ◉

3. For a targeted object, do any of the following:

   Click the **Stroke** and/or **Fill** color listing, then click the color square to open a temporary Swatches panel or Shift-click the square to open a temporary Color panel (**A**, next page). Choose a color.

   To change other stroke attributes, click the under-lined Stroke link, then choose a stroke weight, profile, or other settings on the temporary Stroke panel. To learn about the options on this panel, see pages 122–124 and page 166. Note: If the stroke has a variable width profile, an asterisk will display next to the stroke weight listing when that listing isn't selected.

   To apply a brush stroke, click a Stroke listing, then choose a brush from the Brushes panel or from the Brush Definition menu on the Control panel.

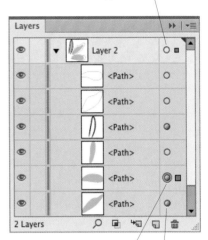

This layer is selected but not targeted, and it doesn't contain appearance attributes.

This object is targeted, and it contains appearance attributes.

This object contains appearance attributes, but it isn't targeted.

A *Learn to "read" the three different states of the target circles on the Layers panel.*

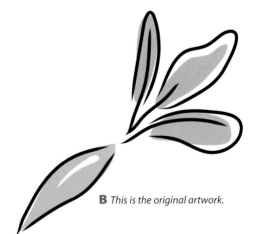

B *This is the original artwork.*

4. For a targeted object, group, or layer, do any of the following:

Click the **Opacity** link to open a temporary Transparency panel, then choose from the Blending Mode menu in the upper left corner and/ or change the Opacity value.**B** (To learn about the Transparency panel, see Chapter 27.)

From the **Add New Effect** menu *fx.* at the bottom of the panel, choose an Illustrator effect, such as one of the effects on the Distort & Transform or Stylize submenu. Choose settings in the dialog, then click OK. The chosen command will be listed on the Appearance panel. (To learn about effects, see the next chapter.)

➤ To target multiple items, Cmd-click/Ctrl-click their target icons.

To untarget an object, group, or layer:

Either Shift-click the gray target circle ⬤ on the Layers panel or hold down Cmd/Ctrl and click a blank area of the artwork.

To choose default appearance settings for new objects:

If the **New Art Has Basic Appearance** command on the Appearance panel menu is on (has a check mark), subsequently created objects will have just one fill and one stroke, in the current colors. If this option is unchecked, the appearance attributes currently displaying on the panel will apply to any new objects you create.

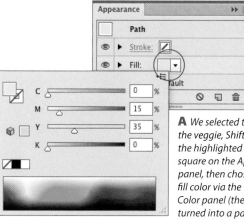

A *We selected the root of the veggie, Shift-clicked the highlighted Fill color square on the Appearance panel, then chose a new fill color via the temporary Color panel (the carrot turned into a parsnip!).*

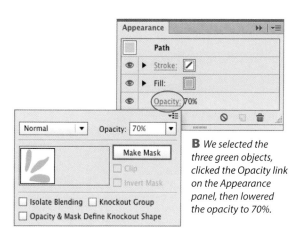

B *We selected the three green objects, clicked the Opacity link on the Appearance panel, then lowered the opacity to 70%.*

Deciphering the Appearance panel

Depending on the entity (an object, group, or layer) that is currently targeted and the attributes it has, you may see one or more of these icons in the upper portion of the Appearance panel:

➤ For a layer or group (not an object), this icon 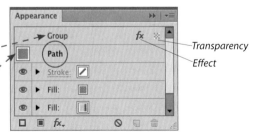 signifies that the item has an added stroke and/or fill attribute, and this icon signifies that it has transparency edits.

➤ This icon indicates the entity contains effects.

The name for the currently targeted entity (e.g., Layer, Group, **A** Path **B–C**, Type, Symbol, Image) is listed in boldface at the top of the Appearance panel.

If you target an object that is nested within a layer and/or group to which appearance attributes have been applied, a "Layer" and/or "Group" listing will also appear above the individual entity (e.g., "Path") listing on the Appearance panel.

If you target a layer or group, a "Contents" listing will also appear on the Appearance panel. Double-click the Contents listing to display Path attributes, click the Layer listing to display attributes that apply to the whole layer, or click the Group listing to display attributes that apply to the whole group. (Yup, this can be mighty confusing!)

<table>
<tr><td></td></tr>
</table>

TARGETING LAYERS FOR APPEARANCE EDITS

Although both selecting and targeting cause objects to become selected in your document, they're not interchangeable when it comes to whole layers:

➤ If you target a top-level layer by clicking its target circle and then apply appearance attributes (e.g., a fill color, an effect, or an opacity setting), those attributes will be applied to, and listed on, the Appearance panel for that layer, and the word "Layer" will appear at the top of the Appearance panel.

➤ If you click the selection area for a top-level layer instead of the target circle, then apply appearance attributes, those attributes will be applied separately to each object or group in that layer, not to the overall layer (they won't be listed on the Appearance panel if you target the layer). To edit those attributes, you would need to target an object individually, not the top-level layer.

Selecting and targeting do work interchangeably for objects and groups. If you click the selection area or target circle on the Layers panel for an object or group, that entity is both selected and targeted.

A When a group is targeted, the attributes that apply to the whole group are listed on the Appearance panel.

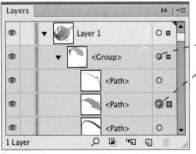

B The path we targeted is nested in a group, which has its own appearance attributes.

C The Appearance panel is listing the attributes for the path, and is also indicating that the group contains effects and nondefault transparency settings.

To apply multiple stroke or fill attributes:

1. Target an object, group, or layer. **A**

2. Do either of the following:

   At the bottom of the Appearance panel, click the **Add New Stroke** button ▢ (Cmd-Option-/; Ctrl-Alt-/) **B** or the **Add New Fill** button ◼ (Cmd-/; Ctrl-/).

   Click a Stroke or Fill listing on the Appearance panel, then click the **Duplicate Selected Item** button ▧ at the bottom of the panel.

3. A new Stroke or Fill listing appears on the panel. Click the new listing, then modify its attributes so it differs from the original one (or modify the original listing instead). Note: For multiple stroke attributes, make sure a narrower stroke is stacked above a wider one, **C–D** so the one on top doesn't obscure those on the bottom. Similarly, for multiple Fill listings, lower the opacity (or change the blending mode) of the topmost one.

➤ You can drag a Stroke or Fill listing upward or downward on the panel. Be aware that this will change the object's appearance in the document.

➤ When you select an object that contains multiple stroke attributes, an alert icon ⚠ may display next to its fill color on the Control panel. If you click the alert icon, the color for the topmost Stroke and/or Fill listing will display on the Control and Color panels.

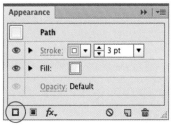

B We clicked the Add New Stroke button.

A The targeted object (the outer circle) has a gray fill and a green stroke.

C We edited the attributes for all three of the Stroke listings. We made the bottommost stroke the widest of the three and applied a Drop Shadow effect to it.

D Our edits display in the object.

Editing appearance attributes

You can use the same convenient in-panel links and menus on the Appearance panel to edit attributes that you used to apply them: the Stroke, Color, Swatches, and Transparency panels; the effect dialogs; and the Brush Definition menu.

To edit appearance attributes:

1. Do either of the following:

   In the document, select an object that contains appearance attributes.

   On the Layers panel, ☰ click the target circle for a layer, group, **A** or object.

2. On the Appearance panel, ◉ click any existing appearance listing to open a related panel (or a dialog, in the case of an effect). **B** If there are multiple Fill or Stroke listings, be sure to click the one you want to modify.

3. Using links or menus on the Appearance panel, make the desired edits **C** (see steps 3–4 on pages 200–201). For example, to modify the setting for a stroke attribute, click the underlined Stroke link to open a temporary Stroke panel and choose options. If the object has a brush stroke, you can click a replacement brush on the Brush Definition menu or change the weight via the Stroke link.

➤ If you use the Brush Definition menu on the Appearance panel and then target or select a different object that doesn't have a brush stroke, the Brush Definition menu will still display. To redisplay the stroke weight controls, deselect the Stroke listing, then reselect it. To learn more about brushes, see Chapter 23.

To add attributes to just an entity's stroke or fill:

1. On the Layers panel, ☰ click the target circle for a layer, group, or object.

2. On the Appearance panel, ◉ click a Stroke or Fill listing, then click the expand arrow. Do any of the following:

   Click the **Opacity** link to open a temporary Transparency panel, then change the opacity value and/or blending mode.

   From the **Add New Effect** menu, *fx.* choose an effect, choose options, then click OK.

   The newly applied attributes will be nested within the Stroke or Fill listing.

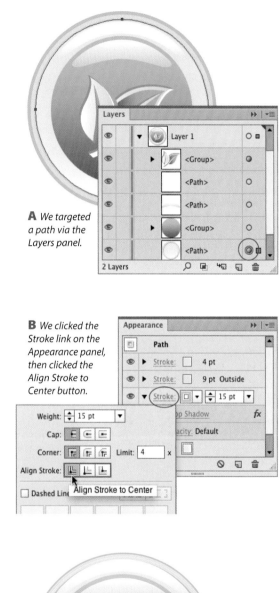

A We targeted a path via the Layers panel.

B We clicked the Stroke link on the Appearance panel, then clicked the Align Stroke to Center button.

C The new stroke alignment displays in the object.

Hiding and deleting appearance attributes

To hide an appearance attribute:

1. Target a layer, group,**A** or object.

2. On the Appearance panel, click in the visibility column to make the icon and the targeted entity disappear **B–C** or reappear.

To delete an appearance attribute:

1. Target a layer, group, or object.

2. On the Appearance panel, click the attribute to be deleted, then click the **Delete Selected Item** button at the bottom of the panel.

➤ The sole remaining fill and stroke appearance attributes can't be removed. You can, however, click the Delete Selected Item button for either of those appearance attributes to apply a color of None.

➤ To remove a brush stroke from a stroke attribute, click the Stroke listing on the Appearance panel, then click the Basic brush on the Brush Definition menu.

if you want to remove all but the basic appearance attributes from an individual object (using either of the commands discussed below), you need to target that object specifically. If you target a layer or group instead, the commands will remove only attributes that were applied to that layer or group, not attributes that were applied directly to objects nested within it.

To delete all the appearance attributes from an entity:

1. Target an object, layer, or group.

2. Do either of the following:

    To remove all appearance attributes from the targeted entity and apply a stroke and fill of None, click the **Clear Appearance** button on the Appearance panel (for type, the fill color becomes black and any stroke color is removed).

    To remove all the appearance attributes except the entity's original stroke and fill colors, choose **Reduce to Basic Appearance** from the Appearance panel menu.

    Note: Regardless of which command you choose, all effects, brush strokes, and added fill and stroke attributes will be removed, and the transparency settings will be restored to a blending mode of Normal and an opacity setting of 100%.

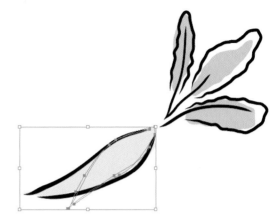

A *We targeted a group.*

B *On the Appearance panel, we clicked the visibility column for the Warp effect to hide that attribute.*

C *The Warp effect is now hidden, but we can redisplay it at any time.*

Copying appearance attributes

To copy appearance attributes from one object or layer to another:

Do either of the following:

On the Layers panel, Option-drag/Alt-drag the target circle from the item that contains the attributes you want to copy onto the target circle for another layer, group, or object.**A**

Choose the Selection tool (V), click an object that contains the attributes to be copied, then drag the square thumbnail from the upper left corner of the Appearance panel over an unselected object in the artwork.**B–C** (Note: If you don't see the thumbnail, choose Show Thumbnail from the panel menu.)

➤ To remove the appearance attributes from one item and apply them to another, drag a target circle from one layer, group, or object to another one without holding down any modifier keys.

➤ To select objects in a document based on their matching appearance attributes, select one of the objects, then choose Select > Same > Appearance.

Expanding appearance attributes

When you expand an object's appearance attributes, the paths that were used to create the attributes are converted into (dozens of!) separate objects, which can be edited individually. When exporting an Illustrator file to a non-Adobe application that can't read appearance attributes, this command may be a necessity.

To expand an object's appearance attributes:

1. Select an object that contains the appearance attributes to be expanded.

2. Choose Object > **Expand Appearance**. On the Layers panel, you will now see a new <Group> (or nested groups). The former effects or other attributes will become individual path and/or image listings. Even the former fill and stroke attributes will be listed as separate paths.

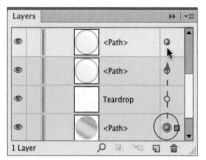

A *To copy appearance attributes, either Option/Alt drag the target circle from one listing to another…*

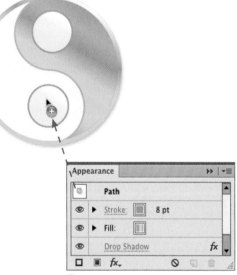

B *…or drag the thumbnail from the Appearance panel over an object (note the plus sign in the pointer).*

C *The appearance attributes were copied to the object to which we dragged.*

Effects apply distortion, texture, artistic, shape, and stylistic changes to objects and imported images, with results that range from subtle to marked. In this chapter, you will apply effects via the Appearance panel, the Effect menu, and the Effect Gallery, and explore a few effects in depth. (Effects can also be saved in and applied via graphic styles. See the next chapter.)

The effect commands change only the appearance of an object — not its underlying path. **A–B** Effects can be edited or deleted at any time without permanently affecting the object they're applied to, and without affecting other effects or appearance attributes in the same object. Moreover, if you reshape the path of the underlying object, the effects adjust accordingly. In other words, effects are live.

Applying Illustrator effects

The Effect menu offers a choice of Illustrator effects and Photoshop effects. Most of the Illustrator effects, which are in the top portion of the menu, are vector based, meaning they can be applied only to path shapes and output as vector objects. The following Illustrator effects can be applied to vector or raster objects: all the effects on the 3D, SVG Filters, and Warp submenus; the Transform effect on the Distort & Transform submenu; and the Drop

Continued on the following page

A *We chose this setting in the Twist dialog.*

B *The Twist effect was applied to the artwork shown at the top of the page, with these results (see page 215).*

15

EFFECTS

Shadow, Inner Glow, Outer Glow, and Feather effects on the Stylize submenu. All the effects itemized above except the 3D, Transform, and Warp effects are rasterized upon output (are converted from vector to raster).

All the Photoshop effects (on the bottom part of the Effect menu) are pixel based, meaning they introduce painterly attributes, such as soft edges or transparency, and are rasterized upon output. They can be applied to both vector and raster objects.

For most Illustrator effects and for some Photoshop effects, an individual dialog opens. Most of the Photoshop effects are applied via the comprehensive Effect Gallery (see pages 217–218).

Keep these basic facts in mind as you apply effects:

➤ You can apply Illustrator and Photoshop effects to an object's fill or stroke (the object may have a brush stroke); to type; or to a group, layer, embedded bitmap image, symbol instance, blend, or compound shape.

➤ If you apply an effect to a targeted layer or group, it will affect all the current and future objects in that layer or group.

➤ If you apply an effect to editable type, the type and its attributes will remain editable.

➤ You can apply multiple effects to the same object. If you do so, the effects may preview more slowly in the dialog (a progress bar may display). Some effects and settings require more memory to process than others.

The Illustrator effects can be applied via the Effect menu **A** or via the Appearance panel. The effects that you have applied to the current selection of objects are listed individually as appearance attributes on the Appearance panel.

To apply an Illustrator effect:

1. Do either of the following:

   On the Layers panel, 🔻 click the target circle for a layer, group, or object (the circle should now have a double border), or click the selection area for a group or object.**B**

   To limit the effect to just the stroke or fill of one or more ungrouped objects, select or isolate them. Display the Appearance panel, 🔘 then click the Stroke or Fill listing.

2. Choose one of the Illustrator effects from the top portion of the **Add New Effect** menu 𝑓𝑥 on the

Effect	
Apply Last Effect	⇧⌘E
Last Effect	⌥⇧⌘E
Document Raster Effects Settings...	
Illustrator Effects	
3D	▶
Convert to Shape	▶
Crop Marks	
Distort & Transform	▶
Path	▶
Pathfinder	▶
Rasterize...	
Stylize	▶
SVG Filters	▶
Warp	▶
Photoshop Effects	
Effect Gallery...	
Artistic	▶
Blur	▶
Brush Strokes	▶
Distort	▶
Pixelate	▶
Sketch	▶
Stylize	▶
Texture	▶
Video	▶

A *Most of the Illustrator effects on the Effect menu are vector effects (but a few are raster effects); the Photoshop effects are all raster effects.*

B *We targeted this entire group of objects.*

Appearance panel, or from the **Effect** menu on the Illustrator menu bar.

3. Check Preview (if available), then choose settings and options.**A** After entering a value in a field, press Tab to update the preview.

4. Click OK.**B** The effect will be listed on the Appearance panel, either above or below the Stroke and/or Fill listings, or nested within one of those listings. Click the expand arrowhead to display it.**C–E**

➤ To apply effects to type, see pages 294–296.

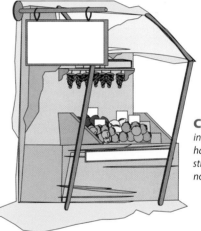

A We chose these values in the Warp Options dialog.

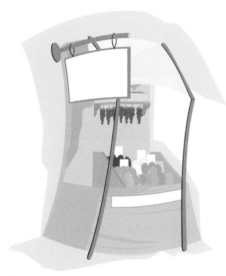

B This is the result of the Warp > Squeeze effect (it reminds us a bit of the artist Chaim Soutine).

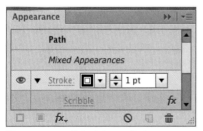

D Because we clicked the Stroke listing on the Appearance panel before we applied the Stylize > Scribble effect, Illustrator nested the effect within the Stroke listing.

C All the objects in this artwork have a black stroke. They're not in a group.

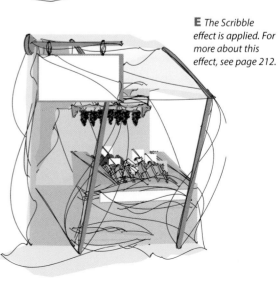

E The Scribble effect is applied. For more about this effect, see page 212.

Editing, duplicating, and deleting effects

To edit an applied effect:

1. Do either of the following:

   Via the Layers panel, ✥ target the layer, group, or object that contains the effect you want to edit.**A**

   If you applied the effect to just an object's stroke or fill, select the object, then expand the Stroke or Fill listing on the Appearance panel.

2. Click the blue underlined effect listing on the Appearance panel.**B** The effect dialog reopens. Check Preview.

3. Make the desired adjustments, then click OK.**C**

➤ When multiple effects are applied to the same object or attribute, you can restack any individual effect by dragging it upward or downward. As a result, other effects may be enhanced or blocked.

➤ To apply the last-used effect and settings to a selected object without opening a dialog, press Cmd-Shift-E/Ctrl-Shift-E. Or to reopen the last effects dialog or the Effect Gallery (if the gallery was used last), press Cmd-Option-Shift-E/Ctrl-Alt-Shift-E. If the object already contains the effect in question, an alert dialog will appear; click Cancel (unless for some reason you want to apply the same effect twice).

To remove an effect:

1. On the Layers panel, ✥ target the layer, group, or object that contains the effect to be removed.

2. On the Appearance panel, ◉ click next to the effect name, then click the **Delete Selected Item** button. 🗑

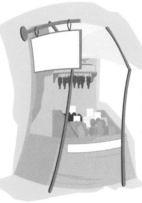

A *We targeted a group to which the Warp > Squeeze effect had been applied.*

B *We clicked the effect listing on the Appearance panel to reopen the dialog.*

CHOOSING SPOT COLORS FOR EFFECTS

You can choose a spot color for the Stylize > Drop Shadow, Inner Glow, and Outer Glow effects. Load the desired swatch(es) onto the Swatches panel. In the effect dialog, click the color square to open the Color Picker. Click the Color Swatches button, if necessary, to display a list of the swatches that are currently on the Swatches panel, and click the desired spot color (then click OK twice to exit both dialogs).

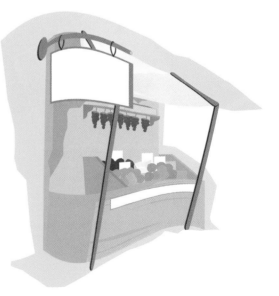

C *In the Warp Options dialog, we changed the Style from Squeeze to Fish.*

A few Illustrator effects up close

On this page and on the next four pages, we have illustrated uses for a few Illustrator effects, just to whet your appetite. In this first task, you will use a Convert to Shape effect to change an object's silhouette to a rectangle, rounded rectangle, or ellipse — without altering the actual underlying path.

To apply a Convert to Shape effect:

1. On the Layers panel, ♥ click the target circle for a layer, group, or object.**A** Or to limit the effect to a stroke or fill attribute, select or isolate an object, then on the Appearance panel, ◉ click the Stroke or Fill listing.

2. From the **Add New Effect** menu *fx.* on the Appearance panel or from the **Effect** menu on the Illustrator menu bar, under Illustrator Effects, choose Convert to Shape > **Rectangle**, **Rounded Rectangle**, or **Ellipse**. The Shape Options dialog opens.**B** (You can also choose one of those shapes from the Shape menu in the dialog.)

3. Check Preview.

4. Do either of the following:

   Click **Absolute**, then enter the total desired Width and Height values for the shape's appearance.

   Click **Relative**, then enter an Extra Width or Extra Height value (a positive value to enlarge the effect or a negative value to shrink it).

5. For the Rounded Rectangle shape, you can also change the **Corner Radius** value to control the roundness of the corners.

6. Click OK.**C–D**

➤ To round the corners of an object without converting its shape, use Effect > Stylize > Round Corners.

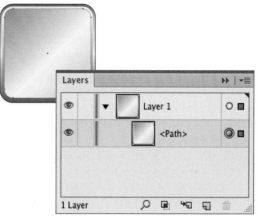

A We targeted an object (this object contains a graphic style; see the next chapter).

B We applied the Convert to Shape > Ellipse effect, choosing these options in the Shape Options dialog.

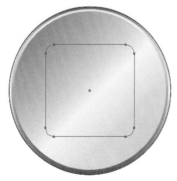

C Although the underlying path remains the same…

D …the outer shape looks like (and will print as if it were) an ellipse.

The Scribble effect makes an object's fill and stroke look as though they were sketched with a felt-tip marker or pen.

To apply the Scribble effect:

1. On the Layers panel,  click the target circle for a layer, group, **A** or object. Or to limit the effect to a stroke or fill attribute, select or isolate the object, then on the Appearance panel, click the Stroke or Fill listing.

2. From the **Add New Effect** menu *fx.* on the Appearance panel, or from the **Effect** menu on the Illustrator menu bar, under Illustrator Effects, choose Stylize > **Scribble**. The Scribble Options dialog opens.**B**

3. Check Preview. Begin by choosing a preset from the **Settings** menu. Follow the remaining steps if you want to choose custom settings for the preset, or if you're satisfied with the preset results, click OK to exit the dialog.

4. To change the angle of the sketch lines, enter an **Angle** value or move the dial.

5. Drag the **Path Overlap** slider toward Outside to allow the sketch lines to extend beyond the edge of the path, or toward Inside to confine them to the interior of the path. Choose a high **Variation** value to produce random variations in line lengths and a wilder, more haphazard look, or a low Variation value for shorter and more uniform line lengths.

6. Under Line Options, do any of the following:

   Move the **Stroke Width** slider to change the thickness of the lines.

   Change the **Curviness** value to control whether the lines angle sharply or loop widely where they change direction. The Variation slider controls the degree of random variation in changes of direction.

   Change the **Spacing** value to cluster the sketch lines more tightly or to spread them further apart. The Variation slider controls the degree of random variation in the spacing.

7. Click OK.**C**

➤ If you change the settings in the Scribble Options dialog and then choose a preset from the Settings menu, the preset values will be restored to the sliders. Unfortunately, custom Scribble settings can't be saved as a preset.

A *We targeted this group of bananas.*

B *We chose these settings in the Scribble Options dialog.*

C *The Scribble effect is applied.*

The Inner Glow effect spreads a color from the edge of an object inward, whereas the Outer Glow effect spreads a color from the edge of an object outward.

To apply the Inner Glow or Outer Glow effect:

1. On the Layers panel, ⬥ click the target circle for a layer, group,**A** or object. Or to limit the effect to a stroke or fill attribute, select or isolate the object, then on the Appearance panel, ⬤ click the Stroke or Fill listing.

2. From the **Add New Effect** menu *fx.* on the Appearance panel, or from the **Effect** menu on the Illustrator menu bar, under Illustrator Effects, choose Stylize > **Inner Glow** or **Outer Glow**.

3. In the Inner Glow **B** or Outer Glow dialog, check Preview, then do any or all of the following:

   Click the color square next to the Mode menu, then via the Color Picker, choose a different spot or process color for the glow.

   Choose a blending **Mode** for the glow color.

   Choose an **Opacity** for the glow color.

   Click a **Blur** arrowhead or enter a value to adjust how far the glow extends inward or outward. The higher the Blur value, the wider the glow area. If you're going to choose the Center option (next), keep the Blur value low.

   For the Inner Glow effect, click **Center** to have the glow spread outward from the center of the object, or **Edge** to have it spread inward from the edge of the object toward the center.

4. Click OK.**C**

➤ To soften the hard edges of a vector object, apply Effect > Stylize > Feather.

A *We targeted the papers in this group of objects.*

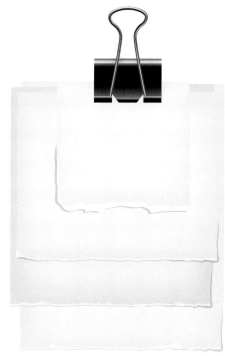

C *The Inner Glow effect is applied.*

B *We chose these options in the Inner Glow dialog.*

The Drop Shadow effect adds soft shadows.

To apply the Drop Shadow effect:

1. On the Layers panel, ≋ click the target circle for a layer, group, or object.**A** Or to limit the effect to a stroke or fill attribute, select or isolate the object, then on the Appearance panel, ● click the Stroke or Fill listing.

2. From the **Add New Effect** menu *fx.* on the Appearance panel, or from the **Effect** menu on the Illustrator menu bar, under Illustrator Effects, choose Stylize > **Drop Shadow**. The Drop Shadow dialog opens.**B** Check Preview.

3. Do any or all of the following:

   Change the blending **Mode**.

   Change the **Opacity** value for the shadow.

   Enter an **X Offset** for the horizontal distance between the object and the shadow and a **Y Offset** for the vertical distance between the object and the shadow.

   Change the **Blur** value for the width of the shadow (change this amount slowly).

   Click **Color**, click the color square, choose a spot or process color for the shadow from the Color Picker, then click OK; or click **Darkness**, then enter a percentage of black to be added to the shadow.

4. Click OK.**C**

To apply the Gaussian Blur effect:

1. Follow steps 1–2 in the preceding instructions, except in step 2, choose Blur > **Gaussian Blur**.

2. In the Gaussian Blur dialog, choose a Radius setting.**D–E** The effect previews in the artwork. Click OK.**F**

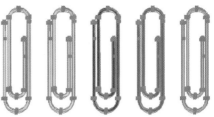

A We targeted these objects.

B We chose these settings in the Drop Shadow dialog.

C This was the result.

D We targeted the yellow ellipse in the center of this group of objects.

E We chose this setting in the Gaussian Blur dialog.

F The blur softened the "light."

The Roughen effect adds anchor points and then moves them. Use it to make an object look more irregular or hand drawn. This effect can be applied to whole objects or to just an object's stroke or fill.

To apply the Roughen effect:

1. On the Layers panel, ● click the target circle for a layer, group,**A** or object. Or to limit the effect to a stroke or fill attribute, select or isolate the object, then on the Appearance panel, ● click the Stroke or Fill listing.

   ➤ Choose View > Hide Edges (Cmd-H/Ctrl-H) to make it easier to preview the results.

2. From the **Add New Effect** menu *fx.* on the Appearance panel, or from the **Effect** menu on the Illustrator menu bar, under Illustrator Effects, choose Distort & Transform > **Roughen**. The Roughen dialog opens.**B** Check Preview.

3. Under Points, click **Smooth** to produce curves, or click **Corner** to produce pointy angles.

4. Click **Relative** to move anchor points by a percentage of the object's size, or **Absolute** to move them by a specific amount, then choose a **Size** amount to specify how far the object's anchor points may move (try a low percentage first).

5. Choose a **Detail** amount for the number of points to be added to each inch of the path segments.

6. Click OK.**C**

The Twist effect twists an object's overall shape.

To apply the Twist effect:

1. For one or more objects, follow step 1 in the instructions above.

2. From the **Add New Effect** menu *fx.* on the Appearance panel, or from the **Effect** menu (under Illustrator Effects), choose Distort & Transform > **Twist**. In the Twist dialog, check Preview.

3. Choose a positive **Angle** to twirl the path clockwise or a negative value to twirl it counterclockwise (–360 to 360).

4. Click OK (see **A–B**, page 207).

A We targeted the green tile objects in this artwork.

Roughen

Options

Size: ──────────── 2%

● Relative   ○ Absolute

Detail: ──────────── 18 /in

Points

● Smooth   ○ Corner

☑ Preview   Cancel   OK

B We chose these settings in the Roughen dialog.

C The Roughen effect is applied.

Rasterizing objects

The Rasterize command converts vector objects to bitmap images. You can use the settings in the dialog to control, on a per-object basis, how an applied stroke, vector (Illustrator) effects, or bitmap (Photoshop) effects on an object will be converted to pixels, to help prevent errors and unwanted surprises upon output.

To rasterize a vector object:

1. Select one or more vector objects, or target them on the Layers panel.

2. Choose Object > **Rasterize**.

3. In the Rasterize dialog, choose a **Color Model** for the resulting object. Depending on the current document color mode, you can choose CMYK for print output; RGB for video or onscreen output; Grayscale; or Bitmap to convert the object to black and white (Photoshop effects won't be available for the resulting object if you choose Bitmap).

4. For the **Resolution**, choose Screen for Web or video output, Medium for desktop printing, or High for commercial printing; or enter a resolution in the Other field; or click Use Document Raster Effects Resolution to use the current global resolution settings in the Effect > Document Raster Effects Settings dialog (see page 439).

5. Click **Background: White** to make any transparent areas in the object opaque white, or **Transparent** to make the background transparent. We prefer the latter option (see the sidebar on this page).

6. Under **Options:**

   For most kinds of objects, you can choose **Anti-aliasing**: Art Optimized (Supersampling) to allow Illustrator to soften the edges of the rasterized shape. Since this option can make type or thin lines look blurry, Type Optimized (Hinted) is a better option for type objects. If you choose a setting of None, objects will remain hard-edged. Note: The setting chosen for type on the Anti-aliasing menu on the Character panel (Sharp, Crisp, or Strong) is honored only for the Type Optimized option.

   If you clicked Background: White and you want Illustrator to add a white border around the object, enter a width for the border as the **Add [ ] Around Object** value.

Check **Preserve Spot Colors** (if available) to preserve spot colors in the object, if any.

7. Click OK.

➤ If the object contains a fill pattern and you want to preserve any transparency in the pattern, in the Rasterize dialog, click Background: Transparent and choose Anti-aliasing: Art Optimized.

➤ The Effect > Rasterize command provides the same options as the Object > Rasterize command, except for the Preserve Spot Colors option. When applied as an effect, the rasterization isn't permanent, and you can edit the settings at any time. However, if you apply the Object > Expand Appearance command after applying the effect, the object will be rasterized permanently using the settings from the effect.

➤ If you save an Illustrator document to the TIFF, GIF, or JPEG format or export it to an application that doesn't read vector objects, the entire document will be rasterized.

➤ If you change the resolution setting in the Effect > Document Raster Effects Settings dialog, all raster effects in the document will be recalculated, but you will see little or no change in how the objects look.

TRANSPARENT VS. CLIPPING MASK OPTIONS

Both the Background: Transparent and Create Clipping Mask options in the Rasterize dialog remove an object's background, but they produce different results:

➤ The Transparent option removes the background by creating an alpha channel. Of the two options, this one does a better job of anti-aliasing. All the opacity settings are restored to the default value of 100%, but the look of semitransparency is preserved. All the blending modes are restored to the default setting of Normal, and their effect is removed from the artwork.

➤ The Create Clipping Mask option turns an object's path into a clipping path. Any existing transparency attributes are applied to the clipping mask, and the transparency settings for the object are restored to Normal mode and 100% opacity. Any stroke or effects that extended beyond the object's path are clipped. If you click the Transparent option, there's no need to check this option.

Applying Photoshop effects via the Effect Gallery

The large Effect Gallery dialog provides access to most of the Photoshop effects and settings. Note: The gallery lets you preview, apply, show, and hide only one individual effect at a time. If you want to apply multiple Photoshop effects, you have to reopen it for each one. To work around this limitation, after applying multiple effects, click the visibility icon 👁 on the Appearance panel for any effects that you want to hide or show.

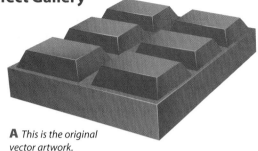

A *This is the original vector artwork.*

To use the Effect Gallery:

1. Select a path object, an embedded image,**A** or editable or outline type.

2. From the **Add New Effect** menu *fx.* on the Appearance panel, or from the **Effect** menu (under Photoshop Effects), either choose **Effect Gallery** or choose an individual Photoshop effect from any submenu except Pixelate, Blur, Sharpen, or Video.

3. The resizable dialog opens.**B** It contains a preview window, effect thumbnails, and settings. If you want to switch to a different effect, expand a category in the middle panel of the dialog, then click a thumbnail, or choose an effect name from the menu on the right side of the dialog.

4. Choose settings for the current effect.

Continued on the following page

B *The Effect Gallery has three panels.*

Click the arrowhead/ chevron to hide or show the middle panel.

Switch to a different effect either by clicking a thumbnail in the middle panel or by choosing from this menu.

Choose settings for the current effect.

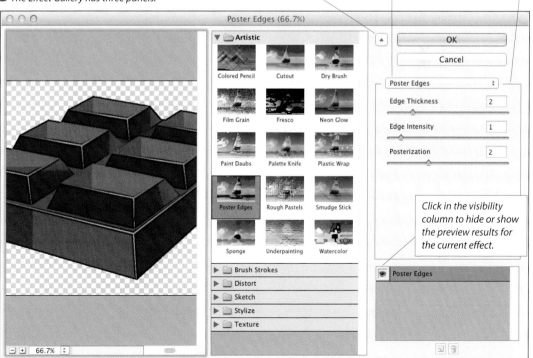

Click in the visibility column to hide or show the preview results for the current effect.

➤ You can change the zoom level for the preview via the zoom buttons or menu at the bottom of the dialog, and you can drag a magnified preview in the window.

5. *Optional:* If you want to see the preview without the effect, click the visibility (eye) icon on the right side of the dialog. Remember to redisplay the effect before exiting the dialog.

6. For some effects, such as Artistic > Rough Pastels and Underpainting, you can choose a texture type from a **Texture** menu. Move the Scaling slider to scale the pattern; move the Relief slider, if there is one, to adjust the depth and prominence of the texture; and choose a Light direction option.

7. Click OK.**A–D**

Note: All the Photoshop effects are rasterized upon output, as are the following Illustrator effects: Stylize > Drop Shadow, Inner Glow, Outer Glow, and Feather. To control which settings Illustrator uses for this process, see page 435.

➤ In the Effect Gallery dialog, you can hold down Option/Alt and click Reset to restore the first effect that was applied when the dialog was opened, with its default settings (the Cancel button becomes a Reset button).

➤ To intensify the results of a Photoshop effect on a vector object, apply an Illustrator effect such as Stylize > Feather or Inner or Outer Glow first to add some variation to the fill color.

A *The Artistic > Plastic Wrap effect is applied.*

B *The Distort > Diffuse Glow effect is applied.*

C *The Sketch > Charcoal effect is applied.*

D *The Texture > Grain effect is applied.*

A graphic style is a collection of appearance attributes that is stored on the Graphic Styles panel and can be applied to an object, group, or layer. Any appearance attributes that can be applied to an object can be saved in a graphic style, such as fills and strokes, Stroke panel settings, Transparency panel settings (opacity and blending mode), and effects.**A**

In this chapter, you will learn how to load graphic styles from a library panel to the Graphic Styles panel; apply, remove, create, duplicate, redefine, and delete graphic styles; save custom graphic styles libraries; and break the link between an object and a graphic style.

Graphic styles basics

To display the Graphic Styles panel, **B** choose Window > Graphic Styles. You can also display a temporary Graphic Styles panel by clicking the Style thumbnail or arrowhead on the Control panel.

Continued on the following page

A *These objects have the same underlying paths, but different graphic styles.*

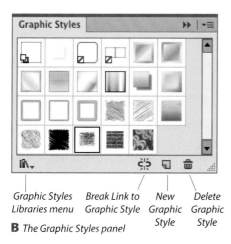

Graphic Styles   Break Link to   New   Delete
Libraries menu   Graphic Style   Graphic   Graphic
                                       Style   Style

B *The Graphic Styles panel*

These are some of the benefits to using graphic styles:

➤ Using graphic styles, you can quickly apply many attributes at once.

➤ Graphic styles change the way an object looks without changing its underlying path.

➤ If you redefine a graphic style, the style will update instantly on any objects to which it's already assigned.

➤ At any time, you can apply a different graphic style to an object, apply additional styles, restore the default style (a 1-pt. black stroke and a solid white fill), or remove the style altogether.

If you're wondering if graphic styles are like paragraph and character styles, the answer is yes—except for one significant difference. If you modify an attribute directly on an object that is linked to a graphic style, that modification effectively breaks the link between the object and the style. If you were to subsequently redefine that graphic style, it wouldn't update on that object.

When an object or a group containing a graphic style is targeted, the style name and its individual attributes are listed on, and can be edited via, the Appearance panel.**A–B**

Note: In this chapter, you will use the Graphic Styles, Appearance, and Layers panels.

The original objects

Blue Neon
(Neon Effects library)

RGB Denim
(Textures library)

Scribble 7
(Scribble Effects library)

Yellow Glow
(Image Effects library)

RGB Dirt
(Textures library)

Metal Gold
(Type Effects library)

RGB Burlap
(Textures library)

A *When an object or a group containing a graphic style is targeted, the style name and its attributes are listed on the Appearance panel.*

B *We applied a few Illustrator graphic styles to these objects, just to give you an inkling of what styles can do.*

Loading graphic styles from a library

The default Graphic Styles panel contains only eight styles, but there are many other predefined graphic styles that you can load onto the panel. The styles on the panel save with the current document.

To load graphic styles from a library:

1. From the **Graphic Styles Libraries** menu ◄ at the bottom of the Graphic Styles panel, ◄ choose a library name. A separate library panel opens.**A**

   Note: User libraries are opened from the User Defined submenu on the Graphic Styles Libraries menu (see page 228).

2. Do one of the following:

   To add a style to the Graphic Styles panel by applying it to an object, select an object, then click a style thumbnail in the library. The chosen style will also appear on the Graphic Styles panel.

   To add a style to the Graphic Styles panel without styling an object, deselect, then click a style thumbnail in the library.

   To add multiple styles, click, then Shift-click a series of consecutive styles on the library panel or Cmd-click/Ctrl-click multiple styles, then choose **Add to Graphic Styles** from the library panel menu.

3. To cycle through other predefined libraries (in alphabetical order), click the Load Previous Graphic Styles Library button ◄ or Load Next Graphic Styles Library button ► on the library panel.

➤ If a style that you load onto the Graphic Styles panel contains a brush stroke (such as the Charcoal style in the Artistic Effects library), and that brush isn't already present on the document's Brushes panel, Illustrator will add it to the Brushes panel.

➤ To change the view for the Graphic Styles panel or a library panel, from the panel menu, choose Thumbnail View, Small List View, or Large List View. Also choose the Use Square for Preview option (the default square shape) or the Use Text for Preview option (to have a "T" character display in each thumbnail).**B**

➤ To load a graphic styles library from another Illustrator document, choose Other Library from the Graphic Styles Libraries menu, locate the desired file, then click Open. A library panel opens.

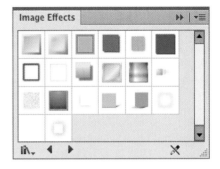

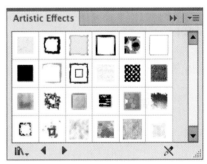

A Graphic styles libraries display in a separate panel.

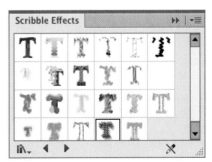

B We chose the Use Text for Preview option for this panel.

Applying graphic styles

When you apply a graphic style to an object, the attributes in the style replace the existing attributes in the object completely. On the preceding page, you learned that a graphic style is applied to a selected object automatically if you click a style on a library panel. In the steps below, you will apply a style via the Graphic Styles panel. The style will remain associated with the object unless you break the link (see page 228).

To apply a graphic style to an object:

1. Display the Graphic Styles panel, 🖾 and load any styles onto it that you want to try out.

2. Do either of the following:

   With the Selection tool (V), select one or more objects in the document window.

   On the right side of the Layers panel, ❧ click the target circle for one or more objects.**A**

3. Do either of the following:

   Click a style name or thumbnail on the Graphic Styles panel.**B–C** The name of the graphic style that's linked to the selected object, group, or layer is listed at the top of the Appearance panel. Some styles take a few moments to process.

   Click the **Style** thumbnail on the Control panel to open a temporary Graphic Styles panel, then click a style on the panel.

   ➤ To view an enlarged thumbnail of a graphic style on the panel, right-click and hold on the thumbnail.

➤ To preserve the existing fill and stroke colors of type when applying a graphic style, uncheck Override Character Color on the Graphic Styles panel menu before applying the style.

APPLYING STYLES TO A GROUP

➤ If you apply a graphic style to a group, it will apply automatically to any objects that you subsequently add to that group. You can also apply a different graphic style or attributes to individual objects within the group (yes, this can lead to confusion!).

➤ If you apply a graphic style to a targeted group and you don't see a change in the artwork, on the Appearance panel, drag the Contents listing below the bottommost Fill listing (note that this will break the link to the style).

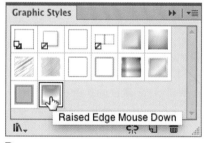

A *Via the Layers panel, we targeted a type object for an appearance change.*

B *Then we clicked a swatch on the Graphic Styles panel (Raised Edge Mouse Down is in the Buttons and Rollovers library).*

C *The graphic style appeared on the object.*

Removing a graphic style from an object

To remove a graphic style that you have applied to an object, use the default graphic style, which applies a solid white fill and a black stroke of 1 pt. (Note: If you need to break the link to a style without changing the object's appearance, see page 228.)

To remove a graphic style from an object and apply the default style:

1. With the Selection tool (V), select the object to which you want to restore the default graphic style, or on the Layers panel, click the object's target circle.**A**

2. On the Graphic Styles panel, click the **Default Graphic Style** (first) thumbnail. **B–C**

If you apply a graphic style to a layer or group and then subsequently decide to remove it, you need to click a different button than for an object.

To remove a graphic style from a layer or group:

1. Target the layer or group from which you want to remove a graphic style.

2. At the bottom of the Appearance panel, click the **Clear Appearance** button.

There are two ways to establish basic style settings for future objects.

To choose basic styling for future objects:

1. Deselect, then choose a fill and stroke color (or None) and choose Stroke Weight, Cap, Corner, and optional Dashed Line settings on the Stroke panel.

2. On the Appearance panel menu, check **New Art Has Basic Appearance**. The current Fill and Stroke colors and the chosen Stroke panel settings will apply to newly created objects (no graphic styles, effects, or extra fill or stroke attributes).

   Note: If you uncheck New Art Has Basic Appearance, the attributes that are currently on the Appearance panel will be applied to new objects instead of the basic Stroke and Fill settings.

To choose the default graphic style for future objects:

1. Deselect.

2. On the Graphic Styles panel, click the **Default Graphic Style** thumbnail.

A *This object has a graphic style (RGB Diamond Plate). We want to restore the default style to it.*

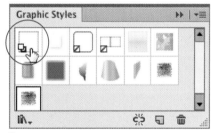

B *We clicked the Default Graphic Style thumbnail on the Graphic Styles panel.*

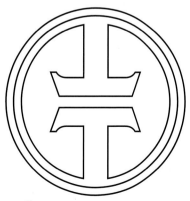

C *The default graphic style has a white fill and a black 1-pt. stroke.*

Applying multiple graphic styles to an object

Instead of letting a graphic style wipe out all the existing attributes on an object, you can add a graphic style to the existing attributes. Styles from the Additive and Additive for Blob Brush libraries must be applied this way, but any other graphic style can also be applied as an additive style.

To add a graphic style to an object's existing attributes:

1. With the Selection tool ▶ (V), click an object to which appearance attributes or a graphic style has been applied, **A** or target the object via the Layers panel.

2. *Optional:* Open the Additive or Additive for Blob Brush graphic styles library or another library (see page 221). The thumbnails for additive styles have a red slash. 🗹

3. On the Graphic Styles panel or on a library panel, Option-click/Alt-click a style thumbnail. **B–C** The new style will be added to the existing attributes.

   Note: If the results are not what you expected, it may be due to the stacking order of attributes on the Appearance panel. For example, a fully opaque fill attribute may be obscuring another fill attribute below it. To change the result, change the opacity and/or blending mode of the attributes that are listed first (see page 378), or restack them. To verify the effect of an attribute, hide and then show it by clicking in the visibility column.

➤ Graphic styles can be applied to symbol instances with the Symbol Styler tool (see page 397).

A *These are the original objects.*

B *We applied the Embossed Blind style (Image Effects library).*

C *And then we added the Drop Shadow style (Additive library) to the existing style.*

Creating graphic styles

There are two ways to create a new graphic style. You can base it on an existing object that contains the desired attributes, or you can duplicate an existing style and then edit the duplicate. The first method will probably feel more natural and intuitive, especially if you want to experiment with various settings for the new style before you create it.

To create a graphic style from an object:

1. Target an object that contains the attributes to be saved as a graphic style. If desired, use the Appearance panel to apply attributes that you want the style to contain, such as effects, additional fills or strokes, or opacity settings.**A**

2. Do either of the following:

   On the Graphic Styles panel,🗃 Option-click/ Alt-click the **New Graphic Style** button,🖽 type a name for the style in the Graphic Style Options dialog, then click OK. The new style will appear as the last thumbnail or listing on the panel.**B–C**

   Drag the thumbnail from the upper left corner of the Appearance panel onto the Graphic Styles panel, or with the Selection tool, drag the object onto the Graphic Styles panel. Double-click the new style swatch, type a name for it, then click OK.

To modify a duplicate graphic style:

1. On the Graphic Styles panel, click the style swatch or name to be duplicated, then click the **New Graphic Style** button.🖽 A numeral will be appended to the style name (e.g., the numeral "1" for the first duplicate of the style).

2. Double-click the duplicate style to open the Graphic Style Options dialog, type a name for the style, then click OK.

3. If you click the duplicate graphic style swatch or name, the attributes it contains will be listed on the Appearance panel. Edit the style by following the steps on the next page.

➤ If you save your favorite graphic styles to a custom library, you'll be able to access and use that library in any document (see page 228).

A *Click an object that contains the attributes to be saved as a graphic style.*

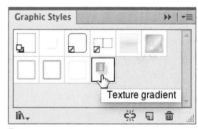

B *The new style appears as the last swatch on the Graphic Styles panel.*

C *We applied our new style to some other objects.*

Redefining graphic styles

Beware! If you redefine a graphic style, your edits will appear in all the objects to which the style is currently linked. If you don't want this to happen, duplicate the style first (see "To modify a duplicate graphic style" on the preceding page), then edit the duplicate.

To redefine a graphic style:

1. Apply the graphic style to be redefined to an object, so you'll be able to preview your edits. Keep the object selected.**A–B**

2. Via the Appearance panel, ⦿ edit the object so it has the attributes you want in the redefined style. Edit or restack the existing appearance attributes, add new attributes, or delete any unwanted ones (see Chapter 14).**C–D** For example, you could apply a different solid color, pattern, or gradient to an existing fill attribute; create an additional fill, stroke, or effect attribute; edit the settings for an existing effect by clicking the effect name; or change the blending mode or opacity via the Opacity link (see Chapter 27).

3. Do any of the following:

   On the Appearance panel menu, choose **Redefine Graphic Style** "[style name]."

   Option-drag/Alt-drag the square from the upper left corner of the Appearance panel over the original swatch on the Graphic Styles panel.

   Option-drag/Alt-drag the selected object onto the original swatch on the Graphic Styles panel.

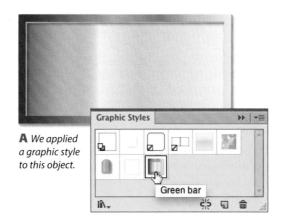

A *We applied a graphic style to this object.*

B *The Appearance panel displays the attributes for the targeted object.*

C *We added the Warp (Rise) effect to the object and a Drop Shadow effect to the upper Stroke listing.*

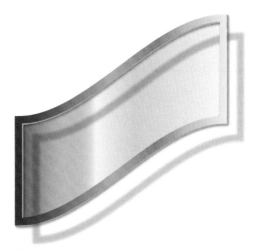

D *This is the object after we edited its style attributes via the Appearance panel.*

Regardless of which method you use, a progress bar may display temporarily, and the style swatch will update to reflect your edits.**A** Any objects to which the style is linked will update automatically.**B**

➤ While editing the settings for a graphic style, be careful not to click other styled objects or graphic style thumbnails, or your current appearance settings will be lost.

Deleting graphic styles from the panel

If you delete a graphic style that's linked to any objects in your document, the attributes from the style will remain on the objects, but of course the link will be broken.

To delete a style from the Graphic Styles panel:

1. Deselect, then on the Graphic Styles panel, click the style to be removed, or Cmd-click/Ctrl-click multiple styles.

2. Click the **Delete Graphic Style** button on the panel.

3. Click Yes in the alert dialog. (If you change your mind, use the Undo command.)

➤ To delete a selected graphic style without an alert dialog opening, Option-click/Alt-click the Delete Graphic Style button or drag the thumbnail to the Delete Graphic Style button.

A *The style updated on the Graphic Styles panel…*

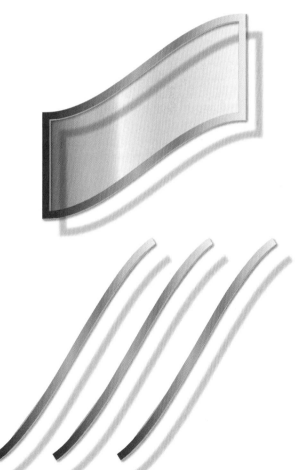

B *… and also updated on all the objects where it was in use.*

Creating a custom graphic styles library

If you save your favorite graphic styles to a custom library, you'll be able to use that library in any document. You can organize and name your libraries in any logical way, such as by theme or by client name.

To create a graphic styles library:

1. Make sure the Graphic Styles panel contains only the styles to be saved in a library.

2. *Optional:* To remove all the styles from the Graphic Styles panel that aren't currently being used in the document, choose Select All Unused from the Graphic Styles panel menu, click the Delete Graphic Style button, 🗑 then click Yes in the alert dialog.

3. From the **Graphic Styles Libraries** menu ᴵⁿ⌄ on the Graphic Styles panel, choose **Save Graphic Styles**.

4. In the Save Graphic Styles as Library dialog, type a name for the library, keep the default location, then click Save.

5. The new library will now be listed on, and can be opened from, the **User Defined** submenu on the Graphic Styles Libraries menu.**A**

Breaking the link to a graphic style

If you break the link between an object and a graphic style, the object won't change visually. However, if you subsequently redefine the style, the style won't update on that object (but it will update on any other objects it's still linked to).

To break the link to a graphic style:

1. Do one of the following:

   With the Selection tool (V), select one or more objects in the document.

   Click the target circle for an object on the Layers panel, or if the style was applied to a group, click the target circle for the group.

2. Do either of the following:

   Click the **Break Link to Graphic Style** button ⊂⌐ at the bottom of the Graphic Styles panel.**B**

   Edit the appearance attributes of the selected item or items (e.g., apply a different fill color, stroke color or setting, pattern, gradient, transparency setting, or effect). Your edits will break the link.

   Note: The graphic style name is no longer listed at the top of the Appearance panel for the selected or targeted object(s).

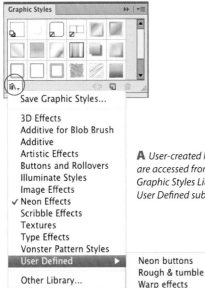

A *User-created libraries are accessed from the Graphic Styles Libraries > User Defined submenu.*

B *Click the Break Link to Graphic Style button on the Graphic Styles panel.*

Using the new Image Trace panel, you can easily convert any digital or scanned photo to editable vector art. The results can range from a close simulation of the shapes and colors in the photo to black-and-white shapes or line **work**. The tracing features do an impressive job, and produce more accurate, cleaner paths and more accurate color than in previous versions of Illustrator. You may still need to do some cleanup or editing work on the resulting vector shapes afterward, but less so than before.

You can use a built-in preset (a set of presaved settings) from the Image Trace panel as a starting point for a tracing and/or choose from a wide array of options. And because traced objects are live, you can also use the panel to refine the results. Among the numerous settings that you can specify are the number of colors used, a color palette, and the precision with which the image is traced.

In this chapter, you will learn how to apply preset and custom tracing settings, as well as create custom tracing presets. After tracing an image, you will use the Expand command to convert the results to editable paths.

Tracing a raster image using a preset

In these steps, you'll trace a raster image using a tracing preset and a few basic controls. Because the results of a tracing are live, you can alter settings on the panel to modify the tracing at any time — even after you close and reopen your document. When you're satisfied with the tracing results, the final step is to convert the tracing to vector paths (see pages 237–238).

To trace a raster image using a tracing preset:

1. With an Illustrator document open, use File > **Place** (with the Link option unchecked) to place a raster image (**A**, next page). It can be a Photoshop EPS, TIFF, JPEG, or PSD image file, or scanned artwork. Note: To learn how to use the Place command, see page 309.

   Note: If the Photoshop Import Options dialog opens, click Flatten Layers to a Single Image to import the image as just one flattened layer.

   ➤ For faster tracing, use an image that has a resolution of 150 ppi or less.

2. Select the image to be traced via the Selection tool ▶ or the Layers panel.

Continued on the following page

17

3. Choose the **Tracing** workspace or open the Image Trace panel. ⚙

4. When you do either of the following, the Preview box is checked automatically:

Click one of the six preset buttons at the top of the panel.

Choose a preset from the **Preset** menu.**B–C**

Note: An alert dialog may appear, informing you that the tracing may proceed slowly. If you want to make it run faster, click Cancel, then reduce the resolution of the image in Photoshop or via Object > Rasterize in Illustrator. Click OK in the alert.

5. A progress bar appears onscreen while Illustrator traces the image, then an "Image Tracing" listing for the traced object appears on the Layers panel.

From the **View** menu, choose an option to view the tracing result, the tracing result with outlines, the source image, or a combination thereof (**A–B**, next page).

6. *Optional:* To change the preset, repeat step 4 (**C–D**, next page).

A *A raster image was placed into an Illustrator document.*

Auto Color High Color Low Color Grayscale Black & White Outline

B *We chose the Low Fidelity Photo preset from the Preset menu on the Image Trace panel.*

C *This is the result.*

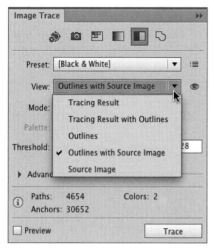

A *Choose a view option for the tracing from the View menu.*

TRACING OPTIONS ON THE CONTROL PANEL

You can also produce a tracing via the Control panel. Select a raster image, then click Image Trace or choose a preset from the Tracing Presets menu. ▼

B *This is Outlines with Source Image view.*

C *We changed the preset to Sketched Art.*

D *This is the result.*

Applying custom tracing settings

Here you will learn how to modify a tracing using custom options on the Image Trace panel, beginning with the options for controlling colors.

To produce a custom tracing:

1. Open a raster image for tracing (see step 1 on page 229).**A**

2. Via the Selection tool ▶ or the Layers panel, select an image object to be traced or an existing tracing.

3. Choose the **Tracing** workspace or open the Image Trace panel. ● On the panel, uncheck Preview.

Choose color settings

1. To control the color of the tracing, from the Mode menu on the Image Trace panel, choose **Color**, **Grayscale**, or **Black and White**.

2. If you chose Color in the preceding step, do one of the following:

   Choose **Automatic** or **Full Tone** from the Palette menu to generate tracing colors from colors in the photo. Use the **Colors** slider or enter a percentage to control the fidelity of the colors — whether they closely (More) or loosely (Less) match the colors in the image (**A–B**, next page).

   Choose **Limited** from the Palette menu to use a very reduced palette of image colors. Use the

Colors slider to set the exact number of colors to appear in the tracing (**A**, page 234).

To control specifically which colors are used for the tracing, create one or more color groups on the Swatches panel, then choose **Document Library** from the Palette menu on the Image Trace panel. If you want to further limit the colors to one color group, click to open the Colors menu, then click a color group (**B**, page 234).

To have Illustrator use colors in a swatch library for the tracing, open a library via the Swatch Libraries menu 🗒▾ on the Swatches panel, then choose the **library name** from the Palette menu on the Image Trace panel.

3. To view your settings in the tracing, click **Trace** or check **Preview**. When the updating is finished, uncheck Preview.

4. If you chose the Mode setting of Grayscale, set the **Grays** value to control how closely each color in the image is matched to one of 256 levels of gray.

   If you chose the Mode setting of Black and White, set the **Threshold** value (the default value is 128). All pixels darker than this value will be converted to black, and all pixels lighter than this value will be converted to white.

Instructions continue on page 235

A *We were curious to see how Illustrator would interpret the bright colors of the cyclist's clothing in this photo, relative to the earthy colors of the dirt and grass.*

RELEASING A TRACING

To restore an Image Tracing to its virgin raster (pretraced) state, select it, then choose Object > Image Trace > Release. The listing on the Layers panel will change from Image Tracing to Image or the file name of the original image.

Use the readout to monitor the current number of Colors in your tracing.

A To have the colors in the tracing closely match those in the photo, we set the Mode menu to Color and the Palette menu to Automatic. Even at a moderate Colors setting of 60, the tracing contains 1,934 colors, enough for a lot of details from the photo to be translated into vector artwork.

B Next, we lowered the Colors value to 8. Although this reduced the number of colors in the tracing significantly, the Palette setting of Automatic preserved the distinct reds and blues in the cyclist's clothing. This version has broader blocks of color and fewer small details than figure **A** (which had a higher Colors setting).

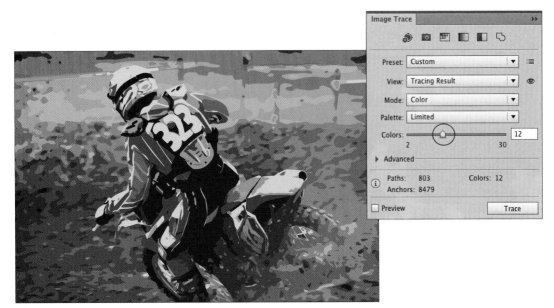

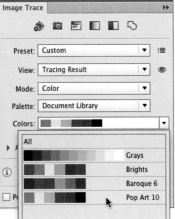

A *For another variation, we tried limiting the colors further by choosing the Palette option of Limited and a Colors value of 12. Although this produced an adequate amount of detail in the dirt track, it eliminated the bright reds and blues in the cyclist's clothing, which are the focal point of the artwork. For this image, these were the least successful settings.*

B *To experiment with a very different color palette, we added a color group from the Art History > Pop Art swatch library to our Swatches panel. On the Image Trace panel, we chose Document Library from the Palette menu, then clicked the Pop Art 10 color group on the Colors menu. The dominant color areas in the photo were redefined using just the six colors in the color group.*

Control the amount of detail

1. If the **Advanced** options aren't showing on the Image Trace panel, click the arrowhead. **A**

2. To control how closely the traced paths follow the edges of shapes in the image, do the following:

   Set the **Paths** percentage to control how closely the tracing translates image details into paths. The lower the Paths value, the fewer paths are generated, and the less precise the detail.

   Set the **Corners** percentage to control the extent to which Illustrator uses corners (More) to define areas in the image versus curves (Less). The higher the Corners value, the more closely the resulting paths will fit details in the image.

   Set the **Noise** value (pixel size) to control the threshold above which small details in the image are traced. The lower the Noise value, the greater the number of resulting paths.

   Click the **Method: Abutting** button to generate adjacent shapes that don't overlap, or click the **Overlapping** button to allow smaller shapes to overlap and be stacked above larger shapes (smaller shapes won't knock out any larger ones below them).

3. To judge your settings thus far, click **Trace** or **Preview** to generate a tracing, then uncheck Preview when the updating process is complete.

4. If the Mode setting is Black and White, you can check Create: **Fills** to produce filled paths and/or **Strokes** to produce stroked paths. If you check Strokes, also specify the maximum **Stroke** width (in pixels) an image area must have to become a stroke; areas wider than this value will become a fill. Also, if you want Illustrator to apply a fill of None to any white areas in the tracing, check Ignore White; those areas will become transparent.

5. *Optional:* Check Snap Curves to Lines to have Illustrator create straight edges from slightly curved lines. (Uncheck this option if small white gaps appear in your tracing.)

6. Check Preview again, and make any needed adjustments to the settings (**A–B**, next page).

7. *Optional:* To save your Image Trace settings as a preset, so you can apply them easily to any image, from the Manage Presets menu, ☰ choose Save as New Preset. In the Save Image Trace Preset dialog, type a name for the preset, then click OK.

Saved presets are available on the Preset menu on the Image Trace and Control panels.

➤ Press and hold the visibility icon 👁 on the Image Trace panel to display just the source image temporarily and hide the tracing.

A *Click the arrowhead to expand the Image Trace panel.*

THE METHOD OPTIONS

➤ If you choose Method: Abutting, expand the tracing (see page 237), then move or delete a shape, the result will be a knockout (blank white) area.

➤ If you choose the Method: Overlapping option, shapes may be stacked on top of one another, depending on the location of shapes that Illustrator detects in the original image. Smaller shapes (generated from small color areas in the image) will be stacked on top of larger shapes (generated from large color areas). If you expand the tracing results, then move or delete one of the smaller shapes, you'll reveal more of the underlying path. If a smaller path is completely within the boundary of a larger path, no knockout will be produced.

A *We reset the Palette menu to Automatic and the Colors value to 60. In the Advanced area, we lowered both the Paths and Corners values to 5%. Even at these reduced settings, the tracing contains plenty of detail. (Compare with figure A on page 233, for which both the Paths and Corners options were set to the default value of 50%.)*

Monitor the number of Paths and Anchors (points) in your tracing via the readouts.

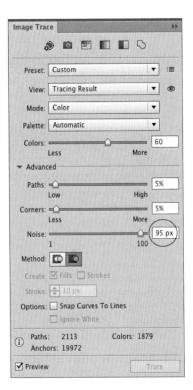

B *Finally, we raised the Noise value to 95 px to eliminate minor extraneous details. We like this tracing version the best because of its loose, hand-painted look (it contains the fewest number of paths, anchor points, and colors, but we don't consider that to be a drawback).*

Expanding a tracing into paths

The Expand command converts a tracing to standard paths, which can then be selected and recolored, reshaped, or transformed like any other paths in Illustrator. Be aware, however, that once a tracing object is expanded, you can no longer change its settings via the Image Trace panel.

To expand and edit the tracing results:

1. Trace a placed image in your document (see pages 229–236).

2. Via the Layers panel, duplicate the Image Tracing object to preserve its live features, and keep the duplicate object selected.

3. On the Control panel, click **Expand**. When the command is done, a group of paths appears on the Layers panel.

4. Deselect. To locate individual paths, turn on View > Smart Guides (with the Object Highlighting option checked in Illustrator/Edit > Preferences > Smart Guides) and pass the Selection tool over areas in the artwork.

5. Click the group, then press Cmd-Shift-G/ Ctrl-Shift-G twice to ungroup it.

6. You can edit the objects any way you like. Here are some suggestions:

   Select or isolate, then recolor or reshape any of the objects.**A**

   To simplify color areas, unite multiple selected paths via the Unite button on the Pathfinder panel (under Shape Modes); see page 362.**B** (See also **A–C**, next page.)

   To delete extraneous paths, select them with the Selection tool, then press Delete/Backspace; or multiple-select their listings on the Layers panel, then click the Delete Selection button. 🗑 Be patient; this can be painstaking work.

➤ To create a color group from the expanded results, select either the whole group or some objects, then click the New Color Group button 📁 on the Swatches panel. In the New Color Group dialog, enter a name, click Selected Artwork, then click OK.

A *After expanding the Image Tracing object, we ungrouped the resulting paths, then deselected them. With the Lasso tool, we selected some of the objects in the upper left area of the artwork.*

B *We clicked the Unite button (Pathfinder panel) to unite the selected objects, then applied a fill color.*

A *We used the Lasso tool and the Unite command to select and combine the expanded objects on the right side of the background, then united the two large objects into one.*

B *Finally, we applied a gradient to the unified background object. Compare this expanded tracing with the original photo, below.*

C *This is the original photo.*

The Live Paint feature provides a novel way to fill paths. To create an "armature" for a Live Paint group, you can either create some open or closed paths with a drawing tool, such as the Pencil or Blob Brush tool, then convert the whole drawing into a Live Paint group,**A** or you can convert a tracing into a Live Paint group and recolor it using Live Paint group features.

With the Live Paint Bucket tool, you simply click or drag across any area that is formed by intersecting lines (called a face),**B** and the current paint attributes are applied. Add to or reshape the Live Paint objects at any time, and the fill color flows into the new shape; that's what makes the whole process "live." Another unique feature of Live Paint groups is that you can recolor (or leave unpainted) individual line segments, called edges.**C** This method for recoloring sketches and tracings is flexible — and fun.

In this chapter, you will learn how to convert ordinary objects to a Live Paint group, apply colors to faces and edges in the group, reshape and move parts of the group, add new faces and edges, and finally, expand or release the group into standard paths.

LIVE PAINT

18

IN THIS CHAPTER

A *We converted this pencil sketch to a Live Paint group.*

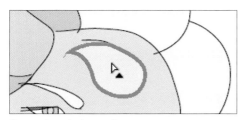

B *We selected a face in the group.*

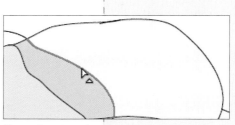

C *We selected an edge.*

Creating a Live Paint group

To create a Live Paint group from your artwork, you can either click on paths with the Live Paint Bucket tool or choose the Live Paint command. Both methods preserve only the basic fill and stroke settings. Other attributes, such as transparency settings, brush strokes, and effects, are removed.

When drawing paths for a Live Paint group, you must allow your drawing lines to intersect, because the Live Paint Bucket tool, which you'll use to color areas of the group, detects and fills only faces (areas that are bounded by intersecting lines).

To create a Live Paint group:

1. Draw some open or closed paths, such as with the Pencil, Blob Brush, Pen, Line Segment, or Ellipse tool, and apply stroke colors and weights. You may use the Paintbrush tool, but the Live Paint command will remove the brush stroke. As you create the sketch, be sure to let some or all of the segments intersect.**A**

2. Select all the paths.

3. Do either of the following:

   Choose the **Live Paint Bucket** tool (K), then click one of the selected objects.**B**

   Choose Object > **Live Paint** > **Make** (Cmd-Option-X/Ctrl-Alt-X).

   If an alert appears regarding object features that may be discarded, click OK. On the Layers panel, the paths will be nested within a Live Paint group.

   Note: If an alert illustrating the steps to create a Live Paint group appears, click OK. Make sure the objects are selected, then follow step 3 again.

➤ To produce a Live Paint group from a symbol or a blend, you must apply Object > Expand first; to produce a Live Paint group from a clipping set, release the set first; or to produce a Live Paint group from type, convert it to outlines via Type > Create Outlines first.

➤ Some Illustrator commands aren't available for Live Paint groups, such as the Clipping Mask, Pathfinder, and Select > Same commands.

A *As you draw a picture, allow your line segments to intersect. This portrait was drawn with the Pencil tool.*

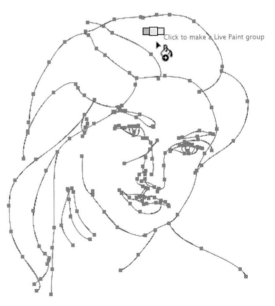

B *Click one of the selected paths or enclosed areas with the Live Paint Bucket tool to convert all of them to a Live Paint group.*

Using the Live Paint Bucket tool

On the next page, you'll learn how to use the Live Paint Bucket tool to recolor a Live Paint group. Before doing so, use the Live Paint Bucket Options dialog to choose settings for the tool.

To choose options for the Live Paint Bucket tool:

1. Do either of the following:

   Double-click the **Live Paint Bucket** tool 🖌️ (K).

   Select the Live Paint Bucket tool (K), then press Return/Enter.

2. The Live Paint Bucket Options dialog opens.**A** In the Options area:

   Click **Paint Fills** and/or **Paint Strokes**, depending on what parts of the group you want the tool to paint. Note: If you're going to recolor faces as described on the next page, check only Paint Fills.

   ➤ If you check just one of these options, you can Shift-click with the tool to switch its function between painting fills (faces) and applying stroke (edge) colors and weights. We actually find this to be the easiest method, because when the tool has only one function, you can't inadvertently recolor a face when you meant to recolor an edge, or vice versa.

   ➤ If you check both Paint options, you can hold down Shift to restrict the tool function to Paint Fills.

   Check **Cursor Swatch Preview** to display, in a tiny strip above the tool pointer, the current color (when using the Color panel), or the color of the last chosen swatch on the Swatches panel and the swatch to its left and right.**B–C** We find this option to be useful.

3. *Optional:* If the current highlight color is too similar to colors in your artwork (or colors you're likely to apply), check Highlight, then, from the Color menu, choose a preset color for the faces and edges the tool will pass over, or click the color swatch and choose a color from the Colors dialog. You can also change the Width for the highlight.

4. Click OK. Now you're ready to use the tool, which we give instructions for on the next page.

   ➤ Choose a different highlight color for the Live Paint Bucket than for the Live Paint Selection tool (by default, they're different).

A *Use the Live Paint Bucket Options dialog to establish default settings for the tool.*

B *If the Cursor Swatch Preview option is on for the Live Paint Bucket tool and you mix a color via the Color panel, that color will display above the tool icon.*

C *If the Cursor Swatch Preview option is on for the Live Paint Bucket tool and you click a swatch on the Swatches panel, that color as well as the previous and next swatches in the Swatches panel will display above the pointer.*

When you apply fill or stroke attributes to a Live Paint group, faces or edges are recolored, but not the actual paths. If you reshape a Live Paint group in any way, such as by editing the paths, colors in the group will reflow instantly into any new or reshaped faces. In the steps below, you will recolor faces with the Live Paint Bucket tool. This technique reminds us of a drawing method we used as kids: We would draw a big swirly doodle on a piece of paper, then color in the shapes. It's so much faster in Illustrator!

Note: You can apply a solid color, pattern, or gradient to faces and edges in a Live Paint group. The term "color" in this chapter is a generic reference to all three kinds of swatches.

To recolor faces with the Live Paint Bucket tool:

1. Have a Live Paint group at the ready (you don't need to select it).**A** Double-click the **Live Paint Bucket** tool to open the Live Paint Bucket Options dialog. Check Paint Fills, uncheck Paint Strokes, then click OK.

2. Organize some colors on the Swatches panel to be used for recoloring, preferably in color groups. You can use the Recolor Artwork, Color Guide, or Kuler panel to create color groups.

3. Click the Fill color square on the Tools or Color panel, then click a swatch or color group icon on the Swatches panel. If the Cursor Swatch Preview option is checked in the tool options dialog, as we recommended, the currently selected swatch will display as the middle color above the pointer.

   ➤ Press the left or right arrow key to cycle through the previous or next swatches on the Swatches panel.

4. Do either of the following:

   Move the pointer over a face that you want to recolor (an area where two or more paths intersect), then click in the highlighted face.**B**

   Drag across multiple faces.

   ➤ Hold down Option/Alt to turn the Live Paint Bucket tool into a temporary Eyedropper tool, and use it to sample (by clicking) a fill color anywhere in your document.

A *This Live Paint group was created from lines that were drawn with the Pencil tool.*

B *When the Live Paint Bucket tool is clicked on a face (an area where paths intersect) in a Live Paint group, the current fill color is applied (**B**, next page, shows this face filled in).*

"FLOODING" FACES

➤ Double-click a face with the Live Paint Bucket tool to fill contiguous faces across all edges that have a stroke of None.

➤ Triple-click a face to recolor all faces that already have the same color as the one you click, whether they're contiguous or not.

You can also use the Live Paint Bucket tool to apply stroke colors and/or stroke settings. Each edge can have a different color, weight, and other stroke attributes, or a color of None. A unique feature of Live Paint groups is that only the edges you click are modified — not the whole path.

To modify edges with the Live Paint Bucket tool:

1. Choose the **Live Paint Bucket** tool, 🪣 and establish the same default settings as in step 1 on the preceding page.

2. Click the Stroke color square on the Tools or Color panel, then choose a stroke color. Also choose a stroke weight and other attributes via the Stroke panel, which you can access via the link on the Control or Appearance panel. Or choose a color of None if you want the edges you click to be "hidden."

3. Do either or both of the following:

   Hold down Shift to toggle the tool function to Paint Strokes (it becomes a brush icon), then click the tip of the brush on an edge.**A–C**

   Starting with the tip of the brush positioned over an edge, Shift-drag across or along multiple edges.

➤ Note that the highlight on edges is thinner than the highlight on faces.

➤ You can also recolor a Live Paint group by using the Recolor Artwork dialog (see Chapter 29).

➤ You can apply transparency settings, brush strokes, and effects to an entire Live Paint group, but not to individual faces or edges. To apply a brush, drag it from the Brushes panel over a Live Paint group.

"FLOODING" EDGES

➤ Double-click an edge with the Live Paint Bucket tool to apply the current stroke color and attributes to all edges that are connected to, and have the same stroke color and weight as, the one you click.

➤ Triple-click an edge to apply the current stroke color and attributes to all edges that have the same attributes as the one you click, both contiguous and not.

A *We are applying stroke attributes to an edge with the Live Paint Bucket tool.*

B *To create more fillable faces, we drew additional paths on the neck, lips, and face.*

C *We used the Live Paint Bucket tool to fill the new faces, and also applied a stroke of None to some edges on the neck, cheeks, and forehead.*

Using the Live Paint Selection tool

With the Live Paint Selection tool, you can select edges and/or faces in a Live Paint group for editing or deletion. Choose options for the tool first.

To choose options for the Live Paint Selection tool:

1. Choose the **Live Paint Selection** tool 🔲 (Shift-L), then press Return/Enter (or double-click the tool).

2. In the Live Paint Selection Options dialog, check **Select Fills** and/or **Select Strokes.A** For example, if you want to select only faces, uncheck Select Strokes to prevent any edges from becoming selected. You can also choose a different Highlight Color and/or Width for the selections (it should be a different highlight color than for the Live Paint Bucket tool). Click OK.

To recolor or delete faces or edges with the Live Paint Selection tool:

1. Choose the **Live Paint Selection** tool 🔲 (Shift-L), and choose options for the tool (see the steps above).

2. Click an edge or face in a Live Paint group (depending on the current tool setting), then Shift-click additional edges and/or faces.**B** The selection displays as a gray pattern. If you need to deselect an individual edge or face, Shift-click it.

3. Do any of the following:

   For **faces**, click the Fill color square on the Tools or Color panel, then choose a solid color,**C** gradient, or pattern. You can modify a gradient fill with the Gradient tool (see pages 351–352).

   For **edges**, click the Stroke color square on the Tools or Color panel, then choose a color. You can also change the stroke weight and other stroke attributes. Apply a stroke of None to any edges that you want to hide.

   To **delete** the currently selected edges or faces, press Delete/Backspace.

   ➤ Press Cmd-H/Ctrl-H to hide or show the gray selection overlay.

4. Click outside the Live Paint group to deselect it.

➤ Select a face and/or an edge with the Live Paint Selection tool, then choose Select > Same > Fill Color, Stroke Color, or Stroke Weight to quickly select all the other faces and/or edges in the group that have matching attributes.

A Use this dialog to control what parts of a Live Paint group the tool may select or to change the highlight color for its selections.

B *We selected three sections of the woman's hair with the Live Paint Selection tool.*

C *We applied a new fill color to the selected faces.*

COMPARE A LIVE PAINT GROUP CREATED FROM PENCIL TOOL STROKES ...

A *When we drew a series of separate paths with the Pencil tool, we made sure the endpoints of each path overlapped another path, in order to create closed areas.*

B *With the Live Paint Bucket tool, we applied fill colors to the faces and stroke colors to individual edges. The fact that we were able to apply a different stroke color to each separate former Pencil tool path proves that those paths became separate edges when they were converted to a Live Paint group.*

...WITH A LIVE PAINT GROUP CREATED FROM BLOB BRUSH TOOL STROKES

C *We used the Blob Brush tool to create a series of separate strokes, which we connected with other strokes in order to create closed areas (faces). In this case, the result is one continuous closed path.*

➤ *When drawing Pencil or Blob Brush artwork for a Live Paint group, avoid drawing lines that may be hidden behind other shapes, which could produce extraneous faces in the resulting group.*

D *With the Live Paint Bucket tool, we applied fill colors to faces, including one fill color to the entire former Blob Brush stroke outline. Because the Blob Brush drawing converted to just faces, we were able to apply stroke colors only to the entire perimeter of a face (orange to the outer edge of the stroke outline and yellow to the edge of the blue-green face). There are no separate edges to recolor or delete, as there are in figure **B**, above.*

Reshaping a Live Paint group

In this task, you will transform or move whole faces in a Live Paint group or manipulate the anchor points on individual edges. Colors will reflow automatically into the newly modified shapes.

To reshape or move areas in a Live Paint group:

1. Choose the **Selection** tool (V), and make sure the Bounding Box feature is on (View menu).

2. Isolate a Live Paint group by double-clicking a face or edge in the group.

3. Do either or both of the following:

   With the **Selection** tool (V), either click a face that contains a fill color or click an edge. A bounding box displays, with star-filled selection handles. Drag the face or edge to move it, or drag a handle on an edge to transform it (see page 147).**A–B** If you want to delete the current selection, press Delete/Backspace.

   With the **Direct Selection** tool (A), click an edge to display its anchor points and direction handles, then reshape it by manipulating the points and handles or by using the Anchor Point tool (see Chapter 12).

   Fill colors will reflow automatically into any areas you reshape or transform (unless the Live Paint group was created exclusively from Blob Brush strokes).

4. To exit isolation mode, press Esc.

➤ To switch quickly between the Direct Selection tool for reshaping and the Live Paint Bucket tool for recoloring, press A for the former or K for the latter.

A *We selected an edge in a Live Paint group with the Selection tool, then lengthened it to make it intersect with another edge; this produced a new face.*

B *With the Live Paint Bucket tool, we applied a fill color to the new face.*

Adding new faces and edges to a Live Paint group

To add new faces and edges to a Live Paint group:

Method 1 (via the Layers or Control panel)

1. Draw a new path on top of or next to a Live Paint group, or select an existing path.

2. Do either of the following:

   On the Layers panel, drag the new path listing into the **Live Paint Group** listing.

   Choose the Selection tool (V), marquee both the new path and the Live Paint group, then click **Merge Live Paint** on the Control panel. Click OK if an alert dialog appears.

Method 2 (in isolation mode)

1. Choose the Selection tool (V), then double-click the Live Paint group to put it in isolation mode.

2. With a drawing tool, such as the Pencil or Blob Brush, or a geometric tool, such as the Rectangle or Ellipse, draw the path to be added.**A** It will automatically become part of the Live Paint group.

3. To exit isolation mode, press Esc.**B–C**

➤ With a Live Paint group in isolation mode, if you create a new closed face then drag it over filled faces in the group, release the mouse, and then move the new face away from the group, any of the following may happen: Some faces may adopt the fill color of another face in the group, some faces may adopt the color of the new face, or the new face may be filled with an existing color from the group. If you don't like a result, undo it immediately.

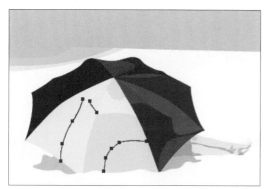

A *With the Live Paint group in isolation mode, we drew paths with the Pencil tool to create some new faces (then we exited isolation mode).*

B *We used the Live Paint Bucket tool to apply fill colors to the new faces.*

C *This is the final artwork.*

Choosing gap options for a Live Paint group

Normally, if you reshape an edge so as to create an opening (called a "gap") in a formerly closed area (face), any fill color in that face will leak or disappear, because in the world of Live Paint, fill colors can't be applied to open faces. Via the Gap Options dialog, you can specify a gap size setting that will stop fill colors from disappearing or leaking into other faces.

To choose gap options for a Live Paint group:

1. Choose the Selection tool (V), then click the Live Paint group that you want to choose options for.

2. Click the **Gap Options** button 📧 on the Control panel. The Gap Options dialog opens.**A**

3. Check Preview, then do any of the following:

   Check **Gap Detection**, then to specify a gap size up to which the fill colors won't leak or disappear, from the **Paint Stops At** menu, choose Small Gaps, Medium Gaps, or Large Gaps, or choose Custom and an exact gap size.**B** The dialog lists the current number of Gaps Found in the artwork, based on the Paint Stops At setting.

   From the **Gap Preview Color** menu, choose a preview color for the invisible (and nonprinting) lines that Illustrator uses to bridge the gaps and prevent paint leakage (or click the color swatch and choose a color via the Colors dialog).

   ➤ The gap lines display in a selected Live Paint group when View > Show Live Paint Gaps is on or while the Gap Options dialog is open.

   Click the **Close Gaps with Paths** button to have Illustrator close up any existing gaps with edge segments (click Yes if an alert dialog appears). This may improve the processing time for further edits you make to the group.

4. Click OK. If you increased the gap size, try using the Live Paint Bucket tool to fill areas that couldn't be filled before.**C** Fill colors will still leak or disappear from open faces that have gaps larger than the current Paint Stops At value.

   ➤ The more you allow lines to intersect in the original objects, the fewer gaps will result when the objects are converted to a Live Paint group. If you want to eliminate any overhanging edges, select them with the Live Paint Selection tool and delete them (or apply a stroke of None to hide them).

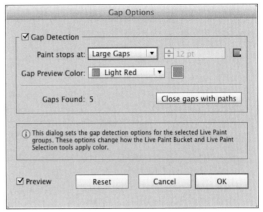

A *Choose gap options to control color leakage in a Live Paint group.*

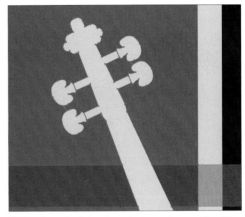

B *We chose the Paint Stops At: Large Gaps option. The gaps are previewing in the current Gap Preview Color.*

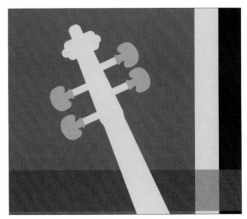

C *With the Large Gaps option chosen, we were able to fill faces that had small to medium-sized gaps.*

Expanding and releasing Live Paint groups

You can't apply appearance attributes (such as brush strokes, transparency settings, or effects) to individual parts of a Live Paint group; you would have to expand or release it into ordinary Illustrator objects first. A Live Paint group may also need to be expanded or released before it can be exported to a non-Adobe application. Use these commands only when you're sure you're done editing the group.

To expand or release a Live Paint group:

1. Using the Selection tool or the Layers panel, select a Live Paint group. *Optional:* To preserve a copy of

the group for future edits, Option-drag/Alt-drag its selection square to a new layer, then hide the copy.

2. Do either of the following:

    On the Control panel, click **Expand** to convert the Live Paint group into two groups of standard paths nested together within a group.**A** One group will contain filled paths made from the former faces;**B** the other group will contain paths with stroke colors made from the former edges.

    Choose Object > Live Paint > **Release** to convert the Live Paint group to separate paths, each with a .5-pt. black stroke and a fill of None, within one group. Use this option if, say, you want to start your sketch over with just line work, and you want to remove all the fill colors first.

➤ After applying the Expand or Release command, you can apply stroke or fill attributes, such as a brush stroke or an effect, to the resulting paths.**C**

A *The Expand command produced two nested groups.*

B *After expanding the Live Paint group, we hid the <Group> layer containing the stroked paths. Now only the filled paths are visible.*

C *Finally, we applied a .3-pt. brush stroke to the group of stroked paths to make the line work look more hand drawn.*

EXPANDING A LIVE PAINT GROUP: THE RESULTS FROM FORMER PENCIL PATHS COMPARED WITH FORMER BLOB BRUSH STROKES

Group of paths, with stroke colors

Group of paths, with fill colors

Group of paths, with stroke colors

Group of paths, with fill colors

When we applied the Expand command to a Live Paint group that we created from Pencil tool strokes, the result was two standard nested groups: one containing stroked paths (from the former edges) and the other containing filled paths (from the former faces).

When we applied the Expand command to a Live Paint group that we created from Blob Brush tool strokes, the result was also two nested groups: one containing the former faces, now filled paths, and the other containing only two stroked paths (because we had applied a color to only two edges in the Live Paint group).

The type controls in Illustrator are extensive, and worthy of the two chapters that we have devoted to them. You will create three kinds of type in this chapter: point type, area type (inside an object), and type along a path. You will also copy type between objects, import type from another application, thread overflow type between objects, convert point type to area type (and vice versa), rotate type, and put type on a circle. In the next chapter, you will learn how to select type and change its attributes.

The type tools

There are three horizontal type tools: the Type tool, Area Type tool, and Type on a Path tool; and three vertical type tools: the Vertical Type tool, Vertical Area Type tool, and Vertical Type on a Path tool. With the exception of the versatile Type and Vertical Type tools, each tool has a specialized function.

➤ With the **Type** tool, $\mathbf{T}$ you can create a free-floating block of type that isn't associated with a path,**A** draw a rectangle with the tool and enter type inside the rectangle, enter type along the edge of an open path, or enter type inside a closed path.

➤ The **Area Type** tool $\boxed{\text{T}}$ creates type inside an open or closed path. The lines of type that are created with this tool automatically wrap inside the path.**B**

➤ The **Type on a Path** tool $\diagdown$ creates a line of type along the outer edge of an open or closed path.**C**

➤ The **Vertical Type** tool $\downarrow\mathbf{T}$ has the same function as the Type tool, except that it creates vertical type.

➤ The **Vertical Area Type** tool $\boxed{\text{↓T}}$ creates vertical type inside an open or closed path.

➤ The **Vertical Type on a Path** tool $\diagdown$ creates vertical type along the outer edge of an open or closed path.**D**

The Type tool creates point type or type inside a rectangle.   **A** *Type tool*

The Area Type tool enters type into a path of any shape. The Area Type tool enters type into a path of any shape. The Area Type tool enters type into a path of any shape. The Area Type type tool enters type into a path of any shape. The Area Type type tool enters type into
B *Area Type tool*

The Type on a Path tool enters type along a path.
C *Type on a Path tool*

T
H
E
V
E
R
T
I
C
A
L
T
Y
P
E
P
A
T
H

D *Vertical Type on a Path tool*

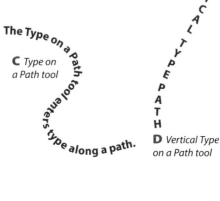

CREATE TYPE

19

Choosing a font and font size for a type tool

In the next chapter, we'll show you how to use the extensive typographic controls in Illustrator to change the attributes of existing type. Here we offer the basic steps for choosing a font family and font size for the type tools that you will use in this chapter.

To choose two basic attributes for a type tool:

1. Choose the Type T (T), Area Type, T Type on a Path, Vertical Type, T Vertical Area Type, T or Vertical Type on a Path tool.

2. Do either or both of the following:

   On the Control panel, **A** choose a font family from the **Font** menu and a style from the **Font Style** menu.

   On the Control panel, enter the desired size in the **Font Size** field (you don't need to reenter the unit of measure), or choose a preset size from the Font Size menu, or click the up or down arrow.

IS IT POINT TYPE OR AREA TYPE?

To distinguish between a point type object and an area type object, look for these clues:

➤ As you enter point type, the only way to produce line breaks is by pressing Return/Enter, whereas when you enter area type, Illustrator creates line breaks automatically to fit the type within the object.

➤ If the View > Bounding Box feature is on and you select a point type object with the Selection tool, the annotator on the right side of the object is hollow, whereas if you select an area type object with the same tool, the annotator is filled (see page 262).

➤ If you scale a point type object, the type also scales, whereas if you scale an area type object, the object scales but the type does not.

| Character: | 🔍 Myriad Pro | ▼ | Bold | ▼ | 12 pt | ▼ |

A From the menus on the Control panel, choose a Font Family, Font Style, and Font Size.

I don't know the key to success, but the key to failure is trying to please everybody.

— Bill Cosby

B This point type was created with the Type tool.

Creating point type

Point type stands by itself — it's neither inside an object nor along a path. This kind of type is most suitable for short passages, such as headlines, titles, or labels for Web buttons. For point type, line breaks are created manually.

To create point type:

1. Choose the **Type** tool T (T) or **Vertical Type** T tool.

2. Choose a font family, font style, and font size (see the steps at left).

3. Click a blank area of an artboard where you want the type to start (don't click an object). A flashing insertion marker appears.

4. *Optional:* By default, Illustrator applies a fill color of black and a stroke color of None to the characters in a new type object. If desired, before you begin to type characters, you can choose a different fill color. If the Stroke square happens to be selected and set to a color of None when you choose your type tool, Illustrator will select the Fill square automatically.

5. Enter type. Press Return/Enter to start a new line.

6. To complete the type object, do any of the following: **B**

   Click a selection tool on the Tools panel (don't use the tool shortcut), then click outside the type block to deselect it.

   Press the Esc key. This will automatically activate the Selection tool and highlight the text. ★

   To keep the type tool selected (so you can continue using it), either click the type tool or Cmd-click/Ctrl-click outside the type block to deselect it (the shortcut gives you a temporary selection tool).

➤ To recolor type, see the sidebar on page 271.

➤ To align multiple separate blocks of point type, use the align buttons on the Control panel or the Align panel (see pages 107–108).

INSERTING AND DELETING CHARACTERS

➤ To add characters to an existing type object, choose a type tool, click to create an insertion point, then type.

➤ To delete one character at a time, choose a type tool, click to the right of the character to be deleted, then press Delete/Backspace. Or to delete multiple characters, select them with a type tool before pressing Delete/Backspace.

Creating area type

In this task, you'll draw a rectangle, then enter type inside it. The type will wrap within the edges of the object automatically. On the next page, you'll learn how to enter type inside an existing object of any shape.

To create type in a rectangle:

1. Choose the **Type** tool 𝕋 (T) or **Vertical Type** ↓𝕋 tool.

2. Choose a font family, font style, and font size (see the preceding page).

3. Drag to create a rectangle. When you release the mouse, a flashing insertion marker will appear. *Optional:* Change the fill color.

4. Enter type.**A** The type will wrap automatically to fit into the rectangle. Press Return/Enter only when you need to create a new paragraph.

5. Do any of the following:

   Choose a selection tool on the Tools panel (don't use a keyboard shortcut to select the tool), then click outside the type block to deselect it.

   Press the Esc key on your keyboard to make the Selection tool active. ★

   To keep the type tool selected (so you can continue using it), either click the type tool or Cmd-click/Ctrl-click outside the type block to deselect it.

   Note: An Out port (overflow symbol) ⊞ on the edge of a type rectangle indicates that the rectangle isn't large enough to display all the type. If you want to reveal the hidden type, click the object with the Selection tool, then drag a handle on its bounding box (View > Show Bounding Box). The type will reflow to fit the new shape. A second option is to reshape the object with the Direct Selection tool.**B** A third option is to thread the overflow type into another object, as described on page 260.

   ➤ To recolor type or a type object, see the sidebar on page 271.

   ➤ If you drag to define an area with the Vertical Type tool before entering type, the type will flow from top to bottom and from right to left.

   ➤ If you click in your document with a type tool unintentionally, an empty type object will be created, which you can delete via the Layers panel. To delete the results of all such clicks, choose Object > Path > Clean Up. In the dialog, check just the Empty Text Paths option, then click OK.

It spoils people's clothes to squeeze under a gate; the proper way to get in, is to climb down a pear tree.

— *Beatrix Potter*

A *Drag with the Type tool to create a rectangle, then enter type. To reveal the edges of the rectangle, either display the document in Outline view or use the Object Highlighting feature of Smart Guides.*

It spoils
people's
clothes to
squeeze
under a
gate; the
proper
way to
get in,
is to climb
down a
pear tree.

B *We reshaped the type rectangle with the Direct Selection tool.*

USING A TEMPORARY HAND TOOL WHILE EDITING TEXT

To access a temporary Hand tool when a type tool is selected and your pointer is in text-editing mode, hold down Option/Alt and drag the document in the window. Release Option/Alt to resume text editing. Note: Don't use the Spacebar to access the Hand tool, or you'll add spaces to your text (or replace selected text with spaces) instead of moving the document in its window. (The Option/Alt shortcut replaces the former — cumbersome — Cmd/Ctrl and Spacebar combo.)

➤ When editing type, keep track of the pointer location. If the pointer is in a panel field, you will edit the panel values instead of the type characters.

When you use the Area Type or Vertical Area Type tool to place type inside a path of any shape or inside an open path, the object is converted to a type object. The type will wrap within the edges of the object automatically.

To enter type inside an existing object:

1. *Optional:* Once you place type inside or along a graphic object, it becomes a type object permanently. To preserve a copy of the original graphic object, hold down Option/Alt and drag its selection square upward or downward on the Layers panel.

2. To enter type inside a closed path, choose the **Area Type**, 🔲 **Vertical Area Type**, 🔲 **Type** 🅣 (T), or **Vertical Type** 🅣 tool; or to enter type inside an open path, choose either one of the Area Type tools.

3. Choose a font family, font style, and font size (see page 252).

4. Click precisely on the edge of a path. A flashing insertion marker appears, and any fill, stroke, or brush stroke on the object is removed. The former path object is now a type object. *Optional:* Change the fill color.

5. Enter type inside the path, or copy and paste some type from a text-editing application into the path. The type will wrap within the object.**A–B** Note that the Layers panel is now listing the first few words in the type object instead of the path.

   ➤ To make the type fit symmetrically within the object, give it a relatively small point size. Also, on the Paragraph panel, check Hyphenate and click either the Align Center button or one of the Justify alignment buttons (see page 282).

6. Do either of the following:

   Choose a selection tool, or simply press Esc, then click outside the type object to deselect it.

   To keep the type tool selected (so you can continue using it), Cmd-click/Ctrl-click away from the type block to deselect it.

   ➤ To adjust the spacing between area type and the object that contains it, see the next page.

   ➤ To recolor type or a type object, see the sidebar on page 271.

   ➤ Type can't be entered into a compound path, an object in a clipping mask, a mesh object, or a blend.

   ➤ When you edit area type in Illustrator CC, it updates more quickly than in prior versions of Illustrator.

COLORING A TYPE OBJECT

When you enter type inside an object or along a path, a fill and a stroke of None are applied to the object automatically. If you want to apply colors to the object, deselect it, click its edge with the Direct Selection tool (you can locate it via the object highlighting feature of Smart Guides), then apply the desired fill and/or stroke colors.

This is text in a copy of a light bulb shape. You can use the Area Type tool to place type into any shape you can create. When fitting type into a round shape, place small words at the top and the bottom. This is text in a copy of a light bulb shape. You can use the Area Type tool to place type into any

A *Area type*

The kiss of memory made pictures of love and light against the wall. Here was peace. She pulled in her horizon like a great fish-net. Pulled it from around the waist of the world and draped it over her shoulder. So much of life in its meshes! She called in her soul to come and see.
ZORA NEALE HURSTON

B *Type in a circle*

To adjust the spacing between area type and the edge of its object, change the Inset Spacing value in the Area Type Options dialog. To reposition the first line of type, change the First Baseline value.

To choose Inset Spacing and First Baseline options for area type:

1. Select an area type object with a selection tool, a type tool, or the Layers panel.**A**

2. Choose Type > **Area Type Options**. In the Area Type Options dialog,**B** check Preview.

3. In the Offset area, choose an **Inset Spacing** value to adjust the spacing between the type and the type object.**C**

4. To control the distance between the first line of type and the top of the object (or the current inset, if the Inset Spacing value is greater than 0), choose a **First Baseline** option (try Ascent or Cap Height, or for the most control, use the Fixed option):

   Ascent to have the top of the tallest characters in the line touch the top of the object.

   Cap Height to have the top of uppercase letters touch the top of the object.

Leading to make the distance between the first baseline of text and the top of the object equal to the leading value of the type.

x Height to have the top of the "x" character in the current font sit flush with the top of the object.

Em Box Height to have the top of the em box in an Asian font touch the top of the object.

Fixed, then enter a Min (minimum) value for the location of the baseline of the first line of text.

Legacy to use the method from previous versions of Illustrator.

Note: If you choose a Min (minimum baseline offset) value above 0, Illustrator will use either that value or the current First Baseline value, whichever is greater.

5. Click OK.

➤ You can select an area type object and then reopen the Area Type Options dialog to view or edit the current settings.

A The type is touching the edges of this object.

C Now this area type object has an Inset Spacing value of 6 pt. The type looks better with some "breathing room" around it.

B We used the Inset Spacing control in the Area Type Options dialog to adjust the spacing between the type and the edge of the object.

Creating path type

Follow these steps to place type in a single line along the inner or outer edge of a path.

To place type along an object's path:

1. Do either of the following (the path doesn't have to be selected):

   Choose the **Type on a Path** or **Vertical Type on a Path** tool, choose a font family, font style, and font size (see page 252), then click the edge of an open or closed path.**A**

   Choose the **Type** or **Vertical Type** tool, choose a font family, font style, and font size (see page 252). Click an open path, or hold down Option/Alt and click the edge of a closed path.

2. The flashing insertion marker appears. If desired, change the fill color. Enter type, without pressing Return/Enter. The type will appear along the edge of the object. The object now has a fill and stroke of None, and any brush stroke was removed.**B**

3. Do either of the following:

   Choose a selection tool, or simply press Esc, then click outside the type object to deselect it.

   To keep the type tool selected (so you can continue using it), hold down Cmd/Ctrl and click outside the type object.

To reposition type on a path:

1. Choose the **Selection** tool or **Direct Selection** tool.

2. Click the type (not the path). Center, left, and right brackets appear.**C**

3. As you do any of the following, be sure to drag the bracket (the vertical bar) — not the little square. If your tool switches to a type tool, choose a selection tool and try again.

   To reposition the type block along the path, drag the center bracket to the left or right.

   To reposition the starting point of the type on the path, drag the left bracket.**D–E** You could also drag the right bracket back across the existing type (this will shorten the amount of type that's visible on the path and may produce a type overflow). For right-aligned type, do the opposite of the above.

   To flip the type to the opposite side of the path, drag the center bracket perpendicularly across the path (see also the Flip option on the next page).

B *This is vertical type on a path.*

A *To help prevent the letters from scrunching together when adding horizontal type to a path, use an object that has gentle curves rather than sharp corners.*

The icons shown below appear next to the pointer when it's moved over a bracket on a selected type path.

C *A left, center, and right bracket will display for path type when it's selected with the Selection or Direct Selection tool.*

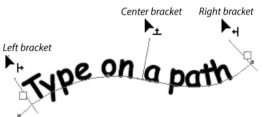

D *We dragged the left bracket to the right.*

E *We released the mouse.*

A *Use the Type on a Path Options dialog to apply a type effect.*

Via the Type on a Path Options dialog, you can quickly change the shape, orientation, and alignment of type on a path. The more curvy the path, the more obvious the changes. The dialog settings are editable and reversible.

To apply options to path type:

1. Do either of the following:

   Choose the Selection tool, ⬉ then click the type on a path.

   On the Layers panel, click the selection area for a path type object.

2. Choose Type > Type on a Path > **Type on a Path Options**. Check Preview in the dialog.**A**

3. Do any of the following:

   From the **Effect** menu, choose Rainbow, Skew, 3D Ribbon, Stair Step, or Gravity.**B**

   Choose **Align to Path**: Ascender, Descender, Center, or Baseline (the default setting) to control which part of the type touches the path.**C**

   Check (or uncheck) **Flip**.

   Choose a positive or negative letter **Spacing** value. Change this value in small increments at first.

4. Click OK. To change or reverse any of the option settings at any time, reselect the object and reopen the dialog.

➤ To shift type upward or downward from its baseline by a specific value, see page 290. To adjust the spacing between a pair of characters, see page 276.

➤ The type effects can also be applied individually via the Type > Type on a Path submenu.

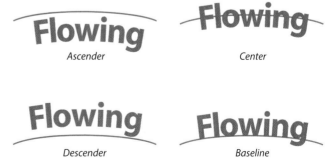

B *The Effect choices in the Type on a Path Options dialog change the shape and spacing of characters on a path.*

C *The Align to Path options affect the position of the baseline of path type relative to the path.*

Copying or moving type characters

To copy or move type from one object to another:

1. Choose the **Type** tool T (T) or **Vertical Type** T tool.

2. Do either of the following:

   Select (drag across) the type characters to be moved.

   To move all the type from one or more threaded objects, click in one of the objects, then choose Select > **All** (Cmd-A/Ctrl-A).

3. Do either of the following:

   Choose Edit > **Cut** (Cmd-X/Ctrl-X).**A**

   Choose Edit > **Copy** (Cmd-C/Ctrl-C).

4. To create a text insertion point in an object, do one of the following (for the first three options, the object doesn't have to be selected):

   To put the type into an existing closed path (area type), click the edge of the object.

   To put the type along the outside of a closed path (path type), hold down Option/Alt and click the edge of the object.

   To put the type along an open path (path type), click the edge of the object.**B**

   To create a new type rectangle to contain the type, hold down Cmd/Ctrl and click a blank area of the artwork to deselect, then drag to create a rectangle.

5. Choose Edit > **Paste** (Cmd-V/Ctrl-V).**C**

Let us spend one day as deliberately as Nature. Let us spend one day as deliberately as Nature, and not be thrown off the track by every nutshell and mosquito's wing that falls on the rails.

A *We selected type, then chose Edit > Cut to put it onto the Clipboard.*

B *We clicked a path.*

C *We pressed Cmd-V/Ctrl-V. The contents of the Clipboard appeared on the path.*

COPYING A WHOLE TYPE OBJECT

➤ To copy a type object within the same document, use any method you would use to copy a path object: Option/Alt drag the object with the Selection tool, or Option/Alt drag the object's selection square upward or downward on the Layers panel (for the latter method, move the copy away from the original afterward).

➤ To copy a type object between Illustrator documents, use the drag-and-drop method (see page 104) or Clipboard commands (see page 105).

Note: When you copy a threaded text object, only that single object and the visible text within it are copied.

Importing text into Illustrator

The Place command lets you import text files in the following formats into an Illustrator document: plain text (.txt); Rich Text Format (.rtf); or Microsoft Word (.doc or .docx). The text will appear in a new rectangle.

Note: To enter text onto or into a custom path, first place it into an Illustrator document by following the steps below, then copy and paste it onto or into the path (see the steps on the preceding page).

To import text into an Illustrator document:

1. Open or create an Illustrator document. Click an artboard in the document or on the Artboards panel.

2. Choose File > **Place** (Cmd-Shift-P/Ctrl-Shift-P). ★

3. In the Place dialog, locate and click the text file to be imported, then click Place.

4. For a file in Microsoft Word or RTF format, the Microsoft Word Options dialog opens.**A** Decide which options you want Illustrator to include. If you want to preserve any text styling, be sure to leave Remove Text Formatting unchecked.

   For a file in the plain text (.txt) format, the Text Import Options dialog opens.**B** Formatting and styling are removed from text in this format.

5. Click OK. The loaded text pointer appears, indicating that there is text to be placed on the page. The icon displays the number of files to be placed (one of one file) and a preview of the text to be placed.**C** ★

6. Click once to place the text at 100% size (determined by the file being placed), or drag to define a new area for the text. You can use the Selection tool to resize it. To restyle it, see the next chapter. If the overflow symbol appears in the lower right corner of the rectangle **D** and you want to thread the type to another type object, see the next page.

A For text in Microsoft Word or RTF format, you will choose settings in the Microsoft Word Options dialog.

B For text in the plain text format, choose settings in the Text Import Options dialog.

1/1

C The loaded text pointer appears.

> Let us spend one day as deliberately as Nature, and not be thrown off the track by every nutshell and mosquito's wing that falls on the rails. Let us rise early and fast, or break fast, gently and without perturbation; let company come and let company go, let the bells ring and the children cry,— determined to make a day of it. Why should we knock under and go with the stream? Let us not be upset and overwhelmed in that terrible rapid and whirlpool called a dinner, situated in the meridian shallows.

— *Henry David Thoreau*

Overflow symbol (in the Out port)

D The placed text appears in a rectangle.

Threading type objects

To reveal overflow (overset) text, you can either thread the type object to another object (see the next task), or simply enlarge the type object via one of these two methods:

➤ Click the type block with the Selection tool. If the bounding box isn't visible, choose View > Show Bounding Box. Drag a handle on the bounding box (the handles on a bounding box are hollow).

➤ Deselect the type object, click the edge of the rect-angle — not the type — with the Direct Selection tool (use the Object Highlighting feature of Smart Guides to locate the rectangle), then Shift-drag a segment.

If your type overfloweth, you can spill, or thread, it into a different object or into a copy of the same object.

To thread a type object to another object:

Method 1 (by clicking)

1. With the **Selection** tool (V), select the original type object.

2. Click the Out port ⊞ on the selected object. The pointer becomes a Loaded Text pointer. **A**

3. Do either of the following:

   To create a new object to contain the overflow type, either click where you want a duplicate of the currently selected object to appear, or drag to create a rectangular type object. **B–C**

   Position the pointer over the edge of a second object (the pointer changes to 🖿), then click that object's path. A fill and stroke of None will be applied to the path.

4. Overflow type flows from the first object into the second one. Cmd-click/Ctrl-click to deselect the objects.

➤ If you double-click an Out port with the Selection tool, the first object will be threaded to a linked copy of that object.

Method 2 (using a command)

1. Via the Selection tool or the Layers panel, select the original type object and a second object.

2. Choose Type > Threaded Text > **Create**.

➤ If you edit threaded type in Illustrator CC, it will update more quickly than in previous versions.

In port

A *To thread text, click the Out port with the Selection tool first...*

B *...then with the Loaded Text pointer, drag (or click) elsewhere on the artboard.*

— *Zora Neale Hurston*

C *The overflow type spills from the first object into the second one, in the direction indicated by the thread arrowheads.*

NOT ALL IS COPIED

If you click to duplicate a type object (step 3 on this page), only the object's shape will be copied, not its fill and stroke attributes. To copy the fill and stroke attributes afterward, choose the Direct Selection tool, click the artboard to deselect, then click the edge of the duplicate object (the handles on the object should be hollow). Choose the Eyedropper tool (I), move the pointer over the background of the original type object (make sure the pointer doesn't have a little "t" in it), then click.

Are you curious to see what's threaded to what? Display the text threads (the nonprinting lines that reveal the links between text objects).

To reveal the text threads:

Select a linked type object via a selection tool or the Layers panel. If the thread lines aren't visible, choose View > **Show Text Threads** or press Cmd-Shift-Y/Ctrl-Shift-Y.

➤ The stacking order of type objects on the Layers panel has no effect on the direction in which text flows between objects.

When you unthread two objects, the chain is broken and the overflow text gets sucked back into the first object of the two. The path objects are preserved.

To unthread two type objects:

1. Choose the **Selection** tool (V), then click a threaded type object.

2. Do either of the following:

   Double-click the object's In port or Out port.**A–B**

   Click an In port or Out port, move the pointer slightly if you want to verify that it has become an unthreading cursor, then click the same port a second time to cut the thread.

Follow these steps if you want to keep the remaining links intact as you release just one object from a series of threaded objects. The type will reflow into the remaining objects.

To release an object from a thread while preserving the remaining threads:

1. Choose the **Selection** tool (V), then click the type object to be released.**C**

2. Do either of the following:

   To unthread the object while preserving it, choose Type > Threaded Text > **Release Selection**.**D**

   To unthread the type object by deleting it, press Delete/Backspace. (Too simple, right?)

➤ To disconnect all the objects in a text thread while keeping the type in its present objects, click one of the objects with the Selection tool, then choose Type > Threaded Text > Remove Threading. The threads disappear, but the type stays where it is.

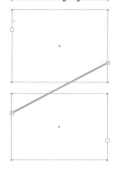

A *When the Out port is double-clicked...*

B *...that type object becomes unthreaded.*

C *Here the middle type object is selected...*

D *...and then released from the thread via the Type > Threaded Text > Release Selection command.*

Converting point type to area type, and vice versa

You're not stuck with point type remaining as point type or area type remaining as area type — you can convert one to the other. The conversion works for both horizontal and vertical type. (Path type can't be converted to point or area type.)

Note: For the tasks on this page and the next page, make sure the Bounding Box feature is on (View > Show Bounding Box or Cmd-Shift-B/Ctrl-Shift-B).

If you convert point type to area type, the text will wrap within the contour of a new rectangle instead of remaining on separate, noncontinuous lines.

To convert point type to area type:

1. With the **Selection** tool (V), select a point type object.

2. Do either of the following:

   Double-click the annotator at the right end of the type object.**A–B**

   Choose Type > **Convert to Area Type**.

3. *Optional:* Reshape the object by dragging a handle on its bounding box. To delete any unwanted paragraph returns, click at the left edge of a line of type, then press Backspace/Delete. (If you want to view the return characters, choose Type > Show Hidden Characters.)

To convert multiple point type objects to one area type object:

1. Do either of the following:

   To select all the point type objects in your document, choose Select > Object > **Point Type Objects**.

   To select two or more point type objects, either use the Layers panel or Shift-click or drag across them with the Selection tool (V).

2. Double-click the annotator at the right end of the type objects.**C–D** Keep the resulting area type objects selected.

3. Choose Type > Threaded Text > **Create** (**A**, next page).

4. Click the artboard to deselect. With the Selection tool, Shift-click to select all the objects except the last one, then press Backspace/Delete.

5. To reveal all the type, click the remaining object, then enlarge it by dragging a handle on the bounding box (**B**, next page).

A *The pointer is positioned over the annotator on a point type object. Note that the annotator is hollow.*

B *When we double-clicked the annotator, it became filled and the object was converted to area type. We reshaped the type object, and the type conformed to the new contour (we deleted some unwanted paragraph returns).*

C *We selected three point type objects, then positioned the pointer over the annotator.*

D *We double-clicked the annotator to convert all the selected objects to area type objects.*

To convert area type to point type:

1. Do either of the following:

   To select all the area type objects in your document, choose Select > Object > **Area Type Objects**.

   Select one or more area type objects via the Layers panel or the **Selection** tool (V).

   Note: If you convert a nonrectangular area type object to point type, the type will be preserved but the object will be deleted. If you want to preserve the original object, duplicate it now.

2. Make sure all the text that you want to display in the area type object is now visible, because all overflow text will be deleted during the conversion. If you need to reveal more text, drag a handle on the object.

3. Do either of the following:

   Double-click the annotator at the right end of the type object.**C**

   Choose Type > **Convert to Point Type**.

   Note: If the original object contained overflow text, an alert will appear, warning you that the overset (hidden) text will be deleted during the conversion. If want to let Illustrator delete the overflow text, click Yes; if you want to preserve all the text, click No, then repeat step 2, making sure to reveal all the type in the object.

4. *Optional:* If you turn on Type > Show Hidden Characters, you will see that Illustrator inserted a soft return after every line of the new point type.**D**

➤ If you convert a threaded area type object to a point type object, that object will be unthreaded from the other objects.

A *We threaded the three objects together.*

B *We deleted the first two objects, then enlarged the last object.*

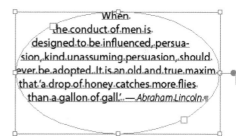

C *The pointer is positioned over the annotator on an area type object.*

D *We double-clicked the annotator; the object converted to point type. Illustrator inserted a soft return after each line (we turned on Type > Show Hidden Characters).*

IMPROVED HIDDEN CHARACTERS ★

The 2014 release of Illustrator CC has improved several aspects of how hidden characters are dispayed. The font has been changed to make the characters more readable, and the end-of-paragraph and end-of-line characters are now indicated by different glyphs (characters). Also, new hidden characters are included to represent the em dash, en dash, diaeresis, and caron.

Rotating type

To rotate type characters at a custom angle:

1. Select a type object with the Selection tool or via the Layers panel, or select one or more type characters with a type tool.

2. Show the Character panel 🅰 (Cmd-T/Ctrl-T). If the full options aren't showing, click the double arrowheads ⬍ on the panel tab.

3. Choose or enter a positive or negative **Character Rotation** value. 🅣 🅐

➤ After rotating type, you may need to adjust the spacing between the characters (see page 276).

To make a whole horizontal type block vertical, or vice versa:

1. Select a type object with the Selection tool or via the Layers panel.

2. Choose Type > Type Orientation > **Horizontal** or **Vertical**.

➤ To rotate vertical area type characters, select just the characters to be rotated. From the Character panel menu, choose Standard Vertical Roman Alignment (to uncheck it).

A *We rotated the orange letter by 15°.*

TRANSFORMING TYPE

To rotate type, as in the numbers on the tickets below, use one of the rotation tricks you learned in Chapter 11 (e.g., manipulate the object's bounding box or use the Free Transform tool).

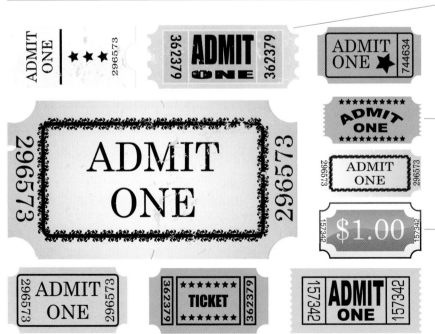

➤ *One way to create a "grunge" effect like this is by drawing strokes with the Paintbrush tool. For the tool, choose the Chalk brush (in the Artistic_ ChalkCharcoalPencil library) and a stroke color that's similar to the background color.*

➤ *Use the Rainbow path effect to produce curved type (see page 257).*

➤ *To carve the corners of a rectangle like this, draw a rectangle, then use the Live Corner options to change the corner effect and the type of corner (see page 78).*

EXERCISE: Putting type on a circle

Create the type

1. Deselect all, click Document Setup on the Control panel, choose Units: Inches, then click OK.

2. Using the Control panel, choose a fill color of None and a dark green as the stroke color.

3. Choose the Ellipse tool ⬭ (L), then click on an artboard to open the Ellipse dialog.

4. Click the Constrain Width and Height Proportions button, enter "3" in the Width field, then click OK.**A**

5. Double-click the Scale tool. ⬚ Enter "68" in the Scale: Uniform field, then click Copy. Cmd-click/Ctrl-click to deselect.

6. Choose the Type on a Path tool. ⬚

7. On the Control panel, click Character to open a temporary Character panel. Enter "28" in the Font Size field and choose the Stencil font from the Font menu. (Note: If you need to use the Stencil Std Bold font instead of the Stencil font, choose a Font Size of 25 pt.)

8. Click the top of the inner circle, then type the desired text (to copy our example, type "RECYCLED 100%"; press the Spacebar; to type an en dash in the Mac OS, press Option- – (hyphen), or in Windows, hold down Alt and enter 0150 on the number pad; then press the Spacebar again. Finally, enter the same type and dash again without the last space).**B** Don't deselect.

9. Click the Selection tool. ⬚ Drag the center bracket (look for it near the bottom of the circle) along the outside of the small circle to reposition the type, so the dashes are positioned at the top and bottom of the circle.**C**

   Note that the left and right brackets are practically on top of each other near the starting point of the type. To avoid causing a text overflow, don't move the left bracket over the right one.

Continued on the following page

A *Create a circle.*

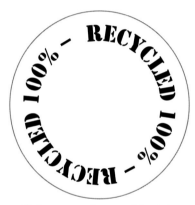

B *Create a smaller copy of the circle using the Scale dialog, then add path type along the edge of the circle (the circle now has a stroke of None).*

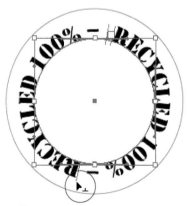

C *Drag the center bracket of the path type to position the dashes at the top and bottom of the circle.*

Refine the type

1. Choose the Direct Selection tool. Click the path for the larger circle. On the Appearance panel, click the Stroke listing, then click the up arrow to set the stroke weight to 3 pt.

2. Click the path of the smaller circle. On the Appearance panel, click the Stroke listing, then click the Stroke color square. On the temporary Swatches panel that opens, choose the same dark green as on the large circle. Click the up arrow to set the stroke weight to 3 pt.**A**

3. Choose the Selection tool and click the type. Display the Character panel. Increase the Baseline Shift value to center the type in the space between the circles (we used a value of 8 pt).

4. If necessary, increase the Tracking value to space the type and the two dashes evenly (see page 276),**B** then repeat step 9 from the preceding page to reposition the type on the circle.

5. Via the Control panel, apply the same dark green to the type. (Keep the stroke color as None.)

6. *Optional:* To add the trees shown in figure **C**, do as follows:

   On the Layers panel, click the New Layer button to create a new layer.

   Display the Symbols panel. From the Symbol Libraries menu at the bottom of the panel, choose Nature. From the library panel, drag the Trees 1 symbol into the center of the two circles.

   To scale the symbol to fit within the small circle, with the Selection tool, Shift-drag a corner handle of the bounding box for the symbol (if you don't see the bounding box, which has hollow handles, choose View > Show Bounding Box).

7. Choose the Selection tool, marquee the two circles and the symbol instance, then choose Object > Group (Cmd-G/Ctrl-G).

8. Cmd-click/Ctrl-click to deselect, then choose Reset Panel from the Character panel menu to restore the default settings to the panel.

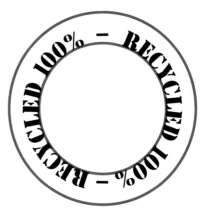

A Apply the same green color and stroke weight to the smaller circle.

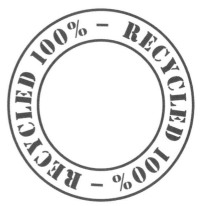

B Use the Baseline Shift and Tracking controls to adjust the type, and apply the same green color to it.

C For the inner graphic, we dragged the Trees 1 symbol from the Nature library panel into the small circle, then scaled it to fit.

In the preceding chapter, you learned how to create type. Now you will learn how to format and refine it. The first step is to learn how to select type, the type object, or both. Once you've mastered those skills, you will use the Character and Control panels to change typographic attributes; the Glyphs and OpenType panels to insert special characters; the Paragraph panel to apply paragraph settings; the Paragraph Styles and Character Styles panels to apply collections of attributes quickly; the Touch Type tool to transform individual characters manually; and the Tabs panel to align columns of text. Finally, you will learn how to convert type characters to paths; wrap type around an object; and apply appearance attributes to type, including multiple strokes and effects.

Selecting type

Before type can be modified, it must be selected. Use the selection method described on this page when you need to move, transform, restyle, or recolor all the type in or on a type object. To reshape or recolor a type object (but not the type), use the first selection method on the next page instead. Or to edit, restyle, or recolor just some of the type in a block, use the second method on the next page.

To select type and its object:

Method 1 (Selection tool)

1. Open the Illustrator/Edit > Preferences dialog. In the Smart Guides panel, check Object Highlighting, and in the Type panel, make sure Type Object Selection by Path Only is off (the default setting). Click OK.

2. Turn on View > **Smart Guides** (Cmd-U/Ctrl-U).

3. Choose the **Selection** tool ▶ (V).

4. Do one of the following:

    For area type (inside an object), click a type character **A** or the outer path.**B** Or if the object has a fill color, you can click the fill.

Continued on the following page

If we shadows have offended,
Think but this—and all is mended—

A *To select type and its object, either click a type character…*

If we shadows have offended,
Think but this—and all is mended—

path

— William Shakespeare

B *…or click the path of the type object.*

For point type, click the type.**A**

For type on a path, click the type or the path.

Method 2 (Layers panel)

Click the selection square for the type on the Layers panel.

➤ If the bounding box feature is on (View > Show Bounding Box), a bounding box will surround selected type.

➤ If the Type Object Selection by Path Only preference is on, you must click the baseline of a point type object to select it. Use the Object Highlighting feature of Smart Guides to locate it.

Use this selection method if you want to recolor or reshape a type object but not the type.

To select a type object but not the type:

1. Choose the **Direct Selection** tool.

2. Cmd-click/Ctrl-click, if necessary, to deselect. Click the edge of an area or path type object (not point type). You can use the Object Highlighting feature of Smart Guides to locate it.**B** Any modifications you make now will affect only the type object.**C**

Use this selection method to select just the type — not the object — so you can copyedit the text, change its character or paragraph settings (Character or Paragraph panel), or change its fill or stroke settings.

To select type but not the type object:

1. Choose a type tool.

2. Do any of the following:

   To highlight one or more words or a line of horizontal type, click and drag horizontally across them.**D** For vertical type, drag vertically.

   To select whole lines of horizontal type, drag vertically. Or for vertical type, drag horizontally.

   Double-click to select a word.

   Triple-click to select a paragraph.

   To select all the type in the block or on the path, plus any overflow type, click in a text block or on a text path, then choose Select > All (Cmd-A/Ctrl-A).

   Click to start a selection, then Shift-click where you want the selection to end. Continue to Shift-click if you want to extend the selection.

3. When you're done editing the type, Cmd-click/Ctrl-click outside the type object to deselect it.

If we shadows have offended,
Think but this—and all is mended—

A *Point type is selected with the Selection tool.*

If we shadows have offended,
Think but this—and all is mended—
path

B *With the Direct Selection tool, a type object is selected. The type characters are not selected.*

If we shadows have offended,
Think but this—and all is
mended—
anchor

C *The type object is reshaped and recolored.*

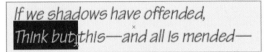

If we shadows have offended,
Think but this—and all is mended—

D *Two words are selected with a type tool.*

SELECTING TYPE FOR EDITING: A SUMMARY

➤ To change character or paragraph attributes for all the text in a type object or on a path, select the object or path via the Selection tool or Layers panel.

➤ To change the attributes of one or more characters, words, or consecutive paragraphs, drag through them with a type tool.

For a description of the Character and Paragraph panels, which are used throughout this chapter, see pages 45 and 51, respectively. You can open either panel from the Type submenu on the Window menu, or temporarily via a link on the Control panel. To open all the type panels quickly, choose the Typography workspace from the Workspace menu on the Control panel.

In the method shown on this page, you will choose a font from the full Font Family menu on the Character or Control panel. In the method shown on the next page, you will choose a font by using a search feature.

Changing the font family and style

To change the font family and font style:

Method 1 (choose from the full list)

1. Do either of the following:

   Select the type to be modified with a type tool.

   Select one or more type objects via the Layers panel or the Selection tool.

2. On the Character panel **A** or the Control panel, click the **Font Family** menu arrow to display an expandable list of available font families and styles.**A** To scroll through the list, leave the mouse button up and press the up or down arrow on the keyboard; the fonts will preview immediately in your document. To expand a collapsed category, position the mouse over the category (mouse button still up), then press Cmd/Ctrl down arrow; scroll the nested list by pressing the up or down arrow. (To collapse an expanded category, position the mouse over it and press Cmd/Ctrl up arrow.)

3. To apply the currently highlighted font and exit the panel, press Return/Enter (or click the font name).**B**

➤ If selected type already contains the desired font family and you want to change just the font style, you can also do so via the Font Style menu or field on the Character or Control panel.

Continued on the following page

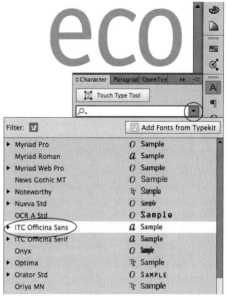

A *We selected a type object, clicked the Font Family arrowhead on the Character panel to display this menu, then pressed the down arrow to highlight the ITC Officina Sans family.*

B *Next, we pressed Cmd/Ctrl down arrow to expand the ITC Officina Sans family, then pressed the down arrow to highlight the Bold style. (Last, we will press Return/Enter to exit the panel and apply the highlighted font.)*

CHOOSING DEFAULT SETTINGS FOR A TYPE TOOL

To choose default settings for the currently selected type tool, deselect all objects, then choose the desired attributes (e.g., from the Character, Paragraph, Character Styles, or Paragraph Styles panels).

Method 2 (via a search)

1. Do either of the following:

   Select the type to be modified with a type tool.

   Select one or more type objects via the Layers panel or the Selection tool.

2. Verify that **Search Entire Font Name** is checked on the search menu $\mathcal{O}\text{-}$ on either the Character panel or Control panel (Search First Word Only uses the method of earlier versions of Illustrator).

3. On the Character panel or the Control panel, click in the Font Family field. If desired, you can clear the field by pressing the. 🔲 Next, do one of the following:

   Start typing a font name.**A**

   Type a generic category, such as "semibold italic," "black condensed," or "ornaments".

Type an abbreviation for a specific font (e.g., "f g" for Franklin Gothic or "my p" for Myriad Pro). Note the inclusion of spaces.

4. A menu displays, listing the fonts that most closely match the letters you typed. To scroll through the list, keep the mouse button up and press the up or down arrow on the keyboard. Fonts will preview immediately in your document.

5. To apply the currently highlighted font and exit the panel, press Return/Enter (or click the font name) **B** (see also **A–B**, next page).

➤ If you want to exit the panel during a font search without changing the font, press Esc.

➤ For another way to change the font, select type characters or a type object, right-click the type, then choose from either the Font submenu or the Recent Fonts submenu on the context menu. You can also choose a recently used font from the Recent Fonts submenu on the Type menu.

A We began typing a font name in the Font Family field, and this reduced menu appeared.

B We highlighted the desired font by pressing the down arrow (to apply the font to our type, the next step would be to press Return/Enter).

CHOOSING AN ANTI-ALIASING OPTION

To learn about the options on the Anti-aliasing menu on the Character panel, see page 448.

STYLING TYPE QUICKLY

The fastest — and most consistent — way to apply type attributes and formats is by using character and paragraph styles. After you master the basic type controls, learn about type styles on pages 284–287.

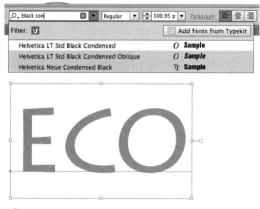

A *In the Character field on the Control panel, we started typing the words "black condensed"; this menu appeared.*

B *We highlighted the desired font via the down arrow (the next step would be to press Return/Enter).*

To apply all caps, small caps, underlining, or other styling:

1. Select the type to be modified with a type tool.

2. On the Character panel, make sure full options are displaying. If not, click the double arrow ⚙ in the panel tab or choose Shop Options from the panel menu.

3. Near the bottom of the panel, click the **All Caps**, **Small Caps**, **Superscript**, **Subscript**, **Underline**, or **Strikethrough** button. (To remove the styling, select the text, then click the same button again.)

➤ For other case options, select some text, then choose Type > Change Case > UPPERCASE, lower-case, Title Case, or Sentence case.

RECOLORING TYPE

To recolor all the type in an object, select the object with a selection tool or via the Layers panel (see the first figure below); to recolor just some characters or words, select them with a type tool (see the second figure below). Choose a color via the Color, Swatches, or Color Guide panel. Note: If type characters are highlighted with a type tool and you want to see how the new color looks, either deselect the object or choose a selection tool. To apply multiple fills or strokes to a type object, use the Appearance panel (see pages 294–296).

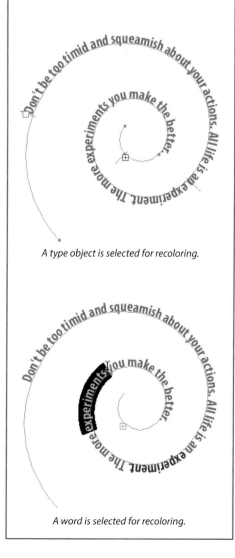

A type object is selected for recoloring.

A word is selected for recoloring.

Working with Typekit fonts

Typekit.com is an Adobe website from which you can purchase font families. As a Creative Cloud subscriber, you have access to over 1000 fonts that can be synced to your computer. To use this feature, you will need to link Typekit to your Adobe ID. Creative Cloud subscribers are automatically enrolled in the Portfolio plan, but you can upgrade to a more robust package by visiting Typekit.com.

Typekit is integrated into all of the Creative Cloud applications, including Adobe Illustrator. Via any of the Creative Cloud applications you can initiate the process of activating additional fonts, you can filter the font menus to display only Typekit fonts, or if the filter is off (fonts of all kinds are displayed), you can identify Typekit fonts by their symbol ⓣ.

Note that although Typekit fonts can be embedded in PDFs, EPUBs, and websites, they are not bundled with other fonts when you use the File > Package command in Illustrator to prepare your files for output. The idea is that if you send a project to someone else who is a Creative Cloud subscriber, they can activate the Typekit fonts on their computer.

To activate Typekit fonts in Illustrator: ★

1. On the Character panel, click to open the Font Family menu. At the top of the menu, click the **Add Fonts from Typekit** button.**A** Your web browser will launch and display the Typekit website.

   The first time you access the Typekit website, you'll need to link your Adobe ID to the Typekit service. Follow the onscreen instructions to link your account.

2. On the Typekit website, you'll see an interface that allows you to preview, search, and filter by classification, and other properties to help you find a font appropriate for your project.**C**

3. Hover your cursor over one of the fonts within the filtered range of fonts displayed, and click the **Use Fonts** button to activate the font.

4. A window will display listing the font faces available. Put a check mark next to each font face that you want to sync, then click the **Sync Selected Fonts** button.**B** A window will appear indicating that your fonts are being synced.

➤ The Creative Cloud desktop application needs to be running in order for fonts to properly sync to your computer.**C**

To view Typekit fonts in Illustrator: ★

1. On the Character panel, click to open the Font Family menu; or choose a type tool, then click to open the Font Family menu on the Control panel. On the menu, activate the **Apply Typekit Filter** button.ⓣ **D**

2. Choose a Typekit font from the list of fonts that you've synced to your computer.

   ➤ You can also search for a specific Typekit font by clicking in the Font Family field, then typing the name of the desired font.

A We clicked the Add Fonts from Typekit button to access the typekit.com website.

B We chose the font faces that we wanted to sync to our computer by enabling the check box next to each font face. Then we clicked the Sync Selected Fonts button.

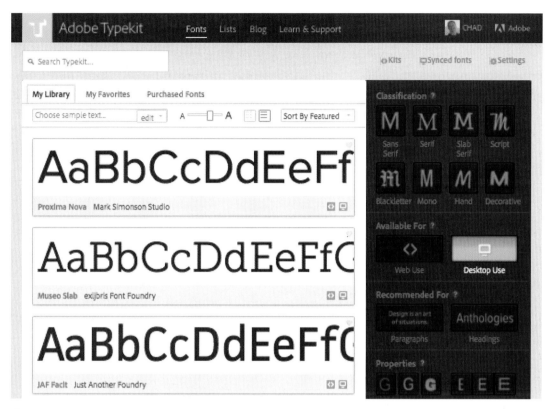

C *Here we accessed the Typekit website and synced fonts to our computer.*

D *We clicked the Apply Typekit Filter button to limit the displayed fonts to only those that we synced from the Typekit website.*

Changing the font size

You can change the font (point) size of individual characters or words, or of all the type in an object.

To change the font size:

1. Do either of the following:

   Select the type to be modified with a type tool.

   Select a type object with the Selection tool or the Layers panel.

2. Do one of the following:

   On the Character panel  or the Control panel, enter the desired size in the **Font Size** field **A–B** (you don't need to reenter the unit of measure). You could also choose a preset size from the menu; or click the up or down arrow; or click in the field, then press the up or down arrow on the keyboard.

   ▶ If the type that you select is in more than one size, the Font Size field will be blank, but the new size you choose will apply to all the selected type. When using the Character or Control panel, you can press Return/Enter to apply the new value and exit the panel, or press Tab to apply the value and highlight the next field.

   Hold down Cmd-Shift/Ctrl-Shift and press > to enlarge the font size or < to reduce it.**C** The type will resize by the current Size/Leading increment, which is set in Illustrator/Edit > Preferences > Type (the default increment is 2 pt). To change the font size by five times the current Size/Leading increment, hold down Cmd-Option-Shift/Ctrl-Alt-Shift and press > or <.

   Right-click the type and choose a preset size from the **Size** submenu on the context menu. (Choosing Other on the context menu highlights the Font Size field on the Character panel.)

   ▶ You can use the Horizontal Scale feature on the Character panel to make type wider (extend it) or narrower (condense it), or the Vertical Scale feature to make it taller or shorter. If you want to minimize the distortion, raise or lower the percentage by just a few points (e.g., 104% or 98%). To quickly reset the Horizontal Scale and Vertical Scale to the default value of 100%, select the type or type object, then press Cmd-Shift-X/Ctrl-Shift-X. Our preference is to use a typeface that has the desired characteristics — and more balanced proportions — in its design, such as Gill Sans Condensed or Tekton Pro Bold Extended.

A *Change the size of type by using the Font Size controls on the Character panel…*

B *… or the Control panel.*

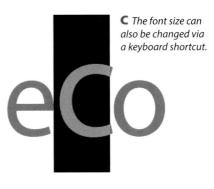

C *The font size can also be changed via a keyboard shortcut.*

SCALING TYPE INTERACTIVELY

▶ To scale an individual path or point type character manually with the Touch Type tool, see page 287.

▶ To scale all the type in a point type object manually, as shown below, select it first with the Selection tool, and make sure the View > Bounding Box feature is on. Drag a handle on the box — or even better, Shift-drag a handle to scale the type proportionally.

Changing the leading value

Leading is the distance between the baseline of each line of type and the line above it, and is traditionally measured in points. (To adjust the spacing between paragraphs, see page 283.)

Note: To change the vertical spacing in vertical type, change the horizontal tracking value (see the next page) instead of using leading. In vertical type, leading controls the horizontal spacing between vertical columns.

To change the leading value for horizontal type:

1. Do one of the following:

   To change the leading for an entire block of type, select it via the Selection tool or the Layers panel. (You can also select multiple threaded or nonthreaded type objects using either method.)

   To change the leading of all the lines in a paragraph, triple-click in the paragraph with a type tool.

   To change the leading of an entire line of type, drag across it with a type tool, making sure to include any spaces at the end of the line.

2. Do either of the following:

   On the Character panel, 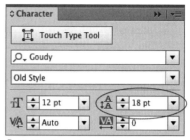 enter a **Leading** value (or click in the field, then press the up or down arrow on the keyboard), **A–C** or choose a preset value from the menu.

   Hold down Option/Alt and press the up arrow on the keyboard to decrease the leading or the down arrow to increase it by the Size/Leading increment, which is set in Illustrator/Edit > Preferences > Type (the default increment is 2 pt). To change the leading by five times the current Size/Leading increment, hold down Cmd-Option/Ctrl-Alt as you press an arrow.

➤ When Auto is the current Leading setting, Illustrator calculates the leading as a percentage of the largest font size on each line (and the leading value is listed in parentheses). The default Auto Leading percentage is 120%; it can be changed in the Justification dialog, which opens from the Paragraph panel menu.

➤ If you change the leading for a threaded type object, only the leading in that object will change. To change the leading for a whole thread, select all the objects or use the Select > All command first.

A On the Character panel, enter a Leading value, or click the up or down arrow, or choose a preset value from the menu.

How can one conceive of a one-party system in a country that has over 200 varieties of cheese?

B *This 12-pt. type has loose, 18-pt. leading.*

How can one conceive of a one-party system in a country that has over 200 varieties of cheese?

— *Charles de Gaulle*

C *This 12-pt. type has tight, 13-pt. leading.*

SELECTING A TYPE TOOL QUICKLY

With the Selection or Direct Selection tool, double-click a character in a type object. The Type tool or Vertical Type tool becomes selected automatically, and an insertion point appears where you clicked.

Applying kerning and tracking

All fonts have specific kerning values built into them to optimize the spacing between specific character pairs (e.g., between an uppercase "T" and a lowercase "a"). These built-in kerning values are adequate for small text, such as body type (see the sidebar on this page), but not for large type, such as headers and logos. To remedy any awkward spacing between a pair of letters in large type, you can apply manual kerning values.

Tracking is the adjustment of spacing between three or more selected characters. It's best used sparingly, such as to spread out the characters in a single line of type (e.g., a header or subhead). Refrain from tracking whole paragraphs.

To move an individual character closer to an adjacent character manually, see page 287.

To apply manual kerning or tracking:

1. Do either of the following:

   Zoom in on the type that you want to kern or track. Choose a type tool, then either click to create an insertion point between two characters for kerning, or highlight a range of text for tracking.

   To track (not kern) all the type in an object, select it with the Selection tool or the Layers panel.

2. Do either of the following:

   In the **Kerning** or **Tracking** field on the Character panel, A **A** enter a positive value to add space between the characters or a negative value to remove space (or click in the field, then press the up or down arrow on the keyboard); **B–D** or choose a preset value from the menu; or click the up or down arrow.

   Hold down Option/Alt and press the right arrow on the keyboard to add space between letters or the left arrow to remove space, based on the current Tracking increment in Illustrator/Edit > Preferences > Type. To kern or track by a larger increment, hold down Cmd-Option/Ctrl-Alt as you press an arrow.

➤ The Tracking and Kerning features affect the vertical spacing of characters in vertical type.

➤ To undo manual kerning, click between a pair of characters, then press Cmd-Option-Q/Ctrl-Alt-Q or reset the Kerning value on the Character panel to 0 (zero). To undo manual tracking, select the characters in question before resetting the Tracking value to 0 or using the above-mentioned shortcut.

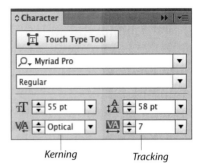

Kerning   Tracking

A *Use the kerning and tracking controls to refine the spacing between characters.*

Simone

B *The original type contains no manual kerning or tracking.*

Simone

C *We tightened the spacing between the first two characters in this word via kerning…*

Simone

D *…then tightened the spacing between the last five characters via tracking.*

THE AUTO KERNING OPTIONS

Via the Kerning menu on the Character panel, you can choose from three kinds of automatic (nonmanual) kerning:

➤ Auto (or "metrics" kerning), the default method, is applied to new or imported text based on the information that is built into each font for specific pairs of characters, such as To, Ta, We, Wo, and Yo.

➤ Optical adjusts the spacing between adjacent characters where needed. It's a good choice for type that is set in a font that has inadequate or no built-in kerning, or that contains multiple typefaces or font sizes.

➤ Metrics-Roman only also uses built-in kerning data, but is applicable only to type that is set in Roman (e.g., non-Asian) language fonts.

The Fit Headline command uses tracking values to fit a one-line paragraph of horizontal or vertical area type to the edges of the object.

To fit type to its container:

1. Choose a type tool.

2. Select or click in a single-line paragraph of area type (not point type or a line within a larger paragraph).**A**

3. Choose Type > **Fit Headline**.**B**

➤ If you scale a type object to which you have applied the Fit Headline command, you will need to reapply the command afterward, because the tracking values won't readjust automatically.

A *Our text cursor is inserted into a line of type.*

B *The Fit Headline command added space between the characters to fit the line of type to the full width of the object.*

WORD AND LETTER SPACING OPTIONS

➤ To change the horizontal word or letter spacing for paragraphs that have a justified alignment setting, choose Justification from the Paragraph panel menu, then in the Justification dialog, change the Minimum, Desired, and Maximum values for Word Spacing or Letter Spacing. The Desired setting also affects nonjustified paragraphs (in fact, we like to reduce the word spacing for subheads and headers, as part of a paragraph style). Glyph Scaling (50%–200%) affects the width of the actual characters.

➤ If you are setting type for online viewing that is 20 pt. or smaller, you may want to turn the Fractional Widths feature off (Character panel menu). To learn about this feature, enter "Fractional character widths" in the search field in Illustrator Help.

Ocean
Body more immaculate than a wave,
salt washing away its own line,
and the brilliant bird
flying without ground roots.

Normal word and letter spacing

	Minimum	Desired	Maximum
Word Spacing:	80%	100%	133%
Letter Spacing:	0%	0%	0%
Glyph Scaling:	100%	100%	100%

Ocean
Body more immaculate than a wave,
salt washing away its own line,
and the brilliant bird
flying without ground roots.

Loose letter spacing

	Minimum	Desired	Maximum
Word Spacing:	80%	100%	133%
Letter Spacing:	5%	10%	20%
Glyph Scaling:	100%	100%	100%

Ocean
Body more immaculate than a wave,
salt washing away its own line,
and the brilliant bird
flying without ground roots.
— *Pablo Neruda*

Tight word spacing

	Minimum	Desired	Maximum
Word Spacing:	70%	70%	100%
Letter Spacing:	0%	0%	0%
Glyph Scaling:	100%	100%	100%

Using smart punctuation

The Smart Punctuation command converts applicable text (listed under "Unsmart type" in the sidebar at right) to professional typesetting characters, when available in the current font. You can apply the command to selected text or, even better, to an entire document. To set yourself apart from amateurs, use this feature (and also use typographer's quotes, which are discussed next). Notes: The Smart Quotes option in the Smart Punctuation dialog overrides the current Double Quotes and Single Quotes settings in the Document Setup dialog. To set ligatures and expert fractions in an OpenType font, use the OpenType panel (see page 280).

To create smart punctuation:

1. To change all the type in your document, deselect;**A** or with a type tool, select the text to which you want to apply smart punctuation.

2. Choose Type > **Smart Punctuation**.

3. Check the desired options in the **Replace Punctuation** area of the dialog,**B** and click Replace In: **Selected Text Only** or **Entire Document**.

4. *Optional:* Check Report Results to have a tally of your changes appear onscreen after you click OK.

5. Click OK.**C**

To specify quotation marks and apostrophes for future type:

1. Deselect, then click **Document Setup** on the Control panel (Cmd-Option-P/Ctrl-Alt-P).

2. Under Type Options, check **Use Typographers Quotes** and choose the **Language** in which the text is going to be typeset. The standard Double Quotes and Single Quotes marks for the chosen language will display on both menus. Click OK.

B *Check the desired Replace Punctuation options in the Smart Punctuation dialog.*

THE SMART PUNCTUATION OPTIONS

Option in the Smart Punctuation dialog	"Unsmart" type	The result
ff, fi, ffi Ligatures	ff, fi, ffi	ff, fi, ffi
ff, fl, ffl Ligatures	ff, fl, ffl	ff, fl, ffl
Smart Quotes	' "	' " " '
Smart Spaces (one space after a period)	. T	. T
En (dashes)	--	–
Em Dashes	---	—
Ellipses	...	…
Expert Fractions	1/2	½

"We are living in a world today where lemonade is made from artificial flavors and furniture polish is made from real lemons."

-- Alfred E. Newman

A *Dumb punctuation: Straight quotation marks, double hyphens instead of dashes, and no ligatures.*

"We are living in a world today where lemonade is made from artificial flavors and furniture polish is made from real lemons."

— Alfred E. Newman

C *Smart punctuation: Smart quotation marks, a single dash, and ligatures (the "fi" in "artificial" and the "fl" in "flavors"). For hanging punctuation, see page 288.*

Inserting alternate glyphs

The OpenType font format was developed jointly by Adobe and Microsoft to help prevent font substitution and text reflow problems in files that are transferred between platforms. The OpenType format also allows for a wide range of stylistic variations, called glyphs, for any given character in a specific font (sounds like something in *The Hobbit*!). For each individual character in an OpenType font, you can choose from an assortment of alternate glyphs, such as ligatures, swashes, titling characters, stylistic alternates, ordinals, and fractions. Fonts labeled "Pro" have an expanded set of characters.**A**

You can insert alternate glyphs manually by using the Glyphs panel (as in the steps below), or automatically by using the OpenType panel (as in the steps on the next page). The Glyphs panel isn't just used for OpenType fonts, though — you can also use it to locate and insert characters in a non-OpenType font.

To replace or insert a glyph using the Glyphs panel:

1. Choose a type tool, then select a character or click in the text to create an insertion point.

2. Display the Glyphs panel 𝓐 (choose Glyphs from the Type menu or from the Window > Type submenu). If you selected just one character in the prior step, that character will be highlighted on the panel.

3. From the **Show** menu,**B** choose a category of glyphs to be displayed on the panel: Alternates for Current Selection,**C** Entire Font, Access All Alternates, or a specific category. Different options will be available depending on the current font and whether you selected a character or just created an insertion point.

4. *Optional:* You can choose a different font family and font style from the menus at the bottom of the Glyphs panel.

5. Double-click a glyph to be inserted in your text or to be used as a replacement for the selected character; or if the square containing the currently highlighted glyph has a mini arrowhead in the lower right corner, you can click the arrowhead and choose a glyph from the menu. The glyph will appear in your text.

➤ To change the display size of the glyphs on the Glyphs panel, click the Zoom Out or Zoom In button in the lower right corner.

SPOT THE IMPOSTORS!

To highlight all the text in which a glyph has been substituted throughout your document (due to the original font not being available), deselect, click Document Setup on the Control panel, then check Highlight Substituted Glyphs.

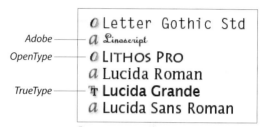

Adobe ——
OpenType ——

TrueType ——

A *When Font Preview is checked in the Type panel of the Preferences dialog, the font type can be identified by its symbol on the Font menu on the Character panel.*

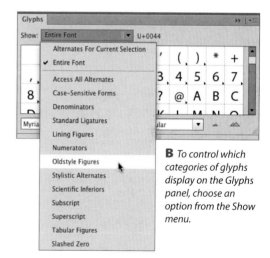

B *To control which categories of glyphs display on the Glyphs panel, choose an option from the Show menu.*

C *We selected the letter "e" in our text (note that we're using a Pro font), then chose Alternates for Current Selection from the Show menu.*

By using the OpenType panel, you can control whether alternate glyphs in OpenType fonts will be substituted for standard characters automatically, where applicable (and if available in the current font). For example, you can choose to have Illustrator insert a glyph for a properly formatted fraction whenever you type the characters for a fraction, such as ½ for 1/2 or ¾ for 3/4. Other options include ligature glyphs for specific letter pairs (such as ff, ffl, and st), swash and titling characters, etc.

To specify or insert alternate glyphs for OpenType characters:

1. As you do either of the following, remember that the "Pro" fonts contain the most glyph options:

   To change all applicable occurrences in existing text, either select a type object with the Selection tool or the Layers panel or highlight one or more characters with a type tool, then style it with an OpenType font via the Control or Character panel.

   To specify alternate glyph options for future text to be entered in a specific OpenType font, choose a type tool, then choose that font on the Control or Character panel.

2. Display the OpenType panel ⬙ (Cmd-Option-Shift-T/Ctrl-Alt-Shift-T),**A** then click any of the available buttons.**B–C** The choices will vary depending on the glyph set of the current font.

➤ The Figure menu on the OpenType panel controls the style and spacing of numerals. The Tabular options insert an equal amount of spacing between numerals, and are designed for aligning columns of numerals in a table. The Proportional options allow for variable spacing based on the actual width of each numeral character, and are designed to improve the appearance of nontabular numerals. Oldstyle numerals are beautiful but, because of their variable heights, are appropriate only in special design settings.

➤ If a font lacks a true superscript, superior, subscript, or inferior glyph, or nonstandard fractions (such as $^5/_{25}$), you can use options on the Position menu on the OpenType panel to produce the needed "faux" glyph. For example, to produce the fraction $^5/_{25}$, we used the Numerator and Denominator options.

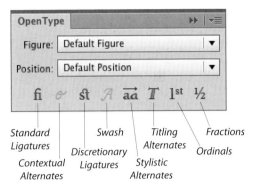

Standard Ligatures · Contextual Alternates · Discretionary Ligatures · Swash · Stylistic Alternates · Titling Alternates · Ordinals · Fractions

A Using the OpenType panel, you can control which categories of alternate glyphs will be used to replace standard characters in current or future text.

Swash

Fluffy

1st 2nd

Ordinal

Fraction

$^5/_8$ *Fact* — Discretionary ligature

Stylistic alternates

friend &

B The OpenType panel inserts alternate characters like these into your text.

 Available

 Selected

1st Not available

C The buttons on the OpenType panel have three states.

Applying hyphenation

You can turn on auto hyphenation for existing type or as a default setting for future type.

To hyphenate text and choose hyphenation options:

1. *Optional:* To hyphenate or change the hyphenation settings for existing text, select it via a type tool, the Selection tool, or the Layers panel.

2. Display the Paragraph panel ¶ and its full set of options. Check **Hyphenate**.

3. If you want to choose hyphenation settings, choose **Hyphenation** from the Paragraph panel menu. In the dialog,**A** check Hyphenation and Preview.

4. In the **Words Longer Than** [ ] **Letters** field, enter the minimum number of characters a word must contain in order to be hyphenated (3–25). We usually enter a value of 6 or 7.

   In the **After First** [ ] **Letters** field, enter the minimum allowable number of characters that may precede a hyphen. We use a value of 3 or 4.

   In the **Before Last** [ ] **Letters** field, enter the minimum allowable number of characters that can be carried over to the next line following a hyphen. We use a value of 3.

   In the **Hyphen Limit** field, enter the maximum allowable number of hyphens in a row (0–25). For the sake of both readability and aesthetics, we use a setting of 2. Oddly enough, a setting of 0 permits an unlimited number of hyphens in a row.

   Or for a less calculated approach to achieving the desired number of line breaks (try this on existing text), simply move the **Hyphenation Zone** slider toward Better Spacing or Fewer Hyphens.

   Finally, decide whether you want Illustrator to **Hyphenate Capitalized Words** (preferably not).

5. Click OK.

➤ Regardless of the current hyphenation settings, you will need to "eyeball" your hyphenated text and, if necessary, correct any awkward breaks using a soft return or the No Break command. To prevent a particular word from breaking at the end of a line, such as a compound word (e.g., "single-line"), to reunite an awkwardly hyphenated word (e.g., "sex-tuplet"), or to keep related words together (e.g., "New York City"), select that word or those words, then from the Character panel menu, choose No Break.

OUR FAVORITE COMPOSER

On the Paragraph panel menu, you can choose a line-composer option for selected type — or for future type, if no type is selected. Note: The line-composer names or options will vary depending on whether Show East Asian Options or Show Indic Options is checked in Illustrator/Edit > Preferences > Type.

➤ Adobe Single-Line Composer adjusts line breaks and the hyphenation for each line without regard to other lines or the appearance of the overall paragraph.

➤ Adobe Every-Line Composer (the option we prefer) examines all the lines in a paragraph and adjusts the line lengths and endings to optimize the overall appearance of the paragraph.

CHOOSING A LANGUAGE FOR HYPHENATION

From the Language menu on the Character panel, you can choose a language for hyphenation in the current document. In Illustrator/Edit > Preferences > Hyphenation, you can choose a default hyphenation language for Illustrator; in that dialog, you can also enter hyphenation exceptions — words that you don't want Illustrator to hyphenate (type a word in the New Entry field, then click Add).

A *in the Hyphenation dialog, set parameters for automatic hyphenation.*

Changing paragraph alignment

Before learning how to apply alignment, indentation, and other paragraph formats, you need to know what a paragraph is, as far as Illustrator is concerned. To start a new paragraph as you enter a block of text (or to create a paragraph break where your cursor is inserted in existing text), press Return/Enter. Every paragraph ends with one of these hard returns.

➤ To reveal the symbols for nonprinting characters, such as paragraph endings,¶ soft returns,↵ spaces,▪ and tabs,➡ choose Type > Show Hidden Characters (Cmd-Option-I/Ctrl-Alt-I).

Note: To create a soft return (line break) within a paragraph in nontabular text in order to bring the text to the right of the insertion point down to the next line, press Shift-Return/Shift-Enter.

To change paragraph alignment:

1. Do either of the following:

   Choose a type tool, then click in a paragraph or drag through one or more consecutive paragraphs.

   Select a type object with the Selection tool or the Layers panel.

2. Display the Paragraph panel ¶ (to access it quickly, you can press Cmd-Option-T/Ctrl-Alt-T or click Paragraph on the Control panel).

3. Click an **alignment** button.**A–B** The first three alignment buttons (Align Left, Align Center, and Align Right) are also available on the Control panel.

   Use one of the keyboard shortcuts listed in the sidebar on this page.

➤ The justify alignment options have no effect on point type (type that's not inside an object), because point type doesn't have a container for the type to justify to.

SHORTCUTS FOR PARAGRAPH ALIGNMENT		
	Mac OS	Windows
Left	Cmd-Shift-L	Ctrl-Shift-L
Center	Cmd-Shift-C	Ctrl-Shift-C
Right	Cmd-Shift-R	Ctrl-Shift-R
Justify Last Left	Cmd-Shift-J	Ctrl-Shift-J
Justify All (including the last line)	Cmd-Shift-F	Ctrl-Shift-F

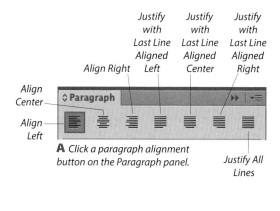

A Click a paragraph alignment button on the Paragraph panel.

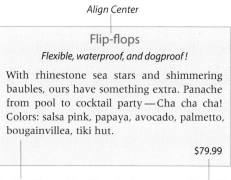

B A few paragraph alignment options are illustrated here.

Changing paragraph indentation

You can apply indentation values to any kind of type.

To change paragraph indentation:

1. Do either of the following:

    With a type tool, drag through the paragraphs to be modified, or click in a paragraph.

    Select a type object with the Selection tool or via the Layers panel.

2. On the Paragraph panel, ¶ do either of the following:

    Enter a **Left Indent** and/or **Right Indent** value, then press Return/Enter or Tab;**A–B** or click the up or down arrow; or click in the field, then press the up or down arrow on the keyboard.

    To indent only the first line of each paragraph, enter a positive **First-Line Left Indent** value.

Changing inter-paragraph spacing

Use the Space Before Paragraph or Space After Paragraph feature on the Paragraph panel to add or subtract space between paragraphs. (To adjust the spacing between lines of type within a paragraph, use leading; see page 275.)

To adjust the spacing between paragraphs:

1. Do either of the following:

    With a type tool, drag through the paragraphs to be modified, or click in the paragraph above which you want to adjust the spacing.

    Select a type object with the Selection tool or the Layers panel.

2. Via the **Space Before Paragraph** or **Space After Paragraph** controls on the extended Paragraph panel, ¶ choose a positive value to move the paragraphs farther apart or a negative value to bring them closer together (if you enter a value, press Return/Enter or Tab to apply it).**C**

➤ Because the Space After Paragraph value for a paragraph is combined with the Space Before Paragraph value from the paragraph below it, you could wind up with more space between paragraphs than you intend. We recommend entering a positive value for just one of the two features, when needed, while keeping the other value at zero.

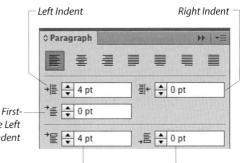

Left Indent · Right Indent

First-Line Left Indent

Space Before Paragraph · Space After Paragraph

A *Choose indentation and/or spacing values on the Paragraph panel.*

> The Mock Turtle sighed deeply, and began, in a voice choked with sobs, to sing this: —
>
> Beautiful Soup, so rich and green,
> Waiting in a hot tureen!
> Who for such dainties would not stoop?
> Soup of the evening, beautiful Soup!
> Soup of the evening, beautiful Soup!
> Beau — ootiful Soo-oop!
> Beau — ootiful Soo-oop!
> Soo — oop of the e — e — evening,
> Beautiful, beautiful Soup!
> — *Lewis Carroll*

B *We increased the Left Indent value for these paragraphs.*

C *We also increased the Space Before Paragraph value for this paragraph.*

CREATING A HANGING INDENT

To create a hanging indent, enter a positive Left Indent value and a negative First-Line Left Indent value. Below, we pressed Tab to align the second column of text with the indent.

Bene.:	Pray thee, sweet Mistress Margaret, deserve well at my hands by helping me to the speech of Beatrice.
Marg.:	Will you then write me a sonnet in praise of my beauty?
Bene.:	In so high a style, Margaret, that no man living shall come over it; for, in most comely truth, thou deservest it.
Marg.:	To have no man come over me? Why, shall I always keep below stairs?
Bene.:	Thy wit is as quick as the greyhound's mouth; it catches. — *William Shakespeare*

Using paragraph and character styles

Now that you know how to style type manually by using the Paragraph and Character panels, you're ready to learn how to format type by using character and paragraph styles. They will enable you to reach the same goal with far less effort. In addition to making the job of typesetting quicker and easier, type styles also help ensure that your formatting remains consistent among multiple artboards and related documents. If you use a word processing or layout program, you may already be familiar with the general concept.

A paragraph style is a collection of paragraph formats, such as hyphenation and indentation, plus character attributes, such as the font family, font style, and font size. When you click a paragraph style, all currently selected paragraphs are reformatted with the attributes in that style.**A**

A character style contains only character attributes and is normally used to accentuate or reformat select characters or words within a paragraph (such as symbols in a bulleted list or boldfaced or italicized words) — not whole paragraphs. Character styles are applied in addition to paragraph styles — they're the icing on the cake. As with paragraph styles, when you click a character style, all currently selected characters are updated with the attributes in that style.

To create, modify, and apply type styles, you will use the Paragraph Styles and Character Styles panels. We'll show you the easiest way to create a style.

To create a paragraph or character style:

1. Display the Paragraph Styles 🔲 or Character Styles 🔲 panel (Window > Type submenu).**B** If this is your first foray into styles, we suggest that you work with paragraph styles first.

2. Apply all the attributes to be saved in the style to some text.

3. With a type tool, click in the type, then Option-click/Alt-click the **New Style** button 🔲 on the Paragraph Styles or Character Styles panel.

4. An options dialog opens. Change the default **Style Name** to a descriptive one that will help you remember the style's function (such as "Subheads" or "Body Indent").

5. Click OK. To apply the new style to some type, see the next task.

To apply a type style:

1. For paragraph styling, click in or select a type object, or drag through some paragraphs. Or to quickly select all the type objects in your document, choose Select > Object > Text Objects.

   For character styling, select one or more type characters (not a whole type object).

2. Click a style name on the Paragraph Styles 🔲 or Character Styles 🔲 panel. How easy was that?

   Note: If the text doesn't adopt all the attributes of the style sheet, follow the next task, then try again.

➤ To choose a paragraph style before you create type, deselect, click Normal Character Style on the Character Styles panel, then click a style on the Paragraph Styles panel.

There is something that comes home to one now and perpetually ▲ It is not what is printed or preached or discussed…. ▲ It eludes discussion and print. ▲ It is not to be put in a book…. ▲ It is not in this book ▲ It is for you whoever you are ▲ It is no farther from you than your hearing and sight are from you ▲ It is hinted by nearest and commonest and readiest…. ▲ It is not them, though it is endlessly provoked by them…. ▲ What is there ready and near you now?

— Walt Whitman

A paragraph style   *A character style*

A *Use paragraph styles to format the main text (body, headers, subheads, etc.), and character styles to format special characters, bullets, or words within paragraphs.*

Character Styles	Paragraph Sty	▶▶	▾≡
[Normal Character Style]			
Triangle symbol			
Italics			

B *Display the Character Styles and Paragraph Styles panel group.*

If you apply attributes to text manually after applying a style, when that text is selected, the presence of those overrides (attributes that don't match the style definition) will be indicated by a + (plus) sign after the style name on the Paragraph Styles and/or Character Styles panel. If you want to force the text to match only the attributes in the style, clear the overrides, as follows.

To remove overrides from styled text:

1. Select the characters or paragraphs that contain the overrides to be removed;**A** or to reset the whole object, select it with the Selection tool.

2. Hold down Option/Alt and click a name on the Paragraph Styles or Character Styles panel.**B** The manually applied attributes in your text will disappear, and the + sign will disappear from the style name on the panel.

   Note: If your text contains both paragraph and character style overrides, you will need to clear them separately via each panel.

➤ If you unintentionally apply a character style to a whole type object and subsequently apply a paragraph style, only the formats from the paragraph style will be applied — not the character attributes — and the override symbol + won't display next to the paragraph style name. To force a paragraph style to override a character style completely, select the type object, then click [Normal Character Style] on the Character Styles panel.

You can copy paragraph and character styles from one file to another. If you're working on a series of documents for the same client or project, using the same styles for all will ensure that your type has a consistent look.

To load type styles from one Illustrator document to another:

1. From the Character Styles or Paragraph Styles panel menu, choose one of the following: **Load Character Styles**, **Load Paragraph Styles**, or **Load All Styles** (to load both character and paragraph styles).

2. In the Select a File to Import dialog, locate and click the Illustrator document that contains the styles you want to import, then click Open. Note: If an incoming style bears the same name as a style in the current document, it won't load, period.

When you edit a style, all the text in which it is being used in your document updates accordingly. There are two ways to edit a type style: by restyling a word or paragraph and then using it to redefine the style (as in the steps below) or by using the Paragraph or Character Style Options dialog (see the next page).

To edit a type style by redefining it:

1. Select a word or paragraph in which the style to be edited is being used. The style name becomes selected on the Paragraph Styles or Character Styles panel.

2. Change any attributes manually via the Paragraph, Character, Control, or Tabs panel.

   Note: Make sure all the type you have selected contains the style you are redefining and the new attributes. If you're redefining a paragraph style, also make sure the type doesn't have a character style applied to it.

3. Choose **Redefine Paragraph Style** from the Paragraph Styles panel menu or **Redefine Character Style** from the Character Styles panel menu. The style will update to include the attributes of the selected text.

GEORGES BRAQUE (1882–1963)

There is only one **valuable** thing in art: the thing you cannot explain (as reported in *Saturday Review*, May 28, 1966).

A paragraph style   A character style

A *The boldfacing for the word "valuable" was applied manually, so Illustrator considers it an override.*

GEORGES BRAQUE (1882–1963)

There is only one valuable thing in art: the thing you cannot explain (as reported in *Saturday Review*, May 28, 1966).

B *We selected the main paragraph, then Option/Alt clicked the paragraph style on the Paragraph Styles panel. This removed the boldfacing override but not the character style that we used to format the words "Saturday Review."*

To edit a type style via an options dialog:

1. Deselect, then double-click a style name on the Character Styles 🅰 or Paragraph Styles 🔲 panel.

2. The Character Style Options or Paragraph Style Options dialog opens.**A** Click **General** at any time to view an expandable list of all the settings in the style. Check Preview so you will be able to preview changes in your document, then to edit the style, click an option set name on the left side:

   Click **Basic Character Formats** to choose basic character attributes, such as the font family, font style, size, leading, kerning, and tracking.

   Click **Advanced Character Formats** to choose horizontal and vertical scaling, baseline shift, or rotation values.

   In the Paragraph Style Options dialog, you have access to the **Indents and Spacing**, **Tabs**, **Composition** (composer and hanging punctuation options), **Hyphenation**, and **Justification** option sets.

   Click **Character Color**, click the Fill or Stroke square, then choose a fill or stroke color for the type. Colors from the Swatches panel will be listed here. For a spot color, you can choose a Tint percentage. For the stroke, you can also change the Weight.

Click **OpenType Features** to choose options to be applied if the style includes an OpenType font (see page 280).

3. Click OK. All the type in your document in which the style is being used updates instantly.

➤ To clear all the settings in the currently displayed option set (in the currently displayed style options dialog), click Reset Panel.

➤ A dash/blue background in a check box signifies that the option won't override any attributes that were applied manually to text in the document.

➤ To create a variation of an existing style, drag it to the New Style button. 🔲 Double-click the duplicate style (labeled "copy"), then follow all the steps on this page. Neither of the Normal styles can be copied.

When you delete a style, the text attributes don't change in the document.

To delete a character or paragraph style:

1. Deselect all.

2. Click a style name (or Cmd-click/Ctrl-click multiple style names) on the Character Styles or Paragraph

---

Paragraph Style Options

Style Name: | Main Body text

General
Basic Character Formats
Advanced Character Formats
Indents and Spacing
Tabs
Composition
Hyphenation
Justification
Character Color
OpenType Features

General

Style Settings: [Normal Paragraph Style] +

▼ Basic Character Formats
    Font Family: Myriad Pro
    Font Style: Bold
    Size: 24 pt
    Leading: 29 pt
    Kerning: Optical
  Advanced Character Formats
▼ Indents and Spacing
    Alignment: Left Justify
  Tabs
  Composition
▼ Hyphenation

☑ Preview   Reset Panel   Cancel   OK

A *The General option set of the Paragraph Style Options dialog lists all the attributes in the current style. Use features in any of the other option sets to edit the style.*

Styles panel, then click the **Delete Selected Styles** button 🗑 (or drag the style name over the button).

3. If the style is being used in your document, an alert dialog will appear. Click Yes (this can't be undone).

➤ You can't delete the [Normal Paragraph Style] or [Normal Character Style].

➤ To delete all the styles that aren't being used in your document, choose Select All Unused from the panel menu, then click the Delete Selected Styles button.

Using the Touch Type tool

With the Touch Type tool, you can quickly extend, condense, lengthen, shorten, rotate, or shift an individual character manually. This will be a fun break from all the technical skills you have learned in this chapter!

To use the Touch Type tool:

1. Click the **Touch Type Tool** button on the Character panel, or choose the Touch Type tool (Shift-T). 🔲 Note: If you don't see the button on the Character panel, choose Show Touch Type tool from the panel menu.

2. Click a type character (try using this tool on large, chunky type). A selection border with handles displays around the character.**A**

3. Do any of the following (if you have a touch screen device, you can use your finger):

    To **scale** the character **proportionally**, drag the upper right handle inward or outward.**B**

    To **scale** the character **horizontally**, drag the lower right handle to the left or right.**C**

    To **scale** the character **vertically**, drag the upper left handle upward or downward.

    To **rotate** the character, drag the little circle (located above the character), to the left or right.

    To **shift** the whole character, drag inside the selection border in any direction.**D–E**

    Note: In vertical type, use the handle that is diagonally opposite each one that is described above.

➤ To reset the horizontal and vertical scale values of a selected character or a selected type object to 100%, press Cmd-Shift-X/Ctrl-Shift-X. To reset the baseline shift or rotation value, enter 0 in the respective field on the Character panel.

A *With the Touch Type tool, we clicked the "R" character.*

B *We dragged the upper-right corner to scale the character proportionally.*

C *We dragged the lower-right corner to scale the character horizontally.*

D *We rotated the character, then moved it to the left.*

E *We also scaled, recolored, and moved the last character.*

Hanging punctuation

The Roman Hanging Punctuation command adds a professional typesetter's touch to your document by forcing punctuation marks that fall at the beginning and/or end of a line of area type to hang partially or fully outside the type block. This feature affects single and double quotation marks, hyphens, periods, commas, asterisks, ellipses, en dashes, em dashes, colons, semicolons, and tildes.

To hang punctuation:

1. Do one of the following:

   With a type tool, select a paragraph in an area type object.

   With a selection tool or the Layers panel, select a whole type object.

   To turn on hanging punctuation as a default setting for future type objects, deselect.

2. From the Paragraph panel menu, choose **Roman Hanging Punctuation.A**

➤ For a more visually pleasing alignment of letters and punctuation at the beginning and/or end of lines in a type object, such as the letters "W," "O," or "A," select the object, then choose Type > Optical Margin Alignment. This command may cause some letters to shift slightly outside the block, but they will print.

Setting tabs

The only way to align columns of text or numerals properly is by setting tabs — not by pressing the Spacebar! The default tab stops are half an inch apart. After inserting tabs in your text by following the steps below, you will need to use the Tabs panel to change their alignment style and/or location. You can also add an optional leader character (such as to create a dotted line in a table of contents).

To insert tabs into text:

1. Do either of the following:

   Press the Tab key as you input copy, before typing each new column (you can change the tab location later). The cursor will jump to the nearest default tab stop.**B**

   To insert a tab into existing text, click just to the left of the text that you want the tab to align, then press the Tab key. The text will move to the nearest default tab stop.

2. To customize the tab settings, follow the steps on the next page.

"Dining is and always was a great artistic opportunity."

— Frank Lloyd Wright

A *If you let it hang out — with Roman Hanging Punctuation, that is — the alignment of your type will look more even. This paragraph is left-aligned, so the punctuation is hanging in that direction.*

	Front·9		Back·9		Total¶
Steve	34		34		68¶
Phil	38		44		82¶
Rory	34		38		72¶
Matt	35		38		73#

B *This text is aligned using tab stops. These nonprinting tab characters will display if you choose Type > Show Hidden Characters (Cmd-Option-I/Ctrl-Alt-I).*

To set or modify custom tab stops:

1. After inserting tabs into your text (see the preceding page), do either of the following:

   Select a type object with the Selection tool or the Layers panel.

   Choose a type tool and select some text.

2. Display the Tabs panel ▦ (Window > Type > Tabs or Cmd-Shift-T/Ctrl-Shift-T).**A**

3. To align the ruler with the left and right margins of the selected text for horizontal type, or with the top and bottom margins for vertical type, click the **Position Panel Above Text** button. ▣

4. Do any of the following:

   To add a marker, click in or just above the ruler (the selected text will align to that stop), then with the marker still selected, click an alignment button in the upper left corner of the panel. Repeat to add more markers.

   ➤ Option-click/Alt-click a selected marker to cycle through the alignment choices for it.

   To delete one marker, drag it off the ruler. Or to delete a marker and all markers to its right, Cmd-drag/Ctrl-drag it off the ruler.

   To reposition a tab marker, drag it to the left or right, or enter an exact location in the X field for horizontal type, or in the Y field for vertical type (or click in the field, then press the up or down arrow on the keyboard). Cmd-drag/Ctrl-drag a marker to move that marker and all the markers to its right by the same distance.

5. *Optional:* Click a tab marker in the ruler, then in the Leader field, enter a character (or up to eight characters), such as a period and a space, to be repeated between the tab and the succeeding text.**B**

6. *Optional:* For the Decimal-Justified tab alignment option, in the Align On field, enter a character for the numerals to align to (such as a period for a decimal point, or a dollar sign).**C** Unlike when you use the Leader option, the Align On character must be present (entered) in your text.

➤ To create a sequence of tab stops that are equidistant from one another, based on the spacing between a selected marker and the one to its left, choose Repeat Tab from the panel menu. *Beware!* This command deletes all existing markers to the right of the one you click before it inserts new ones.

➤ Choose Snap to Unit from the Tabs panel menu to have tab markers snap to the nearest ruler tick mark as you insert or move them. (You can also Shift-drag a marker to invoke the opposite behavior of the current Snap to Unit setting.)

➤ Drag the right edge of the panel to adjust the panel width.

➤ To clear all custom tabs, choose Clear All Tabs from the panel menu.

➤ To change the attributes of the leader characters in your text, use a character style.

Scruffy slaw. 8.95
Slurpy soup. 7.50
Boysenberry bundt. 6.00

B *We entered a period and a space as the Leader characters.*

C *We entered a period as the Align On character for a Decimal-Justified tab.*

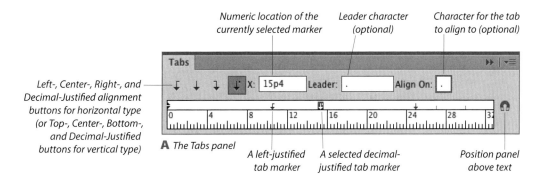

Numeric location of the currently selected marker

Leader character (optional)

Character for the tab to align to (optional)

Left-, Center-, Right-, and Decimal-Justified alignment buttons for horizontal type (or Top-, Center-, Bottom-, and Decimal-Justified buttons for vertical type)

Tabs

X: 15p4   Leader: .   Align On: .

0   4   8   12   16   20   24   28   32

A *The Tabs panel*

A left-justified tab marker

A selected decimal-justified tab marker

Position panel above text

Changing the baseline shift value

By using the Baseline Shift feature, you can shift characters upward or downward from the baseline or, for path type, from a path. Note: To shift whole lines of type, use the leading feature instead (see page 275). To drag an individual character upward or downward manually (using the Touch Type tool), see page 287.

To shift type from its baseline:

1. With a type tool, select the type characters to be shifted.**A**

2. Do either of the following:

   On the Character panel **A** (with its full options displaying), enter or choose a positive **Baseline Shift** value to shift characters upward, or a negative value to shift them downward (or click in the field, then press the up or down arrow on the keyboard).**B–E**

   Hold down Option-Shift/Alt-Shift and press the up arrow on the keyboard to shift the selected characters upward or the down arrow to shift them downward by the current Baseline Shift increment in Illustrator/Edit > Preferences > Type (the default value is 2 pt).

➤ To access superscript and subscript characters in an OpenType font, use the OpenType panel.

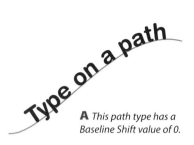

A *This path type has a Baseline Shift value of 0.*

B *We chose a Baseline Shift value of –9 to shift the type downward.*

C *Now the type is straddling the path.*

D *The original artwork contains some type on a path.*

E *To move the type closer to the inner circle, we shifted it downward by –7 pt.*

Creating type outlines

The Create Outlines command converts each character in a type object to a separate graphic object. As outlines, the paths can then be reshaped, used in a compound, or filled with a gradient, like other ordinary paths. You can use this feature to craft custom logos or insignia. Because the outlines are standard paths, they can be printed without your needing to make any printer fonts available.

To create type outlines:

1. Create type using any type tool. Note: All the characters in the object or on the path are going to be converted to outlines.

2. Style the type as desired, including scaling it to the desired size. Once the type is converted into outlines, you won't be able to change the font or other typographic attributes.

3. *Optional:* Type that is converted to outlines can't be converted back to type (unless you undo the conversion immediately), so we suggest that you duplicate the type object.

4. Select the type object with the Selection tool or the Layers panel.**A**

5. Do either of the following:

   Choose Type > **Create Outlines** (Cmd-Shift-O/ Ctrl-Shift-O).**B**

Right-click the object and choose **Create Outlines** from the context menu.

6. Each former type character is converted to a separate compound path and is nested within a group on the Layers panel (see the last tip on page 367). If you want to reshape the points and segments on the resulting paths, you can double-click the group in the document window to put it into isolation mode first.**C**

Note: The fill and stroke attributes and any appearance attributes from the original type characters will be applied to the outlines. If the type was formerly along or inside an object, that object will be preserved as a separate path—unless it formerly had a stroke and fill of None, in which case it will be deleted.

➤ You should avoid creating outlines from small type, for a few reasons: The characters will no longer have the hinting information that preserves the shape of type characters for printing; outline shapes are slightly heavier than their editable type counterparts, so they can be hard to read (even more so if you give them a stroke color); and outlines increase the file size.

A *We selected a type object.*

B *We converted the type to outlines.*

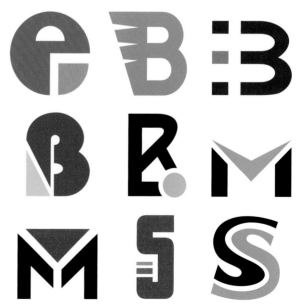

C *Logos like these can be produced using type outlines as a starting point.*

Wrapping type around an object

Type can be wrapped around an Illustrator path, an Illustrator type object, or a placed bitmap image.

To wrap text around an object:

1. Create area type (type inside an object). For the most even-looking wrap, apply one of the justify alignment options to the type (Paragraph panel).

2. Follow this step carefully, or the wrap isn't going to work: Stack the object that the type will wrap around (we'll call it the "wrap object") in front of the type to be wrapped around it, within the same top-level layer, sublayer, or group. (Restack the object via the Layers panel, if necessary.) It can be a vector object, or a bitmap (placed) image that is surrounded by transparency.

3. Select the wrap object.**A**

4. Choose Object > **Text Wrap** > **Make**.

5. Choose Object > Text Wrap > **Text Wrap Options**. In the dialog,**B** check Preview, then enter or choose an **Offset** value for the distance between the wrap object and the type that is wrapping around it.

   Note: To enable text to wrap around opaque (or partially opaque) pixels in a placed image, in Photoshop, put the imagery on a layer that is surrounded by transparency, delete the Background, then save the file in the Photoshop (.psd) format. Import the image into an Illustrator document via the Place command (see page 309).

6. Click OK.**C** Try moving the wrap object slightly, and note how the type rewraps around it.

   Note: If you edit the type in a text wrap in Illustrator CC, the type will update more quickly than in previous versions of Illustrator.

➤ To prevent a text object from being affected by the wrap object, via the Layers panel, restack it above the wrap object or to a different top-level layer.

➤ To change the Offset for an existing wrap object, select it, then choose Object > Text Wrap > Text Wrap Options to reopen the dialog. (In case you're wondering, the Invert Wrap option forces text to wrap inside an unfilled path instead of outside it.)

To release a text wrap:

1. Select the wrap object (not the type).

2. Choose Object > **Text Wrap** > **Release**.

A *Select the object around which you want the area type to wrap.*

B *In the Text Wrap Options dialog, enter an Offset value and check Preview to see the effect in your document.*

Just picture a large sparrow cage made of bamboo grillwork and having a coconut-thatch roof, divided off into two parts by the curtains from my old studio. One of the two parts makes a bedroom, with very little light, so as to keep it cool. The other part, with a large window up high, is my studio. On the floor, some mats and my old Persian rug; and I've decorated the rest with fabrics, trinkets, and drawings. — *Paul Gauguin*

C *The type is wrapping around the palm tree.*

EXERCISE: Create a shadow for point type

A drop shadow that is created using the following method (unlike one that is produced via the Effect > Stylize > Drop Shadow command) is a separate vector object that can be modified via effects, the transform tools, or other methods.

Create type and apply the Feather effect

1. Create some large point type, and select it with the Selection tool.

2. Apply a dark fill color and a stroke of None.

3. Option-drag/Alt-drag the type block slightly downward and to the right.

4. With the copy of the type block still selected, choose a lighter shade of the same fill color.

5. On the Layers panel, ♻ drag the copy of the type below the original, **A** and make sure it's still selected (has a selection square).

6. Show the Appearance panel. From the Add New Effect menu *fx.* on the panel, choose Illustrator Effect > Stylize > Feather. Check Preview, choose a Radius value (try a low value of around 1–4 pt), then click OK. If desired, you can also click the Opacity link to open a temporary Transparency panel, then lower the Opacity setting slightly. **B**

Slant the shadow

1. Verify that the shadow type object is still selected.

2. Double-click the Shear tool 📐 (it's on the Scale tool fly-out menu).

3. Enter 45 as the Shear Angle, click Axis: Horizontal, then click OK.

4. Use the arrow keys on the keyboard to align the baseline of the shadow text with the baseline of the original text. **C**

Reflect the shadow

1. With the shadow type still selected, double-click the Reflect tool 🔲 (it's on the Rotate tool fly-out menu), click Axis: Horizontal, then click OK.

2. Using the arrow keys again, drag the shadow type so its baseline meets the baseline of the original type. **D** You're done!

A *Create a shadow object, then via the Layers panel, stack it below the original type.*

B *Apply the Feather effect and, if desired, lower the opacity of the shadow.*

C *Slant the shadow with the Shear tool.*

D *Reflect the shadow with the Reflect tool.*

A DIFFERENT SLANT

After following steps 1–6 on this page, use the Layers panel to select the shadow object, choose the Free Transform tool, then vertically scale the object by dragging its top center handle upward. If you want to shear it, start dragging the top center handle downward, then hold down Cmd/Ctrl and continue to drag it downward and slightly to the right, all the way across the object. Reposition the shadow object, if needed, then Cmd-click/Ctrl-click the artboard to deselect.

Applying appearance attributes to type

When applying attributes to editable type, such as an added fill or stroke or editable effects, it's important to recognize the difference between selecting the type object and selecting the type characters. This can be made clear by studying the Appearance panel.

➤ When a type object is selected with the Selection tool or via the Layers panel, a **Type** label appears in boldface at the top of the Appearance panel. For basic type, no Stroke or Fill listings display.**A** Any effects that you apply will affect the whole type object (both its fill and its stroke) and will be listed on the panel when the type object is selected.**B**

➤ If you highlight some text characters with a type tool or double-click the word "Characters" on the

Appearance panel, just the original Stroke, Fill, and Opacity attributes for those characters will be listed on, and be editable via, that panel.**C** If you want to redisplay the attributes that apply specifically to the type object, click the word "Type" at the top.

If you find this confusing, just remember that if the label next to the color square at the top of the panel is "Characters," your edits will affect just the selected characters, whereas if the label is "Type," your edits will affect all the type in the object.

➤ To apply transparency settings to the fill or stroke of type, see page 379.

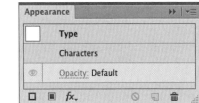

A Because we selected a type object with the Selection tool (above), a "Type" label appeared next to the color square at the top of the Appearance panel (right).

B With the type object selected, we applied two effects: Bulge and Drop Shadow. (Effects can be applied to a type object, but not directly to type characters.)

C Here we selected type with a type tool, so a "Characters" label appeared next to the color square on the Appearance panel, and the Stroke, Fill, and Opacity listings display (not the effect listings).

Next, we'll show you two ways to embellish type, to build on the skills you learned in Chapter 14 (Appearances).

EXERCISE: Add multiple strokes to a character

1. Create a type character in an extra bold, black, or heavy font, approximately 230 pt. in size.

2. Select the type object with the Selection tool.**A**

3. On the Appearance panel, ⬤ click the Add New Fill button. ⬛ A new Stroke and a new Fill listing appear on the panel.

4. From the Swatch Libraries menu on the Swatches panel, ▦ choose Gradients > Metals. On the Metals library panel that opens, click the Gold (first) swatch.

5. On the Gradient panel, ◨ set the Angle value to –90°.

6. On the Appearance panel, click the Stroke listing, Shift-click the color square to open a temporary

Color panel, then enter C 18, M 25, Y 94, and K 0 (press Tab to proceed from field to field). Choose 12 pt from the Stroke Weight menu.**B–C**

7. Continuing on the Appearance panel, click the Add New Stroke button. ⬜ Apply a color of C 0, M 7, Y 51, and K 8, and a Stroke Weight of 8 pt.

8. Click the Add New Stroke button once more. Apply a color of C 20, M 40, Y 96, and K 8, and a Stroke Weight of 2 pt.

9. Click the bottommost Opacity listing on the panel. From the Add New Effect menu, *fx,* choose Illustrator Effects > Stylize > Drop Shadow. Check Preview, choose settings to produce a pleasing-looking shadow, then click OK.**D–E**

A *When we selected the original type object…*

B *…these listings displayed on the Appearance panel. We added new fill and stroke attributes to the type object.*

C *This is the type object after we applied the "Gold" gradient fill preset, a tan stroke color, and a Stroke Weight of 12 pt.*

D *The Appearance panel lists the two new stroke attributes and the effect that we applied to the type object.*

E *This is the final result.*

EXERCISE: Use the Free Distort effect on type

1. Create a type character in an extra or ultra bold font, approximately 230 pt. in size. Choose the Selection tool.

2. At the bottom of the Appearance panel, ⊙ click the Add New Fill button.■ Click the color square for the new Fill listing and choose a light brown color, or Shift-click the Fill color square and mix a light brown via the temporary Color panel.

3. Double-click the Stroke color square and click a dark green swatch. Choose a value of 7 pt from the stroke Weight menu.**A**

4. Double-click the Characters appearance listing, then set both the Stroke and Fill listings to a color of None.

5. Click the Type appearance listing to view the appearance attributes for the type object. Click the Fill listing, then from the Add New Effect menu, *fx* choose Distort & Transform > Free Distort.**B**

6. In the Free Distort dialog, move the top left point downward and to the left. Repeat for the top right point, then click OK.**C**

➤ To edit the Free Distort settings at any time, expand the Fill listing, then click Free Distort.

A We used the Appearance panel to add fill and stroke attributes to this type object.

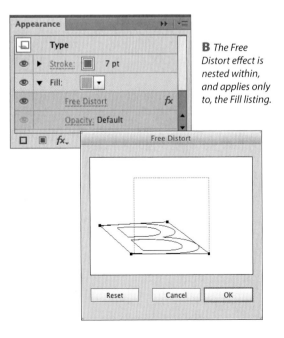

B The Free Distort effect is nested within, and applies only to, the Fill listing.

C The distortion was applied to the fill attribute for the type. (The point type on the bottom has a reddish-brown stroke color and a fill of None.)

Dealing with missing fonts

Fonts, like linked images and graphics, become dependencies when used in an Adobe Illustrator document. This means that those fonts need to be accessible on the computer viewing the document. Adobe Illustrator CC wants to ensure that the fonts used in a document will appear the exact same way when viewed on another computer and will never replace the fonts in a document unless implicitly instructed to do so.

When an Illustrator document is opened and the fonts used in the document are unavailable, Illustrator CC highlights text that uses a missing font in a pink color.**A** Once the fonts are made available on your computer, the text is accessible to Adobe Illustrator and it can display the text using the font in which it is intended to display.**B**

➤ Fonts can be activated on your computer using several methods. Although we discuss below how to manually load fonts onto your computer, many users take advantage of a font management application such as Extensis Suitcase to make the process of activating fonts faster and easier.

To load fonts onto your computer:

1. Do either of the following.

   In the Mac OS, navigate to the ~/Library/Fonts folder (the ~ indicates your user folder). In Windows, navigate to the C:\Windows\Fonts folder. Copy the font files into the Fonts folder.

   In the Mac OS, double-click the font files to launch the Font Book application, then click the Install Font button in the lower-right corner of the window. In Windows, right-click the font files and choose Install.

To identify which fonts are missing in an open document:

1. Choose Type > Find Font to display the Find Font dialog.

2. Choose a missing font from the Fonts in Document section of the dialog.

3. Choose System or Document from the Replace With Font From drop-down menu.

4. Choose a replacement font from the section at the bottom of the dialog, and click Change to change the current found instance of the font or Change All to change all instances of the font.

"Creativity is just connecting things. When you ask creative people how they did something, they feel a little guilty because they didn't really do it, they just saw something. It seemed obvious to them after a while."

A *We opened an Illustrator document that used fonts not found on our computer. This is how the text appears.* ★

"Creativity is just connecting things. When you ask creative people how they did something, they feel a little guilty because they didn't really do it, they just saw something. It seemed obvious to them after a while."

—*Steve Jobs*

B *We then loaded the fonts on our computer, and the text displayed correctly because the fonts were available.*

C *We chose a missing font at the top of the dialog, and we chose System in the Replace With Font From drop-down menu. Then we chose the replacement font at the bottom of the dialog and clicked the Change button.*

Dealing with missing Typekit fonts

Although Typekit fonts can't be packaged and sent to other Illustrator users, subscribers to Creative Cloud have access to needed Typekit fonts as part of their membership. The 2014 release of Illustrator CC introduces an improved workflow for dealing with missing Typekit fonts.

When an Illustrator document is opened and contains text elements that use Typekit fonts not currently activated, Illustrator CC will automatically search the online Typekit desktop font library. If the missing font is available online, you are given the option to sync the missing fonts to your computer.

➤ Although an active internet connection is not required to use Typekit fonts once they are activated on your computer, it is required to actually activate those fonts. So if you're traveling or working without an Internet connection, you'll need to wait until you are "connected" to activate any Typekit fonts.

Activating missing Typekit fonts: ★

1. Open a document that utilizes Typekit fonts that are not currently activated. This will display the Missing Fonts dialog, with a Sync check box next to each font. **A**

2. If Illustrator CC determines that fonts used in the document are available from the online Typekit library, a check mark will display in the Sync box next to each font available to be synced. Make sure that the check mark is chosen for each font, and click the Sync Fonts button in the lower-right corner of the dialog. **B**

➤ Syncing fonts to your computer will take a few seconds to a few minutes, depending on the speed of your Internet connection.

➤ To inspect the missing fonts more closely, click the Find Fonts button to display the Find Font dialog, which will show all missing fonts, including any Typekit fonts.

➤ During Typekit font synchronization, a sync-in-progress icon ⟳ appears as an indicator that font synchronization is in progress.

A We opened a document that utilized Typekit fonts that were not active on our computer.

B We enabled the Sync check box for each font and clicked the Sync Fonts button. The fonts activated and were no longer listed as missing in the dialog.

Mastering the Pen tool — Illustrator's most difficult tool — takes patience and practice.
If you get accustomed to using it, refer to Chapter 12 to learn how to reshape the resulting paths. If you try using this tool but find it to be too difficult, remember that you can create shapes using other methods. For example, you can draw simple geometric shapes (Chapter 6) and then combine them (Chapter 25), or draw in a freehand style with the Blob Brush or Pencil tool (Chapter 7).

Drawing with the Pen tool

The Pen tool creates precise curved and straight segments that are connected by anchor points. You can either click with the tool to create corner points and straight segments without direction handles,**A** or drag with the tool to create smooth points and curve segments with direction handles (the handles look like antennae).**B** The initial shape of the curve segments is determined by the distance and direction in which you drag the mouse, but you can manipulate the direction handles afterward to reshape the curves. You can also use the Pen tool to create corner points, which join nonsmooth curves.**C** The 2014 release of Illustrator CC provides a preview to make it easier to use this tool.

In the instructions on the following pages, you'll learn how to draw straight segments, smooth curves, and nonsmooth curves. Once you master all three techniques, you'll naturally combine them while drawing shapes without really thinking about it: Drag-drag-click, drag, click-click-drag …

PEN TOOLS

21

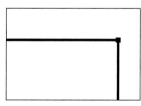

A *This corner point is joining two straight segments, and has no direction handles.*

B *A smooth point has a pair of direction handles that move in tandem. This is a smooth curve.*

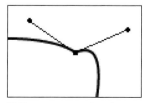

C *This corner point has direction handles that move independently. This is a nonsmooth curve.*

Before you tackle the challenge of drawing curves with the Pen tool, practice the easier task of clicking with the tool to create straight segments.

To draw a straight-sided object with the Pen tool:

1. If the current fill choice is a solid color, a gradient, or a pattern (not None), your Pen path will be filled when you create the first three points. If you prefer to have the segments appear as lines only, choose the desired stroke color and a fill of None.

2. Choose the **Pen** tool 🖋 (P).

3. Turn on Smart Guides (Cmd-U/Ctrl-U), and in Illustrator/Edit > Preferences > Smart Guides, check all the boxes under Display Options.

4. Click to create the first anchor point, then click to create a second one. A straight segment will connect the two points.

5. Click to create additional anchor points. They will be connected by straight segments. You can use the alignment guides feature of Smart Guides to align new points and segments with existing ones or to the horizontal or vertical axis.**A** You can also hold down Shift to constrain the segments to an increment of 45°.

6. Do one of the following:

   To complete the object as an open path and keep it selected, click any tool.

   To complete the object as an open path by deselecting it, Cmd-click/Ctrl-click outside it, press Cmd-Shift-A/Ctrl-Shift-A, or simply press the Esc key.

   To complete the object as a closed path, position the pointer over the starting point (a tiny circle appears in the pointer and an "anchor" label displays next to the point), then click the point.**B–D**

➤ If the artboard starts to fill up with extraneous points as a result of numerous "false starts," choose Object > Path > Clean Up, check just Delete: Stray Points, then click OK.

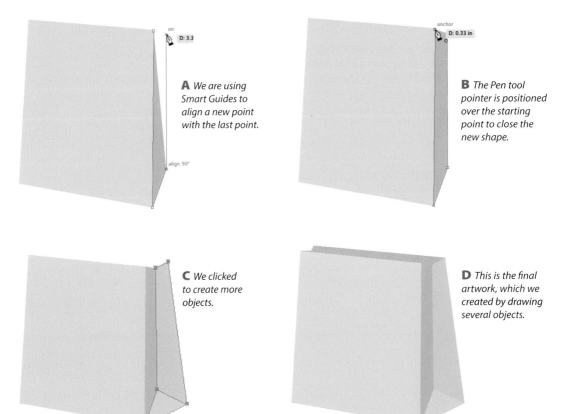

A We are using Smart Guides to align a new point with the last point.

B The Pen tool pointer is positioned over the starting point to close the new shape.

C We clicked to create more objects.

D This is the final artwork, which we created by drawing several objects.

Follow these steps to create smooth curves with the Pen tool. Each smooth anchor point that connects two curve segments has a pair of direction handles that move in tandem. The longer the direction handles, the more steep or broad the curve.

To draw curves with the Pen tool: ★

1. Choose the **Pen** tool  (P).

2. Turn on Smart Guides (Cmd-U/Ctrl-U), and in Illustrator/Edit > Preferences > Smart Guides, check all the boxes under Display Options.

3. Drag (don't click) to create the first anchor point.**A** The angle of the direction handles on the point will align with the direction you drag.

4. To create a second anchor point, release the mouse and move it away from the last anchor point. You'll see a preview showing the general appearance of the next line segment that you'll draw.**B** ★ Drag a short distance in the direction you want the curve to follow.**C** A curve segment will connect the first and second anchor points, and the next pair of direction handles will appear.

5. Drag to create more anchor points and direction handles.**D–F** The points will be connected by curve segments.

   ➤ To produce smooth, symmetrical curves, place the points at the beginning and end of each arc rather than at the middle. You can use Smart Guides to align new points to existing ones.

6. Do one of the following:

   To complete the object as an open path and keep it selected, click any tool.

   To complete the object as an open path by deselecting it, Cmd-click/Ctrl-click outside it or press Cmd-Shift-A/Ctrl-Shift-A.

   To complete the object as a closed path, position the pointer over the starting point (a tiny circle appears in the pointer and an "anchor" label displays next to the point). Drag from that point, then release the mouse.

➤ To keep the curves from looking bumpy and irregular, use just the minimum number of anchor points necessary to define them. Also, drag short distances to produce relatively short direction handles — you can always lengthen them later if needed.

➤ After you draw a line segment, use the Pen tool preview that appears to visualize what your next line segment will look like. ★

A *Drag to create the first anchor point.*

B *A preview of your next line segment appears as you move your cursor away from the original anchor point.* ★

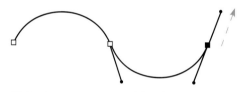

C *Release and reposition the mouse, then drag in the direction you want the curve to follow.*

D *Continue to reposition and drag the mouse.*

E *Continue to reposition and drag.*

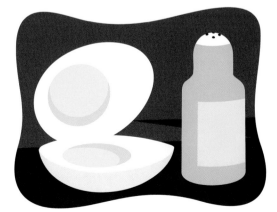

F *Most of the segments in the objects in this illustration are curved. (The large curved shape in the background of this illustration is being used as a clipping mask; see Chapter 26.)*

USING SMART GUIDES WHILE DRAWING A PATH WITH THE PEN TOOL

You can use Smart Guides to align new anchor points with existing points. Although anchor points will align to one another when snapping is enabled, the handles will not snap to other objects, to provide more drawing control. ★

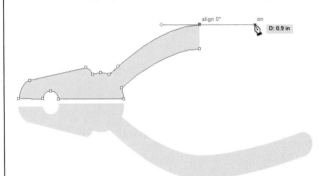

ADJUSTING POINTS AND HANDLES WHILE DRAWING A PATH WITH THE PEN TOOL

► To change the length of the direction handle but keep the direction handles on either side of an anchor point paired, hold down Cmd/Ctrl as you drag a handle. ★

► To reposition the last corner point, keep the mouse button down when you click to create the point, then hold down the Spacebar and drag the point (or do the same for the last smooth point, except drag the direction handle). Release the Spacebar, reposition the mouse, then continue to draw. Practice this; you sort of have to think ahead.

► If the last point you created was a corner point and you want to add one direction handle to it, position the Pen tool pointer over it, then drag; a direction handle appears. Release and reposition the mouse, then continue to draw.

► If you want to convert a corner point to a smooth point while keeping the curve intact, choose the Anchor Point tool and Option-click/Alt-click on a handle. ★

► If the last anchor point you created was a smooth point (two direction handles) and you want to convert it to a corner point (one direction handle), click it with the Pen tool, release and reposition the mouse, then continue to draw. (See also the following page.)

► The Pen tool preview can be quite helpful when you're learning how to use the Pen tool. However, once you are more experienced, you may find it distracting. To disable the Pen tool preview, Go to InDesign/Edit > Selection & Anchor Display and disable the Enable Rubber Band for Pen Tool option. ★

YOU'RE A GENIUS!

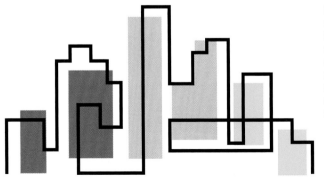

If you get fed up with the Pen tool, create a cityscape like this one and maybe you'll feel better. Draw some rectangles with the Rectangle tool and fill them with a few different colors. Deselect, choose a fill color of None, a black stroke, and the desired stroke weight, then with the Pen tool, click, click, click to create the black lines — using Smart Guides (or hold down Shift) to align them with the horizontal or vertical axis.

Converting anchor points on paths

Yet another use for the Pen tool is to create corner points that join nonsmooth curves—segments that jut out from the same side of an anchor point (unlike smooth curves, which extend from either side of a smooth anchor point). If you move one of the direction handles on a corner point, the contour of the curve changes on just that side of the point.

Note: Smooth points and corner points can be combined in the same path. You can convert smooth points into corner points (or vice versa) as you draw them (as in the steps below) or after you draw them (as in the steps on the next page).

To convert smooth points into corner points as you draw them:

1. Choose the **Pen** tool ✐ (P).

2. Drag to create the first anchor point.**A**

3. Release the mouse, move it away from the last anchor point, then drag a short distance to create a second anchor point.**B** A curve segment will connect the first and second anchor points, and a second pair of direction handles will appear. The shape of the curve segment is controlled by the distance and direction in which you drag.

4. Do either of the following:

   Position the pointer over the last anchor point, Option-drag/Alt-drag from that point to drag one of the direction handles independently, release Option/Alt and the mouse, reposition the mouse, then drag the next point in the direction you want the curve to follow.**C** (So many words to describe a process that becomes intuitive with practice!)

   Click the last anchor point; one of the direction handles disappears from that point.

5. Repeat the last two steps to draw more anchor points and curves.**D–E**

6. To close the shape, do any of the following:

   Drag on the starting point to keep it as a smooth point.

   Click the starting point to convert it to a corner point with one direction handle.

   Option-click/Alt-click the starting point to convert it to a corner point with two direction handles. ★

   To reposition the starting point while closing the path, click and hold down your mouse, then hold down the Spacebar and drag with your mouse. ★

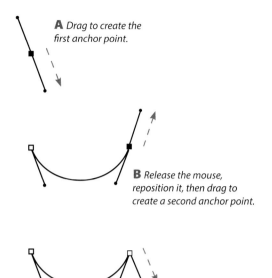

A *Drag to create the first anchor point.*

B *Release the mouse, reposition it, then drag to create a second anchor point.*

C *Option-drag/Alt-drag from the last anchor point in the direction you want the new curve to follow. Both direction handles are now on the same side of the curve segment.*

D *Drag to create another anchor point, and so on.*

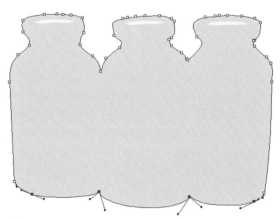

E *We used nonsmooth curves to define the bottom edges of these bottle shapes.*

To convert points on an existing path:

Method 1 (Control panel buttons)

1. Choose the **Direct Selection** tool ⬉ (A).

2. Click a path, then click a point on the path to be converted.

3. On the Control panel, click the **Convert Selected Anchor Points to Corner** button ⬈ or the **Convert Selected Anchor Points to Smooth** button.

   ➤ Read about the Selection & Anchor Display Preferences on page 411. To make it easier to locate anchor points, we recommend checking the Highlight Anchors on Mouse Over preference.

Method 2 (Convert Anchor Point tool)

1. Choose the **Direct Selection** tool ⬉ (A), then click a path.

2. Choose the **Anchor Point** tool ⬈ (Shift-C).

3. To help you locate the anchor points easily, turn on Smart Guides (Cmd-U/Ctrl-U) and in Illustrator/ Edit > Preferences > Smart Guides, check Anchor/ Path Labels.

4. Do any of the following:

   Drag new direction handles from a corner point to convert it to a smooth point.**A**

   To convert a smooth point to a corner point with a nonsmooth curve, rotate a direction handle from the point so it forms a V shape with the other direction handle.**B**

   Click a smooth point to convert it to a corner point with no direction handles.**C–D**

   Option-click/Alt-click a corner point handle to convert the corner point to a smooth point while pairing the handles, maintaining the overall design.**E★**

   ➤ To turn the Pen tool into a temporary Anchor Point tool, hold down Option/Alt. To turn the Pen tool temporarily into the last-used selection tool, hold down Cmd/Ctrl.

   ➤ For more ways to reshape a path, see Chapter 12.

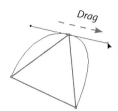

A *A corner point is converted to a smooth point.*

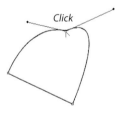

B *A smooth point is converted to a corner point, to produce a nonsmooth curve.*

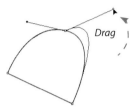

C *A nonsmooth curve is being converted to a corner point.*

D *The path has been restored to a triangle, with no direction handles.*

E *The corner point is converted to a smooth point with paired direction handles.*

EXERCISE: Draw a knife with the Pen tool

Draw the knife blade

1. Turn on Smart Guides (Cmd-U/Ctrl-U) and in Illustrator/Edit > Preferences > Smart Guides, check Alignment Guides and Anchor/Path Labels.

2. Create a long horizontal artboard. Choose the Pen tool 🖊 (P). Choose a light blue-gray solid fill color and a stroke of None.

3. Starting from the left side of the artboard, drag slightly downward and to the right to create the first anchor point. Reposition the pointer on the right side of the artboard and click, move the mouse upward, then click again to create a straight vertical edge.**A–B**

4. Complete the shape by clicking back on the starting point.**C** If necessary, choose the Direct Selection tool ▷ (A) and reposition the handle at the tip of the blade to reshape the blade. Cmd-click/Ctrl-click to deselect.

5. On the expanded Color panel, choose white as the fill color, then add a touch of Cyan or Blue to it.

6. To create the narrow cutting edge of the blade, with the Pen tool (P), click the tip of the blade. Reposition the pointer over the curve of the blade, drag to create a curve that mimics the blade shape,**D** click twice to create a short, straight vertical edge,**E** drag to create a matching curve for the top of the edge of the blade, then click back on the starting point.**F** Reshape the new object, if necessary (as described in step 4).

Draw the knife handle

1. Cmd-click/Ctrl-click to deselect. Choose black as the fill color. With the Pen tool (P), drag over the top right edge of the blade. Working from left to right, drag to create four smooth curve points for the top and end of the handle.**G**

2. Wending your way back to the left, drag to create four smooth curve points to define the bottom of the handle.**H**

Continued on the following page

A *For the blade of the knife, drag to create the first point, then click to create the next one.*

B *Click to create a straight edge.*

C *Click the starting point to close the shape.*

D *For the edge of the blade, click to create a point, then drag to create a curve.*

E *Click twice to create a straight edge.*

F *Drag to create a matching curve, then click the starting point to close the shape.*

G *Drag to create four smooth curve points for the top and end of the knife handle.*

H *Drag to create four smooth curve points to define the bottom of the handle.*

Finally, click near the bottom of the blade, then click the starting point for the handle shape.**A**

Create a shadow for both parts of the knife

1. Choose the Selection tool ⬉ (V). Option-drag/Alt-drag the larger blade object downward and slightly to the left.**B** On the Layers panel, drag the listing for the blade copy to the bottom of the layer.

2. Display the bounding box for the blade copy, then drag the bottom center handle upward slightly to make it more squat. Fill the object with a medium-dark color, and save the color as a swatch to the Swatches panel, if it hasn't already been saved.**C**

3. Option-drag/Alt-drag the handle object slightly downward and to the left.**D** On the Layers panel,

drag the listing for the copy to the bottom of the layer.

4. Fill the handle copy with the shadow color that you saved to the Swatches panel in step 2.

5. Deselect. With the Direct Selection tool ⬉ (A), move the bottom left corner point of the handle copy to smooth the contour between the two shadow shapes (it may help to isolate the object and zoom in).**E**

6. Create a new blank layer, and stack it below the existing ones. With the Rectangle tool ⬛ (M), draw a rectangle behind all the objects, and fill it with a lighter version of the color you chose for the shadows. Time to cook dinner!

A Click to complete the bottom part of the handle, then click the starting point to close the path.

B Option-drag/Alt-drag the blade object downward to copy it. Restack the copy to the bottom of the layer.

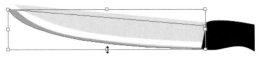

C To scale the shadow, drag the center handle on the bounding box of the copy upward, and fill the path with a medium-dark color.

D Option-drag/Alt-drag the handle object downward to copy it (shown tinted above, for clarity). Restack the copy to the bottom of the layer.

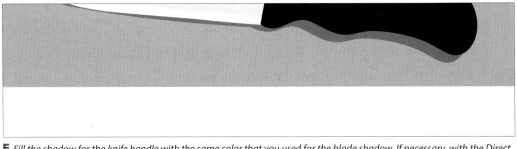

E Fill the shadow for the knife handle with the same color that you used for the blade shadow. If necessary, with the Direct Selection tool, adjust the corner points on the shadow shapes to smooth the transition between them.

If you want to incorporate a photo into your Illustrator design (say, place a photo behind some type for a book cover, poster, or product label) or you want to import a bitmap image or vector artwork for tracing, you will gain the skills you need in this chapter. You will import images into an Illustrator document via the Open and Place commands and via the drag-and-drop method, and you will use the Links and Control panels to edit, replace, locate, update, relink, embed, and unembed your placed images. Illustrator accepts all common graphics file formats.

Note: In this chapter, we refer to linked and embedded bitmap images and vector graphics collectively as "images" or "files."

How images are acquired in Illustrator

The methods for acquiring images or graphics from other applications include the Open command, the Place command, and drag-and-drop. Your choice will depend on what file formats are available for saving the file in its original application and how you plan to use the file in Illustrator.

When you open a file from another drawing (vector) application via the Open command, it appears in a new Illustrator document, and the acquired objects can be manipulated using Illustrator tools and commands. When you open a bitmap image via the Open command, the image is embedded in a new document as a non-vector object.

Via the Place command, an image can be linked or embedded into your Illustrator document. For print output, the recommended formats for linked images — EPS, TIFF, and PDF — preserve the colors, detail, and resolution of the original image. When placing a layered Photoshop (.psd) image into Illustrator, you can choose (via a dialog) to have the image appear as a single flattened object or as separate objects on separate layers.

You can also acquire images or graphics by using the drag-and-drop method. When you drag an image or artwork from one Illustrator window into another, or from a document window of another application (such as Photoshop) into an Illustrator document, a duplicate of that content appears in the target document.

A bitmap image that you acquire in Illustrator via the Open, Place, or drag-and-drop method can be moved, placed on a different layer, masked, modified using any

ACQUIRE IMAGES

22

TRACING IMPORTED IMAGES

If you import a raster image into an Illustrator document, you can convert it to vector art via the Image Trace panel. The artwork shown at the top of this page is an expanded tracing. See Chapter 17.

transformation method, or modified using Photoshop effects. All three methods for acquiring images preserve the resolution of the original image. (For the Clipboard commands—Cut, Copy, and Paste—that can also be used to acquire images in Illustrator, see page 105.)

Using the Open command

The Open command opens an image or graphics file as a separate Illustrator document. For a list of some of the formats that you can open in Illustrator, see the sidebar at right.

Note: To preserve the editability of appearances and text in an Adobe PDF file, use the Open command, as in the steps below, instead of the Place command, which is discussed on the next page.

To import an image into Illustrator via the Open command:

1. Do either of the following:

   In Bridge, right-click a file thumbnail and choose **Open With > Adobe Illustrator CC 2014**.

   In Illustrator, choose File > **Open** (Cmd-O/Ctrl-O). The Open dialog appears. In the Mac OS, choose Enable: All Readable Documents to dim any files that are in formats Illustrator can't read. In Windows, you can filter out files via the menu next to the File Name field, or choose All Formats (the default setting) to display files in all formats. Double-click a file name; or locate and click a file name, then click Open.

2. If you chose a multipage PDF file, the Open PDF dialog will appear.**A** Check Preview, click an arrow to navigate to the desired page (or enter the desired page number in the field), then click OK. Respond to any alert dialogs that appear (see the sidebar on the following page and see also page 63).

   If you chose a Photoshop PSD file that contains layers or layer comps, the Photoshop Import Options dialog will appear. See pages 312–313.

   Other formats may cause a different dialog to appear. Choose options, then click OK to proceed.**B**

   ➤ If you reduce the scale of a linked or embedded image in Illustrator, its resolution will increase accordingly; if you enlarge it, its resolution will decrease.

FILE FORMATS THAT CAN BE IMPORTED INTO ILLUSTRATOR

Image and graphics files in a wide variety of formats can be opened or placed into Illustrator CC. A few examples are BMP, CGM, CorelDRAW, DWG, EMF, EPS, FXG, GIF, JPEG, JPEG2000, PDF, PSD, SVG, SVGZ, TIFF, and WMF (but not SWF). You can also open or place text formats, such as TXT (plain text), RTF, and MS Word. To open native Illustrator files into Illustrator, see pages 55 and 62.

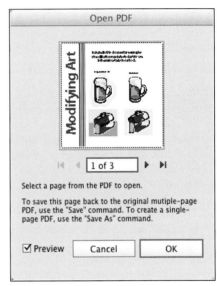

A For a multipage PDF file, navigate to the page that you want to open.

B To produce this artwork, we used editable type as a clipping path to partially mask an imported image. To learn about clipping masks, see Chapter 26. (We also added an object that has a solid white fill.)

Using the Place command

The Place command imports an image or graphic into an existing Illustrator document. You can reposition the graphic on the artboard, restack it via the Layers panel, use it in a mask, transform it, apply any of the Photoshop effects and most of the Illustrator effects to it, or change its opacity or blending mode. Depending on whether you check the Link option in the Place dialog, the artwork will either be linked to your document or embedded into it. Later in this chapter, you will learn how to manage linked images.

To import an image into an Illustrator document via the Place command:

Method 1 (from Illustrator)

1. Open an Illustrator document, and click a layer on which you want the image or graphic to appear.

2. Choose File > **Place**, then in the dialog, click a file to be placed.

3. Do either of the following:

    Check **Link** to place just a screen version of the image file into your Illustrator document, with a link to the original file. The original image file won't be affected by your edits in Illustrator, nor will it be color-managed by Illustrator, but in order for it to print properly, it must be available on your hard disk.

    Uncheck Link to embed a copy of the actual file into the Illustrator document and allow Illustrator to color-manage it. The embedded image will increase the storage size of your Illustrator file.

4. Click Place. An options dialog may appear. For example, if you place a Photoshop PSD file that contains layers (with the Link option unchecked), or that contains layer comps (with the Link option checked or unchecked), the Photoshop Import Options dialog will appear. To learn about this dialog, see the next two pages.

Method 2 (from Bridge)

1. Open an Illustrator document, and click the layer on which you want the imported image to appear.

2. In Bridge, right-click an image thumbnail and choose **Place** > **In Illustrator**. The imported image will appear in the Illustrator document and will be linked to the document automatically.

➤ When selected, a linked image will have an X on top of it, in the selection color of the current layer.**A**

DECIPHERING THE ALERT DIALOGS

When you open or place a file into Illustrator, one or more alert dialogs may appear.

If you get an alert that lists missing fonts and/or objects that have been reinterpreted, like the one shown below, click OK to accept the substitutions (or click Cancel if you change your mind).

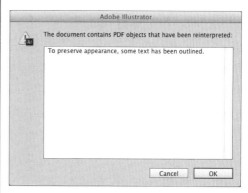

A Photoshop PSD file with a 16-bit depth can be opened into Illustrator only as an 8-bit flat composite image, as the alert shown below will inform you.

To learn about the Embedded Profile Mismatch and Missing Profile alerts, which let you control how an imported image that either contains or lacks an embedded color profile is color managed, see page 63.

A *A linked image is selected in an Illustrator document.*

If you select multiple bitmap or vector files in the Place dialog, the files will load automatically into the pointer when you exit the dialog, and you can drop them into your document in the desired order and location.

To place multiple images into an Illustrator document:

1. Open an Illustrator document, then choose File > **Place**. The Place dialog opens.

2. With Cmd/Ctrl or Shift held down, click two or more file names.**A**

3. Do either of the following:

   Click **Place**. The pointer displays a loaded graphics icon.

   Check **Show Import Options**, then click **Place**.

4. If you checked Show Import Options, and if import settings can be chosen for any of the selected files, the Import Options dialog will appear for each of those files in succession. Choose settings in, then click OK to exit, each dialog (e.g., for a multipage file, use a navigation arrowhead to select the file to be loaded). For a PDF file, choose an option from the Crop To menu (e.g., choose Bounding Box for no transparency in the image, or Art to make the areas outside the artwork transparent, or one of the other options to crop the file).

5. In your Illustrator document, you can press the left or right arrow key to cycle through previews of the loaded images. Display the preview for the image you want to place first (**A**, next page).

   ➤ To view and modify the import options for an image, navigate to its preview by pressing the left or right arrow key, then Shift-click. Change any of the settings, then click OK.

   ➤ If you want to eliminate an image from the loaded pointer, display its preview, then press Esc.

6. To place the image that is currently previewing in the loaded pointer, do either of the following:

   To place the image in its original dimensions, position the loaded pointer in the document where you want the upper-left corner of the image to appear, then click.

   To scale the image as you place it, position the loaded pointer where you want the upper-left corner of the image to appear, then drag. The rectangular bounding box will have the same aspect ratio as the original file.

7. Repeat to place the remaining loaded images. You can align them to one another using Smart Guides (**B–C**, next page).

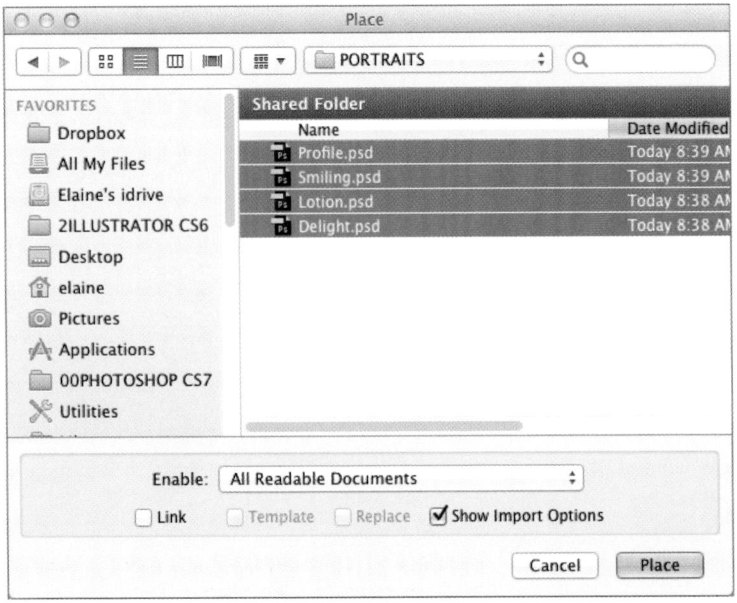

A In the Place dialog, we held down Cmd/Ctrl and clicked four image names.

Loaded graphics pointer

Position of the current image (second) within the total number of loaded images (four)

Preview of the current image

A *When we clicked OK in the Place dialog, the loaded pointer appeared in our document. We pressed the right arrow on our keyboard to select the image we wanted to place first.*

B *We're using a Smart Guide to align the second placed image with the top edge of the first one …*

C *… and then to place the fourth placed image at the intersection of the second and third images.*

Importing Photoshop images into Illustrator

Choosing Photoshop import options

Importing a single-layer image

If you import a one-layer Photoshop PSD image into Illustrator via the **Open** or **Place** command, it will be listed on the Layers panel by its file name on the currently active layer, and no dialog will open (if any alerts appear, see the sidebar on page 309). Illustrator won't generate a clipping mask.

Importing a multilayer image

If you place a PSD file that contains layers with the Link option unchecked, place a PSD file that contains layer comps with or without the Link option checked, or open a PSD file that contains layers or layer comps, the Photoshop Import Options dialog opens.**A** Check **Show Preview** to display a thumbnail preview of the image. The other options are described below.

Importing layer comps

Choose from the **Layer Comp** menu to import a layer comp, if the file contains any. Any comments entered in Photoshop for the chosen comp will display in the Comments window. If you need to import additional layer comps from the same Photoshop image, you will have to use the Place command separately for each one.

If the image contains layer comps and you checked Link in the Place dialog, you can choose **When Updating Link: Keep Layer Visibility Overrides** to preserve the layer visibility (hide or show) state of the layers when you originally placed the image, regardless of any visibility changes you make to the file in Photoshop after it is imported; or choose **Use Photoshop's Layer Visibility** to have any subsequent layer visibility changes that are made to the image in Photoshop also appear in Illustrator (you must click Yes in the alert dialog when you return to Illustrator).

Importing Photoshop layers

If you unchecked the Link option in the Place dialog, you now have the option to keep or flatten the layers. If you click **Convert Layers to Objects**, each object will be nested within an image group on the current layer.**B** Transparency levels are listed as editable appearances in Illustrator. Blending modes that are also available in Illustrator (on the blending mode menu in the Transparency panel) are preserved and are listed as editable appearances. Layer groups are preserved, as are layer and vector masks. A vector mask is listed as a clipping path on the Layers panel, whereas a layer

A When we imported a Photoshop PSD file that contains layers into Illustrator, we unchecked the Link option in the Place dialog, and this Photoshop Import Options dialog opened.

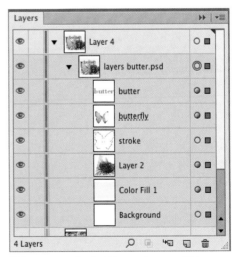

B Because we checked Convert Layers to Objects in the Photoshop Import Options dialog, each Photoshop layer became a separate Illustrator object, nested within one group.

mask becomes an opacity mask and displays on the Transparency panel. Plain type remains editable, when possible (see the last paragraph in this column). Each converted layer from the Photoshop file is listed separately on the Links panel.

If you click **Flatten Layers to a Single Image** instead, a flattened version of the image will be nested within the current layer. All transparency levels, blending modes, and layer mask effects will be applied to the flattened image but won't be listed as editable appearances in Illustrator.

Check **Import Hidden Layers** and/or **Import Slices**, if available (and if desired), to import those elements with the file.

Linked images are flattened automatically (that is, the Convert Layers to Objects option isn't available).

If you click Convert Layers to Objects in the Photoshop Import Options dialog, the Background from the Photoshop file will become one of the nested objects within Illustrator, and will be opaque. You can change its opacity, hide it, or delete it via the Layers panel in Illustrator.

Adjustment layers or effects in a Photoshop file

The position of adjustment layers and effects in the layer stack in a Photoshop document will affect how image layers in that file are converted to objects when the file is placed into an Illustrator document (Convert Layers to Objects option clicked). Any layers above an adjustment layer or a layer containing effects in the Photoshop file will be converted to separate objects in Illustrator. Any layers below an adjustment layer or a layer containing effects in the Photoshop file will be flattened, along with the adjustment layer, into one object in Illustrator, but the appearance of those effects and adjustments will be preserved. Before the image is placed into Illustrator, another option is to merge, delete, or hide adjustment layers in Photoshop (hidden adjustment layers won't be imported, regardless of the Import Hidden Layers setting) and delete all layer effects, then apply any desired effects in Illustrator.

Importing Photoshop type

If you place a Photoshop file that contains editable type into Illustrator (with the Link option unchecked) and click Convert Layers to Objects, the type objects will remain as editable type, provided the type layer in Photoshop didn't contain effects or warp edits.

If you want to import a type layer as vector outlines instead, in Photoshop, apply Type > Convert to Shape,

then import it into Illustrator via the Open or Place command, using the Convert Layers to Objects option.

➤ If a layer in a Photoshop file contains pixels that extend outside the live canvas area, those pixels will be discarded when you import it into Illustrator, no matter which method you use — drag-and-drop, place, or open. Before acquiring an image from Photoshop, make sure the pixels that you want to import are visible within the live canvas area in the Photoshop file.

Importing a TIFF image

When you place a layered TIFF file into an Illustrator document, the TIFF Import Options dialog opens, offering the same options as in the Photoshop Import Options dialog. When you don't have the option to save a document in the Photoshop PSD format for import into Illustrator, TIFF is an acceptable alternative.

CREATING AN OBJECT MOSAIC

To convert a bitmap image into a mosaic of colored vector squares, place an image into an Illustrator document (Link option unchecked). Click the object, then choose Object > Create Object Mosaic. For an easy approach to this dialog, enter a Width value for the Number of Tiles, click Use Ratio, then click OK (unfortunately, the dialog doesn't have a Preview option).

Managing linked images

When you place an image from another application into an Illustrator document, you can either embed a copy of the image into the document (and thereby increase the file size but allow Illustrator to color-manage it) or link the image to your document (and keep the file size smaller but require the original file to be available for print output). For the latter option, a screen version of each image serves as a placeholder in your document, but the actual image remains separate from the Illustrator file. To link an image, use the File > Place command with the Link option checked.

The Links panel **A** lists all the linked and embedded images in your Illustrator document, and provides controls for keeping track of those images. It lets you monitor the status of linked images; restore the link to a missing image (so it can be output properly); open a linked image in its original application (for editing); update a modified linked image; and convert a linked image to an embedded one, or vice versa.

Some Links panel commands are also available on the Control panel when a linked image is selected in your document.**B–D** You can click Linked File to display a temporary Links panel, or click the name of the linked image to access commands.

To edit a linked image in its original application:

1. Do either of the following:

   On the Links panel, click a file name, then click the **Edit Original** button.

   Click a file in the document window, then click **Edit Original** on the Control panel.

   The application in which the linked file was created will launch, if it isn't already running, and the file will open.

2. Make your edits, resave the file, then return to Illustrator. If an alert dialog appears,**E** click Yes. The linked image will update in your document.

   Note: In Illustrator/Edit > Preferences > File Handling & Clipboard, under Files, you can choose preferences for linked images. For example, via the Update Links menu, you can specify whether linked images will update automatically if they are modified in their original application (see also "To update a modified linked image" on the next page, and learn more about these preferences on page 419).

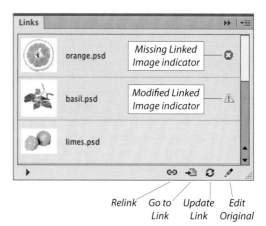

Relink   Go to   Update   Edit
         Link   Link   Original

A *The Links panel provides many useful controls for managing linked images.*

B *When a linked image is selected in your document, you can click Linked File on the Control panel to open a temporary Links panel, or click the image name to access a menu of Links panel commands.*

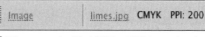

C *When an embedded JPEG or PNG image is selected in your document, you can click Image on the Control panel to open a temporary Links panel, or click the image name to access a menu of Links panel commands.*

D *When any other type of embedded image is selected in your document, you can click Embedded on the Control panel to access a menu of Links panel commands.*

E *This alert appears if you edit a linked image in its original application, then click back in the Illustrator document.*

If you replace one placed image with another, any effects, transparency settings, or transformations (e.g., scale, rotation edits) that were applied to the image in Illustrator are applied to the replacement automatically.

To replace a linked or embedded image:

1. Do either of the following:

   On the Links panel, ⊞ click the name of the file to be replaced, then click the **Relink** button. ⊞ **A**

   Click the image in the document window, then on the Control panel, click the file name or the **Embedded** link (not the Embed button) and choose **Relink** from the menu.

2. In the Place dialog, locate the desired replacement file, then click Place. **B** If another dialog opens, choose options, then click OK.

The Go to Link command simply locates a placed image for you, selects it on its artboard, and centers it within the document window. If your document contains many linked images and you want to locate a particular one, this command may come in handy.

To go to a linked or embedded image:

On the Links panel, ⊞ click a file name, then click the **Go to Link** button. ➡

► If you click the listing for a linked image on the Links panel, then choose Reveal in Bridge from the panel menu, Bridge will open, and the image thumbnail will be selected in the Bridge window.

If you edit an image in its original application and Manually is the current setting on the Update Links menu in Illustrator/Edit > Preferences > File Handling & Clipboard (or Ask When Modified is the preference setting and you click No in the alert), this icon ⚠ will appear on the Links panel. To update the link, follow the steps below. Note: If the preference setting is Automatically, the image will update automatically, without an alert appearing.

To update a modified linked image:

1. On the Links panel, ⊞ click the listing for the modified image. ⚠

2. Do either of the following:

   Click the **Update Link** button ↻ at the bottom of the Links panel.

   Click the image in the document window, then click the file name on the Control panel and choose **Update Link** from the menu.

LINKED VERSUS EMBEDDED IMAGES

► On the Layers panel, a linked image will be listed as <Linked File> or by its file name, within the current layer.

► An embedded image will be listed on the current layer as <Image> or by its file name. A file in the TIFF format will be nested within a group; a PDF file will be nested within three groups, some of which will contain a clipping path.

► Photoshop effects on the Effect menu can be applied to both linked and embedded images and will remain editable.

► You can transform (e.g., move, scale, rotate, shear, or reflect) both linked and embedded images.

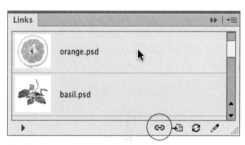

A *Click the linked image to be replaced, then click the Relink button.*

B *We replaced the "orange.psd" image with an image called "apples.psd."*

To locate or replace images upon opening an Illustrator document:

Say you link an image to an Illustrator document, save and close the document, then rename the actual image file or move it from its original location. If you subsequently reopen the document, an alert will appear.**A** Do either of the following:

To locate the missing file or substitute a different image, click **Replace**, locate the missing file or the desired replacement one, then click Replace.

Click **Ignore**. This icon 🞫 will display for the listing on the Links panel. The linked image won't display (but you can locate its bounding box via the object highlighting feature of Smart Guides).

Optional: Check Apply to All in the alert dialog to have the button you click apply to any other missing images.

A *If Illustrator detects that a linked file is missing when you open a document, this alert will appear.*

To locate or replace a missing linked image in an open Illustrator document:

If you link an image to an Illustrator document, rename the image file or move it from its original location, then click back in the Illustrator document, an alert will appear. Do either of the following:

Click **Yes**, then click **Replace** in the next alert dialog. Locate the missing file in the Replace dialog, then click Replace.

Click **No**. At any time, on the Links panel, click the listing that has a missing image icon, 🞫 then click the **Relink** button. In the Place dialog, locate the missing file, then click Place.

➤ If you want to break the link to a missing image completely and prevent an alert prompt from appearing in the future, delete the bounding box and resave your document.

➤ To relink a missing linked image another way, click the image in the document. On the Control panel, click the image link (the file name, not the Embed button) and choose Relink from the menu. In the Place dialog, locate the missing file, then click Place.

VIEWING DATA ABOUT A PLACED IMAGE

➤ The Links panel displays data about the currently selected linked or embedded image (more data is listed for a linked image than for an embedded one). If the data area of the panel isn't showing, double-click the listing for which you want to view data; or click the listing, then click the Show Link Info arrowhead ▶ at the bottom of the panel. The panel expands.

➤ If you want to display the actual folder of the currently selected linked image, click the Show in Finder/Show in File Explorer button 📁 next to the Location data.

➤ To navigate to data for other linked or embedded images, click the Previous or Next arrowhead at the bottom of the panel.

➤ To view other metadata about a linked image (e.g., keywords, copyright info, and IPTC contact info) in a separate dialog, click the file listing on the Links panel, then choose Link File Info from the panel menu.

Embedding and unembedding images

The Embed Image command embeds a copy of an image into the Illustrator document (changes its status from linked to embedded) and breaks the link between the original image file and the Illustrator document. Be aware that this will increase the file size of your document.

To change the status of an image from linked to embedded:

Do either of the following:

On the Links panel, ⛓ click the name of a linked image,**A** then choose **Embed Image** from the Links panel menu.**B**

Click a linked image in the document window, then click **Embed** on the Control panel.

When you embed a multilayer PSD file, the Photoshop Import Options dialog opens; for a multilayer TIFF image, the TIFF Import Options dialog opens. See pages 312–313.

When you import an image into an Illustrator document with the Link option off, the image is embedded into the document. If for some reason you need to unembed an image (say, in the process of preparing your document for output), you can do so via the Unembed command. It saves a copy of the former embedded image as a new, linked document in the Photoshop or TIFF format. In your Illustrator document, the artwork looks the same.

To unembed an image from an Illustrator document:

1. Do either of the following:

   Click an embedded image in your document, then on the Control panel, click **Unembed**.

   On the Links panel, click the listing for an embedded image, then from the panel menu, choose **Unembed**.

2. The Unembed dialog opens. Keep the existing name or enter a new name, choose a location, choose the File Format of Photoshop (*.PSD) or TIFF (*.TIF), make sure Hide Extension is unchecked, then click Save. Note that the file listing on the Links panel no longer has an embedded icon.

A *Click the listing for a linked image on the Links panel, then choose Embed Image from the panel menu.*

Embedded images have this icon.

B *Note that the file name will be listed for all embedded and linked images, but not for embedded images that contain multiple layers.*

Dragging and dropping images into Illustrator

Drag-and-drop is a quick method for duplicating imagery between applications or documents; the copy is created instantly. You can drag and drop (drag-copy) objects between Illustrator documents, as we showed you on page 104, or between Illustrator and Adobe Dreamweaver, Adobe InDesign, or any other drag-aware application. You can also drag and drop a pixel selection or layer from Photoshop into Illustrator, as described in the steps below.

Note: When we need to acquire a Photoshop image for an Illustrator document that is going to be output to print, instead of using drag-and-drop, we convert a copy of the image to CMYK Color mode in Photoshop, save it in the Photoshop (.psd) format, then use the File > Place command in Illustrator to acquire it. The Photoshop Import Options dialog provides an option to convert layers to separate objects and preserve their editability, and the image stays in CMYK mode.

To drag and drop a selection or layer from a Photoshop document to an Illustrator document:

1. In Photoshop, click a pixel layer. *Optional:* Create a selection on the layer.

2. Open an Illustrator document. Arrange the Application frames in Illustrator and Photoshop so both document windows are visible.

3. In Photoshop, choose the Move tool ▶⊕ (V), then drag the selection or layer from the Photoshop document window into the Illustrator document window. A copy of the image appears in the target document, and will be embedded at the resolution and color mode of the original image. In the Mac OS, the image will be nested within a group in the currently active layer; in Windows, it will be listed as <Image>.

▶ The drag-and-drop method doesn't use the Clipboard.

▶ A "dropped" Photoshop selection or layer will be assigned an opacity value of 100% on the Transparency panel in Illustrator, regardless of its

opacity value in Photoshop, but it may look lighter if its original opacity was less than 100%. You can lower the opacity value in Illustrator, if desired. Photoshop blending modes will be ignored visually, and won't register on the Transparency panel in Illustrator.

▶ Layer masks and vector masks from Photoshop will be applied to the "dropped" image (meaning the image will be clipped), and then will be discarded. If necessary, you can create a clipping mask in Illustrator to mask the image further.

▶ If you drag and drop a selection, pixel layer, editable type layer, or shape layer from Photoshop into Illustrator with the Move tool, it will become rasterized (if it isn't already). Any transparent pixels will become opaque white. If you drag and drop a selected path or vector mask from Photoshop into Illustrator with the Path Selection tool, it will become a compound path in Illustrator and won't be rasterized.

▶ Yet another option is to copy a path from Photoshop and paste it into Illustrator, in which case the Paste Options dialog will open. Click Paste As: Compound Shape (Fully Editable) or Compound Path (Faster). The Compound Shape option is recommended for multiple or overlapping paths.

▶ If you have one or more paths in a Photoshop document that you'd like to be able to edit in Illustrator, you can choose File > Export > Paths to Illustrator, which will allow you to save the paths to a separate Illustrator file.

To place an image into Illustrator by dragging it from Bridge:

1. Open or create an Illustrator document.

2. Arrange the Bridge and Illustrator windows so they're both visible. Click in Bridge, then click an image thumbnail.

3. Do either of the following:

   To **link** the image, drag its thumbnail into an Illustrator document window.

   To **embed** the image, Shift-drag its thumbnail into an Illustrator document window.

You can embellish plain vanilla path edges with a brush stroke that looks like ink, paint, or chalk, or that contains a pattern, a bitmap image, or multiple vector objects. The five flavors of brushes — Calligraphic, Scatter, Art, Bristle, and Pattern — are stored on and accessed from the Brushes panel. ✶ A The default panel contains only a small handful of the brushes that are available in Illustrator; we'll show you how to add more.

Not only do Illustrator brushes provide all the advantages of vector graphics (small file sizes, resizability, and crisp output), they're also live. If you edit a brush that's being used in your document, you'll be given the option via an alert dialog to update the paths in which the brush is being used. And if you reshape the path or increase the stroke weight or width, the brush stroke will conform to the new contour automatically.

In this chapter, you will embellish existing paths with brushes; remove and expand brush strokes; create and edit custom Calligraphic, Scatter, Art, Bristle, and Pattern brushes; modify existing brush strokes; add, duplicate, and delete brushes from the Brushes panel; and create and load brush libraries.

There are two ways to produce brush strokes: You can choose the Paintbrush tool and a brush and draw a shape with a brush stroke built into it right off the bat, which we showed you how to do on page 87, or you can apply a brush stroke to an existing path of any kind, as described on the following page.

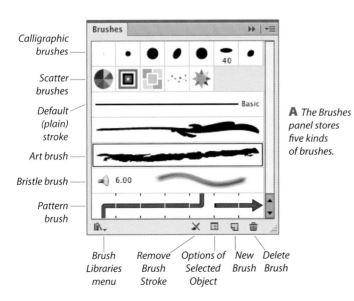

Calligraphic brushes

Scatter brushes

Default (plain) stroke

Art brush

Bristle brush

Pattern brush

Brush Libraries menu

Remove Brush Stroke

Options of Selected Object

New Brush

Delete Brush

A The Brushes panel stores five kinds of brushes.

BRUSHES

23

IN THIS CHAPTER

Applying brushes to existing paths

In these steps, you will apply a brush stroke to an existing path. It doesn't matter which tool the path was created with (e.g., Star, Polygon, Ellipse, Type, Pencil, Blob Brush, Line Segment, or Pen tool).

To apply a brush to an existing path:

1. Do one of the following:

   Select an existing path using a selection tool or the Layers panel,**A** then click a brush on the Brushes panel 🖌 or on the **Brush Definition** menu on the Control panel.**B–F**

   Drag a brush from the Brushes panel onto a path or onto type (the object doesn't have to be selected), and release the mouse when the plus sign pointer is over the object.

   Apply a brush from a library by following the instructions on the next page.

2. *Optional:* You can change the stroke weight or color (a color change won't show up for a Pattern brush). The Align Stroke setting of Align Stroke to

Center (Stroke panel) will be applied to the path automatically; the other Align Stroke settings won't be available.

➤ What's the difference between a Pattern brush **G** and a Scatter brush? **H** For a Scatter brush, you can specify a degree of randomness for the size, spacing, and scatter variables; not so for a Pattern brush. Also, Pattern brushes are made from up to five tiles (Side, Outer Corner, Inner Corner, Start, and End), and are used for creating borders or frames, whereas scatter brushes are made from multiple copies of one object.

A *We selected a path...*

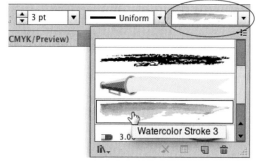

B *...and then clicked a brush on the Brush Definition menu on the Control panel.*

C *The Art brush we chose appeared on the path.*

D *A different Art brush is applied to the same path.*

E *A Calligraphic brush is applied.*

F *A Bristle brush is applied.*

G *A Pattern brush is applied.*

H *A Scatter brush is applied.*

Using the Brushes panel

After opening a brush library, you can either apply a brush from the library directly to any path in your document, or add brushes from the library to the Brushes panel for later use. Furthermore, you can use any brush from a library as the starting point for the creation of a custom brush. After adding a brush to your document's Brushes panel, you can duplicate it, if desired (see page 339), and then customize it to your liking. The brushes on the panel save only with the current document.

To load brushes from a library:

1. Deselect (Cmd-Shift-A/Ctrl-Shift-A).

2. From a submenu on the **Brush Libraries** menu on the Brushes panel, choose a library name.

3. Do one of the following:

   Click a brush in the library. It will appear on the Brushes panel.

   Cmd-click/Ctrl-click multiple brushes in the library (or click, then Shift-click a series of them), then choose **Add to Brushes** from the library menu.**A–B**

   Drag a brush directly from the library onto any object in the document (the object doesn't have to be selected). The brush will appear on the object and on the Brushes panel.

➤ To close all the libraries on a panel, click the close button; to close one library on a panel, right-click its tab and choose Close from the context menu.

➤ Once a library panel is open, you can cycle through the other libraries by clicking the Load Next Brush Library or Load Previous Brush Library button at the bottom of the library panel.

➤ To force a library to display when you relaunch Illustrator, choose Persistent from the library menu. To save the brushes currently on the Brushes panel as a library, see page 342.

➤ To access brushes from another document, for step 2 on this page, choose Other Library on the Brush Libraries menu. Locate the document that contains the desired brushes, click Open, then continue with step 3.

WHICH BRUSH TYPES ARE WHICH?	
Type	Library
Calligraphic	Artistic_Calligraphic, 6D Art Pen Brushes
Scatter	Arrows_Standard, Artistic_Ink, Decorative_Scatter, 6D Art Pen Brushes, Elegant Curl & Floral Brush Set
Art	Arrows_Special, Arrows_Standard, all the "Artistic" libraries except _Calligraphic, Decorative_Banners and Seals, Decorative_Text Dividers, Elegant Curl & Floral Brush Set, Grunge Brushes Vector Pack, Hand Drawn Brushes Vector Pack
Pattern	All the "Borders" libraries, Pattern Arrows, Elegant Curl & Floral Brush Set, Image Brush Library

*To identify brush types by their icons, see **A**, next page.*

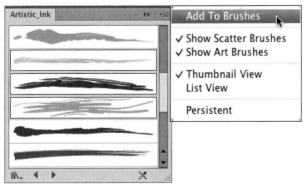

A *To append multiple brushes to the Brushes panel for the current document, Cmd/Ctrl click to select them, then choose Add to Brushes from the library panel menu.*

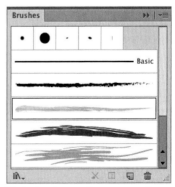

B *The brushes we chose appeared on the Brushes panel for our document.*

To choose display options for the Brushes panel:

From the Brushes panel menu:

Choose **List View** to have a small thumbnail, the brush name, and an icon for the brush type (Calligraphic, Scatter, Art, Bristle, or Pattern) display for each brush on the panel;**A** or choose **Thumbnail View** to display brushes as larger thumbnails without names and icons.

To control which brush types (categories) display on the panel, choose **Show** [brush type] to check or uncheck that option.

➤ You can drag any brush upward or downward on the panel to a different location — but only within its own category. To move a series of brushes, click, then Shift-click to select them, then drag.

Removing brush strokes from objects

When you remove a brush stroke from a path, you're left with a plain vanilla path, in the same color and width as the former path.

To remove a brush stroke from an object, group, or layer:

1. Do either of the following:

Select one or more objects to which a brush is assigned.**B**

Target a layer or group to which a brush stroke is assigned.

2. Do either of the following:

On the Brushes panel, click the **Remove Brush Stroke** button. **C**

On the Brushes panel or on the Brush Definition menu (on the Control panel), click the **Basic** brush.

SETTING UP A PAINTING WORKSPACE

To set up your panel docks quickly so they contain the panels that are customarily used when painting (including the Color, Swatches, Color Guide, Brushes, and Stroke panels), choose Window > Workspace > Painting. You could also create a custom variation of that workspace, then save it by following the steps on page 35.

A When the Brushes panel is in List view, icons for the brush categories display on the right side.

B A brush stroke is applied to this group of paths.

C We removed the brush stroke from the paths.

Expanding brush strokes

When a brush stroke is expanded, it is converted into ordinary editable outlined paths (that is, objects in the shape of the former brush strokes). The stroke will look the same, but will no longer be live, so you won't be able to replace it via the Brushes panel or edit it by editing the brush.

To expand a brush stroke into paths:

1. Select one or more objects that have a brush stroke.**A**

2. Choose Object > **Expand Appearance**. Each brush stroke (and fill, if any) is now a separate object or objects, nested (or double nested) within a group listing on the Layers panel.**B**

➤ To select all of the objects in your document that contain a brush stroke, from the Select > Object submenu, choose Brush Strokes.

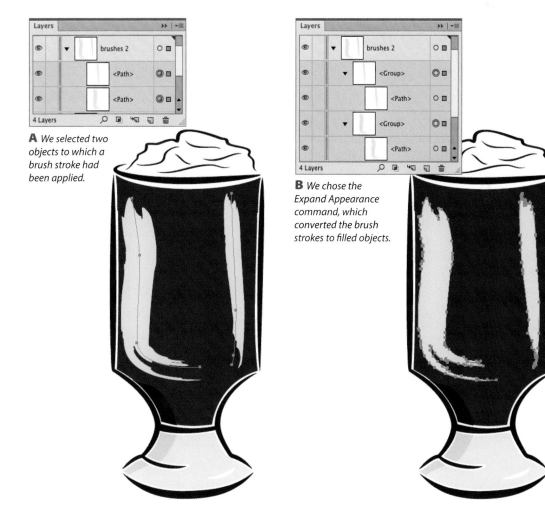

A We selected two objects to which a brush stroke had been applied.

B We chose the Expand Appearance command, which converted the brush strokes to filled objects.

Next, we provide separate instructions for creating
and modifying Calligraphic, Scatter, Art, Bristle, and
Pattern brushes.

Creating and editing Calligraphic brushes

Calligraphic brush strokes vary in thickness as you
draw, as in traditional calligraphy.

To create or edit a Calligraphic brush:

1. Skip this step if you're going to edit an existing
   brush. To create a new brush, click the **New Brush**
   button 🔲 on the Brushes panel. In the New Brush
   dialog, click **Calligraphic Brush**, then click OK. The
   Calligraphic Brush Options dialog opens. Enter a
   Name, click OK, then apply the new brush to a path.

   Note: You will reopen the options dialog in the next
   step, and when you do so, you can take advantage
   of the Preview option, which is available only for
   brushes that are in use.

2. Deselect, then on the Brushes panel, double-click
   the Calligraphic brush to be edited. **A–B** The
   Calligraphic Brush Options dialog opens. **C**

3. Check Preview to view the changes on paths where
   the brush is in use (this option is available only for a
   brush that is in use). The brush shape also previews
   in the dialog.

4. For **Angle**, **Roundness**, and **Size**, choose one of the
   following variations from the menu:

   Fixed to keep the value constant.

A The brush we're going to edit is in use on the thicker
strokes in this artwork.

B On the Brushes panel, we are double-clicking
the Calligraphic brush for which we want to
change the settings.

C In the Calligraphic Brush Options dialog, we changed the Roundness value
from 35% to 9% to make the brush very flat.

Random, click the Variation arrowhead, then move the slider to define a range within which that brush attribute can vary. A stroke can range between the value specified for Angle, Roundness, or Size, plus or minus the Variation value. For example, a 50° angle with a Random Variation value of 10° could have an angle anywhere between 40° and 60°.

If you're using a graphics tablet, choose **Pressure, Stylus Wheel, Tilt, Bearing,** or **Rotation.** Move the Variation slider for Angle, Roundness, or Size to define a range within which that attribute is affected by the chosen stylus feature. For example, with Pressure chosen, light pressure would produce a stroke using the specified Angle, Roundness, or Size value minus the Variation value, whereas heavy pressure would produce a stroke in the specified value plus the Variation value. To learn more about the stylus options, see Illustrator Help.

5. Choose an **Angle** (–180˚ to 180˚) or drag the gray arrowhead on the circle. An angle of 0° produces a stroke that is thinner when drawn horizontally than when drawn vertically; an angle of 90° produces the opposite result.

6. Choose a **Roundness** value (0–100%), or reshape the tip by dragging either of the two black dots inward or outward on the ellipse.

7. For the brush size, choose a **Size** value (0–1296 pt).

8. Click OK. If the brush is already in use in the document, an alert dialog will appear.**A** Click **Apply to Strokes** to update the existing strokes with the revised brush,**B** or click **Leave Strokes** to leave the existing strokes unchanged.

A *When we exited the Calligraphic Brush Options dialog, this alert appeared because the brush we modified is in use in our document.*

B *We clicked Apply to Strokes in the alert dialog to allow the edited brush to update where it is being used in the artwork. The vertical parts of the revised brush strokes are thicker than the horizontal parts — just the calligraphic look we were aiming for.*

Creating and editing Scatter brushes

Objects in a Scatter brush are strewn evenly or randomly along the contour of a path. You can create a Scatter brush from an open or closed path, or from a type character, type outline, blend, compound path, or placed (embedded) image. You can't create a Scatter brush from a mesh object, or clipping mask, or from an object that contains a gradient or pattern.

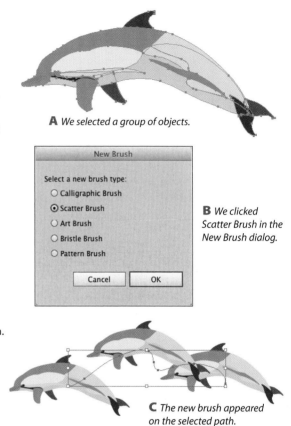

A We selected a group of objects.

To create or edit a Scatter brush:

1. Skip this step if you're going to edit an existing brush. To create a new brush, select one or more objects,**A** then click the **New Brush** button 🗔 on the Brushes panel. In the New Brush dialog,**B** click **Scatter Brush**, then click OK. The Scatter Brush Options dialog opens. Enter a name, click OK, then apply the new brush to any path.**C** (See the Note in step 1 on page 324.) Note: If you try to create a brush from a placed, embedded image and its resolution is too high, Illustrator will stop you via an alert. Lower the image resolution, then try again.

2. Deselect, then on the Brushes panel, double-click the Scatter brush to be edited. The Scatter Brush Options dialog opens.**D**

B We clicked Scatter Brush in the New Brush dialog.

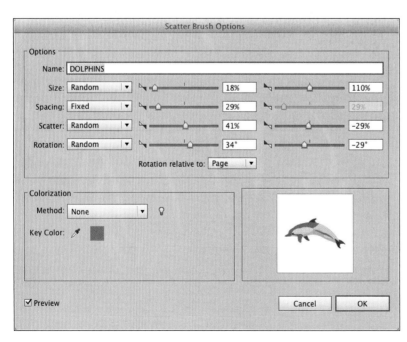

C The new brush appeared on the selected path.

D Use the Scatter Brush Options dialog to adjust the settings for a new or existing brush. These settings produced the results shown on the next page.

3. Check Preview so you will be able to view your edits on paths where the brush is in use.

4. For **Size**, **Spacing**, **Scatter**, and **Rotation**, choose one of the following variations from the menu:

   Fixed to use a single fixed value.

   Random, then move the sliders to define a range within which that property can vary.

   If you're using a graphics tablet, choose **Pressure**, **Stylus Wheel**, **Tilt**, **Bearing**, or **Rotation**. Move the sliders (or enter different values in the two fields) to define a range within which that property can respond to that particular stylus feature. For example, with Pressure chosen, light pressure would use the minimum property value from the field on the left; heavy pressure uses the maximum property value from the field on the right.

   The following is a description of the properties:

   Size controls the size of the scatter objects.

   Spacing controls the spacing between the scatter objects.

   Scatter controls the distance between the objects and the path. When Fixed is chosen as the Scatter setting, a positive value places all the objects on one side of the path, and a negative value places all the objects on the opposite side of the path. The further the Scatter value is from 0%, the less closely the objects adhere to the path.

   Rotation controls how much the scatter objects can rotate relative to the page or path. From the **Rotation Relative To** menu, choose **Page** or **Path**.

5. For the **Colorization** methods, see the sidebar on page 339.

6. Click OK. If the brush is in use in the document, an alert dialog will appear.**A** Click **Apply to Strokes** to update the existing objects with the revised brush,**B** or click **Leave Strokes** to leave the objects unchanged.

➤ To orient scatter objects uniformly along a path, set Scatter to Fixed and 0°, and set Rotation to Fixed and Relative To: Path.

➤ To edit a Scatter brush on a path manually, see page 341.

Adobe Illustrator

That brush is in use and some strokes may have overridden its options. Do you want to apply the changes to existing brush strokes?

[Apply to Strokes] [Leave Strokes] [Cancel]

A *This alert dialog appears if you modify a brush that's currently in use in your document.*

CREATING BRUSH VARIATIONS

To create a variation of an existing brush of any type, duplicate it first (follow the steps on page 339). To create a variation of a brush in a library, add the brush to the Brushes panel first, then duplicate it.

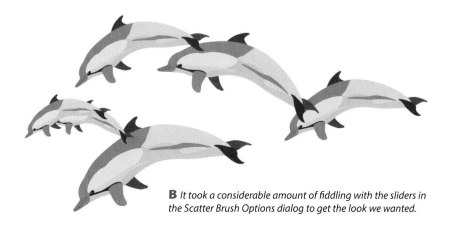

B *It took a considerable amount of fiddling with the sliders in the Scatter Brush Options dialog to get the look we wanted.*

Creating and editing Art brushes

An Art brush can be made from one or more paths (even a Blob Brush object or a compound path), or from a placed, embedded image, but not from a gradient, mask, mesh, or editable type. When applied to a path, an Art brush stroke will conform to the path. If you reshape the path, the brush stroke will stretch or bend to fit the new path contour (fun!). If you browse through the predefined Art brushes, you'll see that some simulate art media brushes and others have recognizable shapes, such as arrows, banners, and ribbons.

To create or edit an Art brush:

1. Skip this step if you're going to edit an existing brush. To create a new brush, select one or more objects,**A** then click the **New Brush** button ▯ on the Brushes panel. In the New Brush dialog, click **Art Brush**, then click OK. The Art Brush Options dialog opens. Enter a Name, click OK, then apply the new brush to any path. (For the reasoning behind this step, see the Note in step 1 on page 324.) Note: If the object is a placed, embedded image and its resolution is too high, an alert will stop you. Lower the resolution, then try again.

2. Deselect, then on the Brushes panel, double-click the Art brush to be edited. The Art Brush Options dialog opens.**B** If you're creating a new brush based on an existing one, enter a new name; or to edit the brush, keep the existing name.

3. Check Preview to view the changes on paths where the brush is in use (this option is available only for brushes that are in use).

4. Click one of the Brush Scale Options: **Scale Proportionately** to preserve the original proportions of the art object as much as possible (**A**, next page); **Stretch to Fit Stroke Length** to allow Illustrator to

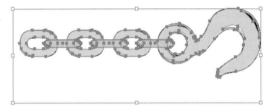

A To create an Art brush, we began by selecting these objects.

B We applied the new brush to a path, then double-clicked the brush on the Brushes panel to open the Art Brush Options dialog.

Art Brush Options

Name: Chain

Width: Fixed ▾   100%   100%

Brush Scale Options
○ Scale Proportionately
○ Stretch to Fit Stroke Length
◉ Stretch Between Guides
Start: 12.253 pt   End: 246.806 pt   Length(X): 427.097 pt

Direction: ← → ↑ ↓

Colorization
Method: None ▾
Key Color: 🖋

Options
☐ Flip Along
☐ Flip Across
Overlap:

☑ Preview   Cancel   OK

stretch (distort) parts of the brush to fit the path **B**; or **Stretch Between Guides**, then move the dashed guides in the preview to define which part of the brush Illustrator can stretch.**C**

5. Click a **Direction** button to control the orientation of the brush relative to the path. The brush will be oriented in the direction the arrow is pointing (this option doesn't preview). The direction will be more obvious for a brush that has a distinct starting and ending shape.

6. Check **Flip Along** to flip the start and end of the brush and/or check **Flip Across** to flip the brush across the path.**D**

7. *Optional:* Change the brush Width slider setting(s).**E** If you're using a stylus and graphics tablet, you can choose an option from the Width menu.

8. *Optional:* Choose a Colorization Method (see the sidebar on page 339).**F**

9. For the Overlap, click the **Do Not Adjust Corners and Folds** button to let the folds and joins in the object fall where they may on the object, with potentially some overlap; or click the **Adjust Corners and Folds** button to prevent folds and joins from overlapping.

10. Click OK. If the brush is in use in the artwork, an alert dialog will appear. See step 6 on page 327.

➤ If you want to apply a different brush to a path while keeping the same brush stroke settings, hold down Option/Alt while clicking the replacement brush.**G–H**

➤ To edit an Art brush on a path, see the following page and page 341.

A *We drew a simple path with the Paintbrush tool, then applied the Art brush. Scale Proportionately is the current Brush Scale option.*

B *We chose Stretch to Fit Stroke Length as the Brush Scale option.*

C *We chose Stretch Between Guides as the Brush Scale option, and moved the guides in the preview to surround just the chain (see figure **B** on the preceding page). The chain stretches to fit the path, whereas the hook does not.*

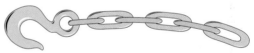

D *We checked the Flip Along option.*

E *We unchecked Flip Along, then changed the Width setting to 195%.*

F *We reset the Width to 100%, then chose Tints and Shades as the Colorization Method.*

G *We selected the path that is shown in figure **A** on this page, then clicked a replacement brush on the Brushes panel.*

H *Here we did the same thing as in figure **G**, except we held down Option/Alt as we clicked the replacement brush to apply the settings from the original brush to the replacement.*

SCALING AN ART OR PATTERN BRUSH STROKE USING THE WIDTH TOOL

If you want to scale a section of an Art brush on a path, in addition to or instead of using the Stretch Between Guides option in the Art Brush Options dialog, try using the Width tool, as shown in the illustrations below. You can also use the Width tool on a Pattern brush stroke.

RESTORING A UNIFORM WIDTH

Say you use the Width tool on an Art or Pattern brush stroke or apply a variable width profile to the stroke via the Control panel or Stroke panel, then decide you want to make the stroke width uniform again. Select the path, then do either of the following:

➤ From the Variable Width Profile menu on the Control panel or from the Profile menu on the extended Stroke panel, choose Uniform. If you used the Width tool, the largest width value that the tool produced will be applied to the brush stroke as one uniform value.

➤ Click the Options of Selected Object button 🖩 on the Brushes panel to open the Stroke Options (Art Brush or Pattern Brush) dialog. From the Width menu, choose Fixed (a change from the setting of Width Points/Profile), then click OK.

USING AN IMAGE IN AN ART BRUSH

We embedded an image into an Illustrator document via File > Place. Next, we created an Art brush from the image, using the Stretch Between Guides option to define the flower stem as only the area to be stretched. Finally, we drew a path with the Brush tool, then applied our new brush to the path. (If you don't like how a brush fits on the curved sections of an object, try changing the Overlap setting for the brush in the Art Brush Options dialog.)

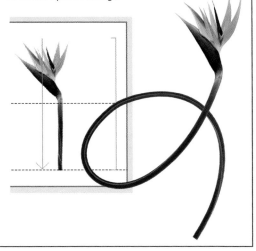

We applied an Art brush to a path, chose the Width tool, and are dragging from an endpoint in a perpendicular direction to the path, so as to create a width point.

That section of the Art brush scaled accordingly.

Creating and editing Bristle brushes

Using the Bristle brushes in Illustrator, you can mimic traditional art media, such as oil paint or gouache. To produce the desired brush characteristics, you can choose from among 10 different shape presets (e.g., Flat Blunt and Round Fan) and adjust many variables, such as the bristle density, thickness, and stiffness. Note: To achieve optimal results with Bristle brushes, Adobe recommends using a Wacom Intuos 3 tablet (or later) and a 6D pen.

To explore the many options for Bristle brushes, you can start by customizing one of the brushes in the Bristle Brush library.

To create or edit a Bristle brush:

1. Deselect, then from the **Brush Libraries** menu ▮▮ on the Brushes panel, choose Bristle Brush > **Bristle Brush Library**.

2. Select one or more paths in your document, then click a Bristle brush in the library panel. The brush will appear on the Brushes panel and on the selected paths.

3. Deselect (Cmd-Shift-A/Ctrl-Shift-A).

4. On the Brushes panel, double-click the Bristle brush that you just applied. The Bristle Brush Options dialog opens.**A** If you're creating a new brush (a variation), enter a new name; or if you want to edit the existing brush, keep the existing name. (The brush will save with your document.)

5. Check Preview so you will be able to view your edits on the paths where the brush is in use (this option is available only for brushes that are in use).

6. Choose a **Shape** preset for the brush.

7. Adjust any of the **Brush Options** settings: Size, Bristle Length, Bristle Density, Bristle Thickness, Paint Opacity, or Stiffness (**A–C**, next page).

8. Click OK. If the brush is in use in the document, an alert dialog will appear. Click **Apply to Strokes** to update the existing objects with the revised brush, or click **Leave Strokes** to leave the objects unchanged.

➤ A document that contains 30 or more Bristle brush paths could cause a printing error. When saving such a file, read the alert that displays. (To see the alerts in Illustrator Help/Help and Tutorials, click Painting, click Brushes, then scroll down to the bottom of the page.) To learn about the Rasterize command, which helps facilitate printing, see page 216.

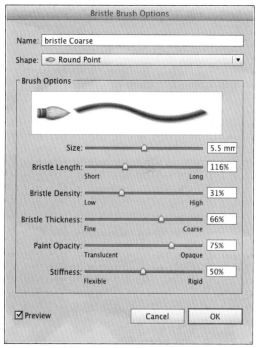

A *Use the Bristle Brush Options dialog to choose settings for a new or existing Bristle brush.*

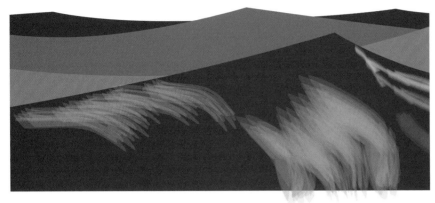

Short Bristle Length   Long Bristle Length

A The Bristle Length controls the width of each flat, overlapping path that forms the paint stroke.

Low Bristle Density   High Bristle Density

B The Bristle Density controls how many overlapping paths pile up within each paint stroke.

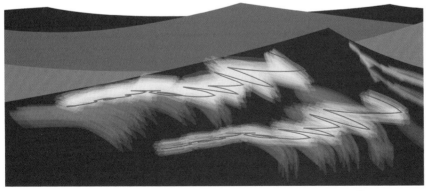

Flexible Bristle Stiffness   Rigid Bristle Stiffness

C The Bristle Stiffness controls how rigidly the bristle paths adhere to the underlying path (here the paths are shown in red).

ENHANCING SOLID-COLOR OBJECTS WITH BRISTLE BRUSH STROKES

In addition to painting a picture from scratch with Bristle brushes, you can draw Bristle brush strokes on top of flat vector shapes to add texture, shading, or depth.**A–B**

A *All the objects in this artwork are crisp, flat vector shapes.*

B *To add shading and texture, we selected each cloud object individually, activated Draw Inside mode, then drew paths with the Paintbrush tool and a Bristle brush. Because we chose this mode, the Bristle brush paths were masked by the crisp vector edge of each object. (To learn about Draw Inside mode, see pages 338 and 371.) To create color highlights on the waves, we drew Bristle brush paths on a new layer above the wave objects.*

CHANGING THE SIZE OR OPACITY OF A BRISTLE BRUSH VIA THE KEYBOARD

Either select paths in which the same Bristle brush is being used, or deselect to choose settings for paths you are about to draw. Choose the Paintbrush tool, then use either or both of these shortcuts:

Change the brush size	Press [or]
Change the paint opacity percentage	Press a number between 0 and 9 (e.g., press 1 for 10%, 9 for 90%, 0 for 100%)

Creating and editing Pattern brushes

Pattern brushes are made from up to five tiles (outer corner, side, inner corner, start, and end), and they always hug the contours of a path (unlike Scatter brushes, which can be offset from a path). You can create a pattern tile from a vector pattern swatch on the Swatches panel or from an embedded image.

In prior versions of Illustrator, it was a challenge to make the corner tiles in a Pattern brush look seamless. Now Illustrator can create seamless corner tiles from a single Side tile. You have a choice of settings for how the tiles fit together in the corners — and you can preview the results.

To create a Pattern brush:

1. Do one of the following:

   Load some patterns onto the Swatches panel (from the **Swatch Libraries** menu ![icon] at the bottom of the panel, Patterns submenu, choose a library).**A**

   Create the artwork to be used as a tile. Select it with the **Selection** tool ![icon] (V), then drag it into the Swatches panel.

Embed a raster image in your Illustrator document via File > **Place** (keep the Link option unchecked); make sure the image doesn't have a high resolution. With the Selection tool ![icon] (V), drag it into the Swatches panel.

2. On the Brushes panel, click the **New Brush** button. ![icon] In the New Brush dialog, click **Pattern Brush**, then click OK.

3. The Pattern Brush Options dialog opens. Enter a Name for the pattern.

4. To have Illustrator generate corners using a single tile (recommended), click to open the **Side Tile** (second) menu, then click a swatch on the menu.**B**

5. On the **Outer Corner Tile** (first) menu, check **Show Auto Generated Corner Tiles**, then choose an option to control how the tiles will fit on the corners of the path when applied as a brush. Your choice will preview both in the menu thumbnail and in the preview area (**A**, next page).

A We're adding a group of objects to the Swatches panel, to be stored as a swatch. (We'll repeat this step for the other two groups of objects.)

B In the Pattern Brush Options dialog, we're selecting a swatch for the Side Tile.

Auto-Centered to bend one Side tile into each corner of the path.**B**

Auto-Between to extend two symmetrical Side tiles into each corner of the path, by stretching and folding.

Auto-Sliced to join two Side tiles at each corner of the path with a diagonal seam, as in the mitered corners of a picture frame.**C**

Auto-Overlap to overlap copies of the tiles at each corner of the path.

6. Repeat the preceding step for the **Inner Corner Tile** (third) menu.

7. *Optional:* From the Start Tile and/or End Tile menu, choose a different tile to display at the start or end of the path. It will display only when the brush is applied to an open path.**D**

Continued on the following page

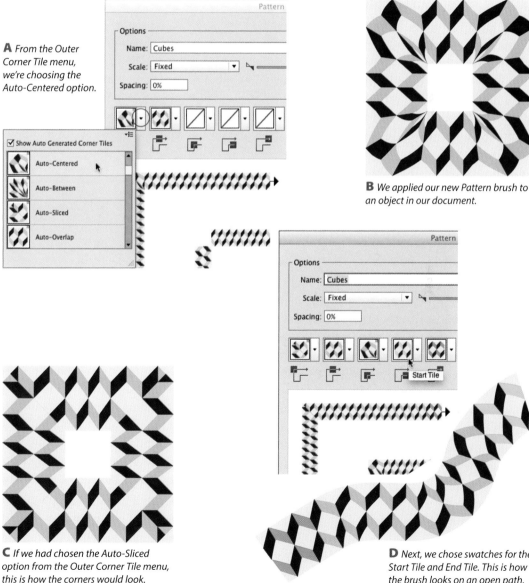

A *From the Outer Corner Tile menu, we're choosing the Auto-Centered option.*

B *We applied our new Pattern brush to an object in our document.*

C *If we had chosen the Auto-Sliced option from the Outer Corner Tile menu, this is how the corners would look.*

D *Next, we chose swatches for the Start Tile and End Tile. This is how the brush looks on an open path.*

8. Do any of the following *(optional):*

To scale the pattern, use the Scale slider.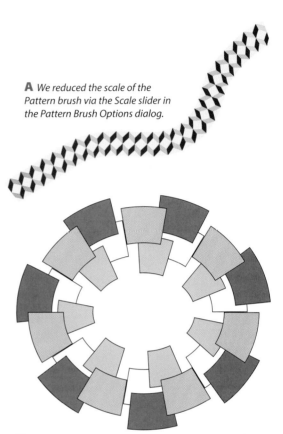**A** If you're using a pen and tablet, you can choose a scale variation option from the menu (e.g., Pressure, Stylus Wheel, Tilt, Bearing, Rotation).

To add space between the tiles, increase the Spacing value.

To change the orientation of the pattern relative to the path, check Flip Along and/or Flip Across.

9. Click a Fit option:

To allow Illustrator to lengthen or shorten tiles to fit the path (permit the tiles to have uneven lengths), click **Stretch To Fit.B**

To have Illustrator apply the pattern proportionally to the path (and add space between tiles, if necessary), click **Add Space To Fit.C**

To fit the tiles on the path without distorting them, while allowing them to be situated slightly inside or outside (instead of centered upon) the path, click **Approximate Path.**

10. For the **Colorization** methods, see the sidebar on page 339.

11. Click OK.

➤ You can use the Width tool on a path that contains a pattern brush (**A–B**, next page). See also pages 167–168 and 330.

➤ You can also quickly create a pattern brush by dragging and dropping artwork directly into the Brushes panel with the Selection tool. The New Brush dialog will open. Click Pattern Brush, then click OK. Follow steps 3–11 in the task above.

➤ If you want to choose an auto-fitting option for inner corners, choose the same swatch for the Inner Corner tile as for the Side Tile.

➤ Don't confuse Pattern brushes, which are used to embellish the edges of a path, with fill patterns, which are used to fill the interior of objects. For fill patterns, see pages 139–146.

A *We reduced the scale of the Pattern brush via the Scale slider in the Pattern Brush Options dialog.*

B *On a path that contains only smooth segments, such as this one, only the Side tile displays (not the corner tiles). For this pattern, we chose the Fit setting of Stretch to Fit.*

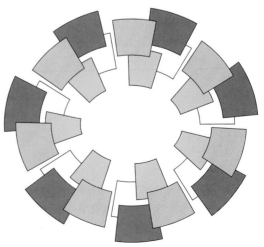

C *For this variation of the pattern, we chose the Fit setting of Add Space to Fit.*

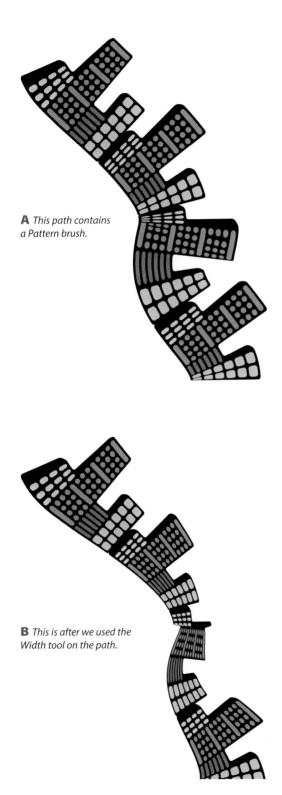

A *This path contains a Pattern brush.*

B *This is after we used the Width tool on the path.*

To edit a Pattern brush:

1. Deselect your artwork, then on the Brushes panel, double-click the Pattern brush to be edited.

2. The Pattern Brush Options dialog opens. Check Preview, then follow steps 4–11 in the preceding task.

3. Click OK to exit the Pattern Brush Options dialog. If the brush is in use in your document, an alert dialog will appear. Click **Apply to Strokes** to update the existing objects with the revised brush, or click **Leave Strokes** to leave the objects unchanged.

USING AN IMAGE FILE IN A PATTERN BRUSH

We placed this raster image in an Illustrator document, then dragged it to the Swatches panel. We clicked the New Brush button on the Brushes panel, then clicked Pattern Brush in the New Brush dialog.

In the Pattern Brush Options dialog, we reduced the Scale value to 43%, chose the Auto-Sliced setting for the Outer Corner and Inner Corner Tiles, and clicked Fit: Stretch to Fit. Finally, we applied the brush to a star-shaped polygon.

Painting brush strokes inside objects

In these steps, you will confine Bristle brush strokes to the interior of a vector object or editable type characters. With your document in Draw Inside mode, as you draw strokes, they will be masked by the edges of a selected object. To learn more about clipping sets, see Chapter 26.

To paint brush strokes inside an object:

1. Choose the **Selection** tool (V) and select an object. It can be a path or an editable type object.

2. From the Tools panel, choose **Draw Inside** mode. Deselect.

3. Choose the **Paintbrush** tool (B). Click a Bristle brush on the Brushes panel and choose a stroke color from the Color or Swatches panel.

4. Paint brush strokes over the object or type characters.**A** Each time you release the mouse, the stroke will be masked by the object.**B**

5. To return to **Draw Normal** mode, press Shift-D.

To edit brush strokes inside an object:

1. Choose the **Selection** tool (V), then double-click the group that contains the brush strokes you want to edit, to isolate it.

2. On the Layers panel, click the target circle or selection square for the brush stroke to be edited.**C**

3. Do any of the following:**D**

    Change the stroke color.

    On the Brushes panel, click the **Options of Selected Object** button to open the Stroke Options (Bristle Brush) dialog, check Preview, then modify any of the brush options. This dialog contains the same options as the dialog shown on page 331. Click OK.

    Drag the brush path to reposition it within the object or type.

    To delete the selected object, press Delete/Backspace.

4. Press Esc to exit isolation mode.

➤ If you want to hide the object that is masking the strokes, on the Layers panel, expand the group, then click the visibility icon for the listing that has an underline (click in the visibility column again when you want to redisplay the object).**E**

A We selected a type object, activated Draw Inside mode, chose a Bristle brush for the Paintbrush tool, then painted some brush strokes across the type.

B Each time the mouse was released, the stroke was masked by the edges of the type characters.

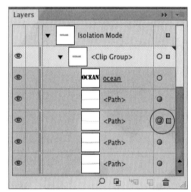

C To edit a Bristle brush stroke, we put the group into isolation mode, and via the Layers panel, we selected a Bristle path.

D An individual brush stroke is edited in isolation mode.

E With the type hidden, we can edit, reposition, or delete individual paint strokes more easily.

Duplicating brushes

Using the Duplicate Brush command as a starting point, you can create a variation of an existing brush, such as a slimmer or fatter version of it.

To duplicate a brush:

1. Deselect all objects.

   ▶ To duplicate a brush that is stored in a library, you must add it to the Brushes panel first.

2. Do either of the following:

   Click the brush to be duplicated, then choose **Duplicate Brush** from the panel menu.

   Drag the brush to be duplicated to the **New Brush** button. **A**

3. The word "copy" will be added to the brush name. **B** To rename it, double-click the brush name, enter a new name in the options dialog, then click OK. To edit the brush, follow the steps for that specific brush type in this chapter.

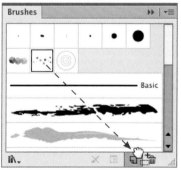

A *Drag the brush to be duplicated over the New Brush button.*

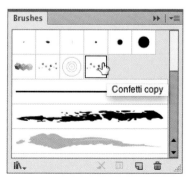

B *The duplicate brush appears after the last brush icon within its category.*

CHOOSING A COLORIZATION METHOD

To change the way a brush applies color, from the Colorization Method menu in the Brush Options dialog for a Scatter, Art, or Pattern brush, choose one of the options listed below.

▶ None to keep the original brush colors as they are.

▶ Tints to change black areas in the brush stroke to the current stroke color at 100% and nonblack areas to tints of the current stroke color. White areas stay white. Use for grayscale or multicolor brushes, or to apply a spot color.

▶ Tints and Shades to change colors in the brush stroke to tints of the current stroke color. Black and white areas stay the same.

▶ Hue Shift to apply the current stroke color to the most dominant color in a multicolor brush (the "key" color) and to change other colors in the brush to related colors. To change the key color, choose the Hue Shift method, click the Key Color eyedropper, then click a color in the preview area of the dialog (not in the artwork). Unfortunately, a Key Color change won't display until you exit the dialog. (The Key Color eyedropper isn't available for the Options of Selected Object feature, which is discussed on page 341.)

To open the Colorization Tips dialog (shown below), click the Tips icon or the Tips button.

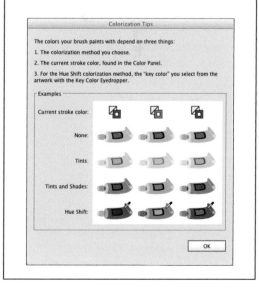

Editing a brush manually

Earlier in this chapter, you learned how to edit brushes via an options dialog. In these steps, you will edit a Scatter, Art, or Pattern brush manually in a document.

To edit a Scatter, Art, or Pattern brush manually:

1. Deselect. If you're going to edit a Pattern brush, double-click the brush and note what swatch is being used for each tile, and whether one of the options for auto generating corners is chosen.

2. Drag a brush from the Brushes panel 🖌 onto a blank area of the artboard.**A–B**

3. Edit the brush objects. To recolor or transform the entire brush, select it (Selection tool) or isolate it first (remember to exit isolation mode when you're done). For a Pattern brush, ungroup the objects so you can edit each tile individually. To recolor or transform individual objects in the brush, select them via the Direct Selection tool or the Layers panel first.

   ➤ You can also recolor the brush objects via the Recolor Artwork dialog. See Chapter 29.

4. Choose the **Selection** tool 🔲 (V) and make sure all the brush objects are selected.

5. Do either of the following:

   To replace the existing brush with the edited one, Option-drag/Alt-drag the modified brush object(s) into the Brushes panel, and release the mouse when the plus sign pointer is over the original brush thumbnail and the thumbnail has a highlight border.**C** For a Pattern brush, be sure to Option-drag/Alt-drag the selection over the specific tile that you want to replace.

   To make the object(s) into a new, separate brush, drag it (or them) onto the panel without holding down any keys. The New Brush dialog opens. Click **Scatter Brush**, **Art Brush**, or **Pattern Brush**, then click OK.

6. The Scatter Brush Options, Art Brush Options, or Pattern Brush Options dialog opens. Keep or change the brush name, then click OK.

7. If you decided to replace the existing brush and it is currently in use in the document, an alert dialog will appear. Click **Apply to Strokes** to update the paths with the revised brush,**D** or click **Leave Strokes** to leave them be.

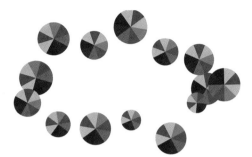

A We applied a Scatter brush to a path.

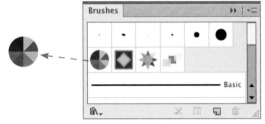

B We dragged the brush from the Brushes panel onto an artboard.

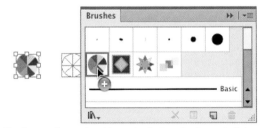

C After recoloring the objects via the Recolor Artwork dialog, we are holding down Option/Alt and dragging them over the original brush on the Brushes panel.

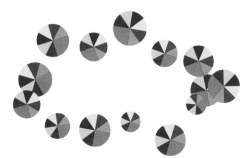

D We clicked OK in the Scatter Brush Options dialog, then clicked Apply to Strokes in the alert dialog to allow the brush to update on the path.

Editing brush strokes on objects

If you edit a brush, either manually or via the options dialog, then click Apply to Strokes in the alert, all the objects in which that brush is being used will update to reflect your edits. If you want to edit a brush stroke on just an individual object — without editing the brush that's stored on the panel — follow these steps instead. You will use the same options dialog controls.

To edit a brush stroke on an individual object:

1. Select one or more objects to which the same brush is currently applied.

2. On the Brushes panel, click the **Options of Selected Object** button. The Stroke Options dialog for that brush type opens. Check Preview.

3. For a Calligraphic brush stroke, follow steps 4–7 on pages 324–325; for a Scatter brush stroke, follow steps 4–5 on page 327; for an Art brush stroke, follow steps 6–9 on page 329 (the Width option becomes a Size option); for a Bristle brush stroke, follow steps 6–7 on page 331; or for a Pattern brush stroke, follow steps 8–10 on page 336.**A**

4. Click OK.**B** Your edits will affect only the selected object(s), not the brush on the Brushes panel.

   Beware! If you use the Options of Selected Object feature on an object, then edit the brush itself and click Apply to Strokes in the alert dialog, your custom options will be removed from that object.

5. For a Calligraphic brush stroke, or for an Art, Scatter, or Pattern brush stroke that is set to any Colorization method except None, you can change the stroke color manually via the usual controls (e.g., Color, Color Guide, or Swatches panel).**C**

   For an Art or Pattern brush stroke, you can also change the variable width profile (see page 166), or use the Width tool (see pages 167–168 and 330).

➤ To restore the original brush stroke to the object, select the object, then click the original brush.

SCALING STROKES AND EFFECTS

If you scale an object that has a brush stroke and Scale Strokes & Effects is checked in the Scale dialog (which you open by double-clicking the Scale tool) or in Illustrator/Edit > Preferences > General, the brush stroke will also scale.

A *We selected some objects that contain brush strokes, clicked the Options of Selected Object button, then reduced the brush Size via the options dialog.*

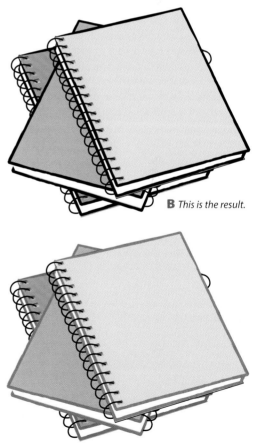

B *This is the result.*

C *After exiting the options dialog, we changed the stroke colors in the artwork via the Swatches panel.*

Deleting brushes

Note: When you delete a brush that's being used in your document, you are given the option via an alert dialog to expand or remove the brush strokes.

To delete a brush from the Brushes panel:

1. Deselect.

2. Do either of the following:

   On the Brushes panel, click the brush to be deleted.

   To delete all the brushes that aren't being used in the document, choose **Select All Unused** from the Brushes panel menu.

3. Click the **Delete Brush** button 🗑 on the Brushes panel.

4. An alert dialog appears. If the brush is not currently in use in the document, click **Yes.A** If the brush is in use in the document,**B** click **Expand Strokes** to expand the brush strokes (they'll be converted into standard paths and will no longer be associated with the original brush), or click **Remove Strokes** to remove the brush from the objects. Note: If the brush is being used in a graphic style, as an alert will inform you, you must delete the style before you can delete the brush.**C**

➤ To restore a deleted brush to the Brushes panel, choose Undo immediately; or if the brush is stored in a library, you could add it to the Brushes panel again (see page 321).

Creating a custom brush library

By saving your brushes in a library, you'll be able to access them easily and load them into any file.

To create a custom brush library:

1. Set up your Brushes panel so it contains only the brushes to be saved in a library. You can create new brushes or add them from a library panel. Delete any brushes you don't want to include in the library.

2. From the **Brush Libraries** menu 📚 at the bottom of the Brushes panel, choose **Save Brushes**.

3. In the Save Brushes as Library dialog, enter a name for the library. Keep the default location, then click Save (for the default folder location, in Illustrator Help/Help and Tutorials, click Painting, then click Brushes, then click Work with Brush Libraries).

4. The library will now be listed on, and can be opened from, the **User Defined** submenu on the Brush Libraries menu.

A This alert dialog will appear if the brush you're deleting is not in use in your document.

B This alert dialog will appear if the brush you're deleting is in use in the document.

C This alert dialog will appear if the brush you're deleting is part of a graphic style that is on the Graphic Styles panel for the current document.

A gradient fill is a soft, gradual blend between two or more solid colors. Gradients can be used to add shading or volume for a touch of realism, or to add volume to abstract shapes. In this chapter, you will load gradients from a library; apply a gradient to an object's fill or stroke; create a simple two-color gradient; add, delete, recolor, and change the opacity of colors in a gradient; save a gradient to the Swatches panel; change a gradient's position, length, shape, or angle interactively by using on-object controls (referred to collectively as the "annotator"); spread a gradient across multiple objects; and expand a gradient into paths.

Applying a gradient to an object's fill or stroke

A gradient can consist of two solid colors (a starting and an ending color) or multiple colors; it can spread from one side of an object's fill or stroke to the other (linear) or outward from the center of an object (radial);**A** and it can be applied to individual objects or across multiple objects in one sweep. You can keep the colors in a gradient fully opaque, or you can make any color semitransparent.

Continued on the following page

A *The sun in this artwork contains a radial gradient, whereas the sky and water contain linear gradients.*

GRADIENTS

24

The first step is to load some predefined Illustrator gradients onto your document's Swatches panel.

To load gradients onto the Swatches panel:

1. Display the Swatches panel. From the Show Swatch Kinds menu, choose Show Gradient Swatches, and from the panel menu, choose Large Thumbnail View.

2. From the **Swatch Libraries** menu ⓘ at the bottom of the Swatches panel, on the Gradients submenu, choose a library.

3. A separate library panel opens.**A** Do either of the following:

   Click a gradient on the panel. It will appear on the Swatches panel.

   Cmd-click/Ctrl-click (or click, then Shift-click) to select multiple gradients, then choose **Add to Swatches** from the panel menu or drag the selected swatches to the Swatches panel.

➤ To view the other gradient libraries, click the Load Next Swatch Library ▶ or Load Previous Swatch Library ◀ button on the library panel.

Now you're ready to apply a gradient to an object.

To fill an object with a gradient:

Do one of the following:

Select one or more objects, click the **Fill** square on the Color panel, then click a gradient swatch on the Swatches panel or on an open gradient library panel.

Select one or more objects **B** and display the full Gradient panel (click the double arrows on the panel tab, if necessary). Click the **Fill** square, click the arrowhead next to the Gradient square to open the gradient menu, then click a gradient. The gradients that are on your document's Swatches panel are listed on this menu.**C–D**

Click the **Fill** square on the Color panel. Drag a gradient swatch from the Swatches panel, from any open gradient library panel, or from the Gradient square on the Gradient panel over any selected or unselected object (plus sign pointer).

➤ You can show the Swatches panel via the Window menu or access it temporarily via the Control panel.

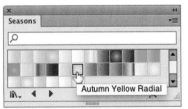

A The gradient library opens in a floating panel.

B We selected the plain vanilla rectangle behind the black objects.

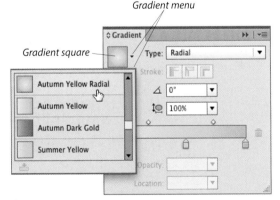

C We clicked a gradient on the gradient menu (Gradient panel).

D The object filled with the soft radial gradient.

You can easily apply a gradient to an object's stroke, and also control the direction of the gradient on the stroke.

To apply a gradient to an object's stroke:

1. Select one or more objects. Give the object(s) a substantial stroke Weight, so it will be easier to see the gradient you apply.**A**

2. Do one of the following:

   Display the full Gradient panel (click the double arrows on the panel tab, if necessary). Click the **Stroke** square, click the arrowhead next to the Gradient square to open the gradient menu, then click a gradient. The gradients that are on your document's Swatches panel are listed on this menu.

   Click the **Stroke** square on the Color panel, then click a gradient swatch on the Swatches panel or on an open gradient library panel.

   Click the **Stroke** square on the Color panel. Drag a gradient swatch from the Swatches panel, from any open gradient library panel, or from the Gradient square on the Gradient panel over an object (the object doesn't have to be selected).

3. *Optional:* To reorient the gradient along or across (instead of within) the path, on the Stroke panel, make sure the path has the Align Stroke setting of Align Stroke to Center. Next, on the Gradient panel, click the Stroke square, then click one of these Stroke buttons: Apply Gradient Along Stroke or Apply Gradient Across Stroke.**B–C**

4. *Optional:* To change the gradient type, choose Radial or Linear from the Type menu on the Gradient panel.**D–F**

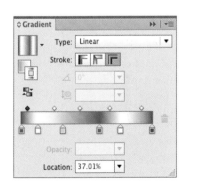

E *We added stops to the gradient and adjusted the location of some of the midpoint diamonds.*

A *A radial gradient is applied to the stroke on this object.*

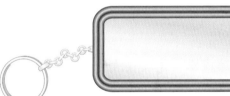

B *We changed the stroke alignment to the Apply Gradient Across Stroke option.*

C *This is the result.*

D *We changed the gradient type to Linear.*

F *This is the how the gradient looks with the settings shown in the panel at left.*

ADDING HIGHLIGHTS USING GRADIENTS IN STROKES

By applying gradients to strokes, you can add shading or graduated highlights to flat objects **A–D** (and **A–D**, next page). You can use the Width tool to widen or narrow sections of the strokes, to echo the contours of the underlying paths.

A *This is the original artwork.*

B *We drew some new vertical paths with the Pen tool, such as on the man's shirt and trousers. (You could use the Pencil tool or another tool.)*

C *To spread the color, we produced non-uniform stroke widths using the Width tool. To widen just one side of a stroke, we held down Option/Alt while dragging with the tool.*

D *We applied gradients (Apply Gradient Across Stroke setting) to the stroke of the new objects and to the large cloud object. The gradients added volume to the flat objects.*

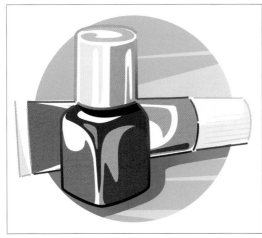

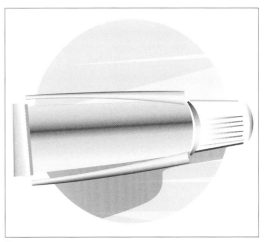

A *In the original artwork, the artist created highlights and shadows using flat objects in various colors.*

B *To create a new version of the artwork, our first step was to apply a gradient to an existing rectangle (the makeup tube). Next, we drew paths to define the ends and sides of the tube, applied gradients to the strokes of those objects (Apply Gradient Across Stroke setting), then used the Width tool to widen one end of each stroke. To delineate the ridges and the contour of the cap, we added some straight and curved paths, and applied still more gradients to the strokes of those objects.*

CONCENTRATE BETTER — WITHOUT CAFFEINE!

When drawing complex artwork, you can simplify what you see onscreen temporarily.

➤ Hide the layers you're not working on.

➤ Lighten the opacity of the objects you're not working on, as we did for the blue objects on this page (see Chapter 27).

➤ Put any object or group into isolation mode.

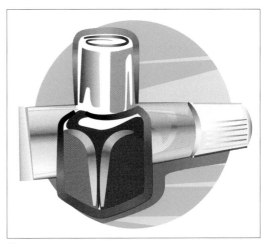

C *We increased the weight of the existing outer strokes on the nail polish jar, then applied a gradient (Apply Gradient Along Stroke setting). We drew more paths — such as the spiral on the lid and the semicircles on the jar — added gradients to their strokes, and made them nonuniform via the Width tool.*

D *The new gradient "reflections" add a touch of glam.*

Creating a two-color gradient

A custom gradient can contain all CMYK colors, all RGB process colors, tints of the same spot color, or multiple spot colors. In these steps, you will change the colors in a simple, two-color gradient.

To create and save a two-color gradient:

1. *Optional:* Select one or more objects.

2. From the **Swatch Libraries** menu 📚 at the bottom of the Swatches panel, Gradients submenu, choose a library that contains two-color gradients, such as Simple Radial.

3. Display the full Gradient panel ■ (click the double arrows on the panel tab, if necessary).

4. Click the **Fill** square. Double-click the left color stop below the gradient bar to display a temporary coloring panel.**A** Click the Color button 🎨 to display Color panel controls or the Swatches button ⊞ to display Swatches panel controls.**B** After choosing a color, click outside the temporary panel to close it.

5. Repeat the preceding step for the right color stop.

6. From the Type menu, choose **Radial** or **Linear**.

7. *Optional:* Move the midpoint diamond (located above the gradient bar) to the right to produce more of the starting color than the ending color, or to the left to do the opposite (the results will be evident if you selected an object in step 1).**C** The diamond indicates where the two colors are equal.

   Note: Although you could add colors or change their opacity via this panel, we think it's easier to use the annotator (see the next page).

8. If you select another object or swatch now, the new gradient will be lost — unless you save it to the Swatches panel by doing either of the following and then resave your document:

   At the bottom of the gradient menu on the Gradient panel, click the **Add to Swatches** button.📥

   To name the gradient as you save it, click the **New Swatch** button 🔲 on the Swatches panel, enter a name, then click OK.

➤ To swap the starting and ending colors (or any other two colors) in a gradient, Option-drag/Alt-drag one stop on top of the other. To reverse the order of all the colors in a gradient, click the Reverse Gradient button. 🔀

A *Double-click a color stop to access a temporary coloring panel.*

B *Choose a color via a coloring panel.*

C *To show more of one color than the other, drag the midpoint diamond.*

Editing gradient colors via on-object controls

Sometimes it can be hard to predict how a gradient is going to look until you actually see it in an object. Using the interactive controls known as the annotator, you can replace, add, move, remove, or change the opacity or spread of any color in a gradient directly in an object. For other annotator controls, see pages 351–352.

To edit the colors in a gradient via on-object controls:

1. Display the full Gradient panel 🔲 (click the double arrows on the panel tab, if necessary), then click the Fill square.

2. Apply a gradient to an object, and keep the object selected.

3. Choose the **Gradient** tool 🔲 (G). The gradient annotator bar should display on the object. If it doesn't, press Cmd-Option-G/Ctrl-Alt-G or choose View > **Show Gradient Annotator**.

4. Position the pointer over the bar to display the color stops, then do any of the following:

    To **recolor** or change the **opacity** setting of an existing stop, double-click it. Click the Color button 🎨 to display Color panel controls or the Swatches button 🔳 to display Swatches panel controls.**A** Underlying objects will be visible below any semi- or fully transparent colors in the gradient. Click outside the panel to close it.

    To **add** a color to the gradient, click below the bar; a new color stop appears.**B** Recolor the new stop as in the preceding paragraph.

    To adjust the **distribution** of two adjacent colors, move a midpoint marker (located above the bar) to the left or right.**C** You can also drag any color stop along the bar.

    To **duplicate** a color stop, Option-drag/Alt-drag it to the left or right.

    To **remove** a color stop, drag it downward off the annotator.

5. To save your edits either to the original swatch or as a new swatch, follow the steps on the next page.**D**

➤ Edits made via the annotator controls also appear on the Gradient panel. To learn more about the panel, see page 353.

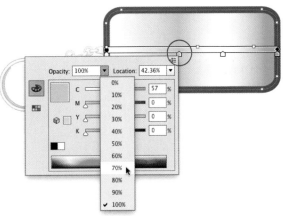

A *Double-click a color stop on the annotator to open a temporary Color or Swatches panel, then choose a new color and/or change the Opacity setting. Note that the Opacity setting can be changed using the scroll wheel on a mouse or using a trackpad.* ★

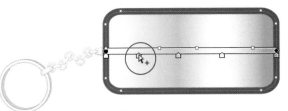

B *Click below the annotator bar to add a color stop.*

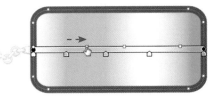

C *Drag a midpoint diamond to the left or right to control the distribution of adjacent colors.*

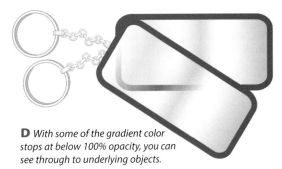

D *With some of the gradient color stops at below 100% opacity, you can see through to underlying objects.*

Saving a gradient as a swatch

To save an edited gradient as a swatch:

1. Edit a gradient by following the instructions on the preceding two pages or in the sidebar on page 353.

2. Read the two methods below before deciding which one to follow:

   To replace the existing swatch with your edited gradient, Option-drag/Alt-drag the **Gradient** square from the Gradient panel to the swatch on the Swatches panel.**A–B** *Beware!* This method will cause the gradient to update in all objects in which it is being used, whether those objects are selected or not.

   To save the modified gradient as a new swatch, at the bottom of the gradient menu on the Gradient panel, click the **Add to Swatches** button 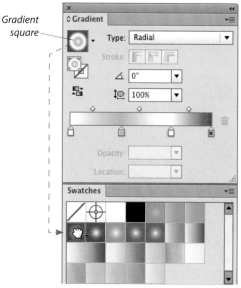 **C**; or drag the **Gradient** square from the Gradient panel to the Swatches panel. The gradient won't update in any unselected objects.

➤ To save gradient swatches as a library, see "To create a custom library of swatches," on page 129. User-defined libraries are listed on, and can be chosen from, the User Defined submenu on the Swatch Libraries menu (Swatches panel).

Gradient square

A *To replace an existing gradient swatch with your edited one, Option-drag/Alt-drag the Gradient square over a swatch on the Swatches panel.*

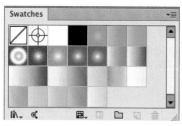

B *The swatch updates on the Swatches panel.*

REAPPLYING THE LAST GRADIENT

To apply the last gradient to any selected object after applying a solid color or a fill color of None, do one of the following:

➤ Click the Gradient square in the upper left corner of the Gradient panel.

➤ Press . (period).

➤ Click the Gradient button (>) on the Tools panel.

APPLYING A GRADIENT TO TYPE

To apply a gradient to type, select the type object via the Selection tool or Layers panel. Click the Add New Fill button or Add New Stroke button on the Appearance panel, then choose a gradient via the temporary Swatches panel on either one of those new listings. If you want to edit the gradient choice at a later time, select the type object and use the Appearance panel again.

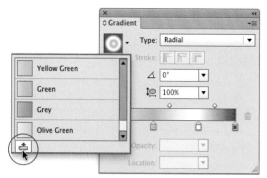

C *To save an edited gradient as a new swatch, click the Add to Swatches button on the gradient menu.*

Changing the position, length, or angle of a gradient in an object

In these instructions, you will change the origin, length, or angle of a linear gradient in a selected object by using the gradient annotator. In the steps on the next page, you will make similar edits in a radial gradient.

To change the position, length, or angle of a linear gradient in an object:

1. Select an object that contains a linear gradient fill.

2. Choose the **Gradient** tool ▣ (G) and click the Fill square on the Tools or Gradient panel. The annotator should display on the object.**A** If it doesn't, press Cmd-Option-G/Ctrl-Alt-G.

3. On the annotator, do any of the following:

   To **reposition** the gradient in the object, drag the round endpoint in a perpendicular direction to the color bands in the gradient. Note: The annotator for a linear gradient always crosses through the center of the object. If you try moving it away from the center (parallel to the color bands), it will snap back.

   To **lengthen** the overall gradient to make the transitions between colors more gradual,**B** or to **shorten** it to make the transitions more abrupt, drag the square endpoint outward or inward.

   To change the **angle** of the gradient, position the pointer just outside the square endpoint, then when the rotation pointer appears, ⟳ drag in a circular direction.**C**

   To change both the **length** and **angle** of the gradient simultaneously, hold down Option/Alt as you drag the square endpoint.

   Note: When the pointer is hovering over the square endpoint (mouse button up), the endpoint will be diamond-shaped; when you start dragging the endpoint, it will become square again.

➤ If you change the position, length, or angle of the annotator on an object and then apply a different gradient fill of the same type (radial or linear) to the object, those custom position, length, and angle settings will be applied to your new gradient choice.

➤ If you scale an object that contains a gradient, the gradient will scale by the same amount.

A *To display the gradient annotator, select an object that contains a gradient fill, choose the Gradient tool, and click the Fill square on the Tools panel.*

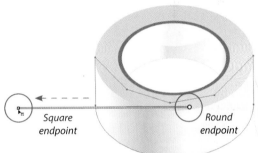

Square endpoint　　　*Round endpoint*

B *To reposition the gradient, we dragged the round endpoint to the left, and to lengthen it, we dragged the square endpoint. Now the color transitions are more gradual, and the gradient extends beyond the object (although it displays only within it).*

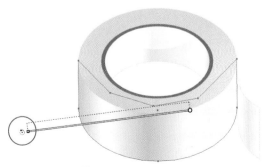

C *To change the gradient angle, we are rotating the square endpoint.*

To change the position, length, shape, or angle of a radial gradient in an object:

1. Select an object that contains a radial gradient fill.

2. Choose the **Gradient** tool ■ (G) and click the Fill square on the Tools or Gradient panel.**A** The annotator should display on the object. If it doesn't, press Cmd-Option-G/Ctrl-Alt-G.

3. On the annotator bar, do any of the following:

   To **reposition** the gradient, drag either the bar or the larger of the two round endpoints.**B** The annotator for a radial gradient doesn't have to remain centered on the object.

   To lengthen or shorten the **radius** of the gradient (scale the gradient ellipse), drag the square endpoint inward or outward. The smaller the ellipse (and the shorter the radius), the more abrupt the color transitions, and vice versa. You can also scale the radius by dragging the dot that

has a white border, located on the edge of the dashed ellipse.**C**

To change the **aspect ratio** of the ellipse to make the gradient more oval or more round, drag the black circle that doesn't have a border (on the edge of the dashed ellipse) inward or outward.**D**

To change the **gradient angle**, position the pointer on the edge of the ellipse, then when you see the rotation pointer,⟳ drag in any direction. An angle change in a radial gradient will be visible only if the gradient is oval shaped.

➤ To move the center of the radial gradient fill without scaling the ellipse, drag the smaller round endpoint on the annotator bar away from the larger one.

A *The annotator is displayed.*

B *To reposition the gradient, drag the large round endpoint.*

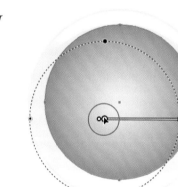

C *To scale the gradient, drag the circle that has a border, located on the edge of the ellipse.*

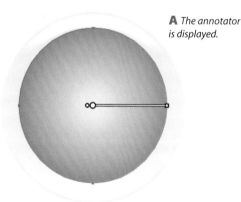

D *To make the gradient more oval or more round, drag the circle that doesn't have a border.*

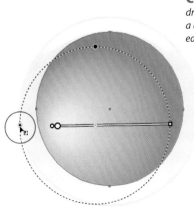

Spreading a single gradient across multiple objects

Normally, when you fill multiple selected objects with a gradient, the gradient fill starts anew in each object.**A** With the Gradient tool, you can spread a single gradient across multiple objects.

To spread a gradient across multiple objects:

1. Select two or more objects, and put them in a group (press Cmd-G/Ctrl-G). Keep the group selected.

2. On the Appearance panel, ⊙ click the **Add New Fill** button. ◼ Click the color square for the new Fill listing, then click a gradient swatch on the temporary Swatches panel. The gradient is applied to the group as a whole.**B**

3. *Optional:* Choose the Gradient tool ◼ (G). The annotator for the entire group displays. Use the controls or color stops on the annotator to edit the gradient. If you want to change a color for a color stop, you will need to do so via the temporary Swatches panel (the Color panel doesn't work).

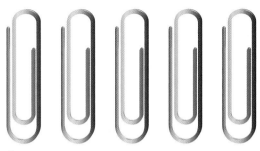

A *A gradient fill is applied individually to each one of these objects.*

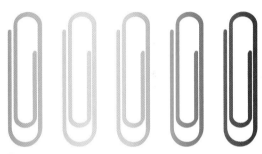

B *We grouped the objects, then, via the Appearance panel, applied a gradient to the entire group. Now a single gradient extends from the first object to the last one.*

EDITING A GRADIENT VIA THE GRADIENT PANEL

The Gradient panel ◼ provides four options that aren't available on the annotator (as noted with asterisks in the figure below), as well as some equivalent controls. To use this panel, either select an object or group that contains the gradient to be edited, or deselect all objects and then click the gradient swatch to be edited. To display the full Gradient panel, click the double arrows on the panel tab.

Gradient menu　　*Type menu* (Linear and Radial options)*

Gradient square

Fill and Stroke squares* (X)

Reverse Gradient* (swaps the order of the gradient colors)

Indicator that the opacity of the color is less than 100%

Opacity level of selected color stop

Location value (positions the midpoint diamond)

Type: Radial
Stroke: ▯ ▯ ▯
◿ 0°
↕⊙ 200%
Opacity: 80%
Location: 0%

Options for aligning the stroke on the path*

Aspect Ratio (makes a radial gradient more oval or round)

A midpoint diamond

Delete Stop (deletes the currently selected stop)

A color stop

*Gradient panel only (not available on the annotator)

Expanding a gradient into paths

The Expand command expands the colors in a gradient fill into a collection of individual paths. One practical reason for doing this might be if a gradient in your document is causing a printing error; simplifying it this way might solve the problem.

To expand a gradient fill into separate objects:

1. Select an object that contains a gradient fill.**A** (If the object to be expanded is in a group, it must be taken out of the group.)

2. Choose Object > **Expand**. The Expand dialog opens.

3. Check Expand: **Fill** and uncheck Stroke.

4. Click Expand Gradient To: **Specify**, then enter the desired number of Objects to be created.**B** To print the expanded gradient successfully, this number must be high enough to produce smooth color transitions (at least 100). (If you want to expand the gradient into obvious bands of color intentionally, enter a value below 20.)

5. Click OK.**C** Note: If the original gradient contained fewer colors than you specified, the resulting number of objects may not match that specified number.

   If you look on the Layers panel, you will see a group containing a clipping path (from the object that contained the gradient fill) and the resulting paths.

➤ To learn about color-separating gradients, see the sidebar on page 427.

To expand a gradient stroke in an object:

1. Select an object that contains a gradient in its stroke.

2. If the Stroke setting (Gradient panel) for the object is Apply Gradient Within Stroke, choose Object > **Expand**. In the dialog, check Stroke, then click OK. The result will be a compound path.

   If the Stroke setting (Gradient panel) for the object is Apply Gradient Along Stroke or Apply Gradient Across Stroke, choose Object > **Expand Appearance**. The result will be a mesh object.

A *The original object contains a linear gradient fill.*

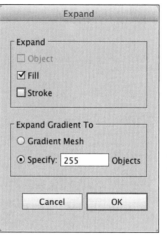

B *In the Expand dialog, we kept the default value for the number of objects to be produced from the gradient.*

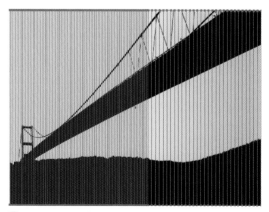

C *The Expand command converted the gradient to a series of separate rectangles, each containing a different tint, within a group, with the outer rectangle serving as a clipping path.*

All the commands discussed in this chapter produce a new shape by combining two or more objects. You will learn about the Shape Builder tool, which unites multiple objects by dragging; the Shape Mode commands, which create one or more standard paths or an editable compound shape from multiple objects; the Pathfinder commands and effects, which produce either a flattened, closed object or a compound path; and the Compound Path command, which joins two or more objects into one object, creating a "hole" where the original objects overlapped. In addition, you will learn how to add objects to, reverse an object's fill in, and release a compound path.

Using the Shape Builder tool

The Shape Builder tool can be used to unite overlapping closed paths, open filled paths, compound paths, or outline type into one shape.**A–B** With this tool, you drag across objects to unite them, in an intuitive way. You can also use it to divide areas that are formed by overlapping objects and to extract (cut out) parts of objects.

Before using the Shape Builder tool, you need to choose options for it, as described on the next page.

COMBINE PATHS

25

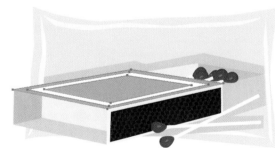

A *We selected three objects.*

B *With the Shape Builder tool, we are dragging across the selected objects. The final, united shape is shown at the top of the page.*

ANOTHER WAY TO WORK WITH INTERSECTING SHAPES

Hide or recolor intersecting faces or edges in a Live Paint group. The result will look similar to some of the Pathfinder commands, but will be easier to edit. See Chapter 18.

To choose options for the Shape Builder tool:

1. Double-click the **Shape Builder** tool 🖲 to open the Shape Builder Tool Options dialog.**A**

2. *Optional:* Check Gap Detection and choose a Gap Length option that best describes the gaps that you see between objects in your artwork. Where the tool detects a gap of this length between selected objects, it will treat areas on either side of the gap as separate, unconnected shapes.**B**

3. Under Options, do the following:

   Check **Consider Open Filled Path as Closed** to have the tool treat filled open paths as separate shapes.**C–D**

   Optional: Check In Merge Mode, Clicking Stroke Splits the Path to allow the tool to split a path when it is clicked on a segment that is formed by overlapping shapes. We keep this option off unless we intentionally want to divide a path into separate segments (see the sidebar on page 359).

   From the **Pick Color From** menu, choose **Artwork** to have the final shape adopt the fill and stroke attributes (including any settings of None) from the object you either click first or from which you start dragging; or choose **Color Swatches** and check **Cursor Swatch Preview** to display, in a tiny strip above the tool pointer, either the current fill or stroke color (if you are using the Color panel) or the color of the most recently chosen swatch on the Swatches panel and the two swatches that are adjacent to it.

4. Under Highlight, do any of the following:

   Check **Fill** to have a gray highlight texture display temporarily within overlapping areas of selected objects as you roll or drag across them, marking the areas that the tool will alter.

   Check **Highlight Stroke When Editable** to have the current highlight color display temporarily on the segments of selected paths you roll or drag across, marking the areas that the tool will alter. (Via the Color menu or swatch, you can choose a different preset color for the highlights.)

5. Click OK.

A *Choose settings in the Shape Builder Tool Options dialog.*

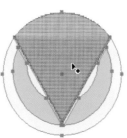

B *Because we set the Gap Length to Medium, the Shape Builder tool is considering the gap between these black and green objects to be a separate shape.*

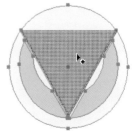

C *Consider Open Filled Path as Closed off: The tool is ignoring the open fill area and selecting a larger shape.*

D *Consider Open Filled Path as Closed on: The tool is recognizing the open fill area as a shape.*

To unite, extract, and divide objects with the Shape Builder tool:

1. Arrange the objects to be united so they partially overlap, and select them all.**A** Note: This tool doesn't work with editable type, blend objects, or Live Paint groups.

2. Choose the **Shape Builder** tool 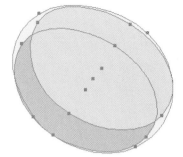 (Shift-M).

3. If the current Pick Color From setting in the tool options dialog is Artwork, position the tool over an object that has the fill and stroke colors that you want to appear in the final shape; or if Color Swatches is the current setting, choose a fill color for the final shape.

   ➤ For the Color Swatches option, after clicking in the Swatches panel, you can press the left or right arrow key to cycle through other swatches (this shortcut works even when the Cursor Swatch Preview option is off).

4. Do any of the following:

   To **unite** some shapes, either drag across the objects to be united **B** or Shift-drag a selection rectangle around them. A closed shape will be created.

   To **extract** a shape, Option-click/Alt-click a non-overlapping area to eliminate it, or Option-click/Alt-click an overlapping area to exclude it (create a cutout).**C–E** Note: If the overlapping area is completely contained within a larger shape (as in a doughnut), the result will be a compound path; see pages 366–367.

Continued on the following page

A *We selected three overlapping ellipses, chose the Shape Builder tool, and in the Shape Builder Tool Options dialog, set the Pick Color From menu to Artwork.*

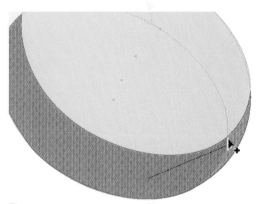

B *As we drag the tool across an area where two selected objects overlap, a gray highlight texture appears in the shapes, indicating that they will be united.*

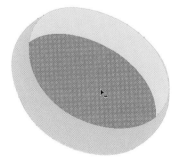

C *Each final, united shape adopted the color of the first object we dragged across. Next, we held down Option/Alt and clicked an overlapping area …*

D *… to extract it, in order to make the center of the ring blank.*

E *Finally, we added an ellipse, converted its stroke to an outlined path (see page 364), then applied gradients to all the objects.*

To **divide** shapes, click an area that is formed by overlapping paths; that area will become a separate shape.**A–B** The current Pick Color From option will control which fill color is applied to the newly divided shape.

B *We dragged the newly divided bottom shape away from the black V shape.*

A *With the Shape Builder tool, we clicked the bottom part of the circle to divide it.*

CREATING AN ILLUSION OF INTERLOCKING SHAPES WITH THE SHAPE BUILDER TOOL

A *Continuing with the artwork shown in **E** on the preceding page, we copied the ring group with the Reflect tool, then repositioned the copy.*

B *We selected all the objects, chose Pick Color From: Artwork for the Shape Builder tool (options dialog), then dragged through three areas to unite them, as shown by the highlight texture, above.*

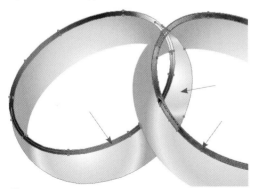

C *We deselected, zoomed in, selected the two outlined paths and a section of the left ring, then dragged in the area shown by the highlight texture.*

D *Now it looks as though the rings are linked.*

USING THE "IN MERGE MODE, CLICKING STROKE SPLITS THE PATH" OPTION OF THE SHAPE BUILDER TOOL

The Shape Builder tool can also be used to split path segments where they touch overlapping objects. To enable this function, in the options dialog for the tool, check In Merge Mode, Clicking Stroke Splits the Path. Also choose Pick Color From: Color Swatches, and check Highlight Stroke When Editable.

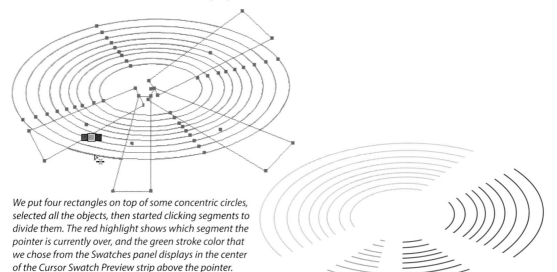

We put four rectangles on top of some concentric circles, selected all the objects, then started clicking segments to divide them. The red highlight shows which segment the pointer is currently over, and the green stroke color that we chose from the Swatches panel displays in the center of the Cursor Swatch Preview strip above the pointer.

When we clicked the segment, it became a separate object, and the tool applied the green stroke color. To complete the artwork, we continued to divide the circles by clicking segments, each time with the desired stroke color selected.

Applying the Shape Mode commands

When you click a Shape Mode button on the Pathfinder panel, ▣ selected, overlapping objects are combined into one or more standard paths—and the result is permanent.

When you Option-click/Alt-click a Shape Mode button, selected, overlapping objects are combined into a compound shape. The objects are nested within a Compound Shape listing on the Layers panel. If you move or reshape an individual object within a compound shape, the contour of the overall shape adjusts accordingly. If you release the compound shape, the objects regain their original attributes.

Here are a few guidelines to bear in mind as you use the Shape Mode commands:

➤ The Shape Mode commands can be applied to multiple standard paths, groups, compound paths, and outline type (not objects drawn with the Line tool). When used with the Option/Alt key, an editable type object or objects in a blend can be combined with other objects into a compound shape.

➤ The Shape Mode commands can't be applied to placed images, rasterized images, or mesh objects.

➤ The original objects can contain gradients, patterns, brush strokes, transparency, effects, and graphic styles.

➤ The Unite, Intersect, and Exclude buttons (if clicked without holding down Option/Alt) apply the color, stroke, and transparency attributes—and any effects—from the topmost object to the resulting path or shape and remove all other color attributes, whereas the Minus Front command preserves the attributes of only the backmost object. To achieve the desired results, remember to put the objects in the necessary stacking position before applying the command.

To combine objects into a path by using a Shape Mode command:

1. *Optional:* Duplicate the objects to be combined, to preserve a copy of them.

2. Select two or more overlapping objects.

3. On the top row of the Pathfinder panel, 🔳 click one of the **Shape Mode** buttons: **A**

   Unite joins the perimeter of the selection into one path, deletes the segments where paths intersect, and closes any open paths (see also page 177).**B**

   Minus Front subtracts the objects in front from the backmost object, preserving the color attributes of only the backmost object. The result is one path or a group of multiple nonoverlapping paths.**C**

   Intersect preserves areas where objects overlap and deletes the nonoverlapping areas. The result is one path.**D** Note: If an alert dialog appears, make sure every object overlaps all the other objects.

   Exclude deletes areas where the objects overlap, preserving only the nonoverlapping areas. The result is multiple nonoverlapping paths nested within a group layer.**E**

➤ You can apply new color or appearance attributes to the newly combined path.

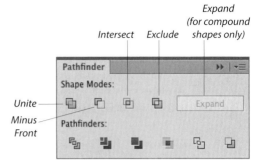

A *The Shape Mode buttons on the Pathfinder panel combine multiple selected objects into a path if you click the button without holding down any keys, or into a compound shape if you click the button while holding down Option/Alt.*

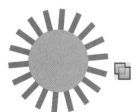

B *These are the original objects.*

Unite joined the perimeter of the selection to produce one path.

C *These are the original objects.*

Minus Front used the frontmost objects like cookie cutters on the object behind it.

D *These are the original objects.*

Intersect preserved only the area where the original objects overlapped.

E *These are the original objects.*

Exclude removed the areas where the original objects overlapped.

When you Option-click/Alt-click a Shape Mode button, a compound shape is produced. Unlike the result that simply clicking the button produces (as described on the preceding page), this method preserves all of the original objects—although this won't be evident unless you view the Appearance panel for a selected object in the shape or release the compound shape.

To combine objects into a compound shape by using a Shape Mode command:

1. Select two or more overlapping objects.

2. On the top row of the Pathfinder panel, ▦ Option-click/Alt-click a **Shape Mode** button:

   Unite joins the perimeter of the selection into one compound shape, applies the attributes of the frontmost object to the result, and hides the object edges in the interior of the shape.**A–B**

   Minus Front subtracts the objects in front from the backmost object, preserving the attributes of only the backmost object. The subtracted objects are hidden.

   Intersect applies the attributes of the frontmost object to just the areas where all the selected objects overlap, and hides all nonoverlapping areas.

   Exclude turns areas where objects overlap into fully transparent cutouts, through which any underlying objects will be visible.

3. *Optional:* Double-click the compound shape to isolate it, then change its color attributes, or move or transform individual objects within it to alter its contour (Selection tool).**C**

When you expand a compound shape, although the artwork looks the same onscreen, only the visible areas of objects remain. If you expand a compound shape that was created via the Unite or Intersect command, the result will be a standard path. If the compound shape was created via the Minus Front or Exclude command, the result will be either a path or a compound path (see pages 366–367).

To expand a compound shape:

1. Select the compound shape.

2. On the Pathfinder panel, click **Expand**.

The Release Compound Shape command restores the original objects and their attributes.

To release a compound shape:

1. Select the compound shape.

2. From the Pathfinder panel menu, choose **Release Compound Shape.D**

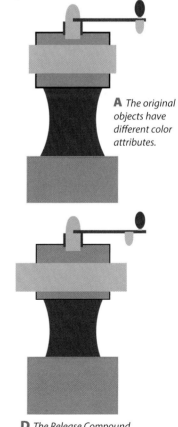

A *The original objects have different color attributes.*

B *We Option/Alt clicked the Unite button to produce a compound shape.*

C *In isolation mode, we used the Selection tool to transform and move objects within the compound shape.*

D *The Release Compound Shape command restored the original object colors.*

Applying the Pathfinder commands

Next, you will use the Pathfinder commands on the Pathfinder panel to divide, trim, merge, crop, outline, or subtract areas from selected overlapping paths. The result will be separate, nonoverlapping closed paths or lines, nested within a group. (To learn how the Pathfinder effects on the Effect menu differ from these commands, see page 368.)

Keep the following guidelines in mind as you use the Pathfinder commands:

➤ The objects to which you apply the command may contain patterns, gradients, brush strokes, transparency, or effects.

➤ Editable type must be converted to outlines first.

➤ Illustrator may take the liberty of closing any open paths for you as it performs the command, so we also recommend closing all open paths first. The steps for converting a stroke or an open path to a filled object are described on page 364.

➤ The original objects can't be restored after you apply the command (unless you choose Undo immediately), so be sure to duplicate the objects first.

➤ Transparency settings are preserved.

➤ For the Trim, Merge, and Crop commands, the original stroke colors are deleted, except from objects that contain an effect or a brush stroke.

To apply a Pathfinder command:

1. Select two or more overlapping objects, and duplicate them.

2. On the bottom row of the Pathfinder panel, click a **Pathfinder** button.**A**

   Divide turns each overlapping area into a separate, nonoverlapping object.**B–C** (Read about the Divide and Outline option in the sidebar at right.)

   ➤ After applying the Divide command, you can double-click the group to isolate it, then apply new fill colors or effects to the individual objects or a fill of None; change an object's transparency settings; or delete an object to create a cutout effect. You can also reposition any individual object with the Selection tool.

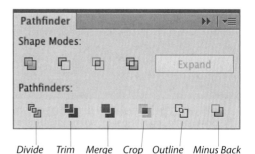

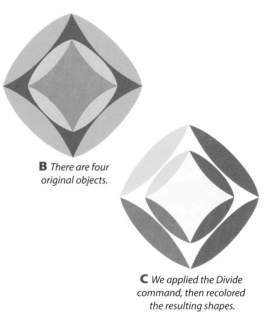

A *The Pathfinder buttons on the Pathfinder panel produce separate closed paths or lines.*

B *There are four original objects.*

C *We applied the Divide command, then recolored the resulting shapes.*

CHOOSING PATHFINDER OPTIONS

To open the Pathfinder Options dialog, from which you can choose the preferences listed below for the Pathfinder commands, choose Pathfinder Options from the Pathfinder panel menu:

➤ The higher the Precision value (.001–100 pt), the more precisely the commands are applied, and the longer they take to process.

➤ With Remove Redundant Points checked, duplicate anchor points in the same x/y location are deleted.

➤ With Divide and Outline Will Remove Unpainted Artwork checked, the Divide and Outline commands will delete any nonoverlapping areas of selected paths that have a fill of None.

Trim preserves the shape of the frontmost object and sections of objects that extend beyond it, but deletes sections of objects that it overlaps.**A** Adjacent or overlapping objects aren't united with one another (the opposite result of the Merge command). Stroke colors are deleted, except from objects that contain an effect or a brush stroke.

Merge preserves the shape of the frontmost object. Adjacent or overlapping objects that share the same fill attributes and uniform stroke widths (but no effects) are united into one or more separate, nonoverlapping objects.**B** Stroke colors are deleted, except from objects that contain an effect, brush stroke, or variable width stroke.

Crop crops away (deletes) areas of objects that extend beyond the edges of the frontmost object, and removes the fill and stroke from the frontmost object.**C**

Outline converts all the objects to segments with a stroke setting of 0 pt. and converts the fill colors to stroke colors.**D** The resulting stroke segments can be transformed, reshaped, and recolored individually. (Read about the setting for Divide and Outline in the sidebar on the preceding page.)

Minus Back subtracts all the objects in back from the frontmost object, leaving only portions of the frontmost object.**E** The color attributes and appearances of the frontmost object are applied to the resulting path.

3. To edit the resulting paths, put the group into isolation mode first by double-clicking it with the Selection tool.

➤ To apply the last-used Pathfinder command to any selected objects, press Cmd-4/Ctrl-4.

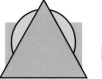 

A *There are three original objects.*

The Trim command was applied (the resulting objects were pulled apart).

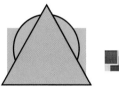 

B *There are three original objects.*

The Merge command was applied (the resulting objects were pulled apart).

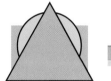 

C *There are three original objects.*

The Crop command was applied.

D *There are two original objects.*

The Outline command was applied (the resulting objects were pulled apart).

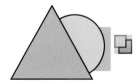

E *There are three original objects.*

The Minus Back command was applied (the objects in back cut through the top one).

Instead of letting a Pathfinder command close any open paths for you, consider using the Outline Stroke command to turn the stroke on a path to a filled object first. Another reason you may need to convert a line or a stroke to a closed path is to prepare it for trapping in commercial printing.

To convert a stroke or an open path to a filled object:

1. Select an open or closed object. Choose a stroke weight, which is to become the width of the final object.

2. Choose Object > Path > **Outline Stroke**. The original stroke and fill areas are now separate objects within a group. The former stroke color is applied as a fill color to the converted stroke.

HOW COMPOUND SHAPES...	...DIFFER FROM COMPOUND PATHS	AND HOW THEY'RE ALIKE
Option-click/Alt-click a Shape Mode button on the Pathfinder panel to produce a compound shape.	Apply the Object > Compound Path > Make command to subtract overlapping areas from the backmost object.	With the Selection tool, you can select or transform a whole compound shape or a whole compound path; or double-click it to isolate it, then click to select and edit any subpath within it.
Subpaths are nested as separate objects within a Compound Shape listing on the Layers panel.	Subpaths become part of one compound path object and listing on the Layers panel. The original objects are no longer listed separately.	Stroke attributes that are applied to a compound shape or compound path will display on the outer edge of the overall shape and on any interior cutout shapes.
The Release Compound Shape command on the Pathfinder panel menu restores the original objects and their appearances (see page 361).	When released, the objects adopt the appearance attributes of the compound path, not their original attributes (see page 367).	

Using the Compound Path command

The Make Compound Path command joins two or more objects into one object. A transparent hole is created where the objects originally overlapped, through which underlying objects are revealed. Regardless of their original attributes (e.g., color, gradient, pattern, brush stroke, transparency, effects), all the objects in a compound path are given the attributes of the backmost object, and form one unit. A compound path can be released at any time, at which point the original object shapes (but not their original attributes) are restored.

To create a compound path:

1. Arrange the objects to be made "see-through" in front of a larger shape.**A**

2. Select all the objects.

3. Press Cmd-8/Ctrl-8 or choose Object > **Compound Path** > **Make**. Or if the objects aren't in a group, you can right-click in the document and choose **Make Compound Path** from the context menu.

   The frontmost objects will cut through the back-most object like cookie cutters.**B–C** A Compound Path listing appears on the Layers panel; the original objects are no longer listed individually.

   The attributes of the backmost object (e.g., fill, stroke, transparency, brush stroke, effects) are applied to sections of all the selected objects. If the see-through holes didn't result, follow the second set of instructions on the next page.

   Note: You can isolate a compound path using the Selection tool, then reshape any of the paths within it using the Direct Selection tool. You can apply different fill, stroke, and other attributes to the whole compound path, but not to any of the individual paths within it.

➤ When combined into a compound path, all the objects are moved to the layer of the frontmost object.

➤ To help prevent a printing error, avoid creating a compound path from very complex shapes, and also avoid creating multiple compound paths in the same file.

➤ Compare this command with the Divide Objects Below command, which is discussed on page 179.

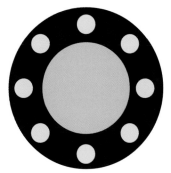

A *Place smaller objects on top of a larger one, select all the objects, then right-click in the document and choose Make Compound Path.*

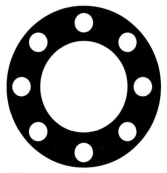

B *The objects are converted to a compound path.*

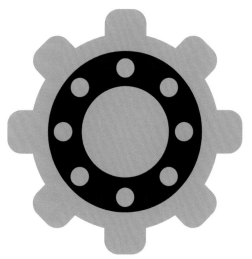

C *We placed an object behind the compound path.*

Working with compound paths

To add an object to a compound path:

1. Move the object to be added in front of the compound path. (If it's in back, its attributes will be applied to the compound path.) You can restack it by dragging its selection square upward on the Layers panel.

2. Select both the compound path and the object to be added to it.

3. Press Cmd-8/Ctrl-8 or choose Object > **Compound Path** > **Make**.

By flipping the Reverse Path Direction switch on the Attributes panel, you can remove the fill color of any shape in a compound path, and thereby make that object transparent, or vice versa.

To make a filled area in a compound path transparent, or vice versa:

1. Deselect the compound path.

2. Choose the **Direct Selection** tool (A).

3. Click the edge of the object in the compound path that you want to reverse the color of.**A** Only that path should be selected.

4. Show the Attributes panel.

5. Click the **Reverse Path Direction Off** button or the **Reverse Path Direction On** button (the one that isn't currently highlighted).**B–C**

   Note: If the Reverse Path buttons are dimmed, make sure the Use Non-Zero Winding Fill Rule button (on the right side of the panel) is activated.

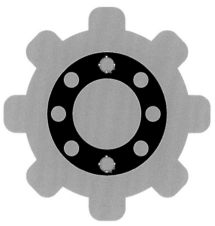

A *Two objects are selected in this compound path.*

B *We clicked the Reverse Path Direction Off button on the Attributes panel…*

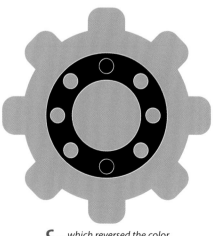

C *…which reversed the color of the two selected holes.*

You can release a compound path at any time, which will restore the original, individual paths (but not their original attributes).

To release a compound path:

1. Select a compound path. **A**

2. Do either of the following:

   Right-click the artboard and choose **Release Compound Path** from the context menu.

   Press Cmd-Option-Shift-8/Ctrl-Alt-Shift-8 or choose Object > **Compound Path** > **Release**.

   All the objects will be selected and will adopt the colors, effects, and other appearance attributes from the compound path — not their original, precompound attributes. **B** If the objects have a stroke of None, you can use the object highlighting feature of Smart Guides to locate them.

➤ All the released objects will be nested within the top-level layer of the former compound path.

➤ The Type > Create Outlines command always produces a compound path. If the former character had a counter (an interior shape, such as in the letters P, A, O, R, or D) and you release the compound path, the counter will become a separate path and will be given the same color attributes and appearances as the outer part of the letterform. **C–D**

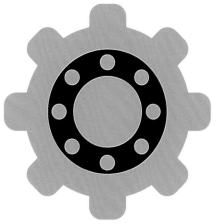

A *We clicked a compound path.*

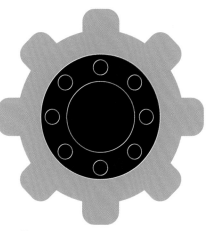

B *We released the compound path, so the holes are no longer transparent.*

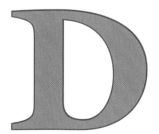

C *All type outlines are compound paths.*

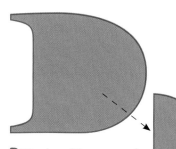

D *We released the compound path to separate objects (then repositioned the counter of the "D").*

Applying Pathfinder effects

The Pathfinder effects function like the commands on the Pathfinder panel, with the following exceptions:

➤ Unlike the Pathfinder panel commands, the Pathfinder effects modify an object's appearance but not its actual path (until the file is flattened for output). For example, the Divide, Trim, and Merge effects don't break up overlapping areas into separate objects (as the commands on the Pathfinder panel do) until the file is flattened.

➤ The effects don't create a compound shape or compound path.

➤ You can easily delete the effect at any time, because it is listed on the Appearance panel as an attribute (see page 205).

To apply a Pathfinder effect:

1. Collect two or more objects into a separate layer or group, then target the layer or group (we do mean target — not select). If you don't do this, an alert dialog may appear when you choose the effect. **A** The objects can be path or type objects, groups, or objects in a blend, and they can contain gradients, patterns, brush strokes, transparency, and effects. They cannot be placed images.

2. Display the Appearance panel. ◉ From the **Pathfinder** submenu on the **Add New Effect** menu, *fx.* choose an effect. **B–C**

➤ To move an object into or out of a group to which a Pathfinder effect is applied, move the object's selection square upward or downward on the Layers panel. Reposition the object, if necessary.

➤ To learn more about effects, see Chapter 15.

➤ If you apply a Pathfinder effect and then apply the Object > Expand Appearance command, the results of the effect will be converted to one or more standard paths.

To replace one Pathfinder effect with another:

1. Target the layer or group to which the Pathfinder effect is applied.

2. On the Appearance panel, click the Pathfinder effect listing. The Pathfinder Options dialog opens. Check Preview.

3. From the **Operation** menu, choose a different **Pathfinder** option, then click OK.

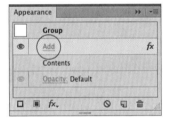

A This alert dialog may appear if you fail to target a layer or group before applying a Pathfinder effect.

B *We applied the Add Pathfinder effect (via the Appearance panel) to unite the objects in this group.*

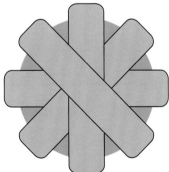

C *When we hid the effect on the Appearance panel, the individual paths redisplayed.*

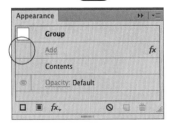

When objects are put in a clipping set, the topmost object (called the "clipping path") crops the objects or images that are below it, like a picture frame or mat. Parts of objects that extend outside the clipping path object are hidden and don't print. This mechanism allows you to fit multiple objects within the confines of a shape without having to spend time cropping and reshaping them. The clipping path and the masked objects are referred to collectively as a "clipping set." The masked objects can be moved, reshaped, recolored, or restacked within the set, and the whole clipping set can be released at any time.

Creating a clipping set

You can create a clipping set from all the objects on a given layer, in which case it is called a "layer-level" set, or from multiple selected objects on one or more layers, in which case it is called an "object-level" set. The methods for creating these two types of clipping sets differ, as do the methods used to select objects within them, but in all other respects they function in the same way.

Before creating a clipping set, review these general guidelines:

➤ The clipping path object (the object that functions as a frame) can be an open or closed path, editable type, a compound shape, or a closed object that was produced by the Unite command (Pathfinder panel).

➤ To help prevent a printing error, avoid using very complex objects in a clipping set.

➤ When you create a clipping set, the clipping path object is listed on the Layers panel as <Clipping Path> with an underline (unless editable type is used as the clipping path, in which case the type characters are listed instead). When you create an object-level clipping set, the objects are moved into a new group automatically.

CLIPPING MASKS

26

IN THIS CHAPTER

When you use the Make Clipping Mask command, the objects to be put into the clipping set can be on any layer. The command moves the objects into a new group within the layer that contains the clipping path.

To create an object-level clipping set from existing objects:

1. Arrange the object or objects to be masked.**A** They can be in a group, or not. Using the Layers panel, stack the clipping path object so it's in front of the objects to be masked.

2. Via the selection area on the Layers panel or via the Selection tool ★ (V), select the clipping path and the objects to be masked.

3. Press Cmd-7/Ctrl-7 or choose Object > Clipping Mask > **Make**. The masked objects are moved into a new Clip Group on the same top-level layer as the clipping path **B–C** and the clipping path is assigned a fill and stroke of None.

➤ If the selected objects aren't in a group, in lieu of step 3 above, you can right-click in the document and choose Make Clipping Mask.

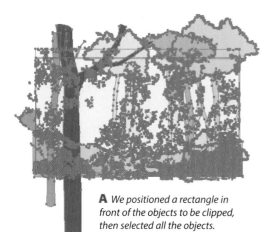

A We positioned a rectangle in front of the objects to be clipped, then selected all the objects.

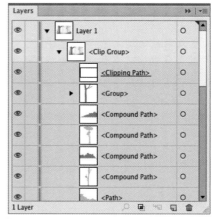

B We chose the Make Clipping Mask command, which put the objects into a clipping set within a <Clip Group>.

C Sections of objects that extend beyond the bounds of the rectangle (the clipping path) are now hidden.

The Draw Inside mode offers a different approach to creating clipping sets. When this mode is activated, new objects that you draw, or objects that you paste from the Clipboard, are clipped automatically by an object that you designate as a clipping path. Unlike when you use the Clipping Mask command, the original stroke and fill attributes of the clipping path object are preserved.

To create an object-level clipping set using Draw Inside mode:

1. With the Selection tool ▶ (V) or via the Layers panel, select an object to become the clipping path object.

2. On the Tools panel, choose **Draw Inside** 🔲 as the drawing mode. A dashed border appears at the corners of the object.**A** Deselect.

3. Choose a drawing tool (such as the Paintbrush, Pencil, Rectangle, or Ellipse tool) and the desired fill and stroke attributes, then draw new objects that intersect with the clipping path object.**B**

   The object that you selected in step 1 is now functioning as a clipping path. That object, along with the masked objects, is nested within a Clip Group on the Layers panel. If you need to reselect a masked object or the clipping path, click its selection square on the Layers panel.

4. *Optional:* You can also paste an object into the clipping set. With Draw Inside mode still active, copy an existing object on the artboard, then press Cmd-V/Ctrl-V to paste it. It will automatically be centered within the clipping path, but you can move it with the Selection tool.

5. When you're done drawing or pasting inside the clipping path, double-click in the artboard with a Selection tool or press Shift-D to return to **Draw Normal** mode.🔲 The dashed border disappears.**C**

➤ To reactivate Draw Inside mode for an object-level clipping set, select the clipping path via the Layers panel (or click its edge with the Direct Selection tool), then on the Tools panel, choose Draw Inside 🔲 mode. The dashed border reappears. Deselect, then repeat steps 3–5 above.

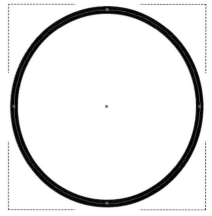

A *We chose the Draw Inside option. A dashed border appeared around our selected object.*

B *We drew an orange ellipse and lines to define the seams. Only sections of the objects that fall within the bounds of the black ellipse are visible.*

C *We put Illustrator in Draw Normal mode.*

The Make/Release Clipping Mask button on the Layers panel clips all the objects and groups on the currently active layer (whether the objects are selected or not) and uses the topmost object in the layer or group as the clipping path.

To create a layer-level clipping set:

1. Put all the objects for the clipping set on the same layer, and make sure they're the only objects on that layer.**A** Stack the object to be used as the clipping path so it's the topmost listing on the layer, and click the layer listing.

2. Click the **Make/Release Clipping Mask** button 🔲 on the Layers panel.**B–C** The clipping path is assigned a fill and stroke of None.

A These are the original objects.

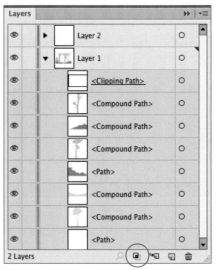

B We clicked the Make/Release Clipping Mask button on the Layers panel, which created a clipping set from all the objects in the currently active layer. The topmost object (the rectangle) became a clipping path.

C This is the artwork after we clicked the Make/Release Clipping Mask button. Sections of objects that lie outside the bounds of the clipping path object are hidden.

Selecting objects in a clipping set

When objects are in a clipping set, only the areas of masked objects that are positioned within the confines of the clipping path are visible (whether the set is selected or not). Follow these instructions to select a whole clipping set, which includes the clipping path and the masked objects.

To select a whole clipping set:

On the Layers panel, 🌣 click the selection area for the clipping set (the Clip Group or layer).

For an object-level clipping set (Clip Group), you could also click a visible part of any masked object in the document with the Selection tool ▶ (V).

➤ The bounding box (if showing) for a selected object-level clipping set will surround the clipping path, not the outermost edges of the masked objects.

You need to use a different method to select individual objects in an object-level clipping set than to select objects in a layer-level set. (To select objects in a layer-level clipping set, see the next page.)

To select objects in an object-level clipping set:

Method 1 (isolation mode)

1. Choose the Selection tool ▶ (V). In the document, double-click a visible part of one of the masked objects to put the group into isolation mode.

2. Use the Selection tool to move or transform the clipping path or any other object in the clipping set, or to select an object for recoloring.**A** Use the Direct Selection tool ▶ (A) for reshaping.

3. To exit isolation mode, press Esc.

Method 2 (buttons on the Control panel)

1. Choose the Selection tool ▶ (V).

2. To select all the masked objects but not the clipping path (perhaps to move or transform all the masked objects as a unit), click any visible object within the set, then click the **Edit Contents** button ⊙ on the Control panel.**B–C**

To select just the clipping path (perhaps to change its color attributes), click any object within the clipping set. By default, the **Edit Clipping Path** button ⊡ becomes selected on the Control panel.

➤ You can also select the clipping path or a masked object in a clipping set by clicking its selection area on the Layers panel.

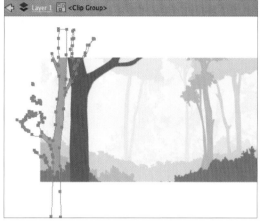

A *When a clipping set is in isolation mode, you can edit individual objects as you would objects in an ordinary group.*

B *We clicked the Edit Contents button on the Control panel to select all the masked objects, so we could move them as a unit.*

C *We moved the masked objects downward within the "frame" of the clipping path.*

To select objects in a layer-level clipping set:

1. Do either of the following:

   Choose the Selection tool ▶ (V), then click an object in the clipping set (either a clipped object or the clipping path).

   ➤ You can use the object highlighting feature of Smart Guides to locate an object.

   On the Layers panel, click the selection area for an object.

2. Do any of the following:

   Use the Selection tool to move or transform any object in the clipping set.

   Use the Direct Selection tool ▶ (A) to reshape a selected object, or the Color or Appearance panel to recolor it.

   To isolate an individual object, double-click it with the Selection tool. If you want to select a different object in the clipping set, click the layer name on the isolation mode bar, then double-click the object. (Press Esc to exit isolation mode.)

RECOLORING A CLIPPING PATH

To apply a fill or stroke color to a clipping path, click its selection area on the Layers panel first.**A–B** The stroke color will be visible no matter what, whereas the fill color will be visible only if there are gaps between the masked objects.**C**

A *This is the original clipping set.*

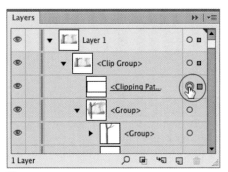

B *To select the clipping path, we clicked its selection area on the Layers panel.*

C *We applied a stroke color (dark green) and a fill color (midnight blue).*

Adding objects to, and deleting them from, a clipping set

To add a new object to a clipping set:

Method 1 (Draw Inside mode)

1. On the Layers panel, click the selection square for the Clipping Path listing.

2. From the Tools panel, choose **Draw Inside** 🖵 as the drawing mode. Deselect.

3. Do either of the following:

   While drawing a new object, make sure the pointer intersects with the clipping path.

   Copy and paste an object.

4. Press Shift-D to return to **Draw Normal** mode.🖵

Method 2 (isolation mode)

1. With the Selection tool ▶ (V), double-click a masked object in the clipping set to put it into isolation mode. Deselect.

2. Draw a new object, making sure the pointer intersects with the clipping path as you do so. To exit isolation mode, press Esc.

To add an existing object to a clipping set:

1. With the Selection tool ▶ (V), move the object to be added over the set.**A**

2. On the Layers panel, 🍂 expand the list for the clipping set, then restack the listing for the object to be added to the set group or layer, placing it below the Clipping Path listing.**B–C**

➤ To restack an object within a clipping set, on the Layers panel, drag the object listing upward or downward within its group or layer (below the Clipping Path listing).

You can take an object out of a clipping set while preserving the object.

To take an object out of a clipping set:

1. Expand the list for the clipping set on the Layers panel.

2. Create a new, blank layer, if necessary, to hold the object you will take out of the clipping set.

3. Drag the listing for a clipped object upward or downward to a different top-level layer.

➤ To remove an object from a clipping set by deleting it from the document, click its selection square on the Layers panel, then press Delete/Backspace.

A *We moved a new circle over the clipping set.*

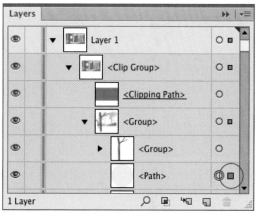

B *We moved the new path to the desired stacking position in the group within the clipping set.*

C *Once in a blue moon?*

Releasing a clipping set

When you release a clipping set, the masked objects regain their original attributes. The former clipping path is listed again as a standard path on the Layers panel, but it will have a stroke and fill of None (not its former attributes) unless you applied a color to it while it was a clipping path. If the clipping path was editable type, it is given a black fill and a stroke of None. The steps for releasing a clipping set differ depending on how it was created (whether it is an object-level or layer-level set).

To release an object-level clipping set:

1. Do either of the following:

    With the Selection tool ▶ (V), click any visible part of the clipping set.

    On the Layers panel, click the selection area for the group that contains the clipping set.

2. Do either of the following (the Clip Group listing will disappear from the Layers panel):

    Press Cmd-Option-7/Ctrl-Alt-7 or choose Object > Clipping Mask > **Release.A–B**

    Right-click in the document window and choose **Release Clipping Mask**.

To release a layer-level clipping set:

1. On the Layers panel, ♦ click the layer that contains the clipping set to be released.

2. Click the **Make/Release Clipping Mask** button ⬚ at the bottom of the Layers panel.

A *This is the original clipping set. The large blue rectangle is functioning as a clipping path.*

B *This is the result after we released the clipping set. The blue rectangle was restored to a standard object.*

The objects in our environment have various densities depending on the type of material they're made of, and may also look different depending on how much light is filtering through or reflecting off them. Take a minute to study the shade on a lamp. You might say "The shade is white" when you describe it simply, but upon closer inspection, you may notice that rather than being a dense, uniform color, it contains several permutations of white. And if the bulb is switched on, the shade will look semitransparent rather than opaque.

By using Illustrator's transparency controls, you can add a touch of realism to your drawings. If you were to draw a window, for example, you could add a tinted, semisheer, diaphanous curtain on top of it. Draw some autumn leaves, and you could lower their opacity to make them look semitransparent. Abstract designs can be enhanced by opacity variations, too.

Changing an object's opacity or blending mode

You can change the opacity of any kind of object, even editable type. You can also choose a blending mode for any object to control how its colors blend with the colors in the underlying objects. Objects that you add to a group or layer adopt the transparency settings of that group or layer. The opacity and blending mode controls in Illustrator are chosen from the Transparency panel. **A** You can open this panel via the Window menu, or access it temporarily via the Opacity link on the Control panel or Appearance panel.

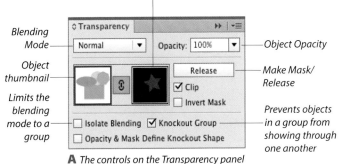

A The controls on the Transparency panel

- Opacity mask thumbnail
- Blending Mode
- Object thumbnail
- Limits the blending mode to a group
- Object Opacity
- Make Mask/Release
- Prevents objects in a group from showing through one another

To change the opacity or blending mode of an object, group, or layer:

1. Do one of the following:

   On the Layers panel, ❧ click the selection area or the target circle for an object, type, or placed image for which you want to change the transparency settings.**A–B** To edit the attributes of all the objects in a group or layer, click the target circle for that entity.

   With the Selection tool, ▸ select or isolate one or more objects in the document.

   Select some type characters with a type tool. (To change the opacity of just the fill or stroke of type, see the second task on the next page.)

2. Do either of the following:

   To change the opacity, enter or choose an **Opacity** percentage on the Control panel.

   To change the opacity and/or blending mode, either click the Opacity link on the Control or Appearance panel to open a temporary Transparency panel or display the Transparency panel. ◉ The contents of the selected or targeted layer, group, or object display in the thumbnail on the panel. Choose from the **Blending Mode** menu and/or change the **Opacity** setting **C–D** (and **A–B**, next page).

   ➤ To adjust the opacity in the Transparency panel, do one of the following: type a value in the Opacity field, click the arrow to the right of the Opacity field and choose a value, or use a trackpad or the mouse. ★

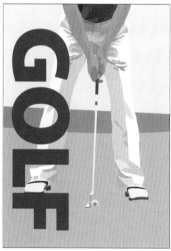

A This is the original artwork.

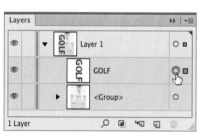

B On the Layers panel, we are clicking the target circle for the type object.

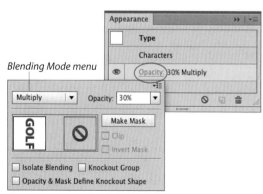

C We clicked the Opacity link on the Appearance panel to display a temporary Transparency panel, then chose Multiply as the blending mode and an opacity of 30%.

D This is the result.

To change the opacity or blending mode of an object's fill or stroke:

1. On the Layers panel, click the target circle for an object.**A** (For a type object, follow the next set of instructions instead.)

2. On the Appearance panel, ⊙ expand the Fill or Stroke listing, then click Opacity to open a temporary Transparency panel. Change the **Opacity B** or **Blending Mode** setting.

If you want to change the opacity of the stroke on a type object separately from the fill, or vice versa (while keeping the type editable), follow these steps.

To change the opacity or blending mode of the fill or stroke in type:

1. Select an editable type object using the Selection tool or the Layers panel.**C** You're going to add an extra fill and stroke attribute, so make sure the type is large enough for both of those attributes to be visible.

2. At the bottom of the Appearance panel, click the **Add New Fill** button ◼ or press Cmd-/; Ctrl-/. A new fill attribute and stroke attribute are created.

3. Click the Fill color square and choose a fill color. Double-click the Stroke color square and choose a stroke color; also use the controls on the panel to adjust the Stroke Weight.

4. Double-click **Characters** on the Appearance panel. All the characters in the object will become selected.

5. Click the **Fill** listing on the Appearance panel, then click the Delete Selected Item button 🗑; do the same for the Stroke listing. Now the fill and stroke of the Characters have a setting of None.

6. Click the **Type** listing at the top of the Appearance panel.

7. Expand the new Fill or Stroke listing, click the Opacity link, then change the **Blending Mode** menu and/or the **Opacity** setting.**D**

A *We selected an object.*

B *We lowered the opacity of the object's fill.*

C *All of the type objects in this artwork have an opacity of 100%.*

D *We reduced the fill opacity of the "0" object to 30%, but kept the opacity of its stroke at 100%.*

EXPORTING TRANSPARENCY

To export a file that contains nondefault transparency or blending mode settings to another application, keep it in the Adobe Illustrator (.ai) format if the target application supports that format or, if it doesn't, save a copy of it in the PDF format (see pages 442–445).

Controlling which objects the transparency settings affect

If you apply a blending mode to multiple selected objects, that mode becomes an appearance attribute for each object. In other words, the objects blend with one another and with any objects that are stacked below them. By applying the Isolate Blending option to a group, as in the instructions below, you can seal a collection of objects so they blend with one another but not with any underlying objects.

Note: The Isolate Blending option affects blending, not opacity. Whether this option is on or off, underlying objects will show through any objects in the artwork that aren't fully opaque.

To restrict a blending mode to specific objects:

1. On the Layers panel, ✿ expand the listing for a group of objects. Apply different blending modes (other than Normal) to all or some of the objects.**A** Click the target circle for the group. Note: To see the effect of this option, stack an object behind the group.

2. On the Transparency panel 🔵 (with full options showing), check **Isolate Blending**.**B** (If this option isn't visible, click the double arrowhead on the panel tab.) Nested objects within the targeted group will now blend with one another, but not with any objects below them.

Note: To reverse the effect, retarget the group, then uncheck Isolate Blending.

➤ This option can also be applied to an individual targeted layer.

SELECTING INDIVIDUAL OBJECTS VERSUS TARGETING A GROUP OR LAYER

We selected multiple ungrouped objects in a layer (above left), then applied an opacity setting of 60% (above right).* The opacity levels are compounded in the areas where the objects overlap (it's as though we piled up sheets of colored acetate). If we were to select any object individually, however, the Transparency and Appearance panels would list its opacity level as 60%.

Above, we targeted a group, then chose an opacity setting of 60%.* The opacity levels aren't compounded in the overlapping areas. If we were to target an individual object in the group, its opacity would be listed as 100%. (We would have gotten the same result had we targeted a layer.)

*This information also applies to blending modes.

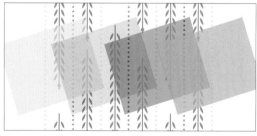

A *The original objects consist of a pattern fill in a rectangle, which is stacked below a group of rectangles. The blending mode and opacity setting of each rectangle are interacting with all the underlying layers.*

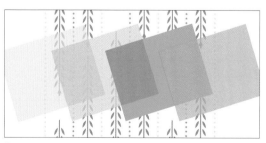

B *We checked Isolate Blending for the group of rectangles. Now the blending modes are affecting only the objects within that group. (Note that where objects in the group don't overlap one another, you can still see through them to the underlying pattern.)*

The Knockout Group option on the Transparency panel controls whether objects in a group or layer will show through (knock out) one another in the areas where they overlap. This option affects only objects within the same targeted group or layer.

To knock out objects:

1. Nest some objects within the same group or layer and arrange them so they partially overlap one another.

2. So you will be able to see how the Knockout Group option works, target some or all of the nested objects individually, then apply an opacity value below 100% and/or apply a blending mode other than Normal.

3. On the Layers panel, ✎ target the group or layer that the objects are nested within.**A**

4. On the Transparency panel, ◔ click the **Knockout Group** box once or twice, until a check mark displays.**B** With this option checked, objects nested in the group won't show through one another, but you will still be able to see through any semitransparent objects in the group to underlying objects.

   Note: To turn off the Knockout Group option at any time, target the group or layer to which the option is applied, then click the Knockout Group box once or twice until the check mark disappears.

➤ ct all the objects in your artwork that have the same blending mode or opacity, select an object that contains the attribute you're looking for, then choose Select > Same > Blending Mode or Opacity.

USING THE TRANSPARENCY GRID

➤ Once you start changing the opacity settings for objects, you may find it hard to distinguish between those that have a light but solid tint and those that have an opacity below 100%. With the transparency grid on (View > Show Transparency Grid or press Cmd-Shift-D/Ctrl-Shift-D), you will be able to see a checkerboard pattern through semitransparent objects.

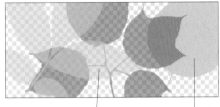

A semitransparent object A light-colored, fully opaque object

➤ If you want to change the colors or size of the transparency grid to make it contrast better with the colors in your artwork, deselect, then click Document Setup on the Control panel. Under Transparency, choose a Grid Size of Small, Medium, or Large. From the Grid Colors menu, choose Light, Medium, or Dark for a grayscale grid, or choose a preset color. (You can also choose custom colors by clicking each color swatch, then choosing a color in the Colors dialog.)

You can also check Simulate Colored Paper in the Document Setup dialog to have objects in your document look as though they're printed on colored paper. The object color will blend with the "colored paper," which will display as the background on all the artboards. The color in the top swatch is used as the paper color. To view the effect of this option, you must hide the transparency grid.

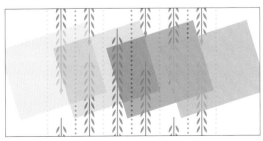

A *The Knockout Group option is off for the group of rectangles (and Isolate Blending is also unchecked).*

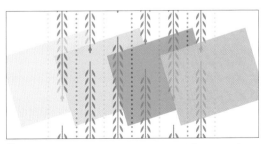

B *We checked the Knockout Group option. The rectangles are no longer transparent or blend with one another (but they still blend with the underlying pattern).*

Creating an opacity mask

Via the Transparency panel, you can apply the gray-scale equivalent of a solid color or gradient colors in an object as an opacity setting to underlying objects. Black applies 0% opacity; white applies 100% opacity.

To create an opacity mask:

1. On the Layers panel, ☟ stack an object to be used as a mask above one or more other objects. To that object, apply solid gray, a solid color, a gradient, or pattern fill, and keep it selected. Note: If you want to have more control over the resulting opacity level, apply a fill of gray (try 20% to 50% gray).

2. Via the Layers panel or the Selection tool, select the mask object and the objects to be masked. **A**

3. On the Transparency panel, ⬤ click **Make Mask. B** If you selected three or more objects, and they weren't already in a group, Illustrator will put them into one. On the Layers panel, a dashed or solid underline will display below the Path or Group listing for the opacity mask.

4. *Optional:* To stop the masking object from clipping the masked objects, uncheck Clip. **C**

➤ To set a default so the Clip option is on for new opacity masks, check New Opacity Masks Are Clipping on the Transparency panel menu.

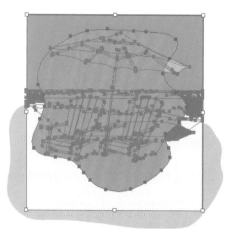

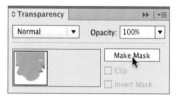

A *We selected several objects, including an object containing 50% gray, which is on top, then clicked the Make Mask button. (The bottommost tan object wasn't selected.)*

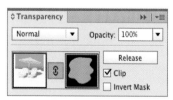

B *Illustrator applied the gray-scale value of the mask object (shown in the mask thumbnail) as an opacity value to the masked objects. (The underlying tan object remains visible because it isn't in the mask.)*

C *We unchecked the Clip option on the Transparency panel. The opacity mask is still in effect, except now areas of masked objects that extend beyond the mask are visible.*

USING A GRADIENT FILL AS A MASKING OBJECT

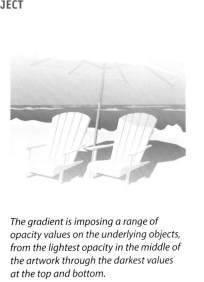

A rectangle was drawn and filled with a gradient (Gradient panel, Type: Linear, Angle 86°). The objects were selected, then Make Mask was clicked on the Transparency panel.

The gradient is imposing a range of opacity values on the underlying objects, from the lightest opacity in the middle of the artwork through the darkest values at the top and bottom.

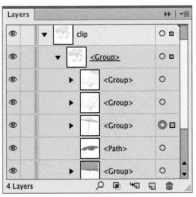

A *To edit masked artwork, select it, then click the left thumbnail on the Transparency panel.*

B *With the left thumbnail clicked on the Transparency panel, only the masked objects (not the masking object) are listed on the Layers panel.*

Editing masked artwork or the masking object in an opacity mask

To edit masked artwork in an opacity mask:

With the Selection tool, ⬚ click the masked artwork in the document. On the Transparency panel, ⬚ click the left thumbnail,**A** then do either of the following:

With the Selection tool, ⬚ double-click the masked artwork to put it into isolation mode. Edit any of the objects, then exit isolation mode. You can also add objects to the mask.

On the Layers panel, click the selection square for one or more masked objects (or for the whole group, if any),**B** then apply edits.

➤ To disable a selected opacity mask temporarily, Shift-click the mask thumbnail on the Transparency panel (a red X appears on the thumbnail).**C** Repeat to re-enable the mask.

C *This opacity mask is disabled.*

To edit the masking object in an opacity mask:

1. With the Selection tool, ▶ click the masked artwork in the document.

2. On the Transparency panel, ⬤ click the opacity mask thumbnail (on the right).

3. Select the masking object via the Selection tool or the Layers panel.**A**

4. Edit any attribute of the object, such as its shape or fill, or for a gradient, edit its gradient settings.**B** Note that the actual fill of a masking object doesn't display. You can also lower the opacity value of the masking object to alter the opacity of the masked artwork.

5. On the Transparency panel, click the left thumbnail.

➤ To display just the masking object in grayscale in the document, hold down Option/Alt and click the mask thumbnail on the Transparency panel. To redisplay the artwork in color, click the left thumbnail.

➤ To reposition one object in an opacity mask, drag it with the Direct Selection tool. To reposition all the masked objects separately from the masking object, click the artwork with the Selection tool, click the Link icon 🔒 on the Transparency panel, then drag the artwork in the document. When you're done, click the icon 🔗 to restore the link.

To release an opacity mask:

1. Via the Selection tool or the Layers panel, select an opacity mask.

2. On the Transparency panel, click **Release**.

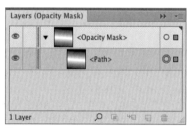

A *When the mask thumbnail is clicked on the Transparency panel, only the masking object is listed on the Layers panel.*

B *If you select a masking object that contains a gradient, then click the Gradient tool, you can move or modify any of the stops on the annotator to control what opacity levels are applied to the masked artwork.*

USING A PATTERN FILL AS A MASKING OBJECT

If you use an object that contains a pattern fill as a masking object, the artwork will be most visible below the lightest areas in the pattern. We recommend using a pattern that has strong light and dark color contrasts.

This is the original artwork.

A rectangle containing a pattern was positioned over the artwork, then it was used as an opacity mask. (A sample of the pattern is shown in the upper right.)

By dragging symbols out of the Symbols panel onto your artwork, you can create complex art quickly and easily. Illustrator supplies hundreds of predefined symbols, and you can also create symbols from your Illustrator artwork.

To place a single instance of a symbol onto the artboard, you either drag it out of the Symbols panel 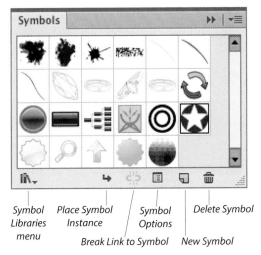 A or click the Place Symbol Instance button. To place multiple instances of a symbol (into what is called a symbol set), you either drag with the Symbol Sprayer tool or hold the tool down in one spot. To create a flowering forest and meadow, for example, you could create a few tree and flower instances by dragging symbols into your document, and create a set of grass symbols by spraying.

In this chapter, in addition to learning how to create symbol instances and sets, you will learn how to replace, create, delete, and edit symbols, as well as expand symbol instances. And by using the Symbol Shifter, Scruncher, Sizer, Spinner, Stainer, Screener, and Styler tools (that's a tongue twister!), you will change the stacking order, position, size, rotation angle, color tint, transparency, and style, respectively, of multiple symbol instances in a selected symbol set. These tools merely alter the way the instances look, without breaking their link to the original symbol. The reverse is also true: If you edit the original symbol to which instances are linked in your artwork, your changes will appear instantly in all those instances.

Continued on the following page

Symbol Libraries menu
Place Symbol Instance
Break Link to Symbol
Symbol Options
New Symbol
Delete Symbol

A *Use the Symbols panel to store symbols, place and replace symbol instances into your artwork, access symbol libraries, and open an options dialog for the symbolism tools.*

SYMBOLS

28

Another advantage of using symbols is efficient storage. For example, say you add a dozen instances of a parking symbol to a map design. Although all the multiple parking symbols will be visible in your document, Illustrator will define the object only once in the document code. This helps reduce the file size and speeds up printing and downloading. File size is especially critical when outputting to the Web in the SVG (Scalable Vector Graphics) or SWF (Flash) format. Because each symbol is defined only once in the exported SVG image or Flash animation, the size of the exported file is kept relatively small, and the download time is minimized.

Accessing the symbol libraries

In these steps, you will learn how to access the Adobe symbol libraries and add some of those symbols to the Symbols panel for your current document.

To access symbols from other libraries:

1. Display the Symbols panel.

2. From the **Symbol Libraries** menu at the bottom of the Symbols panel, choose a library. A separate library panel opens.**A**

3. Do any of the following:

   Click a symbol on the library panel. It will appear on the Symbols panel.

   To add multiple symbols from a library to the Symbols panel, click, then Shift-click a series of consecutive symbols or Cmd-click/Ctrl-click nonconsecutive ones, then choose **Add to Symbols** from the library panel menu.

   Drag a symbol from a library panel into your document; the symbol will also appear on the Symbols panel.

4. To browse through other libraries, click the **Load Next Symbol Library** button or **Load Previous Symbol Library** button at the bottom of the library panel.

▶ To change the Symbols panel display, from the Symbols panel menu, choose Thumbnail View, Small List View, or Large List View. When the panel is in Thumbnail View, you can identify the symbol names via tool tips.

▶ To sort the symbols alphabetically by name, choose Sort by Name from the Symbols panel menu. You can also rearrange the symbols manually by dragging them.

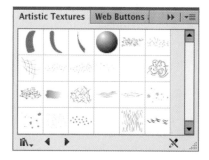

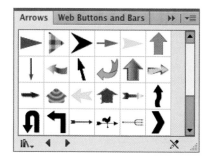

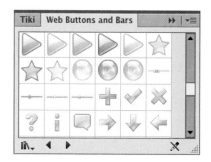

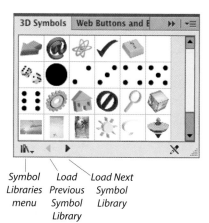

Symbol Libraries menu   Load Previous Symbol Library   Load Next Symbol Library

A These are some of the many predefined symbol libraries that are available in Adobe Illustrator.

➤ To control whether a library panel reappears when you relaunch Illustrator, check or uncheck Persistent on the library panel menu.

➤ To import symbols from another Illustrator file, from the Symbol Libraries menu 📚▾ on the Symbols panel, choose Other Library. Click the file from which you want to import symbols, then click Open. The symbols will appear in a symbol library panel; follow step 3 on the preceding page.

Creating individual symbol instances

In the steps below, you will create individual symbol instances. On the next page, you will place multiple instances of a symbol into a document quickly by using the Symbol Sprayer tool.

To create individual symbol instances:

1. Display the Symbols panel. 🔖

2. Do either of the following:

   Drag a symbol from the Symbols panel onto an artboard. **A**

   Click a symbol on the Symbols panel, then click the **Place Symbol Instance** button ➡ on the panel. The instance appears in the center of the document window.

3. Repeat the preceding step if you want to add more instances. **B**

➤ To demonstrate the fact that each instance is linked to the original symbol, place instances of a few different symbols into your document. Click one of the instances, then look at the Symbols panel. The thumbnail for that symbol becomes selected on the panel.

➤ To duplicate an instance (along with any transformations or other edits that you have applied to it), Option-drag/Alt-drag it in your document. The duplicate instance will be linked to the same symbol on the Symbols panel.

➤ When an instance is selected, a registration point displays in its center (see the sidebar on page 389 and the second tip on page 391).

➤ If the View > Smart Guides feature is on (with the Alignment Guides preference enabled) and you drag an object near a symbol instance, Smart Guides will align to shapes within the instance.

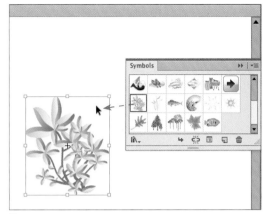

A *We dragged a symbol from the Symbols panel onto an artboard.*

B *This artwork was created from symbols in the Nature library.*

APPLYING ILLUSTRATOR COMMANDS TO SYMBOL INSTANCES AND SETS

➤ You can transform a symbol instance or set by manipulating its bounding box with the Free Transform or the Selection tool.

➤ To undo all the transformations you have applied to a selected symbol instance, click Reset on the Control panel.

➤ You can apply Appearance and Transparency panel settings to symbol instances and sets.

➤ Although you can apply effects (Effect menu) to symbol instances and sets, you'll achieve a smaller file size if you apply them to the original symbol instead.

Creating symbol sets with the Symbol Sprayer tool

The Symbol Sprayer tool sprays multiple instances of a symbol into a symbol set; it can also be used to delete instances from a set. It's easy and fun to use. You can choose from a slew of options for the tool (as we show you on page 392), but first do a bit of spraying with it, just to get the hang of it.

To create a symbol set with the Symbol Sprayer tool:

1. Choose the **Symbol Sprayer** tool 📷 (Shift-S).

2. On the Symbols panel, 🔲 click a symbol.

3. Click to create one instance per click, or click and hold or drag to create multiple instances quickly. **A** The instances will appear in a set, within one bounding box.

4. *Optional:* To create another set, hold down Cmd/Ctrl and click outside the bounding box for the original set to deselect it, then follow the preceding step.

To add instances to an existing set, you must use the Symbol Sprayer tool (not the Place Symbol Instance button).

To add instances to a symbol set:

1. Do either of the following:

    Choose the Selection tool ▶ (V), then click an instance in a symbol set.

    Select a symbol set via the Layers panel.

2. Click a symbol on the Symbols panel. It can be a different symbol than those already in the set.

3. Use the **Symbol Sprayer** tool. 📷 **B**

To delete instances from a symbol set:

1. Select a symbol set with the Selection tool (click an instance in the set) or via the Layers panel.

2. If the set contains instances of more than one symbol, do either of the following:

    To restrict the deletion to instances of a particular symbol, click that symbol on the Symbols panel (or Cmd-click/Ctrl-click multiple symbols).

    To allow instances of any symbol to be deleted, click a blank area of the Symbols panel.

3. Choose the **Symbol Sprayer** tool. 📷

4. With Option/Alt held down, click or drag in the set.

A *We created a symbol set with the Symbol Sprayer tool.*

B *To add instances of a different symbol to a set, select the set, choose the Symbol Sprayer tool, click the desired symbol on the Symbols panel, then drag within the set.*

Replacing symbols in a document

When you replace a symbol in a solo instance or in a symbol set with a different symbol, any transformations, transparency changes, or edits made by a symbolism tool (e.g., by the Symbol Shifter or Sizer tool) that were applied to the original instance or set will appear automatically in the replacements.

To replace a symbol in an instance:

1. With the Selection tool , click an individual symbol instance in your document.**A**

2. On the Control panel, click the **Replace** thumbnail or arrowhead to open a temporary Symbols panel, then click a replacement symbol.**B–C**

When you apply a replacement symbol to a symbol set, all the instances in the set are replaced with the new one, even if they originated from different symbols.

To replace the symbols in a symbol set:

1. Via the Selection tool or the Layers panel, select a symbol set in your document.

2. Click a replacement symbol on the Symbols panel, then choose **Replace Symbol** on the panel menu.

REGISTRATION POINT OR REFERENCE POINT

By default, the transformation of an individual symbol instance is calculated from its registration point. To have Illustrator calculate transformations from a point you designate on the Reference Point locator on the Transform panel instead, uncheck Use Registration Point for Symbol on the Transform panel menu.

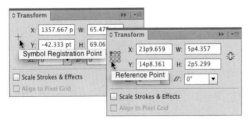

ALIGNING SYMBOLS TO THE PIXEL GRID

To align an individual instance or all the instances in a set to the pixel grid (for Web output), either select the instance or set or select the symbol to which it is linked on the Symbols panel, click the Symbol Options button, ![icon] then check Align to Pixel Grid. Any new instances that you add to the set will also align to the grid. Note that even when aligned to the grid, instances that have been scaled may not output crisply.

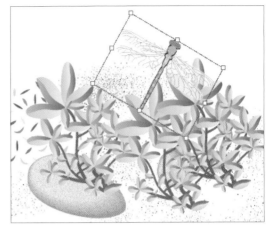

A *Click a symbol instance in your document.*

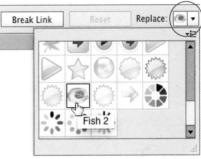

B *Click the Replace thumbnail or arrowhead on the Control panel, then click a replacement symbol on the temporary Symbols panel.*

C *We replaced the dragonfly symbol with a fish symbol.*

Creating symbols

Now that you're acquainted with the Symbols panel, you're ready to create your own symbols. Any Illustrator object(s) can be made into a symbol: a standard path or group of paths, a compound path, an embedded raster image, type. Well…within reason. If you're planning to spray the symbol densely all over a document, try to avoid creating it from complex artwork.

The object from which you create a symbol can contain a brush stroke, blend, effect, or graphic style. Those elements won't be editable in the symbol instances, but you can edit the original symbol at any time (see "Editing symbols" on the next page).

To create a symbol from artwork:

1. Create one or more objects, or a group of objects. Color and scale them as desired, and keep them selected.**A**

2. Choose the Selection tool ▶ (V), then Shift-click the **New Symbol** button 🔲 on the Symbols panel (the Shift key will prevent the original object from becoming an instance).

3. The Symbol Options dialog opens.**B** Enter a name for the new symbol, choose Type: **Movie Clip** if you will be exporting the symbol to Adobe Flash or click **Graphic** if not, click a **Registration** point to establish a reference point (from which transformations are calculated), check **Align to Pixel Grid** if the symbol will be used for Web output, then click OK. The symbol appears on the Symbols panel.**C**

Deleting symbols from the panel

If you try to delete from the Symbols panel a symbol that is in use in your document, you will be given a choice via an alert dialog to expand or delete the instances that were created from it.

To delete symbols from the Symbols panel:

1. Click a symbol on the Symbols panel, then click the **Delete Symbol** button 🗑 on the panel.

2. If there are no instances of the deleted symbol in your document, click **Yes** in the alert dialog.

   If the document does contain instances of the symbol, a different alert dialog appears. Click **Expand Instances** to expand the linked instances into standard objects, or click **Delete Instances** to delete the linked instances.

A Select an object or group in your artwork.

B Choose options in the Symbol Options dialog.

C The new symbol appears on the panel.

RENAMING SYMBOLS AND INSTANCES

► To rename a symbol, click the symbol on the panel, click the Symbol Options button, 🖾 then change the name in the dialog.

► If you're going to export your symbol artwork to the Flash (.swf) format, you can assign names to individual instances. Click an instance, then enter a new name in the Instance Name field on the Control panel.

Creating a custom symbol library

If you save the symbols that are currently on your Symbols panel as a library, you'll be able to access them quickly at any time via the Symbol Libraries menu.

To create a custom symbol library:

1. Make sure the Symbols panel contains only the symbols to be saved in a library. From the top of the Symbol Libraries menu 📚 on the panel, choose **Save Symbols**.

2. In the Save Symbols as Library dialog, type a name for the library, keep the default location (the Symbols folder), then click Save.

3. The new library (and other user-saved libraries) can be opened from the **User Defined** submenu on the Symbol Libraries menu. 📚

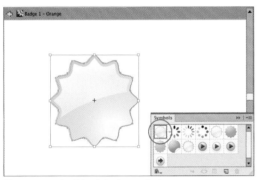

A *When we double-clicked a symbol, a temporary instance of it appeared in the document window, in isolation mode.*

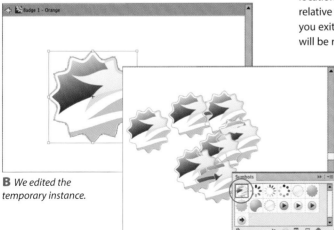

B *We edited the temporary instance.*

C *When we exited isolation mode, the symbol updated on the Symbols panel and in an existing set.*

Editing symbols

Note: When you edit a symbol in the Symbols panel, your edits will be applied to any and all instances in the document to which the symbol is linked.

To edit a symbol:

1. Do either of the following:

    Double-click a symbol on the Symbols panel. A temporary instance of the symbol appears in your document, in isolation mode.**A**

    Click an individual symbol instance in your document, click **Edit Symbol** on the Control panel, then click OK if an alert dialog appears. The instance is now in isolation mode.

2. Select and modify the object(s).**B**

3. Exit isolation mode by clicking the gray bar at the top of the document window. Your edits will be applied to the original symbol on the Symbols panel and to any instances that are currently linked to that symbol.**C** Any transformations that you applied to those instances before the symbol was edited will be preserved.

➤ To create a variation of a symbol, click the symbol on the Symbols panel, then choose Duplicate Symbol from the panel menu. Double-click the duplicate, then follow steps 2–3, above.

➤ When you select symbol instances, or while you edit them with a symbolism tool, a registration point displays at the center of each instance. To reposition the registration point from its default location, after step 1 above, drag the instance relative to the stationary registration point. When you exit isolation mode, all instances of that symbol will be repositioned automatically.

REDEFINING A SYMBOL

To replace an existing symbol with one or more entirely different objects, hold down Option/Alt and drag the nonsymbol object over the symbol on the Symbols panel to be replaced (or select the object, click the symbol to be replaced on the panel, then choose Redefine Symbol from the panel menu). Any instances that are linked to that symbol will update accordingly.

Choosing options for the symbolism tools

In the Symbolism Tools Options dialog, you can choose global settings that apply to all eight of the symbolism tools, as well as settings that apply to one tool in particular. The global settings and the settings that apply to just the Symbol Sprayer are discussed below and in the sidebar on this page; the settings that are unique to other symbolism tools are mentioned on pages 394–397. Note: To keep the symbolism tools readily available, display them in a tearoff toolbar or make them part of a custom Tools panel.

To choose options for the symbolism tools:

1. *Optional:* If you want to change the density for one or more existing sets in your document, select them now via the Selection tool or Layers panel.

2. Double-click any symbolism tool to open the Symbolism Tools Options dialog.**A**

3. To specify a default size for all the symbolism tools, enter a **Diameter** value.

4. The current choice on the **Method** menu applies to all the symbolism tools except the Symbol Sprayer and Symbol Shifter: **Average** gradually equalizes the edits made by the tool, **User Defined** modifies instances based on how the mouse is used, and **Random** applies random values.

5. To adjust the rate at which the sprayer creates instances or the tools produce changes, enter an **Intensity** value (1–10). Or to allow a stylus to control the intensity instead, choose any option from the menu except Fixed.

   ➤ To adjust the Diameter and Intensity values "on the fly," see the sidebar on the next page.

6. To specify how tightly all the instances will be packed within the set when the Symbol Sprayer tool is used, enter a **Symbol Set Density** value (1–10). Note: Changes to this value will also affect the instances within any currently selected sets.

7. Check **Show Brush Size and Intensity** (as we do) to have Illustrator represent the current Diameter setting by a ring around the tool icon and represent the Intensity setting by a shade of that ring (black for high intensity, gray for medium intensity, and light gray for low intensity). With this option off, only the tool icon displays (no ring).

8. Click OK.

A *Use the Symbolism Tools Options dialog to choose global and individual properties for the symbolism tools. The menus in the lower portion of the dialog appear only when the Symbol Sprayer tool icon is clicked.*

USER DEFINED, DEFINED (FOR THE SPRAYER)

For each property of the Symbol Sprayer tool (Scrunch, Size, Spin, Screen, Stain, and Style), you can choose either Average or User Defined:

With Average chosen, the tool adds each new instance based on an average sampling of neighboring instances already in the set, within the current diameter of the brush cursor.

With User Defined chosen, the properties will be based on the following values (to see the changes more easily, set the Intensity value to 4–8):

➤ Scrunch (density) uses the original symbol density, not any density values that were produced via the Symbol Scruncher tool.

➤ Size uses the original symbol size, not modified sizes in the set.

➤ Spin is controlled by the direction in which the mouse is moved.

➤ Screen applies instances at an opacity of 100%, not based on modified opacity values in the set.

➤ Stain applies the current fill color at a tint of 100%.

➤ Style applies the graphic style that is currently selected on the Graphic Styles panel.

Note: The settings chosen from the six individual tool menus are unrelated to the Method setting, which applies to all the symbolism tools except the Sprayer and the Shifter.

Using the Symbol Shifter, Scruncher, Sizer, Spinner, Stainer, Screener, and Styler tools

The tools discussed in this section modify the attributes of individual instances or instances within a set, such as their stacking position, location, size, orientation, color, transparency, or graphic style. Generic instructions for using the tools are given here. On the next four pages, you will find separate instructions for each tool.

To use the Symbol Shifter, Scruncher, Sizer, Spinner, Stainer, Screener, or Styler tool:

1. With the Selection tool ▶ (V) or the Layers panel, click a symbol instance or set.

2. Choose the **Symbol Shifter**, **Scruncher**, **Sizer**, **Spinner**, **Stainer**, **Screener**, or **Styler** tool.**A**

3. *Optional:* Choose settings via the Symbolism Tools Options dialog (see the preceding page) or use the shortcuts listed in the sidebar at right.

4. Do any of the following:

   Click an instance.

   Drag within a symbol set.

   Hold the mouse button down within a set.

   Note: If a selected set contains instances from more than one symbol, and one of those symbols is selected on the Symbols panel, modifications made by a symbolism tool will be limited to instances of that symbol. To remove this restriction so you can modify instances of different symbols, deselect all symbols first by clicking a blank area of the Symbols panel. Or to modify instances of multiple symbols, Cmd-click/Ctrl-click those symbols on the panel before using the tool.

➤ Although the symbolism tools affect all the instances in a set, by choosing a small brush diameter and by positioning your pointer carefully, you can control where a tool has the most impact. The effect is strongest in the center of the brush and diminishes gradually toward its perimeter.

➤ When using a symbolism tool (such as the Symbol Shifter, Scruncher, or Sizer) to modify a set, keep these two seemingly conflicting tendencies in mind: The tool will shift or scale the instances while also trying to maintain the existing density of the set. Yin and yang.

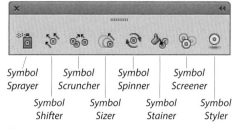

| Symbol Sprayer | Symbol Scruncher | Symbol Spinner | Symbol Screener |
| Symbol Shifter | Symbol Sizer | Symbol Stainer | Symbol Styler |

A *The Symbol Sprayer tool creates symbol instances; the other symbolism tools modify symbol instances in different ways.*

THE SHORTCUTS FOR QUICK DIAMETER AND INTENSITY CHANGES

When using a symbolism tool, you can quickly change the tool Diameter or Intensity without opening the Symbolism Tool Options dialog:

Increase or decrease the brush Diameter	Press or hold down] (right bracket) or [(left bracket)
Increase or decrease the brush Intensity	Press or hold down Shift-] or Shift-[

The Symbol Shifter tool 🖼️

The Symbol Shifter tool has two functions. It either shifts instances in a set on the same plane, based on the direction in which the mouse is dragged, or changes their stacking order from front to back, depending on where you click. Having the ability to bring instances forward or behind other instances would be useful, for instance (pun intended), in a set in which trees are obscuring some figures: You could move the trees closer together to create a forest, then bring the figures forward, in front of the trees.

➤ Drag within a symbol set to move instances on the same plane.

➤ Shift-click an instance within a symbol set to move it forward, or Option-Shift-click/Alt-Shift-click an instance to move it behind adjacent instances. **A–B**

The Symbol Scruncher tool 🖼️

The Symbol Scruncher tool either pulls symbol instances closer toward the center of the cursor or spreads them farther apart. You could use this tool on a symbol set of clouds or fish, for example, to pack the instances more densely or to pull them apart.

➤ For the most predictable results, double-click the Symbol Scruncher tool, and in the options dialog, choose Method: User Defined.

➤ To bring instances closer together, either drag with the tool or hold the mouse button down in one spot. To spread instances apart, hold down Option/Alt while dragging. **C**

A *We clicked the symbol for the plant on the Symbols panel, and with the Symbol Shifter tool, we're dragging to the right.*

B *Some of the plants moved to the right, while the other instances stayed in place.*

C *With the same plant symbol selected on the Symbols panel, we're using the Symbol Scruncher tool (Method: User Defined) with Option/Alt held down to move the plants apart in all directions from the center of the cursor.*

The Symbol Sizer tool

The Symbol Sizer tool scales existing instances by variable amounts. The Method options for this tool are as follows: User Defined scales instances based on how you use the mouse, Average gradually makes variably scaled instances more uniform in size, and Random enlarges or shrinks instances by random amounts.

➤ With User Defined chosen as the Method for this tool, click on or drag across instances to enlarge them, **A–B** or hold down Option/Alt and click or drag to shrink them. Instances closest to the center of the tool cursor will scale the most.

The options dialog offers two extra features for this tool:

➤ Proportional Resizing prevents instances from being distorted as they are resized.

➤ Resizing Affects Density allows instances to move apart when they're enlarged or move closer together when they're scaled down. With this option off, the Sizer tries to preserve the existing density of the set. If the Resizing Affects Density option is on, you can disable it temporarily by holding down Shift as you drag with the tool.

The Symbol Spinner tool

The Symbol Spinner tool rotates instances (changes their orientation).

The Method options for this tool are as follows: User Defined rotates symbol instances in the direction in which the mouse is dragged, **C** Average gradually makes the orientation of all rotated instances within the brush diameter more uniform, and Random varies their orientation at random angles.

As you use this tool, temporary arrows point in the direction the instances are being rotated. If the arrows are hard to see against your artwork, change the selection color for the layer the set resides in to a more contrasting color (double-click next to the layer name to open the Layer Options dialog).

The Symbol Stainer tool

The Symbol Stainer tool colorizes solid-color fills, patterns, and gradients in symbol instances with variable tints of the current fill color, while preserving

A *This is the original symbol set.*

B *This is after we clicked the plant symbol on the Symbols panel, then used the Symbol Sizer tool (Method: User Defined) to enlarge the plants in the foreground.*

C *And this is after we used the Symbol Spinner tool to rotate the plant instances (or was it a tropical gust of wind?).*

existing luminosity values. This is a useful tool because you can't recolor instances via the usual Illustrator color controls. You could use the Stainer to vary the shades of green in foliage, the shades of blue-green in water, etc.

➤ Before using this tool, choose a fill color to be used for staining. Click on, or drag across, an instance or within a set to apply a tint of the current fill color. Continue clicking or dragging to increase the amount of colorization, up to the maximum amount.**A–B** Black and white aren't stained, and the luminosity values of colors are preserved.

➤ Hold down Option/Alt and click or drag to decrease the amount of colorization and restore more of the original symbol colors.

➤ To apply a new stain color only to instances that have already been stained without changing the existing levels of staining, choose a new fill color, then Shift-click or Shift-drag with the tool.

The Method options for this tool are as follows: User Defined gradually applies the current fill color, Average evens out the amount of any existing staining without applying more, and Random applies random variations of the stain color.

Note: The results of the Symbol Stainer tool (and the Symbol Styler tool, which is discussed on the next page) increase the file size and diminish Illustrator's performance. Avoid using them if you're going to export your file in the Flash (.swf) format or if you're having problems with system memory.

The Symbol Screener tool

Use the Symbol Screener tool to fade instances and make them more transparent. The Method options for this tool are as follows: User Defined gradually increases or decreases the transparency of instances, Average gradually makes nonuniform transparency more uniform, and Random varies the transparency by random amounts (for the most naturalistic look).

➤ With User Defined chosen as the Method for the tool, click and hold on or drag across instances to make them more transparent,**C** or hold down Option/Alt and click or drag across instances to progressively restore their opacity.

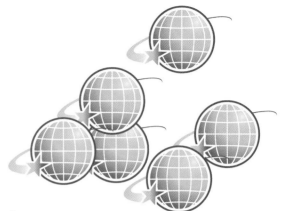

A *This is the original symbol set.*

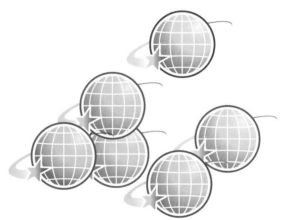

B *We chose a blue as the fill color, then dragged the Symbol Stainer tool (Method: User Defined) across the set.*

C *With the Symbol Screener tool (Method: User Defined), we dragged across the original set (shown in **A**, above).*

The Symbol Styler tool

The Symbol Styler tool applies the graphic style that is currently selected on the Graphic Styles panel to symbol instances. You can apply more than one style to the same symbol set.

➤ Use the Symbol Styler tool in this sequence: Select a symbol instance or set; choose the Symbol Styler tool; click a graphic style on the Graphic Styles panel or choose a style from the Style preset picker on the Control panel; then finally, click and hold on or drag across the instance or set to apply the style. **A–B** The longer you hold down the mouse, the more completely the style settings are applied. Pause to allow the results to process. This can take some time, even on a speedy machine.

➤ Shift-click or Shift-drag with the tool to gradually apply more of the same graphic style or a different style only to instances that have already been styled.

➤ With Option/Alt held down, click or drag to remove styling that you have applied.

The Method options for this tool are as follows: User Defined gradually increases or decreases the amount of styling; Average evens out the amount of styling that has already been applied without applying any new styling; and Random doesn't seem to make any difference, at least in our testing.

Unlinking symbol instances

When you break the link between an instance or set and the original symbol, the instance is converted to a normal object or group of objects.

To break the link between instances and a symbol:

1. With the Selection tool ▶ (V), click a symbol instance or set.

2. Do either of the following:

    Click the **Break Link to Symbol** button ⊙⊙ on the Symbols panel. You must use this method when breaking the link for a set.

    Click **Break Link** on the Control panel.

➤ To select all the instances of a particular symbol in your document, click the symbol on the Symbols panel, then choose Select All Instances from the panel menu.

A *This is the original symbol set.*

B *And this is the set after we applied a few different graphic styles with the Symbol Styler tool.*

Expanding symbol instances

When applied to a symbol set, the Expand command breaks the set apart into individual instances without breaking the link to the original symbol, and nests the resulting instances within a group on the Layers panel. When the command is applied to an individual symbol instance, it produces a very different result: It breaks the link to the original symbol and nests the resulting paths within a group and sublayer on the Layers panel.

To expand a symbol instance or set:

1. Select a symbol instance, multiple instances, or a symbol set. **A** Note that individual instances are listed by their symbol name on the Layers panel, whereas sets have the generic name "Symbol Set."

2. Choose Object > **Expand** (or if you applied an effect or graphic style to the symbol instance or set, simply choose Object > Expand Appearance and skip the next step).

3. In the Expand dialog, **B** check **Object** and **Fill**, then click OK.

4. If you expanded a symbol set, **C** you can now use the Direct Selection tool to move the individual instances apart, or double-click the group with the Selection tool to isolate it, then modify the instances. In either case, they will remain linked to the original symbol.

   If you expanded an individual instance, **D** it will now consist of a group of paths within a sublayer (labeled with the name of the former symbol), and will be unlinked from the original symbol. **E** You can edit the group in isolation mode.

➤ If you use the Symbol Stainer tool on a symbol set and then expand the set, the instances that were modified by the tool will be given a numeric listing on the Layers panel.

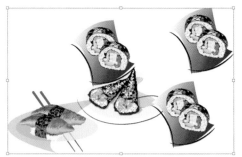

A *We selected a symbol set.*

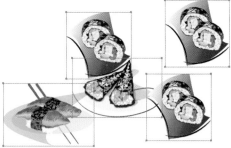

B *We checked Object and Fill in the Expand dialog.*

C *The Expand command divided the set into individual instances.*

D *We selected an individual symbol instance.*

E *We applied the Expand command to the individual symbol instance. (And then we moved the resulting paths apart.)*

Now that you know how to use the basic color controls in Illustrator, you're ready to explore the Recolor Artwork dialog. Using this complex and powerful feature, you can generate color schemes based on a new harmony rule or other variables, reassign specific colors in your artwork, save color groups to the Swatches panel, and, should the need arise, reduce the number of colors in your artwork. The practical applications for this dialog are wide ranging, from improvising to see how your artwork might look in a different range of hues or tints or in a new group of coordinated colors to assigning colors that have been specified for a particular project.

Creating color groups via the Recolor Artwork dialog

There are so many features in the Recolor Artwork dialog, we divided our instructions into four manageable tasks. In this first task, you will save the existing colors in your artwork as a color group (to revert the artwork to, if needed), then change all the colors in the artwork in various ways based on those original colors. Note: Many of the icons in the dialog have changed from Illustrator version CS5. We labeled them to help you identify them.

To create a color group via the Recolor Artwork dialog:

1. Select the objects to be recolored. **A**

2. Do either of the following:

   At the bottom of the Color Guide panel, ◣ click the **Edit or Apply Colors** button. ⬤ The current color group on the panel is applied instantly to the objects, as a preview.

   On the Control panel, click the **Recolor Artwork** button. ⬤ The colors in the selected objects won't change yet.

3. At the bottom of the Recolor Artwork dialog, check **Recolor Art**.

Continued on the following page

A *These are the original objects.*

4. If the list of Color Groups isn't displaying on the right side of the dialog, click the **Show Color Group Storage** button. **A**

5. To create a color group from the selected objects, click the **Get Colors from Selected Art** button at the top of the dialog, and enter a name in the field. Click the **New Color Group** button.

   ➤ To restore the original object colors at any time, click the color group that you created (see above) or the Get Colors from Selected Art button. Keep these options in mind, because you can't undo individual editing steps while the dialog is open.

6. To try out some new colors on the selected objects, do any of the following:

   Choose a rule from the **Harmony Rules** menu at the top of the dialog. You may recognize these rules from the Color Guide panel.

   From the **Color Mode** menu, choose **Global Adjust**, then move the Saturation, Brightness, Temperature,**B** or Luminosity slider.

Click (and keep clicking) the **Randomly Change Color Order** button or **Randomly Change Saturation and Brightness** button.

7. Click the **New Color Group** button to save the active color group to the list of Color Groups. (The colors also appear on the Color Guide panel.)

   ➤ To rename a color group, double-click the current name.

8. Continue to create as many new groups as you like by repeating the last two steps. You can also recolor your artwork at any time by clicking any group on the list of Color Groups.

   To save your edits to the existing group, click the Save Changes to Color Group button.

9. Do either of the following:

   To save all new color groups to the Swatches panel and recolor the selected objects, click OK.

   To save all new color groups to the Swatches panel without recoloring the selected objects, uncheck Recolor Art, then click OK.

   Note: If an alert appears, click Yes to save your edits to the color group.

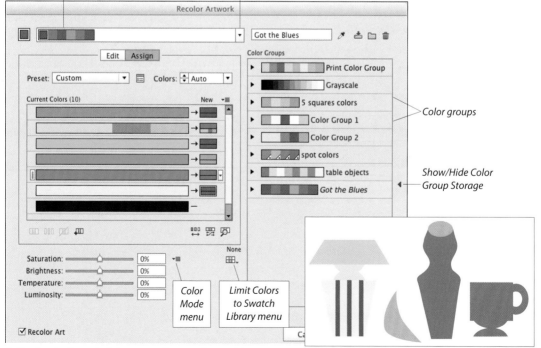

A *The Recolor Artwork dialog is complex — and powerful.*

B *This is after we chose the Left Complement harmony rule and reduced the Temperature value to a chilly −74.*

Using the color wheel in the Recolor Artwork dialog

Next, you will use the color wheel in the Recolor Artwork dialog to adjust the hue, saturation, and brightness of colors in your artwork.

To use the color wheel in the Recolor Artwork dialog:

1. Select the objects to be recolored. **A**

2. On the Control panel, click the **Recolor Artwork** button.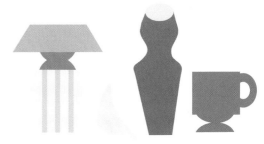

3. In the Recolor Artwork dialog, check **Recolor Art**, then click the **Edit** tab.

4. If you don't see a smooth color wheel, click the **Display Smooth Color Wheel** button.

5. Edits you make to the color wheel will affect the active color group. To choose that group, either click the **Get Colors from Selected Art** button at the top of the dialog or click a group in the list of **Color Groups**. If desired, you can also choose a new rule from the **Harmony Rules** menu.

   Each round marker on the color wheel represents a color in the current group, except for the largest marker, which represents the current base color. **B** The arrangement of the markers is based either on the colors in the selected artwork or on the current harmony rule.

6. When the dialog is first opened (or when the Get Colors from Selected Art button is clicked), the lines connecting the markers to the hub are dashed and the color markers can be moved independently of one another. If you click a color group or choose a harmony rule, the connecting lines become solid, the color relationships are preserved, and the color markers can be moved only as a unit. Depending on how you want to edit the artwork colors in the next step, either click the **Unlink Harmony Colors** button to unlink the markers, or click the **Link Harmony Colors** button to link them.

7. From the **Color Mode** menu, choose **HSB**.

8. To adjust the colors, do any of the following:

   Click the **Show Saturation and Hue on Wheel** button, then drag a color marker to change the hue and saturation **C** (or Shift-drag a marker around the wheel to change only the hue; or release, then drag a marker inward or outward

Continued on the following page

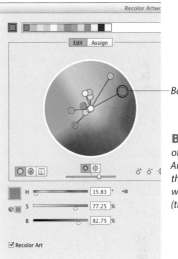

A *This is the original artwork.*

B *In this view of the Recolor Artwork dialog, the colors on the wheel are linked (the lines are solid).*

Base color

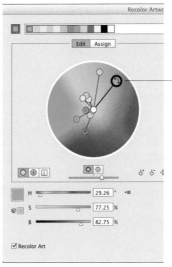

C *To shift all the hues, we're Shift-dragging the base color marker in a circular direction.*

to change only the saturation). To change the brightness of the wheel and artwork, move the **Brightness** slider (located below the buttons).

Click the **Show Brightness and Hue on Wheel** button,✸ then drag a color marker inward or outward to adjust the hue and brightness (or Shift-drag a marker around the wheel to change only the hue; or release, then drag a marker inward or outward to change only the brightness).**A** To change the saturation of the wheel and artwork, move the **Saturation** slider (located below the buttons).

To edit a color or all colors (depending on whether they are linked), click a color marker in the wheel, then adjust any or all of the **H**, **S**, or **B** sliders.**B–C**

To add a new color (and marker) to the group, click the **Add Color** tool,⚲⁺ then click a color area somewhere in the wheel.

To remove a color, right-click the marker to be removed and choose **Remove Color**.

To choose a replacement color, double-click a color marker. Click the Color Swatches button to access the colors that are currently on the Swatches panel, or click Color Models to display the process color controls. Choose a color, then click OK.**D** You could also right-click a marker and choose **Select Shade**, choose a shade, then click outside the shade box to close it.

9. Modify the group name, then click the **New Color Group** button.🗀 A new group appears on the list.

10. Do either of the following:

To save all new color groups to the Swatches panel and recolor the selected objects, click OK.

To save all new color groups to the Swatches panel without recoloring the selected objects, uncheck Recolor Art, then click OK.

A *This is after we changed the hues.*

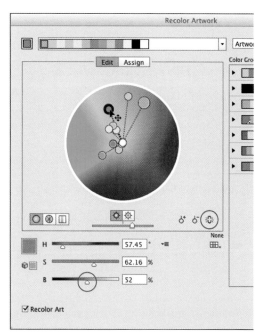

B *We clicked the Unlink Harmony Colors button, clicked the marker for the purple color, changed its hue to olive green, and lowered its Brightness value via the B slider.*

C *This is the result of the changes noted in figure* **B**.

D *And this is after we replaced a few more colors.*

Assigning colors to artwork via the Recolor Artwork dialog

By using the Assign tab of the Recolor Artwork dialog, you can control which colors in a group will replace specific colors in your artwork. The features in this tab can be confusing, so it may take you a few tries to get the hang of them. We will discuss some key features.

To assign colors to artwork via the Recolor Artwork dialog:

1. If you want to access specific color swatches in the Recolor Artwork dialog, they must be in groups in the Swatches panel. To create a color group, deselect, select the desired swatches, then click the New Color Group button. 🗀

2. Select the objects to be recolored.**A**

3. On the Control panel, click the **Recolor Artwork** button. 🌐 In the dialog, check **Recolor Art**.

4. Click the **Assign** tab.**B** Colors from the currently selected objects display in the Current Colors column, and colors from the active color group display in the New column.

5. To change the active color group, click a group on the **Color Groups** list on the right side of the dialog and/or choose a new rule from the **Harmony Rules** menu at the top of the dialog.**C**

6. If the new active color group contains fewer colors than the number of current colors, the current colors that are closest in hue, shade, or tint to one another will be grouped in a multicolor row and will be assigned the same New color (thereby reducing the total number of colors in the artwork). The solid colors and tints that are assigned to each row display in the New column.**D**

   Click a color in the **New** column. A white border displays around it, and the row becomes selected. To edit the color, move the sliders at the bottom of the dialog; or double-click the color, then choose a color in the Color Picker; or click the Color Swatches button in the picker to access the colors that are on the Swatches panel.

Continued on the following page

A *This is the original artwork.*

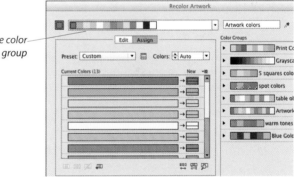

B *We selected all the objects in our artwork, then opened the Recolor Artwork dialog. In the Assign tab, colors from the selected artwork display in the Current Colors column and replacement colors display in the New column.*

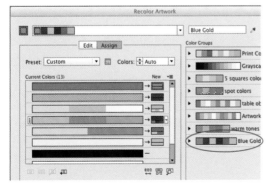

C *We clicked a color group called "Blue Gold." Because that group contains fewer colors than the original artwork, Illustrator combined similar colors into multicolor rows in the Current Colors column.*

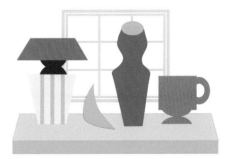

D *The new color group is assigned to the artwork.*

7. Do any of the following:

To reassign a color to a different New color, drag a block from the **Current Colors** column upward or downward to a different row.**A–B**

To reassign a whole multicolor row to a different New color, drag the selector bar (located at the left edge of the row) upward or downward to a different row.**C**

To reassign a New color to a different Current Colors row, drag it upward or downward in the **New** column.

➤ To prevent a row of Current Colors from being reassigned to a New color, click the arrow between the two columns **D–E** (it becomes a dash; to permit the colors to be assigned, click the dash. To prevent an individual color from being reassigned, click it, then right-click it and choose Exclude Colors from the menu; to reinclude it, drag it back over the blank white row.

8. Do either of the following:

If you clicked a color group in step 5 and you want to save your edits to that group, click the **Save Changes to Color Group** button.

To save the active color group to the list of Color Groups, enter a name in the field at the top of the dialog, then click the **New Color Group** button (the new color group will also appear on the Swatches panel when you exit the dialog).

9. Click OK.

➤ To delete a color group, click the group, then click the Delete Color Group button. To remove a color from a color group, right-click the color to be removed and choose Remove Color from the context menu (if you want to expand the color group first, click the arrowhead). Like other individual edits in the dialog, this cannot be undone.

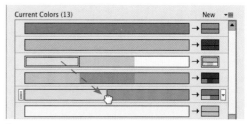

A *We are dragging a Current Color block to another row to assign it to a different New color.*

B *The tabletop and window frame are now blue-green.*

C *If you want to relocate a whole row, drag the selector bar upward or downward.*

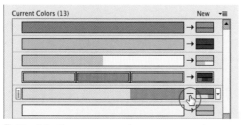

D *We clicked between two columns to remove the arrow, to prevent the colors in that row from being reassigned.*

E *Because we removed the arrow, the original colors for that row are now redisplaying in the artwork.*

Reducing colors via the Recolor Artwork dialog

Yet another use for the Recolor Artwork dialog is to reduce the number of colors in your artwork. You may need to do this if you're planning to print your document using one, two, or three spot colors instead of the standard four process colors.

To reduce colors in artwork via the Recolor Artwork dialog:

1. *Optional:* If you're going to reduce the colors in your artwork to a specific group of process or spot colors, make sure those colors are saved as a group in the Swatches panel. To create a color group, deselect, select the desired swatches, then click the New Color Group button.

2. Copy your document using File > Save As.

3. Select one or more objects.**A**

4. On the Control panel, click the **Recolor Artwork** button.

5. In the Recolor Artwork dialog, click the **Assign** tab. Also check **Recolor Art** to preview changes in your artwork (and to allow your changes to apply to the artwork when you exit the dialog).

6. Do one of the following:

    From the **Colors** menu, choose the desired number of colors.**B–C** That number of colors from the

Continued on the following page

EDITING DOCUMENT SWATCHES

Deselect your artwork, then double-click the icon for a color group on the Swatches panel to edit those colors in the Edit Colors dialog.

LIMITING COLORS TO A LIBRARY

To limit the colors on the color wheel and Harmony Rules menu in the Recolor Artwork dialog to colors in a specific library, from the Limit Color Group to Swatch Library menu, choose a library name (e.g., Color Books > PANTONE + Solid Coated). To remove the restriction at any time, choose None from the same menu.

USING KULER SWATCHES

To recolor your artwork using color themes from the Kuler panel, add them to your document's Swatches panel (see page 134). The color groups will appear on the list of Color Groups in the Recolor Artwork dialog.

A *The original artwork contains 13 colors.*

B *When you select a value from the Colors menu, the Current Colors are reduced to that number.*

C *The number of Current Colors in the artwork was reduced to four colors in the original color group.*

active color group will be applied to your artwork. *Optional:* Click a color group on the list of Color Groups.

If you have a custom color group ready (see step 1), click that group on the list of **Color Groups**.

From the **Preset** menu, choose **1**, **2**, or **3 Color Job.A** From the Library menu 田, in the dialog that opens, choose a matching system library or choose None, then click OK. If you chose a library, the active color group will now contain only colors from that library.**B–C**

▶ To reset reduced artwork colors to all the colors in the active color group at any time, choose Auto from the Colors menu or choose Color Harmony from the Preset menu. Or to restore the original colors to your artwork, click the Get Colors from Selected Art button. ✐

7. Follow steps 6–7 on pages 403–404 to reassign and edit the New colors.

8. *Optional:* Click the New Color Group button 🗀 to add the reduced active color group to the Swatches panel.

9. Click OK.

▶ To control whether black is recolored in your artwork or preserved, click the Color Reduction Options button 🗐 next to the Preset menu in the Recolor Artwork dialog. In the Color Reduction Options dialog,**D** check or uncheck Preserve: Black. This dialog contains the same Preset and Colors menus as the Recolor Artwork dialog, plus some Colorize Methods. To learn more about these options, see Illustrator Help.

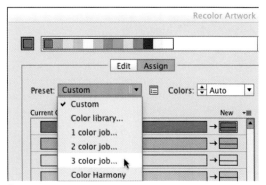

A *You can also reduce the number of Current Colors by choosing a Color Job option from the Preset menu.*

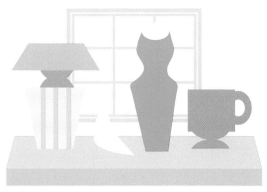

B *We chose the 3 Color Job preset to reduce the number of colors in the artwork to three.*

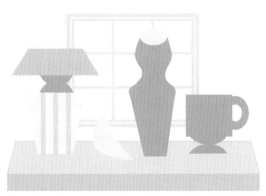

C *Here, we chose the 1 Color Job preset, with a more minimal result. We also changed the sole color in the New column to blue.*

D *In the Color Reduction Options dialog, you can specify whether instances of black in your artwork will be recolored or preserved.*

The preferences are default settings for Illustrator features that apply to the current and future documents. Use this chapter as a reference guide to the options in the 13 panels of the Preferences dialog.

Opening the Preferences dialog

To open the Preferences dialog:

1. Do one of the following:

   Press Cmd-K/Ctrl-K.

   Deselect, then click **Preferences** on the Control panel.

   Choose a panel name from the **Preferences** submenu on the Illustrator/Edit menu.

2. To switch to a different panel, click the name of an option set on the left side of the dialog.

RESETTING THE ILLUSTRATOR PREFERENCES

To restore all the default settings to the Illustrator preferences, quit/exit Illustrator, then relaunch the program while holding down Cmd-Option-Shift/ Ctrl-Alt-Shift.

PREFERENCES

30

IN THIS CHAPTER

General Preferences

Keyboard Increment

This value is the distance by which a selected object moves when an arrow key is pressed on the keyboard. To move a selected object by 10 times this increment, press Shift-arrow.

Constrain Angle

This sets the angle (–360° to 360°) for the x and y axes. The default setting is 0°, which is parallel to the edges of the document window. Edits such as transformations, dialog and panel measurements, Smart Guides, the grid, and the construction of new objects are calculated relative to this angle. See the sidebar on the next page.

Corner Radius

This value controls the degree of curvature in the corners of objects that are drawn with the Rounded Rectangle tool. The default value is 12 pt. A value of 0 (zero) produces a right angle. This value can also be set in the Rounded Rectangle dialog.

Disable Auto Add/Delete

Checking this option disables the ability of the Pen tool to switch to a temporary Add Anchor Point tool when moved over a path segment on a selected path, or to a temporary Delete Anchor Point tool when moved over an anchor point on a selected path. You can hold down Shift to enable or disable this option.

Use Precise Cursors

When this option is checked, the drawing and editing tool pointers display as crosshairs instead of as the tool icon. To turn this option on temporarily when the preference is off, press Caps Lock.

Show Tool Tips

If this option is checked and you rest the pointer on an application feature, such as a tool, swatch, or panel button or icon, a brief description of that feature pops up onscreen. For some features, such as tools, the shortcut is also listed.

Anti-Aliased Artwork

When this option is checked, the edges of existing and future vector objects (not placed images) look smoother onscreen. It doesn't affect print output.

Select Same Tint %

When this option is checked, the Select > Same > Fill Color and Stroke Color commands select only objects that contain the same spot color and exact tint percentage as the currently selected object. When this option is off, the tint percentage is ignored as a criterion.

Use Preview Bounds

If this option is checked, an object's stroke weight and any applied effects are included as part of the object's height and width dimensions. This affects the Align commands, calculations on the Transform panel, and the dimensions of the bounding box. (If you were to select an object, apply a command on the Effect > Distort & Transform submenu, and then turn this feature on and then off, you would see a change in the size of the bounding box.)

Append [Converted] upon Opening Legacy Files

If this option is checked and you open a file that was created in Illustrator version 10 or earlier into a CS or CC version of the application, Illustrator will append the word "[Converted]" to the file name.

Double Click to Isolate

If this option is checked and you double-click an object or group, that entity is put into isolation mode and other objects become uneditable temporarily. To exit isolation mode, click the gray bar at the top of the document window or press Esc. This is a great feature, so we recommend keeping this option checked. To put an object (or group) into isolation mode when this option is off, select the object, then click the Isolate Selected Object button ⛶ on the Control panel.

Use Japanese Crop Marks

Check this box to have Illustrator use Japanese-style crop marks when outputting color separations.

Transform Pattern Tiles

If this option is checked and you use a transformation tool (such as the Scale tool) on an object that contains a pattern, the pattern will also transform. This option can also be turned on or off in the Move dialog, on the Transform panel menu, in the Transform Each and Transform Effect dialogs, and in the dialog for each individual transformation tool. You can also temporarily enable transforming of patterns by holding down the tilde (~) key when using these tools.

Scale Rectangle Corners ★

On Live Rectangle shapes, enable this option so that the corners will be scaled proportionately with the size of the shape. With this option disabled, the corners will maintain their original radius as the shape is scaled.

Scale Strokes & Effects

Check this box to allow an object's stroke weight and effects to be scaled when you scale an object (e.g., via its bounding box, the Scale tool, or the Transform panel). This option can also be turned on or off in the Scale, Transform Each, and Transform Effect dialogs, and on the Transform panel menu.

Reset All Warning Dialogs

Click this button to allow warnings in which you checked "Don't Show Again" to redisplay when edits cause them to appear.

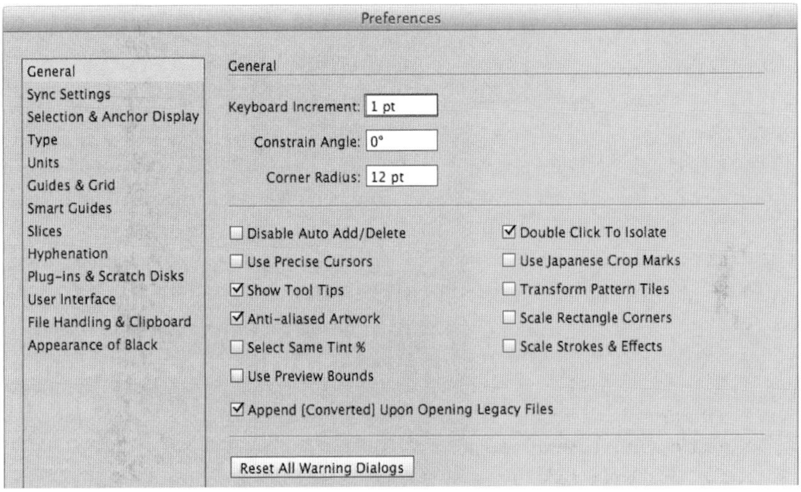

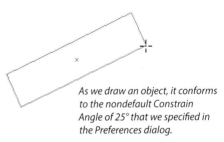

WHAT THE CONSTRAIN ANGLE AFFECTS

➤ Type tools, when you're creating a type object

➤ The Rectangle, Rounded Rectangle, Ellipse, and graph tools (see the figure at right)

➤ Some transformation tool dialogs (Scale, Reflect, and Shear)

➤ The Gradient tool and the Pen tool (if used with the Shift key held down)

➤ Objects that are moved or drag-copied with the Shift key held down or by pressing an arrow key

➤ The grid

➤ Smart Guides (Transform Tools and Construction Guides features)

➤ Readouts on the Info panel

As we draw an object, it conforms to the nondefault Constrain Angle of 25° that we specified in the Preferences dialog.

To establish a constrain angle based on an object that you have just rotated with the Rotate tool or the Free Transform tool, keep the object selected, note the Angle readout on the Info panel, and enter that number as the new Constrain Angle value.

Sync Settings Preferences

On pages 455–457, we show you how to upload your Illustrator CC preferences and presets to the Creative Cloud server, and then sync those settings from the server to one or two computers on which you're allowed to activate your licensed copy of Illustrator CC. In this Sync Settings Preferences panel, you will choose essential settings for that process.

Note: Next to Signed In As, the panel lists the Creative Cloud membership ID of the Illustrator user who is currently signed in. The panel may also list the date and time of the Last Sync.

Sync Settings Options

Sync

From the Sync menu, choose All Settings, Selected Settings, or None. If you choose Selected Settings, also check the categories of Illustrator settings that you want to sync.

When Conflict Occurs

From the When Conflict Occurs menu, choose an option for resolving sync conflicts: Sync Local Settings to preserve settings on the current computer and have Illustrator upload them to the Cloud automatically; or Sync Cloud Settings to have Illustrator overwrite the settings on the current computer automatically with the settings that are stored in the Cloud; or Keep Latest File to preserve the most recent settings (the settings that have the latest date and time) from either the Cloud or the current computer; or Ask My

Preference to be given a choice via an alert dialog to preserve remote or local settings each time you sync settings.

Sync Settings Now

Note: Although this panel also provides a button for actually syncing the Illustrator settings, Adobe recommends using the Sync Settings button ⚙ at the bottom of the document window instead. If you decide to use the button in this dialog, do as follows:

After choosing the desired Sync Settings Options, you can click Sync Settings Now to implement your choices. Settings will either be uploaded from your computer to the Cloud, or downloaded from the Cloud to your computer. Note that if the current date and time display next to Last Sync, the settings were synced and no action is required on your part.

If "Ready to Apply" displays next to Last Sync, settings from the Cloud were downloaded to your computer but haven't yet been applied (note that the Sync Settings Now button isn't available). To apply the settings from the Cloud to your computer, after exiting this dialog, click the Sync Settings button ⚙ at the bottom of the document window, then respond to any dialog prompts that appear (see step 3 on pages 455–456).

Manage Account

Click this button to open your personal storage page on the Creative Cloud website.

Selection & Anchor Display Preferences

Selection

Tolerance
Specify the range within which an anchor point becomes selected when you click near it with the Direct Selection tool. The default setting is 3 px.

Object Selection by Path Only
With this option checked, in order to select an object with the Selection or Direct Selection tool, you must click a path segment or anchor point. With this option unchecked, you can select a filled object in Preview view by clicking the fill area with a selection tool. We keep this option off.

Snap to Point
With this option checked, as you drag, draw, or scale an object, the pointer will snap to a nearby anchor point or guide within the range of pixels that you specify in the field (the default setting is 2 px). This option can also be turned on or off via the View menu.

Command/Ctrl Click to Select Objects Behind
With this option checked, you can Cmd-click/Ctrl-click to select objects in succession below the currently selected object, under the ⬚ pointer.

Constrain Path Dragging on Segment Reshape ★
With this option enabled, the handles of a segment will be constrained in a perpendicular direction when using the Anchor Point tool.

Anchor Point and Handle Display

Anchors
Choose a style for the way Illustrator displays anchor points: small selected and unselected points, large selected points and small unselected points, or large selected and unselected points.

Handles
Choose a display style for the direction points on direction handles: small solid, larger solid, or hollow.

Highlight Anchors on Mouse Over
If this option is checked and you move the Direct Selection tool over an anchor point, the point will become highlighted (enlarged) temporarily. We recommend checking this option, because it makes it easier to locate anchor points on a path.

Show Handles When Multiple Anchors Are Selected
Check this option to allow an unlimited number of direction handles to display on curve anchor points when selected with the Direct Selection tool, or uncheck it to allow a maximum of four direction handles to display at a time.

➤ When using the Direct Selection tool to select an object, you can allow more than two direction handles to display at a time by clicking the Handles: Show Handles for Multiple Selected Anchor Points button on the Control panel, ⬚ or allow a maximum of only four handles to display at a time by clicking the Hide Handles for Multiple Selected Anchor Points button. ⬚

Hide Corner Widgets for Angles Greater Than ★
Enable this option to hide the corner widgets on shapes with Live Corners when the angle of the corner exceeds the value defined in this preference.

Enable Rubber Band for Pen Tool ★
When this option is enabled (it is by default), you will see a preview for each segment that you draw with the Pen tool. Disabling this option hides the preview, which was the default behavior in previous versions of Illustrator.

Type Preferences

Size/Leading, Tracking and Baseline Shift

Selected text is modified by this increment each time a keyboard shortcut is executed for the Size/Leading, Tracking, or Baseline Shift feature.

Language Options

Check Show East Asian Options to have options for Chinese, Japanese, and Korean language characters display on the Character, Paragraph, and OpenType panels, and on the Type menu, or check Show Indic Options to display options in those locations for Indic languages (including Bengali, Gujarati, Hindi, Kannada, Malayalam, Marathi, Oriya, Punjabi, Tamil, and Telugu).

Type Object Selection by Path Only

When this option is checked, in order to select a type object with a selection tool, you have to click precisely on the type baseline. With this option unchecked, you can select a type object by clicking anywhere on or near it. Unless your artwork is very complex, we recommend keeping this option off.

Show Font Names in English

When this option is checked, Chinese, Japanese, and Korean font names display in English on the Font menus. When this option is off, two-byte font names display in their native characters.

Number of Recent Fonts

Choose the maximum number of recently chosen fonts (1–15) that you will permit Illustrator to list on the Type > Recent Fonts submenu (and context menu). The default number is 5.

Font Preview

Check this option to have font family names display in a simulation of their actual fonts, along with the icon for the font type (e.g., TrueType, OpenType) for easy identification on the Type > Font menu (and, in the Mac OS, also in the Find Font dialog and on the Character panel). Choose a Size for the font display of Small, Medium, or Large.

Enable Missing Glyph Protection

With this option checked, if you style type in a Roman font, enter some non-Roman (e.g., Japanese or Cyrillic) glyphs, then restyle all the type in a Roman font, Illustrator will preserve the non-Roman glyphs; with this preference off, non-Roman glyphs will be replaced by blank spaces.

Highlight Substituted Fonts ★

With this option checked, missing fonts that have been substituted with a replacement font are highlighted in a pink color for easy identification.

Units Preferences

To open this panel of the Preferences dialog quickly in the Mac OS, press Cmd-, (comma).

General

This unit of measure is used in entry fields in many panels and dialog boxes in Illustrator, and for the rulers in the document window. (See also the steps on this page for changing the measurement units.)

Stroke

This unit of measure is used on the Stroke panel and in the Stroke Weight field on the Control and Appearances panels.

Type

This unit of measure is used on the Character and Paragraph panels.

East Asian Type

This menu is available only if Show East Asian Options is checked in the Type panel of this Preferences dialog, and the chosen unit of measure applies just to East Asian type.

➤ When entering values in a dialog or panel, you can use any unit listed in the sidebar below, regardless of the current default units. A value entered in a nondefault unit will be converted to the default unit when you press Tab or Return/Enter.

Numbers Without Units Are Points

If Picas is the current Units: General setting and this option is checked, a value typed in a non type- or stroke-related field without specifying a unit will be entered as points. For instance, if you type "99" in a field, it will be entered as points (but will be converted to the current units, so it will be listed as "8p3"); with this preference off, "99" will be entered as picas and will be listed as "99 p".

➤ To enter a combination of picas and points in a field, separate the two numbers with a "p". For example, 4p2 equals 4 picas plus 2 points, or 50 pt. (For your information, 12 points = 1 pica; 6 picas = 1 inch.)

Identify Objects By

Using the Variables panel, you can make objects dynamic by associating them with XML-based variables. Here you can specify whether dynamic objects are identified by their Object Name or an XML ID number. Consult with your Web developer regarding this option.

The measurement unit that you specify for a document in the Document Setup dialog (as described below) overrides the General unit that is specified for Illustrator in the Units panel of the Preferences dialog.

To change the measurement unit for the current document:

Do either of the following:

If the rulers aren't showing, press Cmd-R/Ctrl-R. Right-click either ruler and choose a unit from the context menu.

Cmd-click/Ctrl-click an artboard to deselect, then click **Document Setup** on the Control panel. Choose a unit from the **Units** menu, then click OK.

ABBREVIATIONS TO ENTER FOR UNITS

Unit	Symbol
Points	pt
Picas	p
Inches	" or in
Millimeters	mm
Centimeters	cm
Q (a type unit)	q
Pixels	px

Preferences

General
Sync Settings
Selection & Anchor Display
Type
Units
Guides & Grid
Smart Guides
Slices
Hyphenation
Plug-ins & Scratch Disks
User Interface
File Handling & Clipboard
Appearance of Black

Units

General: Points
Stroke: Points
Type: Points
East Asian Type: Points

☐ Numbers Without Units Are Points

Identify Objects By: ⊙ Object Name ○ XML ID

Guides & Grid Preferences

Guides

Color

For ruler guides, choose a color from the Color menu; or choose Custom or click the color square to open the Colors/Color dialog, then choose a custom color. See page 109.

Style

For ruler guides, choose a Style of Lines or Dots.

Grid

Color

For the grid (View > Show Grid), choose a color from the Color menu; or choose Custom or click the color square to open the Colors/Color dialog, then choose a custom color. See page 112.

Style

Choose a Style of Lines or Dots for the grid. Subdivision lines don't display for the Dots Style (also, dotted gridlines display only on the artboards).

Gridline Every

Enter the distance between gridlines.

Subdivisions

Enter the number of subdivisions to be drawn between the main (darker) gridlines when the Lines Style is chosen for the grid. **A–B**

Grids in Back

Check Grids in Back (the default and recommended setting) to have the grid display behind all objects, or uncheck this option to have the grid display in front of all objects.

Show Pixel Grid (Above 600% Zoom)

To see a representation of the pixel grid onscreen to make it easier to position objects for Web output, check this option, turn on View > Pixel Preview, and choose a zoom level of 600% or higher for your document.

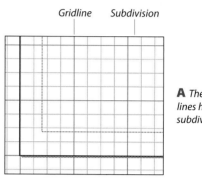

Gridline   Subdivision

A *These gridlines have four subdivisions.*

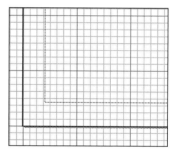

B *These gridlines have eight subdivisions.*

Preferences

General	Guides & Grid
Sync Settings	
Selection & Anchor Display	**Guides**
Type	Color: ☐ Cyan
Units	Style: Lines
Guides & Grid	
Smart Guides	
Slices	**Grid**
Hyphenation	Color: Custom...
Plug-ins & Scratch Disks	Style: Lines
User Interface	Gridline every: 72 pt
File Handling & Clipboard	Subdivisions: 8
Appearance of Black	☑ Grids In Back
	☑ Show Pixel Grid (Above 600% Zoom)

Smart Guides Preferences

To use Smart Guides, choose View > Smart Guides or press Cmd-U/Ctrl-U, and turn off View > Snap to Grid and View > Pixel Preview.

Display Options

Color

Choose a color for Smart Guides from the menu; or choose Custom from the menu or click the swatch to open the Colors/Color dialog, then choose a custom color. (This color can differ from the color that is specified for ruler guides in the Guides & Grid panel.)

Alignment Guides

If this option is on and you create, drag, or transform an object, straight lines will appear when the object's center point or edge meets the center, edge, or bounding box of another object, or the edge of the artboard or bleed region. Alignment guides also appear when you use the Artboard tool to create or move an artboard.

Anchor/Path Labels

Check this option to allow a "path," "anchor," or "center" label to display as you pass the pointer over that part of an object. If the Alignment Guides option is also checked, an "intersect" label will display where two alignment guides intersect.

Object Highlighting

Check this option to have an object's path become highlighted as you pass the pointer over it. **A** This is helpful for locating paths that have a fill and stroke of None (e.g., clipping mask objects) or paths that are stacked behind other paths. The highlight color matches the selection color of the object's layer.

Measurement Labels

If this option is checked and you move the pointer (with the mouse button up) over an anchor point or the center point of a stationary object, the x/y location of that point displays in a label. When an object is moved, the label displays the x/y distance between the object and its original location. When a geometric drawing tool (e.g., the Rectangle tool) is used, or a type tool is dragged to create a rectangle, a label displays the current width and height dimensions of the object. When a transform tool is used, a label displays the transformation values (e.g., the angle of a rotation or shear). When the Pen tool is used, a label displays the distance between the pointer and the last anchor point. And if you press Shift before clicking or dragging with a drawing tool, the starting location is listed.

Continued on the following page

A *An object highlight guide and a text label hint*

Transform Tools

Check this option to have angle lines display as you transform an object with the Scale, Rotate, Reflect, or Shear tool.**A** Choose or create an angles set for the lines in the Angles area (see below).

Construction Guides

With this option checked, if you pass the mouse across an anchor point on a stationary object while drawing a new object or while transforming an existing one, a diagonal angle line emerges from that anchor point.**B** To choose or create an angles set for construction guides, see the next paragraph.

Angles

Choose a preset set of angles from the Angles menu or enter custom angles in one or more of the six fields (press Tab to update the schematic preview).

Snapping Tolerance

The Snapping Tolerance is the distance (0–10 pt) within which the side, corner, or center point of an object you are moving must be from the side or center point of another object for one to snap to the other. The default value is 4 pt.

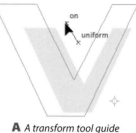 

A *A transform tool guide*   **B** *A construction guide*

Slices Preferences

These preferences apply to creating slices for Web output, a topic that is not covered in this book.

Show Slice Numbers

Check this option to have slice numbers display onscreen.

Line Color

Via the Line Color menu or swatch, choose a color for slice numbers and for the lines that surround each slice.

Preferences	
General	Slices
Sync Settings	☑ Show Slice Numbers
Selection & Anchor Display	
Type	Line Color: ▨ Light Red ▾ ▨
Units	
Guides & Grid	
Smart Guides	
Slices	
Hyphenation	

Hyphenation Preferences

Hyphenation

Default Language

Choose the language dictionary for Illustrator to refer to when it hyphenates words. There are also Indic languages on this menu. Note: From the Language menu on the Character panel, you can choose a different language dictionary for hyphenation that applies to just the current document.

Exceptions

In the New Entry field, enter any word that you don't want Illustrator to hyphenate, then click Add. To remove a word from the list, click it, then click Delete.

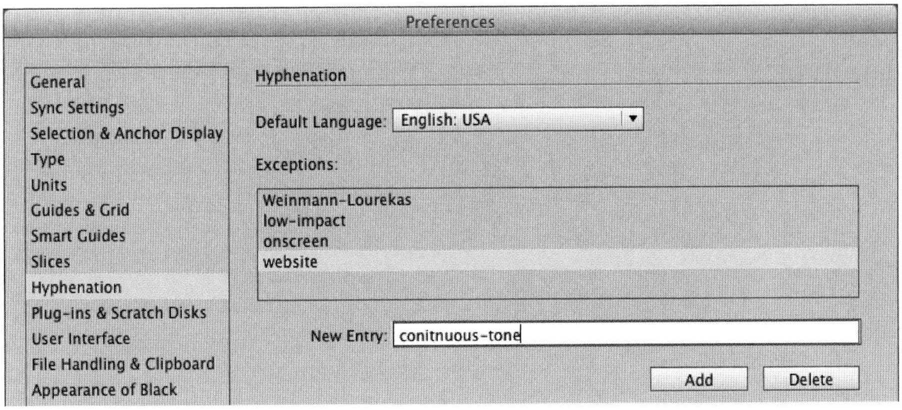

Hyphenation

Default Language: English: USA ▼

Exceptions:

Weinmann-Lourekas
low-impact
onscreen
website

New Entry: conitnuous-tone

[Add] [Delete]

Plug-ins & Scratch Disks Preferences

Note: For changes in this dialog to take effect, you must relaunch Illustrator.

Additional Plug-ins Folder

The core and add-on plug-ins that are supplied with Illustrator provide additional functionality to the main application, and are installed automatically in the Plug-ins folder inside the Adobe Illustrator CC 2014 folder.

If you have additional plug-ins that you want to use with Illustrator but want to store in a separate folder, you must use this Preferences dialog to tell Illustrator where that folder is located. Check Additional Plug-ins Folder, then click Choose. In the New Additional Plug-ins Folder dialog, locate and click the name of the desired plug-ins folder, then click Choose. The new location will be listed in this panel.

Scratch Disks

Primary

Illustrator uses the Primary scratch disk as virtual memory when the amount of currently available RAM is insufficient for processing. From the Primary menu, choose an available hard disk, preferably your largest and fastest one. The default Primary scratch disk is Startup.

Secondary

As an optional step, choose an alternate Secondary hard disk to be used for extra virtual memory when needed. If you have only one hard disk, of course, you can have only one scratch disk.

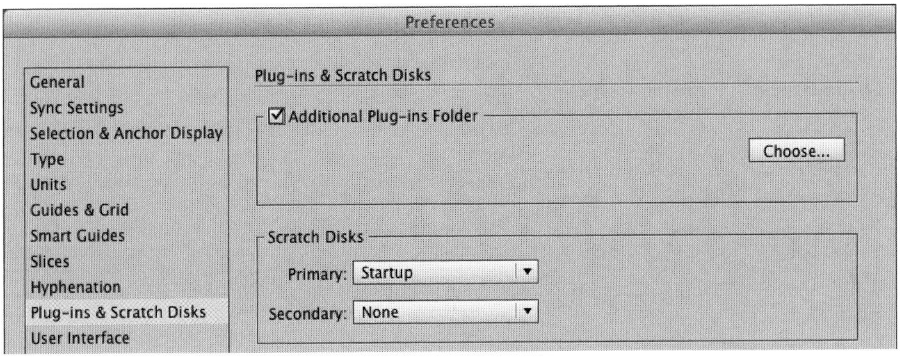

Preferences

Plug-ins & Scratch Disks

☑ Additional Plug-ins Folder

[Choose...]

Scratch Disks

Primary: Startup ▼

Secondary: None ▼

User Interface Preferences

User Interface

Brightness

For the background of the Illustrator panels, Application bar, Control panel, document tabs, dialogs, and Application frame, either choose a preset gray value between Dark and Light from the Brightness menu or move the slider.

Canvas Color

Click Match User Interface Brightness to have Illustrator match the canvas (the area around the artboards) to the current Brightness setting, or click White to make that area solid white, regardless of the Brightness setting.

Auto-Collapse Icon Panels

If this option is checked and you expand a panel that was collapsed to an icon, then click away from the panel, the panel will collapse back to an icon automatically. If this option is unchecked, panels that you expand will remain expanded.

Open Documents as Tabs

If this option is checked (the setting we recommend), multiple documents will dock as tabs into the Application frame or into one floating window when opened. If this option is unchecked, documents will open into separate floating windows.

File Handling & Clipboard Preferences

Files

Use Low Resolution Proxy for Linked EPS
If you work with linked EPS files, you can check this option to have Illustrator display placed EPS images as low-resolution bitmap proxies (screen previews), for enhanced performance. With this preference off, linked EPS images will display at their full resolution. (We keep this option off.)

Display Bitmaps as Anti-Aliased Images in Pixel Preview
If you check this option and turn on View > Pixel Preview, the edges of shapes in raster images that you place into Illustrator look softer.

Update Links
Options on the Update Links menu control whether links to image files that you have imported into an Illustrator document are updated automatically if you modify them in their original application (and then click back in or reopen your Illustrator document):

Choose Automatically to have Illustrator update the linked images automatically, with no dialog opening.

Choose Manually to leave the links unchanged. You can update individual links at any time via the Links panel.

Choose Ask When Modified to have an alert dialog appear, giving you the option to update the links.

Clipboard

On Copy ★
The Include SVG Code option determines whether the SVG code for a copied object will be copied to the Clipboard. If this option is enabled, you can paste the SVG code of the object into a text editor or other application for use on the Web.

On Quit ★
The On Quit options affect whether Illustrator copies artwork in the PDF and/or AICB format to the Clipboard, for pasting into documents in other Adobe Creative Cloud applications. Both formats paste copied content as vector objects, but the AICB option does a better job of preserving the original anchor points. To preserve the appearance of transparency, objects are flattened into nonoverlapping opaque objects; transparency settings in the object don't remain editable in the target document.

Note: If you paste objects containing transparency into InDesign, content in the InDesign document won't show through the Illustrator objects. If you want transparency in your Illustrator artwork to interact with underlying InDesign content, import it using the Place command instead of the Clipboard. Another option is to paste nontransparent objects into InDesign, then use the Effects panel in InDesign to apply the desired transparency settings.

PDF
When artwork is copied and pasted in the PDF format, effects paste as graphics, not as editable paths.

➤ To copy and paste Illustrator objects into Photoshop, check PDF and AICB. To copy and paste Illustrator objects containing effects into InDesign, uncheck PDF and check AICB; the effects will become separate, editable paths.

AICB
For the AICB (PostScript) format, click Preserve Paths to copy objects as a collection of paths, or click Preserve Appearance and Overprints instead to preserve appearances (e.g., effects) and overprints as separate objects.

Preferences

File Handling & Clipboard

General
Sync Settings
Selection & Anchor Display
Type
Units
Guides & Grid
Smart Guides
Slices
Hyphenation
Plug-ins & Scratch Disks
User Interface
File Handling & Clipboard
Appearance of Black

Files
☐ Use Low Resolution Proxy for Linked EPS
☐ Display Bitmaps as Anti-Aliased Images in Pixel Preview
Update Links: Ask When Modified ▾

Clipboard
On Copy: ☑ Include SVG Code
On Quit: ☑ PDF
☐ AICB (no transparency support)
○ Preserve Paths
◉ Preserve Appearance and Overprints

Appearance of Black Preferences

For added depth, black areas in a document can be printed using a combination of CMYK inks rather than just black (K) ink. The first menu in this preferences panel merely controls how black areas in a document are displayed onscreen; the second menu controls how those areas actually print on an RGB or grayscale device.

Options for Black on RGB and Grayscale Devices

On Screen

Choose Display All Blacks Accurately to display blacks onscreen based on their actual values (pure 100% K black will display as dark gray), or choose Display All Blacks as Rich Black to display all blacks as rich blacks regardless of their actual CMYK values.

Printing/Exporting

Choose Output All Blacks Accurately to print blacks on RGB and grayscale devices using their actual K or CMYK values, or choose Output All Blacks as Rich Black to print all black areas as a mixture of CMYK values on those devices. This setting affects the output of composite prints (not of color separations), but doesn't alter values in the document. The Output All Blacks as Rich Black setting produces the darkest possible black on an RGB printer.

Description

To learn about any option in this panel, rest the pointer on it with the mouse button up, and read the pertinent information in the Description area.

Preferences

| General |
| Sync Settings |
| Selection & Anchor Display |
| Type |
| Units |
| Guides & Grid |
| Smart Guides |
| Slices |
| Hyphenation |
| Plug-ins & Scratch Disks |
| User Interface |
| File Handling & Clipboard |
| Appearance of Black |

Appearance of Black

Options for Black on RGB and Grayscale Devices

On Screen: Display All Blacks as Rich Black ▼

Printing / Exporting: Output All Blacks as Rich Black ▼

Example of 100K Black

Example of Rich Black

■Aa   ■Aa

Description

Displaying all blacks as rich black will show both pure blacks (100K) and rich blacks (blacks with mixed CMYK values) as rich black. This will not change color values in the document, but all blacks will appear as dark as possible.

Cancel   OK

In this chapter, you will learn how to print your documents directly from Illustrator, how to prepare them for export to other applications (such as Adobe InDesign and Photoshop), and how to optimize them for Web output. The tasks you will learn in the first part of this chapter include how to print using basic settings, print multiple artboards, specify a bleed region for objects that extend beyond an artboard, prepare a file for color separation, choose flatness settings, choose settings for downloading fonts, use color management in printing, choose overprint options, create and edit print presets, create crop marks, choose a resolution for outputting effects, and use the Document Info panel to get information about a file.

Using the Separations Preview panel, you will preview how the C, M, Y, and K color components in a CMYK document will separate to individual plates during the commercial printing process, check if a particular color is properly set to knock out or overprint other colors, and find out whether a specific black is a rich black (made from a mix of C, M, Y, and K) or a simple black, containing only the K component.

Although Illustrator objects are described and stored as mathematical commands, when printed, they're rendered as dots. The higher the resolution of the output device, the more smoothly and sharply the lines, curves, gradients, and continuous-tone images in your artwork are rendered. The Print dialog contains all the controls needed for outputting a color proof on a desktop printer, and for preparing and printing color separations. To begin, you can output a document using just the basic settings in the dialog, as we show you on the following page. After that, you can delve into the many specialized and advanced controls that are offered.

Later in this chapter, you will learn how to package your Illustrator files for output, save them in the Adobe PDF format, use the Export command, optimize your files for Web output, export text and objects as CSS code, and export Illustrator files into Photoshop.

Note: To quickly open the panels that you will use in this chapter, choose the Printing and Proofing workspace.

PRINT & EXPORT

31

IN THIS CHAPTER

Print dialog: General options

There are seven option sets in the Print dialog. We'll show you how to print a document on a desktop color or grayscale printer using basic settings first.

To print a document on a black-and-white or color printer:

1. For output to a desktop inkjet printer, choose File > Document Color Mode > RGB Color; for output to a desktop color laser printer, check your printer documentation to verify the correct document color mode; for output to a grayscale printer, choose either CMYK Color or RGB Color mode.

2. Choose File > **Print** (Cmd-P/Ctrl-P). The Print dialog opens (**A**, next page). The settings you choose in this dialog will apply to all the artboards in the document.

3. From the **Printer** menu, choose from the list of printers that are available in your system.

   If you choose a PostScript printer, the PPD menu will display the default PPD (PostScript printer description) file for that printer. If your commercial printer supplied (and you installed) a custom PPD file for the chosen printer, choose that file name from the menu instead.

4. On the list of option sets on the left side of the dialog, click **General**.

5. In the **Copies** field, enter the desired number of print copies (you can click in the field, then press the up arrow).

   Click **All** to print all the artboards in the document, or click **Range** and enter the desired artboard number(s). Enter a range using a hyphen, or separate nonconsecutive numbers with a comma. Each artboard will print on a separate sheet of paper.

   ➤ Use the navigation arrows below the preview to display a different artboard.

6. From the **Media Size** menu, choose **Defined by Driver** or a specific paper size.

   Check **Auto Rotate** to let Illustrator orient any landscape artboards automatically to the longest dimension (usually the vertical dimension) of the current paper size, or uncheck it and click an orientation button to print the artboards vertically or horizontally on their respective pages.

7. From the **Print Layers** menu in the Options area, choose which layers are to be printed:

Visible & Printable Layers to print only the visible layers for which the Print option is checked in the Layer Options dialog (which opens from the Layers panel menu). Note: To prevent an object from printing, you have to uncheck the Print option for its top-level layer via the Layer Options dialog before opening the Print dialog (the layer name will become italicized on the Layers panel).

Visible Layers to print only those layers that display a visibility icon on the Layers panel, regardless of their current Print option setting.

All Layers to print all layers, regardless of the current Layers panel visibility and Print settings

8. If you need to change the position of the artboards relative to the paper, do any of the following:

   Click a different point on the Placement icon.

   Enter X and Y values to specify the position of the upper left corner of all the artboards.

   Drag an artboard in the preview area. Note that this will reposition the page borders for all the artboards. Only objects that display within the page area of an artboard will print.

9. From the **Scaling** menu, choose **Do Not Scale** to print each artboard at its current size, even if it exceeds or is smaller than the paper size; or **Fit to Page** to have Illustrator scale each artboard separately to fit the current paper size; or **Custom**, then enter a Scale W (width) or H (height) value to scale all the artboards proportionally. (For nonproportional scaling, deactivate the Constrain Proportions button, ⬚ then enter separate width and height values.) The default Scale value is 100.

   For oversized artboards, read about the tile options on the next page.

10. Click **Print** to print the specified artboards using the current settings (or if you want to save the current settings with your document without printing it, click Done, then save the file).

➤ Adobe recommends choosing all print settings from the Print dialog and bypassing the system options that display when you click the Page Setup or Setup button (in the Print dialog) in the Mac OS, or the Setup button in Windows.

➤ To save a file that contains multiple artboards as a multipage PDF file, see pages 442-445.

A *Via the General option set in the Print dialog, choose basic print settings.*

Access to the option sets

Print preview

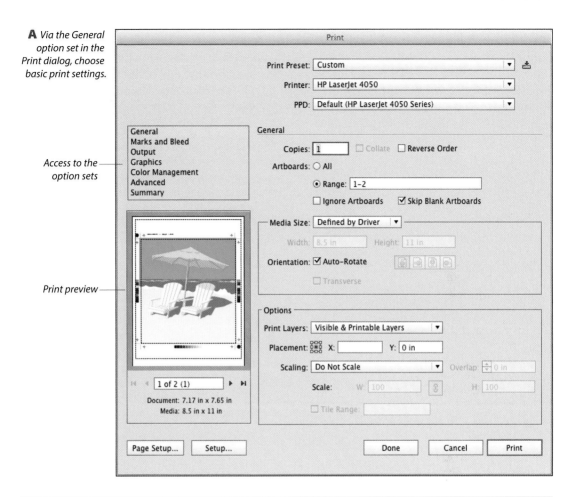

PRINTING OVERSIZED ARTWORK AS TILED PAGES

To print (tile) oversized artwork on multiple sheets of paper based on the printer media size, in the General option set check Ignore Artboards; then under Options, from the Scaling menu, choose Tile Full Pages to divide the artwork into whole pages (with the ability to set an Overlap value for the extent to which pages are overlapped to account for the page margins), or choose Tile Imageable Areas to divide the artwork onto a grid of pages (with no overlap option). See the figures at right. Additional options are as follows:

➤ Drag in the preview to reposition the artwork relative to the tile breaks. To recenter the artwork at any time, click the center point on the Placement icon.

➤ Enter custom Scale: W and H values to scale the artwork to fit the tiles.

➤ To print select tiled pages, check Tile Range, then enter the desired range of pages in the field.

Tile Full Pages

Tile Imageable Areas

Next, we'll explore settings in the six other option sets of the Print dialog.

Marks and Bleed options

Use the Marks and Bleed set in the Print dialog to create marks at the edges of each artboard or the overall printable area (for use by a commercial printer), or to set parameters for outputting objects that extend beyond that area into the bleed region.

To include printer's marks in your printout:

1. To ensure that the printer's marks you opt for will fit within the respective page sizes for the artboards, in the General option set, do either of the following:

   Make sure the chosen output **Media Size** is large enough to accommodate printer's marks for the largest artboard in the document.

   Choose Scaling: **Fit to Page** to allow the artwork and artboards to be scaled down, if necessary.

2. Click **Marks and Bleed** on the left side of the Print dialog (**A**, next page).

3. Under Marks, check **All Printer's Marks**, then keep checked or uncheck any of these options:

   Trim Marks adds thin lines that designate where the printed paper is to be trimmed. The trim marks align with the horizontal and vertical edges of each artboard or, if Ignore Artboards is checked (General option set), with the edges of the tiled artwork.

   Registration Marks adds a target with crosshairs that a commercial printer uses to align the printing plates. They are placed outside the corner of each artboard or, if Ignore Artboards is checked, outside the corner of the bounding box of the tiled artwork.

   Color Bars adds color swatches that a commercial printer uses to judge the density of inks. They are placed outside each artboard or, for tiled artwork, outside the sides of the bounding box.

   Page Information adds a text label containing the file name and specs for the print shop at the top of the printout.

4. From the **Printer Mark Type** menu, choose a style for printer's marks of Roman or Japanese.

5. *Optional:* Via the Trim Mark Weight menu, change the thickness for trim marks. You can also enter an Offset value (0–72 pt) for the distance between the trim marks (and other printer's marks) and the edge of each artboard or the bounding box of tiled artwork. If Fit to Page is the current Scaling choice, the artwork and artboards will be reduced in scale to accommodate a larger offset value.

If you position objects on any artboard so they extend into the bleed region (the area just beyond the edge of the artboard), they will print to the very edge of the final trimmed page. The bleed settings are set initially in the New Document dialog and can be changed in the File > Document Setup dialog. For commercial printing, you should ask your print shop what bleed values to enter for their specific output device, either in one of the above-mentioned dialogs or here in the Print dialog.

To choose bleed values:

1. Follow steps 1–2 in the steps at left.

2. If you have already set the bleed values for the document, in the **Bleeds** area, check **Use Document Bleed Settings** and skip the next step. If you haven't set bleed values yet, uncheck that option and follow the next two steps.

3. Do either of the following:

   With the link icon activated, ⬛ choose or enter a single bleed value (then press Tab) to use that value for all four sides of each artboard.

   To specify asymmetrical bleed values, deactivate the link icon, ⬛ then specify separate **Top**, **Left**, **Bottom**, and **Right** values via the arrowheads or fields.

   Enter a bleed value (or values) to include a bleed amount that will include artwork in the defined bleed area, and thereby print more of the objects that extend into the bleed region. If you chose Scaling: Fit to Page in the General option set, this change will be reflected in the preview. If Ignore Artboards is checked and Scaling: Tile Full Pages is chosen, more tile pages may be produced to accommodate a wide bleed region.

4. Choose any other print settings (see pages 426–427), then click **Print** to print the document; or to save the current settings with the document without printing, click Done, then save your file.

SAVE YOUR PRINT SETTINGS!

Considering how many options you need to choose in the Print dialog, we recommend saving your settings as a preset so you won't have to reenter them each time you print to a particular output device: Click the Save Preset button ![icon] at the top of the dialog, enter a name for the preset, then click OK. Saved presets are accessed from the Print Preset menu at the top of the Print dialog. To edit a print preset, see page 437.

Print

Print Preset: Custom

Printer: HP LaserJet 4050

PPD: Default (HP LaserJet 4050 Series)

General
Marks and Bleed
Output
Graphics
Color Management
Advanced
Summary

Marks and Bleed

Marks

☑ All Printer's Marks

  ☑ Trim Marks   Printer Mark Type: Roman

  ☑ Registration Marks   Trim Mark Weight: 0.25 pt

  ☑ Color Bars   Offset: 0.08 in

  ☑ Page Information

Bleeds

☑ Use Document Bleed Settings

Top: 0.125 in   Left: 0.125 in

Bottom: 0.125 in   Right: 0.125 in

1 of 2 (1)

Document: 7.17 in x 7.65 in
Media: 8.5 in x 11 in

Page Setup...   Setup...   Done   Cancel   Print

A *Via the Marks and Bleed option set in the Print dialog, choose marks for commercial printing and set values for the bleed region.*

Output options

During color separation, each color prints to a separate plate or piece of film. Although the settings in the Output option set of the Print dialog are used primarily by prepress operators to produce color separations for commercial printing (a separate plate is made for each process and spot color in the file), some settings also apply to composite printing.

To output a composite print or color separations:

1. *Optional:* To preview how colors in your artwork are going to overprint and/or separate onto individual plates, click Done to exit the Print dialog, then follow the instructions for the Separations Preview panel on pages 432–433.

2. Make sure your file is in CMYK Color mode.

3. In the Print dialog, show the **Output** option set.**A**

4. On the **Printer** menu, choose a PostScript color or grayscale device that's available in your system.

5. Note: Before choosing settings in this step and in step 6, consult with your commercial printer.

From the **Mode** menu, choose one of the following:

Composite to print all the colors on one sheet (from a desktop printer).

Separations (Host-Based) to allow Illustrator to prepare the separations data and send it to the printing device.

In-RIP Separations to have Illustrator send PostScript data to the printer's RIP* to allow that device to perform the separations. (Available options will vary depending on the type of printer you chose in step 4.)

6. For color separations, do all of the following:

Choose **Emulsion: Up (Right Reading)** or **Down (Right Reading).**

Choose **Image: Positive** or **Negative**.

From the **Printer Resolution** menu, choose the halftone screen ruling (lpi)/device resolution (dpi) that your commercial printer recommends.

For more Output options, see the next page.

A Via the Output option set in the Print dialog, choose settings for color separations.

*The RIP (short for "raster image processor") converts vector data to printable dots.

You can also use the Output option set to turn printing on or off for individual colors or to convert any individual spot color, which is normally printed via a separate plate (in commercial printing), to a process color, which is printed along with other colors via the standard four plates (C, M, Y, and K).

To change the print setting for, or to convert, individual colors in a document:

1. Display the **Output** option set of the Print dialog, then choose a separations option from the **Mode** menu.

2. The colors being used in the document are listed in the Document Ink Options area.**A** To prevent a particular process or spot color from outputting, click to remove its printer icon 🖶 in the left column.

3. Do either of the following:

   Check **Convert All Spot Colors to Process** to convert all spot colors in the document to process colors.

   To convert any specific spot colors to process colors, uncheck **Convert All Spot Colors to Process**, then click the spot color icon ⊙ on the list; it will change to a process color icon. ▨

4. *Optional:* To allow black fills and strokes to overprint any underlying colors, check Overprint Black. To learn more about overprinting, see page 433.

5. Choose settings in other option sets.

➤ To restore all the default ink settings at any time, click Reset to Defaults.

➤ Don't change the Frequency, Angle, or Dot Shape settings unless your commercial printer advises you to do so.

➤ The Adobe Illustrator (.ai) and Adobe PDF (1.5 and later) file formats preserve spot colors and apply overprinting correctly. Spot colors that are applied to objects, raster effects, and grayscale images will appear on separate plates, whether the document is output from InDesign or directly from Illustrator.

COLOR-SEPARATING A GRADIENT

➤ To color-separate a gradient that contains one spot color plus white onto one plate, use the spot color as the starting color in the gradient and use a 0% tint of the same spot color as the ending color.

➤ To color-separate a gradient that contains one spot color as the starting color and another spot color as the ending color, uncheck Convert All Spot Colors to Process (see step 3 at left), and ask your output service provider to assign screen angles to those colors.

➤ To convert a spot color in a gradient to a process color, click that color stop on the Gradient panel, then on the Color panel, click the Spot Color button. ⊙ The color will convert to the current document color mode of RGB or CMYK. Repeat for the other color stops.

🖶		Document Ink	Frequency	Angle	Dot Shape	
🖶	▨	Process Magenta	141 lpi	18.4349°	Dot	
🖶	▨	Process Yellow	141 lpi	0°	Dot	
🖶	▨	Process Black	141 lpi	45°	Dot	
	⊙	PANTONE 1375 C	141 lpi	45°	Dot	
🖶	⊙	PANTONE 173 C	141 lpi	45°	Dot	
🖶	▨	PANTONE 7401 C	141 lpi	45°	Dot	

Printer Resolution: 141 lpi /ProRes 1200 ▾

☐ Convert All Spot Colors to Process
☐ Overprint Black

Document Ink Options   Reset to Defaults

This spot color won't output because we removed its printing icon.

This spot color will output as a process color because we clicked its icon.

A *Via the Output option set in the Print dialog, you can prevent individual colors from outputting or convert spot colors to process colors.*

Graphics options

The Flatness setting in the Graphics option set of the Print dialog controls how precisely all the objects in a document are going to print on a PostScript printer. If your document doesn't print, one possible solution is to increase the Flatness setting.

To change the Flatness setting for a file, to facilitate printing:

1. Open a file that stubbornly refuses to print, choose File > **Print**, then display the **Graphics** option set (**A**, next page).

2. If **Automatic** is checked (under Paths), Illustrator will choose an optimal Flatness value for the chosen printing device. If you have encountered a printing error, uncheck Automatic, drag the **Flatness** slider a notch or two to the right (toward Speed), then try printing the file. If it prints, but with noticeably jagged curve segments, the Flatness value is too high. Lower it slightly by dragging the slider to the left (toward Quality), then print the file again.

➤ To display a numeric readout of the current Flatness setting, with Automatic unchecked, rest the pointer on the slider.

➤ If your document contains 30 or more Bristle brush paths, you will encounter an alert dialog when you try to print it. One solution is to select some of the offending paths and rasterize them via the Object > Rasterize command.

To choose settings for downloading fonts:

1. To manage how Illustrator downloads fonts to the printer, open the Print dialog and display the **Graphics** option set.

2. From the **Download** menu in the **Fonts** area, choose one of the following options:

   None to have no fonts download. This is the preferred setting in a scenario in which fonts are stored permanently in the printer.

   Subset to download only the characters (glyphs) that are being used in the document.

   Complete to have Illustrator download all the fonts being used in the document at the start of the print job. This is effective if you are printing multiple artboards that use the same fonts.

3. Click **Print** to print the document; or to save your settings with the document without printing, click Done, then save the file.

FLATTENING VERSUS FLATNESS

Upon output, Illustrator flattens overlapping shapes in order to preserve the look of transparency. This is a different process from setting a Flatness value (see the steps at left) to control how precisely the curve segments in a document will print. The higher the Flatness value, the less precisely the curves are printed.

OTHER GRAPHICS OPTIONS

Normally, Illustrator sets the PostScript (LanguageLevel 2 or 3) and Data Format (Binary or ASCII) options in the Graphics option set of the Print dialog based on what features the chosen printer supports, so you can ignore them. However, if your printer supports multiple options for those features, you will need to choose settings (decisions, decisions!). For PostScript, we recommend choosing LanguageLevel 3, because it contains the latest definitions for printing transparency and facilitates smooth shading (which helps prevent banding in gradients).

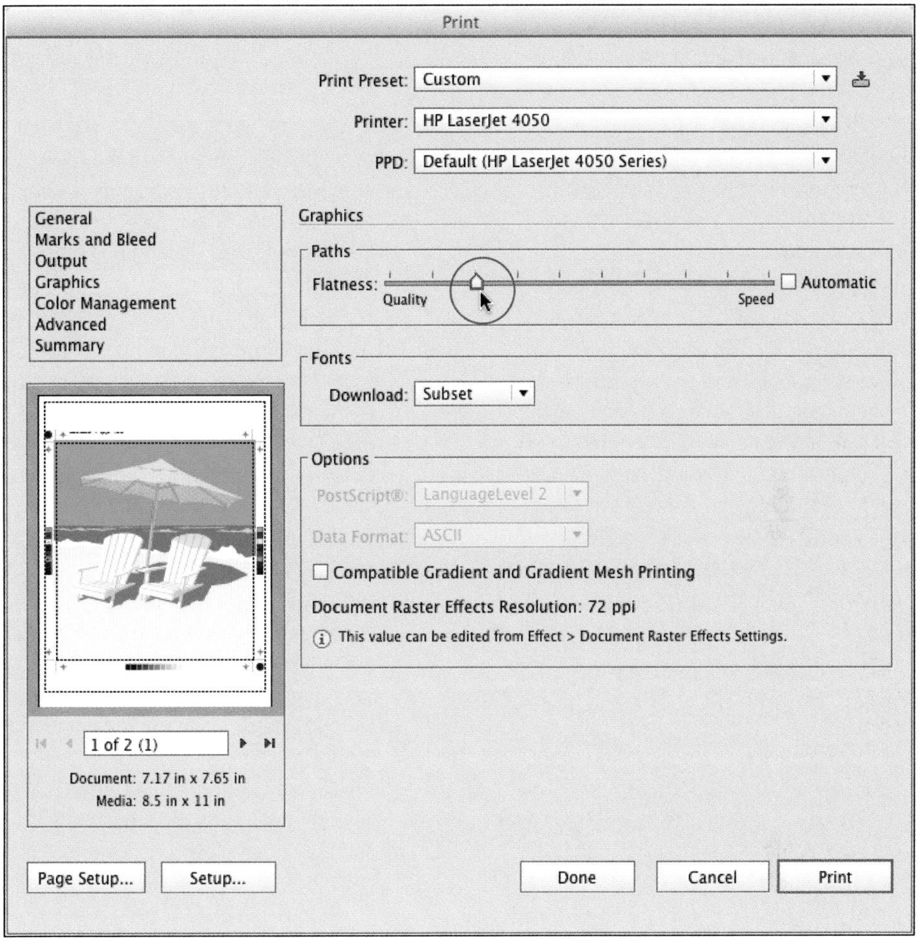

A *In the Graphics option set of the Print dialog, choose a Flatness setting and an option for how fonts are to be downloaded.*

Color Management options

Use the Color Management option set of the Print dialog to control how color conversions will be handled. Note: If you haven't learned about profiles and color settings yet, read Chapter 2 first.

To print using color management:

In the **Print** dialog, display the **Color Management** option set.**A**

Let Illustrator handle the color conversion

1. From the **Color Handling** menu, choose **Let Illustrator Determine Colors** (the preferred choice) to let Illustrator convert document colors to the printer gamut based on the chosen printer profile and send the converted data to the printer. The quality of the conversion will depend on the accuracy of the chosen printer profile.

2. From the **Printer Profile** menu, choose the correct ICC profile for your printer, ink, and paper.

3. Click **Setup**. If an alert dialog appears, click Continue.

4. Turn off color management for the printer driver, as follows:

   In the Mac OS, click Show Details to expand the dialog, if necessary. From the third menu, choose Color Matching or ColorSync (depending on your printer), then choose ColorSync or a similar option (not a printer option). Click Print to return to the Print dialog.

In Windows, see Illustrator Help and refer to your printer manual.

➤ To learn more, search for "Printing with color management" in Illustrator Help.

Let the printer handle the color conversion

1. From the **Color Handling** menu, choose **Let PostScript Printer Determine Colors** to have Illustrator send the color data to the printer and let the printer convert the colors to its gamut.

2. If your printing device requires it, click **Setup**, then locate and turn on color matching or color management for the printer.

3. If the document color mode is CMYK, check **Preserve CMYK Numbers** to preserve the color values of native objects and type in your artwork. For RGB documents, Adobe recommends keeping this option unchecked.

Print the file or exit the dialog

Note: Leave the Rendering Intent on the default setting of Relative Colorimetric unless you or your output specialist has a specific reason to change it. (To learn about the rendering intents, see the sidebar on page 22.)

Choose other print options, then click **Print** to print the document; or to save the current settings with the document without printing, click Done, then save your file.

A Use the Color Management option set in the Print dialog to control whether Illustrator or your PostScript printer will handle the color conversion.

Advanced options

In the Advanced option set of the Print dialog, you can choose overprint settings for fills and strokes in your artwork, to be used for color separations or composite printing.

To choose overprint and flattening options for output:

1. In the **Print** dialog, display the **Advanced** option set.**A**

2. Choose an option from the **Overprints** menu:

   Preserve to use the file's overprint settings for color separations.

   Discard to have the output device ignore the overprint settings in the file.

   Simulate to create the visual effect of overprinting on a composite printer, for the purpose of proofing the document.

   Note: The Overprints setting chosen here doesn't override the current Overprint Fill or Stroke settings on the Attributes panel.

3. *Optional:* Check Discard White Overprint to prevent white objects from overprinting other objects (see the sidebar on page 434).

4. To specify how transparent objects will be flattened for printing, choose a resolution preset from the **Preset** menu (see step 2 on page 434), or click Custom, then choose settings in the Custom Transparency Flattener Options dialog (see page 435).

5. Choose other print settings, then click **Print** or **Done**.

Summary options

Finally, in the Summary option set, you can read a summary of the current Print dialog settings.

To view a summary of the current print settings:

1. In the Print dialog, display the **Summary** option set.**B**

2. Expand any listings in the Options window to view a summary of the settings, and read any pertinent alerts that display in the Warnings window.

3. *Optional:* Click Save Summary to save the current settings to a separate file (enter a name, choose a location, then click Save).

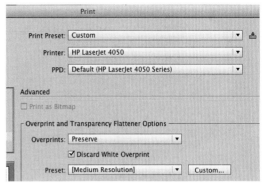

A *Use the Advanced option set in the Print dialog to choose overprint settings.*

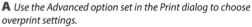

B *In the Summary option set in the Print dialog, you can view a listing of the current print settings.*

ARE YOU USING A NON-POSTSCRIPT PRINTER?

If your document contains complex objects (such as gradients or soft-edged effects) and it generates a printing error from a non-PostScript or low-resolution printer, instead of printing the file as vectors, in the Advanced option set in the Print dialog, check Print as Bitmap. All the artwork in the document will be rasterized upon output. Note that the driver for the chosen printer controls whether this option is available, and most Macintosh printer drivers don't offer it.

Using the Separations Preview panel

The Separations Preview panel lets you see how the C, M, Y, and K color components in a CMYK document will separate to individual printing plates in commercial printing. You can use the panel to check that a color is properly set to knock out colors beneath it in the artwork, or to check whether a color is properly set to overprint on top of the other colors. You can monitor the use of spot colors in the artwork and verify whether a particular spot color is set to knock out colors beneath it. And you can determine whether a specific black is a rich black (a mixture of C, M, Y, and K inks) or a simple black, containing only the K component.

To view individual color plates in a CMYK document:

1. Open a CMYK document,**A** and display the Window > **Separations Preview** panel.

2. Check **Overprint Preview** at the top of the panel to make the list of process and spot colors accessible. With this option on, knockouts and overprints are simulated onscreen.

3. To view a single color plate, Option-click/Alt-click the visibility icon for a color listing.**B** Only the objects in which that color will print are now visible in the document. If an object contains 0% of that particular color, it will display as white.

   To redisplay all the process and spot color plates, Option-click/Alt-click the same visibility icon.

4. *Optional:* Normally, the Separations Preview panel lists all the spot colors that are currently on the Swatches panel for your document, whether or not they are being used. If you want the panel to list only the spot colors that are being used, check Show Used Spot Colors Only.

5. To restore the normal view of your artwork, uncheck Overprint Preview.

➤ If you want to reduce the number of colors in your document to, say, two or three colors, use the Recolor Artwork dialog (see pages 405–406).

➤ There is no set recipe for producing a rich black. Each print shop uses its own formula to produce a warm, cool, or neutral black. Ideally, the shop will adapt the formula to the content of the artwork.

➤ A rich black should not be used for small type. The multiple inks could cause registration problems.

A *We are going to preview color separations for this artwork.*

B *On the Separations Preview panel, we checked Overprint Preview and used the visibility controls to display just the Cyan and Magenta color plates.*

By default, when color-separating a CMYK document for commercial printing, Illustrator knocks out the colors below an object so its colors don't mix on press with the colors it overlaps. Because black ink is opaque (and normally is printed last), and to prevent any potential gaps from showing due to the misregistration of printing plates, it may be preferable to set black fills or strokes to overprint on top of other inks instead. Note: Colors overprint on a commercial press but not on a composite print (proof) that you output from a PostScript color printer.

To preview and change black knockouts to overprints:

1. Open a CMYK document.

2. Display the Separations Preview panel, ◪ and check **Overprint Preview**.

   ➤ Checking this option also checks the View > Overprint Preview command (and vice versa), and "Overprint Preview" will be listed in the document tab.

3. Click the visibility icon 👁 for **Black** to hide that color plate.

4. If a black object is previewing as white in the preview, it means that object is set to knock out any colors below it and that black won't mix with other inks on press.**A** Any black objects that aren't previewing as white are going to overprint on top of other colors, meaning their colors will mix with other inks. Note: If any black objects preview as gray, see the next set of instructions.

5. To make a black fill or stroke overprint instead of knock out, with the Selection tool (V), click the white knockout area (a black area that is previewing as white). Display the Attributes panel, 🔲 then check **Overprint Fill** or **Overprint Stroke** (the part of the object for which you want to enable overprinting).**B**

➤ You can learn more about trapping and overprinting in Illustrator Help > Printing > More, and be sure to ask your output service provider for specific suggestions about your document.

To identify which objects contain rich or 100% K black:

1. Display the Separations Preview panel, ◪ and check **Overprint Preview**.

2. Click the visibility icon 👁 for **Black** to hide that color plate. Fills or strokes containing 100% K (black) ink will now be hidden; fills or strokes containing a rich black (made from a mixture of C, M, Y and K) will display as a shade of gray. If you want to confirm this, click a "gray" object with the Selection tool and view the CMYK settings for the fill or stroke on the Color panel.

3. Click in the visibility column for Black to redisplay that plate.

A *With the Black color plate hidden, black objects preview as white. They will knock out the colors beneath them.*

B *Overprint Fill is checked for the black objects and the Black plate is hidden. Those objects will overprint other colors, so they no longer preview as a white knockout.*

Printing and exporting semitransparent objects

Any nondefault transparency settings in objects, groups, and layers are preserved when a document is saved in the Adobe Illustrator (.ai) format from a CS or CC version of Illustrator, or if saved in the Adobe PDF (.pdf) format with a Compatibility setting of Acrobat 5 or higher. Nondefault settings include a blending mode other than Normal and/or an opacity level below 100%.

When you print a file that contains nondefault transparency settings, or when you export it to a vector format that doesn't support transparency, Illustrator uses the current transparency flattener settings to determine how objects will be flattened, in an effort to preserve the appearance of semitransparency.

During the course of flattening, if Illustrator detects a semitransparent object that overlaps an underlying object, it converts the overlapping area to a separate flat, opaque shape and leaves the remaining, nonoverlapping parts of the original objects as vectors.

Although Illustrator tries to keep flattened shapes as vector objects, if the look of the current transparency settings can't be preserved in the flattened vector object, the program will rasterize those shapes instead. This happens, for instance, when two gradient objects containing nondefault transparency settings overlap; Illustrator rasterizes the resulting flattened shape to preserve the complex appearance of transparency.

To control how transparency is flattened in a document:

1. Deselect, then click **Document Setup** on the Control panel.

2. In the dialog, do either of the following:

   Under Transparency and Overprint Options, **A** choose an option from the **Preset** menu: [High Resolution] for high-quality color separations or color proofs, [Medium Resolution] for desktop PostScript color prints or proofs, [Low Resolution] for black-and-white desktop printing or Web or mobile device output, or [For Complex Art] for artwork that contains multiple areas of transparency. Click OK.

   Click **Custom** to create a custom preset that will save with the file, then follow steps 2–8, starting on the next page.

THE DISCARD WHITE OVERPRINT OPTION

Normally, in Illustrator, white objects don't overprint non-white objects. You could, however, unintentionally create an instance in which a white object is set to overprint (say, by applying a white fill to an object that was previously set to overprint). To ensure that white objects don't overprint, by default, Illustrator turns on these two options: Discard White Overprint in Output in File > Document Setup and Discard White Overprint in the Advanced panel of File > Print (see page 431). If for some reason Discard White Overprint in Output is unchecked in Document Setup, you can override that setting by checking Discard White Overprint in the Print dialog. Note: These options don't affect objects that contain a spot color of white. Also, white overprinting is turned off automatically for files that are saved in the Adobe PDF format.

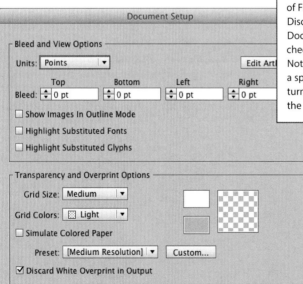

A *Using the Transparency controls in the Document Setup dialog, you can either choose an existing transparency flattener preset or create a custom one.*

To choose custom transparency flattener options:

1. To open the Custom Transparency Flattener Options dialog, click **Custom** in the Transparency area of the Document Setup dialog or in the Advanced option set of the Print dialog.**A** Perform any of the following steps.

2. Move the **Raster/Vector Balance** slider to control the percentage of flattened shapes that will remain as vector shapes versus those that will be rasterized. Vector shapes print with cleaner, higher-quality color and crisper edges. This setting applies only to shapes that are flattened to preserve the look of transparency.

   If you move the slider toward Vectors, more shapes will be printed as vectors (although complex flattened areas will still be rasterized), and the output processing will be slower. If you move the slider toward Rasters, the file will output more quickly at a lower resolution. If a document is very complex and contains a lot of transparency effects, you may need to move the slider toward Rasters to achieve acceptable (not necessarily poor) quality output.

3. During rasterization, the output quality is calculated based on two resolution settings. To specify the resolution for rasterized line art and text, choose or enter a **Line Art and Text Resolution** value. For most purposes, a resolution setting of 300 ppi is adequate, but for small text or thin lines, you should increase this value to 600 ppi. Type objects that have an opacity below 100% are flattened and are preserved as editable type objects. Clipping and masking are used to preserve the look of transparency.

4. For the **Gradient and Mesh Resolution**, choose or enter the resolution for rasterized gradients and mesh objects. Because gradients and meshes don't contain sharp details, the default value of 150 ppi is usually adequate; 300 ppi is considered a high value.

5. With the Raster/Vector Balance slider at a setting between 10 and 90, portions of type that are overlapped by a semitransparent object will be rasterized or converted to outlines and may be thickened slightly. If those areas look noticeably different from type that isn't overlapped by a semi-transparent object, you could **Convert All Text to Outlines** to have all the type within a given font print in the same width or move the type into its own layer above the semitransparent object.

6. With the Raster/Vector Balance slider at a setting between 10 and 90, any strokes that are overlapped by a semitransparent object will convert to outlines. As a result, very thin strokes may be thickened slightly and may look noticeably different from parts of strokes that don't overlap semitransparent objects. If you check **Convert All Strokes to Outlines**, the look of each stroke will be preserved for its entire length, but this option will also increase the number of paths in the file. An alternative to this option is to apply Object > Path > Outline Stroke to selected strokes in the artwork.

7. When a file is sent to print, any areas of semi-transparent objects that overlap other objects are flattened and rasterized. The flattened areas, however, won't match the exact path shapes of

Continued on the following page

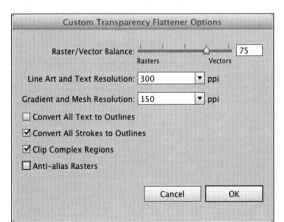

TRANSPARENCY TO ADOBE INDESIGN

When saving artwork for InDesign CS6 or CC, use the native Adobe Illustrator (.ai) format, which keeps transparency settings editable. When placed into InDesign, Illustrator artwork that contains non-default transparency settings will look as intended in the InDesign layout, and InDesign will perform transparency flattening during printing or exporting, if needed.

A *Use the Custom Transparency Flattener Options dialog to choose custom settings for your file.*

the objects. Also, the resulting flattened object may contain a combination of pixel and vector areas, and color discrepancies (called "stitching") between adjacent pixel and vector areas may result. If you check **Clip Complex Regions**, boundaries between raster and vector flattened shapes will fall exactly on object paths. This helps eliminate the signs of stitching but also slows down printing because the resulting paths are more complex. (Note: If an entire document is rasterized, no stitching occurs.)

8. Check **Anti-alias Rasters** to smooth any jagged edges on flattened shapes that will be rasterized on output (based on the current Raster/Vector Balance slider setting).

9. Click OK.

➤ If your document contains a placed linked image that is overlapped by an object containing transparency, before choosing flattener options, make sure the image is embedded into (not just linked to) the Illustrator document.

Via the Flattener Preview panel, you can see in advance which objects in your artwork will be affected by flattening upon output, and you can also use the panel to create flattener presets.

To preview the flattening settings in a document (and create presets):

1. Display the Flattener Preview panel, with full options showing. 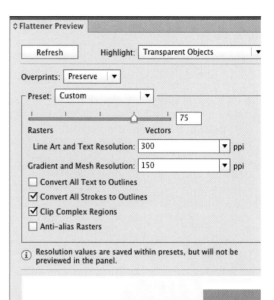 **A**

2. On the panel menu, make sure **Detailed Preview** (not Quick Preview) is checked.

3. On the panel, click **Refresh**.

4. From the **Highlight** menu, choose which category of objects you want the panel to display in a highlight color.

5. Do either of the following:

   Choose a preset from the **Preset** menu (see step 2 on page 434).

   Move the **Rasters/Vectors** slider, if desired; check the appropriate options (see the previous task); then click Refresh again.

6. *Optional:* To save your settings as a preset, choose Save Transparency Flattener Preset from the panel menu, enter a name, then click OK.

➤ To learn more about flattening, search for "transparency flattener options" in Illustrator Help.

A *Use the Flattener Preview panel to preview various flattening settings for semitransparent objects in your document.*

In addition to setting flattening options for an entire document, you can set them for individual objects. When your document is ready to be output, save a copy of it. Select a semitransparent object and any objects that it overlaps, choose Object > Flatten Transparency, then follow our steps on the preceding two pages. The command will flatten (divide) the areas where selected objects overlap into separate, nonoverlapping objects. Although the objects will still look semitransparent, the transparency settings will no longer be editable. (To learn about the Preserve Alpha Transparency and Preserve Overprints and Spot Colors options, search for "Printing and saving transparent artwork" in Illustrator Help.)

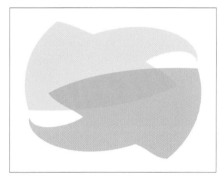

The yellow object in this artwork has a fill color and a stroke of None; the green object has a semitransparent fill and a stroke of None.

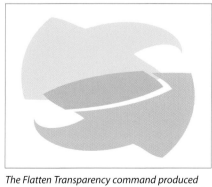

The Flatten Transparency command produced three objects from the original two. (We moved the flattened objects apart to make this obvious.)

Creating and editing presets

By creating a preset for your custom transparency flattener or Print dialog settings, you'll be able to apply the same settings to multiple files quickly. For example, instead of having to tediously choose custom flattener settings for individual files via the Print dialog (in the Advanced option set) or the Document Setup dialog (in the Transparency area), you can create presets for different printing scenarios and use them with any file. Presets can also be exported as files for use by other Illustrator users.

To create or edit a transparency flattener, print, or PDF preset:

1. From the Edit menu, choose **Transparency Flattener Presets**, **Print Presets**, or **Adobe PDF Presets**. A preset dialog opens.

2. *Optional:* Click the New button to create a new preset; or click an existing preset, then click the New button to create a variation (copy) of it.

3. In the next dialog that opens, enter a name for the preset.

4. Choose settings. For the Transparency Flattener Preset Options dialog, follow the instructions on the preceding two pages; for the Print Preset Options dialog, see pages 422–431; or for the Adobe PDF Preset dialog, see pages 442–445. Click OK.

5. To edit an existing user-created preset (one that is not listed in brackets), click the preset name, click the **Edit** button, change any of the settings, and then click OK. Note: You can also edit the settings for either of the [Default] print presets, but not for the predefined transparency flattener or Adobe PDF presets.

6. Do any of the following optional steps:

   To view a summary of the settings in a preset, click the preset name, then view the information in the **Preset Settings** window.

   Click the **Delete** button to delete the currently selected user-created preset.

   Click **Export** to save the settings for the currently selected preset as a separate text file.

   Click **Import** to locate and open a settings file that was previously exported.

7. Click OK.

Producing crop and trim marks

Both the Crop Marks effect and the Create Trim Marks command place four pairs of crop marks around a selected object or group. Print shops use these marks as guides to trim the paper. If you move or transform an object to which the Crop Marks effect is applied, the marks will move accordingly, whereas if you do the same for an object to which the Create Trim Marks command was applied, the actual trim marks will stay where they are.

To produce crop marks for an object or group:

1. Select an object or a group, and make sure there is enough room around it on the artboard to accommodate crop marks.

2. From the Add New Effect menu *fx.* at the bottom of the Appearance panel, or from the Effect menu on the Illustrator menu bar, choose **Crop Marks**. Crop marks will appear at the four corners of the selection.**A–B**

➤ To delete a set of crop marks, select or target the object or group to which the effect is applied. On the Appearance panel, click the Crop Marks effect listing, then click the Delete Selected Item button.

➤ You can apply the Crop Marks effect to a selection of multiple groups (such as a series of business cards), but bear in mind that the effect will produce a separate set of crop marks around each group.

To produce trim marks for one or more objects or a group:

1. Select one or more objects or groups. The Create Trim Marks command will produce one set of trim marks around the entire selection.

2. Choose Object > **Create Trim Marks**. Trim marks will appear at the four corners of the overall selection. The marks will be listed as a group (containing eight separate lines) on the Layers panel.**C**

➤ To delete a set of trim marks, delete its group listing from the Layers panel.

➤ Marks that are produced by the Trim Marks option in the Marks and Bleed option set of the Print dialog will align with the edges of each artboard or the tiled artwork, and are independent of any marks that are produced by the Crop Marks effect or Create Trim Marks command.

A *We applied the Crop Marks effect to this group of objects.*

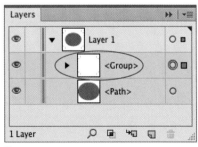

B *The Crop Marks effect appeared as a listing on the Appearance panel.*

C *The Create Trim Marks command produced a group listing on the Layers panel.*

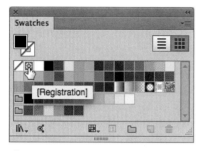
Choosing a resolution for effects

All the Photoshop effects in the lower half of the Effect menu will rasterize automatically upon export or output, as will the SVG Filters and the following effects on the Illustrator Effects > Stylize submenu: Drop Shadow, Inner Glow, Outer Glow, and Feather. By following these steps, you can specify a resolution value for all the raster effects in a document.

To choose a resolution for raster effects:

1. With your Illustrator file open, choose Effect > **Document Raster Effects Settings.A**

2. From the Resolution menu in the dialog, choose a **Resolution** option, or choose **Other** and enter a custom value. The value should be appropriate for the output medium: 72 ppi for onscreen or Web or mobile device output, or 300 ppi for print output. The higher the resolution, the slower the output processing time, but the higher the quality of the rasterized effects.

▶ To learn more about the options in this dialog, see page 216.

▶ The current resolution value from this dialog is also listed in the Graphics panel of the Print dialog.

A *In the Document Raster Effects Settings dialog, choose a Resolution setting for raster effects.*

Packaging files for output

To help you expedite your output workflow, the Package command gathers a copy of your Illustrator document, and depending on what options you check in the dialog, a copy of the linked images and/or fonts used in the file. If desired, you can also have Illustrator produce a text report listing the contents of the packaged file.

To package an Illustrator file:

1. Open the document to be packaged, and apply the Save command if it contains unsaved edits. Choose File > **Package** (Cmd-Option-Shift-P/Ctrl-Alt-Shift-P). The Package dialog opens.**A**

2. Do the following:

   Click the **Choose Package Location Folder** button, choose a location for the package, then click Choose.

   In the **Folder Name** field, keep the default name (the name of the Illustrator file being packaged) or enter a new name.

3. To permit the command to copy linked graphics and files to the package folder, check **Copy Links.**

   Additionally, you can check **Collect Links in Separate Folder** to have Illustrator copy the linked graphics to a Links subfolder within the package folder. With this option off, linked files will be copied to the same folder level as your .ai file.

   Relink Linked Files to Document to link the packaged Illustrator document to the graphics in the new package folder. With this option off, the

packaged Illustrator document will remain linked to graphics in their original location instead (but copies of the linked files will still be collected into the package).

4. Check **Copy Fonts Used in Document (Except CJK)** to have Illustrator copy only the fonts that are used in the document (excluding Chinese, Korean, and Japanese fonts) instead of entire font families.

5. Check **Create Report** to have Illustrator produce a .txt file that summarizes the contents of the packaged files, including the color mode and profile, spot color objects, fonts used (including any missing fonts), and linked and embedded images (including any missing links).

6. Click **Package**. If you checked Copy Fonts used in Document (Except CJK), an alert may appear, warning you to verify that you are complying with your font licensing agreement. If you're authorized to copy your fonts, click OK.

   When the Package command has run its course, another alert dialog may appear (**A**, next page). Click **Show Package** to view the package contents in a window onscreen (**B**, next page), or click OK to close the alert dialog without viewing the package.

   If you checked Create Report in the Package dialog, you can double-click the .txt file to view its contents in a text editor (**C**, next page).

➤ If you want to unembed any files from your document (convert them to linked files) before using the Package command, see the steps on page 317.

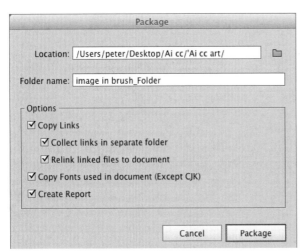

A Use the Package dialog to specify a location and name for your package folder, and optionally, to include linked images, fonts, and a text report.

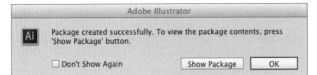

This alert may appear after you click Package in the Package dialog. When we clicked Show Package …

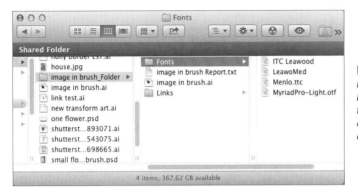

B *… this window appeared. It contains copies of the Illustrator document, the fonts used in the document, and the linked images, plus a text report (.txt file).*

```
● ○ ○                    image in brush Report.txt
Package Report

-----------------------------------------------------------------
Document:
Name: image in brush.ai
Color Mode: CMYK color
Color Profile: U.S. Web Coated (SWOP) v2
Ruler Units: points
Artboard Dimensions: 769 pt x 792 pt
Show Images in Outline Mode: OFF
Highlight Substituted Fonts: ON
Highlight Substituted Glyphs: ON
Preserve Text Editability
Simulate Colored Paper: OFF

-----------------------------------------------------------------
Spot Color Objects:
PANTONE 1225 C (Lab)
PANTONE 171 C (Lab)
PANTONE 7575 C (Lab)

-----------------------------------------------------------------
Missing Fonts:NONE

-----------------------------------------------------------------
Fonts:
ITC Leawood Medium (Type 1)
Menlo Regular (TrueType)
Myriad Pro Light (OTF)

-----------------------------------------------------------------
Embedded Fonts:
NONE

-----------------------------------------------------------------
Missing Links:
NONE

-----------------------------------------------------------------
Linked Images:

/Users/peter/Desktop/Ai cc/'Ai cc art/flowers white.tif
Type: CMYK
Bits per Pixel: 32
Channels: 4
Size: 3971K, 1271 by 800 pixels
Dimensions: 457.56 by 288 points
Resolution: 200 by 200 pixels per inch
```

C *Because we checked Create Report in the Package dialog, this report appeared in our package folder.*

Choosing a file format for export

▶ To export an Adobe Illustrator document to any CS or CC version of Adobe InDesign, your simplest and best option is to keep it in the native **Adobe Illustrator (.ai)** format. In the Illustrator Options dialog, which opens when you click Save in the File > Save As dialog, check Create PDF Compatible File to ensure that the file includes both Illustrator and PDF data. The Adobe Illustrator (.ai) format preserves transparency and live features, such as effects.

▶ To prepare an Illustrator file for a drawing or page layout application that doesn't read native Adobe Illustrator files, save it in the versatile **Adobe PDF (.pdf)** format (see the instructions that begin on this page). Other formats can be accessed via the **Export** command (see pages 446–447).

▶ To output an Illustrator file to the Web, optimize it in the **GIF** or **JPEG** format (see pages 448–451).

▶ To export your Illustrator file to Adobe Photoshop, either keep it in the Adobe Illustrator (.ai) format and open it in Photoshop as a **Smart Object**, or use the **Copy** and **Paste** commands.

Saving files in the Adobe PDF format

The versatile Adobe PDF (Portable Document Format) is a good choice for output to the Web and to other applications and platforms. It is also useful for showing Illustrator artwork to clients, as the only software a user needs in order to view a PDF file is Adobe Reader (which is available as a free download) or, in Mac OS X, the Preview application (the user doesn't need Adobe Illustrator). Plus, your artwork will look as it was originally designed, because this format preserves all object attributes, groups, fonts, and type.

PDF files can also be viewed in Adobe Acrobat X Pro, in which edits and comments can be applied. Acrobat versions 5 and later support transparency; Acrobat versions 6, 7, and 8 also preserve layers; and Acrobat 8 offers support for 3D features. This format also supports document text search and navigation features.

Note: The following steps are long-winded (yawn). If you like, you can end your journey at the end of step 3, after choosing one of the default presets.

To save a file in the Adobe PDF format:

Save as PDF using a preset

1. With your file open in Illustrator, choose File > Save As or Save a Copy.

2. From the Format/Save as Type menu, choose **Adobe PDF (pdf)**, and choose a location for the file. To save each artboard as a separate page, click **All**; or to save only specific artboards as pages, click **Range** and enter a range. Click Save. The Save Adobe PDF dialog opens (**A**, next page).

3. From the **Adobe PDF Preset** menu, choose a preset that is best suited for the output medium (the default Acrobat version for the chosen preset displays on the Compatibility menu):

   ▶ You can read information about the currently chosen preset in the Description window.

   Illustrator Default creates a PDF file that can be reedited in Illustrator or placed into InDesign or QuarkXPress. Fonts are embedded, and bitmap images aren't downsampled or compressed.

   High Quality Print creates PDF files for desktop printing and proofing devices.

   PDF/X-1a: 2001, PDF/X-3: 2002, and **PDF/X-4: 2008** create Acrobat-compatible PDF files that are checked to ensure that they comply with specific graphic exchange and printing standards, to help prevent printing errors. The PDF/X-1a and PDF/X-3 presets don't support transparency (files are flattened); the PDF/X-3 and PDF/X-4 presets support embedded color profiles and color-managed workflows; the PDF/X-4 preset supports transparency (the artwork isn't flattened). If you need the file to remain fully editable in Illustrator, don't choose a PDF/X preset.

   Press Quality produces high-quality files for commercial printing. This preset embeds subsets of fonts automatically, uses JPEG compression at an image quality setting of Maximum, preserves CMYK colors, and converts RGB colors to CMYK. The inclusion of all this data will increase the file size.

   Smallest File Size creates compact, low-resolution PDF files for output to the Web and mobile devices, and for email distribution. Fonts are embedded and all colors are converted to RGB.

   If you're satisfied with the settings in the chosen preset, click Save PDF. Or if you need to choose custom settings, proceed with any or all of the remaining steps.

Save as PDF using custom settings

1. We recommend leaving the Standard setting alone. From the **Compatibility** menu, you can choose the version of Adobe Acrobat with which you need your file to be compatible. Note that not all applications can read files in Acrobat 8 (PDF version 1.7) or later.

   If you choose any nondefault settings for a preset, the word "(Modified)" appears next to the preset name on the Adobe PDF Preset menu.

2. In the General option set, under **Options**, check any of the following, if available:

   Preserve Illustrator Editing Capabilities to save all the Illustrator data in the PDF file. This option will enable the file to be reopened and edited in Illustrator but also will increase its size and limit the extent to which it can be compressed. (This option isn't available for the PDF/X presets.)

   Embed Page Thumbnails to save a thumbnail of each artboard in the file for display in the Open and Place dialogs in Illustrator.

   Optimize for Fast Web View to enable parts of the file to display in a Web browser while the file is downloading.

   View PDF After Saving to have your system's default PDF viewer (most likely Adobe Reader or Acrobat) launch automatically and display the file after you click Save PDF (in step 10). We keep this option checked.

   If the chosen Compatibility option is Acrobat version 6, 7, or 8, check **Create Acrobat Layers from Top-Level Layers** to preserve the editability of top-level layers if the file is opened in one of those versions of Acrobat.

   Continued on the following page

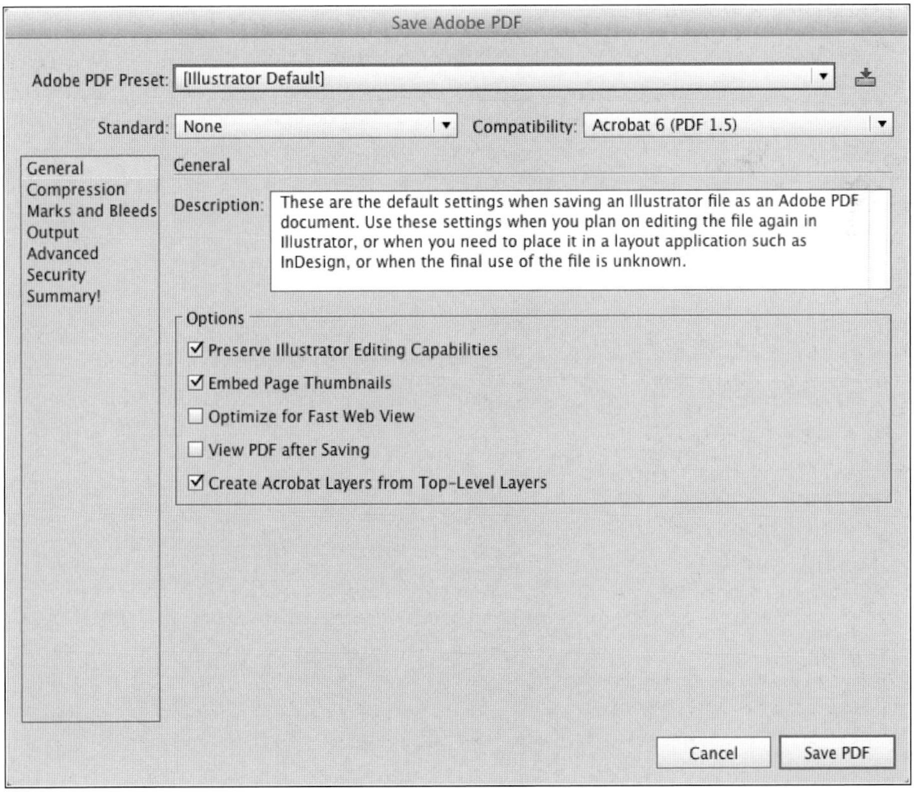

A *These are the [Illustrator Default] settings in the General option set of the Save Adobe PDF dialog.*

To choose further custom options, follow the remaining steps in this task. Otherwise, click **Save PDF**.

3. For online (not print) output, display the **Compression** option set, then choose options to control how bitmap images and raster effects are compressed (downsampled) to reduce the file size.**A** From the menus under Color Bitmap Images, Grayscale Bitmap Images, and Monochrome Bitmap Images, choose an interpolation method to be used for downsampling:

Do Not Downsample preserves the existing size of any bitmap images.

Average Downsampling To divides the image into sample areas, averages the pixels in each area, and substitutes those average values for the original values.

Subsampling To replaces a sampled area with pixel data taken from the middle of that area. It produces a smaller file size but may also diminish the smoothness of continuous tones (e.g., gradients, drop shadows, and raster images).

Bicubic Downsampling To replaces the sampled area with a weighted average of the values in an area and produces smoother continuous tones than the Average Downsampling To option.

For each of the chosen interpolation methods, enter the desired **ppi** resolution and the minimum resolution threshold an image must have in order to be downsampled.

Also choose a compression type from each **Compression** menu: None for no compression, an Automatic option, a JPEG option (which will cause data loss), or ZIP (ZIP compression is usually lossless). If you choose an Automatic option, Illustrator will choose the appropriate compression settings for the artwork: Automatic (JPEG) for the widest compatibility with other applications, or Automatic

A Choose Compression options in the Save Adobe PDF dialog.

(JPEG2000) for equally good compression with progressive display. To learn more about these options, in Illustrator Help, click Importing, exporting, and saving > More > Adobe PDF options.

4. To learn about Marks and Bleed options, see page 424.

5. The **Output** set contains options for controlling the color conversion. Unless you're knowledgeable about setting up a color-managed workflow, it's best to leave these menus on the default settings. For a detailed explanation of these options, see the Illustrator Help reference mentioned in step 3.

6. Display the **Advanced** option set to access font, overprint, and flattening options.

   By default, the PDF presets automatically embed all the characters of every font that is being used in the document. If only a portion of the characters in those fonts is being used in your artwork, you can reduce the file size by embedding just those subsets. To do this, enter a percentage in the **Subset Fonts When Percentage of Characters Used Is Less Than** field. For example, if you enter 50% and more than 50% of a font's characters are being used in the file, the entire font will be embedded; if fewer than 50% of those characters are being used, just the subset will be embedded.

   Acrobat versions 5 through 8 preserve overprinting and transparency settings automatically. If Acrobat 4 (PDF 1.3) is chosen as the Compatibility option and the document contains overprints, from the **Overprints** menu, choose whether you want Illustrator to Preserve or Discard overprints. Similarly, if the artwork contains transparency, choose a transparency flattener preset or custom options (see pages 434–436).

7. Moving right along, display the **Security** option set if you want to restrict user access to the PDF. The following options aren't available for PDF/X files (and some aren't available for early versions of Acrobat):

   To protect the file with a password, check **Require a Password to Open the Document** and type that password in the Document Open Password field.

➤ The password can't be recovered from the document, so jot it down somewhere (yes, we mean on paper!).

If you want to maintain control over your viewers' use of the file, check **Use a Password to Restrict Editing Security and Permissions Settings**. Type a password in the Permissions Password field, and choose or disable/enable these **Acrobat Permissions** settings:

Choose an option from the **Printing Allowed** menu to control whether users can print the file: None, Low Resolution (150 dpi), or High Resolution. The Low Resolution option is only available for Acrobat versions 5 and higher.

Choose an option from the **Changes Allowed** menu to specify precisely which parts of the document users may copy.

Check **Enable Copying of Text, Images, and Other Content** to permit users to copy the document content.

If you unchecked the previous option, you can check **Enable Text Access of Screen Reader Devices for the Visually Impaired** to permit screen reader devices to view and read the file.

To allow the file metadata to be searchable by other applications, uncheck the Enable Copying of Text, Images, and Other Content option, then check **Enable Plaintext Metadata** (available only for Acrobat versions 6 through 8).

8. Click **Summary** on the left side of the dialog to view an expandable list of the settings you've chosen in each option set, as well as any alert warnings.

9. *Optional (but recommended):* To save your custom settings as a user-created preset for use in any file, click the Save Preset ⬇ button in the upper right corner of the dialog. In the Save Adobe PDF Settings As dialog, enter a name for the preset, then click OK.

10. Click **Save PDF**, then give yourself a nice pat on the back.

➤ To edit a user-created preset, see page 437.

Using the Export command

The Export dialog gives you access to other file formats besides PDF.

To export an Illustrator file:

1. With an Illustrator file open, choose File > **Export**. The Export dialog opens.

2. *Optional:* Change the file name in the Save As/File Name field. Illustrator will automatically append the proper file extension (e.g., .bmp, .psd, .tif) to the file name for the format you are going to choose in the next step.

3. Choose a format from the **Format/Save as Type** menu,**A–B** and choose a location for the new file.

   ➤ To create a new folder for the file in the Mac OS, choose a location, click New Folder, enter a name, then click Create. To do this in Windows, click New Folder, then enter a name.

4. If the Use Artboards options are available for the chosen format and you want to save multiple artboards in the document as separate files (they will be labeled with the artboard name), check **Use Artboards**, then click All or click Range and enter a range. Or if you want to combine all the artboards into one file, uncheck Use Artboards.

5. Click Export/Save. Choose settings in any further dialog that opens, then click OK. A few file formats are discussed in brief on this page and the facing page; following that, the GIF, JPEG, and PSD formats are discussed in depth.

A few export formats, in brief

If you choose a raster (bitmap) file format in the Export dialog, such as BMP (.bmp), the Rasterize Options dialog opens. Choose a Color Model for the resulting file. For the file Resolution, choose Screen (72 dpi), Medium (150 dpi), or High (300 dpi), or enter a custom resolution next to Other. Choose an Anti-Aliasing option to control whether pixels will be added along curved edges to make them look smoother: None, Art Optimized (Supersampling) for artwork that doesn't contain much type, or Type Optimized (Hinted) for artwork that contains a lot of editable type. Note: For the Type Optimized option to have any effect, before the Export command is chosen, a setting of Sharp, Crisp, or Strong must be applied to the type via the Anti-Aliasing menu on the Character panel.

BMP (.bmp)

BMP is a standard bitmap image format on Windows computers. After choosing settings in the Rasterize Options dialog and clicking OK, the BMP Options dialog opens. Choose Windows or OS/2 as the File Format and specify a bit (color) Depth. If you chose RGB as the Color Model in the Rasterize dialog, you can access more specific bit depth options by clicking Advanced Modes. Optional features include Compress RLE (available only if you chose Grayscale as the Color Model) and Flip Row Order.

Enhanced Metafile (.emf) and Windows Metafile (.wmf)

In these formats, vector data is stored in a metafile as a list of commands for drawing objects, such as straight lines, polygons, and type, and commands to control the style of the objects. Windows Metafile (.wmf) is a 16-bit metafile format; Enhanced Metafile (.emf) is a 32-bit metafile format that can store a wider range of commands than .wmf and is therefore the better choice of the two. Use these formats, when necessary, only to export simple artwork to the Windows platform.

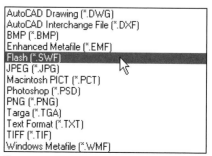

```
✓ PNG (png)
  BMP (BMP)
  AutoCAD Drawing (dwg)
  AutoCAD Interchange File (dxf)
  Enhanced Metafile (emf)
  Flash (swf)
  JPEG (jpg)
  Macintosh PICT (pct)
  Photoshop (psd)
  TIFF (tif)
  Targa (TGA)
  Text Format (txt)
  Windows Metafile (wmf)
```

A *These choices are available on the Format menu in the Mac OS.*

```
AutoCAD Drawing (*.DWG)
AutoCAD Interchange File (*.DXF)
BMP (*.BMP)
Enhanced Metafile (*.EMF)
Flash (*.SWF)
JPEG (*.JPG)
Macintosh PICT (*.PCT)
Photoshop (*.PSD)
PNG (*.PNG)
Targa (*.TGA)
Text Format (*.TXT)
TIFF (*.TIF)
Windows Metafile (*.WMF)
```

B *These choices are available on the Save as Type menu in Windows.*

Flash (.swf)

The .swf format can be used for exporting Illustrator artwork as vectors to Flash-based programs (such as Adobe Flash Professional). An easy way to get Illustrator objects into Adobe Flash Professional is simply by importing your Adobe Illustrator (.ai) file into that program. All paths, strokes, gradients, masks, effects, symbols, and standard type (or type that is designated as dynamic text) are preserved. In the Import dialog in Flash Professional, you can specify whether layers are converted to individual Flash symbols, frames, or a single layer.

Note: Artwork in the .swf format will display only in Web browsers and mobile devices that support the Flash Player plug-in. To learn more about this format, see Illustrator Help/ Exporting artwork.

TIFF (.tif)

TIFF, a bitmap image format, is supported by virtually all paint, image-editing, and page layout applications. It supports RGB, CMYK, and grayscale files, and offers LZW as a compression option. When you choose the TIFF (.tif) file format in the Export dialog, the TIFF Options dialog opens. Choose a Color Model; from the Resolution menu, choose Screen (72 dpi), Medium (150 dpi), or High (300 dpi) or choose Other, then enter a custom resolution; and choose an Anti-Aliasing option. Check LZW Compression if you need to compress the file; this lossless method won't discard or degrade image data. Check Embed ICC Profile if you have assigned such a profile to your file.

Microsoft Office

Choose File > Save for Microsoft Office to save your document in a PNG format that is readable by Microsoft Word, PowerPoint, and Excel. The entire background of the exported artwork will be opaque.

Note: If you want to specify a resolution and background color for the exported artwork, with an option to preserve background transparency, instead of using the Save for Microsoft Office command, choose File > Export, then choose PNG (png) from the Format/Save as Type menu in the Export dialog.

Using the Document Info panel

On the Document Info panel, you can view data about all the objects in the document or about just one or more selected objects.

To view document information:

1. Show the Document Info panel.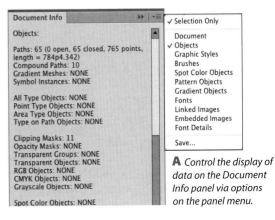

2. *Optional:* Select one or more objects about which you want to read data.

3. To view information pertaining only to the current selection (if any), on the panel menu, make sure **Selection Only** has a check mark, **A** or uncheck that option to display data pertaining to all the objects in the document.

4. From the panel menu, do one of the following:

   Choose **Document** to view a list of document-wide settings (e.g., the color mode).

   Choose **Objects** to view a tally of various kinds of items in the document, such as paths, compound paths, opacity masks, transparent objects, etc., and the number of fonts and linked images used.

   Choose any other category (e.g., **Brushes** or **Linked Images**) to view more detailed data.

5. *Optional:* If Selection Only is checked on the panel menu, you can click another object in the document to view data about that object (the same category applies).

6. *Optional:* Choose Save from the panel menu to save the current data (in all categories) as a text document. Choose a location in which to save the text file, rename the file, if desired, then click Save. Use the system's default text editor to open the text document. You can print this file and refer to it when preparing your document for output.

A *Control the display of data on the Document Info panel via options on the panel menu.*

Optimizing files for the Web

You can use Illustrator to create graphics for a Web page, such as a logo or an illustration, or perhaps some buttons, graphics, or text to be used as navigation devices. Before placing your artwork into a Web page creation program, such as Adobe Dreamweaver, you need to convert it from vector art into pixels, a process known as rasterization, and optimize that raster image to a suitable file size for Web output.

Image size and compression

The length of time it takes for an image to load into a Web page is directly related to its file size. The file size, in turn, is governed by the dimensions of the image (in pixels) and the amount and kind of compression that is applied to it when it is optimized. Vector graphics, in particular, tend to compress well because they contain solid-color shapes. For your Web artwork, resist the urge to use patterns or gradients, which compress less than solid colors. When choosing dimensions for the document, keep in mind that the common Web browsers in which your graphics will be viewed have an approximate width of 1000 pixels; don't let your document width exceed that value.

The GIF and JPEG file formats

GIF and JPEG, the two file formats that are commonly used for optimizing graphics, are suitable for different types of graphics and use different compression schemes. Although those compression schemes cause a small reduction in image quality, it is a price that must be paid to enable your file to download more quickly on the Web.

GIF is an 8-bit format, meaning it can save a maximum of 256 colors. It's a good choice when color fidelity is a priority, such as for artwork that contains type or solid-color vector shapes. Graphics like these contain far fewer colors than continuous-tone (photographic) images, so the color restriction won't have an adverse impact. If your artwork contains transparency, you must choose this format, because it supports transparency, whereas the JPEG format does not. When a file is optimized in the GIF format, a set of colors (called a color table) is generated from it. By reducing the number of colors in the color table, you can shrink the file size and enable the file to download more quickly.

If your Illustrator file contains continuous-tone images (e.g., gradients or imported raster images), the JPEG format, with its ability to save 24-bit color, will do a better job of preserving color fidelity than GIF. Another advantage to using the JPEG format is that its compression scheme can shrink an image significantly without lowering its quality. When saving an image in this format, you can choose a quality setting. The higher the quality setting, the larger the resulting file size.

Unfortunately, the JPEG format, unlike GIF, doesn't preserve transparency, nor does it preserve the sharp edges of vector objects. Furthermore, when you optimize an image as JPEG, some image data is lost; the greater the compression, the greater the loss.

Exporting type to the Web

All the options (except None) on the Anti-Aliasing menu in the expanded Character panel add partially transparent pixels along the edges of the characters to make them look smoother: Sharp may produce inconsistent letterforms; Crisp preserves the weight and curvature of the original letterforms and is suitable for large point sizes; Strong increases the weight of the original letterforms and is best suited for type that has thin strokes. Choose None (no anti-aliasing) only for very small type. If you apply the Sharp, Crisp, or Strong option, you can utilize the anti-aliasing option of Type Optimized in the Save for Web dialog (see pages 449–451).

Note: Before optimizing a file, follow the steps in "Creating pixel-perfect artwork for the Web" on page 84. Regarding symbols, see "Aligning symbols to the pixel grid" in the sidebar on page 389.

THE PNG FORMAT

PNG can be used as an alternative format to GIF and JPEG. It employs lossless compression and supports transparency. For optimizing soft-edged effects (e.g., drop shadows), gradients, and transparency, the PNG-8 optimization options and results are similar to GIF. PNG-24 produces the best optimization results, but at the expense of a large file size. One drawback to PNG files is that older versions of Web browsers may have trouble displaying them correctly. To learn more about this format, see "PNG" in Illustrator Help.

In the Save for Web dialog, you'll find all the controls you need to optimize your Illustrator graphics for the Web. Note the effect in the preview as you test various optimization settings for your document.

To use the preview controls in the Save for Web dialog:

1. Via the artboard navigation controls at the bottom of the document window or via the Artboards panel, display the artboard for which you want to preview optimization settings.

2. Choose File > **Save for Web** (Cmd-Option-Shift-S/ Ctrl-Alt-Shift-S). The current artboard will display in the dialog.**A**

3. Click the **2-Up** tab to compare the original document with an optimization preview. The preview reflects the settings on the right side of the

dialog. As you change the settings, note how it affects the document and its file size (listed below the preview).

Note: There is no longer a 4-Up preview option, nor a preview menu for choosing a download connection speed.

4. For a more definitive test preview, click the **Preview** button at the bottom of the dialog. Your optimized image will open in the default Web browser application that is installed in your system. Or if you want to choose a different browser that's installed in your system, from the **Select Browser** menu, choose a browser name; or choose Other, then locate and open the preferred browser. Quit/exit the browser when you're done admiring your work.

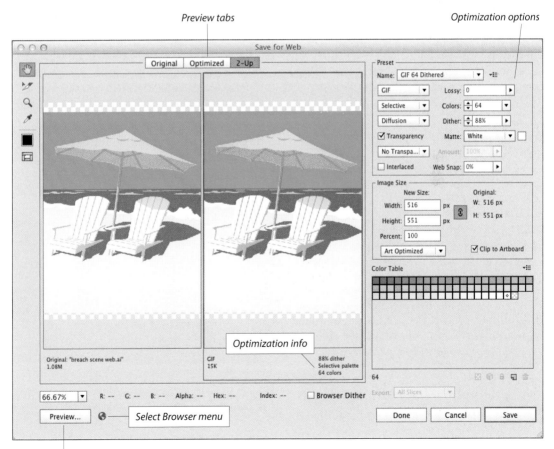

Preview tabs

Optimization options

Optimization info

Select Browser menu

Preview (in default browser)

A *Use the Save for Web dialog to choose and preview optimization settings for your document.*

We'll show you how to optimize files in the GIF format first, because it does a better job of optimizing vector objects and type than the JPEG format.

To optimize a file in the GIF format:

1. If your artwork contains type, apply anti-aliasing to it (not a setting of None) via the Character panel.

2. Save the file and display the artboard to be optimized. Choose File > **Save for Web** (Cmd-Opt-Shift-S/Ctrl-Alt-Shift-S). Click the **2-Up** tab at the top of the dialog to display both the original and optimized previews of the document.

3. Do either of the following:

   From the **Preset** menu, choose one of the **GIF** options. Leave the preset settings as is, then click Save. The Save Optimized As dialog opens. Keep the current name, choose a location for the file, and then click Save.

   Follow the remaining steps to choose custom optimization settings.

Choose GIF settings

1. From the Optimized File Format menu, choose **GIF**. **A**

2. From the **Color Reduction Algorithm** menu, choose a method for reducing the number of colors in the image. We recommend the Selective (default) option because it preserves both solid and Web-safe colors.

3. Next, to remove some colors from the document's color table to reduce the file size, choose 16 from the **Colors** menu. If it looks as though some colors have been substituted (note the optimized preview), you can increase the Colors value to 32.

4. *Optional:* Dithering is a process by which Illustrator mixes dots of a few different colors to simulate a broader range of colors. This option increases the file size slightly but is beneficial for artwork that contains gradients or soft-edged effects (e.g., drop shadows). Choose the Diffusion method from the Dither Algorithm menu, and on the right, choose a Dither value between 50% and 75%. (At a setting of No Dither, gradients may have noticeable bands.)

5. Check **Transparency** to preserve fully transparent pixels in the artwork. By default, the background will be transparent. *Optional:* With Transparency checked, you have the option to define which colors in the artwork will become transparent. To do this, choose the Eyedropper tool in the dialog, click a color in the optimized preview area, then

click the Map Selected Colors to Transparent button below the Color table.

6. If the artwork contains any soft-edged effects (such as drop shadows) on top of transparent areas and you happen to know the background color of the target Web page, click the **Matte** swatch and choose that color via the Color Picker (or click Color Swatches to access colors on the Swatches panel). This will help your artwork blend in with the background. If that color is unknown, set Matte to None; the result will be hard, jagged edges.

   Another option is to choose Matte: None, and with Transparency checked, choose an option from the Transparency Dither Algorithm menu; in this case, the art will look the same on any background.

7. From the menu in the **Image Size** area, choose an **Anti-Aliasing** setting of None, Art Optimized, or Type Optimized. Note: The Type Optimized option works only if an anti-aliasing option was applied to the type via the Character panel (see step 1).

   Check **Clip to Artboard** to clip the optimized image to just the size of the current artboard, or uncheck it to include artwork on all artboards.

   Changes in the Image Size area update instantly.

8. *Optional:* To save the current (Unnamed) options as a preset, see step 8 on the next page.

9. Click Save. In the Save Optimized As dialog, keep the current name, choose a location for the file, and then click Save.

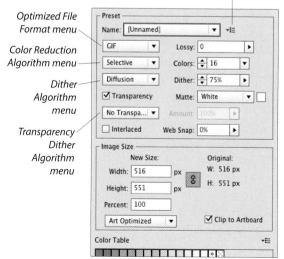

Optimize menu

Optimized File Format menu

Color Reduction Algorithm menu

Dither Algorithm menu

Transparency Dither Algorithm menu

A *Choose optimization options for a GIF file in the Save for Web dialog.*

When a file is optimized in the JPEG format, its 24-bit color is preserved (and can be enjoyed by most of your viewers). If your artwork contains gradients, JPEG is a better choice than GIF. Two drawbacks to JPEG are that its compression method eliminates some image data and that it doesn't preserve transparency.

To optimize a file in the JPEG format:

1. If your artwork contains type, apply anti-aliasing to it (not a setting of None) via the Character panel.

2. Save the file and display the artboard to be optimized. Choose File > **Save for Web** (Cmd-Opt-Shift-S/Ctrl-Alt-Shift-S). The Save for Web dialog opens.**A**

3. Click the **2-Up** tab at the top of the dialog to display both the original and optimized previews of the document.

4. Do either of the following:

    From the **Preset** menu, choose one of the **JPEG** options. Leave the preset settings as is, then click Save. The Save Optimized As dialog opens. Keep the current name, choose a location for the file, and then click Save.

    Follow the remaining steps to choose custom optimization settings.

Choose JPEG settings

1. From the Optimized File Format menu, choose **JPEG.**

2. Do either of the following:

    From the **Compression Quality** menu, choose a quality level for the optimized image.

    Move the **Quality** slider to set the compression level.

    ➤ The higher the compression quality, the better the quality of the optimized file — but the larger the file size.

3. Increase the **Blur** value slightly to lessen the prominence of JPEG artifacts that may be produced by the chosen JPEG compression method, and also to reduce the file size. Be careful not to blur the artwork to the point that sharp vector shapes look too soft.

4. Choose a **Matte** color to be substituted for areas of transparency in the artwork. If you choose None, transparent areas will display as white.

    ➤ To have the Matte color simulate transparency (which the JPEG format doesn't support), make it the same solid color as the background of

the Web page (you need to know what that color is).

5. Uncheck **Progressive** and **ICC Profile**.

6. *Optional:* Check Optimized to produce the smallest possible file size.

7. From the menu in the **Image Size** area, choose an **Anti-Aliasing** setting of None, Art Optimized, or Type Optimized. Note: The Type Optimized option works only if an anti-aliasing option was applied to the type via the Character panel (see step 1).

    Check **Clip to Artboard** to clip the optimized image to just the size of the current artboard, or uncheck it to include artwork on all artboards.

    Changes in the Image Size area update instantly.

8. *Optional:* To save the current (Unnamed) options as a preset, choose Save Settings from the Optimize menu, ▼▤ enter a name, then click Save. Your saved set is now available on the Preset menu in the Save for Web dialog for any file.

9. Click Save. The Save Optimized As dialog opens. Leave the name as is, choose a location for the file, then click Save.

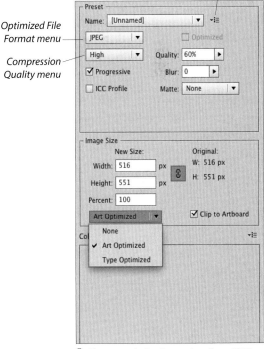

A *Choose optimization options for a JPEG file in the Save for Web dialog.*

Exporting artwork as CSS code

When designing a Web page, some users create a mock-up of their layout in Illustrator, which they submit to their Web developer; the developer, in turn, uses the mock-up as a reference when creating an HTML file. For a faster workflow, and to ensure a closer match to your original design, you can use the CSS Properties panel in Illustrator to generate CSS styling code from the actual objects in your document, which the developer then uses to style the elements on your Web page.

To prepare the initial HTML file:

1. In an Illustrator document that contains only one artboard, create a mock-up of a Web page, including text and vector artwork. Using the Character Styles panel, apply character styles to all the text, and via the Graphic Styles panel, apply graphic styles to all the objects that contain multiple strokes, fills, or effects.

   ➤ Don't sweat over the style names; they will be changed later.

2. Have your Web developer hand-code a layout of your mock-up file. To ensure that each object in your artwork is ultimately linked to the correct element in the HTML file, ask the developer to supply you with the HTML class names that they assigned to page elements.

   Also work with the developer to devise names to replace the temporary character and graphic style names that you assigned to the objects in Illustrator. (Later, the developer will assign those new style names as class names to specific HTML elements.)

3. In your Illustrator document, make sure the name of each individual object, group, and type listing on the Layers panel (not the top-level layer names) matches the corresponding HTML class name that was given to you by the developer.

4. Name the type style listings on the Character Styles panel to match the corresponding names that were devised with your developer. Do the same for the listings on the Graphic Styles panel, for each graphic style that is used in your artwork.

5. Save your Illustrator file, then proceed with the next task.

The next step is for either you or the developer to copy and paste the CSS code into the HTML file using an HTML editor. The class names will provide the link between the attribute descriptions in the CSS code and the HTML elements, so your custom styling is assigned to the correct elements on the Web page. Note: If you're going to use a developer to do the HTML work, they can use the directions in these two tasks as guidelines.

To copy and paste the CSS code for one or more objects into an HTML editor:

1. Show the CSS Properties panel, ▦ then do either of the following:

   To copy the CSS code for one object, select that object.

   To copy the CSS code for multiple objects, select those objects, then click the **Generate CSS** button ▦ on the CSS Properties panel.

2. The code displays in the CSS Properties panel (**A**, next page). Click the **Copy Selected Style** button. ▦

3. In the HTML editor, paste the CSS code into the correct location. Adobe recommends pasting the code inside the <style> tag.

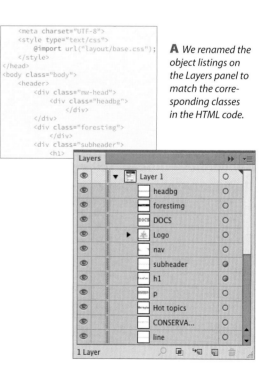

```
<meta charset="UTF-8">
<style type="text/css">
    @import url("layout/base.css");
</style>
</head>
<body class="body">
    <header>
        <div class="mw-head">
            <div class="headbg">
            </div>
        </div>
        <div class="forestimg">
        </div>
        <div class="subheader">
            <h1>
```

A We renamed the object listings on the Layers panel to match the corresponding classes in the HTML code.

To copy and paste character and graphic styles as CSS code:

1. Deselect all objects.

2. All the character styles and graphic styles that are being used in the document are listed in the upper part of the CSS Properties panel. Select one or more style names, then click the **Copy Selected Style** button.

3. In the HTML editor, paste the CSS code into the correct section of code.

To export the CSS code as a file:

1. On the CSS Properties panel, do either of the following:

   To export the CSS code for one or more objects, select those objects, then click the **Export Selected CSS** button.

   To export the CSS code for all the objects in your artwork, choose **Export All** from the panel menu.

2. The Export CSS dialog opens. Enter a name (don't enter spaces), keep the .css extension, locate the folder that contains the HTML file, then click Save.

3. The CSS Export Options dialog opens.**B** Do the following:

   Under CSS Units, click **Pixels**.

   Check which **Object Appearance** attributes you want to include. Keep the **Position and Size** options unchecked.

   Under Options, keep **Generate CSS for Unnamed Objects** unchecked (because you have entered class names for all the objects and styles). To ensure the proper display of your artwork in specific browsers, check **Include Vendor Pre-Fixes**, then check the desired browsers on the list; minor changes will be made to the code for each browser. Check **Rasterize Unsupported Art** to enable complex artwork to be rasterized in the CSS code, either as a JPEG file (with no alpha channel) or as a PNG file (with an alpha channel, if you need to preserve soft-edged transparency); or uncheck this option if you want to optimize and export the art yourself in either of those formats. From the **Resolution** menu, choose Use Document Raster Effects Resolution, or choose Other and enter a value. Click OK.

Continued on the following page

A *On the CSS Properties panel, the character styles and graphic styles that are being used in the file are listed at the top of the panel, and the CSS code that was generated for the currently selected object(s) is shown at the bottom.*

B *In the CSS Export Options dialog, we're specifying the features in the file that we want Illustrator to generate as code.*

4. Have your developer include a link to your CSS file by entering this HTML import rule inside the <style> tag in the HTML file: @import url ("yourfilename.css"). When the HTML file is loaded into the browser, the class names will provide the link between the attribute descriptions in the CSS code and the HTML elements.**A–B**

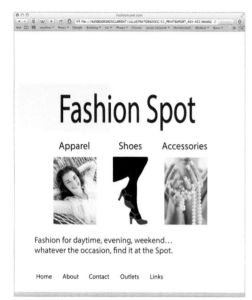

A *This is our original HTML file, viewed in a browser.*

B *This the HTML file after it was linked to our CSS file.*

Exporting Illustrator files to Adobe Photoshop

Creating a Smart Object

When exporting an Illustrator file to Photoshop, for the greatest ease in future editing, your best option is to create a vector Smart Object. A vector Smart Object is created automatically if you do either of the following:

➤ Place an Adobe Illustrator (.ai) file into a Photoshop document via the File > Place command in Photoshop or via the File > Place > In Photoshop command in Bridge.

➤ Copy an object in Illustrator (Edit > Copy), click in a Photoshop document, use the Paste command (Edit > Paste), then in the Paste dialog, click Paste As: Smart Object. Note: To ensure that the Paste dialog displays in Photoshop, in File Handling & Clipboard preferences in Illustrator, check both of the PDF and AICB options.

If you double-click a vector Smart Object thumbnail in Photoshop (then click OK if an alert appears), the embedded file will open in Illustrator. Edit and then save the file, and the vector Smart Object will update automatically in Photoshop — an easy round trip!

For print output, exporting Illustrator objects as Smart Objects has an advantage over exporting a file in the Photoshop (.psd) format. Photoshop prints vector objects and type in a vector Smart Object at the printer resolution, which on a high-resolution PostScript device is typically higher than the resolution of a Photoshop file. Illustrator objects that are saved in the Photoshop .psd format and then placed into Photoshop, in contrast, print at the resolution of the Photoshop file, not the resolution of the output device.

Pasting as pixels, a path, or a shape layer

The Paste dialog offers other Paste As options besides Smart Object. Copy an object in Illustrator (Edit > Copy), click in a Photoshop document, then use the Paste command (Edit > Paste). In the Paste dialog, click Paste As: Pixels, Path, or Shape Layer, depending on how you want to use the object in Photoshop. (See also the Note, above.)

➤ If you copy a compound path or compound shape in Illustrator, paste it into Photoshop, then click Shape Layer in the Paste dialog, it will arrive as multiple paths on a shape layer. In Photoshop, the shape will be filled with the current Foreground color.

Syncing Illustrator settings via Creative Cloud

When you're signed into your Adobe Creative Cloud account, you can sync Illustrator libraries, presets, workspaces, keyboard shortcuts, and application preferences between two computers; manage your files (e.g., post them publicly); and acquire application updates immediately when they are released. Note: Adobe permits each user to activate his or her licensed copy of Illustrator on two computers (e.g., between a desktop computer and a laptop).

To sync the settings on your computers, you upload your custom settings from one computer to the Cloud, (this task) then sync the settings from the Cloud to your second computer (next task).

To upload settings from one of your computers to Creative Cloud:

1. When you sign into Creative Cloud to download (then launch) Illustrator CC, then create or open your first document, an alert gives you the option to sync the default settings to the Cloud. Click Sync Settings Now.A

2. With a document open in Illustrator, create custom settings. You can choose options in the Preferences dialog; save each customized panel (e.g., swatches, brushes, symbols, or graphic styles) as a library (only user-defined libraries can be synced); create and save Print, PDF, or other presets; create and save workspaces; or create shortcuts via Edit > Keyboard Shortcuts. See "Items synchronized using the Sync Settings Feature" in Illustrator Help.

3. To make sure the sync feature is enabled, and to set preferences for syncing, choose Illustrator/Edit > Preferences > Sync Settings or Illustrator/Edit > [your Adobe ID] > Manage Sync Settings. From the Sync menu, choose All Settings; or choose Selected Settings, then check the categories of settings you want to sync. Also choose When Conflict Occurs: Ask My Preference. Click OK.

4. Click the Sync Settings button ⚙ in the lower-left corner of the window, then in the dialog that opens, click Sync Settings Now.B

➤ To verify that you are signed into your Creative Cloud account, click the Illustrator/Edit menu; your account name should be listed on the menu.

➤ To learn more about the Sync Settings preferences in Illustrator, see page 410.

➤ Now that you have uploaded your settings from one of your computers to the Cloud, you can sync those settings to your second computer.

To download your settings from the Cloud to your second computer:

1. On your second computer, launch Illustrator CC. Go to Illustrator/Edit > Preferences > Sync Settings; choose All Settings, or choose Selected Settings and check the desired boxes; then click OK. Open an Illustrator document.

2. In the lower-left corner of the document window, click the Sync Settings button, ⚙ then in the small dialog that opens, click Sync Settings Now.

3. If any of these alerts display and you respond as follows, the settings in the Cloud (that you uploaded from your first computer) will be preserved and your two computers will be synced:

   If a message says "Updated settings are ready," click Apply Now.C Settings from Creative Cloud will overwrite the settings on your current computer.

Continued on the following page

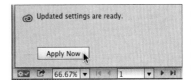

A When we launched Illustrator for the first time, this alert displayed. We clicked Sync Settings Now.

B To upload our settings to the Cloud, we clicked the Sync Settings button, then in this dialog, we clicked Sync Settings Now.

C Click Apply Now to apply the settings that were downloaded from the Cloud.

If a message tells you to relaunch Illustrator, click **Restart Now** (this is needed to sync workspace settings and some presets and preferences).**A**

If the settings on your second computer differ from the settings in the Cloud, an alert will inform you that a sync conflict is detected.**B** To allow the settings in the Cloud to overwrite the settings on your current computer (and to sync your computers), click **Sync Cloud**.

The other sync conflict options

➤ Click **Sync Local** to preserve the settings on the current computer and upload them to the Cloud (and thereby overwrite the current settings in the Cloud). Your two computers won't be synced.

➤ Click **Keep Latest File** to preserve the newest settings (either on the Cloud or on the local computer). Your two computers won't be synced.

➤ If you click **Remember My Preference**, your response will apply automatically to all future sync conflicts. (We keep this option unchecked.)

Note: If, after clicking either Sync Local or Keep Latest File, you want to sync your computers, sync the settings from your current computer to the Cloud, then from the Cloud to your other computer.

A After clicking Sync Settings Now, you may get a directive to relaunch Illustrator.

B This message will appear if a sync conflict is detected.

Importing and exporting Illustrator settings

Via the Export Settings and Import Settings commands, you can export and import Illustrator CC 2014 application settings from one computer to another (excluding keyboard shortcuts). While this method is useful for sharing your settings with other users, to share settings with multiple computers on the same Creative Cloud account, you should use the Sync Settings feature (previous page).

Note: The Illustrator version into which you import settings must have the same locale settings as the Illustrator version on the source computer.

To export an Illustrator settings file: ★

1. Choose Edit > My Settings > **Export Settings**.

2. The Export Settings dialog displays. Choose a location for the settings file, then click OK. Give the file a name of your choice, and save it in a location that will be accessible by the computer on which you want to import the settings.

To import an Illustrator settings file: ★

1. Save your file.

2. Choose Edit > My Settings > **Import Settings**.

3. An alert dialog will appear, indicating that the imported settings will replace the existing settings, and that Illustrator will quit/exit and relaunch automatically so as to activate the imported settings. Click OK.

4. The Import Settings dialog displays. Click the Illustrator settings file that you want to import, then click Open. Pause to allow Illustrator to quit/exit and relaunch.

Managing files via Creative Cloud

One of the benefits of a Creative Cloud subscription is that you are allotted space on your page to store your files (as of this writing, up to 20 GB). Once they're stored in the Cloud, you can access your files from any computer, post them publicly, or email them. You can get to your Creative Cloud page from Illustrator.

To upload files to Creative Cloud:

1. Choose Illustrator/Edit > [your Adobe ID] > **Manage Creative Cloud Account**.

2. Your personal Creative Cloud page displays in your browser. Do either of the following:

From the Actions (blue) menu, choose **Upload**. In the dialog, locate and click a file name (or Cmd/Ctrl click multiple file names), then click Choose.

Move the Creative Cloud window slightly to the side, then drag a file thumbnail (or multiple selected thumbnails) from Bridge into the Creative Cloud window.

3. A progress bar will display at the top of your Cloud page while the files are uploading. When the uploading is finished, thumbnails of the chosen files will display on the page.

To share, rename, move, or archive files via Creative Cloud:

1. Choose Illustrator/Edit > [your Adobe ID] > **Manage Creative Cloud Account**.

2. On the View menu, make sure **Mosaic** is checked.

3. From the menu in the lower-right corner of any file thumbnail, choose any of these options:

To share the file via Behance, choose **Post Publicly** (if available for the current file format), enter a title, then follow steps 4–8 on page 458.

To email the file, choose **Send Link**. Click Make Public to unlock the file; if desired, check Allow File Download; enter the email address of the recipient; then click Send Link.

To put the file into a folder on your Creative Cloud page, choose **Move**, click a folder name in the dialog, then click Move [#] items. (If you need to create a new folder, from the Actions menu, choose Create Folder, enter a name, then click Create Folder.)

To rename the file, choose **Rename**, enter the desired name, then click Rename.

To archive the file (move it to an Archive page, for potential future deletion from the Cloud), click **Archive**, then click Archive again. To display all your archived files, click the **Archive** button. 📁 Check the box next to the files that you want to restore or permanently delete; from the menu 🔽 above the list, choose Restore or Permanently Delete from the Cloud; then click the button of the same name.

➤ To find how much of your Cloud storage is currently being used, click the ⚙ icon in the upper-right corner of the page.

To access additional commands for managing an individual file:

1. On your Creative Cloud page, click a file thumbnail.

2. An enlarged view of the file displays, and information about the file displays in the sidebar on the right (if you don't see the sidebar, widen your browser window).

3. Do any of the following:

To display file specifications, as well as swatches of colors that are found in the artwork, click the **File Information** button. ⓘ If desired, you can click Download ASE (Adobe Swatch Exchange File) to create an .ase file of the swatches that can be loaded into any Creative Cloud application that has a Swatches panel; or you can click View on Kuler to view the colors on Kuler.adobe.com (see pages 133–135).

To manage comments about the file, click the **Activity** button. 🗨 Type a comment in the field, then click Add Comment. To delete a comment, click the X, then click Delete Comment.

To manage the visibility of layers in the file, click the **Layers** button, 🗹 then click the visibility icon for each layer you want to show or hide. (The button will display only if the file contains layers.)

If the file contains multiple artboards, you can cycle through them by rolling over the image, then clicking the arrow to the left or right of the image.

➤ Via the Share menu, you can access the Post Publicly and Send Link commands. And via the Actions menu, you can access the Download, Rename, Archive, and Search commands.

4. To return to viewing multiple thumbnails, click **Files** on the menu bar.

To sign out of your Creative Cloud page:

From the menu 👤 in the upper-right corner of the menu bar, choose **Sign Out**.

Sharing your artwork on Behance

Behance, an online image-sharing service, is accessible directly from Illustrator CC 2014. Once you upload artwork for a project on the Behance website, viewers can search for, view, and comment on your work and you, in turn, can track and monitor their comments.

To share a file on Behance:

1. In Illustrator, open either a new file to be uploaded to Behance, or a variation of an image that you have already uploaded. Display an artboard.

2. Click the **Share on Behance** ⬀ button in the lower left corner of the document window (or choose File > Share on Behance). Note: If you haven't yet linked your Adobe ID with Behance, either click Start Your Public Portfolio, or enter your Behance email address and password and click Link Account.

3. A JPEG version of the file opens in the Share on Behance dialog. On the Enter Information screen, do either of the following:

   If you're adding a new image, click **New Work**, then in the **Title** field, enter a title for the work.

   If you're uploading a variation of an image that is already on Behance, click **Revision**, click to open the **Choose Existing** menu, then click the existing image to link it to the variation.

4. To make the work searchable, enter a keyword in the **Tags** field, then press Return/Enter; repeat, if desired, to attach more keywords. (To delete a keyword, click its X.)

   In the **Post a Comment to Start the Conversation** field, you can enter comments about the image.

   To choose a visibility setting for the image, click Edit to display the **Visible To** menu, then choose Everyone or (your user-created) Feedback Circle.

5. Click Continue. The Select Cover Image screen displays. To define the area for the preview of your work in progress, position the crop box over the image. If you also want to scale the crop box, drag a handle (it will scale proportionately). Click **Crop Cover & Publish**. Your work is now live on Behance.

6. Click **View & Share on Behance** to launch Behance.

7. On the Request Feedback screen, click one of those "Sign In" links to announce your work, or click Skip.

8. Your Behance page displays, along with the currently uploaded image. *Optional:* To edit the current image information, click Edit Info (above the image), make the desired edits, then click Save.

To log out of or into Behance:

To log out of Behance, choose Me > **Log Out**.

To get to your Behance page without using Illustrator, go to Behance.net, click Adobe ID, enter your ID and password, then click Sign In. In Behance, click Done if the Find Creatives to Follow screen appears, then choose My Portfolio > **My Work**.

To create a project on Behance:

1. In Illustrator, export some Illustrator files as images in the JPEG, GIF, or PNG format.

2. In Behance, choose Add Work > **Add Project** (or on your My Work tab, click Create Project). Click **Upload Files**; select your JPEG, GIF, or PNG files; then click Choose. If desired, use the buttons to embed media or add text. Click **Save**, then click Continue.

   On the Cover screen, enter a project title, click **Upload Image**, locate a JPEG, GIF, or PNG image for the cover, then click Choose. Adjust the crop box, if desired; click **Crop**; then click Continue.

   On the Settings screen, choose or enter **Creative Fields**, **Project Tags**, and **Project Description** info. Use the links on the right side to add or edit information, such as Credits and Copyright settings. Click **Save Changes**, then finally, click **Publish**.

To display your My Work page:

From the My Portfolio menu in Behance, choose **My Work**. To display your current projects, click the **Projects** link; or to display all your images in progress, click the **Work in Progress** link. To access available options for managing your projects or images (e.g., edit, view, promote, clone, unpublish, or delete), roll over any image thumbnail.

To view comments about your work:

To view any comments that have been posted about your work, choose Activity > **Activity Feed**. Click **Comments on Your Work in Progress** or **Comments on Your Projects**.

➤ To locate your URL on Behance (for use in promoting your work), choose My Portfolio > My Profile. Your address should be listed under Profile URLs.

INDEX

Unless noted otherwise, the entries in this index pertain to Illustrator.